# CONFLICTS OF INTEREST

Tony Benn, who first entered Parliament in 1950, has been the Labour MP for Chesterfield since March 1984. He was elected to the National Executive Committee of the Labour Party in 1959, and was the Chairman of the Party in 1971-2 has been a Cabinet Minister in Labour Government since 1964, holding the positions of Postmaster General, Minister of Technology and Minister of Power. From 1974-9 he was Secretary of State for Industry, later Secretary of State for Energy and one-time President of the Council of Energy Ministers of the European Community. He contested the leadership of the Labour Party in 1976 and in 1988.

He is the author of eleven books, including *Arguments for Socialism*, *Arguments for Democracy*. The previous volumes of his Diaries, *Out of the Wilderness*, *Office Without Power* and *Against the Tide*, have all been published to great critical acclaim. He holds four Honorary Doctorates from British and American Universities. He is married to Caroline, and they have four children and six grandchildren.

D1099103

# TONY BENN

## Conflicts of Interest

### DIARIES 1977 – 80

Edited by Ruth Winstone

ARROW BOOKS

Arrow Books Limited
20 Vauxhall Bridge Road, London SW1V 2SA

An imprint of the Random Century Group

London Melbourne Sydney Auckland Johannesburg
and agencies throughout the world

First published by Hutchinson 1990
Arrow edition 1991

© Tony Benn 1990

Printed and bound in Great Britain by
The Guernsey Press Co. Ltd
Guernsey, C.I.

ISBN 0 09 989870 5

# Contents

This volume is dedicated to Caroline with love; her knowledge of, and contribution to, the ideas of socialism have been the greatest single influence in my political life.

# Acknowledgements

This is the fourth volume in a series of political diaries which span nearly twenty years and which are themselves drawn from political and personal records encompassing nearly half a century

A project of this magnitude could not possibly have been undertaken without the support of a team of people who have worked together to turn the raw material into the published text.

Ruth Winstone, the Editor, has been in overall charge of the series from the beginning, and her role has developed far beyond the usual editorial tasks of checking facts and preparing notes, background and biographical material and appendices: her judgment in discussing and recommending passages for inclusion, ensuring continuity and intelligibility without compromising the original much lengthier account, has made these books very much her own.

Sheila Hubacher and Ruth Hobson again undertook the awesome job of the transcription for this volume of almost two million words, and were invaluable in their informed criticism and comments throughout; as was Linden Stafford, who had editorial responsibility for preparing the final text for the printers. Her meticulous eye and her suggestions and advice added significantly to the quality of the finished book.

I have also to record again my thanks to Random Century who took on this long-term series in 1986, particularly to Richard Cohen who has overseen the unfolding saga and to all those in the company who have worked on the project.

Having said all that, the final responsibility for this volume, and for any errors that may have crept in, rests with me alone.

Tony Benn
1990

# List of Illustrations

Being framed by Denis Healey *(Private Eye)*
Paul Foot and Tariq Ali *(Benn Archives Collection)*
Rosalind Retey Benn
Michael Meacher and Les Huckfield *(Chris Mullin)*
Tony Banks *(Chris Mullin)*
Frances Morrell with Geoff Bish
Ayatollah Khomeini *(Popperfoto)*
President Reagan *(Popperfoto)*

### *Cartoons*

© Nicholas Garland, *New Statesman* (p.54, p.158, p.258); © Les Gibbard, *Guardian* (p.544); Nicholas Garland, © *Daily Telegraph* (p.481, p.513, p.570); Jensen, © *Sunday Telegraph* (p.539); Cummings, © *Sunday Express* (p.493), *Daily Express* (p.292); Franklin, © *Sun* (p.375).

# Editor's Note

The fourth volume of Tony Benn's political diaries has the distinction of being the only published contemporaneous account of the Callaghan Government's last years, and of Labour's first twelve months in opposition to Margaret Thatcher's administration.

As with previous volumes, I have tried to maintain the balance of the daily record of a Member of Parliament engaged in the activities of Government and Party at the highest level. *Conflicts of Interest* was planned to include Michael Foot's three years as Leader, ending in 1983. However, this would have required such drastic paring of the original diary transcript that it was decided to end this volume in May 1980, at the point when the pressure for democratic reform in the Party was building up. Even so, two million words of transcription had to be reduced to *one-eighth* of that total, so that inevitably certain themes have had to be omitted; while the meetings, decisions and events included represent only a fraction of Tony Benn's actual prodigious daily activity.

Ensuring continuity and intelligibility has as a result proved increasingly difficult, and notes, linking passages and appendices have been designed with this problem in mind. I have, as before, assumed that readers have a basic background knowledge of recent political events; nevertheless, it was still a lesson to me to discover that the expression 'Selsdon man' was unknown by one colleague; indeed, when Edward Heath held his famous meeting at Selsdon Park Hotel in 1970, most A level students now studying that period of British Government were not born! So I should apologise for omissions of explanation which I should have foreseen, and for any errors of spelling in names which it proved impossible to check despite Tony Benn's formidable collection of papers, press cuttings and manuscript notes and books.

I could not have managed without the support of Linden Stafford who, in addition to copy-editing, took over many of the functions of advice and criticism formerly provided by Hutchinson's editor, Kate Mosse, who went on maternity leave. Also, Hugh Scott provided invaluable and reliable assistance at later stages in checking and in preparing appendix material.

Ruth Winstone
July 1990

# Foreword

The last years of the Seventies and the beginning of the Eighties marked the end of one political era and the start of a new one.

In 1977, as these Diaries open, the Labour Government was attempting to survive without a parliamentary majority, at the mercy of the Liberals, and with its economic policies determined by an agreement with the IMF to cut public expenditure.

When, in 1978, these IMF cuts began to bite and the Government sought to limit wages in the public and private sector, relations both with the trade unions and with industrialists deteriorated: the so called Winter of Discontent led inexorably to Labour's defeat and to the election of Margaret Thatcher's monetarist administration, committed to upholding and strengthening British capitalism by quite different means.

While economic and industrial problems preoccupied Jim Callaghan's Cabinet, we were also concerned with Britain's relations with the European Community – in particular our attitude to the direct election of representatives to the European Parliament and our stand on the European Monetary System. As Energy Secretary seeking to control our own natural resources, I was also brought into direct conflict with the Community Commissioners in Brussels whose exercise of powers under the Treaty of Rome was contrary to Britain's interests.

This debate about Britain's relations with its Community partners is still in progress, and at that time the Labour Party was explicitly opposed to the process of integration which has since intensified. My membership of the National Executive and of its Home Policy Committee enabled me to participate in that debate from within the Cabinet and the Party.

The Conservative Government that came to power in May 1979 has been widely characterised as 'Thatcherite', but, as my Diaries show, many of the principles and policies of the Labour Government – particularly in respect of the adoption of monetarist measures, its commitment to the EEC, and its maintenance and modernisation of nuclear weapons – suggest that 'Thatcherism' had become the philosophy of the British establishment long before Margaret Thatcher became Prime Minister, and had paved the way for the intellectual dominance of right-wing ideas throughout the Eighties.

The story of the fall of the 1974–9 Labour Government is one which has been subject to many, many misconceptions, encouraged by the establishment and accepted as fact, thus influencing the thinking of a generation. *Conflicts of Interest*, the only Cabinet diary so far published of this period, reports my observations of, participation in, and reactions to political activity at the time as accurately as I was able to make them, interspersed with contemporary comment which reflected my own assessment of the political situation.

With Labour in opposition there emerged through the NEC and Conference a movement aiming to make the Party a more democratic one by, among other things, requiring the Leader to be accountable to the Party membership so as to ensure that the alternative policies adopted by Conference would be advocated in Parliament and implemented when Labour returned to office.

Future volumes of the Diary will record the success of this strategy – rejecting the Cold War, seeking an open relationship with the whole of Europe, opposing the destructive effect of market forces, and supporting groups subjected to discrimination and prejudice – and its subsequent reversal after 1983.

The original diary for the period 1977–1980 is two million words long, and, as the Editor's Note explains, the substantial cutting required to reduce it to managable proportions has had its effect on the shape of the published book.

However, the uncut text has been made available to those serious researchers who wished to look at the record in detail to amplify their work or to help them to reach conclusions different from those that appeared at the time. Those who come to write a more definitive historical work may possibly see the arguments afresh instead of simply translating from the headlines into the history books the conventional views of the rich and the powerful.

I hope that, by recognising and understanding Labour's recent history in the light of this perspective, future Labour Governments can be armed against making the same mistakes again.

Tony Benn
July 1990

# 1
# Windscale Crisis
## January–March 1977

*Tuesday 11 January 1977*
I left for the Orkneys with James Bretherton (my new Private
Secretary) and Bernard Ingham. Dr Armand Hammer and his third
wife were at Heathrow, having flown in on their personal jet, and a host
of other people were waiting to fly to the Orkneys for the inauguration
of the Flotta oil terminal.* Hammer is of course a mythological figure
and every passenger on the plane was given a copy of a biography about
him.

His great-grandfather was a shipbuilder in Odessa; his grandfather
put his money in the safest thing possible, salt, which was evaporated
from the Black Sea, but owing to severe typhoons and storms he lost it
all and emigrated to America. Armand Hammer's father became a
socialist under the influence of Daniel De Leon.

Armand qualified as a doctor, and after the First World War decided
to visit Russia. He was so overcome by the terrible conditions of famine
that he bought up a hospital and transported it to Russia. He also
imported food, and under these circumstances he met and became close
friends with Lenin. Hammer said that Lenin had told him that
communism was no good, that the Soviet Union would need to start
again with capitalism, and a new economic policy, and asked Hammer
if he would be the first business concessionaire. Hammer agreed to do
so out of a mixture of human sympathy, socialist understanding,
internationalism and, of course, the entrepreneurial nose. He set up a
pencil factory to service the huge educational programme. Many years
later Brezhnev, of whom he is a great admirer, told him he was
educated at a school which used Hammer pencils.

When Stalin came to power, Hammer left for Paris. In 1956 he
retired, at the age of fifty-eight, and, because he was bored, bought a
little oil company for $50,000 and built it up into Occidental, one of the
largest oil companies in the world. He also, of course, has this fabulous

* Hammer's Occidental Group developed and operated two North Sea oilfields, Piper
and Claymore, for which Flotta was the pipeline terminal.

art collection. He's a historical figure, very charming, extremely modest.

On the plane he showed me a couple of little films about the development of shale oil, which he thinks is the answer to the world's oil problem. Tonight he is going to speak on the telephone to James Schlesinger, the new US Secretary for Energy, to try to persuade Carter to take it up. Hammer likes Carter because he is prepared to do something about energy.

He was angry about the build-up towards rearmament. He said that communism hadn't solved the problems and capitalism couldn't distribute the wealth and some new scheme would have to be worked out. As always, shrewd enough to see what the really big long-term problem was, I thought.

Well, we got to Orkney, then by helicopter to Flotta, and went round in buses – it was pretty cold – and assembled around this installation. The whole thing, if you include the Piper and Claymore fields, has cost $1.3 billion, which in current prices would be about £600 million, and they will get their money back in two years, and we'll get 70 or 75 per cent of it through the petroleum revenue tax.

During the opening ceremony John Foster, the former Tory MP for Northwich, was sitting opposite me and we chatted. He talked to me about the deal of 1941 under which the Americans gave us some of their destroyers in return for leasing them bases on British territory. President Roosevelt was ready to do it but was afraid it might be a breach of the Neutrality Act, and he was particularly afraid that Wendell Wilkie (the Republican candidate in the 1940 presidential election) might make political capital out of it. So he sent somebody to see Wilkie but the deal had been reported in the *New York Times* before he got the secret message.

John Foster was in the States, in Colorado Springs, heard Wilkie was there, rang up Wilkie's HQ, and Wilkie invited him over straight away. John persuaded Wilkie that it was necessary to supply the destroyers to save the British from being absolutely swamped by the German fleet. Wilkie said, all right, I give you my word, 'but don't forget that Roosevelt will always see that I get the shitty end of the stick.' Foster sent a cable back to the British Embassy in Washington asking for this to be relayed to Churchill and Roosevelt, and when he later arrived in Washington John was rebuked for using the phrase 'the shitty end of the stick' and embarrassing the decipher girls. That made him laugh.

The other story he told me was terribly interesting – it concerned Edward VIII's abdication.

In 1936, two or three days after the Bishop of Bradford, Dr Blunt, had made his famous sermon – as a result of which the whole story of Edward VIII's affair broke – Foster went to dinner with Ernest

Simpson and his brother in London and of course they talked about the divorce. It turned out that Ernest had admitted to a completely fraudulent adultery with the wife of a friend of his, to give Wallis Simpson her freedom – he hadn't committed adultery with her at all. Foster realised he had in his hands information which would have prevented the divorce from going through.

So a message was sent to the Prime Minister, Baldwin, about this evidence, pointing out that Ernest Simpson's decree nisi would not be made absolute and would be cancelled, and that would mean the King couldn't marry Mrs Simpson and therefore the abdication would be off. What did Baldwin think?

Baldwin sent a message saying: Do nothing. So in effect that little story, if it's true, suggests that Baldwin wanted to get rid of the King; Foster said it wasn't a bad thing because actually the King was very sympathetic to the Germans.

I also talked to an Air Vice-Marshal, a naval captain from Rosyth and one or two people about the physical security of the oil. One of them said to me, 'Well, I understand that every single person who works on the oil installations is regularly monitored by the police.'

He didn't say any more, but if that's true it's another pointer towards the supervised society and another warning about civil liberties.

*Occidental, Armand Hammer's oil company, was one of a number of powerful multinationals with which I had to negotiate after I became Secretary of State for Energy in June 1975. The Government's relationship with the oil companies at that time was still being developed. Our job was to make sure that the resources of the North Sea were exploited for the benefit of the nation as a whole and not solely for the benefit of a handful of multinationals controlled mainly from America. But at the same time we did not want to prevent the flow of capital and technology that the oil companies could bring to the North Sea for its development. We needed to establish a relationship with both finance and the oil companies on a basis of trust and confidence.*

*Some oil companies are comparable in strength and wealth to national governments. In 1977 Shell earned $55 billion from 4.2 million barrels per day, while Exxon earned $58 billion producing 4.9 million bpd. By contrast, the revenues of Saudi Arabia were only $38 billion producing 9.2 million barrels per day, and the revenues of Iran were $23 billion producing 5.7 million bpd. As Secretary of State, I learned that relations between governments and oil companies were rather like treaty negotiations.*

*The Conservative administration gave a large number of licences to oil companies to develop the North Sea without any provision that any oil be directed to meet United Kingdom needs. There was no proper statutory framework and no petroleum revenue tax. The Labour Government had introduced a very complex petroleum revenue tax which differentiated between the marginal and the profitable fields and gave us an average 70 per cent return. We also passed the Petroleum and Pipelines Act, which gave the Secretary of State enormous powers over depletion and control. Thirdly, in 1975, we established the British National Oil Corporation (BNOC), to which Lord Kearton was appointed Chairman and Thomas Balogh Deputy Chairman.*

*At first we faced a pretty hostile atmosphere from the oil industry itself, which was not really ready to make distinguished oilmen available to work on BNOC. What we wanted was access to the oil. We set ourselves as an objective the right to buy at market prices 51 per cent of the oil. Secondly, we sought a seat, voice and vote on the operating committees so that the BNOC would be able to enter, slowly but steadily, into a position where it would know what was going on in the oil companies licensed in 1972. These discussions were extremely detailed and complex and we found it necessary to vary the agreements to meet the different circumstances of each individual company.*

*We tried to enter into what were, in effect, treaty arrangements with them – provisions over and above access to knowledge and access to oil. One of these was that proper consultative arrangements must be set up with the companies which would maximise both the use of UK oil and the benefit to the UK balance of payments deriving from the oil.*

*All multinationals, but especially oil companies, move cash and technology across the world in a way that has considerable impact on the rate of world development. However, unlike the sheikhs of forty years ago, we were not prepared to allow them free rein without safeguarding our interests. The treaty arrangements, which we called participation agreements, were the method we adopted. After long hours of discussion we did reach a position where almost all the major oil companies agreed.*

*We did not – and no British Government would – adopt the rule of confiscation or damage the legitimate interests arising from a round of licences already agreed. We made it clear from the outset that the Government's revenue interests would be met from taxes and royalties and not through the participation agreements.*

*In 1977 we were about to embark on the fifth round of licences, which was deliberately made smaller than the 1972 round. This was because, when the 1972 round was announced and the allocations were made, the stress and strain upon the British industrial equipment industry was such that it was simply unable to meet the demand. We wanted to ensure as far as we could that orders for such equipment were brought to the UK in order to create jobs. But, of course, smaller rounds were also a form of depletion control that would not raise the problems of cutbacks, which if introduced arbitrarily might affect the confidence of companies operating in the North Sea.*

### Wednesday 12 January

To Dublin for talks about EEC energy policy, my first call as President of the Council of Energy Ministers. Fitzpatrick, the Irish Minister, is a nice, gentle, conservative solicitor of about fifty-eight. His room was low-lit, and had panelled walls, and there was an open fire with blocks of lovely-smelling peat burning.

I got him to tell us what the Irish interest was: to secure supplies of oil in a crisis, to get ahead with their nuclear programme, to achieve the maximum production of indigenous resources, to make use of all the money available from the EEC in grants, loans and price support.

The British Ambassador, Robin Haydon, a big, red-faced, red-haired man, drove me in his Ford Granada, which had double bullet-proof windows, steel on the sides and underneath; it weighed two tons. There were three car-loads of the Gardai, the police, all armed to the teeth, one car in front and two behind. Since the murder of Ewart-Biggs, the British Ambassador, in the summer, apparently the security for the British Ambassador is greater than for anyone in the Republic, including the President. The Irish were very embarrassed by the assassination. Haydon said he couldn't go into his garden without having men with machine-guns keeping an eye on him. This is an aspect of modern diplomatic life which is perhaps not fully recognised. I felt awfully sorry for him.

On the way back from the Ministry to the airport, we were caught in a most terrible traffic jam and the lights were out because of an unofficial strike by power engineers, so we went through these darkened streets with little candles flickering in the newsagents' windows; it was very Edwardian.

*Thursday 13 January*
Cabinet at 10.30 dealt with an item which wasn't properly on the agenda, namely the question of how we should handle the commitment we made in the summer, during the public expenditure cuts, to look at long-term economies in the Department of Health.

David Ennals had suggested that a charge should be made through insurance companies to pay for the cost of medical treatment arising out of road accidents.

When you look into it, it is an extremely difficult thing to do; there has been a committee under Merlyn Rees trying to find an answer, and they have failed to come up with a solution. We had a discussion for nearly an hour, and it was suggested that the alternative was to put a charge on Vehicle Excise Duty. Denis Healey resisted this bitterly on the grounds of hypothecation.

I didn't make a careful note as the discussion went round, but Jim Callaghan was very peppery about it. I should add that it was in his brief today that he is going to take charge of economic and industrial strategy. Denis Healey, therefore, must have felt rebuked. Harold Wilson used to do it to me in the past, and I somewhat sympathised; Eric Varley has been a complete failure at the Department of Industry and everything has been controlled by the Treasury, and Jim has no love of the Treasury.

I think Jim may feel that after all the bloodshed over the cuts last December things are going well and he wants to take charge. In so far as that really represents an advance in anything like our manifesto policy, it's a good thing.

We came to the parliamentary situation and Jim said he wanted to say one or two words.

First, on Tuesday morning in committee the Government's bill to take away the right to unemployment pay for occupational pensioners between sixty and sixty-five had been defeated.

Second, last night (while I was in Ireland) seventy-four people had abstained in the defence debate, or had voted for a motion calling for further cuts in defence. These included seven PPSs, three of whom were attached to Cabinet Ministers. In addition, on the main question where the Tories had voted against us and therefore our position was more vulnerable, three MPs, Reg Prentice, I think Dick Crawshaw and John Mackintosh, had abstained.

Jim thought the right thing to do was to sack all the PPSs immediately because the Party was fraying at the edges. (I heard later from Stan Orme that all the letters of dismissal had actually been drafted and were ready for signing.)

Michael Foot intervened to say he thought a warning would be sufficient and Stan Orme agreed.

I didn't say anything because I was in some difficulty over Brian Sedgemore, Jim having tried to stop me appointing him as my new PPS. Mike Cocks then said he had to warn the Cabinet that there was a large core of people who had come into the Party in 1974, some of whom didn't have any real links with the Party, who were really tough, and so on. Real McCarthyism beginning to develop.

Denis Healey thought a warning would be appropriate, and Crosland said, 'You know there have always been fifty to seventy people in the PLP who have been in favour of defence cuts and it is no worse than ever before; I think a warning would be sufficient.' I was slightly surprised at Crosland, but actually it was a shrewd comment.

Then John Silkin said, 'Well, as a former Chief Whip at the time that Harold Wilson sacked seven PPSs, I can tell you it led to a great row', and Peter Shore said, 'Anyway, you don't get much out of being a PPS', and Jim interrupted him, 'Oh yes you do, you get into the very centre of ministerial work.'

Roy Hattersley said, 'If you do warn them you have got to let it be known there has been a warning.'

In the end Jim concluded, 'Well, I've been persuaded not to do what I wanted to do', and David Ennals said, 'Thank you very much indeed for giving us the chance to comment, Prime Minister.' The most revolting bit of fawning I've heard for some time.

I went back to the office, and when I reflected on it I had a slight feeling that the Cabinet was moving to the right – Jim having become confident enough to take charge and impatient with those who are causing trouble.

*Saturday 15 January*
Caught the train to Bath for the Avon County Labour Group meeting in preparation for the county council elections this spring.

There is a complete transformation in the leadership of the Party locally. There are still one or two of the old boys but the youngsters who have come up are marvellous. I say youngsters, they are people of forty or below, but they are principled, are keen on democracy, and care about education, planning and democratic control of the council.

*Sunday 16 January*
Amazement of amazement, the *Sunday Times* had two leading articles today, one saying that the motorcycle co-operative at Meriden must be saved, and the other singling me out for favourable mention for my open government policy at the Department of Energy.

The background to this is that I had called in the Nuclear Inspectorate to ask them questions about the fast breeder, like 'What would happen if a fast breeder blew up?' They had answered, Well 10,000 (or whatever) would be killed, and I had stopped the discussion and said, 'I really cannot be told this in private, and know it privately; do you mind if I put the questions in writing to you and publish the answers?' So the answers were published this week.

It must be the first time in history, I think, that the Nuclear Inspectorate have been cross-examined by their responsible Minister, or indeed that the Minister has ever revealed in public the interrogation of his officials about nuclear policy, or about anything.

*Monday 17 January*
I had an hour with Reg Underhill [the National Agent] about the Andy Bevan case.[1] Reg is a funny chap; he is 100 per cent against Andy Bevan, he loathes Militant, he is a Party disciplinarian, but told me rather pathetically that he regarded himself as left of centre and had always been in the Party and would fight for the Party; he has been a pacifist, but he would not tolerate people taking over the Party organisation. He described at great length how these guys were taking it over and was furious that the Executive had not looked at his report.

I am apt to be pretty relaxed with Reg, and told him I didn't think Militant could take it over, but I recalled the attempt to get rid of the

Bevanites and said I was really an old-fashioned liberal about this. It was partly the young against the old, and wasn't really what lay behind the Reg Prentice-type problems.

I asked him whether he thought Reg Prentice would stand against the Party in a by-election. He thought it was possible and that Neville Sandelson [MP for Hayes and Harlington] would too. I pursued the question of expulsions – we never expelled Jim Sillars,* I said, we just don't expel MPs.

Back to the office and had a very interesting meeting on refinery policy. The Department was trying to get me to abandon our objective that 66 per cent of refining must be carried out in the UK. They asked me before Christmas and I refused, and the following day the *Financial Times* reported that I was going to do it, so obviously they had already briefed the *FT* in anticipation that I would accept it.

We had a real argument about this. I said it must be to our advantage to have the refining here, and they said, 'Well, BP would make more profits if it put its refinery in Rotterdam,' and I said, 'Maybe they will, but the whole point is to harmonise the interests of the British national balance-of-payments investment against the interests of global companies.'

With Caroline to *Tribune*'s fortieth birthday party at Number 10 – it was immense fun. Jim was charming and had baked a cake which said, 'Happy Birthday *Tribune* – Life Begins at Forty', with a red ribbon round it. He made a little speech saying he read *Tribune* and had done for years, and yearned for the day when he would agree with it.

Then Jim took us down to the Cabinet Room, which I wanted Caroline to see. We all stood there – all the wives and Dick Clements, the editor of *Tribune*, and his staff. Jim told me to stand behind my usual seat. 'Now, where do we all sit?' he asked. So I began going round and we could remember our side of the table, but when it came to the other side Jim couldn't remember. I went through them. 'There's Harold Lever, and next to him Fred Peart. Next to him David Ennals, then John Silkin . . .' When we got to the end we couldn't think of anybody else. So Jim pulled out his diary and said, 'Well, let's look it up and see who else is in the Cabinet.' 'Don't tell me,' I said, 'we forgot Edmund Dell.' In the far corner was Bill Rodgers's seat. We'd all forgotten about him. There was a great deal of laughter, and it was very agreeable.

We had a word with Denis and Edna Healey. Denis gave a good imitation of Mike Yarwood. He was full of *bonhomie* and goodwill.

---

* Elected Labour MP for South Ayrshire in 1970; formed the Scottish Labour Party and resigned the Labour whip in 1976; defeated in the 1979 General Election. In 1988 he was elected Scottish Nationalist MP for Glasgow Govan.

*Tuesday 18 January*

I worked until 2, then up at 6.30 to go off to begin my tour of European capitals as President of the Council of Energy Ministers.

I took my own mug and lots of tea bags. When we arrived in Paris we were met by the Ambassador, Nico Henderson, a tall, grey-haired, scruffy man, almost a caricature of an English public schoolboy who got to the top of the Foreign Office. I don't think I had ever met him before; he was rather superior and swooped me up in his Rolls Royce.

My first call was on the French Minister, Michel d'Ornano. I quite like him. He's a bit of a playboy, Giscard's favourite son, though he did say to me when he was in London in November that he felt himself more in accord with the likes of Roy Jenkins and Jimmy Carter. He's a sort of civilised man of the centre – absolute dream coalitionist of all time, really. I began by asking him about the mayoralty of Paris, which has not had a democratic constitution since the Commune of 1871. It is an amazing story – a hundred and six years of punishment for the Commune.

I must say, the more I hear about the details of French democracy the more terrifying they become. What interests me is that d'Ornano himself picks the entire slate of candidates – 109 – for the Paris municipal elections. It is as if Herbert Morrison, as Leader of the LCC, had been able to pick the candidate for every ward in London, or as if Jim Callaghan could pick all the candidates for Parliament, and it has nothing to do with democracy at all; it is a total patronage system.

We left Paris at about 4 o'clock and flew to The Hague, where the British Ambassador, Sir John Barnes, met me. These ambassadors all live in great luxury.

In half an hour I am going to have dinner with Ruud Lubbers, the Dutch Minister of Economic Affairs, and a team of Dutch officials and Ministers, and go over it all again. . . .

Well, it is now about a quarter to midnight, and I have just come upstairs after a very long session with Lubbers.

He's quite a young man – just under forty – has a family engineering business, and is a progressive employer type, bright, with a broad range of responsibilities.

Max van der Stoel, the Dutch Foreign Minister, was present and he said that Kissinger had argued the case for east–west interdependence. I pressed this question: Should we not have an opening of some kind to the east? Barnes joined in and made it clear that he didn't want an eastern policy such as the Russians were seeking.

I asked about the Economic Commission for Europe. 'Well,' they said, 'we'll look at that but that is just a UN thing.'

There is no doubt whatever that this reflected an inflexibility towards the east.

I asked what they thought was going to happen. 'Don't you think there is going to be some easement of the relations between east and west? Some break-up of the Soviet empire so that we will have a new Yugoslavia when Tito dies. What about Czechoslovakia?' and so on.

I couldn't get any change out of them and Barnes was most passionate about it, but the Foreign Office is utterly rigid. Compare this with the French, who are always popping backwards and forwards to Moscow. It's a completely different tactical position. I get this feeling of a deep and continuing Cold War mentality among our people; the Dutch were pretty negative too. But I think this tour will help towards an understanding of the positions of the various governments.

The end of another day of negotiations, and I enjoyed it very much. In a way it's very relaxing not to be a British Minister, just a European one.

But I must admit that the standard of living of, for example, the Ambassador – a Rolls Royce, luxurious house, marvellous furniture, silver plate at dinner – is indefensible. Ours is a sort of corporate society with a democratic safety valve. What a long time it will take to put it right. And how do you get measured steps of advance? Undoubtedly openness is one, and negotiations and discussions with the trade unions is another. Nobody should have power unless they are elected.

*Wednesday 19 January*

At 7 in came the butler and the sub-butler with the silver salver and silver teapot and China tea and lemon, scrambled egg, crispy bacon, toast and marmalade.

We flew off to Brussels and went to the international press centre.

They hadn't really opened by 10.30 but we found a little corner in this lush building, had a cup of coffee, and who should buzz in but Sir Donald Maitland, our Ambassador to the EEC, who always looks very busy.

We sat and talked for a bit and the journalists, who had arrived by 10.45, were drinking at the bar. I had been warned that not many people would come to a press conference but about thirty-five journalists, French and British and from all over the Community, turned up. I simply told them what I had told every Minister.

Maitland looked terribly agitated. I think it was partly at the idea of the Community having an eastern policy, which has terrified the Foreign Office – because they know nothing about it. I asked permission from nobody to broach the subject.

We went off from there for a lunch with the Belgians given by Sir David Muirhead, our Ambassador to the Brussels Government, who lives in another of these great fancy houses with a butler, a sub-butler, a log fire and God knows what. I found the Belgians terribly funny, by which I mean that they laughed at my jokes.

The truth is that everyone who works at Brussels, be they Ministers, bureaucrats, representatives of the delegations or the press, have just got used to the fraud of it all, the muddle, the confusion and the obscurity. So, when someone comes along and says Ministers must be in charge and they must meet a directive and do things openly, then it is like saying the emperor has no clothes on. That is really the reaction.

We flew to Luxembourg, a ghostly airport which was absolutely empty. A snow plough or something had been along the runway, a large wartime runway built for the B52 Flying Fortress bombers. Gradually we saw these tiny figures in the snow waiting for us. It was like an exchange of prisoners in a spy story.

The Ambassador, Antony Acland, a relation of Richard Acland* of the famous Devon family, was there and we drove off, together with the Permanent Secretary, into this idyllic little town and up to the twelfth floor of a tall office block. There was Monsieur Mart, who is actually called the Minister for the Middle Classes, Economy, Transport and Energy! He is a jolly man, and I liked him.

Luxembourg would really like to be a province in a bigger Europe. The people don't like the way the big nations fight for their own interests. Mart interpreted my informality and particularly my external perspectives as being far-sighted and bold and leading only to common policies. Although I wasn't really deceiving him – I don't believe in a federal Europe – I do believe in harmonising our approach one way or another by agreements, as long as we don't get all these directives and regulations; that is what I object to, the power of the Commission and the law-making. But as to agreements – I'm all for those.

Back to the airport and flew back to Northolt in the snow. Lovely to be home.

*Thursday 20 January*
I got into the office at 8.30 this morning. Brian Sedgemore, whose appointment as my PPS was announced today, was there; we had a talk and went over a speech I am giving at a Tribune Group meeting tonight.

Cabinet, and we had a revealing discussion on the Bullock Report on industrial democracy which has just been published. [2] Jim said this was an explosive issue. It could be like the Tory Industrial Relations Act. He was afraid it would cause polarisation.

* Christian socialist, Liberal MP for Barnstaple 1935–45, but founded the Common Wealth Party in 1942 and fought Putney as the Common Wealth candidate in 1945. Fought and won Gravesend for Labour in 1947, resigning in March 1955 over the hydrogen bomb. Between 1942 and 1945 the Common Wealth Party won Eddisbury, Skipton and Chelmsford.

Edmund Dell thought the defects were that multinationals must be allowed to control their own investment and if they couldn't (because of interference from employees) they would stop investment here and move money out. The election of workers couldn't be left to the trade unions because the House of Commons wouldn't accept it. The draft statement we put out, said Edmund, should not reject the minority report with its proposals for two-tier boards.

Then we came to devolution and I raised one point – that in the provision for a referendum there should also be a referendum for electors in England. I said I forecast that we wouldn't get through a bill under which the English were not also allowed to vote.

On the extent to which Scottish and Welsh MPs' representation should be concomitantly reduced at Westminster, it was suggested there should be a Speaker's Conference to consider it.

'That is not going to discuss proportional representation, is it?' I asked. No, I was told.

*In its attempt to provide devolved political powers to assemblies in Edinburgh and Cardiff, through the Scotland and Wales Bill, the Government got itself into a great mess in the course of 1977.*

*The pressure for devolution was not new. In Scotland, which is a nation, calls for Home Rule go back to the days of Keir Hardie and the ILP, although there have also been some notable Conservative proponents of devolution. In Wales devolution has more often been argued on cultural and linguistic grounds, parts of Wales having large Welsh-speaking communities. In 1964 a Secretary of State for Wales (Jim Griffiths) was appointed to put the administration of the principality on a more equal footing with Scotland.*

*By 1976 successive Labour Conferences had agreed on the principle, and a commitment to elected assemblies for the Scots and the Welsh appeared in our 1974 manifesto. As Leader of the House, Michael Foot was put in charge of the formidable task of preparing legislation, and John Smith, who had been Minister of State in my Department, was transferred to work with him. The Scotland and Wales Bill, providing for separately elected assemblies in Edinburgh and Cardiff, was introduced into Parliament at the end of 1976.*

*The principle of a referendum of the voters in Scotland and Wales, to be held once the bill was law but before its implementation, was also included in the bill. But so strong was the opposition to the bill during the committee stage in February 1977, not least from English MPs fearing the diminution of Parliament, that a 'timetable motion' or guillotine to limit the legislation time for the bill's passage was defeated by 29 votes. The bill was thus seriously delayed. Subsequently the Scotland and Wales Bill was abandoned, and bills dealing with devolution in Scotland and Wales separately were introduced in late 1977 and passed in 1978.*

At the end of the Cabinet I passed a note over to Jim. Yesterday he had sent round a minute to all senior Ministers:

10 Downing Street

19 January 1977

**BREVITY**

The papers which I see – memoranda and reports addressed to me personally, as well as papers for Cabinet and its Committees – are too long; and they seem recently to be getting longer. . . .

We cannot afford inflation in words and paper, any more than in our currency. It is often harder work to be brief – but only for the writer. We shall all benefit as readers. Let us adopt again in our Ministerial papers the habit of setting out in plain words, and in short paragraphs, the main points (detail in appendices, if need be) and the recommendation. The same discipline should apply to memoranda etc. addressed to the public bodies outside Government and to the public. Please take any necessary action in your Department to achieve this. Your Permanent Secretary should inform the Head of the Civil Service of what has been done and he will report to me.

L.J.C.

So in reply my note said:

Secretary of State for Energy

P.M.

BREVITY

O.K.

AWB
19.1.77

and I attached to it an extract from Mao's collected works which began: 'Let us now analyse stereotyped Party writing and see where its evils lie.'

I feel my relations with Jim are improving. I think maybe he needs me on the industrial democracy front, and now that Sedgemore is appointed I feel more cheerful.

After lunch I had a meeting with Friends of the Earth, and we had a fascinating discussion about civil liberties and nuclear power. They put a lot of questions to me; I said I would get them answered and write to them.

With Caroline, Stephen, June, Hilary and Rosalind to the Central Hall for the Tribune Group meeting. The whole left was there: Ian Mikardo in the chair, Neil Kinnock, Dick Clements, Mark Saunders, Lawrence Daly, Barbara Castle, Jack Jones, myself, Michael Foot, Fenner Brockway, who made a marvellous speech, Jimmy Reid and Donald Soper. A tremendous turnout.

*Friday 21 January*
Got up at 6.30 and caught the little Hawker Siddeley 125 to Rome. There we were greeted by the British Ambassador, Sir Alan Campbell, with the inevitable Rolls Royce, and a police escort driving at speed through the streets of Rome to the Department of Industry, a Mussolini building of massive proportions, designed to reduce man to just a speck, with huge, ugly, stained-glass windows greeting you half way up the marble staircase. A typical Italian office – no women, and lots of soldiers saluting with guns.

We got there early and the Minister for Industry, Carlo Donat Cattin, was late because the Italian Cabinet was having a long and bitter discussion about economic cuts.

We had translators, and it is difficult having a discussion in translation because you don't look at each other; when you are capable of understanding what is being said it is coming from the interpreter and not the other Minister, and when he is speaking there is no reason to look at him because you are not expected to understand. But it is courteous to listen – I pick up a bit and get the flavour from the man's face, but Donat Cattin did not look at me at all while I was speaking, and I tried to watch him while he was speaking but he was looking at the interpreter, and at a piece of briefing material he had.

He said that the Italians want a complete Community energy policy – that is to say regulations and harmonisation, and a full policy in which the Community controls all the energy. So I thought very carefully as I listened to this and, though I disagreed with it and could knock it to pieces, I decided to say, 'This is a marvellous subject for a discussion. Will you please publish it and we'll have a discussion about it; it is just what I need in my public debate on Community energy matters.'

He was vaguely hostile, ordered a cup of coffee for himself but none for us, wasn't at all friendly.

Got to London about forty minutes ahead of schedule, and my driver Ron Vaughan zipped me to Paddington, for a train to Bristol.

*Saturday 22 January*

Up early for my surgery all morning, then to the hall where the all-day policy conference of Bristol Labour Party was being held.

I stayed for about three hours, shivering in this icy-cold, bare hall.

But the meeting was a display of basic democracy and basic decency. There was the chairman sitting on the platform entirely by himself and a chap sitting at another little table who was the head of the standing orders committee. He had a little handbell which he announced he would ring after three minutes, and twice after five minutes if the speaker didn't stop, then he would blow his whistle. Everyone laughed.

Most of the people were delegates and the agenda dealt just with Bristol issues. The first part was housing and the homeless, then direct labour, then resolutions about the Lord Mayor's office, and so on.

It was a mixture of socialists, Marxists and Christians, with powerful speeches about the immorality of evicting families: seven families have been evicted in Bristol, they said. One was an old man dying of cancer, another was an old man with asthma, another a battered wife with two children.

One of the delegates, a Bakers' Union shop steward, who has lost his job in one of the big mergers of the local bakeries, got up and said, in an Irish accent, 'It's the morality of housing that we're after. Society is a chain, and the strength of a chain is its weakest link, and the wealth of a society is the wealth of its poorest members.' Tremendously moving.

Herbert Rogers made a brilliant speech attacking the quarter of a million pounds wasted on the Lord Mayor – which infuriated some of the old councillors.

*Monday 24 January*

The *Daily Mail* this morning had a picture and story under the headline 'The Day Wedgie Sent in the Marines' with an account of my allegedly having ordered the marines to seize a German trawler in December. It was carefully designed to do damage to me in meetings later today with German Ministers.

I sent for the relevant documents and discovered that some German trawlers had violated the safety zone around the oil rig *Beryl* last December. A note had been sent to my Minister of State, Dick Mabon, who had said, 'See what else you can do', and the Navy had been asked to send in a patrol. I suppose one shouldn't get excited about these things, but when you are attacked you do get angry.

Went over to Number 10 and waited until about 11.55 for Helmut Schmidt, who had come in by helicopter to Battersea heliport and was being brought by car accompanied by Jim.

The discussions covered Portugal, Rhodesia, the forthcoming summit and the economic situation, and Schmidt then said he would like to mention one question about the debate going on in Britain on co-determination – this was a reference to the Bullock Report. He said he understood that industrial democracy was a big problem in the UK: he knew the CBI was opposed to intellectuals and the trade unions, and there were risks and problems here, and he thought it only fair to warn the British Government that, whereas co-determination in industry, ie worker representatives on company boards, worked easily when there was growth, in a recession it made the unions more defensive and there were dangers of communists, Maoists and Trotskyites among the rank and file wrecking it all. This is the group that Schmidt calls 'the Chaotics'.

Crosland remarked that the Japanese were committed to 7.6 per cent growth and the trouble with Japan was that their aid levels and their defence spending were so low. So Schmidt said, 'How can you force the Japanese to rearm? Or to increase their defence expenditure?'

I was asked to comment on energy and I said I had had good discussions during a series of meeting of all the energy Ministers. We had identified the germ of objectives – conservation, nuclear power, refinery, coal and coke, European Atomic Energy Community (Euratom) and so on.

We moved upstairs and I had a word with Schmidt. I asked, 'How's your nuclear debate going?'

He replied, 'Only the communists in West Germany, the Chaotics, are against nuclear power.'

I said, 'The Russians told me they are a bit worried about it too.'

'Ah well, they have a big programme.'

He takes the view that nuclear power is absolutely right and that anyone who is against it is part of the sandals and brown bread brigade, as they are called. Very interesting. In a way, nuclear power is a left–right issue, with CND, those concerned about radioactivity and most of the miners lined up against the scientists.

We went into lunch and I was at a table between Herr Günther van Well, the Deputy Secretary in the Foreign Office, and Georg Leber, the Defence Minister. The Ambassador was there, plus Jim's Private Secretary Ken Stowe, and Tom McCaffrey, the Press Secretary at Number 10.

I talked to Leber a bit over lunch. I thought I might as well take advantage of his presence. I said, 'I am trying to understand the parliamentary and political systems on the continent. Tell me about your party. How does it work? First of all, how do you select a candidate?' He described the German system, which is more democratic than the French. Then I asked him about Cabinet meetings and he said, 'We try and reach a consensus. We don't actually vote. We put our hands up, but it is a collective decision, not like the French Cabinet, where Giscard simply decides what to do and everybody takes their instructions from the top.'

### Tuesday 25 January

The press was full of hysteria today. *The Times* had a headline, 'Benn Backs Labour Marxists', quoting an interview I had given to the *Cambridge Review*. There was an item claiming that the National Executive Committee was trying to set up a Marxist party with me as leader and that this called for a democratic anti-Marxist coalition; and Joe Haines had a huge piece in the *Mail* saying 'only a coward or a fool could ignore' the Trotskyite challenge.

There was also a small item stating that Jim Callaghan and Jack Jones were working together to change the composition of the National Executive.

This evening I had a long talk with Eric Heffer, Brian Sedgemore and Audrey Wise and the good old left. We mainly discussed how to handle Militant at tomorrow's NEC. Then I went up and dozed a bit. Finally the House rose at about 4.45.

### Wednesday 26 January

After very few hours' sleep, I got up at 8; my first meeting was the National Executive.

The first item of any substance was the resolution by Tom Bradley that we note with concern a number of newspaper reports of entryist activities and instruct the National Agent to update his paper on the subject, if possible by the next meeting of the NEC. Eric Heffer moved an amendment that the reports were Tory-inspired and designed to damage the Party: 'The movement should not assist the media in their campaign; we welcome the unity of the Party and must not condone constitutional irregularities in our search for a democratic solution.' Eric said he had known the Militant Tendency for a long time and the issue had been blown up out of proportion.

Frank Allaun said we couldn't get into the position where we started interrogating everyone – did you sell, did you buy, did you read, did you contribute to *Militant*? Why not *Tribune*? That was the sort of thing that would happen if we passed this.

Joan Lestor said she hadn't read the reports but an inquiry would cause damage and the press would love it.

Michael Foot said we were in a fine old muddle; we were helping our opponents, it was a mistake not to look at Reg Underhill's report, and the Tribune Group had been an *open* conspiracy. He suggested there should be a sub-committee of five to look at it.

Kinnock feared an exodus from the Party, not entryism into it.

Shirley Williams said that Tribune and the Manifesto Group were different from Militant. Joan Maynard observed that these were not new problems; there had always been groups in the Party, and we wanted to continue the debate on ideas.

I said that nobody wanted a witch-hunt or expulsions, we had all been through that before, and we all wanted to help the Party and resist attempts to undermine it; the Tories and the press were more our enemies. We couldn't suppress Reg Underhill's views or reports and we should automatically make available all the material he has. I went on to say that there were many tendencies in the Party and they all enriched us; I didn't want to harass or suppress any of them, even if they were critical of me.

'What really worries me is that there is such a vacuum of ideology or thought and discussion in the Party that any little sect can fill it, but it can't *control* the Party – I've never known a *Leader* who could control the Party. So what we should do is to open up the problem and have confidence in our capacity and strength to deal with it.'

Tom Bradley summed up that he was disappointed with the reaction, that penetration was the problem, that Militant talked about revolution in the streets. He supported Michael's proposal.

It was agreed by 10 votes to 9 that there would be a special committee to look at it.

Foot was wobbling about, Hayward was all over the shop, and Bradley and John Chalmers were for rigorous action.

I had clearly voted against Jim and against Michael Foot on the sub-committee proposal, on the principle that I do not want it focused on a particular issue.

Then the Agee and Hosenball business came up.[3] Judith Hart reported on a meeting with Merlyn Rees, who had said he could do nothing. Would Jim receive a deputation because the law was so insufficient, and couldn't there be judicial procedures?

Jim said he couldn't accept judicial procedures where lives were at stake, any more than in Northern Ireland.

After that I came back to the office and had a meeting with Kearton and Dick Mabon about how to deal with Amoco. The President of Amoco Europe, Mr Aune, who is apparently a discourteous and offensive guy, has declined to give us the voting we want, participation in all fields, and special arrangements. We agreed to have a meeting next Monday to try to clinch it.

*Thursday 27 January*
Cabinet, where we discussed health and safety representatives at work. Albert Booth, having been rebuffed in the autumn about implementing the Act passed in 1974, came back and said we really *must* do something, and he started very sensibly by stating the problem. Eight workers a day are killed in industry, there are 3000 accidents a day, 23 million man days lost by accidents – which is four times as many as by strikes – at a cost of £200 million a year in industrial injury benefit.

Albert said the number of people employed was dropping but the number of accidents was not, and therefore the rate of accidents was increasing. He said the Health and Safety Commission and the TUC were implacably opposed to any delay or phasing of the implementation of the Act and he was prepared to find £12 million from his own resources in order to finance some of the costs which were alleged to be necessary.

Alan Watkins of the *Observer* was coming to lunch and I had very mixed feelings about seeing him. He's very rumpled and messy and he said to me, 'I'm pretty cynical really, you know. I like the eighteenth century.' I asked him about the eighteenth century. 'Well, you know there was a great flowering of the arts and reason and writing, and London society was much more disrespectful than it is today.' I've never studied the eighteenth century at all, I know nothing about it, and he recommended me to read J. H. Plumb.

Then he went out of his way to say things designed to be friendly. He observed, 'The Common Market has been a disaster, hasn't it?', and I said, 'Well, it's very bureaucratic.' Then he went on, 'You know, your articles in the *Guardian* in 1963–4, when you were expelled from Parliament, were the best I ever read in that series.' Well, that was unnecessarily friendly. He added, 'I've got your book of speeches. You speak for the Seventies in a way that no one else does; you understand, and speak for the aspirations of the people. Did it worry you when you were criticised violently by Bernard Levin and all that?' I said that it wasn't very pleasant but I was glad it happened early in my career because it makes one more serious.

I felt it wasn't just flattery on his part. He continued, 'You see, I feel myself to be a craftsman, I am a writer and I polish everything I write, and I say to myself when I publish it, Is it the best I can do? I try to make it that, and I'm proud of what I write', and then he began bemoaning the way that craftsmanship is being driven out by modern society. I said, 'Well, the cash society has no room for the craftsman.' Then we talked about the sovereignty of Parliament and about lawyers and politicians, and he remarked, 'You know, if I had to choose between being governed by Dennis Skinner or by the Master of the Rolls I'd rather have Dennis Skinner' – a curious comment from somebody whom I think of as a moderate. Lord Denning, he said, had got some idea that the sovereignty of Parliament was not part of the British constitution; that there was some moral law which overhung everything.

I got an insight today, which really made me feel quite disposed towards him. He is a cynic, he is not enthusiastic, he writes for the establishment, not for the public, but he was undoubtedly trying to be friendly.

This evening to Copenhagen, where we were met by the first British woman Ambassador, Anne Warburton. She is an economist, was in America during the war, went to Somerville, joined NATO as an economic analyst, then to the United Nations and in 1960 joined the Foreign Service. She lives a life entirely remote from other people's daily lives, in a beautiful eighteenth-century house, owned by successive British Ambassadors since 1850, with beautiful paintings, and a beautiful ballroom. I was put in the royal suite.

### Friday 28 January

Went down to breakfast and found a photographer from *Woman's Own* who was photographing the Ambassador for a piece in the magazine. I was asked to take part in that, so I was photographed with her. Then I went to the Ministry of Commerce, where Per Haekerup, the Danish Minister, and various of his colleagues were waiting for talks.

The Danes are extremely worried about energy. They want conservation to be in a way imposed on them, because they have had a problem with an energy tax which they couldn't get through their Parliament.

We flew back to London Airport. Ron Vaughan was waiting at the bottom of the aircraft steps, and I jumped into the car and we raced to Reading, where I caught my train to Bristol with half a minute to spare.

To the Tobacco Workers' Union, where I did a fantastically long surgery full of the most tragic problems, then went to a ward meeting, which was extremely interesting because there were a lot of young people. This young couple, Dawn and Mike Primarolo, have really made that ward party come to life. It was an excellent meeting – criticism and discussion of the Government, and what the Party should do and how to keep it together.

### Monday 31 January

I went over at 4 o'clock with Jack Rampton to Number 10 for nearly two hours with the PM and the Chairman of GEC, Arnold Weinstock, and the Deputy Chairman, Lord Aldington. We were really there to discuss nuclear power, but Weinstock began by saying there had been great negligence on energy.

He was completely out of his depth, and I was asked to comment. I said that I didn't agree at all, we had a very active energy policy, but what we didn't have was a nuclear decision. Then he went on about the PWR, which he wants for GEC, he attacked the SGHWR, he attacked the AGR, he attacked previous Governments, he attacked the industry, the unions, the select committee – he had a case but he overdid it. I said, 'Look, the fact is that we are the strongest energy country in Europe. We don't need as much nuclear power as the French or the Germans or the Italians. How much do we need and what do we use to fill the gap? There is a choice between three systems', and so on.

Jim is clearly much impressed by Weinstock, and I had a strong feeling of the power of the industrial/political complex – this great industrialist and a right-wing Labour Prime Minister and the whole of the Civil Service behind them. I felt very powerless. But I will try to stave it off.

*As Secretary of State for Energy I was faced with major decisions relating to the future direction of the nuclear programme, including the type of thermal reactors to choose. Having abandoned plans to continue with the costly steam-generating heavy-water reactor (SGHWR) in 1976, we had opted for two new advanced gas-cooled reactors (AGRs), a model which had been operational for over two decades and in which we had invested heavily. But the AGR was opposed by those, including Weinstock, who favoured the pressurised water reactor (PWR) on the basis of its export potential and lower production costs.*

*There were known safety problems with the PWR and little experience of the larger-capacity models which would be required to meet Britain's energy needs. I favoured delaying any plans to build the PWR until further research had been done. The PWR was subsequently rejected, to re-emerge as an issue for the Conservative Government after 1979.*

*During my period in office, I also had to decide whether to go ahead with a commercial fast breeder reactor programme. One FBR, which unlike thermal reactors uses 50 per cent of the potential energy in uranium and in effect breeds its own fuel, was already operating experimentally at Dounreay.*

*I was not against a prototype commercial fast breeder, provided that it did not commit us to a large programme before the problems of reprocessing, waste disposal and safety had been properly addressed through an inquiry. There were also the wider implications of security and civil liberties that such a dangerous programme would inevitably involve.*

*The report of the Royal Commission on Environmental Pollution, chaired by Sir Brian Flowers, had been published at the end of 1976, and it reflected a general and growing concern over the whole nuclear programme, questioning the desirability of large quantities of plutonium in an unstable world, and of depending for our energy supplies on such hazardous materials.*

### Tuesday 1 February

At 9.30 this morning, Frances Morrell's daughter Daisy, who is three and a half, came to the office. She had her hair done in little bows, and a red coat and a red anorak, and she was all shy. I showed her round the office and took lots of photographs of her and Frances.

Had a meeting of the North Sea Renegotiation Committee, which I chaired. We came to the impact of our participation policy on Common Market legislation, or rather the impact of the Treaty of Rome on our participation policy, and the lawyers who have been studying it say the deal I made with Shell-Esso under which I let them have the oil on a buy-back arrangement is a breach of the Treaty.

The Attorney-General, Sam Silkin, who hadn't read his brief, was simply bloody awful. He was obstructive, difficult, negative, but I have seen him do it before: he makes these pompous statements but if you listen respectfully and then sum up he always accepts the summing up, so I wasn't unduly worried.

### Wednesday 2 February

Home at 6 after a late sitting. Got up at 8 for a meeting of NEDC at 9.30 chaired by Jim Callaghan. He began by saying that it was a very important meeting, that the working parties of each sector of NEDC (engineering, manufacturing, etc.) had been very valuable, and that we had enough analysis and now we wanted action. There were certain more favourable factors – sterling was more stable, there was a more general realisation of the need for a strategy, world trade was weak, and only the United States was likely to see unemployment fall in 1977. The level of unemployment was a great handicap to what we were trying to do, but he said it was not just a British phenomenon.

Lord Watkinson, who is President of the CBI, said he knew this was not the place to discuss Bullock but he must speak; the Government had said that it wished to get away from the policies of confrontation and that we would need a united effort; employee involvement was a part of it but it must be based on consent. He said the CBI could not accept the majority report of the Bullock Committee: it wouldn't win consent, and therefore legislation on it would be divisive and unworkable and would prevent economic growth; this was the view of his membership.

Jack Jones then said he regretted the matter had been raised – there had been no indication that it would be discussed, and the TUC would make no comment on it whatsoever.

I'll just record a few thoughts about Neddy today because I believe it will provide interesting material for students.

First of all, who was on it? There were seven Ministers, five trade-unionists, seven members of the CBI (if you include the bankers and the independent people), three chairmen of nationalised industries, the Chairman of the National Consumer Council and the Director-General. If you analyse it by political allegiance, there were thirteen Labour and eleven non-Labour, and if you look at it another way there were four ex-communists – Len Murray, Hugh Scanlon, Edmund Dell and Denis Healey. The other fact about it was of course the very strong corporatist strain. Here are these top chaps who meet together and are going to decide at the top and then tell people down the line what they have to do, and try and involve them. It is no doubt how good kings fended off democracy, and it has nothing whatever to do with democracy. The third point is this obsessive secrecy, combined with hand-wringing that they couldn't get through to people.

Well, I went back to the office and had a sleep and at 2.45 we had a discussion on how the National Economic Development Office report on nationalised industries should be handled.

It was a fascinating discussion because NEDO had suggested a two-tier board and various other things, all designed to stave off any real industrial democracy, and to avoid Government interference. The Treasury meanwhile are working on a new White Paper on the financing of nationalised industries, which is going to incorporate all of the doctrine; I remember that the last one, which Otto Clarke, my old Permanent Secretary at Mintech, had worked on, became our bible.

The Treasury had come up with a new concept of financial return called an RRR – a realisable rate of return. So I said, 'Well, I'm in favour of a CSF', and they asked, 'What's a CSF?' I said, 'Common sense factor – I don't believe in all this jargon.' It turned out that Fred Atkinson, my Chief Economic Adviser, had invented the RRR. 'Well, whatever you do,' I added, 'leave it flexible in some way. Bring in some common sense, particularly on how to get energy policy matters somehow integrated into the pricing structure.'

Afterwards I went down to a party in the office for journalists. I wandered round and talked to them in a friendly and informal way and it certainly was a much nicer atmosphere than a year ago. I made a little speech saying how important their work was and how there are various theories about who runs the Department. If you read the *American Energy Review* you would think the Department was run by the NUM and the Friends of the Earth. If you believe the editor of *The Times* you would think the Department is just the sub-branch of the National Youth Office at Transport House, and if you read Ray Dafter in the *Financial Times* then you will know that, of course, officials run the Department.

'Actually,' I said, 'the truth is that it is run by the Press Office. They get all their information at the Christmas party, they think about it for a month and then they feed it all out during January, and the rest of the year we just do silly things like have energy conferences, publish brown books and statistics. To prove it's all run by the press I will read the minute which my Press Office sent round about this meeting. "Tonight's party for the Press Office will give journalists the full opportunity to explore through casual conversations with Ministers and officials progress on two oil-related items which are currently topical, the announcement on fifth-round licensing, and our participation talks with Amoco. Since all who will be representing the Department tonight will no doubt wish to maintain a consistent line if asked about these issues, it might be useful if I describe the line that the Press Office has been authorised to take."'

I said, 'I have to stop there because the last two paragraphs – which tells you the Press Office line – have been classified top secret by Sir Jack Rampton.' There was a lot of giggling and amusement.

Went home exhausted.

*Thursday 3 February*
To Cabinet at 10.30. It was pouring with rain and there was a big traffic jam, due I think to a bomb scare in Whitehall. I had to run the last couple of hundred yards from Birdcage Walk to Number 10.

Unfortunately I have lost the notes I made at Cabinet – whether I left them at the Cabinet Office or dropped them somewhere I don't know. Anyway I shall have to dictate it from memory.

First of all next week's business, then a long discussion about how to handle the Scotland and Wales Bill because the Chief Whip reported that on his best estimate, after a great deal of lobbying and canvassing, we would be defeated by 39 votes on a timetable motion (guillotine). Michael Foot said it might be better to advance the referendum issue in the bill and get that out of the way, and then proceed to the guillotine later.

The draft wording of the question which would be on the ballot paper for the referendum was read out: 'The Government has suggested the establishment of a Scottish Assembly under devolution proposals contained in the Scotland and Wales Act, under which Scotland would remain a part of the United Kingdom. Are you in favour of the implementation of this Act in Scotland?' And the same for Wales.

Third item was the defence White Paper and we went through some discussion about it. We are spending much more of our GNP on defence than everybody except the Americans.

Fred Mulley made one complaint about how he had to pay 8 per cent VAT on fixed-wing aircraft he bought for the services but 12.5 per cent VAT on helicopters. So I said that it would be wildly popular if the

Chancellor announced a cut in VAT on helicopters in the Budget – which caused some amusement.

Came back and had lunch with David Wood of *The Times*. He was born in Grantham, I think, and knew Margaret Thatcher's father, a local shopkeeper who became an alderman; he remembered the daughter when she was a little girl. We had a long talk about the Samuel Smiles Victorian ideals of self-help, duty, etc., which David Wood believed in.

He remarked, 'Margaret Thatcher's a very cautious woman, you know, very cautious. She will have to get rid of Airey Neave and George Gardiner* and broaden her base; she may be bold in thought but in action she will be very cautious. She wants to get on with the trade unions very much and thinks she can: she sees no reason why she shouldn't. She knows they are powerful and she has got to learn to live with them. That's the way the Tories operate.'

I said, 'Well, Wilson tried the same thing with the CBI, but when it comes to the Election they all vote against you and organise against you.'

Then I had a three-hour meeting with David Owen and Ruud Lubbers, the Dutch Economic Affairs Minister, and Hans Matthöfer, the German Technology Minister, and officials, about Urenco, the Dutch/German/British uranium enrichment consortium which we are currently chairing. We had a long discussion about export policy, where the Dutch are very much against the German deal with Brazil under which the Brazilians would get equipment to reprocess their own fuel elements and create weapons-grade plutonium. I think it is a most revolting deal but I was heavily briefed against criticising it publicly. The Prime Minister has expressed some doubt but we have never criticised it openly.

I was sickened by this and I decided I would do something about it. I had to go over to dinner with Caroline in the House, and afterwards Brian Sedgemore came up and expressed great interest in what had happened and asked if I had been in touch with Jim. So during the next Division I went up to Crosland, then to David Owen, then to Jim; I said to Crosland and Owen that I felt very uneasy about this Brazilian affair and I wanted it to be discussed by Ministers because I thought we ought to consider the likely implications of all this.

Crosland looked bored and said, 'Well, I'm in favour of that', and Owen said, 'Yes, very strongly.' I mentioned it to Jim, and later that night I drafted a minute to him suggesting a talk.

* Two Conservative MPs on the right of the Party, very close to Margaret Thatcher; Neave, head of her Private Office, was assassinated in March 1979.

*Friday 4 February*

The press today had a number of items I must record. The Social Democratic Alliance* has published a paper suggesting that Jack Jones, Hugh Scanlon, Ray Buckton of ASLEF and other trade union leaders were traitors and didn't believe in parliamentary democracy and so on; this was taken up by the front page of the *Sun* and became a great big story in the *Telegraph*. It's just an indication of what will happen. Once they have got rid of Andy Bevan, then they will go for the unions and then for the Party as a whole – you can't buy them off.

Donald Maitland, our permanent representative in Brussels, came to see me. He said, 'After your press conference in Brussels, they all took up the point you made about the difference between centralisation and progress.' This was taken as a significant comment, apparently – that the strengthening of Common Market institutions and devolution were compatible.

I said, 'Well, it isn't the case really. We spent hundreds of years building up all our hopes of making the House of Commons the instrument of the popular will, and if you now say that a Scottish assembly that hasn't been established and a Common Market parliament that hasn't been elected are to wield great powers, you are throwing away our history – you are substituting voting for democracy.'

The next item I had to deal with was Amoco. In effect, the long discussions with Amoco which went on until midnight on Monday night and which were supposed to be concluded on Tuesday had foundered on the simple point that the President of Amoco Europe, Mr Aune, the Amoco executive, Norman Rubash, and the lawyer, Ed Bissett, had declined to accept the form of words that Shell and Esso had accepted: namely that they would have a statement of intent as to their refinery policy in Britain and their readiness to try to optimise the use of North Sea oil; and that they would conduct their trade in a way that would maximise the benefit to the United Kingdom. They would not accept this because they claimed it would commit them legally to a £100 million investment in the Milford Haven refinery and they were not prepared to do that.

So I said to Frank Kearton, 'Will you stick with me if I am strong?' Frank was terribly keen and the officials did in effect agree, so I called in Aune and Rubash at 11.15 without any of the others. They had been warned of the attitude I would adopt and I think they wanted to test it.

With me I simply had James Bretherton (taking notes), Frank, and John Liverman, and I asked Aune and Rubash what had gone wrong. They produced a long explanation about how the whole thing had

* A right-wing pressure group in the Labour Party, led by several GLC councillors, 'accusing' union leaders of 'pro-Soviet' sympathies.

changed, they had never understood that what was wanted was this, and they had produced another draft. I said, 'Look, I am not negotiating it. We were going to settle the whole thing on Friday and we went through the words very carefully.' They said that the board of directors would never yield their powers over investment.

So I said, 'You told me you were fully authorised to discuss it.'

'Well,' they said, 'will you look at this new draft?'

'No. I cannot go beyond the Shell-Esso arrangements.'

Rubash looked absolutely white. Aune looked shifty.

I continued, 'That is it. You are dealing with Her Majesty's Government and these participation talks are intended to make a real difference. We are not prepared to be pushed. You are not dealing with a sheikh in the 1940s, you know, you are dealing with the British Government in the 1970s.'

'Well,' they said, 'This hundred million clause . . .'

'I never mentioned a hundred million,' I said. 'You invented it and then you say it is a barrier. We have never asked that, but it is intended that there should be deep discussions about your market policy – that is what the whole thing is about. You have to value the goodwill of the host government, and, if you don't attach importance to that goodwill, that is a matter for you. Will you please let me know by tonight.'

While we were talking, messengers came in with tea, so I turned round and waved my hand and they took the tea away. I was just coming to the end of the discussion and inside I was boiling with rage – I felt like the president of a banana republic dealing with a multi-national company. I'll never forget that experience with Amoco. If they won't co-operate they won't get participation, and they won't get the licence, and that's it.

*Saturday 5 February*

At 9.30 a producer from the BBC came to discuss the Edmund Burke programme I have been asked to make. It will be recorded on a Sunday in June. I am going to look at Burke's Bristol period and the four issues he took up in his life – America, the French Revolution, Catholic emancipation, and his attitude, as an MP, towards Parliament.

I got home and worked like a fiend from about 1.30 to about 7.30, did my red box, signed all my letters, then put a few things in my satchel, put on my anorak, went to Liverpool Street and caught the train to Southminster, not having told Caroline, Lissie and Joshua, who were at Stansgate for the weekend, that I was coming.

I thought I would walk all the way to Stansgate but it would have taken about an hour and a half and I didn't think I would make it so I rang Caroline from a call box. Actually she had been asleep for an hour but wouldn't hear of me walking all the way and got out of bed. I had got about a third of the way to Stansgate when they picked me up. It was lovely, and I would have been absolutely miserable at home on my own.

### Sunday 6 February

I am reading the *Life of Edmund Burke* by Philip Magnus written in 1939, in preparation for the television lecture. It is a lyrical biography, full of praise for Burke's principles and oratory and philosophy, yet even an author as uncritical as he cannot but acknowledge the fact that Burke was the most corrupt man, always looking for places for his relatives, supporting his brother, who was a no-good, in his ventures in the West Indies and India. His support for the American colonists was the sort a British Tory would have given Ian Smith in Rhodesia. His connection with Bristol was most fortuitous. He was invited to Bristol in the middle of elections and held the seat from 1776 to 1780, when he withdrew, knowing he would be defeated, and went on to represent Malton, a pocket borough of Lord Rockingham's.

Burke emerges as a most unsympathetic, reactionary, decadent man. Still he was a great writer and he influenced his times; and there is no doubt he is one of the few of that period whose names have survived because of their writings.

Came back to London, and I just caught the end of Colin Morris's TV programme *Anno Domini* interviewing Enoch Powell, in which he absolutely massacred Powell. Enoch had been comparing the role of the politician to that of a prophet, challenging authority and being persecuted because of the unpopularity of his views. Then at the very end Morris asked, apropos immigration, 'Where do you inject moral values into what you say?', and Enoch was completely lost for words. He had allowed himself to be led on, and when it came to applying Christianity to the black family next door he couldn't answer. It was most effective.

### Monday 7 February

Joe Haines's book, *The Politics of Power*, is being serialised in the *Daily Mirror* and included a slashing attack on Marcia Williams. Marcia, who is in bed with a slipped disc and can't get up, issued a statement saying that Joe Haines had once had a whisky bottle broken over him and she had had to sponge his coat. So it looks as if the gang has fallen out. Apparently this afternoon Harold went to visit Marcia at her bedside.

### Tuesday 8 February

The Marcia Williams/Joe Haines/Harold Wilson row continued today. Haines alleges that a Tory MP, Captain Henry Kerby, had asked Wilson for a peerage in return for secrets from the Tory Party. Wilson denied that he ever knew the story. George Caunt, one of Wilson's old aides, supported Haines and said he had had to throw Marcia across the room and on to a couch to shut her up. It is doing such harm to Wilson, which gives me wry pleasure. But it is also damaging the image of people at the top and gives an insight into the way leadership operates.

Had a meeting with Roy Hattersley and Joel Barnett about coal prices. Put broadly, I want to preserve the investment programme for the mining industry but don't want to price it out of the market. Barnett wants high prices to ensure there isn't a claim on the contingency fund and Roy Hattersley wants to keep prices down.

At 12.15 Frank Kearton came into the office to discuss Amoco and we agreed that he write to withdraw the offer to volunteer participation. I said I would note that and I got clearance from the Prime Minister, subject to David Owen's and Harold Lever's agreement, to announce the fifth round without Amoco tomorrow.

At 2.15 Arthur Scargill came along with an anti-nuclear campaigner from Cornwall, and Arthur was telling me about his anti-nuclear campaign, which he said would grow into as big a movement as CND.

I went over to the House, had a short briefing meeting, and discovered that BNFL had been given approval to continue taking fuel for reprocessing to be stored in cooling ponds until the oxide plant at Windscale (Thorp) was approved.[4] I was cross that it had been done without my really realising what had happened.

Went into the Chamber and there was a tremendous row. First of all Jim Callaghan asked Mrs Thatcher to condemn the fascists in her party if he was to condemn the Marxists. She said, 'I regularly do', and Jim said she didn't. But why he should have to condemn Marxists I don't really know. We don't condemn people for their opinions but for what they do.

*Wednesday 9 February*
Up early, and my first appointment after a brief talk with Bernard Ingham was a TV interview with the BBC's Michael Charlton about nuclear power. He was very pro-nuclear, pro-American, and he flushed up quite a lot during the interview. I hope I was calm. I tried to be reasonable and said we must have time before we went ahead, this was a very awesome responsibility, and so on.

At 10 I had a Japanese delegation enquiring about reprocessing at Windscale; they are afraid they are not going to get their waste reprocessed. I said we were partners with them, and we wanted it settled quickly.

I had been told that, after I had seen the Japanese Ambassador on a previous occasion about Windscale, the message the Japanese sent back to Tokyo had been very full and accurate, which confirmed that we have a way of intercepting messages from the Japanese Embassy back to Tokyo. It also indicated that the Japanese must come in with little tape recorders secreted about their persons which pick up everything said by anyone they visit, because the information is so accurate. I asked why I couldn't have one – it would be rather handy!

At EY [the Cabinet Economic Committee] we came to a paper on international aspects of unemployment. To cut a long story short, the paper said there was nothing you could do about unemployment – it was an international problem. Then it listed a lot of measures we should urge on other countries.

I said that it was all very well saying unemployment was an international problem but what was the impact of this on domestic politics? Whereas a few months ago the Tory papers were calling for cuts in public expenditure, now for example they were running a campaign about the poor quality of hospitals, which implied we needed more public expenditure; we were now likely to be attacked for higher unemployment by the very people who have called for it, and we wouldn't be able to get away with it.

It was a friendly meeting, but what interested me was that not one of the members of a Labour Government – senior members of an economic committee of a Labour Cabinet – mentioned socialism or the socialist analysis once in their discussions. I tried to raise – though not explicitly – that the crisis of capitalism, the effect of democracy and the need for intervention are socialist points.

Today I announced the fifth round of North Sea licences for oil. My statement was long and boring and there was no cheering when I sat down. Then Tom King, the shadow spokesman, got up and attacked it, and I clobbered him. I clobbered every Tory who got up and criticised it. Patrick Jenkin [Conservative MP for Wanstead and Woodford], who had been Minister of State at Energy, was quaking. It cheered the Party up no end because it hadn't heard a Labour Minister hammering the Tories for ages.

Caroline came and watched from the Gallery, and then we went to a dinner which Tony and Susan Crosland were giving for the US Ambassador, Anne Armstrong. Henry Moore, the sculptor, was there – I've never met him before, but years ago he wrote me an awfully nice letter about my peerage case. He is eighty; his wife is Russian by birth, and left Russia when she was five.

Also there were Hugh Trevor-Roper, Daniel Bell (Professor of Sociology at Harvard), Harold Lever, Michael Palliser from the Foreign Office, David Basnett and his wife, and the Labour MP for Belper, Roderick MacFarquhar. Tony made a speech for which he actually had a text – it was very unusual. He was funny about George III and former ambassadors who had become presidents and so on.

I went with Roderick MacFarquhar to the House to vote and then returned, and had a little talk with Anne Armstrong. I asked her if she was going to put life back into the Republican Party.

She said the Republican Party was quite different from any of the parties here, and that the Republican philosophy was of course for less government. She is a real Republican committee woman, absolutely done up as if she has come out of a bandbox.

*Thursday 10 February*
Cabinet, and Jim said, 'Before we start I would like to mention the Silver Jubilee; the Cabinet ought perhaps to consider giving a gift to the Queen – a token of some kind.' So Shirley Williams suggested a saddle, because Jim had said we want to give her something she would really use. Someone else said don't forget that Parliament gave Charles I a saddle, at which there was a lot of laughter.

I said, 'We are a Labour Cabinet, so if we are going to give her something shouldn't it be uniquely Labour?' I added, 'I am not suggesting a leather-bound volume of our Constitution' – at which there was a sort of groan around the whole Cabinet. Fred Peart put his head in his hands and Jim said, 'Let him finish.' I continued, 'Well, I think we should perhaps give her something that comes out of the labour movement. I have got in my office a vase, given me by the Polish Minister of Mines, carved out of coal by a Polish miner. What about that?'

Elwyn Jones said, 'Well, in Wales we have beautiful clocks set in carved coal', so the suggestion wasn't entirely ridiculed. But I was interested in the reaction to the idea that we should give her something representing the work of working people.

Peregrine Worsthorne came to lunch; he is the associate editor of the *Sunday Telegraph*. I asked him about his work. He said he wrote on a Friday, and tomorrow he was going to write about Marcia and Joe Haines, and that the whole story reveals how corrupt government is, and why it should not have too much power. His article will show in effect how unfit for government Labour is, that respect for authority has been eroded by it, and this is damaging.

I told him my theory of the forty-year cycle: that there have to be real radical reforms about every forty years – 1832, 1867, 1906, 1945, 1980. He said, 'Yes, but next time they will be right-wing. Mrs Thatcher will tear up the welfare state by its roots, and the health service and education. That's how the radicalism will manifest itself.'

I said, 'Maybe you are right, you know. It is going to be pretty disruptive.'

He added, 'She is prepared to deal with the unions as a power but with no social contract or wage control – she doesn't believe in all that; she will just deal with them as a power in a monetarist society.'

So I said, 'Well, you know Heath tried that with his monetarist policy, but he had to reverse it, and I think she will have to reverse it too.'

He asked me, 'Aren't you worried about the power of the unions?'

'I know what you mean – the middle class is worried – but if I look at the powerful groups I have to deal with, the unions are only a part. All right, Jack Jones is powerful, but that's nothing compared to what Fleet Street can do – it pillories you, holds you up to excoriation, Bernard Levin says you are mad. I feel like poor old Solzhenitsyn in Russia, except that Fleet Street can't actually put me in a lunatic asylum. There is the power of the big oil companies who operate here, and are bigger than nation states. There is the IMF, which forces us to cut the welfare state. In that jungle of power I don't see the unions as being dominant.'

Worsthorne told me, 'I am not in favour of a further stage of reform. I think that the establishment now needs to be defended, needs to have some backbone put in.'

I said, 'In 1970 the establishment thought: when Heath comes in he will know all the answers, he'll take us into Europe and discipline everybody. But by the time we came to power in 1974 the establishment was totally demoralised.'

To ENM, the Cabinet Energy Committee. We had a sort of very neutral and inadequate paper from officials suggesting the response the Government might make to the Flowers Report (the Royal Commission on Environmental Pollution). I referred to one paragraph on security and civil liberties in which Brian Flowers had implied that there might be some problem of security in a plutonium society and of countervailing restriction of civil liberties in dealing with it.

They said that we had to have some defence machinery for plutonium, and I said, 'Of course, I appreciate all that; indeed, I introduced the Atomic Energy Authority Armed Constables Bill.'

'So what are you worrying about?' they asked. 'You're not suggesting that anyone should be able to go into a plant and pick up plutonium!'

'No, you must have protection, but then if you do that what effect does it have on civil liberties? What I'm saying is that we have always been against an armed police force, and now we have got guys going up and down the country with sub-machine-guns guarding plutonium when it is on the move – that is a problem. And there are surveillance problems around the power stations and Windscale.'

Merlyn remarked, 'Look at all the security we have in Northern Ireland; you have to get used to it.'

I said, 'That is the whole problem, Merlyn – in Northern Ireland a civil war makes it necessary, but the English people might not want Northern Ireland security standards introduced into Britain *without* a civil war, merely as a by-product of nuclear power.'

Shirley supported me a bit, as did Albert. Anyway we agreed to come back to it, and they asked, 'Well, what's your suggestion?'

'Very simple – we should say that Parliament must look at these matters.'

'Interesting for a seminar,' said Bill Rodgers, 'but I don't see the point of it.'

It was a most revealing discussion. I think they were only just waking up to what the whole thing is about – what I call the nuclear police state.

The next question was on the National Waste Management Corporation; the officials suggested that the corporation should be under Peter Shore's control. This matter is actually under consideration by the Prime Minister, and my officials don't want waste management handed over to Peter Shore. But I do, because, as I said, the Minister promoting nuclear power shouldn't be responsible for disposal of its waste.

Dick Mabon spoke passionately against me, although he is my Minister of State, so I said, 'I must make this absolutely clear: I have seen the paper, I have considered it, and this is my decision.' Merlyn said a minute had gone from the Cabinet Secretary to the Prime Minister along the same lines. At least I had the Prime Minister on my side.

They said, 'You can't hold up nuclear power just because the problem of waste hasn't been sorted out.'

'That is exactly the point – indeed the *Financial Times* this morning made it clear that the German courts had ruled that the Germans couldn't start more nuclear power stations until they knew how the waste could be dealt with.'

Albert Booth said that they hadn't solved the problem of vitrification, they didn't know where to put the waste, and this was an absolutely major matter.

In the end, after a discussion of about forty minutes, we decided to adjourn it. I must say I was absolutely thrilled.

*Sunday 13 February*
Had a late lie-in. There was another extract from Joe Haines's book in the *Sunday Times*, describing in detail how the Treasury had effectively organised a coup in the summer of 1975 by failing to buy sterling, in order to create circumstances in which the Cabinet would agree to statutory pay policy. It threw such doubt on the way in which officials behaved that it made the Haines memoirs worth reading just for that alone.

Hilary looked in yesterday. He has been elected political education officer of his local party and delegate to the GLRC of the Labour Party.

John Cunningham rang to say he had spent the weekend at Windscale trying to sort out a strike there; he is trying to head it off. Of course as the local MP he also has a constituency interest in it.

In the evening Peter Shore (without Liz), the Baloghs, the Booths and the Foots came for dinner. We began discussing the Haines thing, inevitably, and the scandal of the Treasury coup and all that.

I said I thought this was the moment for open government, and Michael Foot blazed with anger. 'What do you mean, open it up? We are fighting for our lives, we have got to defend ourselves. Do you want Thatcher in for a generation? Have the *Daily Mail* sitting in on the Cabinet? Is that what you are arguing? It would destroy us for ever. Drive discussions into secrecy.'

He went on, and was red-faced and angry, and it was a bit of a shock. I was calm, and said I wasn't saying that, I was saying we should identify the choices. 'Aren't you prepared to defend the Government?' accused Michael.

We went on to discuss pay policy; I said I didn't think we were going to get away with a pay policy, we were going to have to change it, because the unions wouldn't give us a pay policy without the alternative strategy, so we came back to that. Michael was furious about that too. He is sensitive because his policy is failing. Otherwise it was quite a pleasant evening.

*Monday 14 February*

This morning the papers reported that Tony Crosland was in hospital having been taken ill yesterday, and as the day proceeded it became clear that he was critically ill.

He evidently had a stroke and is deteriorating. Later in the day Bob Mellish came up to me and told me he was not expected to live. I asked Roger Stott, Callaghan's PPS, and he confirmed that in fact he might well die tonight, but that in any case he could never come back to work. I must say, looking back on it all – though I mustn't assume the worst – he really is my oldest political friend. I have known him since 1943 when he came back to Oxford on leave from the paratroopers and we spoke together in a debate. That is an enormous length of time and, although he has been arrogant and on the right of the Party and difficult and supercilious and so on, I recognise that underneath it all there has been a kindness of heart and gentleness of manner and personal sympathy which I found immensely comforting and helpful. He supported me on a number of occasions, although we have been on entirely opposite sides of the Party. I really feel very sad for him,

Foreign Secretary for less than a year, at the peak of his parliamentary career at fifty-seven.

More revelations in the papers this morning by Joe Haines, including that the CBI and the City demanded my dismissal as Secretary of State for Industry: this is not anything new, but just confirming it.

In the afternoon I was interviewed for the BBC *Europa* programme. The interviewer began by asking, 'How is it that you, a bitter anti-European, can . . . ?' Next question: 'Why does someone who is bitterly anti-European . . . ?' So I stopped the discussion and said, 'Look, it is entirely up to you what questions you put to me and I am not trying to change them, but I don't have to do the interview and quite frankly all that presentation does is to destroy my credibility before I even begin.' I added, 'Let's drop it.'

They got into a panic and suggested leaving out that question. I said, 'Well, I don't mind a question at the end about my own opinion, and I will tell you what my view is, but don't put me on a charge right from the start.' They were thoroughly embarrassed and conducted it as I wanted.

I had a brief word with Frances Morrell and Francis Cripps about a minute from Walter Marshall proposing that we go in with Iran and supply them with sensitive technology on nuclear matters. I have no intention whatsoever of doing that. They suggested I take it up with David Owen and Fred Mulley.

At the Commons, Dennis Skinner came up and said, 'Crosland is dying and there'll be a reshuffle. Watch out because they may well try and move you away from Energy to Trade.' I think the miners realise I have done a good job for them. I told Dennis I hadn't really thought about it, which is true – though I am beginning to think of it now.

I heard that the Tribune Group met this evening and decided to put down a motion at the next PLP meeting about the election of the Party Leader by Conference.

Johnny Prescott, the MP for Hull East, who is also the leader of the Labour Party delegation in Europe, came to me tonight in the Tea Room and said the Party had to take very seriously the European direct elections because £2 million each year was being tucked away by the European Parliament and would only be available to finance parties which fought the European elections.

Well, once you accept financing from the centre you are establishing a completely new convention, namely that democracy is funded by bureaucracy, and thus the corporate state becomes complete.

*Provision for the election of representatives from each European Community country to the European Parliament by direct voting had been made in the 1957 Treaty of*

*Rome. But by February 1977 no system had been introduced, representation up until this point being by nomination from each national parliament.*

*The Community saw Britain's acceptance of direct elections as central to our commitment to the European idea, and indeed Harold Wilson had agreed to the principle at the Paris summit meeting of heads of government, in December 1974, before the Common Market Referendum, without consulting the Cabinet. By July 1976, a 410-seat Parliament had been agreed upon and elections were planned to take place simultaneously throughout the Community in every country in 1978 (this was later changed to 1979).*

*Many members – if not a majority – of the Parliamentary Labour Party opposed direct elections because they were seen as consolidating the EEC and giving it a veneer of popular support, as well as establishing a second parliament challenging, or undermining, the authority of the House of Commons.*

*When the European Elected Assembly Bill came before Parliament in 1977, there was much dissent. The first bill had not completed its passage before the end of the 1977 session and had to be re-introduced and debated a second time. The following pages record repeated arguments in Cabinet and elsewhere over the principle and particularly over whether or not collective Cabinet responsibility would be enforced at various stages of the bill.*

*Tuesday 15 February*
Derek Ezra (Chairman of the NCB), Alex Eadie and a number of Labour MPs from mining constituencies – Neil Kinnock, Alex Wilson, Gwilym Roberts, Peter Hardy, George Grant, Joe Harper and others – came to lunch. We discussed the mining industry and the problem of incentives, and it was useful, although Neil Kinnock and Gwilym Roberts did all the talking, and infuriated the real miners – the clever boys dominating the discussion against those who had real experience. Here were two young men whose fathers and uncles had been miners pitched against men who had themselves once been working miners. Interesting.

During lunch I slipped out and spoke to the Administrator of the Radcliffe Infirmary at Oxford and there is no doubt Crosland is dying – they don't know when. Later I heard from David Owen that he had never heard doctors so pessimistic about a stroke patient. Susan is with him and apparently is all right unless she meets friends and then she breaks down.

It's 2 and I am going home. I forgot to mention that at 7.30 for half an hour Frank Muller, from the Australian Labour Party, came to see me. He's an environmentalist and he told me briefly about the Australian labour movement's growing determination to stop uranium mining in Australia. He said the mining is of no particular benefit to Australia, it benefits the international uranium companies, and he thought there was a possibility that those interests had contributed to the overthrow of the Prime Minister, Gough Whitlam, in November 1975. He knew something that indicated that the companies were discontented with the Labour Party and the trade union attitude towards uranium before the election following Whitlam's removal.

It was a bit conspiratorial, but it was interesting, and I described the position here frankly – the enormous power of the nuclear lobby in Britain and my fear that we would go under to it. I wondered if Australia would be able to hold out so long on uranium that it could impose a moratorium worldwide. It has opened up as a left–right issue in Australia.

The facts are fascinating and I do find it one of the most interesting arguments at the moment. He was a serious, bearded, sensitive guy, a zoologist by training, employed by an environmentalist group financed by the Government. It gave me a new dimension to it all. There's a lot to be said for not being dependent on officials.

### Wednesday 16 February
First engagement was at Number 10 for a joint meeting of the Cabinet and the NEC. Tony Crosland absent of course, and the latest news is that he has died mentally. He is really a breathing corpse. It's tragic.

Jim Callaghan began by saying that this should be one of a series of meetings between the Cabinet and the NEC. We would only win the Election if we got closer. That was the desire of both the Cabinet and the NEC too, and was a good start. But, he said, the NEC had been too negative and should tell the country more about the Government's achievements.

Eric Heffer spoke. 'As to the role of the NEC, Jim says it is being too negative, but I do not agree with that. Conference decides our commitments; the publicity put out by Transport House is positive; the Executive is not made up of left-wing crackpots. But what do Ministers say on unemployment? The Tories will call us the party of unemployment. Job creation is not enough and the first sub-committee we set up here should be on unemployment. The Tories will deserve to get in if we don't solve that problem. As to prices, Shirley did nothing on prices in her first year: we must have working-class interests at heart, and prices are the key. Some people don't have working-class mothers-in-law as I do, and action on unemployment and prices is essential.'

Frank Allaun thought the cuts and the job creation schemes together meant we were sacking people from real jobs and creating unnecessary ones. 'The TUC and Labour Conferences won't accept cuts.' He said he was reading the Crossman *Diaries* for 1967 which said that we would lose the next Election because of the cuts. If tax relief was possible, why not withdraw the cuts?

Denis Healey said, 'You can't run the finances of the country any differently from the way you run the finances of the Party. The trade unions are not satisfied with the Party finances.' He was just being provocative, really, about Norman Atkinson, the Party Treasurer.

Then Denis added: 'After the cuts we will still be borrowing £8.7 billion on the PSBR next year, and I am nobody's slave, neither the slave of the civil servants nor of Transport House nor of Ron Hayward. But the rules of arithmetic are inexorable and they cannot be compromised. Creditors fix the value of our money. The Labour Conference pushed the pound down. Shirley did all she could on prices, and so, now, is Roy Hattersley. Don't bleat to the Government about things we can't control. To move half way towards each other from opposite sides of the Grand Canyon would be a disaster. The alternative strategy would be to abandon the international approach in favour of the siege economy. Jack Jones and Hughie Scanlon are helping the Government; why can't the Executive?' Well, that was Denis, clear, strong and provocative.

When it came to my turn, I said, 'We have a common interest in sustaining the Government, implementing the manifesto, developing a common programme for the next Election, winning the next Election and implementing the programme; and the Tories want to divide us, destroy the Government, frustrate the manifesto, make a common programme difficult and defeat us at the Election. It is hard for the Government. We haven't a parliamentary majority. There is the slump and international pressures and difficult negotiations with the TUC. The Tory appeal now is that if you get rid of the Government you will have free collective bargaining.'

Finally Jim spoke. 'We are all aware of the joint responsibility of this meeting. Barbara asked me to withdraw the word "negative" about the Executive but I won't withdraw it. I shall never forget the public demonstration organised by the Party against the Government.

'The difficulty is that the Cabinet thinks that the economic policy is right. The Cabinet has talked it through honestly. You can't talk Denis Healey out of his policy. You can't ask the Cabinet to adopt a policy it doesn't believe in.

'Now,' said Jim, 'I don't say I was always right. The National Enterprise Board* is valuable and I was wrong in opposing it. But the Government cannot be shifted on the kernel of economic policy; the trade union leaders may find it difficult and may fear they are being confronted with suicide but there is no reason why we should hand them the knife.

* The NEB was set up by the Labour Government in 1974 with powers to channel public funds into industry and to acquire key companies for public ownership where the national interest required it. Its powers were progressively weakened between 1975 and 1979. See *Against the Tide 1973–76*.

'Industrial democracy is important, and we have got to look at tactics and objectives. The CBI accepts legislation and worker directors, but participation in the body of the company is the starting point. This is the best way to get the CBI to talk. The nationalised industries can certainly go ahead with worker participation, for example in the Post Office. Yes, we should have an unemployment working party, yes, one on industrial policy, but a manifesto committee – not yet.' Jim hoped the response would be constructive and said we should continue joint meetings. Well, that was all.

One of the advantages of doing a diary is that when you dictate it from notes at night, or in this case the following morning, you do get a slightly different feeling about it. I came away feeling that Jim had absolutely clobbered the Executive and that there had been a lot of ill will, but it was just a debate, a regular old Labour Party discussion. The fact that we met together I think was worthwhile. I've been through so many periods when one thinks there is going to be trouble but in the end there never is.

Anyway I went back to the office and Robin Day came to lunch, the first meal with him for ages. I have known him for years, since 1945.

Over lunch he said he didn't like Mike Yarwood imitating him because Mike Yarwood had him on TV more often than he was on himself. I asked him what he would like to do in the future. Apparently he applied for the job of Director-General of the IBA and of the BBC and was turned down. He said he thought there was too much trouble whenever he got involved in anything.

I asked him if he would like to go into the House of Lords, an idea which excited him very much. He is fifty-two or fifty-three, a year older than me, and we all have to begin looking forward. I think Crosland's illness and impending death is making everyone think a bit about the future.

Then he talked a little bit about politics, about how Mrs Thatcher was a radical, that John Biffen would probably be Chancellor, Howe would get the Woolsack and that she would be a great reformer. This is the Tory line now. He didn't think there was a shift to the right at all, and of course he is the great architect of the notion of 'left-wing extremists' and all that. In all his broadcasts it is always the left-wing, the left-wing, the left-wing.

I didn't try to be provocative and it wasn't a very memorable lunch, but an agreeable one.

I had a word with Dick Mabon – he was angry that I had cancelled a meeting about Marshall going to Iran. I said I was not going to be pushed into a great nuclear deal with Iran just because Marshall had initiated it. Marshall had absolutely no right. The story is that he went to Iran and talked to Dr Etemad, Minister of Nuclear Energy, whom I have known for years, and Etemad had suggested a complete linked nuclear deal in which Iran would put in money in return for a huge nuclear programme – of course the real object is military nuclear technology. It is quite clear that in the end that is what they want – the power to make the bomb. Nuclear policy does have its own foreign policy; it makes you do deals with Brazil, with Iran, with South-West Africa on uranium. It is something that moves you to the right on everything – very interesting, fascinating.

Brian Flowers came at 6.15 and stayed for an hour and a half; I really enjoyed it and I somewhat poured my heart out to him. 'Look, I really want your help because the whole nuclear thing is getting out of control. The lobby has got me by the neck; I don't know what to do about it. But I do want a new scientific adviser.' He said, 'You're right to remove Marshall – you can't have Marshall as scientific adviser and Deputy Chairman of the AEA.' He suggested Sir Hermann Bondi from Defence, who would like to come, but Rampton doesn't want him.

We talked about civil liberties, the way in which the lobby was working, and how it might be checked and watched. It was candid and extremely friendly.

*Thursday 17 February*
Cabinet began at 10.50. Devolution came up under parliamentary business and Michael Foot told us there would be a timetable motion for Tuesday to limit the debate on the Scotland and Wales Bill. Mike Cocks said, 'It's too risky.'

Jim said we had to go all out to win. 'What if we lose?' David Ennals asked. 'Have we thought about that? Before we decide to go ahead with it, oughtn't we to consider what we do if we lose?'

So Jim replied, 'Well, I am afraid I am not prepared to have that discussed in Cabinet. Cabinet is a very leaky place.'

On foreign affairs, David Owen sat in for Tony, who is lying literally on his death bed in Radcliffe Infirmary. David said that messages had reached him that Vorster, the South African Prime Minister, thought that Smith would accept black majority rule in Rhodesia in two years.

On President Idi Amin of Uganda, Peter Shore asked for more information about the killing of an archbishop and two Ministers, in effect by Amin. The men had 'confessed' to plotting against Amin, and I think he had then arrested the three men, and said later they had died trying to escape.

Peter asked, 'Do we have to have Amin at the Commonwealth Prime Ministers' Conference?'

So Jim said, 'Well, there is not much we can do. We are not the ones who invite people to the Conference. It is the Commonwealth Secretariat.'

Of course in the back of our minds is the possibility that if we did keep him out, which I suppose we are entitled to do, he might kill every English man and woman in Uganda as a reprisal. He is a brute.

Back to the office, and Alastair Burnet of ITN came to lunch – part of Frances Morrell's veto-lifting campaign (getting me to talk to people in the media) – and he was extremely friendly, indeed he went out of his way to be. He came in beaming and charming, and I sat him down and gave him a drink – he drank gin, I think. He said, 'You must be busy with the Agee and Hosenball case', so I said, 'We haven't discussed it in Cabinet. We don't discuss the prerogative issues.' He didn't realise that. I said a lot of industrialists couldn't believe we didn't debate the Budget before it was announced to the House of Commons. But it's true.

Then we talked about the House of Lords. He said that Mrs Thatcher believed very strongly in hereditary peerages, and she might reintroduce them. I commented, 'Well, Home could be made an earl again, you know – a *life* earl', and I went into all the peerage complexities. He asked me if I would go on ITN to discuss the result of the Stechford by-election, which was called after Roy Jenkins got the Presidency of the European Commission. I said it would depend on Transport House – they would decide who was the best person. Probably they would want Roy Hattersley, who knew the Midlands much better. He has asked John Biffen on and I said I'd like to do it very much with Biffen but I was not good at all the electoral statistics. So if that comes off it will be very nice.

At the end of lunch I said, 'You know all the interesting political discussions are now in the theology programmes, because that is where you can have a discussion without being bullied by Robin Day and all that. Colin Morris's *Anno Domini* has the best serious interviews.' Then he came back to the point that Robin Day had made the other day – that in fact *News at Ten* was meant to be a series of interviews.

I had a long talk with David Owen about the Marshall proposal for a deal with Iran on nuclear technologies and nuclear co-operation, and David agreed to send a minute out on it. I would write a report and that would take it out of the hands of the Department of Energy. I was very pleased about that, and he said he would see Michael Palliser, head of the Foreign Office, who would have a word with the Prime Minister or the Cabinet Secretary, Sir John Hunt.

Well, then we had a little bit of a talk about his own position and I said I didn't think he would get the Foreign Office but I was interested to know what job he would like. He said Environment or Health or something, as long as he got in the Cabinet.

At the PLP the question of Agee and Hosenball was raised by Stan Newens [MP for Harlow], who said, 'I don't want to go into the merits of it, though there is an absolute sense of outrage, but we must have a debate, just as in Opposition we forced one on the Tories when they expelled Rudi Dutschke.' After a couple of other points were made, Merlyn said, 'Well, I am afraid I can't say more than I've said, namely that I looked into it very carefully, it was a matter for me alone, I was advised that these men were a security risk, this is not a political deportation but a security deportation', and that they had been in contact or whatever with enemy agents or something – he got quite a reasonable hearing from the Party.

*Saturday 19 February*
Heard on the 7 o'clock news that Tony Crosland died earlier this morning. It is extremely sad. He was so very good to me, taught me economics, helped me get a seat, was kind to me in Parliament, and under that gruff and arrogant exterior he really had a heart of gold. I liked him very much. I know other people didn't, and I was often critical and scornful of him and thought all this intellectual stuff was much overdone, but he did, through his book, have a profound influence. He was the high priest of revisionism or social democracy in the Labour Party for a generation, and the book will be studied and read long after his death.

*Sunday 20 February*
Melissa's twentieth birthday, bless her. She is such a lovely girl and she is a great source of pride to the family. She got all her presents and was thrilled.

The papers today are jampacked with obituaries and tributes to Tony Crosland.

Roy Jenkins rated him above any living socialist philosopher. The rest of the papers went into an emotional spasm about him. I must say when I read it all it struck me that, all right, he was a very nice guy, he wrote a good book, but if I look back over his political career I can't honestly say his judgement was particularly good. Certainly *The Future of Socialism* misread the underlying crisis in a capitalist economy.

And, I had better be candid, I felt a twinge of jealousy at the thought of the guy who was going to be appointed to the Foreign Office tomorrow by Jim Callaghan. I suppose like anybody else I am ambitious and feel it is a bit hard to take if others are jumped above me.

*Monday 21 February*
We had my weekly Ministers' lunch which Brian Sedgemore, Dick Mabon and Alex Eadie attended. I must say it was amusing. We just joked most of the time. We talked about this right-wing group which met on Saturday with Bill Rodgers in the chair. Dick Mabon had

attended it. About a hundred people turned up and they decided to set up the CLV, Campaign for a Labour Victory, a cover for a right-wing organisation designed to clear the National Executive of some of its left-wing members, of the women's section, and so on.

Dick, whom I like personally very much, was talking about the 'legitimate left', and I said, 'Am I a member of the legitimate left?'

'Oh yes, but the legitimate left has got to be careful it doesn't pave the way for others to come in.'

So I said, 'Well, if I am the legitimate left I regard you as the authentic right.'

I addressed the Tribune Group later and said there was a rift between the Party and the Government, which had peaked during the IMF discussions. The Cabinet and the Executive were now meeting to try to resolve it, and working back from next Election polling day we had to reach an agreement. The dilemma for the social democrats was that high public expenditure based on full employment, which would thus redistribute wealth, was no longer an option. There was a harsh choice to be made between monetarism and the Labour manifesto, and that meant investment and public accounting and industrial democracy. I said we had to win the argument because the centre had fallen away, and inequality could no longer be accepted as an engine of capitalist growth. We should work for a united Party and deal with some crucial questions – the machinery of government, parliamentary democracy in dealing with appointments, the House of Lords and Party democracy.

After I had spoken a succession of points was made.

Audrey Wise said all credibility had disappeared; there was a terrible deterioration of morale in the Government.

Dennis Skinner said that we must have a debate which raised the level of the argument. That is what the manifesto was for. We must argue about issues including those which the Government wanted to ignore. The situation was absolutely chronic; a change of attitude by Labour voters was very evident. We must argue about the manifesto, about the House of Lords. The Tories if they got back could be so incapable of dealing with the situation that there would be a further swing to the right.

I went from there straight to Broadcasting House to participate in a tribute to Tony Crosland, beginning with a profile and then a discussion.

Then to the House, and heard that David Owen had been made Foreign Secretary at the age of thirty-eight – a fantastic promotion. I must say it entertains me slightly that Roy Hattersley, David Ennals, Eric Varley and even Merlyn Rees and Shirley Williams have not got that job. Jim has created a new star in the labour movement and he has got another twenty-five years to go. If you begin as Foreign Secretary at thirty-eight you are an absolutely dominating figure.

Well, had a chat in the House of Commons, came home. Judith Hart has been brought back in as Minister of Overseas Development, and Frank Judd has been moved to the Foreign Office as number two to David Owen, which was quite a skilful move, and Joel Barnett has been put in the Cabinet.

I saw Merlyn as I was leaving and he said, 'What do you think of what Jim has done? Don't you think it proves that foreign affairs don't matter any more, compared to the economy?' I said, 'Not at all. Of course they're important. First of all, economic problems are now very largely seen as international, and secondly the Foreign Secretary has got an absolutely crucial job to do in setting our relationship with the Common Market. Are we to be a major nation or are we going to be submerged into a federation? These are crucial questions.' Merlyn was taken aback a bit, and I said I was delighted for David.

*Tuesday 22 February*
In the Commons there was the vote on the guillotine motion to limit the time available for the Scotland and Wales Bill and we were defeated by 29. Twenty-two Labour MPs, I think, voted with the Tories, quite a number abstained, and we were absolutely smashed.

It is a very big political event because we won't get the bill through now. The Government will have to think about what it is going to do. It is a major defeat. The Scottish Nationalists are absolutely furious. Quite what will happen in Scotland and Wales I don't know. It could become a nasty situation, very quickly.

Afterwards Michael Meacher looked in, very discouraged generally. I think we must have a little group of people to sit and discuss what we should do politically, such as Judith Hart, Eric Heffer, Norman Atkinson, Ian Mikardo. I feel very negative because the trade union leaders are so hostile to any criticism of the Government, which they take to be criticism of themselves.

Came home and began on my red box. Today the magazine *Theology* arrived with my review of Milan Machovec's book *A Marxist Looks at Jesus* and comment by the editor, David Jenkins.* It is going out next week. I wasn't brought into socialism by Marxism, but I am trying to introduce Marxism into the mainstream of the British Labour Party debate because, frankly, without it I believe the Party has no political future.

---

* Joint editor of *Theology*, 1976–82; Bishop of Durham since 1984.

*Wednesday 23 February*

The NEC had a long discussion following up the joint NEC–Cabinet meeting last Wednesday. Ian Mikardo said he greatly regretted Jim's comments that the Executive was negative, and Mik went on and on and on. Frankly, if the Government is going to be attacked by the Executive, the Executive can't be too sensitive if it is attacked by the Government.

I said I thought we ought to be practical; we were going to have a campaign committee and we should have these sub-committees which were agreed to. For my own part I thought it would be a good idea if we moved towards a manifesto fairly soon, so that we could campaign on it and address the public and not just ourselves.

Jim, who was a bit more conciliatory today, said, 'Well, I really don't want the manifesto looked at yet; it is too early.'

Came back to the office, and had a meeting on oil depletion policy. In effect the Department said: Don't intervene, because there is not going to be as much oil coming on as quickly as we thought. Francis Cripps had suggested we delay it a little bit. In the end I summed up by saying that we would stimulate the exploration programme, that BNOC should play a part, that we should aim for an annual forward look at production based on home use and the export need. We should then negotiate company by company on the development plan, cutbacks, refineries, the development of smaller fields, and we should keep all our instruments available for use. There was general agreement on that.

Francis Cripps came to see me in the office. Frances Morrell had not come across with him, which is strange, because normally they hunt in pairs. I think Frances was upset about yesterday's *Morning Star* report of my speech to the Tribune meeting. I had said the middle ground had faded away and there was a choice between monetarism and the manifesto, and she thought that was awful, that I was scaring the centre of the PLP. Then she had been angry, I think, about my review of the book *A Marxist Looks at Jesus*.

Francis Cripps had come across in effect to say the same thing. He thought people were getting nervous; they didn't like the feeling there was a stark choice, and he told me I mustn't use language which was frightening, or be abrasive. He said, you are a very valuable instrument, you must use your skill in order to meet this middle-class anxiety. And he was worried about the book review as well. He argued, 'Look, the rehabilitation of Karl Marx has got to wait.'

Well, then in came Brian Sedgemore, and he warned me that the press would blow up my piece on *A Marxist Looks at Jesus*. He said, 'You haven't put your own position in it. It will look as if you are a Marxist; indeed, it might even look as if you were attacking Jesus. Nobody will read it, it will just be built up by the popular press', and so on.

Well, by this time I felt pretty discouraged. If Francis Cripps, Frances Morrell and Brian Sedgemore all say I am wrong, it does just blank me out a bit. And Michael Meacher said last night that he thought I had really been effectively destroyed by the mass media. I feel very depressed by it all.

Anyway, Caroline came in, bless her heart, and we went to dinner with the Speaker. First time I had ever been to the Speaker's flat in the House of Commons – you go up in a little lift above the state rooms. The other guests were Bill Rodgers, Merlyn, Cledwyn Hughes, Joel Barnett and wives. I felt a terrible sense of gloom. There were all the pro-Market people, all Cabinet Ministers, and I didn't enjoy it; I don't think Caroline did much either. I do like George Thomas, and I get on well with Joel and the others, but I felt the one thing you couldn't discuss was politics. Here we were at a political dinner and there was no possibility of a really political discussion between us. I was very quiet.

### Thursday 24 February

My first meeting was at the Economic and Industrial Pay Committee on police pay which was held in Room A of the Cabinet Office. I found myself sitting next to Merlyn Rees, and I asked him what he was going to do about Amin coming to Britain for the Commonwealth Prime Ministers' Conference. So Merlyn pushed across to me the departmental brief from the Home Office, and the key words were these:

Normally heads of state are exempted from immigration controls. The Immigration Service still shudders at the memory of the uproar that followed when a new immigration officer tried to make General de Gaulle fill in a landing card.

That really must have been a story in itself.

At Cabinet we discussed what to do about the Scotland and Wales Bill, now that we have been defeated on the guillotine motion to restrict the bill's timetable.

Michael Foot circulated the draft of a statement he would like to make today which would confirm the Government's support for devolution, propose all-party talks on the bill, and suggest that we should proceed without a guillotine and that we should have a motion which would carry the bill forward to the next session. Jim said that the alternative would be an immediate referendum bill, but there would be constitutional dangers in that; and the vote for independence might be inflated by the disappointment of the last few days.

The SNP wanted to see Jim, so did the Welsh Nats, and, said Jim, we *must* respond. He thought the lesson we should learn was that we would not get the bill through in its present form now or even in the next session. The English dimension had now emerged, UK feeling had been stirred, and the question was whether this bill could survive even if amended. Do we continue with the bill? Our objective must be to hold our political position, and remember the electoral considerations.

Merlyn Rees said he thought the Government could be brought down. He was not against a select committee but we must kill the independence theme. Denis Healey argued that to hold a referendum now before the bill was through would be a disaster and would maximise the separatist vote.

Shirley said she was afraid of violence in Scotland and asked, Couldn't we consider Heath as chairman of a select committee? Roy Mason said the Party was demoralised. The English MPs were sick of it all; we couldn't legislate this session or next, therefore he suggested a consultative referendum. Fred Mulley was very gloomy. Jim encouraged everyone not to be gloomy.

Bruce Millan favoured an immediate referendum. Bill Rodgers said we should abandon the bill, proceed with caution and get our parties to fight against Scottish separatism. John Silkin said there were two pluses. First of all there would now be room in our programme for other things; second, we could have longer recesses, and he favoured a referendum now.

I spoke next and I said I was not gloomy, but we must get it right next time to avoid another defeat. I said, 'We can't take it back to the House of Commons, we haven't got a parliamentary majority on the floor, and we couldn't be sure of control of a select committee. Second, we shouldn't have a referendum because with no bill or no majority to allow us to implement the decision it would be useless. Remember de Gaulle lost the Presidency by staking it on a referendum on regionalism: one can imagine circumstances, for example, where the Scots voted for independence and we couldn't help them, the Welsh voted for the status quo and repudiated our bill and the English seethed because they haven't been allowed to vote at all – which I warned of earlier. Third, I don't want all-party talks. The Tories want to weaken us, they want to obscure, as far as the public are concerned, their opposition to devolution, they want to paper over the cracks in their own party, and they want to retain their complete freedom to issue an attractive manifesto commitment whenever they like. We would lose control.

'Where have we got full control? The only place we have got full control is in the Cabinet: therefore we should have a Cabinet commission to hear evidence in public. It is a standard practice to have Cabinet commissions to look at constitutional matters, and the Home Secretary has done it in the past, in respect of the constitution of the Channel Islands. We should publish the evidence and an interim report, and the Party meanwhile would campaign for devolution.'

I passed a note to Michael Foot saying such a commission could consist of the Lord President, Home Secretary, Environment Secretary, Scottish and Welsh Secretaries, and the terms of reference would be to consult with representatives of public opinion on the Government's devolution proposals.

Poor old Michael Foot is in a real difficulty. As Leader of the House he has got us into a situation from which it doesn't seem easy to extricate ourselves.

Jim summed up. 'Well, we haven't got a majority, so whatever we do can only be done by consent, and we must allow the evolution of thought to continue. Michael should make a statement.' Jim didn't rule out the idea of a Cabinet commission, it needed time, but he queried the extent to which we should progress with the bill, and it was agreed to defer the matter.

David Owen was at Cabinet in his first appearance as Foreign Secretary; he reported that the talks on Rhodesia at official level between the United States and the United Kingdom had begun. Amin might not in fact come to Britain for the Commonwealth Conference because he might not dare to leave Uganda, but we had taken soundings among Commonwealth members about whether we should keep him out, and we wouldn't get a majority if we tried.

That was the end of the Cabinet, and I went straight to Broadcasting House to make a programme with Keith Joseph. Lunch first with Greville Havenhand, the senior producer of *Analysis*, and Sir Keith Joseph and his researcher. Frances was unable to come because she had a bad cough. Keith is an absolutely tortured soul – he was in agony, his face twisted in anxiety, his head in his hands. He was scribbling notes, and worrying; he really is a sick man. We talked about Heath, and the U-turn, and what Heath's Cabinets were like; Keith said most discussions took place in Cabinet committees, there was a sort of Inner Cabinet and the Cabinet as a whole did not discuss very much. Keith Joseph himself realised his mistake about policy and now favoured more open government. I tried to be jolly and cheerful. Then we went and recorded a forty-five-minute discussion.

### Friday 25 February

Saw my Under-Secretary Chris Herzig about a minute I wrote yesterday to the Prime Minister in which I spelt out some of the problems in the nuclear policy field. It pointed in quite a different direction from that of the officials and of course, when I come to think of it, the fact that the Department was asked to supply Number 10 with a background paper indicates that they were seeking to bypass me. It is the policy considerations, not the nuts and bolts, that we have got to look at carefully. These are very grave issues and I am determined to deal with them.

Cabinet at 10, and we spent the whole morning, and half an hour after lunch, on the direct elections to the European Parliament.

Roy Hattersley told us that when Wilson was Prime Minister he had promised that Britain would agree to all the elections taking place on a single day. 'There is a danger of us welshing on our commitment,' said Roy. All the Welshmen shouted, and Roy said, 'I didn't know the word "welsh" had anything to do with the Welsh', so I added, 'You had better scotch that.'

Jim mentioned that five out of six of the most senior members of the Cabinet are Welsh members: himself, Merlyn Rees, Elwyn Jones, David Owen and John Morris – which is an indication of the extent to which he has used his powers to get Welsh people in.

Anyway, Roy Hattersley continued, 'The next thing we can do, therefore, is to try and fail.' I interrupted again: 'I suppose your motto could be, if at first you don't succeed, fail and fail again.' Everybody laughed. But Roy's remark did do him an enormous amount of damage. It created the impression, as many others said in the course of the day, that he had been too clever by half.

I said I wanted to look at the politics of direct elections. We had to consider the impact on the British constitution itself. The British labour movement had traditionally put its hope in Parliament, using the vote to bring about action, and this direct connection between government and people was going to be diverted by assemblies in Edinburgh and Cardiff and Strasbourg; these were untried vehicles or vessels for expressing the democratic purpose. It would be very serious if there was a malrepresentation of this country. It might be under Thatcher, or it might be us, but it would be extremely serious, and the Tories would very quickly regard a victory at home in direct elections as being grounds for saying *they* really represented England.

We had to consider whether if we made this first faltering step towards direct elections we wouldn't end up with absolutely full constitutional harmonisation, with fixed elections every five years for the European Assembly, the House of Commons and local government – as in the United States. That would destroy the responsibility of the Cabinet to the House of Commons. Were we going to go for harmonisation or federalisation? If we chose federalisation, then of course the main vehicle of democratic control would be the European Assembly. I said I was a harmoniser, I had tried to be constructive in the energy field through harmonisation and I had got a good response, but inevitably it would mean that Section 2 of the European Communities Act would have to be amended at some stage.

'That's all very well,' said Jim, 'but where does it lead us now? What do we do now?'

'Well, certainly no bill this session, and much more discussion.'

Shirley passed me a little note afterwards saying she thought it was terrific. She certainly is trying to be friendly at the moment.

Peter Shore said he saw the risk of a separate 'European Labour Party' emerging in Britain.

Fred Mulley thought we must grasp the nettle of proportional representation. He favoured a regional or national list; he warned us that the high salaries of European MPs – which, it is alleged, will be £20,000 per year – were already causing resentment in the House of Commons. He said we did not want election dates coincidental with a British General Election.

We adjourned for lunch and talked about Reg Prentice,* who should have had his constituency annual meeting a couple of nights ago. Apparently Reg was hoping he would be thrown out of the local Party so that he could stand again, and he was very cross to find that the meeting was postponed. Reg is all set on forming a new party.

The subject of the French Revolution arose, and Bill Rodgers asked Michael Foot why Danton and Robespierre were guillotined and how Napoleon rose up. Denis Healey commented, 'The extreme left is always so incompetent, it paves the way for a dictator.' I asked him, 'Are you the candidate for being so incompetent or the candidate for the dictator who follows?' He did actually laugh.

There was the vote on the second reading of William Benyon's bill on abortion this afternoon. We lost by 38 votes. As soon as I had voted, I jumped in the car for Paddington and caught a train to Bristol.

*Sunday 27 February*
London, and Caroline and I went to the Foots' for dinner. The Baloghs were there, and Judith and Tony Hart, welcome back after Judith left the Government nearly two years ago. The Shores came in later.

We talked over dinner about Ministers dying early, about abortion – it was a morbid discussion, really. Then Michael said he was keen on my scheme for a Cabinet commission on devolution. After dinner I raised a couple of issues. On civil rights, I said I was worried about the Agee and Hosenball case but I got absolutely no response at all. Michael seems an extinct volcano. He said, 'Oh, Merlyn is very decent, I've got no complaints against Merlyn', then he began to move on to open government, but it's got nothing to do with open government. I think Michael is quite content to be a Minister in the last few months or years of this Government and doesn't want to fight for anything particular.

* In July 1975, Newham North East Labour Party requested their MP, Reg Prentice, to retire at the next Election as a result of dissatisfaction with his activities and statements. He refused, ultimately joining the Conservatives (see Principal Persons).

*Monday 28 February*

Cabinet Energy Committee (ENM) at 3. On the agenda was the response of the Government to the Flowers Report. We had already dealt with civil liberties, and on radioactive waste I said that we should set up a National Waste Corporation under the responsibility of Peter Shore, who now has strategic responsibility.

Dick Mabon bitterly opposed me again, which caused some shock, as he is my Minister of State. David Ennals supported me and thought Environment should have it. So Dick Mabon came back and said, 'All I can tell you is that Department of Energy officials agree with me', and he quoted the Permanent Secretary.

I replied, 'I am all for free discussion, but *my* view is the Department of Energy view and it isn't really right to quote officials against me in a committee.' It absolutely shocked people.

During the course of the discussion I wrote a little note out to Peter:

Three constitutional problems.

Am I right to give Dick Mabon freedom to attack my view?

Second, is he right to quote my Permanent Secretary's views from a minute sent to him but not to me?

Third, is my Permanent Secretary right to brief my Minister of State to defeat me?

Peter wrote 'No' against all three questions. I passed it to Merlyn too and he wrote against it, 'Incredible'. And so it was. Quite incredible.

Frances rang me at home to say she had had a word with Tom McNally, Jim's political adviser, who very much liked my minute on nuclear issues and thought Jim would agree with it.

Did my box, and found a letter from Sir Peter Ramsbotham, our Ambassador in Washington, to Sir Jack Rampton, saying he had seen Schlesinger, who stated that the fast breeder programme would be sharply cut back. That is really very important, marvellous news. So I might win.

In the office today I had a talk about Windscale, where BNFL has precipitated the most appalling strike, entirely the fault of management, and John Cunningham has been dealing with it. I should just touch on what happened.

The changing-room attendants at Windscale were fed up with staff coming in and throwing their radioactive white coats and gloves on the floor instead of putting them in the bins provided. They raised it more than once with the management and nothing happened, so they went on a one-day token strike. As a result, a wide range of staff and manual workers were laid off at a few minutes' notice, with an hour's pay for the manuals and full pay for the staff. The manuals wouldn't have this and stayed on strike. Then the changing-room attendants put in for an increase, which was outside pay policy, and the manuals put in a similar bid for a pay increase, so now we have had a five-week strike of a thousand people.

Unfortunately, the union national officials led by Gavin Laird of the AUEW went to see BNFL management, said it was an unofficial strike and they wouldn't talk to the workers. So we have a situation where an initial strike provoked by management, and nothing to do with pay, has escalated into an unofficial strike by a thousand workers for five weeks, in which the full-time officials are in effect supporting the management, and which has now become an issue of pay. God knows how we get out of it; the problem for me if we don't resolve it is that I may have to send troops in with emergency supplies to deal with safety. It is an outrage and I won't send troops in; I just won't do it. I shall send a minute if necessary to the Prime Minister because it has tremendous potential dangers.

*Tuesday 1 March*
The first meeting this morning was about this hideous dispute at Windscale. I called in Con Allday, the Managing Director of BNFL, and his chief industrial relations officer, and the national union officials, Jack Biggins of the GMWU, Peter Adams of the ETU and Gavin Laird.

After I had welcomed them, I said, 'You probably realise that if anything goes wrong I shall be in the position of having to use troops, and therefore I would really like to know what the background is.'

So Con Allday began with a tremendous technical explanation. He said they hoped it would not be necessary, but they had got to be prepared for the use of the army. The pickets had stiffened recently, the police were helping to get staff in, but no materials were getting through. He said Windscale needed constant supplies of $CO_2$ and nitrogen. It needed $CO_2$ to top up the AGR in order to keep steam on the site: the plant safety requires steam in the event of a leak of toxic wastes. The next supply of $CO_2$ would be needed by the end of this week. He told me that if water or air got into the reactor it could be closed for four years.

Nitrogen was required by the AEA laboratories on the site to prevent a flare-up in the glove boxes through which radioactive plutonium particles are handled: BNFL had got plans for alternative supplies of $CO_2$ and nitrogen. 'We are giving pickets the chance to let these in and we hope the unions will support the company. BNFL have ordered a tanker of nitrogen for Thursday or Friday and the TGWU say they will let it in if it is for safety use.'

Gavin Laird said that troops would not be needed – that was very emotive language to use. The police would do the trick.

Adams commented, 'We will ensure the $CO_2$ will go in. We are confident it can be done without troops or police. The unions will tell the men the equipment has to go in.' He hoped a resumption of work would be agreed, but the unions would not be supporting the men in the dispute.

Jack Biggins said we had to offer the lads on the site a way out; we didn't want to snub the men.

Allday added that industrial relations had been bad at Windscale, the lay-off had been on the basis of company policy, and they had offered alternative work where possible.

Peter Adams gave further details of the dispute. The changing-room attendants had said conditions were intolerable, and the men had organised a four-shift withdrawal of labour, as a result of which the company had laid off a thousand people twenty-four hours later. Those who were laid off asked for payment for the lay-off and later a wage claim was made. A claim of 30p an hour for those inside and 20p for those outside the radioactive area was put in. The company was given an hour to respond, then a strike notice was issued and 3000 went off. The company offered £15 lay-off money but a mass meeting rejected it. BNFL has offered an increase of 1p an hour, which has incensed the workers, and the unions are unable to move the company. 'As national representatives we are bound by the Social Contract,' Adams pointed out.

John Cunningham, my Parliamentary Under-Secretary, who is the local MP and a GMWU member, interrupted. 'The account of events given does not correspond to my knowledge.'

So Gavin Laird retorted, 'I'm not having this. I'm not staying on that basis, with MPs and Ministers muddying the water.'

I said I must defend John Cunningham. All we wanted to know was the cause of the dispute. Was it originally a pay claim? It appeared not, but it had become a pay claim. As the owner of the company I had ultimate responsibility for safety, and with the local MP, who went in with my authority, I must be free to ask questions.

So Gavin Laird said, 'I am not here to listen to talk like that.'

'I have said nothing; no statement has been made. I didn't want to make a statement, and I thought I had better have a word with you first,' I replied.

Gavin Laird then apologised, so that was all right.

I summed up. On the safety aspect the unions obviously had the first-line responsibility but the Government was ultimately responsible. 'I am tied like you to the Social Contract, but that is not what this was about originally, and only the unions can resolve the dispute.

*New Statesman*, 1 April 1977

Would the Conciliation Advisory Service [ACAS] help?' No, said Adams.

To the Cabinet Economic Committee, and we came to a paper on micro-measures and unemployment. The paper described a 300,000 increase in unemployment this year. Albert Booth said employment was 138,000 up on a year ago, and 122,000 of these were in the sixteen to eighteen age group; 242,000 had been unemployed for more than twelve months; 83,000 were men between twenty-five and forty-four. The trend was worsening. He went through all the items in his paper and said he would prefer a link with education, that he wanted to sustain training and to continue our work experience programme. He wanted coloured unemployment to be dealt with by putting more effort into high-immigrant areas.

Denis said, 'I can stimulate the economy a bit in the Budget by tax cuts but I would like all this extra expenditure to be taken out of the contingency fund.'

I should add that Rampton, my Permanent Secretary, had written on my brief in his own hand, 'Why don't we have national service? We are the only country in the whole Community who don't have a year's national service.' So progressively the idea of dealing with the unemployment problem by rearmament – it would be a form of mobilisation – is beginning to emerge.

The final item was the OECD pledge not to introduce import controls. Edmund Dell said we could renew it; we would lose nothing, and the IMF forces us to accept it anyway. He added, 'I have not changed my view', and Michael Foot said, 'I hope you aren't still holding the views you held in the CP?' Edmund coloured up, so Jim said, 'Right, once and for all, all those who were in the Communist Party please hold up their hands.' Denis and Edmund held up their hands, and I said, 'I hope you are not going to be too hard on the communists because at least they are taking cheap butter from the Common Market!'

I saw Frances and we talked about the Civil Service; if civil servants want to have any influence with the Minister they have got to try and see the world through the Minister's eyes. It's a bit of an anxiety that they just pursue their own policy, because it means that I don't listen to their advice. They know perfectly well what I want on nuclear energy, on coal, because I have been absolutely specific and categoric about it, but they don't want to help.

### Wednesday 2 March

Frances Morrell had been to Number 10 yesterday or the day before and she told me that the only thing worth my doing was to become Leader of the Party. I said there was another choice, to influence the Party, and she said there was no real influence except as Leader. But I've seen so many lives wrecked by ambition and I don't intend to do that.

I forgot to mention that I had a forty-five-minute interview with Nigel Hawkes of the *Observer*, a meeting which Bernard Ingham fixed up. Had a very candid talk telling him everything, including my anxieties about nuclear energy. He told me that Walter Marshall had said to him, 'I don't know anything about this nuclear lobby', so I said to Nigel, 'He shaves the main member of it every morning!'

### Thursday 3 March

The editor of the *Daily Telegraph*, Bill Deedes, came to lunch. I've always liked Deedes. He told me that F. A. Hayek, the author of *The Road to Serfdom*, had come to see him the other day, and Hayek had said, 'You know, my view is that Britain ought to pursue an effective monetarist policy – but I'm very worried about unemployment; it's on such a scale now.'

Well, if Hayek is worried about unemployment, and the editor of the *Daily Express* is worried, and Bill Deedes is worried, why isn't the Government worried?

At the very end Bill said, 'You know, you are a very thoughtful guy, you've a lot of experience, you can obviously manage your Department, and you have got a lot more supporters in the *Daily Telegraph* than you might think.' He was frightfully nice.

At 5 David Basnett, Jack Biggins and Peter Adams came along to discuss the Windscale dispute. Apparently the strike committee are ready to recommend that the safety cargoes go through, and they will check it tomorrow. I said no attempt was to be made to get a driver through without my consent.

My Deputy Secretary, Brian Tucker, was in a great tizzy, and indeed one of the union officials told me that they had word that 'your Department has got into a panic'. I think that's probably true; I think they are pushing me into using troops, which I don't want to do.

I decided to talk to the PM.

*Friday 4 March*
Visit to Maerdy Colliery in the Rhondda. I was extremely tired, and when I arrived I was called away immediately to the phone to be told that approaches were being made today to get the shop stewards at Windscale to agree to the delivery of safety materials – $CO_2$ gas and nitrogen.

Of course it was in the Rhondda that Churchill used troops in the General Strike. It was a strange feeling, being a socialist Secretary of State ringing from the same place to my office in London with instructions intended to avoid the use of troops at Windscale.

*Saturday 5 March*
The strike committee had not been able to be gathered together yesterday but they are meeting tomorrow.

*Sunday 6 March*
I had a letter from Number 10, sent at Private Secretary level. The Prime Minister insisted that all books written by Ministers had to be approved by Number 10, and had to be in line with Government policy. Once again the thing is tightening up.

A phone call from James Bretherton saying that after a great debate the strike committee at Windscale had agreed to let the emergency supplies in, so in fact the Windscale crisis is postponed for a few days.

We had a party this evening, and I had a long and interesting talk to Dudley Bahlman, a relation of Caroline's, about Gladstone and his Secretary, Hamilton. Dudley is editing Hamilton's diaries – well, he is analysing, footnoting and indexing them. It is going to involve, in the end, five volumes of diaries, a work of scholarship which he has been engaged on for five or six years.

*Monday 7 March*

No reference in the news to Windscale except in the *Daily Express*, which had a banner headline, 'Windscale Supplies – Benn Acts', and an account of how I had sent in $CO_2$ gas yesterday. This means that the media are now alerted to it. I wondered how it had got through to the *Express*. I think probably the security services are tapping the phones of the strike committee and have a regular link to the *Express*.

Tony Crosland's memorial service was held in Westminster Abbey. It was a tremendous event, as you would expect for a Foreign Secretary dying in office. The Abbey was packed, the Cabinet in the choir stalls on the left, where as a Westminster schoolboy I used to sit every day for Latin prayers. Opposite were all the other Ministers and Ambassadors. There were three former Prime Ministers over on the right – Heath, Wilson and Home – and Princess Alexandra was there representing somebody.

It was the establishment recognising and at the same time burying the idea of social democracy. First of all we had the Dean saying a few words about Tony's incisive and lively mind, about his passion for a just and equal society, his unfaltering desire to raise up the under-privileged and to care for the less fortunate. Then we had the national anthem, then Derek Gladwin, southern regional secretary of the GMWU, described in the programme as Grimsby-born, who read Ecclesiasticus, 'Let us now praise famous men.' Of course we had the hymn 'Jerusalem'. Then a reading by Dick Leonard, a past PPS of Tony's, from *The Future of Socialism*, in which the first passage read was as follows:

> It is not only dark satanic things and people that now bar the road to the new Jerusalem but also, if not mainly, hygienic, respectable, virtuous things and people, lacking only in grace and gaiety.

The most astonishing thing to read, that the only bar to socialism was now hygienic respectability and virtue. Later came a passage attacking the Webbs and continuing:

> Today we are all incipient bureaucrats and practical administrators. We have all so to speak been trained at the LSE, are familiar with blue books and white papers and know our way around Whitehall.

An absolutely élitist view of politics; then finally the famous phrase:

> Total abstinence and a good filing system are not now the right signposts to the socialist utopia, or at least, if they are, some of us will fall by the wayside.

After an address by Lord Donaldson, his old friend Jack Donaldson, we had the prayer for Parliament, which contains these words –

> That thou wouldst be pleased to direct and prosper all their consultations to

the advancement of thy glory, the good of thy church, the safety, honour and
welfare of our sovereign and her dominions

and so on – the parliamentary prayer which of course is absolutely pre-
parliamentary, let alone pre-democratic.

That memorial service really could be published as a Gaitskellite
pamphlet. It was the Gaitkellites mourning their dead.

Geoff Bish, Brian Sedgemore and Frances and Francis had a
sandwich with us. Geoff has started drafting the manifesto and we
agreed that the right line now was to make full employment in the 1980s
the centrepiece. If the Party doesn't speak about full employment it is a
terrible hostage to fortune because it leaves it to the Tory press, who
demand public expenditure cuts, and to Mrs Thatcher, indeed to
everybody to speak about it except us.

At 3.15 I had a meeting of the Civil Contingencies Unit (CU), which
comprises officials from the Home Office, the Ministry of Defence and
no doubt the security services, under the chairmanship of the Home
Secretary. I have never attended it before. It is an important committee
in my opinion because you are actually meeting there the men who
would run Britain in the event of a breakdown of law and order, a
general strike. At my request three other Ministers were added.

I looked round the table and I just saw these hard-faced regional or
national controllers. We are normally represented there by Brian
Tucker. The Ministry of Defence was represented because it was
necessary to consider the possibility of using troops.

I briefly reported roughly what had happened. Albert Booth then
said he hoped we could avoid taking action because he felt it might
escalate the situation. One of the Home Office people said there was a
great reservoir of goodwill in the area which we hadn't yet fully tapped.
I agreed with that.

Then Merlyn turned to me. 'Is there any alternative to using troops?
I know that the Ministry of Defence will say they don't want to be
involved.' No, obviously they don't want to send in army drivers, as it
just gets them involved in an industrial dispute. He said, 'You did
mention to the Prime Minister that you might go up there yourself.'

I said I wasn't looking for a job but if it were possible to settle it
without sending troops I would be very pleased.

Then the question of keeping in step with the trade union leaders –
Len Murray, Jack Jones, David Basnett, John Boyd – was discussed,
including how to separate the safety issue from the industrial dispute.

We had a great discussion about deadlines. It became clear that the
$CO_2$ gas which had got in on Sunday has extended the safety deadline
to 15 March. Although there never has been a leak from a toxic tank, it
would be a serious risk to remove the capacity of the $CO_2$ to deal with

leaks of toxic waste, and that would involve a real hazard to the neighbourhood. You would have to evacuate houses.

The nitrogen supplies now available would last until Saturday 12 March. If this nitrogen is not used, the plutonium will ignite and start a fire, and then you would have a very difficult and unpleasant job cleaning up the contaminated areas. If we could get more nitrogen in today or tomorrow that would push the date back to 1 April; thereafter you would need $CO_2$ every five days.

So the immediate deadline is 12 March.

Having discussed the timetable, we then considered what would happen if the voluntary scheme failed. One official said, 'Why don't you use non-union labour?' Well, that was absolutely ruled out.

Then the question of using the army was considered. Army drivers, possibly from the Royal Corps of Transport, would have to pick up the gas from the suppliers, Air Products, and get it through the picket line. The alternative would be to use a helicopter – which would mean transporting the gas in smaller containers, three or four times a day.

I was told to get in touch with Len Murray to discuss voluntary methods, consultations on the spot, how he could help with back-up, and whether he would have a preference for sending an army lorry through the picket lines or using a helicopter.

It is an extremely worrying and difficult issue. I am sure the men at Windscale are highly responsible and must not be conned under any circumstances. They must be told the truth; they will know about the deadlines and they will know what the risk is. On the other hand this is the thing they are clinging to in order to preserve their own standing in the dispute.

*Tuesday 8 March*
Had a word with Bernard Ingham, who told me that the office had asked him two weeks ago to prepare a statement for feeding through the press to prepare the public for the use of troops at Windscale. I was never consulted about that, and Bernard said he hadn't actually done it. Interesting.

To the Economic Committee (EY), where we talked for two hours about the Budget, and Denis gave an awful lot of figures, some of which I wrote down; we were told afterwards to leave notes behind – the first meeting at which I haven't been able to keep notes, except for the Budget meeting itself.

Denis announced that the Treasury had miscalculated the PSBR by £1 billion and he went into the ways in which this could be given back in taxation.

I asked, 'Assuming, therefore, that our present policies succeed, what is our strategy for a return to full employment? As far as the

Budget is concerned, it would seem to me that public investment is better than tax relief because it has less import potential. The tax on big firms has been relaxed very much and we should help small businesses; and, third, we should consider subsidies to keep down prices.'

Well, Jim went very red at all this, and in effect he said you can do nothing about unemployment; indeed, he remarked: 'Looking at the Eighties we shall be in a new ball-game, with high unemployment.'

Then Denis went on about industrial performance, design and marketing, just mouthing the phrases; in the end what we're saying is it's the working class that are responsible for all the troubles. I actually came away from the EY more depressed than I have ever been. Full employment is no longer on the agenda of a Labour Government. They haven't even got a strategy for the Eighties. They simply haven't got a strategy.

I had Dick Mabon, Frances Morrell, Alex Eadie and John Cunningham in to discuss Windscale, and while we were talking we heard that an attempt to get the supplies in today had failed. So it seemed we were back where we started.

But then I heard that the deadlines had changed. It now turns out the deadlines are entirely different. I have got another week, until Wednesday 16 March. That made me hopping mad because it destroyed my credibility – having pulled out the safety stops early, I find out it wasn't necessary.

We spent an hour considering whether I should go up to Windscale. John Cunningham thought it was sensible, Dick Mabon said it would be better than sending troops, Alex Eadie said it would be a disaster because the trade union leaders would never forgive me for doing a deal (but they couldn't do one). It was eventually agreed I would call in David Basnett and tell him he must get the supplies in somehow and, if not, ask him to confirm that I will have to get them in. If I could be of any help I would go up with him.

So I had a word with Basnett on the phone. Biggins has been busy all the time but he's just got stuck. The workers there have decided not to let safety materials in. I gathered that the shop steward from Air Products turned up but wouldn't go in, so the whole situation is jammed up.

I went over to the House of Commons and David Basnett and Jack Biggins came to my room. David had several whiskies, and a number of points came out. First of all, I'd been misled about the deadlines, Basnett had been misled, and it had destroyed both our credibilities, and it was due to the management of BNFL who, quite frankly, are in cahoots with the Department and were pushing me to use the safety argument too early and then to put soldiers in. It was partly panic and partly mischief really. They thought: Oh well, why bother to tell the

Secretary of State, because he will do what we tell him anyway. Now that I know this I am simply furious.

David Basnett was furious about it too, because of course the shop stewards know better than anybody else that in fact there are extra reserve supplies at Windscale, which management never disclosed to me. So I said to David, 'Well, look, you'll have to get it all sorted out by Sunday. After that it will have to be understood that I must take the necessary action. I'm at your disposal if I can help you, if you want me to come up with you.'

At that moment Brian Tucker interrupted to say that John Dunster, Deputy Director-General of the Health and Safety Executive, had been telephoning the shop steward, Bill Maxwell – not even the national or regional official in Windscale – and had offered to write a letter saying that it would be in the interests of safety if the dispute was settled. That made David Basnett even more angry – the thought that a civil servant in the Health and Safety Executive had been intervening directly with the stewards. It all confirmed very much what Alex Eadie had said earlier, that if I got involved it would be possible only at the request of the general secretaries of the unions concerned and not on my own initiative.

We agreed to leave it, but I am going to put a bit of pressure on Allday to help to settle and we've got about a week to do it.

I saw Robin Corbett [Labour MP for Hemel Hempstead] in the corridor and I congratulated him on the line he was taking on the defence of Agee and Hosenball. He said to me, 'Do you know that everybody involved in that case has had some security incident? For example, a woman on the committee who had the cheque book for the Agee and Hosenball fund found her handbag pinched. She was desperate. It came back the following day and the only thing missing was the cheque book containing the names of the people to whom money had been paid or a receipt book or something. Another man put down his briefcase and it disappeared.'

With the NCCL being raided too, it causes me deep anxiety.

*Wednesday 9 March*
Caroline is going to Paris today to participate in Unesco discussions as part of the British Unesco Commission to which she was appointed two years ago.

I went to the Committee of the Civil Contingencies Unit and reported on Windscale. 'The union general secretaries have been told they've got until Sunday, and after that I am free. At today's meeting we shall have to prepare for the army but I don't want any helicopters. We need a contingency plan ready to be activated on Monday, but I think we also ought to have a court of inquiry to bear on the dispute.'

Harold Walker, who was there representing the Department of Employment, is not the most imaginative man, and raised all sorts of difficulties.

Dunster said we needed plans now for approaching the companies covertly. John Gilbert reported on behalf of the Ministry of Defence that the army had no $CO_2$, but they did have nitrogen at non-standard pressures. By Puma helicopter you would need 103 sorties a week, and at £1300 an hour that would be extremely expensive.

As to tankers, the army had no chemical tankers for liquid fuels, but cylinders could be transported in ten-ton lorries at the rate of fifteen deliveries a week; it would be best to have Service drivers in civilian trucks. He said we would need forty-eight hours for reconnaissance. Since he would like a green light on Sunday, it was agreed that we would keep everything quiet until Sunday evening.

It was also agreed that Dunster should talk to the Air Products management in Surrey. A number of people around the table said that telephone conversations were not secure because they go through switchboards (and no doubt for other reasons).

Merlyn said, 'Right, now "Butch" Baker, Assistant Under-Secretary of State at the Home Office, will be in charge of this. We will meet again tomorrow. Defence will report on their preparations, Labour will report on the possibility of a court of inquiry, and I will report on events. As to public opinion, we will stay completely private until Sunday, completely private, and then we will go public, if we do go ahead, to prepare people. Meanwhile there should be a complete question-and-answer statement prepared in case it is necessary.' I then learned that it was the Civil Contingencies Unit (CU) which had ordered the press statement to be prepared by my office three weeks ago.

Went to lunch with the *Sunday Times* journalists Harold Evans, Hugo Young, Keith Richardson, Frank Giles and Michael Jones; next to me Ronald Butt. I knew them all.

We talked about the market economy and I said Fleet Street didn't really operate under a market economy, nobody believed in it – the proprietors didn't, the editors didn't, the unions didn't. They said, well we all live in an atmosphere of a market economy. I replied, 'I accept that; we all live under the stars and the sun, but we don't worship them.'

Then we went on to discuss Labour politics. Ronald Butt said I wanted a small clique of people unrepresentative of the Labour Party to dominate it. I said not at all, I wanted an expanded Party membership, and a very active Party. He asked, What about Marxists? I said a lot of people have been Marxists – Ramsay MacDonald, Herbert Morrison, Crosland. You can't repudiate the contribution Marx has made, although as a matter of fact British socialism goes back to the Levellers and much beyond that.

*Thursday 10 March*
Merlyn, Albert and I had a word, and Albert said he would be ready to come to Windscale as soon as necessary.

At 11 Sheikh Yamani, the Saudi Oil Minister, came to see me and I asked him about the king's health because apparently many Saudi Ministers are in London seeing the king in bed in a clinic somewhere. I fixed up my visit to Saudi Arabia next month. But the real intention was to find out about likely oil price increases after the OPEC meeting in Doha.

I like Yamani and I often compliment him on his help; and he always announces to others in the room, 'Mr Benn says that so often that one day I'll believe it.'

After that I had Ronald Gausden, the new Chief Nuclear Inspector, come to see me, and what he said was really sensational. He said that the liquid nitrogen supplies which we thought would not run out until Wednesday 16 March, giving me till next Monday to bring the army in, would in fact run out tonight at midnight. On Saturday night even the bottles of gas might run out, because he wasn't sure how much was in each. Therefore he couldn't guarantee there wouldn't be a fire some time after Saturday night. This, then, indicated the need for the army to get the cylinders from Air Products tomorrow.

This meant I would have to tell the trade union leaders that the deadline had moved back to tonight instead of Sunday. I rang Basnett and told him this. We had a long discussion about it, and I worked out a programme, namely that we would await the result of the delivery today, and the mass meeting. If either or both are negative then Albert would agree to ACAS being brought in, and I would go to Windscale. On Friday I would meet the strike committee and men and make a final appeal on safety. I would have to make a parliamentary statement. After the CU meeting this afternoon I will call the general secretaries into the office with Albert and tell them their phase is over, the Government is in charge, we have decided to bring in ACAS, and are making military preparations.

I went across to the CU meeting and we sat right through lunch – John Grant standing in for Albert, and John Gilbert, myself, Merlyn in the chair and officials. I brought them up to date and told them that the HSE had given us new deadlines and that I was to go to Windscale as a last attempt; if that failed, the army was to be brought in, after a parliamentary statement. Basnett, Biggins and Len Murray all supported this.

The Deputy Chief Constable of Cumbria said he hoped for a delivery today and there was a lot of goodwill. Gausden reaffirmed that there could be fires possibly from Saturday night, and so Merlyn said, 'All right, we offer conciliation, and if the deliveries fail then Tony will go up. After that the army must be ready.' John Gilbert said the army would prefer cylinders. Air Products can deliver them to an army camp and the army can deliver them on Saturday. Also there is reserve provision at Lakenfield for making nitrogen.

I then went back to the office and really waited for things to happen. I got a succession of contradictory messages, but I heard that the mass meeting had not taken place and it became absolutely clear that I would have to go up. I asked Gausden to give me the latest deadlines and I got a note this time to say the supplies would not be exhausted till *Sunday* night, so the deadline was extended a day: they go backwards and forwards, backwards and forwards. I called him in and he said, 'Well, there may be a bit more in the bottles than we originally thought', so in fact I have got an extra day, which is quite convenient, and the army won't have to rush in quite so quickly.

It was agreed we would book rooms in the hotel in Whitehaven in the name of one of my Private Secretaries, Colin Ambrose.

I wanted to be ready to make a parliamentary statement tomorrow afternoon, but Michael Foot told me you couldn't interrupt business for it, and I said I must. He asked, 'Why can't Dick Mabon make the statement at 11 in the morning?' I said, 'No. I can't have anyone else make the statement while I'm at Windscale because it would be reported while I was in the middle of negotiations.'

I was told I had to clear it with the PM in Washington. So I dictated the text of a parliamentary statement and it was telexed to the Prime Minister.

Bernard Ingham, Frances Morrell, Brian Sedgemore, James Bretherton, myself and seven others left the office and took off from Northolt and arrived in Carlisle at 8. We were driven from Carlisle to Whitehaven, to the Waverley Hotel; nobody knew we were there.

I went into a room immediately and there were Sir John Hill, Chairman of BNFL, and other management people, Con Allday, Thompson Reid, the district secretary of the GMWU, a very solid guy, and a younger chap called Leo Goldsworthy from the AUEW. John Cunningham and his press officer, Heather Lancaster, had also arrived.

While I was there I got a message from Washington – which was a great relief – to indicate it was all right to make the statement; but Jim said he wanted it played down and wanted full trade union support.

I learned from Allday that BNFL have 8 tons of bottles of $CO_2$, two weeks' supplies, at a depot in Leigh in Lancashire, so the great problem of the army getting hold of them tomorrow is over. I told them to arrange for these to be delivered to the army depot. Once the army have got the bottles they can defer their deliveries till Sunday. It is a very important piece of information, in fact, because it gives me more time to play with.

Thompson Reid described the history of the problem, said there were seventy pickets, not 500, and that any driver with a solid working-class background would not wish to cross the picket line. He said, 'We can't influence the stewards and the pickets and if you succeed' (that was me he was referring to) 'it could damage the trade union movement.' He added, 'If the Queen or a distinguished gentleman like yourself comes, it could damage the movement.' Then Leo from the AUEW said that the chances were nil: 'If the national officers can't solve it neither can we.'

Reid said, 'You had better see all of the stewards in the Miners' Hall in Whitehaven tomorrow and be guided by them.'

We spent the next two hours exploring the situation. It is undoubtedly true that BNFL hope to starve the men into submission. The trade union leaders feel bitter on behalf of their men, who have been out for six weeks. One has been thrown out of his accommodation, and they are really angry and hungry. The whole plight of the working class up against management, particularly when management is backed by Government and when the whole thing is concreted in by pay policy, is very rough. I thought Reid and Leo spoke with dignity and integrity and I just listened. Hill was quite sensitive in the end. He said, 'Remember this is a mining area with the loyalty of a mining area.'

I have a very strong interest in not sending in troops – they know that – because it would do damage to the trade unions, damage to me. It would highlight the dangers of a nuclear plant and might well kill Windscale off as a reprocessing centre, and it would of course indicate the serious civil liberties risks of nuclear power. So we are all in a mess and the question is: Can we together get out of it? Of course I can't offer more money, but the conciliation would have to be real.

Allday doesn't think that any more money will be necessary; he thinks if they had a private ballot they would vote to go back to work, because they are near to being starved out. The men have achieved a great deal, of course, by declining to admit safety supplies and getting me up to Windscale. But I feel very calm and experienced in these circumstances.

About midnight I came up to my room and listened to the 12 o'clock news. There was nothing on the news, although the *Daily Express* are apparently going to send someone up tomorrow.

*Friday 11 March*
I was woken about 6.30 to find a telegram from Ken Stowe, the PM's Private Secretary, in Washington:

The PM has asked me to say that he hopes that all the Ministers concerned will endeavour to avoid overdramatising the situation. He recognises that the assessment set before the CU on 10 March calls for speedy decision and positive actions but he would want these to be taken in the closest consultation with the trade union leaders and in agreement with the Ministers concerned. He notes that the Secretary of State for Energy has thought it necessary to visit Windscale. Having previously discussed this with the Secretary of State the PM was surprised at this decision, since it can only tend to dramatise the matter. Nevertheless he agrees that action will be necessary to ensure that essential supplies are delivered through the picket lines in the very near future, and he also agrees that a statement explaining the situation should be made to the House. The tone of the statement should be agreed between the Ministers concerned – namely Home, Employment, Defence and the Lord President – and should in the Prime Minister's view make it clear that the action authorised by the Government for the delivery of essential supplies by servicemen has the full backing of the trades unions concerned. As to the timing of any such announcement, if it is essential that emergency action be taken this weekend the PM agrees that the statement should be made on Friday, although he regrets the need to interrupt business for this purpose, since this can only serve to heighten the tension. He would prefer it if this could be avoided.

At the bottom James Bretherton had added:

You should also know that Len Murray phoned the office about midnight. He said he would do anything he could to help and hoped that the national officers had not been dragging their feet. I gather that Mr Boyd has expressed doubt as to whether sending in the troops could have trade union endorsement.

I thought about this and drafted the following telegram to the Prime Minister in Washington which was sent at 9.55:

After advice that the deadline for the delivery of supplies had been brought forward to Saturday and the unions had exhausted their resources in getting in supplies or resolving the dispute the CU decided that the Ministry of Defence must take action early today which might become public. It was agreed that I should come for talks in Whitehaven designed to secure the delivery of supplies by agreement and if possible get conciliation accepted. The unions concerned are being most helpful. I am keeping Len Murray and the general secretaries informed. It now appears we may be able to hold any decision about the use of an army driver until Monday morning and no question of a parliamentary statement today therefore arises. I am still hopeful that some solution can be found.

I must admit I was not very pleased to get that telegram from the Prime Minister which seemed to me to be singularly unhelpful, since I had asked him last Thursday about it. Although he had given his view then – that it might be a gimmick to come to Windscale – the minute of that meeting contained a clear statement by his Private Secretary, who was present, that he would leave the decision to me. In fact I had not taken the decision alone but in consultation with the CU, and Albert Booth himself offered to come, though I did not think this necessary. But to be told from Washington, such a very long way away, that what I was doing did not meet with the approval of my boss didn't exactly improve the situation, although I decided I had to handle it in my own way, and I knew I had the support of those concerned.

At any rate, I don't know how much of that was really the PM's opinion or whether it was the Number 10 view, expressed by Ken Stowe after a brief word with the PM. I might add that in the course of the day messages came from the Number 10 Press Office to the effect that I should not meet the press or radio or television while I was here, which was an absurd statement, since the television units and press arrived in droves during the day. But I did decide not to meet them till the end of the talks, although of course they covered my walking through demonstrating crowds to meet the shop stewards.

Peter Adams, Jack Biggins and Laurie Smith of the AUEW had arrived from London on the sleeper, and I had breakfast with them.

At 8.30 Sir John Hill, the Chairman of AEA, and I think Con Allday, and Dr Thackrah, the nuclear inspector for this area, came to see me and I went in great detail into the safety argument with them. In effect I was told that the $CO_2$ was a second line of defence, for getting steam that might be needed from the reactor to move the toxic wastes from one tank to another, and that the first line of defence was in fact an emergency generator which could raise the steam itself.

Secondly I was told that the plutonium carbide in the AEA plutonium lab, which is nothing whatever to do with BNFL though it is on the same site, might catch fire and it was this that needed the nitrogen. They all stressed that the real safety problem was not a risk of catastrophe but a steady deterioration of the double or treble banking of safety arrangements which had always been maintained at Windscale.

I was told that the liquid nitrogen would now last until Friday, that is today, that they had ninety-six bottles of nitrogen gas which would last until Monday, that they had tested the argon, that is another inert gas, which they could vaporise and feed through to the plutonium lab, and that could last for another three days. When that ran out it would still be possible to pump dry air into the plutonium lab and that would last indefinitely. And if that was not working they would have a few hours in which to identify the emergency and deal with it.

This was a very important statement, because it told me in effect that there was no immediate risk of catastrophe that would justify the use of troops and there were other things that could be done. And it seemed to me that the management, at least as much as the men, had been using safety arguments to try to find a way of ending the dispute in their own favour. A very relevant fact. Also they told me that the pickets were letting the safety staff through, and that although the staff were getting tired their morale was high. It was agreed that I would see the staff associations in the course of the day.

At 9.30 Hill and Thackrah came to me and said that they could postpone the deadline for the introduction of the nitrogen gas until Tuesday evening. Given all the circumstances, I could postpone the army until Monday. I therefore sent a message through to the army indicating that they could delay their action. I asked BNFL to arrange for some of the bottles to be moved from Leigh to the army barracks so that the army would have the $CO_2$ gas in case it was needed over the weekend, without actually having to order it themselves, which might be held to be provocative.

At 10.30 James Bretherton, Bernard Ingham, John Cunningham, Brian Sedgemore, Frances Morrell, Dr Howser from my Department and I discussed it among ourselves, and we recognised that there were two new factors which we ought to consider. When the debate on the Windscale reprocessing project (Thorp) goes to the House of Commons on Wednesday night, I would have to say something, and I would be confronted with two arguments. First, that this proved Windscale was unsafe and therefore a bill should not be proceeded with until these matters had been settled. The second would be from the Conservative side who might argue that to make so much money available to a plant where there was so much industrial relations trouble would be as wrong as to do the same for Leyland. Therefore the passage of the bill would in some way be endangered. At any rate that was the discussion we had, and we agreed that management would have to be made aware that the problems were wider than simply relying on the Government to force the men into a settlement.

At 10.35 I had a message that the tanker containing the liquid nitrogen which I had ordered to stand by in case it was possible to get it through the picket lines had in fact broken down and another liquid nitrogen lorry was being made available. This was just another of the frustrations of the whole day.

I went across from the Waverley Hotel to the General and Municipal Workers' Union office in Whitehaven to meet the negotiating committee comprising Bill Maxwell (the chairman), Thompson Reid, Leo Goldsworthy and others.

Maxwell said there was a general desire to resolve the dispute. The workers at Windscale had suffered wage restraint since 1968, there had been a deterioration in industrial relations especially in the last three years, and communications were very bad. He then described the history of the dispute. He concluded: 'If the men returned it would be with their heads held high. The shop stewards have tried to stress the need for peaceful picketing but the membership now would almost prefer troops, and probably a battalion would be needed to get a lorry through the picket line.'

Bernard Owen, a member of the GMWU in the fire station, said there were no really clean areas at Windscale: the drains were contaminated, there were fire risks; he had seen a special report which underlined all this. There were many incidents not reported, the men and the fire officer didn't agree, and management must see that this was a special site because of the radioactive materials.

George Lilley remarked that Allday had accepted that it was a unique site and that the Windscale management were very naïve in their handling of the men.

Gibson, a sheet metal worker, said there were two classes of workers: the industrials, who got nothing; and the staff, who could always get regraded to get more money.

Derek Thompson of the ETU stressed the loyalty of the workers to the plant and the Government but he said the pay policy was the cause of the trouble.

Robin Simpson of the AUEW said rents and gas were going up – that was a reference to the announcement in the news that I had to override the price code in raising gas prices. The present Cabinet was the best Tory Government they had ever had.

Bill Maxwell stressed that there should be a recognition that the original lay-off had been wrong, a recognition of the low wages, full payments for the lay-offs, 30p per hour Windscale allowance, and meaningful talks.

By now it was after 12, and I thanked them very much for letting me listen. I said I would now proceed with them to the Miners' Hall to meet the full shop stewards' committee of seventy people.

Peter Adams took the chair and I will report what was said there too because it was so important.

Mike Pyke of the AUEW, working on the cooling ponds, said that the status of staff and industrials was different and they wouldn't accept this industrial apartheid: there was different pay for basic, for overtime, for allowances, for sickness and holiday pay. There should be a common rulebook and common conditions and a common date of settlement. It was the most bitter strike he had ever experienced.

John Armstrong of the GMWU said he had been a member of that union since 1931 and before that a member of the NUM, and this was the fifth strike in which he had been involved. The Government were only interested in Cumbria in wartime and at elections. He said nothing would be going through.

Another shop steward, who was a radiation worker and a member of the AUEW, said he had received an overdose of radiation in 1973; as a result he had had to be moved into another area of the site and had lost between £1500 and £2000 a year. The management had promised compensation for cases of this kind but he had not yet had it after nearly four years.

Derek Murray, one of the health physicists, observed that the management had been inept for years. 'It is our factory and our works and it is time they took some notice of us. It is a culmination of irritation and bickering and the labour department don't have any proper personnel training. The staff expansion is going on all the time at the expense of the workers.'

An AUEW radiation worker said that after eighteen years he got less money and more radiation than ever before.

Well, after everyone had spoken, I replied briefly to say I realised there was very great bitterness, I took it they would not allow the emergency supplies to be sent in, and I promised to go back and see the management. I suggested a meeting at 4.

I should add that as I entered the building and as I left there were lots of people shouting, and others were holding up posters saying 'Send in the troops' and 'Tory con trick' and so on. It was very unpleasant. I suppose I should have stopped to speak to the guys standing there but I didn't. One of them shouted, 'Why don't you make a speech?' But I got in the car and went back to the hotel. I think on reflection it was a mistake; I ought to have stayed on to talk to them.

I might add that about this time two or three things happened. First I heard a report that the BBC were broadcasting a story that there was likely to be an explosion at Windscale; secondly, I was told that the army would not take the bottles till Monday; thirdly, I heard that Peter Mummery, the General Manager of Windscale, was going to be moved or sacked today.

We were in the hotel, and sandwiches and tea were brought in all the time. I hardly budged from that room.

Jack Biggins, Peter Adams and Laurie Smith came back, and Peter Adams reported that a substantial sum would be needed. I said, take the three areas: bad management would require looking at; lay-off pay, whether you called it recommissioning pay or whatever – it didn't involve the Social Contract – would have to be agreed; and, on the Windscale allowance, the principle had already been conceded and if need be the amount could go to arbitration.

At 3 o'clock Hill and Allday came back. I reported on my talks and really formulated, with them, my proposals: that talks be resumed at once; that the prime objective was to get an agreed settlement; that everyone knew the safety supplies must be allowed into the site, but that management would meanwhile only act on deliveries in conjunction with the unions concerned; and that John Hill would report to me on Monday morning.

I did also say, 'I hear you are thinking of removing Mummery. Don't do it today because it will look as if I was responsible. It would be very complicated.' They replied, 'Well, we were going to do it anyway. We are going to put him in charge of the inquiry to look at the Windscale planning application.' I said it was for them to decide but I thought it would be unwise to do it today.

At 3.40 the national officials came back, and Peter Adams said, 'The local unions think you should involve yourself.' I replied, 'I am afraid that having put this to you I have changed my mind because it has been put to me [by Frances and John Cunningham] that it would be a great mistake for me to get involved in negotiations. First of all I would in some way be committed to the outcome, and, second, when we got back to London I would find it harder to describe what had been settled because I would have been a part of it. I think it would be better if I stayed out of it.' In the end I talked them round on that. So it was agreed that we should tell the stewards that the talks must go ahead and that I would have a report on Monday morning.

On the Mummery question they agreed with my view that it would be a mistake to remove him today.

At 4.20 I went back to the shop stewards, all of them in the Miners' Hall, and I was shouted at again as I went in. This time I made a speech. I said that I had listened to everyone, I had taken care, I had the safety problem to consider. I said I had reported what they had said to the management. Talks should be resumed, but I had no cash to offer, no money on the table, nothing at all, but in view of the need for urgency and the problem of safety, and the Windscale Bill coming up on Wednesday, I'd asked for a report in my office on Monday morning.

Then I was asked, 'If the industrials get the 40p an hour Windscale allowance which we are demanding, will the Government and the pay board accept it?' I said, 'I am not here to offer money. I don't want anyone to say Tony Benn came here and made promises. We must be absolutely clear, I am saying no such thing, making no promises about cash.' Someone shouted, 'You're evading the question.' I said, 'No, I am not evading the question, I am giving a very clear answer. There has got to be a measure of mutual confidence at this stage.' I am very glad I said that in the event.

They gave me a bit of a cheer as I left and I went back through the pickets again to the hotel and gave a press conference to the BBC, ITN, Radio Carlisle.

I had a last talk with Hill and Allday, and the interesting thing was that Hill said to me, 'If there is one lesson we have learned it is that we have got to design a new plant when it has expanded so this safety question can't arise.' It was an amazing comment really, because to the last these scientists and engineers think that there is a technical solution by which they could get out of their dependence on their workforce, which they really don't like.

I said, 'John, you can't do that. Nuclear power has been recommended to me on the grounds, sometimes, that it gets away from the dependence on the goodwill of the miners, and look what happens.'

'Well, we'll get round that by redesigning.'

'And what do you do when one of Frank Chapple's electricians turns off a switch in Carlisle and all your computers stop? You'll be in exactly the same position.' They still hadn't got the point.

*Saturday 12 March*

Home. The *Guardian* had a good piece describing the technical background. A photo in the *Mail* showed Brian Sedgemore and myself being heckled outside the shop stewards' meeting. I was reasonably content.

I had a bath and Caroline and I went and bought a couple of vases and drove to Woolwich Town Hall at 10.30 for my driver Ron Vaughan's marriage to Peggy. It was a lovely day and we went to the reception in the Star Hotel.

There was a succession of telephone calls. I rang Merlyn Rees this morning to report that I had left it to negotiation over the weekend. John Cunningham rang to say that an offer had been made by the management. I think this morning it was going to be put to the men – £120 lay-off money, raising the Windscale allowance from 1p to 2½p and arbitration on the rest, and an inquiry into management.

Albert was worried that this was outside the Social Contract. But that is his problem really. My problem is the troops. I am actually a bit anxious in case it is argued that I have breached the Social Contract. I haven't of course; I simply told them to get on and find their way of settling it.

But I was concerned about having helped cause settlement over the odds, in case it becomes tied up either with claims by other workers on AEA sites, or with the Leyland situation. But the alternative is troops going in. This is the bargaining power of nuclear workers. We have to accept they are going to have an even greater bargaining power than miners – a very important consideration.

*Sunday 13 March*

Caroline and I picked up her cousins, Jean and Dudley Bahlman, and drove to Number 10.

We looked at portraits of all the Prime Ministers which Hamilton, Gladstone's secretary, had arranged would be put on the stairs. I had my polaroid camera and took pictures of Dudley beside Gladstone's portrait and sitting at Gladstone's desk.

I should think Heath had spent millions redecorating the place – a fantastic amount of redecoration. We looked into the 'Garden Room' and there was one of the famous Garden Girls, high-society typists and secretaries who work for Number 10. There are thirteen of them and one is always on duty. She was working at a Singer sewing machine. It was just like drifting into a country house, the last remnants of Edwardian England. These girls are from 'good' families, having been to Roedean and other girls' public schools, because class is seen as the ultimate safeguard of national security.

Then we went into Number 11 and Number 12 Downing Street and in Number 12 we saw pictures of the Government whips in 1910, including Father, who was then in the Liberal Party.

Came home, and John Cunningham telephoned to say the offer had been put to the men at Windscale this morning and after a very difficult meeting they had agreed to it – £120 lay-off money and £1 a week Windscale allowance against the £12 which they had claimed. I rang Merlyn Rees, who was extremely pleased and he said, 'You've handled it very well.'

Brian Sedgemore rang up to say how glad he was about the settlement, but he wondered about the pay policy implications.

I feel in a way it has been a success, though there will be criticism on the pay side. My answer is that I wasn't asked about the amounts involved, I simply said there had to be a settlement, and it was agreed that was the object. The lay-off money is of course nothing whatever to do with the Government.

There was no reference on the news to the fact that I had been up there, and I think on the whole the more I am disentangled from this whole story the better. The fact that Bill Maxwell, the shop steward, stated that it was only because they had withheld the safety supplies that they had got the extra money was both true and embarrassing; the fact that it was embarrassing didn't make it any less true and the fact that it was true made it all the more embarrassing. But the reality is that Governments do give way to pressure – look at the whole IMF story. We are lectured all the time on the need to be realistic; they'll have to be realistic about guys at Windscale just as we had to be realistic about the IMF. I feel quite firm in my own mind about the matter – no apologies whatever to make. There may be some repercussions with the Leyland toolroom workers, or other parts of the AEA, but the plain fact is that the pay policy is breaking down, and it is breaking down because you cannot hold the line in that particular way. We have got to rethink our position on it and find some new way of making the Social Contract credible, by giving something in return.

One way of doing it would be to provide very big subsidies again in the Budget to achieve a third year for the pay policy.

Got to Peter Shore's at 10 for dinner. Michael Foot and Tommy Balogh were there. Peter thought there might be more in the safety thing at Windscale than I had argued, and it was quite obvious Michael thought I had broken the pay code. But I did get a bit of propaganda in about nuclear power and the need for greater security and safety. I described how my officials had behaved in the Civil Contingencies Unit and so on.

Thomas described the conduct of Jack Rampton and argued that I should sack him. I said I just didn't believe in that approach: you have got to live with the people who are appointed to work with you and you can't do better than that. You have got to get everybody to work together and if the Cabinet pursued the right policy Permanent Secretaries wouldn't matter.

I got home very late, worked till about 2 o'clock, just exhausted.

*Monday 14 March*
At 9 John Hill came in with Peter Adams. Hill said it was a very difficult situation: the emotion was higher than he had realised; it was an unusual area, cut off on a coastal strip; grievances had built up and fed on themselves; and the site was more exposed to the media than most. We talked about the settlement and then I asked about the origins of the Windscale allowance. He said it was originally given to those inside the chemical plants because, since the 1973 incident, they had to monitor the workers' hands all the time for plutonium. It was also given to certain categories at Harwell, Dounreay and Chapel Cross.

He explained that Windscale was unique because

1.   Reprocessing was being done only at Windscale, since Dounreay had been closed for two or three years. It would reopen later this year.
2.   The £140 Windscale abnormal-conditions allowance had originally been for the chemical plant and labs exposed to fissionable products but not for the reactors, but it had been established recently for the AGR staff, and there was a similar payment in Dounreay.

I asked, 'What are the real hazards there?', and he told me something extraordinary. 'Well, there's activity everywhere you dig on that site. Don't forget that after the war Windscale started as a weapons site. We would be pushed to produce 20 kilograms of plutonium before the Russians marched on Berlin; Windscale was given top priority. Whenever we had a spill we just covered it up. For example, in 1957 one of the reactors caught fire and we simply poured in 300,000 tons of water which went right through the plant and into the ground. You can't dig anywhere without the soil producing a radioactive response.'

He said the plant itself was built to two standards of containment: there were the double-clad, no-leak tanks; and there was the low-activity waste. There was always some seepage from all of it but there were inspection checks. He then said that a special feature of the plant was that the media created an aura of danger. He said the mood locally was that of a mining community and he was afraid, had troops been used, of the risk to the industry and the credibility of the company, and that the planning application could not have gone on. Con Allday had taken the view that troops would have killed off Windscale.

*Tuesday 15 March*
Cabinet discussed the proposed sale of BP shares which had been agreed as part of the IMF deal in December and I was called on to speak first. I said that, as the Cabinet would remember, I was strongly opposed to the sale of shares and the public reaction had also been adverse; 100 Labour MPs of the left, right and centre, including John Cartwright, Phillip Whitehead and Jeremy Bray, had signed a motion against it, and Len Murray had reminded us that it would be a breach of the Social Contract.

Then I read the paragraph from the Public Accounts General Purposes Sub-Committee criticising the sale of the shares. We might lose the lawsuit over Burmah shares,* which would mean we were down to a 31 per cent holding of BP if these shares had to be given back to Burmah, and if there was a rights issue our holding would drop to 25 per cent and we wouldn't control BP.

I said that this sale made a nonsense of our oil policy, people did think we should have a majority shareholding, and BNOC could borrow and buy.

Finally, we now knew that the PSBR was a billion pounds out since December and there was a £2 billion margin of error either way. You couldn't use that argument.

Going round the table, Harold Lever and Edmund Dell were of course in favour of selling the shares. Denis Healey said it would cost us 2p on income tax if we didn't. Peter Shore wanted to leave it a bit and Bruce Millan said something helpful. I said at the end that the argument that it would damage BP if we had a big shareholding was nonsense; they had always complained about it, but no one had ever mentioned it to me. If we did reduce our holding and a foreign government bought the shares, it would be awful. People said that the North Sea was in hock and mortgaged up to the hilt and this would reinforce that view. Why not defer it?

* In 1974 the Burmah Oil Company got into financial difficulties and the Government purchased the company's BP shares at a low price. The price subsequently rose considerably and Burmah shareholders then sued the Government over the transaction.

But I was defeated. Denis said we had to know today in time for his Budget.

Later in the day I had a talk with Francis and Frances and Brian Sedgemore, feeling tremendously gloomy about the Government. It was triggered off by the news that Eric Varley had authorised British Leyland to make a statement in conjunction with the Confederation of Shipbuilding and Engineering Unions that if the toolmakers at Leyland didn't return to work on Monday they would be sacked. We are destroying the cohesion of the trade union movement by its association with a Labour Government. We have to think the whole thing out again; the division is between the top and the bottom and the trade union leadership is now part of the establishment. In the process it is in danger of destroying its credibility with the workforce. I think the 'new' Labour Party will have to appeal to shop stewards joining the Party as individuals.

### Thursday 17 March

Cabinet at 10. The first thing was that Jim said, 'I told the Cabinet I would buy a gift for the Queen and I asked her what she would like and she said she would like something she would use personally, something she really could use herself.' So Peter asked, 'Well, what is it?' He said, 'A silver coffee-pot.' Everyone laughed, because the one thing she must have a million of is silver coffee-pots. So anyway, Audrey Callaghan had gone out and found one and it was brought in and put on the table. It is Victorian and, since it will cost each member of the Cabinet £15, it is worth at least about £370.

I said, 'I assume that as it is a Cabinet coffee-pot it won't leak?' Jim said, 'You can say that to the Queen yourself.'

Then we had a number of items. First, the support plan to allow Shell to buy their tankers from Harland & Wolff instead of from Japan. I had advocated this very strongly, but Harland & Wolff were not satisfied with the arrangement and they didn't accept the deadline that Shell had given for a decision at 2 on Friday afternoon.

We went on to Carter, and Jim reported on his trip with David Owen to the United States. He said Jimmy Carter is a very fast reader, has an amazing capacity to absorb his briefs; he reads at something like 3000 words a minute. 'About the same speed that Harold Wilson writes his books,' I said. Jim went on to say Carter was a great supporter of the Labour Party, and when Jim had told him, 'Well, we may save the country but lose the Election', Carter had replied, 'Well, I hope you succeed with both.'

At 8.30 Robin Cook, the MP for Edinburgh Central, and Brian Sedgemore came in. Robin is an environmentalist, very opposed to nuclear power. We had a candid discussion and I said that first of all they should try to interest the press in the problem, and send little groups of people to talk to members of the Cabinet about it. That is the most influential thing they could do. I told Robin about the enormous strength of the nuclear lobby: we would have to have a second system, or a new system of thermal reactors, but the fast breeder I was determined not to have.

In the Commons, after the debate on public expenditure, we knew we were going to be defeated in the vote because the Tories, the Scot Nats, the Liberals and everybody were going to vote against us and the whips weren't sure whether even all our MPs would support us, so we moved the adjournment of the House and the SNP forced a division. We all abstained and the motion was carried by 293 to 0. Mrs Thatcher got very excited and demanded a motion of confidence next week. So the Government looks shaky in the extreme.

We simply cannot rule out the possibility that there may be a General Election quite soon; not at all impossible.

*Friday 18 March*
To Bristol, and was met at Temple Meads by someone from the Independent Businesses Association. I had geared myself up to sympathise with small businesses and at the same time I was rather nervous of them because I thought they would all be potential National Front people.

Well, I couldn't have had more of a surprise because Mr Tucker, who met me, a man of about sixty-five, born in Bristol, couldn't have been nicer or more politically sympathetic. He hated the Common Market and had been Labour all his life. We and his son, who looked like a really tough self-made Tory businessman, drove in a Rolls Royce to Transport House, Bristol, where I met the small businessmen in the company of Harry Wright of the CSEU. It was an absolutely fascinating hour.

They talked about being inadequately represented. Their voice was not heard. They can live with a lot of legislation, but, said Mr Tucker, the big firms control the paper-money empires and they want recognition of their role.

A printer who employed thirty-five people said, 'I may look wealthy on paper with my premises and plant but I work very hard. I want to pass it on to my sons, but the business would have to be sold to pay for death duties.' He stated that half the people in this country are employed by small businesses; but corporation tax, VAT, PAYE, CTT, CGT, masses of civil servants and a huge inflation of tax levels made things very difficult.

Then Mr Tucker's son said, 'Equality and fairness are not the same. We are not speculators or big businessmen, we are all professional managers, and we are oppressed by the weight of the legislation. We want to be reasonable but it is a weight, and we would rather employ more people than pay more tax.'

It was a very useful meeting; I thoroughly enjoyed it.

At 7 to Brislington Ward, with about twenty-five people there. It is a serious ward and they had a mass of questions for me: first my attitude to the monarchy and the House of Lords, then education, then direct elections to the Common Market, Eurocommunism, small businesses, Russian attitudes to dissenters, and civil liberties in Britain, juggernaut lorries on the roads, comprehensive schools, Windscale and the Severn Barrage. For two and a half hours I was subjected to the most tremendous scrutiny and cross-examination.

The big news of course at the moment is the way in which Mrs Thatcher has picked up our refusal to be defeated in the House on Thursday night and her demand for a vote of confidence, which will take place on Wednesday. It is quite possible at the moment that the Government may be defeated; I think Enoch Powell would want to support us but the Ulster Unionists want to get rid of us; the Scot Nats think they would do very well in a General Election now that devolution has been defeated. The only thing is, the Liberals would be massacred in an Election, or so they think, and David Steel with the help of Reg Prentice and others is trying to force us to abandon our manifesto and go, in effect, for a coalition with the Liberals.

I think this latter development would be a very dangerous situation for us, though in fact there would be practically no difference because the Labour Party hasn't got a majority and therefore wouldn't get any legislation through. I think, frankly, we should make it clear that there will be an Election only when the House of Commons passes a resolution calling for a General Election and the Dissolution of Parliament, and until then there shouldn't be one. We are heading for a period of extreme complexity and if we do a deal with the Liberals, which I am sure will happen, or Jim makes a tacit agreement with them which Michael Foot will go along with, then it is all the more important when we come to the Election that we should extricate ourselves from that Liberal connection and fight on a radical programme. There is going to be a tremendous battle over the manifesto because Jim will want to make a deal with the Liberals and a watered-down manifesto the basis of our appeal to the country.

If he does that and wins, then we have the basis of a Labour Government which will have abandoned entirely the argument for reform. Revisionism will have won. If we try that and are defeated it will open the way for the Party to go left, so it is important that one should be free to argue the case for socialism openly.

*Sunday 20 March*

The clocks went forward today to summer-time. The news is full of the possible deal between David Steel and Michael Foot.

Caroline and I went up to the Baloghs' to join Albert and Joan Booth, Peter and Liz Shore and Michael and Jill Foot. At dinner we talked, inevitably, about how to get a deal on Wednesday and of course Michael Foot had been on the phone all day.

The Liberals have gone out on a limb. The Ulster Unionists want more Ulster MPs, they want to devolve local government and have tighter security measures, so Michael is obviously going to try for that and get their support. But the Government has to accept the fact that it may now be facing the abyss.

I tried to introduce the argument about full employment – that we've only ever had full employment since 1931 when we were either arming or, in the postwar years, when our competitors were destroyed.

Michael said the situation was nothing like 1931, that I was oversimplifying it, and Tommy Balogh said, 'No, that is absolutely right, that is exactly the position.'

I tried to argue that, if we were defeated on Wednesday, instead of resigning we should announce that the Prime Minister would only ask for Parliament to be dissolved if the House of Commons passed a resolution asking the Queen, in a humble address, to dissolve Parliament.

Michael declared, 'We can't do that – we are committed to resign if the Commons rejects us.'

I said, 'Think about it for a moment. Jim might not get a dissolution.'

'The Queen would have to give him a dissolution,' Michael answered.

'She might ask Mrs Thatcher to form a Government without an Election.'

'Oh, maybe in Australia, but they wouldn't do that here.'

So I said, 'Do we *want* an early dissolution? Surely we want to go on.'

I don't think he quite got the point; he hadn't really thought it out. Anyway there might have to be an Election. The question is when would be best. It might be better to have it now rather than later. If we lost it would be the end of the Government, but by God at least things would be clarified a bit.

It wasn't as disagreeable a dinner as I suggest, actually. Thomas told us that Mrs Thatcher had been to dinner with the BNOC board and told them that within a week of coming to power she would abolish them. Peter came out with his proposal for dealing with Europe by changing the Treaty of Rome and calling for legislation to change Section 2 of the European Communities Act, and restore power to the House of Commons. I agree with that absolutely.

*Monday 21 March*

The papers are full of Election fever. Everybody is steamed up about it but I am rather calm because I am absolutely sure a deal will be done (Michael made it pretty clear last night) and because if there isn't a deal and there is an Election we won't do all that badly.

Also in the papers today, the *Cambridge Review*, to which Francis Cripps contributes, forecasts a rise in unemployment to about 2 million; and the press has given it very little coverage.

The Labour Party–Trade Union Liaison Committee met at 10.30. It was agreed we would set aside the agenda and discuss the current parliamentary situation. Jim was asked to speak, and began, 'Well, Chairman, I think . . .' And Barbara as usual said, 'Would you speak up, Jim.' Barbara's a bit deaf, I think.

So Jim continued, 'Well, I was trying to think of what to say – I've had a weekend of work. We have got to preserve the integrity of the movement, it is not the best time for an Election, but the real question for the Government is will we have time to do a proper job? If we have to fight we will fight to win.'

I said it seemed idle to speculate about the outcome of Wednesday or about the timing or result of an Election. The real problem is that we did not have and do not have a majority in the country and this is what we have to correct. If we had a majority in the polls, Wednesday's vote wouldn't matter; if we can win public support we will reduce the risk to us.

Ron Hayward spoke up. He is a bit unimaginative. 'Our polls from Stetchford show us to be where we were in February 1974; housewives are anti, Leyland is the key, and people don't want an Election now, and I must warn you that proportional representation would mean a permanent coalition in this country. Prices and the dole queue are crucial matters; the Common Agricultural Policy is the key.' Then he added, 'I must tell you the *Daily Mirror* cannot be relied upon to support us this time. They had a board meeting recently and there has been a change at top level.'

Jim looked sick. Jack Jones said, 'We need a statement today. As to prices, I would have liked a freeze, but we have got to remember the Tories would abandon prices control if they got in.' Len Murray wanted a combined statement.

Jim said we must make a move to the Liberals and the Ulster Unionists – there is some give.

Listening to the discussion, I came to this conclusion. David Basnett, Len Murray, Hugh Scanlon and Jack Jones all want the Government to survive and would be perfectly content to do a deal. They are critical of the left because they think the left would bring the Government down.

So the trade union leaders ask what is the lesser of two evils in the present situation. Well, the Labour Government is the lesser of two evils compared to the Tories, and Labour with a bit of Liberal support is still the lesser of two evils. No doubt they would carry it further and say, 'Look, if you put up with the Common Market, which limits the freedom of action of the Government, and with the IMF, which limited the freedom of action of the Government, then clearly the Liberal limitation on freedom of action will be less.'

If you take that view – that Jim must be kept as Prime Minister (which is different now from having a Labour Party in power) – that is the only conclusion you can reach. I might add that the trade union leaders are terrified that their own position will be put at risk, if their members say: Well, you delivered us tied hand and foot into the hands of the Tory Government.

At 2.30 Mr Smith, Deputy Chairman of the Gas Board in Northern Ireland, came to see me. He is a young man, and I liked him very much. We had a most interesting discussion about Northern Ireland.

He told me he went to Ulster four and a half years ago, his first time. 'What I discovered was that it was like being in Scotland before the First World War.' (He is Scottish.) 'There is a tremendous gap between the Protestant middle class who run the country, with their golf clubs and wealth and absolute separation from the violence, and the violence of the Shankhill Road and the Falls Road, that is to say the Catholic and Protestant areas.'

He said that the Protestant middle class have been sheltering behind the loyalty of the loyal Orange working class and in that way keeping the Catholics down, but now that the IRA are beginning to shoot businessmen in Northern Ireland the Protestant middle class will get frightened and want an accommodation. Very shrewd. He also said if you could disarm the RUC to do regular police duties they would be accepted in the Catholic areas and then the army could do the military work and gradually be withdrawn. Very sensible.

I went over to the EY Committee which was held in the Cabinet Office (which I've never known happen before), with Denis Healey in the chair, the PM being, as Denis said, 'at the pictures'. Of course Jim is engaged in long discussions with the Ulster Unionists, with David Steel and so on.

First of all we had a long debate about the salaries of nationalised industry board members, and enormous increases were recommended. Albert Booth said this would wreck pay policy. Joel Barnett argued that we mustn't prejudice the pay talks. Hattersley supported Booth. Healey to begin with said: Decide now. Bill Rodgers, Eric Varley, Elwyn Jones and Edmund Dell were in favour of paying the full increase now.

One Minister did say, 'I asked the Treasury to tell me how much my salary was worth compared to ten years ago, and in real terms it is 58 per cent below what it was in 1967. I would now need £79,000 a year gross to have the same real income as in 1967, as a Cabinet Minister.' Anyway it was agreed after a long discussion that we would minute our desire to implement the increase on 1 August and consult the unions.

Went back to the House and, as I entered the Chamber with Brian Sedgemore, John Pardoe was standing behind the Speaker's chair. So I said, 'Well, John, what are you going to do?', and he replied, 'It all depends on *you* personally', meaning either I've got to accept the end of socialism or perhaps that I was going to be booted out of the Cabinet. So I said, 'We want an Election, and we'll win it too', or something like that. Pardoe added, 'I've always thought you were the cause of the trouble; you want a Thatcher Government.'

As I walked away, Brian told me, 'That was a silly thing to say to Pardoe because he will go round saying you want an Election, you want the Government to be defeated.'

If Pardoe spreads it around I shall just stick to the story – that he appeared to imply that I was the price that had to be paid for Liberal support, and so I had responded that if they took us to an Election they would be beaten.

*Tuesday 22 March*
I had a morning at home till 11.30. More speculation about the deals that are being done, and I am quite clear in my mind that one *is* being done. It is interesting that the Cabinet hasn't been consulted about it. The Prime Minister will announce it in the House of Commons tomorrow presumably, and we will hear it from the Front Bench. Then the Cabinet will confirm it on Thursday morning. That is what happens with coalitions: you trust your Leader and he does deals and you follow him out of loyalty. Much new thinking needs to be done.

At 12.40 Francis and Frances came in and we had a blazing row because I said I thought that in my speech to the trade union group of MPs this evening I should say something that bore upon the current political situation. Frances disagreed. She was going to have lunch, so I worked in my room and wrote a few things and had some sandwiches, then she came back and we went over it again. She said, 'Let them discredit themselves. Just sit back and do nothing, say nothing.'

'That's very cynical,' I replied.

'Well, being in this place has made me cynical.'

So I said, 'Well, surely we must sustain the Government campaign for our policies and get re-elected with a big enough majority to implement them?'

'No, no, if you go along with this, you are going along with a coalition.'

'Well, shall I resign?'

'No, don't resign. Just stay there.'

It was an awful meeting, and she was very upset and left the room.

Francis Cripps stayed and I talked to him, probing him. He said, 'You can't put it right with a speech. You have got to quietly make contact with all the people in the labour movement who are thinking it out for themselves and support them and encourage them and gradually re-create a new Labour Party from inside the wreck of this one.' He was quite sensible. I'm sorry I was cross with Frances Morrell, but she is a difficult woman and I am a difficult man, and when I think I am right I am usually wrong.

Caroline and I went together to the Waldorf for the annual party given by the Thompson brothers, the Labour Party's solicitors. The general rumour is there is a deal and we heard on the 10 o'clock news that Pardoe had said there would have to be a written deal.

## NOTES
*Chapter One*

1.   (p. 7) Militant was a Trotskyist movement within the Labour Party, particularly strong among the Young Socialists. One of its supporters, Andy Bevan, was appointed National Youth Officer of the Labour Party in 1976 but his position was a continual source of controversy and there were numerous attempts to remove him from the post and to discredit Militant's activities. This hostility to the movement culminated in the wave of expulsions of Militant sympathisers from the Labour Party in the 1980s.

2.   (p. 11) The Bullock Report was the outcome of a committee of inquiry set up under Harold Wilson in August 1975 to consider how best to extend employee control over management within individual companies. The Government Committee on Industrial Democracy was headed by Sir Alan Bullock and reported in January 1977.

The committee accepted that workers' representation could only be achieved through established trade union structures, and their main recommendation was that, in companies employing more than 2000 people, employees could choose to adopt a scheme involving equal representation of employees and shareholders on a unitary company board. The reaction from employers was predictably hostile, and some industrialists who had actually sat on the committee issued a minority report opting instead for a two-tier board with representation for workers on a supervisory board which could influence management but would be kept separate from it. They particularly opposed a trade union channel of representation and favoured the West

German system of works councils separate from the trade union negotiating machinery. The recommendations of the Bullock Report were never implemented.

Members of the committee were: Sir Alan Bullock, Professor George S. Bain, Norman P. Biggs, Sir Jack Callard, Barrie Heath, Clive Jenkins, Jack Jones, David Lea, John Methven, Professor K. W. Wedderburn, Nicholas S. Wilson. Biggs, Callard and Heath were signatories of the minority report. Nicholas Wilson signed the majority report but submitted a note of dissent.

3.  (p. 18) Mark Hosenball and Philip Agee were two Americans working in Britain, eventually deported by the Home Secretary. Hosenball was a journalist and had published articles giving the location and functions of British Intelligence communication centres. Agee was a former CIA operations officer who wrote a book exposing CIA activities. Their deportation threat aroused much protest from civil liberties groups, the NUJ and the TUC because of the insubstantial nature of the allegations against them and the issues of freedom of speech raised.

4.  (p. 29) In 1977 Windscale, renamed Sellafield in the 1980s, housed BNFL's Calder Hall nuclear reactor for producing plutonium for nuclear weapons use and for generating electricity. It also had facilities for reprocessing spent nuclear fuel from other reactors to recover residual uranium and plutonium for re-use as well as other radioactive wastes for 'safe' storage. The complex additionally housed research laboratories run separately by the AEA.

A thermal oxide reprocessing plant (Thorp) was also planned for Windscale, and in early 1977 BNFL was waiting for approval of the planning application from a Department of Environment planning inquiry, that Department, under Peter Shore, having assumed general responsibility for the disposal of nuclear waste in 1976. Thorp was specially designed for reprocessing oxide fuels which were more highly radioactive. In addition to handling spent fuel from British nuclear reactors, Thorp was contracted to reprocess 3000 tons from Japan.

Objectors argued that oxide fuel reprocessing was technically unproven. Moreover, Britain's claim that it must recover plutonium for civil uses could legitimate other countries' production of plutonium and lead to the proliferation of nuclear weapons.

The application was eventually approved and building went ahead.

# 2
# The Lib–Lab Pact
## March–September 1977

*Wednesday 23 March*

A momentous day. As you might expect, the press was full of rumours of deals and talks. I thought about it again this morning, and after talking it over with Caroline I decided I would oppose any long-term deal with the Liberals. I had a message before I left at 9.30 to say that the Cabinet had been called for 12.

At the office I drafted a statement on a possible Liberal deal. I drafted it carefully, laying out my whole argument, which is that the objectives of the movement are to sustain the Government, to win a majority in an Election, to campaign from now till then to increase Labour support, to reduce support for the Tories, Liberals and Nationalists and to prepare relevant policies for the next Parliament. Any tactical decision made now should be judged against these objectives.

Then I went through the arguments for a pact. Would it sustain the Government? Yes, but only till the pay policy was through. Would it help us win an overall majority? No, because it would give the Liberals credibility and downgrade the influence of the trade union movement, thus damaging the integrity of the Party and Government. Would it reduce the strength of the Tories? No, because the Liberals would now present themselves as the only credible alternative to Labour, not to the Tories, whereas we would gain from a Liberal–Tory split of the right-wing vote. The Liberals would argue in an Election for a greater Liberal showing to tame Labour and keep Thatcher out, and the movement would be disheartened by the fact that we would be fighting on a Lib–Lab and not a Labour record. Would it help us to prepare a credible manifesto? No, because the Lib–Lab understanding would accentuate the difficulties of a Labour manifesto relevant to full employment and the welfare state.

I recommended that we accept the verdict of Parliament on our legislation after seeking wider support for it. Secondly, we should announce that if we are defeated in the vote of no confidence tonight there will be an Election on our record and programme. Thirdly, we should prepare our manifesto, and, fourthly, we should campaign now for support for the Government without a deal with the minority parties.

I went to the Cabinet at 12 and there were crowds of people in Downing Street, including hundreds of photographers.

Jim opened the Cabinet absolutely red-faced. I have never seen him so red. It was strange; he was scarlet. Michael was white and drawn.

Jim said the Cabinet would recall that last week the Chief Whip reported we would lose the vote of confidence tonight, and that at the TUC–Labour Party Liaison Committee last Monday it was clear the trade union leaders did not want an Election. They had encouraged us to hold discussions with other parties while preserving the integrity of our Party. 'In the last two days,' he said, 'I have been engaged in talks and plans, including contingency plans for an Election on 5 May and the Budget problems associated with that. I am grateful for the forbearance of colleagues and I will now report the result of these discussions.

'We began with high hopes for the support of the Ulster Unionist MPs and it is not clear yet what they are going to do. Jim Molyneaux [UUUC MP for Antrim South] and Enoch Powell would like to support us, and in these discussions we have not neglected the interests of Gerry Fitt and the SDLP. The Ulster Unionists have proposed that we recommend to a Speaker's Conference that there should be more Ulster Members, and legislate to that effect.'

'Now,' said Jim, 'I won't take the Cabinet through the long discussions which took place, but last night an agreement was reached with the Liberal Party which I will read, and will circulate. I would ask members of the Cabinet to return their copies.' He said the documents would be signed by himself and David Steel; then he went through the details of the agreement. The substantial points were:

A consultative committee between the two parties will be set up which will examine Government policy before it goes before the House.

There will be regular meetings between our respective party leaders and economic spokesmen.

We will present legislation on direct elections to the European Parliament this session and we will consult with the Liberals on the electoral system adopted. The Liberals 'reaffirm their strong conviction' in favour of proportional representation for these elections.

We will progress legislation for devolution for Scotland and Wales and in any debate on proportional representation for the devolved assemblies we commit ourselves to a free vote in Parliament.

On this last point Stan Orme asked if that included a free vote for Ministers. Jim said, 'Yes, the Cabinet would recommend, and then Ministers would be free.'

Jim went on to say that Michael would chair the consultative committee, which would consist of the two leaders and the two Chief Whips. Eric Varley asked, 'How do you intend to consult the PLP?'

'Well, Cledwyn Hughes, the Chairman of the PLP, has already been consulted and has played some part in the discussions. No alteration is possible, however, if agreement is not given by the PLP.'

Stan Orme said, 'You *must* consult the PLP.'

'If you want my opinion,' said Jim, 'there will be relief tonight and agitation tomorrow.'

Shirley Williams thought we must explain it to the PLP and defuse the anxiety. Fred Mulley and Peter Shore said we must consult the PLP.

Denis Healey said, 'You can't rely on the minorities – the Nats and the nutters will want to bring us down. We have to choose between an *ad hoc* arrangement and a permanent arrangement and under this agreement we get a guaranteed survival till autumn; it is much better than before and I approve it. We can't consult the PLP because only the Prime Minister can speak for the Party; there can be an inquest later.'

Michael Foot said we couldn't have a PLP meeting before the agreement – the only alternative would be a General Election. We shouldn't be afraid of that, but looking around the world all governments which had recently come up for re-election had been beaten – Mrs Gandhi in India, the Swedish Government, Ford and so on. 'Therefore we are carrying out the will of the Party in endorsing this agreement. As to the direct elections, the document provides for a free vote. We can emerge from this stronger and stay longer.'

When I think that at dinner with Michael on Sunday he made no reference at all to the Liberals, just to the Ulster Unionists, I feel totally misled. This does mark a change in my relationship with Michael, I'm afraid.

Anyway, we went round the table, starting with Michael Foot, who approved the agreement.

Peter Shore said it went far beyond anything he had expected, would do untold damage, consultation with the Liberals would be unspeakable or impossible, proportional representation would be dangerous and the idea of the Chancellor talking to Pardoe stuck in his gullet; he was against it.

Fred Mulley said the Liberals would help us, and he was for it.

Roy Hattersley said his constituency Labour Party wanted it and he was in favour.

Stan Orme appreciated that the situation was very difficult but he was against it.

Albert Booth thought it was the best agreement we could get and he was for it. I thought Albert would be against, but obviously Michael Foot, and perhaps the TUC, had influenced him.

Bruce Millan said it was the best possible agreement we could get and we didn't really want a General Election, 'but', he said, 'the danger is so great to the Party that I am against it.'

Sir John Hunt was saying something to Jim at that point and Jim asked, 'What was your vote, Bruce – you're for the agreement?'

'No,' said Bruce, 'I am against it.'

Well, I was as surprised about Bruce as I was about Albert Booth.

Roy Mason said, 'My local Party wants it; it is only an experiment. This is a moment of truth.'

I said, 'This is a parliamentary coalition, institutionalised by a consultative committee. It means the Liberals will penetrate the Official Secrets Act and know what we are doing before we tell anybody else. There is no guarantee the Liberals will support us on any issue. There will be no consultation with the NEC. Direct elections will split the Party and proportional representation would put our long-term survival at risk. It is called temporary but it would in fact be permanent.'

I argued that our job was to sustain the Government, to win a majority next time and to campaign for that victory. The truth was that the establishment only wanted this Government to remain in power until the working-class movement was tied into Phase 3: 'Then they will destroy us or have a real coalition.'

'Second,' I said, 'it will give the Liberals credibility now and in the Election and, whereas in the old days Liberal support came from a Tory split and helped us, now it will come from a Labour split and help the Tories. Third, it will damage the integrity of the Government and the Party; and, fourth, it will damage our capacity to have a manifesto which is radical and relevant. Therefore I think we should say to the House this afternoon that we will accept the verdict on legislation we bring before Parliament – we have no option. We should announce that if we are defeated a General Election will follow, and we should start preparing for that Election now.'

I remarked that, in my judgement, the whole PLP would vote for the Government in the lobbies tonight because a vote of confidence in the Government would always attract support, but if the PLP were asked to give a vote of confidence in a Lib–Lab coalition I couldn't speak for them. I was against it.

Shirley said the arrangement on direct elections was right and we must consult the PLP afterwards – after the statement, perhaps at 6 o'clock. It was painful and difficult for the Party but there would be serious repercussions if Thatcher won. Shirley feared that a Thatcher victory would lead to such a confrontation with the trade union movement that it would be a threat to democracy.

David Owen simply said, 'I support the agreement.'

Next was Healey, who said consultation meant nothing; we consulted all sorts of people – the TUC, the Liaison Committee, Jack Jones, Hugh Scanlon. They wanted it and so did he.

Merlyn Rees was in favour and added, 'I hope we are going to remember to tell the General Secretary of the Party and the trade union leaders.'

Elwyn Jones agreed with it for the reasons that Michael Foot had given and thought that otherwise we would be certain of defeat. 'I think that Shirley Williams put the case best.'

Eric Varley was in favour of it, as was John Morris, who supported it because we were only committed to talks and it was the cheapest buy ever.

Edmund Dell said that this agreement was of enormous significance. The Liberals would expect results and he hoped we'd do no deals with the Ulster Unionists.

Joel Barnett said Clause 4 of the agreement (at which there was some laughter) committed us to nothing.

Bill Rodgers thought the agreement had positive merits and would give us credit in the country; it was openly arrived at and he was in favour.

'It only lasts for this session, and we can make the session as long or as short as we like,' said John Silkin in support.

David Ennals was in favour because it preserved our freedom of action and would do us credit. Fred Peart was in favour, and Harold Lever not only supported it but congratulated Jim on having achieved it.

Jim wound up. 'I am in favour of it, obviously, because of the advantages it will bring to the British people, the unions and the Party. The Tories will either move towards the Liberals or attack them, but we must show good faith with the Liberals.'

Thus by 20 votes to 4 – the four being Peter Shore, Stan Orme, Bruce Millan and myself – the Cabinet consented to the Lib–Lab Pact.

It was now about 1.20 and Jim said, 'I must now ask those who have voted against it if they are prepared to go along with it.'

Stan Orme said, 'Yes, Prime Minister.'

I said, 'I can't answer that question because, despite Denis's comment that the Prime Minister speaks for the Party, all you can do round this table is commit the Cabinet. You can't commit the Party. The Cabinet does not control the Parliamentary Party, or the National Executive, or the Party in the country, and therefore the best I can say to you, Prime Minister, is that there will have to be consultations with the PLP, with the Executive and, in my case, with my own constituency Labour Party, and I am afraid I cannot answer your question until those consultations are complete.' He didn't press me.

That was it and, feeling very sick, I went over to my office. Frances was in the canteen and I scooped her up before she began her lunch and we had a talk. She was immensely agitated about the whole thing. 'This is the left losing again and we must do something immediately,' she said.

Got to the Commons at 2 and wandered round a bit. I found Mik in the Smoking Room with Jo Richardson [Labour MP for Barking] and asked him to come and see me. I had, I might add, kept the documents from the Cabinet meeting because I saw no reason whatsoever why a document signed by the Prime Minister and to be placed with the Liberal Party within half an hour of the Cabinet adjourning should not be available to me to discuss with my political friends.

Mik came up, and I read it to him and asked, 'What shall we do?'

'Well, it is very foolish. When I bargain with a chap I see what strengths that man has got, and I know if there was a General Election the Liberals would be lucky to get three seats. So in fact we have given away a lot for nothing.'

I rang a whole host of other people asking them to come and see me and they came in one after the other – Norman Atkinson, Eric Heffer, Michael Meacher, Judith Hart; everybody was pretty shocked. Michael Meacher just couldn't make it out. Judith was terribly upset but she favoured it because of course her seat would go to the Scot Nats if a General Election were called. She said, 'This is necessary, it means nothing, we must do it.' Norman was cautious. Eric was upset, though he has been saying friendly things about it on television all day. Brian Sedgemore came too, also very shaken.

There is a difference here, and I've noticed it in a number of political crises, between middle-class and working-class people. Middle-class people tend to intellectualise it, think it through, carry it forward, work out what it means and then say it is awful or it is wonderful. Working-class people have quite a different approach. Had Jim any choice? What was best? Here's a bargain. How does it affect us now? Their instinct is in some ways a surer one, more down to earth.

After that, I went into the House and Mrs Thatcher was just coming to the end of an awful speech. Then Jim announced the agreement and got a tremendous response from the House. I was standing with Stan Orme, Harold Wilson and Peter Shore behind the Speaker's chair in front of the box where the civil servants sit. The Tories erupted, throwing their order papers in the air and waving pointedly at the Liberals, who just sat there smirking nervously. The Labour Members were largely silent, sullen and sad.

By this time it was about 5 o'clock. Frances was in my room and we went and had a talk. She was very keen, in effect, on resignations, so we went to Peter's room, where he was talking to Jack Straw, and we brought Stan Orme in and discussed it in detail again. Peter thought it was different for me because I had another power base, whereas he hadn't. Stan said he would talk to his local Party; we had to listen to people, not tell them. Frances hammered home the point about the responsibility of the left to stand up and be counted, and to fight for the things we believed in, even if we were all driven into a corner. But I think even she was a bit shaken by it.

I rang Mother and she was very clear. 'I knew you would be worried,' she said, 'but it isn't a coalition, it is a way through. Don't resign now on this, on something that might go right. Resign only if you think you have to when things go wrong.'

I took a lot of notice of her advice because she had been through it so many times with Father. Anyway I didn't go and hear the debate; I couldn't bear to hear Michael. I went downstairs and, as the Division doors opened for the vote of confidence put down by the Tories, I got in and came out first.

I should add that I rang Herbert Rogers and he hadn't quite taken it on board; when he rang me later he agreed we should discuss it at a special meeting of the general management committee at 10.45 on Saturday morning.

So that is it. Without any consultation with Cabinet colleagues as a whole, Jim and Michael have negotiated something absolutely contrary to what Michael had told me on Sunday night. It was an agreement which we couldn't change in the Cabinet and which had been referred back and forth to the Liberals. It does mean of course that the Liberals will be in a dominant position in discussions with the Government; we shall, in effect, be unable to do anything without their approval. We shall find it extremely difficult to carry out our manifesto.

The National Executive now becomes of supreme importance because it is the only uncommitted part of the Labour Party, and I shall work like anything on the NEC for a really radical programme.

I also think that Jim will now find it that little bit harder to get rid of the left and ignore the National Executive; I can see a certain freedom coming out of this, and it is a pyrrhic victory for the right. They think it is the big rebirth of a social democratic party but it isn't. The Liberals have nothing to offer, they have no power base, and the Party is beginning to understand now what it is all about.

As with all these things – the Common Market, the IMF and now this – I think there will be a temporary euphoria followed by deep disillusionment. I don't want it to, but I think Government support will fall away as a result of this agreement.

*Thursday 24 March*
On the way to the office I went to Metyclean, which is one of my

favourite ports of call when things are going wrong. I bought myself a Casio quartz clock computer which has the most fantastic facilities – gives you the time, works as a stopwatch and as a calculator, and has four alarms. It weighs 4 ounces and fits into your pocket. I was thrilled with it.

At Cabinet, under foreign affairs, David Owen said nothing, so Jim asked, 'Don't you think you ought to mention the letter from Giscard which has just come in?' David replied, 'Well, if you like. Giscard has written to say he does not want Roy Jenkins to be at the European Council meeting in Rome this week.'

I marked in my notes, 'Hurrah!' The French are absolutely determined not to have Roy Jenkins because they don't want the Commission involved when the EEC heads of state meet. I must say the French are totally illogical; two years ago we couldn't get a separate seat at the summit because it was *only* to be the Community that represented us.

There was some reference to a leak in *The Times* today giving details of the split in Cabinet over the Lib–Lab Pact, and John Morris said it was disgusting. In the middle of the Cabinet someone brought in a note telling Jim that there was a Private Notice Question being put down by Ian Gow [Conservative MP for Eastbourne] asking whether, in the light of the story in today's *Times*, the Prime Minister was satisfied that Cabinet security had been preserved.

Jim said, 'If anyone round the table can help me, I would be very grateful.'

Well, I hadn't spoken to a journalist; but of course Jim thought it was me. I just sat tight. Some people explained what had happened and he just thanked them and said again that he would be grateful if any colleagues could help him. I sensed a violent hostility.

Got back to my room at 7.40 and the phone rang. It was Jim. 'There's a letter going round criticising the arrangement with the Liberals,' he said. 'I just want to tell you that, if you sign it, it will be incompatible with your membership of the Government.'

So I said, 'Well, I've already signed it.'

'In that case I want your resignation.'

'I had better think about it,' I replied.

'You know you have been sailing very close to the wind.'

'Jim, all it says is that we should have a special meeting of the Executive. It doesn't comment on the Liberal thing.'

'Yes, but it has been started by Mikardo, and anything Mikardo does is bound to be damaging to the Party.'

I said, 'Actually Eric Heffer asked me to sign it at the Party meeting.'

'Well, that's it,' he said. 'I want your resignation.'

I told him I wanted to think it over and he continued, 'I know you saw Mikardo yesterday and it was a pretty uncomradely thing to tell him what went on in the Cabinet. And it was pretty uncomradely to tell the newspapers.'

I said it wasn't a very comradely thing for me to hear about the deal with the Liberals from Pardoe forty-eight hours before the Cabinet was told.

'Well, we were very busy,' said Jim.

'Maybe you were. If you want to get rid of me I fully understand; perhaps having done a deal with Steel you don't need me any more.'

Jim insisted that that wasn't the case but he wanted an answer by tonight, as he was leaving for Rome in the morning.

I said I would think about it but that it might not be easy. The letter was already signed and if I did decide to withdraw my name it might still get out.

'Well, give me a message by tonight. I am going out to dinner.'

I thought about it, drafted a few letters and tore them all up. I rang Frances and she said I shouldn't have signed it. She may be right, but only yesterday she was saying I should have resigned and asking when the left was going to stand and fight.

I thought, to hell with it, and went to see Michael Foot. He was in a meeting, probably with David Steel. I rang Ron Hayward at home, and he said it would be a forty-eight-hour wonder and then forgotten. 'You are better off in the Government.' So there was no help from him, though I can't say I expected any.

I had a message that Michael Foot was free and he was in his room with Jill. I went over and said, 'You may have heard, Michael, that I have signed the letter calling for a special meeting of the Executive, and Jim says he will sack me. I thought I'd just report to you that I have decided to withdraw my name. I don't often feel like resigning but I did think about it yesterday. However, I've decided to stick with it.'

He asked Jill to leave us and then declared, 'Look, it was the leak to *The Times* that made him so angry. He was certain it was you; he thought you came straight out of the Cabinet and told the press.'

I said, 'I didn't, but I was bloody angry because Pardoe had told me two days before what was going to be in the deal.'

'Ah, but Pardoe didn't know,' he said. 'Pardoe made it up. It wasn't settled till 11 o'clock the night before.'

'Maybe, but Pardoe thought he knew; he pretended to know.'

'You shouldn't have let Pardoe provoke you,' Michael remarked.

I told him that in any case there should have been a meeting of the Executive – that's what it was really about. We were told nothing that morning.

'Oh, you don't realise, this is so difficult, so dangerous; the Government is on a knife edge and if this arrangement with the Liberals goes down we are finished. The Tories are on the defensive now but they'll come back and make something of the fact that you are asking for a meeting of the Executive. You shouldn't do it.'

I said, 'I know you are in a difficulty, Michael, but I just get the feeling that Jim, having got Steel on the hook, wants to get rid of me anyway. It's just not rational to get rid of me for the reason he gave.'

'No, it is just the leak.'

I explained, 'I came out of the Cabinet, I told Norman Atkinson, I told Mik, I told some other people. I didn't see why the Liberals should have the agreement on paper at 2.15 when the Party was going into the debate on the vote of confidence not knowing about it. I didn't think that was right.'

Well, then he said, 'Now look, now look, I'll go and see Jim. You will be Leader of the Labour Party in time, I am sure of it; you speak for the movement, they believe you and trust you, they have faith in you. Don't get into trouble over this.'

'Well, I've said I'll withdraw my name. Leave it to me.'

Then I left. In a way you can see Michael's point – he had to do a deal, the Government has to survive, and someone's got to do the fixing. It isn't all that disreputable – I can see myself in a similar position – but still he didn't tell the Party and it isn't just about the deal. The Cabinet sees it as the birth of a social democratic group, that is what it's really about, and there will come a point when the Party has got to be brought in. It has got to work out this problem.

Came home and at 11 o'clock I rang Mik and said, 'By the way, that letter about the special Executive, I had a phone call from Jim saying that if I signed it I would be out.'

He told me, 'I haven't seen the letter myself. It was Eric's idea and he asked me if I would sign but I haven't seen it yet.'

'Well, your name was on it.'

'Then it was a forgery,' he said, 'but I am in favour of it!'

So then I rang Eric and said, 'Can you find somebody else to sign, Eric? I tell you quite candidly, Jim said if I sign it he'll sack me tonight and it doesn't seem sensible. It shows how jumpy he is and what it is really all about.'

'All right,' Eric replied, 'I'll find somebody else.'

Then I rang Ron Hayward again and said, 'If my name appears on the letter when it reaches you, will you strike it out?' At that moment, Michael Foot rang on the other phone to say he'd been to see Jim and told him that there was no conspiracy, that it wasn't all part of a great plan and that he had given Jim my side of the story. 'Have you withdrawn your signature?'

'Yes.'

'That's all right, then,' said Michael.

I rang Number 10 and asked to speak to the duty officer. After a long pause, Jim came to the phone.

'Oh, Jim – Tony Benn. I've withdrawn my signature.'

'Well, I appreciate that very much,' he said. 'If it comes out that your name was withdrawn, will you say it was a mistake?'

I told him I hadn't spoken to anybody about it and I added, 'It might interest you to know that it wasn't Mik who started it – it was Eric Heffer.'

Then I rang Frances and told her it was all over. 'You should never have signed it,' she said. 'It has weakened your position.'

'Don't attack me, please, Frances. Don't criticise me.'

Actually she is under pressure at the moment. She told me this morning she couldn't go on, the strain was too great.

That's the end of another immensely eventful day.

When I reflect on it, I probably should not have signed that letter.

*Saturday 26 March*

We had a two-hour meeting of my general management committee, called by Herbert Rogers at my request. About fifty members – two-thirds of the whole GMC – turned up at twenty-four hours' notice.

I began with a long speech describing the events leading up to the deal with the Liberals; I said that the trade unions had wanted it, what the alternatives were and what the consequences would be. I dealt with the wider issues of the Common Market and the IMF, with full employment and how it had to be achieved. Then at the end I said we must have a big membership campaign to get support for the manifesto.

Mr Dunn, a retired civil servant, asked if it was really necessary to have the deal with the Liberals. Bryan Beckingham quoted *The Times* that the deal was only to get Phase 3 from this Government and to stop Labour's legislation.

Cyril Langham argued that this situation was due to the failure of the Party to control the PLP and he quoted Wilson's Referendum slogan, 'It's good for Britain, good for labour, good for the country.' Cyril said we must elect the Party Leader at the Conference. He admitted a minority government couldn't have survived and thought I should not resign but stay on to vote against direct elections and advocate a withdrawal from the EEC.

George Staples said, 'I joined the Labour Party, not a coalition. I would have liked an Election on a socialist programme.'

Peter Hammond, the YS delegate, described the reaction among the Young Socialists as one of anger and disgust. He believed we should have called the Liberals' bluff. He doubted if they would have voted against us because business circles didn't want Labour defeated. We should campaign for a socialist alternative. This coalition would provide neither jobs nor houses.

Mr Tarr, who is nearly seventy, agreed with me: we must learn the lessons of history, we must have our eyes on the future, we didn't like the deal but we must accept the position and use it to our advantage. Britain had never solved unemployment – it was the last war which solved that – and he wanted to see a shorter working week, and to start building socialism now.

Celia Roach thought the Lib–Lab agreement was unacceptable. She was worried about certain trends; for example, the media were now trying to make us ashamed of being socialists. She said the magistrates' magazine was recommending resolutions from the magistrates' conference in favour of a sterner view of truancy.

Irving Rogers, Herbert's son, said a recall Party Conference was necessary. The present Government was not socialist, the Stock Exchange wanted Labour to go and the Government was working within capitalism.

Herbert Rogers said the EEC was a centralised capitalist bloc with financial controls. We didn't need a recall Conference and, if we had one, he feared manipulation by the big union leaders, who might use their block votes to support Callaghan. We didn't need a new Conference – we already had a clear manifesto.

I spoke a second time, and said it was not for me to decide what the resolution from this meeting should be but I would have thought it would be sufficient to reject the deal, to campaign, to oppose a special Conference for the reasons given and to make a special point of opposing direct elections. As to my personal position, I said I would like advice later, but I was working on the basis that they wanted me to stay in the Government and fight from the inside. I told them to be ready for an Election, which could even come in July. The meeting ended.

I have recorded it in some detail because frankly these guys are at least as well informed as Cabinet Ministers. The Bristol South East Party is a remarkable Party, with a serious and dedicated membership – many of them youngsters.

### Sunday 27 March

There was quite a bit in the papers about the events of the week, including an article by Hugo Young saying 'Thatcherism' and 'Bennery' have now both been displaced in favour of this new centre arrangement.

Caroline and I decided that we would not attend any more of the Sunday night dinners. I'm not saying some of the participants couldn't be brought in in some way – Stan Orme and Peter Shore certainly could

– but it must be on the basis that we really are trying to work out how to re-create the Party and not just stumbling on.

*Monday 28 March*
I was half an hour early for Cabinet so I went and had a cup of tea in a café by Old Scotland Yard. At Cabinet we had the usual Budget security warning and were told not to take notes. I didn't take any papers or anything; I just sat there, and Denis announced his Budget.

The Cabinet lasted fifty-eight minutes and afterwards I went back to the office and had a talk with Francis and Frances. They had been discussing the coalition, and Frances is convinced I should resign. Francis has been persuaded.

So after three years during which Frances Morrell was dismissing futile gestures she has suddenly swung completely and says there is an overwhelming case for resigning. 'What is the case for staying in?' she asked me. 'Well,' I said, 'what is the case for getting out?' She said that the coalition was different.

Got in the car and drove to Northolt, and there was the little 125 jet to take us to Brussels – Peter Le Cheminant (a Deputy Secretary in the Department), Bernard Ingham, Frances Morrell, James Bretherton and myself. We drove straight to the international press centre, where I gave a press conference as President of the Energy Council, without being diverted on to British policy, and the journalists were furious. They wanted the usual secret briefing, full of gossip and malice, which I wasn't prepared to give them.

After a BBC interview I came back to the Embassy residence where Lady Maitland provided the same room for me. They had very kindly given me a kettle, so I made myself a cup of tea before going down for dinner with the EEC Energy Ministers.

We had the most serious discussion on economic policy that I have ever attended in the Community, but on openness there is not a single one of them prepared to support me.

I said we ought to talk about nuclear problems in the restricted sessions and they agreed. The Germans are in terrible trouble with their nuclear programme and even Brunner, the Energy Commissioner and a German himself, said this was because they were not heeding the advice that I was always giving about taking people into their confidence. This is something I am going to raise in the course of the discussions.

Donald Maitland said it was the best discussion on energy policy he had attended.

I came up, dictated my diary and made a mug of tea, and at about 12.15 Frances Morrell and James Bretherton came into my room for a chat.

*Tuesday 29 March*

I had breakfast in my room in Donald Maitland's beautiful house. The room had heavy shutters which opened on to a balcony, overlooking a lovely garden bathed in bright spring sunshine. It was very cold, however, and flurries of snow were settling on the frozen grass.

We sat from 7 in the morning until 5.30 the following morning, but frankly I don't think the discussions were interesting enough to relate in detail. I took my white mug and got tea brought to me throughout the day.

I took the chair, and the first thing I did in the session was to ask whether Ministers would agree to having the Energy Council conducted in the open. I went round each representative in turn and every one of them found reasons why it couldn't be done – except Dick Mabon, bless him, who said yes. So that disposed of that idea.

We agreed the agenda and then had a discussion in restricted session on energy policy. Guido Brunner introduced a paper: what was really interesting was the tremendous anxiety in the Common Market over nuclear power and the forecast of a fall in demand for it. Reference was made to fusion and to conservation.

I now know these Ministers by their Christian names and I tried to conduct the session informally, calling them Hans and Ivor and so on; maybe I was too matey and not quite dignified enough because they all addressed me as 'Monsieur le Président', 'Herr Präsident' and so on. Still, it was a genuine attempt on my part to introduce a new atmosphere of cordiality.

We moved on to other items which were coming up – conservation, refinery policy and coal.

At lunch we sat with an interpreter who last year had been in Uganda on a Common Market mission and acted as an interpreter for Idi Amin. He said Amin was an enormous man, six foot four and a mountain of flesh, and he entertained the delegation around his swimming pool at his house at Lake Victoria, which he had taken over from a rich British colonialist. At the end of the visit the delegation held a farewell party in Kampala and invited Amin, who said he couldn't come, but in the middle of the party out of the sky came a helicopter and out of the helicopter jumped Amin with a gun in his belt and he stayed for two hours, talking. The interpreter told us that Amin was absolutely charming and he had tried to forget that Amin had killed 20,000 people, but many of the others were very frightened of him.

In the afternoon Gerald Kaufman, who was there representing the Department of Industry, chaired the session and we had the question of the siting of the Jet project.[1] Somehow I felt things were going wrong. By the time we adjourned for dinner I knew we had lost our case for having it at Culham.

I went to see Gerald Kaufman, who was using this long break from about 8 till 10.30 to consult, and he had come to the same conclusion. He was marvellous. We both felt the important thing now was not to allow a vote, in order to preserve the possibility of success, and we identified the points to be made but agreed that as a candidate country for Jet we ought not to come on too strong.

When we got back, Gerald dismissed everybody from the session except Ministers. He was absolutely brilliant – bright, cheerful and really good. He thanked everybody for their contribution, then restated their position in a way that highlighted the differences between the delegations and between the allies of the siting of Jet at Garching in Bavaria. His chairmanship was outstanding, even driving the Germans to the point where they challenged his ruling, but he never allowed anything they said to upset him.

The real lesson is that one should never give up a point in return for goodwill. One should assemble all the possible elements and negotiate it openly as a package – cover it all in Community language maybe. But I am never again going to try, which as an anti-Marketeer I did try, to be constructive and then find that I have lost. That was a tremendous mistake.

What was also highlighted was the strategy of winning by bargaining, legislating by bargaining, getting money by bargaining, which is something that the trade union movement is good at because they do it all the time – threaten something really damaging and then get your way by lifting the threat. This is a technique which has to be used in government but I have had no experience of it whatsoever. As for the civil servants, they are no good at bargaining, their advice is poor, and in any case they have transferred their allegiance to Europe so they are not the best guides on getting a good deal for Britain.

One has to rethink tactics and strategy. I have been through my short constructive period; now I am going to play hard to get and develop a completely different strategy for Britain in Europe.

The French are so good at it. I do admire them. They are clear-headed, logical, quiet, and they present their arguments in a Community spirit. The Germans, on the other hand, are blunderers and end up banging the table. The little five hate the big countries and band together to keep us in order, but they are frightened of the industrial and economic strength of Germany, whose geographical position allows her to dominate Denmark, the Netherlands, Belgium and Luxembourg. Everybody worships France because of her skill in diplomacy and her grandeur. Italy is just a beggar on the southern flank, a transparently devious beggar.

I'm being very blunt because I'm angry! The Irish are trying to be helpful, but they don't want to be thought of as an appendage of

Britain. Indeed, to be lined up with the British all the time is a slight embarrassment for Dublin on the continent, and so we can't really rely on them for support.

Anyway, bed at 5.30 am.

### Thursday 31 March

I went at 9.30 to a highly important meeting of a Cabinet committee called GEN 74 about the international implications of nuclear policy. David Owen was in the chair. Alan Williams, Minister of State in the Department of Industry, Sir Hermann Bondi from the Ministry of Defence, Sir Kenneth Berrill from the CPRS, Walter Marshall from my Department, Dr Robert Press from the Cabinet Office scientific staff, and Goronwy Roberts, Minister of State at the Foreign Office, were present. Goronwy said to me, 'May a member of your praetorian guard reach you?'

We had a thrilling series of papers. David Owen began by explaining the importance of the committee. He said we were concerned with non-proliferation and not with energy policy as such, and that we had to look closely at the spread of nuclear technology, step back a bit from it and take the biggest political view.

The first paper set out existing limits and controls on nuclear safeguards, and we had a brief discussion. I suggested that we make a political assessment of the countries with which we do nuclear business – Brazil, Namibia and Iran in particular.

We moved on to the American statement on nuclear power, sent to us in draft form two days ago and due to be published on 20 April. We have been asked to give our view by 1 April. In fact, Carter is saying exactly what I am saying, namely that we could halt the fast breeder, look very carefully at reprocessing and stop proliferation. If that is to be done, it will require a complete change in our nuclear thinking.

The officials had prepared the most formidable rebuttal of this statement, and were pressing hard for the fast breeder. I felt that, with Peter Shore, Fred Mulley and David Owen, we had at least managed to get a political response from the nuclear lobby, which after years of isolation were finally being forced to defend their case.

What is happening is that there is a very big change in the world's attitude to nuclear power. Thinking it through gives me a chance to argue it out within the Department and, once again, I feel that my main contribution to politics is just being a couple of years ahead of the conventional wisdom.

Marshall told us not to bother with the American attitude to nuclear power because it would have changed back in twelve months' time. I don't believe that. He is a self-satisfied and pompous man with poor political judgement. Anyway, we modified the officials' response.

Cabinet, where we heard the hilarious news that the Liberals had decided that they would vote against the Vehicle Excise Duty increase, that is the rise in car tax of £10 a year and the 5p a gallon increase on petrol. Their reasons are that many Liberals represent rural areas and they don't think they would be able to survive if they voted with the Government. This will lose us £670 million in revenue.

Well, after all that has been said over the Liberal deal, it really made me laugh inside. I said absolutely nothing but I sure noted it down. To see Joel and Denis, so tough against the PLP and yet prepared to crawl to the Liberals – the Party will soon get the message on this.

We went through next week's business. On Tuesday night there is a debate on Agee and Hosenball. Michael Foot stressed how important it was to get all the Ministers there to protect Merlyn Rees. Jim said if we were defeated on Agee and Hosenball then Merlyn's position would be intolerable. We couldn't have Ministers picked off one by one.

So there was Michael, on the one hand suggesting we abandon our economic policy under Liberal pressure, and then urging us to stand firm against any liberal civil rights pressure that might come from Labour MPs over this case. Michael is effectively finished.

On the United Nations, David reported that the Carter administration was producing what he called 'alarming resolutions' on South Africa, including a suggestion that Britain might actually be asked to introduce economic sanctions against South Africa, which would be impossible because of our economic interests there. It appears we now have a Labour Government on the right of an American Government – my God, I feel so out of sympathy with this Cabinet.

In fairness, though, David did say our economic interests in Nigeria were much greater than we realised and we mustn't alienate the blacks in Africa. But basically the British establishment is pro-nuclear when Carter is getting anti-nuclear, and pro-South Africa when the American Government is getting anti-South Africa. It isn't a socialist administration, it isn't even a Labour administration, it is a right-wing Liberal or Heath-like administration. It is awful.

After Cabinet I had a brief word with Albert Booth. After the Windscale settlement I had seen John Hill and the others and I was then asked to send a letter round Whitehall pointing out that there might be repercussive effects. The officials in Whitehall were furious that I had avoided the use of troops in Windscale by encouraging a settlement, and it is clear that they are now trying to frighten Ministers into saying disputes at nuclear installations should be banned. Albert had received a minute from his own officials saying my Department had been in touch with BNFL, who fully expected the Government to block the 2½ pence an hour increase at Windscale as soon as I left the Department. His Department had apparently persuaded the TUC to say that the settlement was outside pay policy. I told Albert that this really wasn't on.

I came back to the office and decided to dictate a very tough letter to Albert explaining that the situation was unique and so on, and sent it off.

Watched the by-election result in Roy Jenkins's old seat, Stechford. There was a 17 per cent swing against Labour, which in a General Election would leave us with fifty seats in the House of Commons. The National Front got 2900 votes, but, like the Liberals, the IMG and the SWP, they lost their deposit. It was a terrifying result because it showed how the country is absolutely fed up with the Government and our people just abstained. The Labour vote dropped drastically and the Tory vote picked up. On TV Angus Maude, Merlyn Rees and David Steel discussed the result with Robin Day. At one point, all three were talking about the need for an incomes policy and Robin Day said, 'Well, gentlemen, what is the real difference between you? What policies do you differ on?'

The political situation at the moment is critical and I don't know if standing out against it can be anything more than an investment in my future credibility. I feel deeply gloomy. If I had resigned from the Government, the Stechford result would have been blamed on me. But the reality is that it was a right-wing candidate, a right-wing Budget and a right-wing Lib–Lab deal. That by-election was really a test of the Callaghan approach – an approach which is absolutely fatal.

*Friday 1 April*

I went into the office for an appointment with John Hill at 9. He said he didn't feel we kept in touch enough. His reappointment as Chairman of the AEA comes up in September and he must have sensed that the officials want to get rid of him. I am going to be a bit clever about this one. I think I will give the Department the impression that John Hill is going, and on that basis remove Walter Marshall from my office and replace him as Chief Scientific Officer with Hermann Bondi. Then I'll keep Hill, and that will leave Marshall as his number two in the AEA.

At 9.30 I went to a meeting of the Cabinet committee GEN 73 at the House of Commons to discuss the plans for selling off our BP shares. It was humiliating and I loathed it, but I did succeed in getting the plans for the sale deferred till we had seen the alternative set out. I also got it agreed that, if the takeover panel were not prepared to let the Government keep 51 per cent of the shares with full voting rights, then I would take it back to the Cabinet. Finally, I persuaded them not to offer early information to the Common Market governments and I got a special arrangement giving preference to UK residents in the sell-off.

*Sunday 3 April*
My fifty-second birthday.

At about 12.30 I boarded a jumbo jet with Sir Jack Rampton, Philip Jones (a Deputy Secretary), Bernard Ingham and James Bretherton and we had a seven-hour flight to Dulles Field, Washington, where we were met by Colin Brant, the energy counsellor at the British Embassy. Washington looked beautiful. It was a warm spring day and there was still some cherry blossom after the recent bad weather. People were fishing by the river and, being a Sunday, it was very quiet.

One thing I noticed while talking in the car to Colin Brant was the slight tinge of dislike of the new administration. There is no doubt that Carter's stand on human rights, not only in the Soviet Union but also in South Africa, his disarmament proposals, his anti-nuclear policy which dominates his thinking on energy and his particular hostility to the fast breeder reactor have led the British Embassy to drop some slightly disrespectful remarks about him.

I have kept a pretty open mind about Carter. I like him for his Niebuhr quotes and for the informality of his approach, and of course I like him because he replaced Ford, but, as I found in Cabinet last Thursday, he is just too radical for the British establishment. But now we are members of the Common Market, our eyes are fixed more on Brussels than they are on Washington. Up to now the Americans have been happy to let this happen – indeed, they encouraged it because the Kissinger–German link was already a strong one. The German–American alliance has increasingly replaced the special relationship which used to exist between America and Britain. But now there is a bit more warmth from Carter for the Callaghan administration and consequently some apprehension on the part of the British establishment towards Carter.

At 5 I met with the Ambassador and all the senior officials and we discussed energy. They kept on coming back to Carter's questioning of the role of nuclear power and in particular of the fast breeder, which really worries them more than anything else.

*Monday 4 April*
Up at 6.30, had a bath and a lovely breakfast and at 7.30 went to do an interview on energy policy for *The Today Show*, which I believe has an audience of about 40 million.

Came back to the residence and had a briefing discussion with all the Embassy people – about twenty-five in all. I hadn't realised how deeply agitated they were about my own views on nuclear energy until I heard them talking about Carter.

I had an exceptionally interesting meeting with Jack O'Leary, the Federal Energy Administrator. O'Leary had been with the Bureau of

Mines and was booted out allegedly for insisting on the implementation of the mines safety regulations. He was also in the Atomic Energy Commission at one stage.

I asked him about energy policy and he said, 'Well, in the old days we worked on a least-cost, *laissez-faire* and rely-on-OPEC policy. Now we recognise that it has all got to change. I must tell you that there is great disenchantment with nuclear power among the utilities due partly to the high capital cost.'

He said some of the criticism was based on environmental problems, but also there was a feeling that in terms of economic performance the nuclear industry had not delivered what it had promised and there was a desire to shift to other fuels. He felt we had to re-examine the whole question of size. The programme was based on what they called the '2000–2000 syndrome', ie 2000 reactors in the year 2000. Now it was much more likely to be 350 light water reactors.

He commented, 'We don't want to move into a society in which there is plutonium in your desk drawer' – which was a vivid way of describing it. He was neither pro- nor anti-nuclear *per se* and he felt that the problems of waste disposal were soluble, but he said the chickens were certainly coming home to roost.

It was a fascinating discussion – tough and to the point.

After lunch, I went to call on Dr Schlesinger, presidential adviser on energy affairs, in the west wing of the White House. I wasn't taken in through the main entrance by the front lawn, which of course I would have liked, but through the side entrance; it was very much like an ordinary house, with a little lobby. There were some guys with mobile television cameras filming a week in the life of the President.

During the interview with Schlesinger, a woman brought in a note which I thought must be telling him to wind up the discussion, but after reading it he passed it to me and it said, 'The film unit would like to take actuality.'

'Do you mind?' Schlesinger asked.

'Not in the slightest.'

Schlesinger is a tough cookie. It was very hot and he wasn't wearing a jacket so I took mine off and we sat with a few officials in this little room – no bigger than our front room at home.

On oil conservation he told me he intended to make huge savings, and on nuclear power they were definitely going to do a deal with the environmentalists under which they could press ahead with the light water reactors in return for downgrading the fast breeder.

I didn't like him to begin with, and I didn't think he liked me, so I decided to play it very cool, argue with him and test his thinking. I did, after all, have the advantage of two years' experience in the field while he had only just started in the job, although he had worked in the

Atomic Energy Commission. He was a serious guy and the meeting did confirm my feeling that American thinking is very much like our own, which does enormously strengthen my hand in dealing with the nuclear establishment in Whitehall.

Dinner at the Embassy with a huge crowd – my officials and lots of people from the Energy administration, plus Lord and Lady Bridges, Colin Brant and his wife, Senator Tom Eagleton, Michael Howard, whom I hadn't seen for ages, and a few Washington friends I asked to be invited.

Michael is a military expert, studying the role of British Intelligence, and I spoke to him briefly after dinner. He said he didn't think the university authorities or television services were too harsh on the Trots. They would get over it.

'That's the children of the establishment protecting their own,' I said. 'It is not so easy further down the line.'

He thought I was overdoing it. 'I don't think of you as a socialist, more of a liberal,' he told me. I said there was something in that but that there were some pretty radical liberals in the old days. Still, if that is what the Intelligence service thinks of me then I feel reasonably content. There is an element of truth in it.

I had a briefing meeting with the Ambassador afterwards in which he said that he thought the talks had gone well. There was some anxiety, which Philip Jones mentioned, that if we tried to develop a special relationship with the US in the nuclear field this would alarm the Europeans. But I don't think so, and I will suggest we invite Schlesinger over to Europe; there is no reason why we shouldn't.

*Tuesday 5 April*
Today nearly knocked me out, it was so busy.

Up at 6.30, looked through my papers and left at 7.30 for the Hyatt Regency Hotel for breakfast with Representatives John Dingell, Clarence (Bud) Brown, Walter Flowers and George Brown and a number of their staff.

We talked for an hour about how Congress was going to handle President Carter's energy message. There are something like seventeen congressional committees concerned with energy matters, so the Speaker of the House has suggested setting up an *ad hoc* committee, made up of the leading members of these others, to assess the energy bill before it goes before Congress.

They were obviously very concerned about the anti-nuclear nature of the President's message. I must say, I become more and more puzzled by the intense commitment of the establishments of the world to nuclear power. In Britain the academic establishment, the Royal Society, the electricity establishment, the Whitehall establishment and the Tory Party are all fiercely committed to nuclear power. It is partly based on energy needs but I think it also has a lot to do with a strong attachment to technology, and of course the civil nuclear industry has been used for military purposes and that defence connection makes their commitment even firmer.

I was so tired I was hardly able to keep my mind focused on the various meetings throughout the day. Very foolish to come to America as tired as I was – I had a headache just from exhaustion.

Just before dinner, the President of Amoco came over and apologised for the behaviour of the men I negotiated with in London on the participation issue. I said they had been very difficult to accommodate because they were so nitpicking. He said, 'Well, we want to live with you. We want to be in Britain for a long time. There was a misunderstanding and I would have signed.' I thanked him for telling me; he kept coming back and repeating it.

### Wednesday 6 April
I had a long sleep and woke up thoroughly refreshed.

I forgot to mention that last night, when I arrived back at the hotel, I saw Gordon Richardson, Governor of the Bank of England. He always gives you such a glinty smile. I suppose he was negotiating the sale of the Government's British Petroleum shares; one has no real sense that the Government is in charge of these matters. There are all these fringe people around in the establishment with their own close contacts and they get to handle these things. Richardson is always friendly to me and must have it in the back of his mind that one day he might have to work with me in some way.

The plane bound for London was jampacked and the stewardesses worked like beavers through the night. I had a meal and then slept most of the way home.

### Thursday 7 April
To Number 10 for a meeting of the Cabinet Energy Committee to discuss the Drax B coal-fired power station.

*My Department was faced with the decision on whether to bring forward the order for Drax B in the light of a worldwide slump in electricity demand. The UK turbo-generator industry, which provided equipment for power stations, faced order book problems in the 1976–80 period, and the CPRS ('Think Tank') had recommended in October 1976 that the order be advanced to secure jobs and skills in the industry, provided that the industry was restructured. Eric Varley as Secretary of State for Industry consequently stipulated that orders for turbo-generating equipment for Drax B would be conditional on a merger between Weinstock's GEC and C. A. Parsons, together with the boilermakers Clarke Chapman and Babcock*

*& Wilcox, giving GEC overall control over the turbo-generating industry with a shareholding for the NEB. Parsons had agreed in principle to a merger but demanded an independent chairman, which Weinstock refused.*

*I favoured a contract with Parsons partly to safeguard jobs in the north-east but also on the grounds that a privately controlled monopoly of the industry would open up tendering to overseas competitors. The only way of preserving jobs was to place the order for Drax B by single tender with Parsons in collaboration with Babcock & Wilcox. I supported restructuring in principle but not if it simply meant creating a GEC monopoly for Weinstock.*

I conceded at the committee that the industry had to be rationalised but we had to maintain steady orders, links with the CEGB, exports and National Enterprise Board involvement without undue costs to the consumer. Parsons would agree to rationalisation, but Weinstock wanted to kill Drax B. If he gained overall control of the turbo-generating industry he would simply switch over to a nuclear power station on American lines.

I said the CEGB had admitted that it was the cheapest to install. I was for advancing Drax B, and I reminded the meeting of our experience of GEC mergers – they gobble up, they rationalise, they don't necessarily go for export markets and they think only of maximising their profits. I added that the trade unions were deeply suspicious of GEC's long-term strategy.

After some discussion, Jim suggested a statement should be published in ten days saying we would order Drax B subject to the completion of the necessary negotiations.

*Saturday 9 April*
Slept till after 10, had a mug of tea and dictated my diary for the last four days.

I should mention that on Thursday night President Carter announced that the Americans were going to wind down their reprocessing operations and stop work on the fast breeder reactor because of the risk of proliferation from the manufacture of plutonium. It was a tremendous statement, and the BBC took it up immediately. John Hill attacked it on Friday's 1 o'clock news, while Brian Flowers welcomed it.

I had a message from Number 10 that I was not to comment on it, which made me very angry – a British Energy Minister forbidden to comment on American energy policy! The nuclear lobby has obviously got at Jim, saying it will wreck our relations with the Common Market and upset the French and the Germans.

So I sent a message back saying that I wouldn't comment on the non-proliferation aspects but I would like to comment on the energy implications. I got a message back that I wasn't to do that either. It really is insulting, and I'm beginning to wonder whether Energy has now become far too important for me to remain in charge, and whether Jim might not try to move me to another Department.

### Thursday 14 April
Up at 7, packed, and at 9 Ron Vaughan picked up Caroline and me and, with James Bretherton, we drove to Northolt. We flew across the North Sea to Oslo for energy talks, and were whipped over to the Embassy residence, built about 1800 I suppose and overlooking one of the fiords. As I sit here in the evening dictating, I can see ships and islands and the sun setting – it is quite lovely. Just opposite is the Russian residence. This part of Oslo is very chic and is not allowed to be built on any more – a beautiful place.

Caroline and I went to have dinner with Prime Minister Nordli in his official residence, a rather gloomy nineteenth-century building made mostly of gilded wood rather than stone because there was so much wood in Norway, and with ornate French ceilings and chandeliers.

Nordli is a tall, shy, serious man but under that grave exterior is a great sense of humour. He took me aside after dinner and we had a good hour and a half's talk. He expressed his real anxiety about unemployment. He said that Schmidt was one of the most reactionary men he had ever met, and he much preferred Willy Brandt – as indeed I do. Norway had been lucky; it could survive by subsidising farmers and fishermen. 'In Norway,' he said, 'we have a saying – that the fishermen fish when there is a good fishing season, but when the fishing season is bad they fish from the Treasury and do just as well.'

His main anxiety, which he described at enormous length, was the development over the last five years of the Soviet naval and air base up in the north at Kola. With the Soviet fleet coming up the Kattegat, down the Skagerrak and soon from the Kola base, they would be enclosed in a ring of steel behind the Soviet Union. He was afraid that western Europe would try to make its northern defence line on the Skagerrak and Kattegat and leave out Norway. He had raised this with Kissinger, who had said, 'Well, about a month ago we set up a working party in the Pentagon to assess the significance of the Kola base.' Nordli said he couldn't believe that the Pentagon had only just begun to take this seriously – after five years. Nor did he think the British took it seriously; he would have raised it with Callaghan but he hadn't had the opportunity. He linked all this up with the need for full employment, saying if we didn't get full employment in the west, the structure of our societies would be destroyed.

'We want détente,' he said, 'of course, we want good relations with eastern Europe, because when the communists in Russia have got enough to eat and better clothes they will want a little more freedom. We must preserve the vitality of the west by dealing with this terrible problem of unemployment.'

It was a most interesting and convincing talk, and I said I would report all this to the Prime Minister on my return; he was obviously a worried man. I think being out of the Common Market, which he had been in favour of joining, has made him feel even more isolated. Still, he was charming.

*Saturday 16 April*
We said goodbye to the Norwegians after a very pleasant visit. They have a great deal of sympathy with the United Kingdom, particularly I'm sure with Scotland, arising from their long historical links. Scandinavia is gentle and civilised, and, as Nordli said yesterday, the Norwegians trust British democracy but are not so sure about French and German democracy. I think that's wise.

The weather was lovely and sunny as we flew back home. I unpacked and started to prepare for my trip to Saudi Arabia on Monday.

*Monday 18 April*
To Saudi Arabia for talks on oil policy.

In the VIP suite at London Airport I saw Mario Soares, the Prime Minister of Portugal, with his Foreign Minister, so I walked over and introduced myself – I had met him before at the Party Conference. I don't like Soares but I daresay he is struggling to keep Portugal on the right course during this very difficult period.

At 11 we arrived at Frankfurt, and the British Consul-General had booked a table for lunch at a restaurant by the airport hotel for me to meet Manfred Stephany, Managing Director of Nukem, the German equivalent of BNFL.

I was a bit cross actually to find this had been done without my permission, so until he arrived I went and sat in another corner of the restaurant for nearly an hour correcting the chapter on the peerage case in Robert Jenkins's biography.*

Stephany turned up at 12.20 just back from America and our talk turned out to be most informative.

He said Carter's statement had greatly upset the Germans, who saw it as discrimination against them and a breach of the Non-Proliferation Treaty, which guaranteed and controlled access to nuclear technology. He believed the effect would be to rally German opinion behind Schmidt.

The Tehran Conference resolution had condemned the American

* *Tony Benn: A Political Biography* (Writers and Readers Co-operative, 1980).

decision, and, Stephany revealed, Dr Walter Marshall had worked on the draft. I didn't even know Marshall was in Tehran, and he certainly didn't consult me.

He said Schlesinger was in fact pro-nuclear and had opposed the policy announcement but Carter had forced it on him. Stephany had heard off the record that the Americans had tipped off Urenco to start high enrichment of uranium in Europe, even though the Americans wanted to restrict their own programme.

He derided Canada's safety regulations on handling nuclear materials, and said they caused great offence in the Community. German opinion was solidly behind nuclear power, he said, and the German Government was afraid that if they didn't have a big nuclear programme there would be high unemployment, which would threaten democracy. They greatly admired the vitality of British democracy because it allowed us to deal with our problems as a united society. In Germany they couldn't do that.

He said Germany was a long way off the fast breeder but they wanted to keep the option open. He personally regretted that the German Government had agreed to supply Brazil with enrichment and reprocessing facilities, but that was spilt milk now and they had to go ahead, otherwise Germany's credibility as a trading nation would be at stake. In any case, he said, anyone could make a bomb nowadays – the Indians had done it in their backyard.

He believed Euratom safeguards were the best in the world, with 500 inspectors operating the treaty. I asked what would happen if somebody breached them.

'Well,' he said, 'that's a very interesting point. We have asked ourselves what we at Nukem would do if the German Government asked us to evade the safeguard system in order to provide high-enriched uranium. We discovered that we would need to tell fifty people what we were doing and the inspectors would be bound to find out.'

'But then what?' I asked.

'That's the problem,' he said. 'Even if it is known, what could you do anyway?' He agreed with me that everyone assumed Israel had the bomb, and what could anyone do about that?

Coming back to Brazil, he thought the best guarantee was to engage in the nuclear trade so that participants could keep an eye on what was happening; for example, Russia was enriching uranium for Germany.

The key to American policy for Stephany was whether Carter would allow the United Kingdom and France to reprocess Japanese fuel. All in all he was very frank and open and he gave away perhaps more than he realised.

At 1.30 we flew to Dhahran, and I talked to Bernard Ingham

throughout the five-and-a-half-hour flight. He advised me to see more of the City and financial people to persuade them of what I was trying to do.

To bed at midnight Saudi time in my room at the Damman Hotel, after an extremely interesting day – just travelling and meeting people.

*Tuesday 19 April*
Another remarkable day. It was hot and the smells through the window reminded me of when I was in Egypt during the war.

I had breakfast in the hotel coffee shop with Jolyon Kay from the British Embassy, and at 8.45 we were greeted by Abdul Aziz al Turki, the Deputy Minister, and another Minister, Dr Fahd al Khayyal, and taken to see the Emir of the Eastern Province.

The palace was built only thirty years ago, yet it looked exactly like those old Turkish palaces you see in Palestine, with slightly peeling white walls and huge wooden doors. We were shown into the Majlis Room, which was laid with the richest carpets and furnished with deep, luxurious armchairs.

The Emir, a handsome man in his fifties I should think, rules over about 200,000 people. He advanced towards us, followed closely by eight or ten bodyguards with swords, who then sat on the floor at the end of the room.

We sat down for the coffee ceremony; I had been told to wave towards him for the first cup, drink it, then take another cup, shake it in my hand, and it would be taken away. Then tea came round, followed by more coffee – that was the ritual. I talked to him through an interpreter but it was very difficult.

Ritual is entirely destructive of any real contact because you sit there wondering if you are behaving correctly while he tries his best to put you at ease. I called him 'Your Highness', though I don't know if that was the right thing to do.

Afterwards in the car, I asked if the Emir was a magistrate as well. He wasn't, but Khayyal told me he could put people in jail. For example, if a man was suspected of being a communist, he would be jailed until the charged was proved. If it turned out to be true, of course he would be sentenced at once. That was just given as a casual example!

It's a case of one faith not tolerating another, because communists are feared as alien and dangerous to the established faith – I suppose in the same way that the communists in Russia fear the Muslims as dangerous to the communist faith.

Well, we went to the new University of Petroleum to see the Vice-Rector, a distinguished Arab, who had been to an American university. I was told there are 13,000 Saudi students coming back from American universities this year alone, which in a country of 7 million is pretty amazing. In this university, money was no object. We were taken around and shown some fantastic equipment.

I would think the Americans in Saudi Arabia are performing very much the same role as in China before the revolution – principal advisers, principal traders and principal beneficiaries, having captured the loyalty of most of the intellectual élite.

Later we took a plane out to sea and looked at some of the industrial development. I was told that about 40,000 people were required for the construction of the gas-gathering pipeline, which will cost between 12 and 16 billion dollars – four times as much as the one in the North Sea. The work will be completed in 1980 or 1985. It was an amazing spectacle.

Back to Dhahran, where we boarded Yamani's G2 jet, a marvellous machine, bigger than the HS125. I was so tired that I dozed off. Yamani was at the airport in Riyadh with a tremendous reception party. He took me to a suite in the Intercontinental Hotel where I am now dictating this.

Yamani invited us to dinner with him, so after I'd slept for half an hour we all went over to the Awami Hotel, of which Yamani occupies a whole wing. The garden was full of armed guards because of the threats to his life.

His wife was there, a beautiful woman of about thirty with long hair, a biologist trained at the American University of Beirut. He has two sons and two daughters, and I think he may have been married before.

The Minister and Deputy Minister of Planning and Abdul Aziz al Turki were there with their wives, who are all highly educated. It was a splendid evening and we stayed till after midnight.

Yamani has a passion for electronic apparatus. He had a cordless radio-controlled telephone with a little aerial, a videotape machine and a huge library of mainly American videotapes. He had a closed-circuit television on which he could check any room in the house and the surrounding area and record it on to videotape. It was really rather amusing.

I had quite a talk with the Minister of Planning. 'Would you say Saudi Arabia was feudal?' I asked.

'No,' he replied, 'it is tribal, not feudal. We have a tremendous sense of individualism, and a collective sense of compassion and family feeling. It is not feudalism with absentee landlords and so forth, it is tribal.'

We compared tribalism with feudalism and capitalism, and we discussed this in terms of the mood of the people in Saudi Arabia. I can see a certain rapport between the British aristocracy – or the Oxbridge establishment – and the Arabs. Law and order and the lack of democracy attract the British establishment.

On the other hand, I can see how the rough-and-ready tribal culture in Saudi Arabia, with its distrust of authority imposed from outside, could create an atmosphere favourable to collectivism. In Saudi Arabia all medical treatment is free; you just ring up for an ambulance. The Government provides an extensive range of services – education and health are absolutely free – but the Minister of Planning felt that this was dangerous because it gave the impression that the Government owed people a living – a rather conservative view.

We went in to dinner, and half a lamb had been prepared with rice. I got to talk to Yamani, and asked him what I should call him.

'Call me Zaki.'

I said, 'You're a commoner, aren't you?', and that really started him off. 'There are families I know,' he said, 'who wouldn't allow their children to marry into the royal family; I can trace my family back to the Prophet Mohammed. The royals seized the country and captured Riyadh with forty troops, gradually extending their control, but they are not really a royal family.'

I got the impression that the Saudi princes, of whom there are 4000, are very hostile to commoners like Yamani who have done well, and Yamani was slightly contemptuous of the royal family because he didn't think they were up to it. He said he wouldn't mind not being in the Government because he would really like to write. But he has been a Minister for a long time and maybe he is just tired of it. It was interesting to get that flavour of the social life and of how it looked from the top.

*Wednesday 20 April*
Breakfast in my room, and then we went to the Ministry of Petroleum, a beautiful building, where we were met by Yamani. He took us into his room, which was decorated in the French Empire style with panelling, gold décor and green leather work – very grand indeed. We sat and talked for two hours. Sheikh Abdul Aziz al Turki was there too.

Yamani said that discussions with Aramco were going well and a new Saudi oil company would be taking over from Aramco. The oil companies would provide technical and exploration services in return for access to oil. The technical section of his own Ministry, set up shortly after he had become Minister in 1963, had given him enormous power over the companies because he knew as much as they did about the oil business.

The national oil company would own more than half of the new refineries, allowing Saudi Arabia to get a much bigger profit. He said the oil companies were powerless against him. He predicted an oil shortage by 1979 and said the Saudis could easily cut back production and get the same income because of a rise in price.

We covered the whole range of energy policy, oil and nuclear, and he was interested in our North Sea prospects. He had mentioned to me on Tuesday that the French were going to handle their nuclear programme for them.

I came on to the theme of an energy forum, which I thought we needed in order to discuss the American domination of uranium, the Saudi strength in oil and the need for conservation. He was attracted by the idea – it is something I have hammered and hammered.

At 12.15 we went over to see the Minister of Planning, Dr Nazer. We got talking about the Arab–Israel question. I said Carter had made a good start, and Brezhnev had made a reasoned speech on the issue. Nazer said, 'We have never really understood why the west was so hostile to us', meaning the Arabs. 'We have studied it more recently and we are horrified by the tremendous Jewish influence there is over the British Labour Party.'

He referred to the emotional welcome that Wilson gave to Golda Meir in London. I told him it was more complicated than that; there had been a lot of anti-Semitism in Britain because we are a Christian country, there was a lot of hostility to the Jews who came over from Russia in the 1890s, and the fascists of course played on anti-Jewish feeling. However, people in the west knew that an injustice was being done towards the Palestinians and that they were entitled to a home of their own.

I think the Israelis, who have always argued that the Arabs don't want peace with them, will be put on the spot if the PLO and the Arab countries take this new line. I believe the Arabs are serious about this. There are Palestinians all over the Middle East whose impetus of exile and desire to come home are in a sense motives that are identical to those of the early Zionists. But the Israelis will not even agree to go back to their pre-1967 borders.

At 1.30 we went to the Equestrian Club, where Yamani had laid on lunch for us. Having flown in yesterday, met me at the airport, given a dinner party, had two hours of talks today and then hosting the lunch, he must be absolutely exhausted.

We got on to the subject that fascinates me most about Saudi Arabia – religion. I asked, 'Are the religious leaders – the Ulema – the people who run the state?'

'No, no,' they said, and anyway, they said, the Ulema were not spiritual leaders like our clergy. Muslims believed that everyone had direct access to God, their own hotline to Allah, and therefore they didn't need a priest. The Ulema, however, had studied Islam most carefully and therefore their interpretation had to be taken seriously.

The religious council was really made up of the elders or wise men of the tribe, whose job was to interpret the Koran and the religious laws specifically, and that gave them a special position. They seemed rather like a bench of bishops or judges from the House of Lords. The Minister of Justice is the only Minister who sits with them.

'So, is it like the Pope in relation to the Government of Italy?' I asked.

'No, certainly not,' they said, and they repeated that they didn't have priests.

'Is it like the Communist Party in relation to the Russian Government?'

'No, because the Government decides: these people only advise.'

It reminded me of the Labour Government back home, with the National Executive observing ideological purity, and administrative responsibility vested in the Cabinet. The showdowns that the Saudi Government has with the religious leaders are probably like the showdowns Callaghan has with the NEC.

I asked if the king was divine.

'No, indeed not. He is an ordinary mortal and he can be sued in the courts for any misconduct.' They told me he had in fact recently been sued.

'But is he leader of the church?' I asked.

'No, he is the person selected by the people as best symbolising the attachment of the administration of the state to the faith. He has a very modest role assigned to him.'

Well, that may be the role assigned to him, but I can't believe that's the role the king believes himself to be performing.

The Saudis attach great importance to the family. Yamani said that every day, even if only for a minute, he calls on his mother on his way to and from the office. He visited people all the time to maintain his family links. This was the most important thing in his life.

At 5.30 I went with Kay and the others to the old part of Riyadh. I took my movie camera but Kay advised me not to film, so we just looked around. We went to the square, known as Chop Square because it is there that they execute people publicly, cut off their hands or flog them, though not very often nowadays. There are about three public executions a year now and they hardly ever cut off people's hands.

We wandered round the old shopping areas, just like the old city of Jerusalem – a huge arcade with shops at each side where you could pick up a gold bracelet for £3000. If you grossed up the value of the stock in one shop alone, I should think it would be worth a quarter of a million pounds – yet there was no real security. They just pulled down the blind and went off to prayers, leaving the place completely unattended. Amazing.

Kay told us about the religious police from the Committee for the Prevention of Vice and Promotion of Virtue, who knocked on shopkeepers' doors if they didn't come out for evening prayers. Religion is to Saudi Arabia what communism is to Russia, a continuing presence in the background which I think will survive for hundreds of years, maybe for ever, just as in the Soviet Union I doubt you will ever shift the effect of those early years of socialist education.

*Thursday 21 April*
We boarded the Saudia Boeing 707 and found they had overbooked the first-class seats, so Jack Rampton, Bernard Ingham and James Bretherton went back to the second class and I was put on a little couch in the bar. I had a table which was right up against my knees, and no head-rest. It was agonising. It was hot and miserable, my head rolled all night and I dreamed of awful tortures in Saudi Arabia. I slept most of the time and woke up with terrible cramp.

We got in just after 8, went to the VIP room and then home. It was wonderful to see Caroline.

Cabinet at 10.30, and just before I went in Jim came up to me. 'I got your speech for the Scottish TUC.' Well, I had dictated a first draft before I left and marked it 'Not to be circulated', but apparently Number 10 had asked for the text of what I was going to say, and someone in my Private Office had innocently sent it. The draft contained the whole of my strategy, namely putting full employment back into the heart of our programme. I told Jim it was very much a first draft but he said he wanted to see me about it this evening.

The direct elections took up most of the Cabinet, mainly the questions of the free vote and whether we should adopt proportional representation. Merlyn said his draft bill had been based on a first-past-the-post voting system but Jim made it clear that he felt committed to giving very serious consideration to the Liberals' desire for proportional representation, using the single transferable vote. Jim was trying to make the Cabinet accept that he had given his word on PR.

Michael said he took a very serious view of the whole direct elections issue and felt that there had to be a free vote in Parliament.

Stan Orme remarked, 'You know some people won't accept it', and Jim said, 'Well I must make my position clear. I am afraid that I couldn't continue as Prime Minister if Cabinet could not discharge this solemn obligation, this international obligation.'

It was very difficult. I hung on for a bit and predictably Shirley Williams said, 'You can't have a free vote', and Harold Lever agreed. John Morris wanted a free vote for junior Ministers, Denis Healey said it was a bore and didn't matter, and Fred Mulley agreed. Joel Barnett said junior Ministers didn't matter because nobody had ever heard of them.

Feeling frightfully tired, I said, 'It seems to me that this is a matter of

Party management. Rightly or wrongly this is a deeply divisive issue' –
Jim had said there was a profound lack of interest in it – 'and there are
people who feel that on the one hand direct elections pave the way for a
united Europe and on the other that they are destructive of national
identity, and if we introduce proportional representation it would mean
the Party would never get into power again.'

I said that we had always followed the principle of respecting
differences of opinion and warned of the loss of credibility involved in
forcing a Member to vote for something to which he was completely
opposed.

Peter just said, 'This is not the moment to decide what to do and
that's why I am keeping my mouth shut.'

But the four of us – Michael, Peter, Stan and myself – will fight very
hard against the direct elections. I think Michael will give way because
he has to. Peter will find a way round, and if Stan went it wouldn't be
very significant and Eric Heffer would be offered his job. So I don't
know whether Jim takes it all that seriously yet. I cannot vote for it and
I shall just have to abstain because if I vote against it it will be too
defiant.

I had a long talk with Frances and Francis, who were chirpy after
their holidays. They had seen the note from Number 10 saying that my
speech repudiated the Government's industrial strategy, and that I
must pledge myself to pay restraint, do this, endorse that. Frances said,
'Don't get into a row', so I wrote a little note to Jim:

Dear Jim,

Thank you for your letter. It is too late to change the speech, but I will make
a speech on energy policy and boost the Government's achievements.

Yours
Tony.

### Friday 22 April

Caught the sleeper to Glasgow, with Bernard Ingham and one of my
Private Secretaries, Sandra Brown, for the Scottish TUC Conference
and arrived at 6.30 in Glasgow Central Station.

We got on the ferry for the Isle of Bute, where the conference was
being held. There were some helicopter pilots from Aberdeen waiting
at the ferry to petition me about their dispute with Bristow, their
extremely anti-union boss who recently dismissed a thirty-two-year-
old captain for being a member of the Air Line Pilots' Association,
BALPA, and when sixty-five other pilots came out in sympathy he took
action against them all.

Well, I had a lovely quarter of an hour with them on the boat –
missed the sights going across the bay, but I heard their demands.

We arrived and I made my speech, in which I said simply that the unions and the Government must stick together. I also raised the helicopter pilots' dispute, and this was well received.

To dinner at Leith Labour Party, my father's old constituency, and after the meal I was asked to sing a song for the first time in my political career. So I sang:

> 'Just a wee deoch an doris,
> Just a wee 'un that's a',
> Just a wee deoch an doris
> Afore ye gang awa'.
> There's a wee wifey waiting
> In a wee but 'n' ben.
> If you can say "it's a braw bricht moonlicht nicht",
> Then you're a' richt, ye ken.'

It was all very cheerful and friendly.

Went back to Waverley Station and caught the sleeper for London.

### Saturday 23 April

Arrived home at around 7, talked to Caroline, and I was just about to have a bath when the phone rang. It was James Bretherton to say there had been a blowout in the Ekofisk field and 4000 tons of oil had bucketed into the sea in just twenty-four hours. I said I might go up there, and much of the morning was spent on that.

Jim rang me. 'Your phone has been off the hook.'

'I was just using it.'

'Well, it was,' he said. He was very shirty. 'If you are going to look at it, why don't you go to Norway?'

I decided I would and sent a message.

Apparently the blowout is huge, there's a force 10 gale and low cloud, but aircraft can't fly lower than 5000 feet in case there is an explosion, and ships have been banned for 25 miles around. I shall fly over the field and then go on to Stavanger or Oslo.

### Sunday 24 April

Up at 6.30, and left for Northolt. I boarded an RAF Andover with James Bretherton, Bernard Ingham, Henry George, our Director of Petroleum Engineering, and a guy from the Board of Trade Marine Division, and we headed for the Ekofisk field.

We were kept at 3000 feet and five nautical miles and it was a most remarkable sight – a great jet of oil and spray and the slick spreading sheen over the water. A number of vessels were standing by, including a warship.

We cruised around for about half an hour, before going on to Oslo to meet the Industry and Foreign Ministers. We talked for two hours at the airport hotel and they reported what had happened and went into all the other aspects – terrorism, fire, cost, fisheries and research.

Flew back, gave some more interviews at Northolt and came home. There was some coverage on the news but not much.

*Tuesday 26 April*
First meeting this morning was at the Cabinet Office at 9.30 for the Legislation Committee of Cabinet. I was only there because there were some EEC documents on energy for consideration. I report this minor incident in a busy life because yesterday, for the first time, I was asked by the Cabinet Office to see Jo Grimond, Liberal energy spokesman, before reporting to the committee. I must say I was annoyed at the thought; Frances Morrell suggested I get Dick Mabon to see Grimond.

In fact, Dick Mabon saw David Steel and the Liberal Chief Whip because Grimond was in the Orkneys, and Dick later told me that Grimond didn't want to see me either; he was sick of the whole arrangement. The Liberals are apparently fed up with Grimond as energy spokesman. Whether it's because they dislike working with me as part of the arrangement, or because Grimond dislikes energy, or because Grimond dislikes the arrangement, I do not know.

I heard tonight that the Bristow helicopter pilots, whom I met in Scotland, have now got the support of the Scottish labour movement, which is blacking all work involving the rigs. That means North Sea oil operations will come to a halt. James Bretherton came to see me and said a committee of the Civil Contingencies Unit may be necessary. I said, 'Fine.' They all know my view.

'Yes,' he told me, 'but you had better get on to Albert Booth quickly because the Employment officials are planning to undermine the strike.'

I said, 'That can't be. I told Rampton that we support the strike.'

'I thought I had better tell you,' he said.

So I wrote Albert a note. He is, of course, sympathetic, and so is Gregor MacKenzie, Minister of State in the Scottish Office, so Bristow has a real fight on his hands. The oil companies will bring pressure to bear on him and he will have to give way. The Government will be 100 per cent on the side of the strikers because the dispute doesn't involve pay policy, the Social Contract or anything like that – just the principle of trade union recognition.

*Wednesday 27 April*
One item I forgot to mention yesterday was that Kirkby Mechanical Engineering (KME), the co-operative in Liverpool which was on the brink of collapse, was saved yesterday by a Cabinet committee. What was interesting was that there had been strong opposition to it within

the committee but in the end they decided that they could not risk killing it off in the middle of the pay negotiations with the TUC. This, of course, is one of the great powers that the trade union movement has over a Labour Government, even a Labour Government as reactionary as this. Hence the importance of maintaining the Social Contract.

At 12.30 Walter Patterson came with a group from Friends of the Earth and a photographer, to present a letter asking the Government to give them money to prepare their case for the Planning Inquiry Commission against the expansion of Windscale. They knew that I couldn't consent but I had agreed to see them, and I was photographed receiving their letter, in front of my Workers' Union banner on the wall of my office.

I made a little statement in which I said the Government did not give money to political parties or pressure groups but that I was anxious that the inquiry should have before it all the possible evidence, and I was grateful to Friends of the Earth for their constructive role in the energy debate. I also said that, as they knew very well, last March I had authorised the go-ahead on technical grounds of the expansion at Windscale.

Although I wasn't able to help them very much, at least in this country nuclear protestors can come and talk to the Minister as friends instead of being beaten down by riot police as they are in Germany.

*Thursday 28 April*
Cabinet at 10.30. Jim said he wanted to thank all of those colleagues who had made speeches over the weekend supporting the pay policy. Well, I hadn't done that but nor had I made one against it, so I suppose I was included in that embarrassing tribute.

Secondly, Jim reported that the threatened strike organised by the United Unionist Action Council, which Ian Paisley is supporting, is causing a lot of anxiety. Fresh troops are being sent over.

Stan Orme intervened. 'May I be allowed to say this – that I think it is just possible that the right thing to do would be *not* to provide support for essential services and let them realise what damage they are doing to themselves.'

Jim said that line had been considered but rejected, but I see great advantages in another Protestant workers' strike, if it sickens the British people with the whole Ulster situation. I am now entirely persuaded that union with the UK was a disaster and we must find a new framework for Ireland with all its problems.

David Owen reported on Pakistan and the Middle East. He had been to Egypt and Syria and said the prospects of a settlement in the Middle East were better than they had been for some time. But it was difficult to get the Israelis, before their election, to agree to the Palestine

Liberation Organisation being represented at the talks, and they were in favour of a homeland but not necessarily a separate state.

David Ennals interrupted in his odiously helpful way. 'I would like, Prime Minister, if I may, to intervene for a moment to say how well I feel David Owen has done in his recent visits to Africa and the Middle East, and perhaps it would be in order, since we don't thank each other very much, for this to be said.'

So Jim observed, 'Well, I said how well David had done last week. I can't say it every week.'

I said, 'I take it this is the equivalent of Idi Amin eating his Cabinet Ministers' – referring to a story in today's paper from a Ugandan defector that Amin had killed a member of his Cabinet, had his liver cut out and mixed with his lunch.

'If I started eating my Cabinet I don't know who I would eat first,' said Jim, looking around the table and settling on me.

The rest of the Cabinet was devoted to the direct elections issue.

Merlyn Rees presented a paper in which he had, at Jim's request, taken on board the Liberals' demand for PR. He recommended that we adopt a regional-list system. He said the figures suggested that we could do very badly with the first-past-the-post system.

Michael thought we should ask the PLP if they wanted the direct elections bill, and Jim said, 'You can't do that; we are committed to it, we are committed by the summit, committed in the Queen's Speech, committed with the Liberals; we are bound to pass a bill.'

Peter Shore argued that the PLP must have a chance of looking at it, and then Jim said, 'I can tell you, if the PLP turns down the principle of direct elections, then I will resign. I cannot introduce a bill when I don't even have a majority in the Parliamentary Party.' He was beginning to panic – it was the second time he'd threatened to resign.

And so it went on. In the end, Jim said it was clear we couldn't decide it today. I was highly delighted because that was the second Cabinet we had got through without a decision. I am clear in my own mind that, without making a fuss about it, I am not going to vote for the second reading, nor for the ratification of that procedure. Jim will then have to determine what he wants to do about it. If I hadn't made a fuss, he couldn't justify a sudden decision to dismiss me, whereas if it becomes a big issue beforehand then the Prime Minister will have to be seen to win.

To the House at 2.30 for an absolutely fascinating meeting of GEN 74 – the committee dealing with nuclear policy, nuclear exports and so on. This is the committee at which you get a genuine ministerial view forming against that of the officials and, in particular, of the nuclear lobby. David Owen was in the chair. The first paper, on uranium demand and supply, had been put in by my Department.

Their first draft hadn't included what I wanted at all, namely a comparison between forecast demand for uranium and forecast supply, particularly over the last four years. Forecast demand had far exceeded forecast supply in the first half of the 1970s but, with the drastic cutback in nuclear installed capacity, the forecast supply now exceeded forecast demand, which meant that availability of uranium was not as tight as anticipated.

So I got the Department to put in a second paper for this committee, and this time it was full of incomprehensible figures. 'Take a pencil and circle the following figures,' I said. Pointing out the key figures, I absolutely destroyed the officials' case. Moreover, I said there had been no reference to my talks with the United States, who have agreed to have discussions about uranium demand and supply. We did have time, I said, that was the important thing.

Walter Marshall was reluctant to defy his Secretary of State, and David Owen said, 'Well, we must have a look at this again and get further figures.'

Immediately after that, I had a meeting to review the case of a Mr Gillen, who died in the early Sixties of leukaemia, having worked for three years for the AEA. His widow was claiming that his illness was due to his work.

Jack Jones had written to me several times about it, so in the end I called this meeting with the AEA legal, professional and medical staff, and the Department of Social Security sent their administrative and medical people along. Alex Eadie was there with me – which was a great comfort because, having been a miner, he was familiar with the whole question of compensation cases. I didn't have much of a leg to stand on, to be candid, but I went into it very carefully. At the tribunal in 1964 the whole thing had hinged on whether it was probable or merely possible that this guy had contracted leukaemia from his work in the AEA. The judgement had been that it was only possible.

But on questioning them I was told that Japanese survivors from Hiroshima and Nagasaki had suffered this particular type of leukaemia; secondly I drew out that there had been some marginal change in diagnostic and analytical skills since 1964; thirdly, that the National Radiological Protection Board had been set up since 1964; fourthly, that an appeal had actually been heard since 1964.

I decided to write to David Ennals and ask him to get the matter looked at again. I have never seen so many glum faces in my life.

*Friday 29 April*
We had an unbelievable by-election defeat at Ashfield yesterday. It is of extreme interest because it was formerly a safe mining seat – David Marquand's – with a Labour majority of 22,000. Nobody had

contemplated that Ashfield could be lost, and if we were to lose on that basis throughout the country it would be a total disaster.

That was the news this morning and it will affect the Lib–Lab Pact; the Liberals have done badly in both seats and I don't think they are going to benefit from the pact at all.

*Monday 2 May*
First meeting at 10 was to prepare for the Downing Street summit with Carter.

The second item on the agenda was the implications of President Carter's statement on energy, and David Owen had presented a paper which had been written by his officials. David declared at the beginning that the paper was too complacent – which it was.

I said, 'I wasn't consulted about this and my officials tell me they weren't fully consulted. It is based on the assumption that there are no defects in our policy. We ought to be a bit more modest. What is happening now is the first serious re-examination of nuclear power; there are problems of plutonium loss and uranium loss, of toxic waste, the destination of which is undecided, of large-scale plutonium handling, of uranium supplies, of what to do about the fast breeder and about the export of sensitive technologies. We ought to have considered all this.'

David Owen thought we should welcome the Carter proposals and study them, we should link up with the USSR, and we should have some links with the IAEA and the nuclear suppliers group.

I added, 'We are highly trusted in the United States through our scientific knowledge and technical capacity in nuclear matters, but we are not America, we are independent, unless we upset the EEC countries.' All the officials nodded because they are determined that Britain must not alienate the French or the Germans. That is the main concern of the British establishment – to bow and kowtow to Europe.

Came back and had a talk to Francis and Frances about direct elections. I am getting increasingly steamed up at the possibility that I may be asked to vote for this in the House of Commons. Frances and Francis were quite relaxed about it; of course it is possible that this is one of those historic changes towards a Europe with real power in Brussels, and Frances said what Caroline has always said, namely that it is not easy to make a stand against democratic elections. At 10 o'clock I went to see Michael Foot. Peter was with him and the real purpose of the meeting was to get me to agree to Jim Callaghan's new proposal to solve the problem of direct elections. Michael had officially taken the position that he could not vote for direct elections in the second reading, but Peter is more ambivalent.

Michael has been to see Jim, who is very worried. Jim's solution was to go to the PLP meeting with three propositions. One, to ask MPs if they wanted direct elections, to urge them to vote for it, then have a vote on it at that meeting, where Cabinet Ministers would be expected to support the Prime Minister. Two, to ask whether they wanted direct elections in 1978 or later (according to Michael, Jim wanted them deferred so that the issue wouldn't come up in this session). Three, to ask MPs which voting system they would prefer – PR or first past the post.

So Jim has evidently persuaded Michael that it will be all right and the whole thing will be deferred. I don't believe that for a minute.

I went back and talked with Michael Meacher till after midnight. He has been involved with Ian Mikardo in setting up this letter to Jim Callaghan, signed by at least fourteen people, saying that unless they are consulted on the same basis as the Liberals they are not prepared to continue to support the Government. I said I thought a general threat like that was a bit incredible.

Today I got a present from Yamani, a complete sheikh's outfit – a brown robe, a little white cap, a red head-dress, and a black thing you put around the head-dress to keep it in place. It was huge fun.

*Tuesday 3 May*
Sir Douglas Allen, the Permanent Secretary at the Civil Service Department, came at 11 to discuss Hermann Bondi's impending appointment as my scientific adviser.

Allen implied that Bondi was disorganised and not very popular and the Minister of Defence would like to get rid of him. I disagreed. I think he is just what I want at the moment. He said he would speak to Sir Frank Cooper, the Permanent Secretary of Defence, and I will have a word with Fred Mulley.

I suggested that we might try to get a knighthood for Marshall when he is pushed out, but Douglas said it would be difficult. I said, 'Well, how does the Honours List work?'

All of a sudden this languid man with his nervous twitch leapt into life and went on for twenty minutes about the Honours List. 'The Honours come in and they go to Number 10, committees are set up to look at each one, the Permanent Secretaries are in charge of committees, they all meet under me, I see the Prime Minister, he can knock suggestions out, we can put things in.' I had hit upon the one thing that really excites the head of the Civil Service – the Honours List. Amazing.

To Paddington to get the train to South Wales for the Miners' Conference in Porthcawl. Just as I got to the station a chap from my Private Office arrived on a motor bike with the proof of my article on the centenary of Father's birth, which is to appear in *The Times* on Saturday. I should add that I had a very nice handwritten letter from

William Rees-Mogg this morning saying how much he had enjoyed reading it, and what a delight it was to publish it. I had a similar letter from the arts editor, so I was awfully pleased, really thrilled about it.

Got back this evening and there were two votes that really turned my stomach. A three-line whip for Ministers – but only two-line for everybody else – on, first, the Criminal Trespass Bill, a hideous bill which makes it a criminal offence to sit in or occupy premises; and, second, on the expulsion of Agee and Hosenball, an even more odious bill. There are many votes I have to cast with which I disagree, but these two were really sickening. We are a most illiberal Government.

Of course, I hadn't taken part in any discussion of these bills because they never came to Cabinet. The Criminal Trespass Bill was raised momentarily but no details were given, and the expulsion of Agee and Hosenball was a discretion exercised by Merlyn Rees as Home Secretary.

### Wednesday 4 May

Over to EY, the Economic Committee, where we were discussing a paper Sir John Hunt had been asked to put in by Jim Callaghan, and also my paper 'Nuclear Policy: The Case for a Pause', which I had written only the day before yesterday.

Jim opened, 'We have two papers, one from the officials, which I commissioned, and one from the Secretary of State for Energy. I would like to ask the Secretary of State to begin, but I hope that although we may talk about a pause we don't just delay decision by default, and I hope that Tony recognises that these decisions are so important that they have to be put into commission. They cannot be taken by a single Minister alone.'

'Prime Minister,' I said, 'I hope you will acquit me of any delays because I have been sending you minutes on this setting out my views clearly, and as far as I am concerned I greatly welcome a collective decision because this is an extremely important matter and it concerns many Departments. I have been trying to get ministerial minds brought to bear on problems which have previously been handled technically.'

Then I went through my paper, line by line, pointing out all the new factors. I concluded by saying, 'We want an early thermal reactor decision, but we don't want to hurry on the fast breeder.'

On the whole I didn't do too badly.

Denis Healey said he didn't disagree with the way I put my case, and the question of using the oil revenues was a very important one; he was going to put in a paper on this. But he thought we must use some of the revenues to create new energy resources, notably to expand nuclear power. He said he was recently in the United States where the

Secretary of State, Cyrus Vance, had great doubts about President Carter's nuclear policy, and France and Germany were also upset. He thought officials had identified a number of detailed decisions which had to be taken.

Peter Shore regarded this as merely a preliminary discussion because of Carter's initiative. He said Brian Flowers's report had drawn attention to the very important question of waste (which I had mentioned), and we should not aim to reach decisions before the end of the year.

Sir Kenneth Berrill said there was a sea change taking place in public opinion on nuclear power and we had to be careful that this didn't lead to a chronic world shortage of energy. Non-proliferation policies could, if wrongly applied, actually lead to proliferation. The problem for the Government was how to get the British people and the world to live with nuclear power, even though they didn't like it. (I thought that was most revealing.) It was vital, he said, that the planning case for a reprocessing facility at Windscale be put very strongly by the Government, and we must remember that the thermal system we adopted would be the basis of our power plant in the future.

Shirley Williams said there could be a very fierce public reaction to nuclear power, and renewable energy sources were very important, but there was a lot of German resentment at the US attitude to the Brazilian deal. We needed international guidelines. She referred to the Flowers Report and the dangers of transporting plutonium.

Shirley is a sort of half-ally, an unreliable social democratic ally, but preferable to these toughies, like the officials and Healey and Mulley, who just want everything now.

After the discussion, Jim said, 'Well, my guess is that we should proceed as follows: a decision by the end of July on the thermal stations; early progress on reprocessing at Windscale; on non-proliferation, let the Germans make the running against the Americans; on Iran, let's keep the door open because the thermal decision might be affected by it.' David Owen is going to Iran next week.

Michael Foot, Peter Shore, Shirley Williams, David Owen and I will be quite sufficient to check a mad rush. There will be no fast breeder reactor while I remain Secretary of State for Energy. I simply won't go for it.

Westminster Hall had been all set up for the Queen's Jubilee address, and I went and sat in the second row on the right-hand side, plum behind the Prime Minister. Next to him was Maggie Thatcher, then Harold Wilson, Ted Heath and Harold Macmillan; then Willie Whitelaw, David Steel, Denis Healey and so on.

I had had very mixed feelings about going but I am glad I did because it was another reminder of how totally undemocratic British democracy is, both in its outward appearance and in reality.

I watched the Lords troop in; it was like Madame Tussaud's with all these figures I hadn't seen for years, some of whom I thought were dead – Derick Heathcoat Amory, Hailsham and others all coming down the steps from the top of Westminster Hall, many of them looking very poorly.

Prince Charles was in a morning coat, looking like a tailor's dummy. I shiver at the thought that that man will one day be King. Finally the Queen and the Duke of Edinburgh came in.

The Lord Chancellor read the most grovelling address about Her Majesty's tremendous contribution, how the monarchy was responsible for the rights of our people. George Thomas said much the same thing, and then the Queen addressed us. She spoke as if Britain were a constitutional monarchy rather than a democracy. The Crown always talks about a constitutional monarchy, the establishment talks about a parliamentary democracy, but nobody talks about a democracy as such. Still, I'm glad I went, just to get the feel of it.

It was very cold and I muttered, 'I've got cold feet', and Maggie Thatcher turned round and said, 'So have I.'

After lunch, I went for a cup of tea in the Tea Room, and I got into a fierce argument with James Johnson [Labour MP for Hull West]. I had confided to him my view that the humble addresses were grovelling.

'Ah yes,' he said, 'but that is what the British people like.'

I said, 'Maybe they do, and maybe the Russians like Brezhnev, and maybe the Ugandans like Amin.'

'Well, democracy means following,' he responded.

'Not at all; democracy means governing yourself, and all the liberties of this country were won by people who fought against the Crown, not by the people who grovel at its feet.'

Alex Lyon was sitting beside me and he made the point that the Cavalier–Roundhead division was still strong within the Party: the moderates were the Cavaliers and Loyalists while the left were the Roundheads.

To Bristol at 5.20 for two meetings on the eve of the council elections. I have to be back in London early tomorrow morning for Cabinet. What a life. I really am exhausted. I have done nothing but travel in the last three months.

*Thursday 5 May*
Left at 5.45 and drove all the way back to London.

Cabinet began at 10.30. As we were sitting down, Shirley said to me, 'Your paper on nuclear policy was the most brilliant paper I have ever seen' – referring to the one we discussed on Monday. So that strengthened my feeling that the social democrats are potential allies against nuclear power.

Jim referred to the summit of the industrial nations in London at the weekend and Carter's visit to north-east England tomorrow. Carter would be tremendously well received, but he hadn't realised what a row there would be over which colliery band should be chosen to play. I said, 'Why don't you pick the Ashfield Colliery Band, on the grounds that it has already selected itself!' – a reference to the by-election result.

'As for meeting Carter,' Jim said, 'Tony Benn specially asked if he might have the opportunity of meeting him so I have laid on drinks for members of the Cabinet at 12.30 on Saturday at Lancaster House.'

We had a disastrous day in the local elections.

*Saturday 7 May*
At 12 Ron Vaughan came and drove me to Lancaster House to meet President Carter at his drinks party. It was absolutely jampacked with journalists and ambassadors wandering about, but I went through to the little room where we normally receive guests. Carter's son Jeff was there; he is twenty-one, doing Geography and Geology at Washington, and wants to get involved in the International Geophysical Year. He was a real southern lad from Georgia and he looked a bit awkward, yet you could see he was having the time of his life. He was obviously very proud of his dad and I rather liked him.

Well, I had to catch a train to Swindon at 1.20, and Carter still hadn't arrived at 1 o'clock. It was clear that I wasn't going to see him and I asked the people there whether I should go or stay. Some said I should stay, and that it was a great opportunity. But I decided to go and do my May Day meeting. Someone else said, 'I am sure the President would expect you to keep in touch with the grass roots.'

So I said to young Jeff Carter, 'Well, as I am going to miss your father, can I give you a message? I am the Secretary of State for Energy and, first of all, I hope he won't be pressured into giving up his nuclear policy.'

'Oh no, he won't,' he said.

'And, secondly,' I went on, 'tell him we are old family friends of the Niebuhrs' – at which point he interrupted and said, 'Ah, my father has read every single word that Reinhold Niebuhr has written.'

'Well,' I added, 'we used to stay with him in New York', and I quoted Niebuhr's remark that man's capacity for evil makes democracy necessary and man's capacity for good makes democracy possible. 'Remember two Ns,' I said. 'Nuclear and Niebuhr.'

I had brought a copy of my Levellers pamphlet to give to Carter, so I put on the front 'To President Jimmy Carter from Tony Benn' with a little note saying that this traced our common heritage from Amos to Micah through the English Revolution and the American War of Independence and so on. I scribbled on the back, 'Sorry to have missed you and I have sent a message through your son.'

Had a mug of tea and some sandwiches on the train and arrived in Swindon just after 2. We marched through the town with the band, and I made a speech in the park. Afterwards I was driven to Reading, and then I came home, so exhausted that I couldn't work, so I watched the Eurovision Song Contest and went to bed.

*Monday 9 May*
Arthur Hawkins from the CEGB came to say goodbye. I have had some tremendous clashes with him, he is such a difficult man, and I thought it would be rather a painful goodbye. I asked after his health, and then blow me down if he didn't say how much he enjoyed the article on Father. He said Father was an old Victorian Nonconformist and that I was a chip off the old block. So that was a nice surprise.

We went on to talk about his experience and he said, 'You know what is doing you down – it is the Civil Service. They're growing in size, they get in our hair, they interfere, they make my job impossible.'

Then he mentioned by name one civil servant in my Department and suggested I get rid of him. He said that this man was disloyal to me and could not be trusted. 'He said to me once, "Arthur, I would very much like a holiday. Can you arrange a trip?"' Arthur said he wouldn't do it. 'You check the contracts he awards,' he told me. It was really rather frightening but I didn't pursue it further.

Jo Grimond came in for a discussion about whether the North Sea defences were sufficient to cope with an oil slick. He was very agreeable and, as we left, I asked him to come and have a talk. He said, 'I don't believe in all that – smoke-filled rooms – I don't believe in it.'

I told him I didn't either. 'Come and have a talk anyway.'

He said, 'If the Liberals are to be involved, we ought to be in the Government, or nothing. At present we have the worst of both worlds.' An interesting comment.

At 12 I had a short security briefing on my visit to Moscow. It was the usual stuff: watch out for the KGB, they have much more sophisticated equipment than ten years ago, don't leave any papers about, they must always be in locked boxes, there are microphones everywhere and bugs in the cars, the servants in the Moscow Embassy are agents of the KGB, and so on. It left me feeling thoroughly unsettled.

Incidentally, Cledwyn Hughes came up and told me how much he had enjoyed the piece about Father and what a marvellous man he was. He came up a second time and said, 'I forgot to tell you, twenty years ago I saw you kiss your father in the Central Lobby and it brought tears to my eyes because I used to kiss my father too.' He was most friendly, and he said Father's values were worth keeping; they were relevant a hundred years ago and they will be relevant a hundred years from now. It was really lovely. Cledwyn's an old Nonconformist.

At 10 o'clock David Owen came to my room about the Soviet Union. Nice of him to come, as he is now senior to me in the pecking order. I told him that when I got to Russia I wanted to probe the possibility of developing the Economic Commission for Europe at the ministerial level, and he said that was all right.

I asked him if there was anything he wanted me to raise with them, and he suggested proliferation and fuel cycle safeguards.

Then I asked, 'How did you get on with Carter at the summit?'

'Oh, very friendly. The French are angry that it's been such a big thing for Jim, and we dealt with nuclear proliferation, which they say is a matter for Euratom; they have been very difficult. But Carter is an idealist, a tough and a nice idealist. I'm sorry you missed him, but you will see him and get on with him.'

### Tuesday 10 May

Three-hour plane journey to Moscow with Caroline, accompanied by Sir Jack Rampton. I read the brief carefully and the dominant theme throughout was a steady determination not to open energy discussions with the Russians on a pan-European basis. The reason for this was not clear until I talked to Sir Howard Smith, the British Ambassador, later in the evening. It was presented as a rejection of the Brezhnev proposals for three pan-European congresses: one on the environment, one on energy and one on transport, all of which are perfectly logical. The Foreign Office view is that until human rights are dealt with by the Russians we can't talk about matters such as these, and that the Economic Commission for Europe is the right body. That is all very well, but we don't even want the ECE to be real. I stored all this in the back of my mind.

At the airport in Moscow we were greeted by Kirillin [Chairman of the State Committee on Science and Technology], Sir Howard and Lady Smith and many people I knew from previous trips, including Anna Santalova, who has been an interpreter for many years. Kirillin said, 'Let's get straight to the cars; time is money.' I said, 'That's a very capitalist phrase', at which he laughed.

Anyway we drove to the British residence on the river just opposite the Kremlin – a most beautiful position, though the house itself is a vulgar extravagance built in the 1890s by a sugar merchant. We were told again about bugs, not to leave any papers around, about the servants working for the KGB, and you had this nightmarish feeling of being under siege, which, in a curious way, is just what the establishment wants. It doesn't want normal relations with the Soviet Union and I am sure the Russians are very suspicious of visitors as possible agents, which in a sense they are. It is one of those self-perpetuating fantasies.

We talked for a bit and then went to the State Committee for Science and Technology, into the very room where I had met Kirillin ten years ago. I said how much I valued our work over the years, how energy was important, and I was really there to explore the development of their energy policy and to answer any questions they might have. I wanted particularly to see how we could build closer links with the Soviet Union as a major producer and consumer and as a great source of new technology – indeed, a crucial player on the world energy scene. I said, 'What about your own plans?', and Kirillin launched into a tremendous speech which, with translation, lasted about an hour and a half.

At dinner I sat next to Lady Smith, and all she did was talk about the servant problem in Russia – how difficult it was to get servants at the Embassy and how British Embassies in other capitals had better servants. It was so boring.

On my other side was Gvishiani, Kosygin's son-in-law, a highly intelligent man and Deputy Chairman of the State Committee. I raised the question of the pan-European congresses, and he mentioned this to Kirillin, so I have got that through. We must beat the Foreign Office on this matter, and that is now my objective.

Back to the Embassy and talked to Sir Howard. It was then that I discovered what the objection to these talks was. From an energy point of view, it is obviously right to have these discussions – it is in our interest, in their interest, in the world interest. But the Foreign Office just sees it as giving way to Soviet propaganda. Smith said, 'They will never tell you anything because everything is a state secret.'

'Well,' I said, 'we have state secrets too, and our biggest state secret is that we don't know what is going to happen.'

He said that the Russians weren't interested in energy; it was all flummery – talking about things that would be of advantage to them and not to us.

This is the standard FO attitude. How any Foreign Secretary can ever get control of it now and really shift it, I just don't know, but it has to be done. There is this deep hostility within the British establishment towards Russia, and it is clearly reflected in our Embassy there. The FO loathes the communist world and everything to do with it, and now that they have transferred their loyalty from the Americans to the Europeans they are no longer interested in east–west relations. Smith said that the Community didn't want east–west congresses; they had very reluctantly agreed to go along with the environmental one, which is pretty meaningless, but they didn't want one on energy. That is what I am going to try and change when I get back, though Smith said that would be most unwise.

Well, there we are. It is midnight in Moscow. I have the radio on –

partly to prevent this diary being bugged, partly in the hope of hearing the news from London, where the NATO heads of state have been meeting today. It is lovely looking across the river at the Kremlin, which is all illuminated.

*Wednesday 11 May*
Had breakfast at the residence and then at 10 I left for the Ministry of Oil, to begin my serious discussions on energy policy.

I was met there by the Oil Minister Maltsev, a plump, friendly chap in his late forties – described in the Embassy brief as uncommunicative and forbidding.

He began by saying that Russia was the greatest oil producer in the world, and how impressed he was by the UK's achievements. When we moved on to a discussion of world energy resources, I put to him what the CIA had claimed – in effect that Russia was running out of oil – and he commented, 'What would they have said ten years ago? All forecasts have their political objectives.'

Then I went to see Neporozhny, the head of the Soviet Electricity Grid – a most dramatic man with white hair. He received me in a huge room with a massive wall chart showing the entire electricity grid of the Soviet Union; it was like a scene from the command headquarters of NATO or the Pentagon, with lights and computers flashing. Neporozhny was absolutely drunk on his own power. There is nothing like a big organisation for producing would-be popes and dictators. He showed me the chart and a digital clock indicating total power consumed, and he pointed to an innocent-looking little man, and said, 'There's the engineer in charge; he is a Hero of the Soviet Union and if he fails he will lose his medal.'

He said nuclear was carrying the base load, and explained the great benefit of the integration of grids for the Comecon countries on the 'sleeping continent' principle: that's to say the nine-hour time gap across the countries allowed them to spread the peak. Coal was cheap in the east and high-voltage lines were the quickest way of transferring it. There was a Minister of Electricity and five deputies responsible for their own power plants – production and distribution, research and so on – and they employed 2 million people: fantastic. But it was very difficult to get money from the Ministry of Finance. He said the cost of producing electricity was immaterial, since the State Committee set fuel prices, and gas and oil prices were higher than atomic.

On nuclear power forecasts, he was sure that in the west all power would eventually be nuclear and that in a planned socialist economy there was no conflict of interest as in the west. He agreed with Jim Stewart of the British Nuclear Forum that we should stop frightening each other with safety factors. He mentioned an American woman who had managed to hold up plans for a nuclear power station for three years, and he said environmental factors could raise the price of nuclear power. The Soviet Union's atomic power stations were inspected for safety; there were some accidents, but it was safer than coal.

We went for lunch at a restaurant and I mentioned my belief that we should make east–west contacts through the European Commission for Europe.

'Well, we have no contact with the Common Market,' said Neporozhny. 'We think it was forced on Europe by the businessmen, and the only economic advantage to the Soviet Union is cheap butter.' He said the risk of proliferation of arms was a very real one, but Carter's line was not serious; it was just designed for American public opinion, and to cater for American commercial interests. Whatever does emerge, he said, must be genuinely international.

He told me that the Ministry needed lots of money, and I said, 'Why don't you arrange for a blackout and then you will get it immediately.'

'Ah,' he sighed, 'the next Minister would get the money, not me!'

I remembered that quotation from Lenin, 'Communism is Soviet power plus the electrification of the whole country'. Then I quoted from *Das Kapital*: 'Technology discloses man's mode of dealing with nature, the means by which he earns his living, the mode of his social relations and the mental conceptions that flow from it.'

'I don't take any notice of that,' he said. 'I remember, when I was a student, another student was always getting up and quoting Marx at the teacher, but we didn't listen. We checked once and the quotations from Marx were incorrect. Marxism bored us very much.'

I recalled that when I was at the Royal Naval College in Greenwich I was told by an old naval officer that the Russian Revolution had come about because they stopped saluting in the Tsarist navy. 'Well,' he said, 'there might be something in that.' He had been a navy man too.

Went off in the afternoon to talk to Morokhov, the Deputy Chairman of the State Committee for Atomic Energy. He stressed that nuclear power was crucial, that natural resources were in the east, and almost exhausted in the west. He said the European Soviet Union depended on nuclear power for their industrial development. By 1985 nuclear power would double (he was reading a long statement which had obviously been prepared for him), and the Soviet reactors were perfectly safe.

On the crucial question of non-proliferation, he said we could not delay nuclear power because there was no alternative. The use of plutonium was serious because of the risk of the spread of nuclear weapons. But that was why the Non-Proliferation Treaty was the key. If you had strict non-proliferation controls, accepted by all countries, then the problem of proliferation would be solved. But not all countries had signed the NPT and we had to make them join.

'How?' I asked.

'Well, it is hard to go back, but we must first agree entirely on controls, export controls and safeguards for all future contracts, and then when we have got that agreement we can bring it back to cover the existing treaties.'

We talked for two hours. He was an intelligent man and, like all these Soviet Ministers, confident – not hostile to the west, not anxious to make a political point; just confident that he was doing the right thing. I was highly impressed by him.

Back to the Embassy and changed for an evening at the Bolshoi Ballet. In the interval, who should come up but Armand Hammer. We talked and he told me that when he was first there in 1921 there were no cars, and orphans were running wild attacking people for food. The Government couldn't control them.

'Of course,' he said, 'that was before Lenin introduced the New Economic Policy. There was nothing in the shops at all.' He took my arm. 'Look at them now, so prosperous, so many cars, lovely clothes, no unemployment – it's an amazing achievement.'

I asked him what he thought of Carter's statement. 'Well,' he said, 'he started it the wrong way, and it thoroughly upset the Russians. The idea that the west is more moral than the east is not true. The Russians were deeply affronted.'

He told me he had been talking today with Promissov, the Mayor of Moscow, who is an industrialist running all the enterprises in a city of 8 million people. Brezhnev was ready to go to the US in the autumn and Hammer had advised Promissov to make some conciliatory gesture because the Jews had such a dominating position in the American Congress and in the media. Hammer suggested reopening the Israeli Embassy in Moscow and getting Golda Meir to come back, or going to Tel Aviv and reopening the Russian Embassy there; that would completely deal with the Jewish lobby. Promissov said he would be seeing Brezhnev in a day or two and he would suggest this.

At 9.45, after a beautiful performance of the *Nutcracker Suite*, I went back to the Embassy and was greeted by Howard Smith. 'Have you heard that Peter Jay has been made our Ambassador in Washington?' He and Rampton are hopping mad about it!*

We talked about that and about my chat with Hammer. Smith is worried about Mrs Thatcher's ignorance of the Soviet Union and he is trying to get the Conservatives to think more about it. He thought

---

* The appointment of Peter Jay (Douglas Jay's son) in place of Sir Peter Ramsbotham was a controversial one, not least because he was the Prime Minister's son-in-law, married to Margaret Callaghan. At the time of the appointment Jay was economics editor of *The Times*, having previously worked for the Treasury.

Brezhnev was a man who really cared and didn't understand why the dissidents were so dissatisfied.

Reflecting more on Jay's appointment, it has got certain interesting features. On the negative side is the fact that Peter Jay is a pessimistic monetarist and a very bad person to have in Washington, and it may prove to be an error of judgement on Jim's part. The positive feature is that it does restore the special relationship between Downing Street and the White House, and also Peter Jay is very anti-Common Market – which will infuriate the Foreign Office.

### Thursday 12 May

A beautiful sunny day. I held a press conference at 9 and then went to see Tikhonov, the First Deputy Prime Minister, in the Kremlin. I was disappointed I couldn't see Kosygin, but I was told he was 'on holiday'.

Lunch at the Embassy with Kirillin, and there was some discussion about Mrs Thatcher; Howard Smith thought she would quickly come to understand the realities of dealing with the Soviet Union. I asked about Eurocommunism and Kirillin said it had some positive features, some negative, at which point Howard Smith broke in saying he didn't want me to establish a serious discussion about that. He was very negative. British Ambassadors in Moscow just are; I think they have a horrible time and they don't like Ministers coming in and thinking they can get on better than they really can with the Russians. But God, I wish we had Jack Jones or somebody in the Moscow Embassy.

Kirillin made a friendly speech, and afterwards I sat and talked to him and Suzlov from the Soviet Foreign Ministry. We discussed disarmament, and I said I thought the Americans and the Russians should play the leading part. They said, 'Well, we think we should talk to you as well.' Suzlov couldn't understand why the west wouldn't give a pledge not to use atom bombs first.

Then I spoke of my fear that unemployment in the west might lead to rearmament. Kirillin said that unemployment was due to our economic system being defective; they, on the other hand, were socialists.

'You mustn't forget that socialism has a long history in Britain too,' I said.

Flew back to London and spent the evening unwinding at home. I had not been to the Soviet Union since my visit in 1969, a few months after the invasion of Czechoslovakia. Then, they were embarrassed, as I was, and the situation was difficult; I didn't enjoy it much. This time it was different. I didn't go on a lot of trips and I spent most of the time just talking to Ministers. I think they know I am anxious to have good relations with them and don't like the Cold War stuff. I can't see any merit in the Foreign Office's approach to the east. Britain is represented in Moscow by one class, namely the upper class.

*As part of my determination to investigate every aspect of nuclear energy policy, I had organised for the weekend of 13 and 14 May 1977 a major seminar on nuclear policy at Sunningdale Park, Berkshire. The seminar, which included the widest range of opinions and interests, was the first of its kind, held at a time when important decisions about Britain's programme were necessary, when the US Government had announced its intention to re-examine its nuclear programme and the Flowers Commission had expressed environmental concerns about nuclear power generally.*

*The sessions were chaired by me and the participants from outside the Government included: Sir Brian Flowers, Sir William Hawthorne of Churchill College, Cambridge, Sir George Porter of the Royal Institution, Professor Cassels of Liverpool University – a great heat and power man – Lord Todd of the Royal Society, Sir John Hill, Con Allday, Sir Alan Cottrell of Jesus College, Cambridge, who is against the PWR, Dr Ned Franklin and Jim Stewart of the Nuclear Power Company, Sir Kelvin Spencer, retired Chief Scientist at the Ministry of Power, who I was told was gaga but was marvellous, Frank Tombs of the Electricity Council and Walter Patterson from Friends of the Earth, who was excellent.*

*In addition to my officials and colleagues from the Department of Energy, we also had: Gregor MacKenzie, Minister of State in the Scottish Office, Sir Kenneth Berrill, Sir Hermann Bondi, Bill Simpson and John Dunster from the Health and Safety Executive, John Hannam representing the Conservative Party, Arthur Palmer, Chairman of the Parliamentary Select Committee on Science and Technology, and Mr Lewis from the Central Unit on Environmental Pollution at the Department of Environment.*

## Friday 13 May

Arrived at Sunningdale in time for dinner with most of the participants.

After dinner, the first session was taken up with a general discussion on the role of nuclear power in society, and the contributions dwelt mainly on options and cost. John Hill said there was no alternative to nuclear power but it required wise provision and an open approach. Brian Flowers believed there were economic uncertainties and we should keep our options open, but democratic control was important.

Walter Patterson doubted the economic arguments for nuclear power and queried the technical choice. Bill Simpson said public fear of the unknown had to be considered. Alan Cottrell agreed that we should keep all our options open, including nuclear. Arthur Palmer was in favour of nuclear power and thought we shouldn't allow US policy to dictate ours: 'Europe does not have to be dictated to by a passing enthusiasm of President Carter's.'

Hermann Bondi warned of the security implications of handling plutonium, and Sir George Porter was worried by proliferation in a world of instability; unilateral action by the UK would not be effective in checking proliferation.

Sir Kelvin Spencer drew our attention to the political consequences of an accident, and the growing power and knowledge of the grassroots environmental organisations.

Frank Tombs said that nuclear power had been cheaper in the UK and that an energy shortage would develop at the end of the century. The dangers were exaggerated, in the opinion of Lord Todd, and nuclear power must be available until fusion was ready. Dr Dunster pointed to the risk of accidents in other areas – greater than for nuclear accidents.

Brian Flowers commented that the dangers were not so much of accident but of proliferation of nuclear weapons; there was a case for waiting.

I asked if we could be wrong about the energy gap, and George Porter said, 'Keep your options open; don't assume there are long-term alternatives; we have no choice.' Arthur Palmer told us that the Select Committee had taken evidence on alternative energy sources and they didn't see much in it. Alan Cottrell differentiated between secure alternative sources and those which were just speculative.

Kelvin Spencer suggested that if we put more money into alternative sources, such as wave power, we could do more with them, and Walter Patterson pointed out that it hadn't been market forces that had built up the nuclear industry.

Berrill said the question was how to live with nuclear power.

I asked about investment in conservation methods, and William Hawthorne said the Government should spend large sums on energy conservation ideas.

It was an extremely interesting session.

*Saturday 14 May*
I introduced the morning session, recommending that we focus first on reactor systems and then, after coffee, on reprocessing.

We had a long discussion about thermal reactor systems, how exports were crucial and so on. Patterson and Spencer were the only consistently anti-nuclear participants and they made a solid, well-informed case without upsetting anybody.

We had lunch and then I came back to London, absolutely exhausted but feeling it had been well worthwhile.

*Sunday 15 May*
I lay in bed till 12. There is a huge row about Peter Jay's appointment as Ambassador to Washington. It will weaken Jim's position on the direct elections issue and may make it harder for him to sack me.

*Monday 16 May*

My first appointment today was a visit from Ray Vouel, the Luxembourg Commissioner for Competition Policy.

I had been told he was a difficult man and the one real problem we anticipated was over interest relief grants, which we have had since 1972 and which have created many jobs in Scotland as a result of orders from the North Sea. These grants were intended to match assistance given by other countries. But the Commission objected to them, although they hadn't objected in 1973. So we have been fighting a rearguard action; my officials are now in a state of paralysis at the thought that the Commission might take us to court. I didn't get the brief on this till five past ten, but they came in all wobbling and I said, 'Leave it to me.'

Well, Vouel came in, looking like a sort of younger version of Goering, accompanied by a tough bureaucratic-looking German who I think is his *chef de cabinet* or Director-General and his deputy.

'Well, tell me how you see competition policy developing,' I said.

'You should read the Six's report on competition.'

'Of course,' I agreed, 'but I'd like to know how *you* see it all.'

'Well, as far as we are concerned, we are trying to bring about true competition in the Common Market and get rid of all aids to industry, and we have to consider energy as well. As for this interest relief grant, we do not regard it as satisfactory.'

'But you approved it in 1973 and it is increasing our share of the market – the market share of the other Community countries has risen already. It also helps to fight off the Americans and the Japanese.'

'Yes,' he said, 'but it is an aid.'

'Have you had complaints about it?' I asked.

'Yes, we have.'

'Did you stimulate complaints or did they just come in? And what were they anyway?'

'We do not release the complaints we receive.'

'Well,' I said, 'as the Commission believes in transparency perhaps it would be a good thing if we did know what the complaints were. Perhaps the Council of Ministers could ask about it; that would seem a sensible way of doing it.'

'That would be interfering with the autonomy of the Commission.'

I tried to be courteous but the more I listened, the more I felt like someone in an occupied country receiving a Gauleiter. It was revolting.

It is nothing to do with him what we do. He said we looked at it from a purely British point of view, while he had to take a Community view.

'I look at it from a British point of view because we want to use our oil to industrialise and benefit our country, like any OPEC Oil Minister.'

'Yes,' he said, 'and the Community is prepared to see you give help to the oil companies, but not just in order to create jobs.'

This went on for about an hour. I put all the arguments but he was absolutely impervious, and at the end he said we had to proceed. I wanted more discussion about it but he pressed me. I said, 'You invented the system in the Community of stopping the clock – not us.'

'We don't want confrontation,' my Deputy Secretary, Peter Le Cheminant, said. Vouel agreed, 'but we must apply the treaty.'

'You must have some discretion,' I said.

'No.'

'But that's very mechanistic and it doesn't take account of the political realities. There may be an explosion if you deny jobs in Scotland, with unemployment being so bad.'

Vouel, looking horrified, told me that he had had a similar conversation with John Prescott the other day and Prescott had told him that he didn't believe in competition.

'Neither do I,' I said. 'The achievements of the British labour movement over the last seventy years have all been won by restricting competition in favour of basic human values.'

Well, Vouel looked as if I had cast a spell in the middle of Holy Communion in St Peter's in Rome on Easter Sunday. I didn't care for him at all and I don't think he cared for me. He is supposed to be a socialist and I was told he was on the left of his party. But he was odious.

Afterwards I talked to James Bretherton and Frances and Francis, and we discussed how to follow up Sunningdale, for example a paper on costing alternative power sources, on seeking self-sufficiency by the year 2000 and on ways of filling the energy gap. We considered holding a seminar on alternative strategies and international co-operation on the fast breeder. It was very useful.

At Questions in the House Jim Callaghan sat between me and David Owen. Jim had to answer a question about Peter Jay, and he got a very rough hearing.

At last Thursday's PLP, Jim had apparently threatened to resign if he didn't get his way on Peter Jay. The fact that there is so much bitterness over this does suggest that Jim's spell is broken now.

Later I had a deep discussion with Frances and Francis about the whole affair. Sir Peter Ramsbotham has made a skilful statement in Washington saying what a brilliant and imaginative choice Jay was, how the handover would be smooth and so on. It is ironic that Ramsbotham has come out of this so well while Jim has been made to look an absolute swine. As somebody said, why didn't Jim just appoint Ramsbotham as Governor of Bermuda and *then* replace him with Jay, instead of the other way round?

*Tuesday 17 May*

Walter Marshall, Lord Aldington, Chairman of the National Nuclear Corporation, and Ned Franklin, Chairman of its operating arm the Nuclear Power Company, arrived at the Department for a meeting on Iran. I simply read to them the brief which stated that Walter Marshall had been asked in February whether we, in concert with the NNC and NPC, would co-operate with Iran on the possibility of providing twenty PWRs, but only on condition that we included the PWR in our domestic programme and that there would be satisfactory non-proliferation arrangements. David Owen had seen the Shah last week, said we were interested, and would the NNC please advise?

Well, Aldington was knocked sideways by this – twenty PWRs is a massive order and his tongue was hanging out at the thought of it. I must say, I loathe having to do this and of course it will inevitably leak, though I did ask them to keep it to the chairmen of the individual companies in the consortia.

Then Walter Marshall said, in his usual arrogant and insensitive way, that as safety adviser to the Shah he would have to approve the safety regulations of the reactors.

In the evening I saw Eric Heffer at the House and he told me that the NEC inquiry into the Trots had gone absolutely soft. Underhill had been outvoted by Eric and Michael Foot, John Chalmers had not turned up, and Tom Bradley was unhappy. Ron Hayward had helped, and it ended up with no witch-hunting. Couldn't be better.

Eric is on the committee dealing with the leadership election with Mik and Frank Allaun, and they are coming up with the idea of an 'electoral college' in which Labour MPs and candidates, constituency parties and the trade unions would have a role in choosing the Leader. It is an interesting idea.

*Wednesday 18 May*

I had a curious nightmare last night. I was standing by a deep concrete pit in a prison with a noose round my neck. I swayed over this pit, looking down and knowing that with the drop the rope would break my neck, and there was this tremendous compulsion to jump, but I didn't. I woke up in a sweat and found it was 3.50. Perhaps it meant that I have managed to control my self-destructive urges; or maybe I was visualising in dramatic form the problems of resignation or dismissal from the Cabinet over direct elections.

I had a long and extremely interesting talk to Clive Jenkins in my office. We discussed security and what had been happening in Australia. Incidentally, today an Australian Minister has confirmed that someone named by Philip Agee was indeed an Australian CIA agent. This has created a storm in Australia. It is clear that the CIA played some part in getting rid of the Prime Minister, Gough Whitlam.

Clive told me he believed his phone was bugged because on a couple of occasions a voice had broken in and said, 'Look out, Clive, look out.' I did tell him that Harold Wilson had informed the CBI in March 1971 that trade union leaders' telephones were tapped. Clive and I have a sort of understanding on this.

### Thursday 19 May

At Cabinet, the sale of our BP shares came up and I introduced the paper calling for postponement of the sale. I said this was the third discussion so far and there were new factors to consider – economic, oil and political. It would cost us £20 million to the jobbers for selling the shares and it is unpopular across the board. We might make a mistake about the price, and be faced with a real scandal.

I said we had decided to sell the shares as part of the crisis measures last year, but we now knew that the PSBR had been overestimated by £1 billion from December to March. The PSBR for 1977–8 was uncertain, but with nationalised industry profits up, a huge sale of gilts, stronger exchange rates and capital inflows – all of which were partly due to oil – the PSBR was likely to be lower than forecast.

Joel Barnett made a very strong speech in favour of selling. Peter Shore agreed with me that it was the sale of the century but thought we had to sell. Denis said something about confidence being shaken if we didn't, and Harold Lever supported the sale. Jim Callaghan did suggest we split the sale into two parts, which was half a victory, but Joel Barnett said that would be impossible.

Anyway it was agreed that it should go back to a committee to be considered again and Denis proposed Harold, Merlyn and Joel. I said, 'I hope you will include me in the committee', and Jim replied, 'Only if you will accept the final Cabinet decision and not argue against it.' When you actually push your full weight behind something and lose, it damages you, and I was cross.

### Friday 20 May

EY Committee lasted for two hours and was one of the most interesting Cabinet committees I have attended for some time because of the light it threw on the nature of the Labour Party.

Edmund Dell introduced his proposal for industrial democracy, which was an immensely watered-down version of Bullock, proposing that worker participation should be established below board level for a couple of years, and then we would move slowly towards a voluntary arrangement whereby workers would constitute one-third of the top tier of a two-tier board. It was absolutely wrong that Edmund should be in charge of this because he is the Minister representing capital; it should have been the responsibility of Albert Booth, the Minister representing labour. Edmund himself is completely opposed to industrial democracy, along with the rest of his Department and Whitehall.

Albert Booth said that Edmund Dell had not really discussed the policy and the key to it all was making sense at the workshop level, which was one of the major problems.

Jim asked, 'What effect would industrial democracy have on business confidence at this moment when we are hoping for investment?' Edmund Dell said it would be disastrous, and Shirley Williams added, 'I can confirm that; it would have a disastrous effect on confidence, particularly on international investment.'

I said we were getting into a muddle because, in effect, we were discussing two things: one, what we would like to do; the other, what we could get through Parliament. For some of us they were quite different things, but not for Edmund Dell, who had honestly admitted that what he wanted to do was whatever would get Liberal support – namely a watered-down version.

I went on to say that the only choice we were making was how to handle the increased power of the trade unions. There were several ways of doing that. One was to drive it back using either unemployment, which had failed because the interdependence of the labour movement had enabled it to maintain its bargaining power even when unemployment was high, or the law, which was also ineffective as shown by the failure of the Industrial Relations Act, which the British public rejected.

The second course of action was to head it off through participation and involvement at board level – a sort of public relations window-dressing with nothing whatever to do with democracy.

The third way to deal with trade union power was to institutionalise it and, through it, create democracy, which meant real control, shifting the balance of power and responsibility in favour of labour. I recommended that we make a clear statement of policy in support of Bullock.

Peter Shore said Dell's paper had disappointed him. The CBI had retreated from their former position in favour of industrial democracy; the TUC were completely unrealistic about the nature of the problems. We must try to relate the issue to the massive decline of UK industry over the last few years. Unless we were convinced it would favour our recovery, we shouldn't go ahead with industrial democracy – we could be sunk by it. The real problem was the balance between capital and labour in the private sector, and we were moving too fast.

Jim summed up, saying we had benefited from the new thinking, we needed a little ministerial committee to look at it – that is Edmund,

Albert, Peter Shore, Roy Hattersley, Eric Varley and Tony Benn – and would Shirley chair it?

I should add that throughout the whole of the meeting, on a very hot May day, there was a band in Horse Guards Parade practising for the Trooping of the Colour. It was a most extraordinary situation – there were we abandoning basic socialist principles in the face of the multinationals' sensitivities, while the band prepared for the Queen's Jubilee. It was a classic case of what is wrong with Britain.

I went straight to the House of Commons for a meeting of the GEN 74 Committee. We had a couple of papers before us: one on how we should handle the follow-up to the summit on proliferation, the other on the transportation of plutonium. On the latter, I asked three questions.

'How is plutonium actually moved at the moment – is it by sea, land or air?'

I was told that it was moved by sea in steel canisters actually welded to the side of the ship, transported by land in this country, and that small quantities were moved by air.

'What protection is given, particularly as it crosses from one country to another?'

'We protect it till it passes out of our hands and then another country takes it in.'

'What effective safeguards are there that the plutonium we send abroad, for fast breeder reactors, research or whatever, is actually used for the purpose intended? For example, do the French account for the use they make of our plutonium?'

I was told that under the Euratom Treaty they didn't.

I think I put my finger on three important questions that officials, technicians and scientists – but not Ministers – have considered.

Peter Shore mentioned the possibility of our dumping at sea and Fred Mulley talked about 'silly pressure groups'.

*Sunday 22 May*
Melissa and I went to Hyde Park. It was a beautiful day and we walked for an hour. We paid 75p and took a boat out on the Serpentine. It was marvellous.

At 12 I had to leave for lunch at Chequers with Prince Fahd, Crown Prince of Saudi Arabia, Prince Saud, the Foreign Minister, Sheikh Yamani, Minister of Petroleum, Sheikh Muhammad, Minister of Finance, Qusaibi, Minister of Industry, Sheikh Wahab, Head of Royal Protocol, and the Saudi Ambassador.

The party was on its way to the United States to discuss with the new administration relations with Saudi Arabia, and particularly the Palestine question. At lunch I found myself sitting opposite Jim, with

Yamani on my left and the Ambassador on my right. It was a very friendly occasion, and Jim said, 'I see we have got a lot of sunshine', which I said had been laid on by the Department of Energy. Then he declared, 'I hear we have as much sunshine and solar energy in Britain as Saudi Arabia', and I commented that that sounded like a Treasury forecast.

Yamani talked mainly to Denis Healey and I talked to the Ambassador, a lawyer, only the third Ambassador since the 1920s, when Saudi Arabia first established diplomatic relations.

I asked him about his faith, and he replied that he himself said prayers five times a day, in the morning, at noon, at sunset, an hour after sunset and before he went to bed. He explained that you had to wash each time before praying – Muslims must wash their hands and forearms, their ears, eyes, mouth and so on – five times a day, which was very hygienic. He pointed out that when a Muslim bows and puts his brow to the floor it restores the circulation of the blood to the brain, as in yoga, and was very good exercise.

He said the Muslim faith was interesting because everybody had direct access to Allah; there were no priesthoods. 'Of course, the Muslim faith has not had any contact with England, unlike the Jewish faith. Since the confrontation of the crusades there has been really no contact with the Muslim world. Later the Turks took up the Muslim faith but they didn't understand it, and distorted it and were cruel. Actually the Muslim faith is a generous faith with a lot of compassion.'

He said the great thing about his faith was that it tried to integrate religion and daily life, rather than separating it off into a priestly practice. It was extremely interesting, and he was most agreeable.

After lunch Jim and Frank Judd went off for a long talk with Saud and Fahd about President Amin's proposed visit to the Commonwealth Prime Ministers' Conference, because Saudi Arabia represents Ugandan interests in the UK at the moment. The rest of us went into the garden.

Yamani described the kidnapping of himself, the Iranian Minister Amouzegar and other Ministers by the terrorist known as Carlos at the OPEC meeting in Vienna in December 1975. I had heard an account from Amouzegar but Yamani went into much more detail. He said only two policemen had been provided at the conference venue by the Chancellor of Austria, Bruno Kreisky. Carlos was with another man and a woman, and one of them had come and asked the police, 'Is the OPEC meeting still going on?', and they were let through into the conference without being asked to prove their identity.

When they got inside, they fired machine-guns up at the ceiling to capture attention, and one of the participants struck Carlos and knocked him down. Another terrorist fired on to the table and wounded an economist from the Qatar delegation. One of the Libyan delegation picked up the machine-gun but didn't know how to work it, and Carlos killed him. Then one of the policemen, an old man due to retire in two months, came up in the lift to find out what was happening, and the girl waited for him to open the lift and shot him down.

The terrorists took their captives in a bus to a plane. In the plane, Carlos asked who was the number two of the Saudi delegation, and al Turki, whom I met last month, very courageously said, 'I am.'

Carlos talked to them a great deal, with a machine-gun on his knee, and Yamani said he was absolutely calm. The girl, however, wept at one stage, and the other boy vomited with nervousness. Carlos even gave Yamani his mother's telephone number in Venezuela so he could ring her and tell her her son was all right! He was an amazing man. Qusaibi thought they were just a murder gang, mercenaries without much political motivation. But Carlos was courteous to Yamani and Amouzegar.

Anyway, they were put in seats which had explosives fitted underneath them so that they could be blown up immediately. When they landed in Algiers and it was clear that they were not going to be allowed to continue their journey, Carlos told Yamani, 'I am going to kill you. I may not get you now, but I am going to kill you. You are a criminal. It won't be long before you are killed.' Then he said, 'I am leaving the plane now, and you can come out in five minutes.'

Well, they didn't know whether the plane was going to be blown up after Carlos left it, but they stayed for five minutes, after which Yamani said, 'I will go down.' 'No, I will go,' al Turki said, 'they may be waiting at the bottom of the steps to shoot you.' Yamani thought al Turki was immensely courageous. They got out and everything was all right, but it was a terrifying experience.

They asked me if I had any security, and I replied, 'No, but some Ministers do.'

'Have you ever been threatened with death?'

I said, 'Yes, I had a policeman with me once for a couple of weeks, after a number of serious death threats, but other than that, no.'

Yamani told me his children had to have police guards; one of his daughters is at Newnham College and she has a policeman with her all the time. They agreed that kidnapping wouldn't make any difference to any Government's policy, but it did give publicity to a cause.

Jim and the Crown Prince came back and then the Saudi party left. Jim suggested we have a talk, so Varley, Healey, Dell, myself, Frank Judd and others went and sat in the great hall.

Jim said, 'Let's talk about Leyland.' A big scandal has broken over bribes given for contracts in the Middle East. This arose after a forged letter purportedly from Don Ryder to the Chief Executive of British Leyland was published in the *Daily Mail* last week.[2]

'Everybody does it,' said Denis, 'jobs are at stake, and we don't want to prejudice the interests of the UK or the nationalised industries by appearing to take too moral a position over this. One of the problems is of course the Swiss banks, which have these numbered accounts.' He was in effect playing it down.

Dell agreed with Denis, and Eric Varley said, 'I have a case now whereby British Shipbuilders have been told they can only get an £80 million contract in Nigeria if they bribe an official, and they don't want to be involved in that.'

Denis thought that the press would suffer because David English, editor of the *Mail*, could be presented as the forger's friend.

I said, 'Everybody knows that it happens; indeed, when I was in Riyadh last month, someone from the Embassy told me that the princes sit around at the end of the day, and one of them says, "It's my turn to award the contract", and the firm he sponsors gets the contract and he gets his cut.' I hoped this would destroy the credibility of the *Daily Mail* generally; as to Leyland, we could leave that to Ryder to deal with.

I said I assumed there was activity of this kind going on here; I had always suspected the oil companies of financing the SNP in Scotland.

Denis interrupted, 'They'd bribe anybody.'

I argued that we should be in favour of international guidelines and maybe bring in the Swiss banks. But also there should be some UK action within our own area of control. Companies operating here should be required to give an assurance that they did not make special payments, and we should register all commercial agents from other countries, in the same way as the American Government registers lobbies. Secondly, we should say that when the Bank of England is asked to give its approval to these special payments – which they do – a full register of what these payments are, and to whom, should be kept.

Generally we should take a stand against it. I don't think British firms like doing it – the ones I have spoken to do it with great reluctance – but they often have no choice. Perhaps we could get them to identify these practices among our competitors.

Jim invited us to stay for a swim but I had some work to do, so I went home.

### Monday 23 May

President Carter made a speech at a university yesterday declaring that American foreign policy was going to be reshaped on the basis that the Cold War was over. America, he said, was no longer prepared to support any dictatorship that called itself anti-communist, because America was no longer frightened of communism and wanted a new international system based on confidence and faith in free societies.

It was a most important statement. It goes far beyond anything

Nixon has done and puts Mrs Thatcher completely out in the cold on rearmament.

I went over to Transport House at 10.30 for a meeting of the TUC–Labour Party Liaison Committee – the first for a very long time. A tribute was paid to Danny McGarvey,* who has died.

I recommended we start work now on a new joint paper by integrating the policies contained in the TUC Economic Review with the policies contained in *Labour's Programme for Britain* of 1976, thus providing a document which would look beyond the end of this Parliament and into the next.

Jack Jones saw some danger in allowing the Liaison Committee to 'fall through the roof' (I think he meant 'floor'). The committee was intended to be a partnership, it had achieved some of its objects, and we must find common ground for the Election campaign; he thought that ground would be youth unemployment, prices and pensions.

Hugh Scanlon said that what with all the uncertainties of Phase 3, and the Lib–Lab alliance and the Government's future, continued promises with no guarantee of fulfilling them could not rally the movement and would be a recipe for disaster. We were on a hiding to nothing; he saw no resurgence in the future.

Typical Scanlon pessimism – he really is a defeated man.

Michael Foot said the proposed document was the key, and the Lib–Lab Pact would condition the nature of the commitments made in it.

Jim did not doubt the value of this committee. He remembered times when the TUC did not want to know the Party, and those were bad years for us. The link between the Government and the TUC was obvious, but this Liaison Committee helped to strengthen it, and he thanked the TUC for its involvement.

He went on to say we couldn't improve living standards before the next Election. We had hit rock bottom and we couldn't expect to go up fast. The pact with the Liberals would continue and in July there would be discussions with them on the contents of the Queen's Speech. Devolution and direct elections were their main demands; if they didn't get direct elections the Pact would end, and, to be frank, there would then be a General Election. This was his dilemma. He said he was not rushing direct elections – and he recognised how passionately both sides felt – but those who felt passionately against it had better face the fact that it would mean going into opposition and fighting direct elections from there.

The document I had suggested worried him because the question was which policy would be adopted. He made it clear that the

---

* President of the Amalgamated Society of Boilermakers, Shipwrights, Blacksmiths and Structural Workers, 1965–77. He was given a knighthood shortly before his death.

Government's policy would continue, and if the document meant a battle then it wasn't worth it.

It was a full and candid statement, and, I must say, to know precisely what Jim is thinking at this moment is important.

I had to leave just at the point when Barbara was beginning to speak and I heard her say, 'I hope what I say won't be taken as a criticism', which meant that that was exactly what it was.

In the afternoon I went over to Number 10 for a meeting with Jim that I had requested, and I stayed for forty minutes. He said, 'How are you?'

I said, 'I'm fine, very well indeed: I got up yesterday morning and went for a row on the Serpentine and a three-mile walk with my daughter. How do you feel, Jim?'

'I'm fine.'

'You always look so cheerful.'

'Under the surface it isn't like that.'

I said I knew how he felt; I was the same. Then he half apologised for having been rough with me. I said, 'Well, I much prefer working with you than with Harold – I must make that clear.'

He then asked if I wanted to talk about energy, and I replied, 'No, I don't want to bother you on that question, but can we talk about the political situation? You and I are obviously committed to the Party and we both want to win the next Election. I want nothing personal from you and I don't suppose you want anything personal from me, and that is the basis on which I begin.'

'Okay,' he said, 'what do you think?'

'I have turned my mind to three aspects of winning the Election. How do you bring about recovery? How do you engage in damage limitation in areas that are difficult? And how do you motivate the Party to fight for us in an Election?'

'Well, on recovery,' he said, 'I would like to repeat what I said a year ago. I feel it strongly, and I want you to appreciate it is not a personal request. We must have some co-ordination of all the industrial Ministers against the Treasury. They are much too powerful, and what we require is a new look at the planning agreements via an agreement to plan – that is, company working parties. That's the way to deal with Bullock. And we have got to deal with small businesses, which I know you are interested in, and so am I.'

I said, 'You could certainly have an industrial committee of the Cabinet with a chairman.'

'Do you mind my writing this down?' he asked.

'Not at all. I won't even say to you, "If you weren't writing down so much you would listen to me" ' – which is what he had remarked to me in Cabinet.

He said, 'Well, it is not for my memoirs.'

I went into the direct elections. 'You know my view, but I am not making a case on the grounds of personal passionate feeling; I am saying that you will split the Party on the vote, and you will split the Party in the direct elections themselves, and after all this pulling together to survive you will find that you have destroyed yourself when it comes to the General Election.'

'What do you suggest?'

'I think you should defer the decision as long as possible, perhaps wait till Conference, and let the French take the brunt with the Germans.'

He was happy to postpone it till 1979 or 1980, and I said, 'That's all right so long as you don't introduce a bill in the next session because it is there that the difficulty will arise. I am assuming you don't really want to get on with it but you feel you have to.'

'You are not far wrong,' he said. Then he asked, 'What are you going to do with your Home Policy Committee?'

'I am going to try and produce a document that will buckle this Parliament to the next one, as I want to do at the TUC–Labour Party Liaison Committee.'

'Well, you know you have a much better chance of being Leader if we win than if we lose the Election. I am not saying you will be Leader, but I shall certainly give up a year after we win.' I told him I didn't believe that. 'Oh,' he said, 'I shall certainly give up after a year and there will be a chance for you.'

'Well, if we are defeated I won't be there anyway. I shouldn't bother about me. The PLP would not elect me as Leader, you know that. I am not going to ruin my life by worrying about that; I have got a different role.'

### Tuesday 24 May

Josh took me into his office this morning in the Kensington and Chelsea Town Hall – very lush. I was there for about an hour and I met all the people in the development planning office. It was nice to see Josh at work enjoying himself and popular with everybody.

Alex Eadie came to see me just before noon, and he said to me in his quiet way, without any fuss or bother, 'I don't mean to trouble you in any way, Tony, but I can't go along with direct elections. I don't know whether I will vote against them or just abstain, but all my life the people I have represented have had their hopes raised by the prospect that Parliament would speak for them, and if you decant the powers of Parliament over to Brussels I would be living a fraud.

'I can't twist and turn and lie and cheat in order to remain in office. Anyway I have got my Coal Bill through and therefore in a way I feel I have done my work as a Minister, and on the back benches I'll see that bill on direct elections never gets through.'

Of course, that is exactly how I feel, and this is where the Common Market and the Lib–Lab Pact and everything come together – in the realisation deep down in the heart of the Party that this is a betrayal. I admired Alex for saying that.

### Wednesday 25 May

My first engagement was at 9, when Michael Pocock, Managing Director of Shell, and Jim Dean of Shell-Esso came to see me at my request to discuss the need for speed in completing the participation agreements with the Government and BNOC.

The Department had pushed me into putting on some pressure and had given me a list of fourteen differences and difficulties, some of which the Department thought were just a nuisance, so I told them, 'I don't want to go into detail but we do want to move quickly, so let's set aside a complete day in mid-June to go through it all. Meanwhile I would be grateful if you could clear up as many of these points as possible.'

It was a short, friendly meeting, at the end of which we had a brief discussion about Russian oil demand and supply. Mike Pocock thought the CIA forecast was politically motivated to produce the result that Jim Schlesinger wanted in America (which is exactly what Maltsev, the Soviet Oil Minister, had said to me in Moscow). They thought there might be some rundown of existing oil and they would build up later with new oil sources, but they didn't think the Soviet Union would be net importers for any period of time.

I went over to the National Executive Committee, where we elected Joan Lestor as Chairman to replace John Chalmers, who resigned in order to succeed Danny McGarvey as General Secretary of the Boilermakers' Society.

We came to the report of the special committee set up to examine Reg Underhill's documents on entryism, that's to say Trotskyite influence in the Party. It was an interesting discussion. Michael Foot moved the report – he had in effect been in the chair most of the time – and it did say a number of helpful things from my standpoint.

It described the intentions of the Militant Tendency and listed the Militant documents which Reg Underhill had 'received'. In combating Militant it recommended a membership drive, that the Party must develop political education, that GMCs must be properly constituted; and that, in recognition of Militant's claim that the LPYS are under its control, the LPYS must have a wider membership. CLPs should be reminded that the LPYS are responsible to their general management committees.

It also recommended that we didn't publish all the documentation that had 'poured in' to Reg Underhill. Reg said that it came 'in plain envelopes', but I think the security services raid Militant's office, pick up documents and hand them over to him.

The inquiry committee had concluded, significantly, that a lot of it was trash, and their report reiterated that they were against witch-hunting. Nick Bradley of the YS said there *were* Marxists and Trots in the Party and the Party needed dialogue. 'What about Reg Prentice's activities,' he asked, 'or the Social Democratic Alliance, what about the Campaign for Labour Victory, or the CIA in Australia? Aren't we interested in all of that?'

John Cartwright accepted the recommendations but said he had read all of the documentation and he wanted it circulated. Joan Lestor pointed out that every member of the Executive could go and examine it if they wanted to.

Michael Foot said there were always Marxists in the Party; there always had been and always would be. There was no witch-hunt, and we shouldn't publish the material.

Mik reminded us that Clem Attlee had endorsed the role of Marxism in the Labour Party; as for publishing, we didn't publish all the reports we had about possible corruption in local parties.

Brian Stanley thought we should accept the report but circulate the documents to the Executive.

The argument whether to publish went back and forth, and I pointed out that, if we did publish, it would be the first time we had ever published non-Labour Party material under an imprint from the Labour Party; if we were to publish the regional organisers' report on Militant activity that would be very serious, particularly if they criticised specific local parties.

They said, 'Oh, there is no suggestion of that', so I said, 'If we are not going to publish the regional officers' comments, we can't publish the rest. The press are not a bit interested in Militant; they just want to damage the Labour Party.'

Anyway it was decided by 13 votes to 10 not to make available the documents, and by 21 votes to 1 to accept the report, Nick Bradley being the one against. I was much encouraged because I don't think we are going back to the old days.

By this time, Jim had arrived and we moved on to the Lib–Lab Pact. I found the discussion riveting.

First of all, Eric Heffer said we didn't need a pact with the Liberals and he didn't want to condemn it now but he thought we should consider what to do for the future.

Michael Foot defended it vigorously. It bought us time; there was nothing permanent in the arrangement, but it meant *we* would fix the Election date instead of Mrs Thatcher.

Jim Callaghan said, 'I haven't got much to add. No one can know whether it is right or wrong.' It was a parliamentary arrangement; the NEC could certainly make a comment about the next session, but, as to the future, that was for the PLP and not the Executive. 'In principle, I would like a renewal of the pact. As to direct elections, we pledged ourselves in the Queen's Speech, and there is a very large PLP group in favour of them, but we'll have a free vote on the electoral system adopted – that has been made clear.'

He went on to say that he and Michael recognised that on both sides there were deep convictions – indeed fanatical zeal – about direct elections, and he did not want to break the Party up over this issue. The Conference had voted against by 4 million to 2 million, but he had given assurances to heads of government that there would be direct elections, and he wanted to narrow this gap.

Barbara Castle said, 'Well, there should be a free vote on the principle of direct elections', and Sam McCluskie added, 'Will there be a free vote in the Cabinet?' Jim replied, 'It is not decided and I couldn't tell you; I could really only tell the Parliamentary Party – I would have to tell them first.'

Well, then we went on to discuss the International Committee. There was a proposal from Shirley that we should have some discussions with Georges Marchais, the French Communist Party leader. Mik said, 'Oh yes, Mitterrand is in favour and in any case we are having discussions with the Italian Communist Party', so gradually this opening up between the British Labour Party and the Euro-communists has begun. Very important.

Incidentally, I got a minute today telling me that when some uranium disappeared in 1968 from France – 200 tons of it – it was never reported to British Ministers. We weren't in Euratom, that is true, but 200 tons of uranium disappearing is extremely serious. And until 1972 there wasn't even a safeguards officer in the Department of Energy. So, in focusing political attention on the whole nuclear power issue, we are gradually discovering all sorts of appalling gaps in our procedures.

I went to the party given by the heads of the African missions in Britain, held at the Egyptian Embassy.

I was introduced to Andrew Young, the black American just appointed Ambassador to the UN by Carter, to deal with Africa. He didn't know who I was, and as I talked to him his eyes kept looking over my shoulder to see if there was anyone more interesting to meet. Anyway, I said, 'If you see Vice-President Mondale, tell him he made a very good speech in the Kansas Law School seminar on civil rights.'

'Who are you anyway?' he asked.

I said, 'Well, I'm Schlesinger's opposite number, the Secretary of State for Energy.' Then he did see someone more interesting and I slipped off.

## Thursday 26 May

It was a very crowded day today. It began with a couple of press stories, one about the NEC having fought off the attempt to expel Militant, and the second on the Tribune Group of MPs having come out officially in favour of withdrawal from the Common Market.

At 9.30 we had the Cabinet committee which deals with Common Market issues (CQM), and pig-meat was on the agenda.

The Commission had appealed to the European Court to rule out of order the pig-meat subsidy that John Silkin had agreed, and the court had ordered that this subsidy cease forthwith. John Silkin reported that he had met Gundelach, the Commissioner for Agriculture and Fisheries, to try to get him to prolong the subsidy till 11 June to give time for it to be phased out.

Frank Judd intervened to say that Foreign Office advice was that 'forthwith' meant at once. The Attorney-General (Sam Silkin) thought it would be wiser to stop anyway now, because we had to challenge the court and if the court thought we had been dilatory in obeying their interim injunction it might damage our case.

I asked whether this was the first time that a European Court decision had been taken against the British Government, and I was told it was. Then I asked what would be the political effect of this on pig producers in the UK. John Silkin said it would mean in effect the destruction of our industry, the mass slaughtering of pigs and the abandonment of our processing plant in favour of the Danes. All in the name of free competition!

I just wanted to be told explicitly – as I was – that I was a member of the first British Government in history to be informed that it was behaving illegally by a court whose ruling you could not alter by changing the law in the House of Commons. That was an absolute turning point, and of course it could happen on grants, on oil policy, on intervention to support industries and so on. At a moment of great excitement, with the Tribune Group coming out against the Common Market and the direct elections brewing, here was an example of direct Community damage to a basic British interest.

At Cabinet during a discussion on the forthcoming Commonwealth Conference, Jim asked if Ministers would accompany him to London Airport to meet the heads of state. So I said, 'Can I meet Amin?' Jim replied, 'Even if you do, he will get all the headlines', and there was a lot of laughter.

Then Jim said, 'I want to say a word about direct elections. There are very serious difficulties here and we must recognise that there is a possibility that, if we don't move on this, there will be a vote of censure tabled against us by the Tories for not producing the bill, and the Liberals would have to support the motion. The Liberals care very much about this.'

He said the Government wanted to introduce a bill providing for direct elections after Whitsun, with the proportional representation clauses and a schedule attached. If it passed the second reading, the committee stage would be on the floor of the House. The Tories would oppose PR, and if the PR system was rejected we would then fall back on the first-past-the-post or simple-majority system at the report stage, and we wouldn't then be forced to have an Election in 1978.

He added, 'Of course there would be a free vote for the Party, and, after the most serious consideration, I have decided to give Cabinet members a free vote.'

Well, Michael said he greatly appreciated what Jim had done and he hoped people wouldn't be too worried about it. For example, in 1910 Lloyd George had voted opposite Asquith on the question of the Conciliation Bill, which gave some political rights to women. Jim said, 'Yes, I would accept a vote against the principle. I hope people won't do it and I hope abstention will be sufficient – I hope they will consider what they are going to do – but they can vote against.'

There was some debate about Jim's announcement, and I expressed my thanks to Jim for giving Cabinet a free vote, knowing how very strongly he felt about this on constitutional grounds. But I could see a time, I said, if we did get direct elections, when there would be two Labour candidates in every constituency, one pro-federal and one anti-Market. I didn't think we could get it through without a guillotine and that would be very difficult. Therefore in my view the wisest thing was not to introduce the bill at all.

Roy Hattersley thought the Prime Minister had produced the best solution. He had warned that the pro-EEC Labour MPs were worms that would turn, and the Cabinet free vote would certainly anger them seriously.

Joel Barnett said, 'I don't want to break up the Government, but if there isn't a bill the Liberals will withdraw, and if there isn't a free vote the Cabinet will split.'

David Owen said very fairly that it would be difficult for him to explain to Europe, but he would do his best, and he didn't want to use those explanations in order to tie people to what they wouldn't have.

Peter Shore believed in collective responsibility but the European case was exceptional. He thought that we might be laying a gunpowder trail, if, as he thought likely, the bill became law.

As Jim summed up, I had to leave to go to Paris. Ron picked me up from the office with James Bretherton and Frances Morrell. I told her at the airport what had happened – it is the most amazing change. The whole political perspective has altered now. Here we are entering upon an issue on which I had absolutely made up my mind that I was not prepared to vote for the Government and I have been reprieved. I have to handle myself with considerable dignity and skill at this particular moment.

*Friday 27 May*
Stayed in the French Embassy and had breakfast at 7.45 with Jacques Delors, a leading figure in the French Socialist Party and apparently very close to Mitterrand.

One of the Embassy staff translated and we sat for an hour in the breakfast room, with bacon and eggs on the heater at the side, coffee and tea, toast, butter and marmalade – just like being in an English country house.

Delors is my age, born in 1925, the son of a Christian trade-unionist. He had worked in the trade union movement and was a trade union militant for many years; he said he'd been a socialist from his youth but moved into the Bank of France and then worked in the personal Cabinet of Chaban-Delmas, the Prime Minister who was sacked by Giscard and replaced by Chirac.

I asked him what the prospects were in the French elections, and he said, 'Oh, the left will win, they're very optimistic.' He told me that they were developing an industrial policy and I asked about the nationalisation of the banks and enterprises. 'Oh,' he said, 'the French people expect that. They don't have the same feeling about national-isation as exists, for example, in Britain, and in any case we want the nationalised industries to be run very much as if they were private businesses, with complete managerial independence.'

'So what is the difference between public and private enterprise, then?'

'Two differences,' he replied. 'First of all, we want to develop *autogestion*, which is workers' control, to prevent them from becoming corporatist. Secondly there would be better motivation in those industries.'

I asked him about the Communist Party and he said that it was very important to bring the Communist voters in France into the main-stream of French politics. Clearly Mitterrand's interest lies much more in the Communist voters than in the Communist Party leaders. Delors said that relations with the Communist leader Georges Marchais were good, they were discussing policy problems, and there would not be too much difficulty in updating the 1972 Common Programme.

I went on to ask him whether Mitterrand might form a coalition with

Giscard and the right instead of the Communists. He said no, because the Communists would do well in the first ballot. This indicated to me that the Socialists might be using the coalition with the Communists simply to draw upon their considerable support and thus get the Socialists into power. With Communist support in the country, Mitterrand would be in a much stronger bargaining position to strike a deal with Giscard – a typical case of the right using the left to get into power and then dropping them. The left has nowhere else to go, so they just have to put up with it. I thought it was most significant.

We came on to Europe, and he didn't think there would be any federalisation of the Common Market. Hadn't I heard the French Government's declaration to the effect that there would be no federal Europe? I had.

Delors believed that, unless there was some impetus towards the development of European institutions, within twenty years the Common Market would be decadent, or decayed. What was really needed was some sort of French Fabian Society to provide ideas for the French Socialist Party. He said the PSF had close relations with the SPD in Germany, discussing economic and social policy, and the problems of the Third World.

Obviously the SPD in Germany, reflecting the growing strength of the German state and the money available to it, is busy building up its own influence over the socialist parties of western Europe, just as the German Government is building up its influence over the governments of western Europe. The German recovery now contained within the Community may be a major factor in making the Community into a German organisation. Indeed, it is one of the reasons why the French feel close to us; they need us in a sort of latterday *entente cordiale* to contain the power of Germany. This is a factor we cannot ignore. The Germans are pro-federal not only because they could dominate a federation, but also because the German leaders are afraid of their own people.

Delors was perfectly cordial, a sort of Roy Hattersley/Shirley Williams figure.

It's like swimming in treacle, trying to be an effective socialist Minister in the bureaucracy of the Common Market at the moment. This cloying bureaucracy has got to be driven back in a major way, otherwise the political impulse of the labour movement will be completely lost. It is not just about the public having lots of forms to fill in; it is about the absolute naked political power of unelected people. This is the dominant political question. I know you can argue that a strong Minister can deal with his Department, but the weapons at the disposal of civil servants are enormously powerful and we have got to get them under control. I am determined to make this a major part of our next Election manifesto.

There was a piece in today's *New Statesman* written by Paul Johnson called 'An Open Letter to Tony Benn', praising me to the skies and asking me to resign from the Government so as to extricate myself from the Tammany Hall politics of Jim Callaghan. It was a shrewd letter, apart from the embarrassing advice on resignation, because every word of criticism of the Government was absolutely true. On the other hand it comes from a man who hates the trade unions and hates the left – a most extraordinary mix-up.

I caught the train to Bristol for my surgery. A folk evening had been organised by Mike and Dawn Primarolo, a young couple who came to Bristol about three years ago and joined the Labour Party in Windmill Hill Ward. They breathed vitality into it, organising surgeries, a city farm and so on.

Anyway, it was a marvellous evening.

*Saturday 28 May*
Today the Government's response to the Flowers Report was the main news, and the *Guardian* and *The Times* concentrated on the pledge that we would not go ahead with the fast breeder reactor without a proper inquiry. This was a phrase over which we had fought very hard with officials. I had been to see Peter to fight for some changes to the official recommendations, because he didn't fully appreciate at that stage the significance of what was being agreed. And I must give Frances Morrell the credit for having identified the changes that were needed and for pointing out to me, with James Bretherton, that even at the last stage, after the EY Committee had considered it, there had been an attempt to change one key phrase in our response in order to alter its meaning. The phrase was that there would be no authorisation even of the prototype fast breeder reactor until the method of the public inquiry itself had been agreed. When it came back in its final draft, the Department officials had changed it to say there would be no authorisation of the construction of fast breeder reactors until the prototype had been agreed – which meant giving the go-ahead for the prototype without saying in principle that we would do it.

When I asked why the phrase had been changed, an official in my Department said, 'Because I don't think Ministers knew what they were doing when they agreed it.' Well, I knew what we were doing. It was a last-minute attempt to change, by stealth, the whole meaning of the response I had fought for and carried through, and it was a reminder of the terrifying power of officials.

*Monday 30 May*
I dictated to my secretary, Julie Clements, the text of my proposed statement to the Common Market Safeguards Committee press

conference on Thursday for circulation because I was rebuked by Jim last year for not circulating a draft speech on the same subject. But I am not going to be driven off the main issue, and if Jim says I can't make the speech I am going to stand firm.

*Wednesday 1 June*
Went into the Department for the signing of the BP participation agreement, the full formal agreement. Sir David Steel, head of BP, Frank Kearton and I sat at the table and signed all these documents with crests on them. I have the gravest doubts whether it has any real meaning, but it is a start and it is the best deal I can get; the fact that the oil companies, even BP, have gone along with it convinces me that it doesn't mean very much. But it has given birth to a national oil corporation which in time could be used in substantial ways.

After that, I had a meeting with the Tory Prime Minister of Australia, Malcolm Fraser, the Australian High Commissioner and Sir Donald Tebbit, our High Commissioner in Australia. Fraser is a farmer, a sort of Ian Smith figure, except that he has a more aristocratic background. He worked with Kerr, the Governor-General of Australia, to oust Gough Whitlam, the Labour Prime Minister, at the end of 1975. The circumstances of that have now been more fully revealed and it appears that the American CIA played some part in bringing about the change of government. It is not at all inconceivable that Whitlam's

*'Once more unto the breach, dear friends, once more . . .'*

opposition to the sale of uranium, supported by the Australian labour movement, was a factor.

Caroline and I visited Peckham Manor Boys' School in Southwark in the evening to give away prizes. We took our places on the platform and the parents and prizewinners were sitting at tables for coffee and biscuits. It was organised by a Parent–Staff Association which includes school workers such as caretakers and cleaners – a most attractive idea. Harvey Hinds conducted the prize-giving and paid the warmest tribute to Caroline. I was extremely proud. He said I was there basking in her glory.

Afterwards we went to talk to the parents and prizewinners, and over half of them were West Indian, Asian, Greek Cypriot and so on. It was a lovely evening, the band was super and the kids were great.

*Thursday 2 June*
The papers this morning had a trailer of the Common Market Safeguards Committee press conference at the Waldorf Hotel. The *Telegraph* had the biggest story: 'Benn Challenges Callaghan on the EEC'.

To the Waldorf Hotel. I announced that I *wasn't* going to talk about direct elections, and then gave a statement quoting figures on price increases, the trade deficit and job losses due to our membership of the Common Market. I put forward four options for Britain: to do nothing about membership, to organise a new campaign to leave, to press federalisation in a United States of Europe, or to work for fundamental reforms in Britain's relationship, including the amendment of the 1972 Act.

The press were difficult and aggressive but I was extremely uncommunicative, and the tension was electric. The press are hired men who *have* to get the Market case across, and they will not allow any other view to be seriously expressed.

When I got home at 5.30 I heard the BBC News, which began with 'Mr Benn gave his reasons today for Britain leaving the Common Market', and followed with a long interview with John Davies, former Conservative Industry Secretary. On the *Newsday* programme Clement Freud, Liberal MP for Ely, had a debate with Bryan Gould, Labour MP for Southampton Test, and Bryan was brilliant – clear-minded, straightforward, knew all the answers. He said, 'Well of course we are constitutionally entitled to have another referendum on whether we wish to come out.'

Clement Freud replied, 'This is unbelievable – we are constitutionally entitled to have a referendum to hang Tony Benn and I am sure there would be a great majority in favour of that.'

On the ITN *News at Ten*, Peter Walker called for my dismissal because of my statement.

*Friday 3 June*

The papers this morning were entirely taken up with the press conference. The tabloids led with 'Sack Benn' stories, in an attempt to revive the spectre from the 1975 Referendum of the man who wanted to split the Party, who wanted the Party to be defeated, and indeed was leading it to defeat. The tone of the heavies, however, was quite different.

I am keen that this issue should be presented as reuniting the Party around a free vote, and winning the next Election by defending our national interest. Those two things must be done.

Caroline thinks there is a difficulty in my being opposed to direct elections, given my views on extending democracy and on internationalism. She suggested I make it clear that I would be in favour of direct elections to the UN General Assembly. That would allow us to say: we want direct elections in Russia to the UN Assembly, direct elections in South Africa to the UN Assembly, until a world assembly of peoples was established.

*Tuesday 7 June*

Jubilee Day and Mother's eightieth birthday.

Ron Vaughan picked us up at 9.30 and we drove to St Paul's Cathedral for the Jubilee service. It had been pouring this morning and was still chilly. When we tried to get down Constitution Hill we were turned back and told to go along Piccadilly. In Piccadilly we saw a great Daimler with a flag and a police escort, so Ron decided to follow it. It turned down St James's, which is normally one-way, and into Lancaster House, and we realised that all the heads of state were meeting at Lancaster House before going *en bloc* to St Paul's. So we had to wend our way back up St James's. We finally got through and drove down the Strand.

The streets along the route were packed with people behind crush barriers, which I don't think were there in 1935, and there was sand on the roads and soldiers and Gurkhas, airmen and sailors, some with fixed bayonets, facing inwards. Crowds and crowds, all waving Union Jacks and cheering. Rather fun, to be honest.

Up Fleet Street and towards the cathedral, and we walked the last few yards. I was wearing a slightly old but warm suit with my medals – Melissa had said I looked like a member of the National Front – and as we walked along a few people cheered me and gave a special wave, but one or two shouted, 'Rubbish!'

We went into the cathedral and found ourselves sitting under the North Dome about five rows back. We were next to the Masons, the Mulleys, the Morrises and other Cabinet members. On my right was Merlyn Rees's wife – he couldn't come because he was waiting for Amin to arrive; this is a great story just now, that Amin is supposedly trying to make his way here. Saw Jim and Audrey, and behind us were the former Prime Ministers, Wilson, Heath, Home and Macmillan; and, behind them, former Commonwealth Prime Ministers – Gough Whitlam, John Gorton and so on.

Then the processions came in: the Gentlemen at Arms, the Beefeaters, the Speaker, the Lord Chancellor, the choir, the Archbishop of Canterbury, the Clerk of the Closet, the minor canons and deputy canons and deputy minor canons, and the Gold Stick in Waiting. After about an hour and a quarter the royal family began arriving, then the Queen and the Duke came in. It was extraordinary.

It is an aspect of the British establishment which you have to see. They haven't got much power, since that has been taken over by the bankers and the businessmen, but many of the individuals are also in banking and business. The peers are bankers, or the bankers are made peers. And some of these landowners, the Duchess of Grafton or the Duke of Beaufort, who look quite harmless, are in their own areas still feudal landowners. Of course if they own property in London they are enormously wealthy.

We haven't removed the grip of this crowd from British society, far from it, but on the other hand the public accepts it all and the press plays it up to divert people from unemployment and the cost of living and the EEC and so on. It is a very important ingredient in British life and it has to be thought about. I am glad I went.

The Archbishop of Canterbury gave an awful sermon, full of the old reactionary ideas, prayers about the Commonwealth and prosperity, trust in God and so on – awful opium of the people stuff.

On our way out, we saw the Russian Ambassador, who was dressed in topper and tails.

*Wednesday 8 June*

At 9.30 we went off to Buckingham Palace. I suppose Caroline and I have been invited to evening parties there before, but we never actually went to one, though I have been to a garden party and to audiences of the Privy Council over the last thirteen years.

The Commonwealth Prime Ministers were there and we went into one of the reception rooms overlooking the garden, where we were offered drinks. I fell in with Paul Martin, the High Commissioner for Canada and a former Foreign Minister, who is always terribly friendly.

By this time we were beginning to string out and we formed a receiving line to be introduced to the Queen and the Duke. I gave an inclination of my head and shook the Duke's hand.

We were ushered into another long chamber and there were the people who had had dinner – Prince Charles, Princess Anne, the

Duchess of Kent, the Duchess of Gloucester, Princess Margaret, Mountbatten and the whole royal family, along with Macmillan, Wilson and Home. We saw the Harts, the Booths, the Healeys and the Owens but I didn't see any others.

Anyway we found Ruth and Seretse Khama and they gave us a great hug. Seretse is very sick; he looks thin and old and has a pacemaker and a hole in his chest where they had to put a wire to his heart. God, it was awful.

We had a word with Hastings Banda, whom I knew years ago when he was in London. He is of course something of a tyrant now, but his story is an interesting one. He left Nyasaland for South Africa, where he found a job as a waiter, before going on to Rhodesia, where he worked in a hospital as an orderly. That gave him the idea of becoming a doctor, and he somehow got to America and went to the University of Chicago and then to Nashville, Tennessee, where he qualified. After that he came to Britain and practised as a doctor in Willesden in London.

It was very interesting from our discussions to find out how the IMF is really squeezing everybody. The Sierra Leone President said the IMF was forcing him to close schools and putting him under very heavy pressure.

As we were talking to Kenneth Kaunda, one of the equerries came up and said, 'Princess Alexandra would like to meet you.' I think she must be the daughter of the late Duchess of Kent.

But fortunately, or unfortunately, as we were moving in that general direction, someone told us that Princess Anne wanted to meet us. So we went over to her. She is interested in anything to do with horses. So I asked her about royal carriages and how they were built, and their springing, and whether they made you travel-sick.

We slipped away, avoiding Prince Charles, and sat on a couch, and at that moment we saw the Queen and the Duke just talking to each other. Caroline thought they were going to come over but the equerry swooped on them with Judith and Tony Hart.

Audrey Callaghan came up and had a long talk with Caroline. Then Mary Wilson came up; I gave her a big kiss – I do like Mary. She said, 'I am so pleased about your speech on the Common Market; the one hope for Labour in the next Election is if we fight against the Common Market.' So I said, 'Don't tell Harold that', and she announced she had told Harold what she thought of my speech and he didn't mind at all.

We talked a bit about the terrible treatment by the press, and she said how awful it was to be distrusted and to have to distrust everybody in case they write down your confidences; how awful to be in a Cabinet and have everything you say written down.

'Well,' I said, 'in the Crossman *Diaries* the gossip wasn't interesting really, neither was it interesting in Haines's book; but they are significant books. It is important that people should know how they are governed. But you are a deeply admired figure, and it has all passed over you, Mary; it is like water off a duck's back.'

'But it is painful,' she said. She looks so happy since Harold has given up the premiership, and somehow the fact that I am in a continual struggle, even now, with Harold doesn't really affect our relationship. She is an extremely nice woman.

Audrey invited Caroline for lunch at Chequers on 26 June while the Cabinet are there for political discussions.

We slipped out of the Palace. They hadn't given the drivers anything to drink and Ron had just been sitting in the car for two and a half hours. Very inconsiderate.

That reminds me: one of the flunkey equerries in uniform was bowing and scraping as he brought us in and Caroline said, 'It is awfully cold in here', to which he replied, 'I am afraid the temperature of the boiler is set by those who work here and they wear a heavy uniform of livery and they think it is too hot.' So Caroline said, 'Well, that's all right because I am all for working conditions being determined by the shop floor. If that's what it is about, then I understand.'

### Friday 10 June

Two-day trip to Scotland. Caroline and I arrived in Edinburgh at 6.40 off the sleeper, and Mick McGahey, the Scottish Miners' President, took us to the Esso Hotel. I just had time for a bath and then we went down and had breakfast with him.

Jim Carver, the Chief Mining Inspector, was there with his wife. He is retiring this month, and I had heard from Alex Eadie about tremendous tensions that had built up between the Mining Inspectorate and the Health and Safety Executive, under whom they were placed by the 1974 legislation.

The mining inspectors have always been highly regarded by both the Coal Board and the NUM because of their absolute independence. They visit each pit once a fortnight, and each inspection involves a representative of both management and the NUM. Any complaints have to be resolved within seven days. The Mining Inspectorate doesn't normally prosecute; rather it makes recommendations on the basis of evidence given at hearings, though it has been known to remove individual mine managers from their posts. But Carver is worried now that the level of safety in mines has been reduced as a result of the change. He said that the Chief Inspector of Nuclear Installations was equally concerned, and there was a terrific battle going on.

Carver had gone down the pits at fourteen, and his wife's mother had lost all four brothers in mining accidents. He said to me, 'I feel mining safety, I feel it in my bones.'

Anyway, the NUM are going to try to get the Mining Inspectorate out of the Health and Safety Executive and I shall see Albert Booth about it. The miners will need TUC support if they are to succeed.

We were taken to Longannet Colliery and went down a mine.

We walked down a steep incline, deep into the earth, for about 1000 feet. It was two and a half miles to the face, and there was a man-carrying car for part of it, but we walked most of the way. It was immensely hard going. My boots were too big and my feet slid about inside, and I got blisters. The roof was low and there was a lot of water around so you kept putting your feet into potholes. Caroline was pitched off the conveyor, and fell forward on to her shoulder. It was really tough – I was exhausted when I got to the coalface. After that, lunch was laid on in the canteen with Mr Bell, the mine manager, Mick McGahey, who had not come down the pit with us, and the managers and leading union officials from the pits in the Longannet complex.

We went back to the hotel and Caroline had a sleep. I was equally exhausted but I had to see the delegation from Lothian Regional Council, who had come with the full-time officials of the Confederation of Shipbuilding and Engineering Unions and shop stewards from three plants – Motherwell Bridge, who produce offshore equipment, Parsons Peebles, the company producing turbo-generators, and Robb Caledon, a shipyard in Leith that will be taken over by British Shipbuilders on 1 July. I won't go over the details, but it was a classic case of three more chunks of British manufacturing industry on the point of decline, more people being laid off, and the manufacturing base being eroded. It really made me weep.

*Saturday 11 June*

At 9.45 we went down to catch the bus to the Miners' Gala. It was about 34° Fahrenheit and pelting with rain; we froze for most of the day.

At 11 we marched out with Mick McGahey, Bill McLean, General Secretary of the Scottish Miners, Peter Heathfield, Secretary of the Derbyshire Miners, and Ray Buckton of ASLEF, and several pipe bands. We marched through Edinburgh, down the Royal Mile, through the courtyard of Holyrood House and the beautiful park overlooked by rocky high hills, and finally on to the stage. We were covered but there was no shelter for the audience; it was still freezing and raining, but it didn't deter them. The people gathered out there, many of them old retired miners, must have had an agonising time.

After a thrilling morning, despite the weather, we were picked up and driven to Bannockburn for tea with Dennis Canavan, the MP for

West Stirlingshire. We arrived early, so we went to the Golden Lion Hotel in Stirling and looked in vain for a warm radiator.

We rounded off the evening in the Thirteen Fourteen pub, within a stone's throw of the site of the Battle of Bannockburn, where Robert the Bruce beat Edward. I went into the lavatory and an old man came in, a bit the worse for drink, saw me, poked his finger in my chest and said, 'You're bloody like Benn.'

'I'm not surprised – I am.'

He shook me by the hand, pumped it indeed, and limped off.

By God, we were tired by the time we caught the sleeper, but it was warm.

### Sunday 12 June

One interesting thing at the moment is the way the flamethrower of the press is being turned on me again as it was during the Common Market Referendum campaign. They have five lines of attack: that I am mad, ambitious, incompetent, a hypocrite and a red. This week I appear to be all of them at once. Alan Watkins describes me as a boy inventor – the next thing to a mad professor.

### Monday 13 June

At 11.15 I went to GEN 86, the Cabinet committee on industrial democracy, with Edmund Dell, Albert Booth, Bill Rodgers, Roy Hattersley, Denis Healey and Shirley Williams in the chair. Edmund has now produced a paper proposing that the legislation should go back beyond elected workers on the board, to a secret ballot to elect the participation committees. He said it was fundamental to have statutory criteria, including elections, and though Jack Jones would not accept them it was vital to safeguard the rights of non-unionists.

I said the system of joint shop stewards' committees and combines had developed naturally, after months and years of work to get them organised. They had grown naturally within firms. 'If you attempt to bypass all that, you are giving to the inactive people a role which only the active people have worked for. This is what we should be saying. Trade-unionism is an indication of stage one of people's desire to have some part to play in their firms.'

I said Edmund's paper would be seen as anti-union; since wages and conditions were the key to the trade union role, you would simply be building in a new source of conflict between these artificially created participation committees and the trade unions. That was why the TUC couldn't agree to it.

I didn't actually say – though it was clearly the case – that Edmund's purpose is to *weaken* the trade unions, that his interest is with management rather than the unions.

At 2 Red Adair came to see me – the great Red Adair from Texas who handled the blowout at Ekofisk. He was a modest guy, and with representatives from the UK Offshore Operators' Association (his biggest customers) also present he was not prepared to be too critical of their standards. He said, 'Minister Benn, they are doing the best they can, and I don't want to tell them what they ought to do.' Unfortunately he declined to have his photograph taken with me!

This evening I flew with Peter Le Cheminant, Bernard Ingham and James Bretherton, through the most fantastic lightning, to Luxembourg for tomorrow's Energy Council meeting.

Waiting there in the rain was Donald Maitland with an umbrella, and we came back to the Holiday Inn and went through the agenda. At about midnight I tried to get a cup of tea but room service was closed, so here I am, an hour later, still working and quite unable, in this modern, expensive, international hotel, to get so much as a cup of tea after midnight.

### Tuesday 14 June

Went over to the Council Chamber; my last period as President.

I was asked to give a report and we then moved on to a very interesting debate on nuclear energy and coal.

At the end I thanked the Commission and my colleagues for their great courtesy and I said we mustn't think we weren't making progress in Europe, because everybody had difficulties – the Americans, north and south, east and west, and so on. The Belgian Ambassador thanked me for my perseverance and zeal, and Brunner thanked me.

Flew home. Audrey Wise and Jeff Rooker [MP for Birmingham Perry Barr] voted four times tonight on amendments, which the Tories supported, knocking £440 million off the Budget tax revenue provisions by raising the tax threshold. It has created a great panic and it looks as if the Government is falling apart at the seams.

### Wednesday 15 June

I had a long struggle today with Shell-Esso, who are being very difficult and trying to pull back from the Memorandum of Understanding which they have with us concerning their North Sea operations. I was courteous but Dick Mabon was much more aggressive, as we agreed he should be. I felt at the end we were losing; Frank Kearton was absolutely furious at the way the companies behaved.

### Thursday 16 June

Cabinet, and another discussion on the direct elections bill. Then foreign affairs, and David Owen paid a tribute to Jim's brilliant chairmanship of the Commonwealth Conference, at which point David

Ennals said, 'I met twelve presidents and heads of state recently, and I must say it was absolutely brilliant, absolutely brilliant, your leadership, Prime Minister.' I do really dislike David Ennals. He is so obsequious.

Finally there was a discussion about transport policy. Bill Rodgers has produced a most reactionary paper which hands railway closures of rural lines over to local authorities which are mainly Tory, and Michael Foot tried to stop it being published. But in the end Jim summed up in favour of publication.

PLP after that. The liaison committee of the PLP had summoned Audrey Wise and Jeff Rooker to report on why they had voted against the Government. So Audrey and Jeff, far from being apologetic, said, 'We'll discuss it at a Party meeting', and Cledwyn said, 'Oh no we won't, we can't; I have only invited you to come here.'

So they asked, 'Did you ask John Mackintosh [MP for Berwick and East Lothian] why he voted against the Government defence expenditure? Do you always ask Members when they vote against?'

Came home and worked late. Caroline came down at midnight precisely and reminded me that it was our wedding anniversary.

### Friday 17 June

Yesterday Julie brought in the most fabulous birthday cake in the shape of an 80 for Mother, who is having a party at the House of Commons this afternoon.

I had rung a translation agency to help me with a speech I am making to the French Socialist Party Congress tomorrow, and a young man came to the house and translated it into perfect French. It took him all morning, and he sat in the kitchen and discussed the meaning of certain words with me. Then he very kindly dictated it himself on to tape and I listened to it about a dozen times. He worked for four and a half hours on a four-minute speech, but it was idiomatic and extremely good.

It is tremendously foolhardy to deliver it in French to a French audience but I am determined to do it. It sets out a number of principles for Europe: that we believe in trade unions and links with the labour movement; that we are opposed to capitalism and in favour of socialism; that we are in favour of democracy and freedom, and we see it all as international.

Then Steve and June, Hilary and Rosalind and Melissa and Josh, who by the way has passed his driving test, all turned up and went off in the car with Mother's present. Got to the House and about 180 people turned up for the party. It was pouring with rain, and cold as anything, so there were heaters in the marquee on the terrace. Elsie Chamberlain, whom Father appointed as first woman chaplain to the armed forces, was there, and the Chief Rabbi, the Lord Chancellor and his wife Polly Binder, friends from the Council of Christians and Jews, the Council for the Ministry of Women and the Congregational Federation; really it was so friendly and Mother was marvellous. Father's old secretary, Miss Knox, came – I hadn't seen her since I was six.

*Saturday 18 June*
Picked up from home at 6 and I listened to the tape recording in French over and over again in the car. On the plane, it was tremendously nerve-racking to contemplate addressing 2000 Frenchmen in their own language, not speaking French myself. Mik was at the airport and we travelled to Nantes, where we were met by George Walden from the British Embassy and his wife, Sarah. She is the sister of Marigold Johnson, Paul Johnson's wife, and she works restoring paintings at the Louvre.

We were taken to this huge aircraft hangar with a high platform and the symbol of the French Socialist Party – a clenched fist holding a red rose.

On the platform were the Central Committee or Secretariat of the Socialist Party, minus Mitterrand, who didn't turn up until after lunch. The media, as always at conferences, appeared to dominate the political process. The noise of the loudspeakers was deafening; it was torture to the ears, and you couldn't escape from it wherever you went.

George Walden, a right old Tory, spent a year at the École Nationale d'Administration (ENA), and looking at my translation he said that one passage was open to considerable misunderstanding. It was a passage in which I had said the time was ripe for liberalisation in the Soviet Union and eastern Europe; it had been translated as saying liberalisation was just about to occur.

It was the first Socialist Party Congress for two years; the big issues were the revision of the 1972 Common Programme with the French Communists, and the policy upon which the party will fight the legislative elections in March next year. The question was whether the CERES group, the left-wing grouping within the Socialist Party, would be admitted back into the Secretariat of the Party. The press stories indicated that Mitterrand was determined to show his strength and impose his will on the Party, whereas CERES had a number of more radical proposals and wanted them to be synthesised into the majority resolutions.

The atmosphere was heady. In the course of the day the *Internationale* was sung five times, whenever the opportunity presented itself. On the other hand there were no trade unions there, so that ballast and stability which the trade unions give the Labour Party was absent. This is the enormous strength of the Labour Party, but it also explains its exceptional conservatism.

George Walden went to great trouble to introduce me to people. I met Jacques Delors and saw Michel Rocard, who has shifted to the right of the Socialist Party but still tries to stay in with the left.

To lunch about 1.30. Walden talked to me for most of it about the importance of the ENA, which produced the high-level civil servants known as the Enarques; he talked about how powerful France was because of its enormous administrative capacity and said this was what we needed in Britain too.

Well, I am getting a bit too old for that sort of crap, so I said, 'The trouble is not that the British Civil Service is not efficient. It is just obstructive, and prevents Ministers doing what they want to do. I have never known such working to rule and obstruction as when I was at the Department of Industry.'

He was terribly taken aback.

'Moreover,' I said, 'the problem with Britain is not the lack of an élite but the fact that we haven't solved some political problems which have been resolved in other countries, with the French Revolution, the American Revolution and so on.' I didn't want to, but I did upset him.

I went back into the hall at 3.15 thinking the conference would resume on time, but, as Mik had predicted, it began an hour late. We were all summoned on to the platform to be introduced to the Congress, and I only just heard my name. There was moderate applause, because they aren't wildly interested in the British Labour Party. All the other delegations had given the clenched fist but I didn't. The Third World delegations were introduced and the biggest cheers were for Spain, Chile and so on.

Mitterrand came and sat on the platform, and then I heard, 'Et maintenant, Tony Benn', so I put on my tape recorder. By this time I was extemely nervous. There was this huge delegation and I had a four-minute speech to make in French and I didn't know if I was going to get through it.

Mitterrand stood up and we shook hands, and I pitched into this event, with a great battery of microphones, bright lights and media people. I plucked up courage and thought I simply had to do it with force and real feeling, so I just hammered through it. I got a little applause for my reference to the racists' days in Africa being numbered, and a little more when I said the multinationals couldn't decide the future for us. Then at the end I said, 'Le Parti Socialiste est l'espoir, et plus que l'espoir, c'est l'avenir de la France et de l'Europe', and they cheered very much. It was such an ordeal, like making my first speech in public, but it was intelligible, I heard later.

While I was standing with Jenny Little [International Secretary of the Labour Party] and George Walden and his wife, there was a tremendous flashlight – it was Felipe Gonzalez of the Spanish Socialist

Party arriving. As he walked up the centre aisle all I could see from where I was standing was a camera moving on a dolly and a dazzle of flashbulbs. Then Gonzalez came into sight – a man of about thirty-five with long hair, wearing a leather jacket and open-necked shirt – and he made his way to the platform to the sound of the *Internationale*. He made the clenched-fist sign and then gave a most impassioned speech. It was very moving that after forty years of Franco's dictatorship Spain's freedom had returned.

Mitterrand spoke, paying tribute to the work done by the French Socialist Party on behalf of Spain, and the courage of the Spaniards, many of whom had died in the struggle.

Walden by this time was getting increasingly Tory in his comments, and when one man in a blue shirt began speaking he said, 'You had better listen to him; he is one of the three proletarians in the Party', which did make me laugh.

By the evening I was exhausted and had a thumping headache from the noise of the loudspeakers. But I did meet twenty or more of the key figures in the French Socialist Party and it was extremely useful.

### Sunday 19 June

Up at 6 and made some tea. The water from my thermos was still just warm enough to infuse a little bit of tea, and I had some powdered milk with me. You have to take a lot of care to get yourself tea or food when you're in politics because you are often entirely at the mercy of people who just don't think about feeding you.

Outside the hotel there was a Frenchman waiting to take me to the airport. I didn't know who he was and I said, 'Qui cherchez-vous?' 'Un ministre anglais,' he answered, and I said, 'C'est moi.' I told him that unfortunately I had no French money for a taxi, to which he replied, 'O, je suis militant, le Parti Socialiste de Nantes', and he was very proud to take me in his Citroën. He told me he was a cook at a local school.

Got home about 11.30. In my box I had a letter from Jimmy Carter thanking me for the Levellers pamphlet I sent him when he was in London. It was probably signed by a machine, but still nice to have.

### Monday 20 June

At lunchtime we had a Private Office party financed by what is loosely known as the slush fund; when I travel abroad I get a living allowance but I never spend a penny of it – I never buy a bottle of whisky or cigarettes or anything. So the allowance goes into the Private Office fund. There were about forty people there.

Walter Marshall came to see me in the afternoon. I had decided some time ago to replace him as scientific adviser and I wanted Hermann

Bondi. The Department want me to get rid of Sir John Hill and put Marshall in his place as Chairman of the AEA, and I won't do it.

I said, 'I'll tell you why I have asked you to come and see me. In a nutshell, I want you to go back to the AEA full-time as Deputy Chairman, and I want a full-time scientific adviser.'

'I had thought of a lot of things you might want to see me about, but I didn't expect the sack,' he said.

I went over the arguments briefly: that the AEA had been through a difficult period and the decisions coming through now needed to be revitalised and so on, and that he was the man to do it – a great scientific manager. But I didn't offer him Sir John Hill's job as Chairman, and he won't get it. I told him I wanted a different type of scientific adviser. He was severely shaken but he got the message and left.

At 5 o'clock we had a meeting on future offshore licensing. I wanted to be sure we weren't committed to another round of licences until BNOC could do more, and that is just what Frank Kearton wants – for BNOC to play a larger part and possibly have some more licensing later. The Department wants a sixth round but Frank is flexing his muscles for the BNOC, and rightly so.

Frank stayed for a moment. He said, 'You know you are getting a bit of a bashing at the moment, but it is an indication of your strength. Many industrialists come to me and say you are the most powerful figure in British politics. They greatly respect your views and work.'

I thanked him for his encouragement. I do need it! He also advised me to make a change in my Permanent Secretary, who follows a policy entirely of his own. He is the second nationalised industry chief to say this.

*Tuesday 21 June*
Went to the PLP meeting about recent parliamentary rebellions at which Jim was going to lay it on the line. I missed the first half-hour and came in just as Jim was saying that the future depended on the Lib–Lab arrangement and defeats weakened the Government.

A lot of points were raised about the free vote on the direct elections, and Jim replied that he had been drawn to the limit in accepting a free vote for Cabinet Ministers, but Europe was unique, and if it was a sign of weakness then it was weakness to help the Party. It was an excellent meeting actually.

Bernard Donoughue came to see me about something, and stayed on for a chat. He is most courteous and respectful. I cross-examined him carefully on the way the Number 10 machine worked. In his own team he has several people working for him, plus an outer team including consultants who put in a brief to Jim on all Cabinets or Cabinet committees, setting out the political points.

I questioned him about the CPRS, and he told me that under Kenneth Berrill it was becoming increasingly an agency of the Cabinet Office and only two or three members were sympathetic – he mentioned someone called Tessa Blackstone, who had written a report attacking the Foreign Office. But the CPRS was Sir John Hunt's political voice; he put people in the Think Tank and through Berrill told them what to do and say. Hunt has ceased to be a functionary and has become a ventriloquist speaking through a dummy.

I also asked him about Tom McNally's role at Number 10, and he said Tom was just a Marcia Williams, running the political office with four secretaries and doing the Prime Minister's correspondence. We discussed the role of political advisers generally throughout Whitehall, and I agreed we should certainly build them up but there was a danger of creating Watergate-type conspirators. I thought we should use MPs more for advice.

Just before Bernard left, Bryan Gould turned up for a talk about the Common Market. Bryan had calculated that the direct elections bill would be carried by two to one, 400 to 200 MPs. I thought this was an overestimate, and he revised it to about 150 against.

Bryan, I had not realised, had been in the Civil Service and is very respectful, like a civil servant.

After that I went and had tea, and talked to Brian Sedgemore and one or two others. There was an all-night sitting and I lay down in my room at midnight with a notice on the door saying 'Please Wake For Division'. I put a handkerchief over my face and left the door open so everybody could see me. Between 12.30 and 7.30 we voted about six times.

## Wednesday 22 June

At the House this evening, Audrey Wise told me all about Grunwick.[3] She had been down there supporting the strike and she saw a policeman pulling a girl's hair, so she put her hand on the policeman's arm. He immediately released the girl and said to Audrey, 'You'll do, love', bundled her into a Black Maria and charged her.

She was shocked; she had never been in an incident like that in her life and she didn't know what to do. She was discussing how she should handle her defence, and I said, 'Why don't you try saying you were arresting the policeman for assault and battery?' Brian Sedgemore is helping her to find a good lawyer.

I should mention that the fighting this week on the picket line at Grunwick has been on a massive scale. The police have been behaving abominably, plucking people out of the crowd. It has attracted thousands of people from all over, including five MPs today. Roy Grantham, General Secretary of APEX, thinks it is getting out of control. Some of the police are just National Front men, and it is alarming because it is reminiscent of the 1930s.

Then Jim Sillars came up for a talk. I hadn't spoken to him for a long time. His Scottish Labour Party in fact is a non-event.

Sillars is a proud man with charisma and appeal; he knows how to use the press, and of course he has been taken up by the media. He thought he would be Prime Minister of Scotland, but actually the press are only interested in him because he split the Labour Party. It shows how easy it is to go wrong, mainly by being misled by a sense of your own importance.

*Thursday 23 June*
Went to the Cabinet, and after another discussion on the direct elections bill we came on to education. Shirley introduced a paper. I had shown it to Caroline to give me comments, and she had suggested three points.

1.   We say we will end selection: when are we going to deal with the education authorities still practising it?
2.   When are we going to get the common 16+ examination?
3.   It doesn't make sense to risk a teacher shortage by closing teacher education colleges – in particular, because two years ago it was thought that if you sacked teachers they would go into industry; now we know that if you sack teachers they go on to the unemployed register along with people from industry.

Shirley, sitting beside me, was nervous about answering these questions, so clearly Caroline's points had been extremely effectively directed.

First, she said, 'The 1976 Act is defective and you can't enforce it on rebel authorities.'

Secondly, on the common 16+ exam, this had to go to the Waddell Committee considering technical college qualifications. As to the closure of colleges of education, that was dealt with under the Public Expenditure Survey Committee.

Jim thought the paper was too turgid, so Shirley was pressed on all sides to rewrite it as representing her philosophy, and Jim said, 'I want you to make it a monument of your work at the Department of Education.'

Well, Shirley was flattered by this and she will now go away and write something herself which will reveal her own thinking.

At the PLP Max Madden, the MP for Sowerby, and Ian Mikardo raised many questions in relation to Grunwick. Why wouldn't the police allow a picket to board each bus? Mikardo said the buses were being driven recklessly – you had to jump out of the way. One driver was a director of Grunwick and didn't have a PSV licence. Further-more, Grunwick had not filed company accounts and may be in breach of the law.

Merlyn gave a most unsatisfactory, waffling answer. He should call in the Commissioner of the Metropolitan Police and tell him he wants the situation brought under control, with a committee of police and trade unions to meet each day and decide how to control the crowd. He should be saying he wants the pickets to be allowed to reason with the workers every day.

### Friday 24 June

To Glasgow overnight; the sleeper pulled in at 7 and I went to the Central Hotel, had a bath and brought my diary up to date.

The day began with a meeting at 9.10 which went on till 11. The AUEW and the CSEU were there to discuss the fact that John Brown Engineering, part of the John Brown Shipyard which was hived off when Upper Clyde Shipbuilders was brought into public ownership, had been left out of an order by the oil companies, led by BP, for some modules for Sullom Voe terminal.

Joe Black of the CSEU, Alex Ferry of the AUEW and Gavin Laird, who is on the board of BNOC, simply blew their tops because it means a thousand men will be sacked and the firm will probably close. Joe Black said the trade unions would not accept it and they would bring the whole of the North Sea to a standstill unless these contracts were allowed.

Ferry said it was a bloody disgrace, the imputations against John Brown which lost them the contract were unfair, there had been full union co-operation.

I listened carefully, and the general feeling was that my Depart-ment's Offshore Supplies Office had let the unions down and had let me down. I ordered a telex to go to BP saying that they were to hold the letters of intent for the contracts on the grounds that I had reason to believe that the Full and Fair Opportunity Memorandum had not been correctly applied, and there were to be urgent talks before the letters were confirmed. Secondly, full and fair opportunity must mean that all bids from all British companies are looked at on their merits, ie price, and, if reasons other than price are held to be a factor, Government should be informed, to provide time for proper tripartite meetings between the Government, management and the unions. My officials were shaken by this, but the unions were pleased. More unemployment in Clydeside is simply not acceptable, but I shall have a hell of a struggle on Monday.

I walked across to the Scottish Amicable building, where the BNOC occupies beautiful new offices on the fourth, fifth and sixth floors. The board were already gathered – Frank Kearton, Tommy Balogh, Dick Briginshaw, Denis Rooke of British Gas, Gavin Laird, Alastair Morton and so on.

I congratulated them on their achievements and requested a BNOC strategy paper. I warned them explicitly of the threat that was coming from the Common Market to our participation policy and the attitude of the oil companies.

They reiterated that they wanted to be sole licensees, but the office is very cautious.

We had lunch, and I heard an amazing story that the European Commission called a meeting some time ago, to which they invited BNOC and other state and private oil companies, to announce that the Commission had decided to do some drilling for oil off Rockall in the South-Western Approaches, in areas contested between France and Britain, and between France and Ireland. Apparently everybody present had been opposed to it but they were still going ahead and BNOC had just heard that drilling had started. This is without any consultation with me and it is a bloody disgrace. The BNOC people were very angry. I have asked for an immediate report from Brunner and I will have that stopped on Monday while I am still President of the Council.

I also heard that the Commission, which has lots of money at its disposal, has offered to lend BNOC money for oil development. Well, they don't need money; they have raised it all on the American market. Of course, the payoff would be that the Commission would demand oil in proportion to their loan. The thing is outrageous, and this is how the Commission is eating and eating away at independent control of our oil resources.

Home, and I found that the BP share offer had been oversubscribed within one minute of opening because of the discount. Every single BP share could be sold in Britain. This means we don't have to sell them in America, but of course we feel committed, so the jobbers will be refusing British bids for BP in favour of New York. The National Iranian Oil Corporation, ie the Shah, is trying to buy 1 per cent so he can get a foothold in the North Sea. The whole thing is a disgrace. Compared to the $853 million that BNOC has raised at a cost of $1 million, the BP sale will raise £535 million at a cost of £20 million to the jobbers, and, because it is being sold at a discount, £100 million has been written off straight away. It is an absolute scandal.

We have handed some of the most valuable assets of this country to the Shah, to the Americans and to private shareholders, and I am ashamed to be a member of the Cabinet that has done this. I am going to put in a full report to the Cabinet so they know exactly what we have done. We have provided a blueprint for selling off public assets in the future and we will have no argument against it. It is an outrage.

At Grunwick, the police have now arrested Arthur Scargill and a Labour MP. The PM is telling everybody to cool it, and Scargill has called on Cabinet members to join the picket. Mick McGahey says he will bring the Scottish miners out if it isn't settled.

*Sunday 26 June*
Slept very late, and at 9.30, on a beautiful summer's day, Ron arrived and we drove off through the countryside to Chequers.

We began at 10.35 and we had three papers – one from the CPRS, one from Denis and one from Donoughue. Jim told us that no officials had been invited, and Bernard Donoughue said he had managed to keep Sir John Hunt and Sir Kenneth Berrill away. There was only one chap taking notes. So apart from Tom McNally, Tom McCaffrey and Donoughue it was just Cabinet.

The first question, said Jim, was do we want to go on and under what conditions? The Lib–Lab alliance had got to be renewed in July. Could we extend the session? Was our authority draining away? He said we must add some excitement; we wanted someone to set the Thames on fire. He then invited Denis to report briefly on pay.

Denis said, 'The inflation battle prospects are better, but if pay goes up inflation will take off again and therefore we should stick to ceilings.' Hugh Scanlon was privately sympathetic, though his union wouldn't help him, and Jack Jones was trying to get it through the TUC. David Basnett and Alf Allen of USDAW were being helpful, but the problem for the trade union movement was that they weren't sure they could deliver. He only had £300 million to play with immediately.

Michael Foot of course believed we should go on; the Lib–Lab Pact helped us.

Roy Mason made a speech of the worst kind. He has always frightened me, but his experience in the Ministry of Defence and in Northern Ireland has converted him to an extreme right-wing position.

He referred to all the polls in Bernard Donoughue's paper and said the NEC was an absolute bogey for us all, and the PLP was riddled with mavericks. Even the Cabinet couldn't be relied upon and we had to look for ways of winning friends.

Of groups we should win over, he put at the top of the list the police and the forces, both of whom had serious pay problems. We needed their support to deal with picketing. Then we should get the disabled on our side, and the pensioners. He said unemployment was not an issue any more and we should stop all these research papers prepared by Transport House and the Executive, and use the Executive to feed the achievements of the Government through to the Party.

He attacked the trade unions, saying they were deeply conservative and not a single socialist idea had come out of them.

Then he said we should turn our minds to winning the support of the Ulster Unionists. We should hold on hard to Enoch Powell and Jim Molyneaux. But he warned us that 11.2 per cent unemployment in Northern Ireland was a serious problem.

It was a confused, right-wing, deeply pessimistic speech, totally out of touch, in my judgement, with what people feel.

Jim thanked Roy for his 'vigorous speech'.

Then John Silkin spoke. 'People vote Labour out of hope, and lack of self-confidence is our problem. We must do something about un-employment.'

Stan Orme stressed that we all wanted to go on – there was nobody in this Cabinet who didn't. (I was very grateful to him for that comment.) 'Nowadays,' he said, 'you have to govern by consent. We are not an oligarchy. The incomes policy was what did us in in 1970 because of its injustice.'

Roy Hattersley wanted us to go on as long as we could; the Lib–Lab Pact was essential for this, and he was prepared to pay a price for it.

David Owen said we should avoid an unnecessary Election and the TUC was the key to this. March 1979 would be the right date.

I was called to speak at about 12.40 and I said that the attitude of the labour movement was quite clear: to sustain us, to re-elect us and to argue with us – and this will was undiminished. The attitude of the labour movement towards the Labour Government was rather like their attitude towards Parliament; they would never turn away to destructive or revolutionary methods but they would use it to get their way.

It was important to realise what would happen if we lost an Election. It would do terrible damage to Britain, not because there would be terrible confrontation under Mrs Thatcher – if she won a huge majority, she could get away with it – but because we would continue to decline, Britain would become the Northern Ireland of the Common Market, selling oil and buying cars from abroad with the proceeds.

I said it would damage the Party desperately. This theory that we would all be in 'unity in opposition' was wrong. 'I disagree with you, Prime Minister, when you said this. There would be ghastly recrimi-nation in the Party, not unity at all. There would be great argument about who was to blame – was it Denis, was it Jeff Rooker?'

'Well, I'd blame you,' said Denis, and there was a lot of laughter.

I went on, 'National self-confidence is desperately needed. The Jubilee was not a particularly attractive way of expressing the desire for national self-confidence but it was the only one the press would allow to let the British people out of their cage of denigration. If pessimism is going to be spread from the top, we're finished. People want to feel that there is a vigorous defence of our national interest. We mustn't always be turning on the TUC as if they were the cause of the trouble.'

On the tactics of how to survive as a minority Government, I said my view on the Lib–Lab Pact had not altered and I was glad we were allowed to talk about it now. I didn't believe in government by coalition; I favoured government by negotiation, which was what a minority Government had to do.

I said we had to negotiate with many interests, including the Liberals. We had to negotiate with the TUC, for example, and on pay they had asked for very little. Indeed, the astonishing thing about the British working-class movement was how little it asked.

Mine was a long speech, and I even made an allusion to Christ and the money-changers. I was quite satisfied with it, I must confess.

After me came Merlyn Rees, who also doubted the exclusivity of the Lib–Lab arrangement. He was worried about bureaucracy. He thought education used to be a good issue for us but not now, and taxation was too high. We must stage-manage the next Party Conference to be sure we got the right message across, and law and order was a crucial question.

As we left for lunch at 1.20 I had a word with Jim. I said it had been a good morning and I was glad we had dealt with the canard that there were people who wanted us to lose the Election. I deeply resented that suggestion, which was simply not true.

'I know that, I know that,' he said, 'but the Party wants unity. I noted what you said about there being no unity in opposition, but all I meant was that there would be unity against the Government of the day.'

Jim is just a right-winger who argues with you if you get in his way, but he doesn't nurse personal grudges.

Went out on the terrace and I took three or four minutes of movie film. Then upstairs I took some movie pictures of the Cabinet gathering and four flash photos of the Cabinet sitting round the table – the first time I have ever succeeded in doing that. People were saying, 'Oh my God, our official photographer', and Roy Mason added, 'It is only because we like you so much that we let you get away with it.'

After lunch, we began again. Shirley Williams said the Lib–Lab Pact should go on for a year. We had made terrible mistakes on prices, for example with gas increases. A TV programme by the Prime Minister would be very helpful. The Government should deal with youth unemployment, show we were a caring society, deal with industrial democracy and build up confidence overseas. In order to win the Election, we must have new target groups. We had tended to neglect women, the young and ethnic minorities.

In the longer term, she thought we must aim at a mixed economy that avoided both the exploitation of capitalism and the dreariness of nationalisation. We should go for small businesses and co-operatives and concentrate on the role of the individual – more like Denmark, Yugoslavia and Sweden. There were many people well disposed to us but they feared their freedom might be undermined by the power of the trade unions against the individual.

As with all Shirley's speeches, though there are things you can agree with, the general impact is always right-wing. There was nothing there that David Steel wouldn't have said.

Elwyn Jones began his contribution. 'There is an old Chinese saying that if you see the bird of sorrow flying overhead there is no reason why you should ask it to nestle in your hair, and the Jubilee year has shown what a bizarre recovery there has been.' He was worried about public order; the courts were faced with enormous problems of crime, disorder and urban violence, which might require very unpalatable measures to deal with them. The Home Secretary had serious problems with the police, the prison warders were angry because of overcrowding, and probation officers were not being helpful.

Harold Lever was for staying in, with Liberal support. In his view unemployment was the greatest vote-loser but it was a purely economic matter.

Then Denis summed up. A change of mood was perceptible, an agreement with the TUC was worth a great deal, but the problem was they didn't have the capacity to deliver. All public expenditure meant more bureaucracy, and he repeated that we couldn't have more than a 10 per cent rise on earnings. On reflation we dare not risk another cuts exercise; something like £2 billion of reflation was going through right now and there would be another billion in November, and £3 billion more in April. Could we offer a perspective that would be compatible with our inflation target?

Jim said, 'Well, Denis, thank you for your contribution; it sounded to me very much like the old Chancellor's speech after all.' So I said, 'I am afraid the bird of sorrow that Elwyn spoke about has actually nested in Denis's tiny Chinese mind.' There was some laughter at this.

Jim wound up. 'We should go on, and I agree with what Stan said: we should all work together; nobody should be looking over their shoulder to see if they would benefit by a defeat. We should plan for victory, and we must have the Liberals. Pay is important, and we might consider a standard of living guarantee. Full employment is central.'

At 4.45 we adjourned, and I dashed out and came back in the car with Ron. A very long day.

There is no doubt that the Cabinet is at its best when it hasn't got a decision to reach. Everybody there has got something interesting to say, and I enjoy listening. We are an experienced, competent team now, but there are some very serious decisions to make. The Cabinet does include people like Edmund Dell whom I would regard as right-wing conservatives. Shirley masks it all in liberal language, but she is a right-wing liberal, which in many ways is worse. Michael is a front man for decent ideas. Peter is thoughtful; Stan is very trade-union-orientated and clear and principled. Albert always skirts around issues but he is a powerful ally. John Silkin is thoughtful, Roy Mason is an extreme right-winger, Mike Cocks is a cynic, Elwyn Jones and Sam Silkin are conservative lawyers. Bruce Millan is thoughtful and sensitive; John Morris and Fred Peart are just makeweights and yes-men to the Prime Minister of the day. David Ennals is unbearable. David Owen is young, bright and intelligent, a civilised man about town who votes Labour. He has some ability and instincts which are discernible under the surface. Harold Lever is a City man sitting in the Cabinet – as absurd as Dennis Skinner sitting in Mrs Thatcher's Cabinet – but at least he always fights for those whose interests he serves.

*Monday 27 June*
Arising out of my meeting in Glasgow last Friday with the unions from John Brown Engineering, I met Sir David Steel and Mr Cooper of BP. I was really trying to bring John Brown back from the dead.

The officials from the Offshore Supplies Office were very uneasy about what I was doing because the truth is that they too had concluded that John Brown Engineering was no good. It was the effect of that tough meeting in Glasgow on Friday which drove me, out of a sense of obligation, to fight for the men concerned, who would otherwise be unemployed.

I knew very little about the issues involved but I did interrogate Cooper in great depth. I discovered, for example, that John Brown Constructors, parent company of John Brown Engineering, had themselves put their engineering firm fourth on the list. And BP had played on the rumours and criticisms from the other oil companies in the consortium who just didn't want this particular company to get the contract. So I played it heavy. I asked them to meet both management and unions. My interest was primarily in maintaining jobs in Clydeside, but I also wanted to help the firm and the management. I felt BP had behaved improperly, and, I might add, my attitude to BP is changing now. They always used to say I couldn't risk twisting their arm because of the big Government holding, but that is now being sold off, so I can be much tougher with them.

At 7.30 I was guest at a dinner with the IPC Mirror Group, and I took Brian Sedgemore and Bernard Ingham along. This is part of Frances Morrell's veto-lifting campaign.

Brian Sedgemore hammered them on their conduct as newspapers, which meant I didn't have to do it and it made me appear moderate in the discussion.

They asked, 'Why can't the labour movement run a paper?'

'Well,' I said, 'what I wonder is why you don't deal with some of the big and really interesting issues of our time.'

'What do you mean?'

'The Common Market, for example – how it really works. Then there's the whole question of bureaucracy, particularly in the Common Market. And you ought to deal with industrial affairs in greater depth, and with civil liberties, telephone tapping and police activities.'

To be fair, Geoffrey Goodman did say that Jack Jones's telephone was tapped by the Tories in 1971.

*Wednesday 29 June*
NEC, deferred from last week. We came to an extremely interesting resolution moved by Nick Bradley – an absolute copy of the resolution calling for an inquiry into Militant entryism, but the word 'CIA' had been substituted for 'Militant'. He was making a political point about entryism not being confined to the left, but he is also concerned, as I think everybody is, about the activities of the CIA.

Well, he moved the resolution, and I intervened. 'Look, I had a word with Nick about this last week and my own opinion is that it would be better not to go for this particular wording. You can't start an investigation into the CIA.' But there was a massive problem of the use of the world's security services to subvert civil and political liberties and democratic freedoms. 'You've only got to read what Vice-President Mondale said about it during the American elections, or look at what BP have been doing, to realise what a huge matter it is.'

I suggested we refer the whole question to the Home Policy Committee. Everybody agreed with me – even Nick Bradley – so that was accepted.

At 7 Caroline turned up and we went off to the US Embassy reception. Unfortunately we hadn't known that it was evening dress, and all the other women except Caroline were wearing long dresses. She could have absolutely bashed me, but she was awfully sweet about it.

Peter Preston, editor of the *Guardian*, was there, tortured by the increasing pressure on him from the trade unions whenever they think the paper is being unfair, as for example in the Grunwick case. I said, 'Don't you think it would be a good idea if complaints were channelled through the printers?' That idea absolutely terrified him.

I continued, 'Well, I would never go to the Press Council or the courts in these matters. Surely it would be better to discuss it with the printers.'

'Oh, it would interfere with editorial freedom.'

'Well, look at me,' I said. 'I am constrained by an enormous number of commitments and pledges – Privy Councillor's oath, oath of allegiance to the Crown, Clause 4, our manifesto and so on – but I have to work my way through. There is conflicting accountability and nobody is absolutely free.'

Had a long talk to John Davies, my predecessor at Industry – the 'lame-duck' Minister, as he was known. John told me that even during the last Tory Government of 1970–4 Maggie Thatcher and Ted Heath loathed each other – so the hatred is not born out of her becoming Leader but is deep-seated. I daresay Heath doesn't like women and she probably doesn't like men who don't like women.

### Thursday 30 June

Frances came and sat in my room for nearly an hour. She told me I had reached an age in life where I should not be rushing into things but standing back more and assessing carefully what was happening before giving my judgement. In effect, she was telling me as politely as she could that I am not a bright, thrusting young politician any more; I'm a statesman, and I have to be much more measured.

She was also saying – which I think is true – that the labour movement proceeds very slowly and collectively; it moves anonymously and it doesn't like publicity or drama. Steadiness was what was required.

In the evening, only ten minutes after I'd got home, the front door bell rang and who should it be but Mark Arnold-Forster. He came in and had a whisky.

He wanted to tell me that he had been alerted by friends in the EEC Commission that Roy Jenkins was going to deliver a tremendous attack on me in a speech in Glasgow tomorrow. This was causing great pleasure in the Jenkins camp. He said Roy had been absolutely sick at the European Council; he had put in proposals for dealing with unemployment and these had been turned down by Helmut Schmidt on the grounds of cost. All his resentments were boiling up, and that included resentment at the anti-Market campaign.

I must say it occurred to me that if Roy does attack me on Europe it would be a marvellous way of getting the debate going; it might even give me an opportunity to say *more* than I would otherwise have done about the EEC.

### Friday 1 July

Bristol for the GMC. Maurice Rea, sporting an APEX picket badge, reported what had happened at Grunwick, having been there today. The Special Patrol Group come in and pull people's hair and kick them about. He and others thought the Northern Ireland situation had been a dry run for what is going to happen in Britain.

Les Rexworthy, a quiet, modest postman, was concerned about the attempt to prevent the postal workers from blacking the mail to Grunwick. He mentioned the defects in the Employment Protection Act and said, if the Government couldn't act to protect working-class interests, what was the point of having a Labour Government at all?

Cyril Langham thought there should be an inquiry into violence on both sides. Maurice Rea said the young policemen, who are themselves engaged in a pay claim, looked uncomfortable when they were told by the pickets that they needed the right to trade union organisation.

Herbert Rogers said, 'What do you expect in capitalism? The police are maintaining the system, and when I hear about law and order I always ask, "Whose law and order?" We must discuss the general politics of the situation and the reason why the Government is carrying out Tory policy.'

Jack Watson, a member of the TGWU, and an old friend, spoke. He said what we needed was working-class people in Parliament, people from the housing estates who really know what life is about, not middle-class people. 'I am not being personal about Tony,' he said, 'but we are paying for the gross errors of the Government and we have to listen to the railwaymen and miners and others. What the movement needs now is leadership, and, as in 1940, somebody must stand up and grasp the nettle. Tony, come out of the Government; the movement wants you and needs you, and this is what you should do.' It was the most direct appeal to me to resign for a very long time.

I made a final statement in which I discussed the problem of coming out and thinking one could solve it alone. It had to be done together.

*Saturday 2 July*

Caught a train to Hull for the Yorkshire women's rally. It was a special holiday train and was jampacked. There wasn't even a buffet car.

In my carriage there was a retired civil servant who said how interesting it was that a real aristocrat should have joined the Labour Party. I disabused her of that idea when I told her that Father was a Labour MP who became a peer towards the end of his life.

Then a woman from the Stock Exchange said, 'I suppose you still have to devote a lot of attention to the business.'

'What do you mean?'

'Wedgwood, the pottery.'

I told her I had no connection with that, so that was two myths destroyed.

Then a Dutchman in the carriage, who spoke very good English, said, 'You can't be a Minister travelling in a train. No Dutch Minister goes anywhere except by private jet.' He told me he was a lorry driver and I asked him which union he was in.

'Oh, we don't believe in unions.'

'Why not?' I asked.

'Take this train,' he said. 'There is an engine driver and a fireman and yet it is a diesel train.'

I said, 'Well, it is quite a comfort to me that with a thousand people aboard we have two drivers.'

'Well, that is the British. They are overmanning.' He laughed.

### Sunday 3 July

Caroline is working on the latest bulletin on comprehensive education. She writes a lot, including the recent NUT pamphlet which was published anonymously. She is in tremendous demand.

She is a marvellous woman and I am quite exceptionally fortunate in being married to her.

Dinner with the Baloghs, the Shores, the Harts and Jill Foot. Judith was very sharp, directing criticism, I thought, at me.

We talked about Tom Driberg's book, *Ruling Passions*, for which Michael Foot has written the Postscript. Tommy Balogh said one night when he was in Malta he stopped in a club for a drink and there was Tom Driberg chatting up a sailor at the bar.

After dinner we sat round and Judith said that a proposal was coming up in Cabinet on Thursday that a Commonwealth force should be set up to go to Rhodesia for the six-month transitional period from white to black rule.[4] Well, Thomas Balogh nearly blew his top – it was absolutely fatal, impossible to do, and so on. Caroline and I both attacked the proposal.

### Monday 4 July

To a meeting on the Falkland Islands at Number 10 after Questions. David Owen has suggested a sell-out because of our great defensive weakness: ie give Argentina an economic zone of 200 miles around the islands, and keep the islands on a three-mile fishing limit. Then we would just hope that the problem could be resolved peacefully.

My Department has briefed me strongly against this on the technical grounds that, if we concede a difference between the economic zone of 200 miles and the land mass of the Falkland Islands, that could be used against us in our median line disputes with the French and the Irish over the Scilly Isles and the Channel Islands.

But the plain truth is that if the Argentinians wished to attack the Falkland Islands they could easily crush them. Fred Mulley pointed out that the Argentinian Government, a ghastly fascist military dictatorship, had ordered £700 million of warships from Vosper Thorneycroft, so they would be crushing the Falklands Isles with British warships.

The Argentine Government is determined to get hold of the islands, even though they are 400 miles away, and the arms trade, the total spinelessness of the Foreign Office and the general decay of Britain will have combined to put us in a position where we will be unable to do anything to defend the 1950 people who live there.

### Tuesday 5 July

Economic Committee at Number 10. Just as we were about to leave for the Palace for the coffee-pot presentation, the PM told Shirley, Michael and me, 'I would like you to stay behind for a moment, as members of the Executive. I have had a talk with Jack Jones and we all agree we cannot have another Party Conference like the last one, and I wondered if you would give your mind to how we should deal with it. Perhaps we should have a great statement of confidence in the Labour Government on the Monday, at the beginning of the week. What do you think?'

I said I thought the whole Party wanted to support the Government, to see it succeed. 'But', I said, 'there will be two other things the delegates will be wanting to do at Conference. One is to express their anxieties and criticisms of the Government, and that must be permitted. We are hammering out a new Labour Party policy for fighting the next Election and to be implemented in the next Parliament, and we mustn't use loyalty to blank out policy making. I'm only giving you a snap view, but I don't think we should stage-manage the Conference because it could blow up and create ill will.'

Then I went over to the Palace. It was a beautiful sunny day, not a cloud in the sky, and we drove through the Palace yard while the guards in their red jackets were conducting their manoeuvres. There weren't as many soldiers as there used to be, but it was fun. There are tourists all over London and it makes the centre of London impossible for ordinary travellers.

We gathered and talked a bit, then we all lined up in a great semicircle and the Queen and Duke of Edinburgh came in. The coffee-pot was on the table and Jim stood there and said, 'Ma'am. The Cabinet considered how we should record your Jubilee with respect – and affection, if I may say so. We decided to give you a gift and I looked up the precedents, and on Queen Victoria's Golden Jubilee in 1887 the then Prime Minister, the Marquis of Salisbury, decided to give her a portrait of himself.' Everyone laughed.

'This time,' he said, 'we thought it would be better to give you something useful and although Tony Benn wondered whether the coffee-pot would leak, unlike the Cabinet' (laughter), 'we thought this would be what you would like.'

The Queen, who can't say good morning without a script, referred to a bit of paper and said, 'Prime Minister, thank you very much indeed. I feel sure the coffee-pot will be more useful than a picture.' More laughter.

We had all been correctly positioned in strict pecking order – that is to say Foot, Healey, Elwyn Jones, David Owen, Shirley Williams, myself and so on. In the Palace protocol is everything. Shirley gave a low curtsy.

After the presentation we were chatting, when Jim came up. 'Come and have a word with the Queen.' He ushered Shirley and me over to her. She didn't look frightfully well; her face was pale and she said she had a cold, possibly pneumonia. Roy Mason was also standing there and, in a booming voice, he declared, 'Ma'am, the whole of Yorkshire is looking forward to your visit.'

I said, 'Do let me ask you this. When were Privy Councillors' uniforms last worn at Privy Council?' Well, she didn't seem to know much about the Privy Council. I added, 'I think they are the House of Windsor uniforms, Windsor jackets and livery with knee breeches and a sword and so on.'

'I don't think my father wore it,' she said. Well of course her father wouldn't have worn a Privy Councillor's uniform. But in the Thirties Ramsay was always photographed at the Palace wearing it with a cocked hat and a sword.

Then Shirley said, 'Ma'am, I have often thought that, in addition to reading the papers, which we know you do so carefully all the time, you might occasionally have audiences with Ministers, say two or three Ministers every few months, and then you would understand Ministers' policies. Because of course, Ma'am, you are so much closer to the people than we are, you know how the people feel, and you may like to know how Ministers feel as well.' The Queen said she read the papers very carefully.

I remarked jokingly, 'The only interest my officials seem to think you take in our activities is when we leave the country – because Private Secretaries always come in hot foot and say, "The Queen has given permission for you to go to Brussels."' I said she must be frightfully busy. She told me that she did take an interest.

Then the Duke of Edinburgh joined us and I told him that Shirley Williams had been persuaded of his idea, which he had voiced ten years ago at a lunch at Winfrith, that the Queen should attend Cabinet and that the Ombudsman should be a member of the royal household.

'Oh yes,' he said, 'a very good idea.' Well actually it was a lousy idea because, as I had said at the time, if the Queen attended the Cabinet, when the Cabinet became unpopular she would become unpopular, and she didn't want to be mixed up with us. Secondly the idea of an aggrieved citizen writing to a member of the royal household was absurd.

'In Saudi Arabia, you know, King Khalid holds court every day. People come and say, "Your Majesty, I haven't got a telephone", and he raises it with his Ministers. That is what the monarchy should be like,' said the Duke.

The Queen did make one interesting comment. 'We had the heads of the Common Market here to dinner the other night, and Helmut Schmidt was so rude.'

I said, 'He always is.'

'Yes, but they were all so cynical and disillusioned and he was so rude and unfriendly.'

That confirmed what I have long suspected: that the royal family loathe the Common Market because they have no role in it. There is no European President's Council in which Queen Juliana can meet the Grand Duchess of Luxembourg: they have no forum and therefore are driven back into a quaint tourist role.

*Wednesday 6 July*

I should mention that Jack Jones was defeated overwhelmingly at the TGWU Conference. They voted for no pay restraint or limitation on free collective bargaining whatsoever in the coming year. Jack took it well.

*Thursday 7 July*

Cabinet. On foreign affairs it was reported that we were reinforcing Belize against a possible attack from Guatemala. David Owen reported that the military in Pakistan, who have overthrown Prime Minister Bhutto, are hoping to restore elections. David introduced a paper proposing a Commonwealth force to supplement British troops in Rhodesia, along with a British Resident Commissioner. He said the alternative to a settlement would be a bloodbath, and a Zimbabwe development fund would be helpful.

I welcomed the discussion on the paper before a policy was developed because I was extremely uneasy about it. There were aspects of the proposals that were not clear: one was that, if we sent a Commissioner, once the rebellion had ended we would have restored legitimacy to the Rhodesian defence forces and would be accountable in the House of Commons for what they did. We would also be answerable for the deaths of white farmers and their families who might be attacked by guerrillas. I said it was a lobster pot – easy to get into, hard to get out of. British public opinion could easily swing towards the 'kith and kin' argument, and we had better be absolutely clear as to the differing reasons why the frontline presidents and the white Rhodesians want us in.

I said the frontline presidents wanted us in because they had never accepted our argument that we could do nothing in 1965 when Smith announced UDI. The whites wanted us in so that once British troops were there, however small in numbers, then the Rhodesian defence forces would be legitimised and white Rhodesians would expect to be defended.

I favoured a United Nations force, despite the Soviet veto. In any case, the Soviet veto was already effective in a physical sense in sending arms and supporting the guerrillas. Therefore we should favour a UN solution and not get involved ourselves.

David Ennals supported the Foreign Office line. Merlyn Rees and Edmund Dell agreed with me, as did Stan Orme; we should avoid giving the white Rhodesians any opportunity to suppose they could rely on us.

Denis Healey supported me: the pressures existed already, namely South African sanctions, and did we really want to be in there physically ourselves?

Harold Lever, Roy Mason, Fred Peart and Roy Hattersley supported me. Roy Hattersley said the whole object of the exercise was to get the white settlers out and not to get white troops in.

Michael Foot and Shirley Williams supported David Owen, and Elwyn supported the Foreign Office on legal grounds. David Owen said, 'Well, the US Congress has refused to authorise troops, and I suppose I could be in a similar position.'

I said, 'I hope people won't think that those of us who take a contrary view are in favour of a bloodbath, but we aren't really persuaded that a bloodbath will take place.'

There was such overwhelming support in the Cabinet for the view that I had put that David Owen realises, I think, that he can't go ahead.

Went back to the House. Lissie came in and we had something to eat on the terrace. At about 9.40 we went into the debate on the European Elected Assembly Bill (the direct elections bill). I told her to wait behind the Speaker's chair, and thought I'd just poke my head round to see if there was any room under the Gallery, which is much the best place for visitors.

As soon as I did, there was a tremendous roar from the Tories – like huntsmen spotting the fox – so I withdrew. When I appeared at the other end of the Chamber, they all shouted again. I ignored it, put Melissa under the Gallery and stood at the bar listening to David Owen wind up.

It was a tremendous day. In forty-six years, since the protection vote in 1931, I don't think there has been an occasion when Cabinet Ministers have been in opposite lobbies. The figures were roughly 394 for the bill, 147 against – a majority of 63 per cent in favour. Of the Parliamentary Labour Party, 127 were for, 124 against, including thirty-two Ministers, of whom six were Cabinet members. So in the PLP only about 40 per cent voted for the bill, 40 per cent voted against and 20 per cent abstained, which means in effect in the PLP it was 60–40 against. I think in these circumstances Jim simply cannot get it through. Best endeavours founder when you can't carry a majority of your own Party.

*Friday 8 July*
I rang Douglas Jay's wife Mary, and she told me that Peter Jay had in fact decided to leave *The Times* before he was appointed Ambassador in Washington. He was going to work at Nuffield for three years on his book, *Market Socialism*, to replace Tony Crosland's *The Future of Socialism*, which Peter thought was out of date, and provide a synthesis for the left in Britain with a view to resolving the 'futile arguments' between the Croslandites and the Clause 4 people.

Mary told me that a whole group of industrialists were very interested in Peter Jay's ideas, notably Arnold Weinstock, who had clearly come to the conclusion that something had to give in order to preserve capitalism and, of course, their privileges. They thought that industrial democracy of a modified kind would be the best way, providing that it was only consultative in character and that the forces of production were still to be imprisoned within the market economy.

Now the fact that Weinstock and Peter Jay have been meeting to discuss this confirms my belief that, far from writing a book about market socialism, Peter Jay is the most advanced member of the vanguard of conservatives who are beginning to realise that concessions need to be made to preserve capitalism. This is partly a product of the great pressure for fundamental change which has come from the trade union and labour movement, with which I have been associated. Therefore the idea that Peter Jay and I, because we are both in favour of co-operatives, are part of the same tradition is quite wrong. Jay is a new-wave conservative; I am part of the challenge to which his market socialism is a response.

*Sunday 10 July*
Got to BBC Bristol, where an army of sound and camera men, researchers and studio managers had gathered to record my lecture on Burke. I did a runthrough before lunch and worked in an office rewriting it and getting it into shape. At about 2.15 I recorded it and was finished by 5. I must say it came across in a relaxed, measured way, and to be able to pay a tribute and describe so clearly the qualities of a Conservative philosopher and his attitude towards life in the late eighteenth century was great fun.

*Monday 11 July*
At the office I was told that British Ambassadors – Nico Henderson in Paris, Wright in Bonn, Maitland in Brussels – are sending in reports saying in effect what a disaster our EEC Presidency has been. They are the most arrogant telegrams. Henderson said that the French were angered by the attention we had given to the Jubilee and the meeting of the Commonwealth heads of government, implying that Britain should sever all its connections with the Commonwealth and America and the Queen in order to prove we are good Europeans. Wright said that the German view on the termination of our Presidency was 'good riddance'. Yet the Queen's review of the Army of the Rhine had been a sensational success, contrasted with the behaviour of British Ministers in Europe. Maitland sent a long and boring telegram implying that we had failed to secure British interests in the Community by appearing to defend them too aggressively. Really the flood of Common Market official opinion against Britain is unbelievable. We are becoming the pariah of Europe to the Common Market élite.

*Tuesday 12 July*
The papers were full of Grunwick, where about seventy people were arrested yesterday. As Francis Cripps said, the working class knows whose side it's on when it comes to an issue like this.

At 9.15 Jasper Cross, my Under-Secretary in charge of the coal industry, came to the office. He is a sort of right-wing Fabian.

We talked a bit about the general state of the industry, and I said, 'Don't you agree, there is really no difference between Healey and Heath?'

'Well, there is. Heath didn't control the money supply and Healey has.'

'Yes, but if Heath had won the Election in 1974 can you think of many changes there would have been between then and now?'

He said, 'No, I think the Government have done what Ramsay MacDonald failed to do in 1931 – persuade the British people to reduce their standard of living.'

I agreed, but argued that in 1931 we ended up in opposition, whereas now we had stayed in and the movement had kept together. But of course, in general, he is not wrong.

After a meeting in my office this afternoon, John Lyons, the General Secretary of the Power Engineers' Association, asked me if I was intending to appoint Walter Patterson as my scientific adviser, which was a joke about Walter Marshall. I told him I was sorry that Marshall had put it about that he had been sacked when I had in fact appointed him as Deputy Chairman of the AEA.

'I suppose you didn't like his nuclear advice?'

I said, 'He was not supposed to give me any nuclear advice – that's Sir John Hill's job. But the AEA needs a full-time Deputy Chairman and I need a full-time scientific adviser.'

There is tremendous tension within the nuclear lobby at the moment. They can't fault me, but they are very uneasy.

*Wednesday 13 July*
EY at Number 10 against the background of rumours in the papers of the breakdown of the Social Contract.

Denis Healey said that no real progress was made last night at the meeting with the TUC to agree a further period of wage restraint. The only thing we appeared to have achieved was the so-called twelve-month rule, which limits unions to putting in no more than one pay claim per year. What could we salvage from the situation? The twelve-month rule, no wage explosion, and a fall in inflation on the way, so we should be able to avoid a further fall in living standards.

I said I was puzzled about the inflation rate. The forecast we had been given a couple of weeks ago was 15 per cent and the Prime Minister had told us we had to keep it quiet. Now the forecast is 9 per cent. I said there was a terrible danger of setting a target for inflation and a ceiling for wage settlements of 10 per cent which could not be realised. Where would it lead? What would happen when the 10 per cent was breached, as it would be? We would be in a siege economy. The analysis in the draft White Paper on pay and prices was pure Heath, and we were facing the end of the Social Contract.

'Wait a minute,' Jim said, 'you are going too wide.'

I replied, 'I only want to make a general point. The other thing is, if inflation is the cause of unemployment, why is unemployment so high in countries that have half our rate of inflation? It is a failure of investment, and we have to consider the effect on jobs of what we are now proposing.'

'Well,' said Jim, 'can we have an answer to this question about the disparity in the inflation forecasts?'

Denis responded, 'The RPI forecast for the rest of this year is going to be helped by the tax changes; for 1978 we did the best we could but we have come up with a different forecast.' I was not at all satisfied with this.

Eric Varley said we should put the 10 per cent ceiling in and meet the TUC again.

Roy Hattersley wanted an agreement with the TUC, especially on the twelve-month rule, but he said the TUC could not carry their membership. 'What I notice', he said, 'is that the trade union leadership is demoralised, their Economic Committee is demoralised, because they are afraid of a defeat by their own membership.' We should stick to the 10 per cent for inflation and wage settlements.

That was the first time since 1974 that I have heard anyone say that the trade union leaders were demoralised. The truth is, when we came to power it was the CBI that was demoralised, the Civil Service, Fleet Street, the City: we were powerful. Now that's been reversed.

Kenneth Berrill said that our job was to give an explanation to the rank and file of the unions. What they were saying was the rate of inflation was now 17 per cent so why should they settle for less? We had to approach the rank and file and explain why. As if Berrill would recognise the rank and file if he met them.

I came in again. 'What about the facts? Inflation in July and August will be 18 per cent. The press, which is entirely unreliable, will already be attributing that to the miners' pay claim even though not a single claim is in yet. There is a passage in the White Paper saying employment will be going up, but we have all been told that unemployment is going up.'

'Employment *is* going up already,' said Denis. 'The trouble is there are a lot more people coming on to the labour market.'

I said, 'People aren't fools. The shop stewards read the *Financial Times* and the *Morning Star*. They know what is going on. If you tell them employment is going up when in fact unemployment is going up, then they will feel you have deceived them. We must be credible. You can't use phoney forecasts. Let's postpone the White Paper.'

I added that I was nervous because of our electoral strategy.

'What do you mean, nervous?' asked Jim.

'Well, I am afraid we are going to precipitate a situation in which everything that happens will be attributed to the trade unions; it is a complete set-up for Thatcher. The Tories will say you argued you could get to 9 per cent inflation, provided you got less than 10 per cent settlements; you won't get inflation to 9 per cent, and settlements will be above 10 per cent. So you are creating a benchmark against which our failure will be judged.'

We agreed that Jim would meet the TUC tonight. The package has still not been disclosed and the crisis atmosphere is building up.

Jo Grimond came to see me and I tried to square him on the reorganisation of the electricity supply industry, on which Frank Chapple had given his agreement today. Jo doesn't like the Lib–Lab arrangement any more than I.

### Thursday 14 July

Cabinet. I was summoned to Number 10 fifteen minutes early and found that we were asked to read a second draft of Denis's White Paper on pay and prices, the printed first draft of which arrived last night.

Cabinet began at 10.30. Jim said how much the Queen had enjoyed the visit of the Cabinet to Buckingham Palace to present her with the coffee-pot. Then on to next week's business, and it was clear that the debate on counter-inflation policy set for Wednesday 20 July will become a vote of confidence.

We came on to the bill on abortion, which the Conservative MP William Benyon is sponsoring. It aims to reduce the time limit for abortions and strengthen the conscience clause for medical staff. Shirley Williams said she very much regretted that the Labour Women's Conference had sent her threatening letters telling her she would have to vote for the status quo on abortion, against the Benyon Bill. Jim said that was disgraceful.

I wonder if they really are 'threatening letters' or whether they are simply reminding her of the policy of the Party, which is a reasonable thing to do. At any rate, Shirley feels strongly about this – which I understand – because she is the leading Catholic in the Cabinet.

Anyway, Michael Foot said there was no Government time available for the Benyon Bill this session. A number of people spoke on this. John Morris said that religious differences were beginning to rear their heads in Wales, and Jim said he had noticed that too – in Cardiff a very good local Party chairman had been defeated because of his line on abortion.

I note this because I think abortion is going to be a major issue in the future. How particular Members react to it now is of interest.

Then we came on to inflation and the draft White Paper.

Jim reported on his meeting with the TUC last night. He thought they had not considered fully the implications of a return to collective bargaining on pay. There was no hostility but the TUC were very much against publishing precise figures in a White Paper.

I was next to speak, and I urged very strongly that we did not publish a White Paper. 'This paper will be the electoral strategy of the Government and Labour Party on which we shall in effect be fighting the next Election. It will be cited by us in order to justify what we are doing, and it will be argued about by the industrialists and trade unions over the next twelve months and used against us by our opponents.

'We are setting out the criteria by which we invite the public to judge us. The whole thing is hopelessly rushed. We got an amended draft late last night which I read at 8.30 this morning. Then we get this draft at 10.15. If we compare this with our response to the IMF, for which we had weeks of discussion, even though we were under immense pressure, we are rushing into this statement and it is absolutely wrong.

'We need only say that moderate inflation will require moderate pay rises and that the two are linked. In effect, an orderly return to collective bargaining means that we just negotiate each case on its own merits. We can, however, announce our fiscal measures and our social programme today, or tomorrow, in order to create the right climate for the pay negotiations in the coming year.

'This White Paper is not intellectually credible. It makes no reference, for example, to North Sea oil, which is a crucial new ingredient in our economic situation. The analysis is superficial and the figures are extremely suspect. It is a hostage to fortune and it pinpoints the trade unions as being responsible for what is wrong with Britain. The whole emphasis is on the unions and wage claims. We have all been along this road before and I just do not believe that all that has gone wrong with Britain since 1945 can be attributed to the level of wage settlements.'

Jim said he had some sympathy with my arguments, particularly about the figures. Denis suggested that, if the Cabinet agreed, a general statement in the House tomorrow would do.

So it was agreed, without further discussion, that we would not publish the White Paper – the first victory of the day. Then we paused to read a statement which Denis had included at the back of the draft White Paper.

Jim said, 'I would like to focus on whether we publish figures or not. The TUC are of the opinion that publishing figures will defeat our objective.'

'But we must publish them,' Denis replied. 'They are already widely known – I have been making speeches about 10 per cent for weeks.'

Eric Varley said that the TUC wanted the Government to manage the economy; they didn't want us to ask them what to do all the time. He favoured publishing the figures.

Peter Shore said Phase 3 was the key and we didn't want to box ourselves in – a shrewd comment. David Ennals thought we were in a hell of a mess and we would be playing into the hands of the militants if we didn't have the 10 per cent wage ceiling.

Roy Hattersley suggested setting an overall figure, that is to say looking at the wage bill for the whole economy over the next ten years, rather than applying the 10 per cent in each particular case.

I agreed with what Jim had said earlier: that the public were very realistic, but we had to recognise that the national pay policy had broken down and national pay bargaining was going to be devolved down to specific cases. It was easier to be tough in general than in individual cases. I said if we did try to be tough we would have to either go for a statutory pay policy, which none of us accepted, or retreat altogether. The only alternative was to negotiate each case on its merits.

Michael Foot said, 'We are trying to run a voluntary policy and we must stay with the TUC. We don't want a statutory policy, and published figures will get hostile TUC comment.' He favoured a low pay floor and if we must have figures he preferred the Hattersley approach.

It was now 1.10 and it was agreed that we would meet again in the evening.

At 6.30 the Cabinet resumed in Jim Callaghan's room at the House. Cabinets are always very different in the House – the table is smaller and we crowd round it; it is hot and the sun pours in across New Palace Yard. There is an air of crisis when we meet there.

I launched in and said, 'I realise that mentioning full employment now is provocative but it ought to be in the statement because that is what we are all about.' In the end it went in – another victory.

We went through the statement paragraph by paragraph and got parts of it toned down. When we got to the conclusion, I said, 'Let us be clear: we have boxed ourselves in very seriously and I want to include a get-out clause, because there will be a dispute and we will have to consider whether or not it is to our advantage to concede. I suggest a phrase like "The Government intends that these pay guidelines will be applied flexibly, sensibly, realistically", or "The Government is determined to apply this with realism".'

Denis was against that. 'You can't do that – it will weaken the whole statement.'

But Jim said, 'Half a minute. You know, it might be that or a defeat in an Election.'

In the end, I think Jim coined a phrase that met this point: 'The Government hopes and intends that all concerned will apply this policy with common sense and realism.' So we ended up with an enormous improvement on the original statement.

*Friday 15 July*

Went in to hear Denis make the statement. The Tories tried to clobber him, but he came across well and the Party was pleased, while the Tories didn't know what to do about it. Denis laid into the Tory side with his usual brutality and vulgarity. Indeed, when Reg Prentice got up and said, 'Wasn't the original Treasury paper for a 5 per cent limit on wage rises, and isn't this a capitulation to the TUC and Tribune?', Denis replied, 'The Right Honourable Gentleman . . .'

'Not Right Honourable Gentleman, Right Honourable Friend,' the Tories shouted.

Denis repeated pointedly, 'The Right Honourable Gentleman, who on one occasion has had responsibility for trade union affairs in a Labour Government, will know that relations with the trade unions are not like that.'

So Reg has now alienated Denis. Reg is an isolated and lonely figure, in trouble even with the moderates in his own constituency.

I went to see Mother briefly. Elsie Chamberlain was with her and they were going to the International Congregational Fellowship

Service in Westminster Abbey. Mother is blossoming at the moment. I
have never seen her so well and happy and amusing. It is lovely to see
her at eighty coming into her own. I hope I live to that age and enjoy life
as much as she does.

### Monday 18 July

Lunch at 1 with Jon Akass, political correspondent of the *Sun*, and an
old *Herald* man. He regards himself as a left-wing columnist but he
quite likes Murdoch, who he thinks is anti-establishment. A couple of
pieces Jon wrote on MI5 appeared today following the big weekend
story about MI5 blunders. When Harold was Prime Minister he was
told that David Owen and Judith Hart had 'connections with Warsaw
Pact countries'. MI5 had confused them with Labour MP Will Owen
(who was acquitted of spying for Czechoslovakia in 1970) and Mrs J.
Tudor Hart, a member of the Communist Party.

The trouble with journalists of his kind – and I have a higher regard
for him than for most – is that they are creatures of the current
philosophy, that is to say the philosophy of profit; and views on
rationalisation, cutting jobs and so on are just mouthed and mouthed
without being thought out.

He told me that people in the pubs were saying, 'Well, let's give Mrs
Thatcher a chance, and if that doesn't work let's give Tony Benn a
chance.' I found that interesting, and in line with my general theory
that things will have to get worse before they get better. In fact the big
reforms I am interested in are mid-Eighties reforms and can't be
implemented before then because the Government doesn't believe in
them and the public isn't ready. They can only be carried through
when we have seen the full meaning and effects of Thatcherism.

### Tuesday 19 July

I had a talk with Harry Evans of the *Sunday Times* in the evening. He
thought the Government would fall this autumn and that Thatcher
sensed power; without Phase 3 there would be nothing to keep Labour
in power. There was a chance Thatcher would be in power by
Christmas but he wasn't sure whether she would win if we stayed in for
another year. He thought the Lib–Lab Pact might fold. We are in
difficulties over wage claims; there is no doubt about that.

After he had gone I saw David Owen about breaches of sanctions of
BP in Rhodesia. He wanted to know whether it had been brought to me
personally; I said it had and I had asked for names.

### Wednesday 20 July

This evening I saw Bill van Straubenzee, the Tory MP, walking by
Mother's flat. We had a chat and he thought there would be an Election

this winter. 'Mrs Thatcher is much better than people imagine. Now there is no pay policy and she has nothing to lose, she will be dead set on being Prime Minister, and the City and the businessmen will support her in that. She is a very competent woman indeed.'

I asked him if he thought Ted Heath would get a job under Mrs Thatcher.

He said, 'No, he has behaved very badly.'

'If Thatcher were defeated in an Election, would you get rid of her?'

'Oh, yes,' he said, 'we are much less generous than you are.' He was certain that Ted Heath wouldn't succeed her but Willie Whitelaw might. 'The man to watch', he said, 'is Francis Pym.'

'I presume that if Carrington were in the Commons he would get it?'

'Yes,' he said. 'But Francis Pym is a quiet chap coming up.'

### Thursday 21 July

On foreign affairs, a small item came up which I should note. Jim is afraid that Schmidt will come out against Carter's human rights policy. Schmidt has problems because he has negotiated with the Russians to get 70,000 East Germans a year into West Germany; any tightening of the Cold War would make that more difficult.

Then the next item was devolution and, after the previous muddle, the question was whether we would have two separate bills for Scotland and Wales. Everybody agreed we should have two bills.

The last item was a ghastly paper called 'Industrial Strategy – The Wider Implications', presented by Denis Healey and Eric Varley, and clearly an attempt to make every other bit of our policy fit into the industrial strategy. Schools must prepare children for industry, we must be less worried about pollution, we must commit ourselves to less industrial legislation and so on. It was really concreting us into a Tory position. It made no reference to the National Enterprise Board or to planning agreements; just rubbishy Tory stuff. I hadn't read it properly because it only came last night but the only analysis I could see was that Governments since the war had been hostile or indifferent to industry and that wealth creation had not been taken seriously – which was another way of saying profits had been too low. It was a punk piece of official analysis in line with the whole con-trick of the industrial strategy.

After Denis had made a very ordinary speech about performance and competitiveness, and Eric Varley had given an abrasive speech criticising Windscale inquiries and plutonium worries, Jim said, 'It is a bit difficult, you know, to have to read this overnight.'

I said I was glad the PM had made this point and I didn't think we should publish it. It should go to a group of Ministers to be looked at very carefully. But, if it were to go on today, I had sixteen substantial amendments to bring forward.

When I said that, Albert Booth supported me and the thing was killed – the second White Paper I have killed in a week. I was pleased about that.

I was late back for my meeting with Lord Rothschild – Victor Rothschild – but I had about forty minutes with him. He was pleased that I had moved Marshall because he hates the AEA and thinks it is dishonest.

In his view Marshall was a man without any political judgement; when Rothschild left the Think Tank, he was afraid that his successors might take some AEA papers seriously and so he did 'a most unusual thing' – he personally shredded them. Well, you couldn't have had a more violent denunciation of the AEA than that.

What I like about Rothschild is that he deeply distrusts expertise; he is a blunt, rude man, and so there is no monkeying about. I told him that since he had left the Think Tank it hadn't been the same. 'Berrill is the political voice of Sir John Hunt.'

'Well,' he said, 'I noticed they changed the headed notepaper from "Central Policy Review Staff" and then underneath "Address: Cabinet Office", to "Cabinet Office" as the main heading and underneath "Central Policy Review Staff".' He thought that was very symbolic.

*Friday 22 July*
The photos of the Cabinet meeting at Chequers came back today – they must be the first photos ever taken of the Cabinet in session. They are not marvellous but I can see their being used for books, articles or audio-visual explanations of how Government works. I am tempted to take my camera into Cabinet committees; the Cabinet are very jolly with me and don't seem to mind much.

I went to the Department and had a talk with Frances Morrell in preparation for Roy Jenkins's visit today. It must be awful for Roy, with his dreams turning to dust, hoping to be a President Carter and ending up as an ambassador. It is his first official visit to Britain since he became President.

I thought as a courtesy I would wait for him downstairs at the door. He arrived with Crispin Tickell, a real deadbeat right-wing Foreign Office man who has been appointed as Jenkins's *chef de cabinet*. I decided to have Frances Morrell in to talk to him because I was hoping for a political discussion, but I didn't get one. I brought him up and got him a cup of tea, which he sent away because he wanted it without milk.

'Nice of you to come,' I said. 'How are you getting on?' I was jolly and friendly. Roy was red-faced and embarrassed throughout, no doubt because of his attack on me in Glasgow recently when he said anti-Market Ministers in the Cabinet had wrecked our reputation in Europe.

But I decided to be nice and, on energy, I said I had no problems, it was going very well, but it took a long time.

I asked him about his perspective, but he told me he had a press conference in eleven minutes. However, he did say that after direct elections he wanted economic and monetary union. 'I know you won't agree, but it is absolutely essential, and a great benefit; we can't have all this business over the green pound and monetary compensation agreements. It would be of benefit all round, with special regional compensations built in and that sort of thing.'

Then he said, 'Of course the EEC will enlarge. Greece is all right, and Spain, but the French are a bit doubtful about Portugal. Still, we must allow it in order to consolidate democracy in those countries.'

I argued we would need to have long transitional arrangements with them because they weren't strong enough to be in the Community at the moment. I asked Roy, 'Enlargement might tend to dilute the Community; do you feel that would have to be compensated for by some strengthening at the centre?'

'Yes, most certainly.'

So Roy is in favour of direct elections, economic and monetary union, and enlargement on the basis of a two-tier Community. I asked about Austria joining.

'They can't because of the treaty with the Russians,' replied Roy.

'What about Switzerland?'

'They wouldn't do it; they are owned by the United Nations.'

'Let me ask you this, Roy.' By this time he was looking at his watch every few minutes and puffing like an old train. 'If Mitterrand and Marchais win in France and Berlinguer gets into the Italian Government, do you think that is going to alter the perspective for European unification?'

'No,' he said, 'I don't see why it should.'

I don't think there was anything else. He admired my office and looked at the banner, and then I took them down and saw them to their car. They had to wait for a break in the traffic to get out. It was a very hot day and the car windows were wound down. I was standing on the pavement a few yards away, and his driver just could not get out – the traffic was just pouring past. It was actually quite funny. Roy kept waving me off but I stood there resolutely and smiling. It was obviously both an embarrassment and a bore but they finally got away and I gave a friendly wave.

Of course he should have arrived in a much more modest way, or perhaps a much grander way, but he just didn't get it right. I felt I was one up and he was awkward.

He did say, 'The Community is taken very seriously in the world, in the developing world and in America. And the Russians – they have to deal with us, you know. We are much stronger outside than we might appear inside.' Well, if that makes him cheerful so much the better.

*Sunday 24 July*
There was an extraordinary article in the *Observer*, clearly arising out of recent reports from British Ambassadors in Europe, about Britain's Presidency of the EEC. The article criticised Labour Ministers for having let down or betrayed officials who had been doing the best job they could; it claimed that officials were out of sympathy with their Ministers. Of course, that is what the Common Market is all about – officials running it and Ministers getting in the way.

At 12.30 Caroline, Melissa and I went off to see Ruth and Seretse Khama and their son Ian at the Hyde Park Hotel. Seretse, who is only in his mid-fifties, looked really old – skinny and poorly. Ian is about Hilary's age and when we last saw him he was at Sandhurst; now he is a brigadier-general and the Deputy Commander of the Botswana Defence Force, which doesn't really exist. Apparently the Bamangwato tribe have proclaimed him chief and he will be installed some time this year. Botswana is three times the size of England and has a population of only three-quarters of a million.

Seretse said that Ian Smith was completely out of touch with reality, but that Vorster, the South African Prime Minister, was much more realistic in that he recognised that he would have to let Rhodesia be settled on the basis of black majority rule and that Namibia would have to be independent. Of course South Africa will want to retain its very considerable commercial interests, notably uranium in Namibia.

He thought David Owen had created a favourable impression. Seretse is himself highly non-political; he doesn't really follow things carefully. Incidentally, Jim Callaghan had been to see him in hospital.

We sat down, had a marvellous lunch, and we joked and laughed. He said Ted Heath had been cold to the Commonwealth heads of government when he was Prime Minister, and that Mrs Thatcher had impressed the Belgian Prime Minister recently as being brilliant, charming and beautiful but cold as a fish. I think human qualitities cannot be underestimated in personal contact.

Caroline commented afterwards that she sensed a slight resentment by Seretse that he was being edged out; Ruth spoke about Ian all the time and Ian was answering all the questions. Seretse would say, 'Let me answer that', and Ruth would insist on Ian answering. Seretse is proud of his son but he feels that he is being pushed a bit to one side. He did look very sick and I presume it's only a matter of years before Ian will become President of Botswana – I should think before he's thirty. The vulnerability of Botswana to the cross-influences from white South Africa and Rhodesia and Marxist Russia and Cuba must be enormous.

We told lots of jokes. Seretse said that one of the chiefs in Botswana still required people to abase themselves before him, and food was brought in and taken out by people on their knees. Seretse has rid himself of all this and he and Ruth enjoy a sort of bourgeois life. They were happy in the old days in Croydon when Ian was at the local school and they used to go to the pub and drink and dance. Ruth will be remembered throughout the whole history of the country as the great white woman. She is such a nice woman, with a tremendously strong character.

Anyway Melissa thoroughly enjoyed it. She found Ian more responsible now.

*Friday 29 July*
Today the *Daily Express* had a fantastic story – Chapman Pincher saying that MI5 had bugged Harold Wilson. The whole security story is now breaking, and this was bound to come to the surface one day.

The Cabinet met at Number 10 for a discussion on Europe which I had suggested at Chequers, and it was one of the most remarkable Cabinets I have ever attended.

I took my cameras because I do feel at this period in my life that I should go on recording various events. So I was feeling cheerful, but we'd only just sat when Jim said, 'Well, I think it's hardly worth having this meeting at all. The whole document that we are discussing today has been leaked to the *Financial Times*, clearly by a member of this Cabinet. And there is an article in today's *Guardian* in which John Silkin has said that the Common Agricultural Policy proves that crime does pay.'

I hadn't seen the articles, and John Silkin said, 'Well, since you refer to me, Prime Minister, this was an interview I gave some time ago on the whole area of agricultural policy. I'm always being asked by journalists whether, as an anti-Marketeer, my views have altered, and what am I to say? I don't think it's very serious.'

So I said, 'It's a very serious thing to say that a member of the Cabinet has given a document to the press. I haven't seen the article but there are a lot of other people who have an interest here. There was an article in the *Observer* last Sunday saying that a Common Market official had reported that British Ministers had betrayed their officials.' I pointed out to him that there might be others who wanted to undermine us.

'Well,' replied Jim, 'that article was written by a pro-Marketeer in my opinion to undermine the authority of David Owen; perhaps it was jealousy because he's been promoted at such an early age, and I'm not having it.'

Stan Orme said, 'I hope we don't let this argument prevent us having this discussion on Europe, because that would be a very great pity.'

Just at that point, when tempers were at fever pitch, somebody came in and said there was another closure vote at the House. So we all scooped up our papers and leapt into our cars like a lot of Hell's Angels to go over to the House of Commons.

I talked to David Owen there and he said, 'I don't take this very seriously. I think this is psychological warfare by Jim to get us all to pull together.'

I went back to Number 10 at about 11 and sat around with the rest of the Cabinet. Then I realised that Jim hadn't arrived yet and I had a supreme opportunity. So I took my first movies and a few stills in the Cabinet Room.

It soon became clear that we were not going to meet again in Number 10, so we were all moved back to the House and finally began at 11.30. Jim opened by saying the most important thing was Party unity and that we must preserve our internationalism.

David Owen then introduced his paper, which did represent an important move towards an agnostic position on the Market.

He said the Labour Party could not be the Euro-party as Mrs Thatcher had described it. We must be in favour of reform from the inside, and the Government must and indeed was maintaining very close links with the European Labour Parties. Parliament could not at the moment perform its proper function in assessing Common Market legislation because of the 'in' or 'out' debate, and the people who were in favour of getting out were just wrecking everything.

However, primary legislation would be necessary to make any substantial change in the powers of the Common Market, and this could not be handled by short debates.

He went through a range of issues – CAP, enlargement, the necessity of a separate seat for Britain on the Energy Council and so on. He hoped that this paper would provide the basis on which we could come together.

When he had finished, Jim Callaghan asked, 'Does the Cabinet agree with this approach?'

We went round the table and people gave their views. At one stage Jim had to leave because Mrs Thatcher had demanded an immediate statement about the bugging at Number 10. Jim said, 'I don't want any of you to come to the House – it will make it too big an event. I want to go in alone, deal with the question and leave.'

So the rest of us went over to Number 10 for drinks, and I had a word with David Owen and Merlyn Rees about the bugging. David controls MI6 and Merlyn MI5 and they both said, 'We control the security services completely; the people at the top are very decent; you would be surprised about how good and decent they are. Some of them you would know, but of course you wouldn't know what they did. It is quite untrue and Harold Wilson is absolutely paranoid.'

'Of course,' said Merlyn, 'there is electronic surveillance at Number 10 but that is so nobody can get in.'

'How did the story come out?' I asked.

They said MI5 were angry that Harold Wilson appeared to be going to dinner parties, getting tight and telling people that MI5 had muddled up David Owen with Will Owen and Judith Hart with Mrs J. Tudor Hart. 'It's quite untrue,' said David Owen. 'They never muddled us up. They are getting back at him to frighten him by saying they bugged him.'

I said, 'I hope you do keep them under control. I was at a dinner in 1971 when Harold told the CBI that the Government bugged the TUC.'

'Oh,' said Merlyn, striking his head with the palm of his hand, 'how awful; he should never have said that' – which indicated that Merlyn knew.

I went on, 'Bryan Stanley told Ray Buckton in the 1972 strike that the ASLEF locomen were bugged.'

'Well, it may be true that at some periods in industrial disputes that does happen,' Merlyn replied.

'Yes,' said David, 'I always thought during the seamen's strike it was done.'

So I pursued it. 'Take another case. When I wanted to appoint Jack Jones to the National Enterprise Board, I was told he was a security risk. When I asked to see the report they withdrew their objection. And in the *Sunday Times* the other day it said all the trade union leaders are bugged. You've got a lot of experience of it, Merlyn, you have been in Northern Ireland, where the situation is kept under very tight control. You must know how these things happen.'

'Yes, I am sure I am told.'

David added, 'I have been through it very carefully, and nothing would be done without my knowing.'

Of course I don't believe that, but I wouldn't have dreamed of mentioning my own experience to them.

Cabinet resumed at 2.45 in the PM's room and we were told to limit ourselves to three minutes each.

Joel Barnett thought there would have to be a genuine compromise over Europe, but tighter federation was not possible. He opposed the EMU and said the CAP was the only common policy there was. It would be a looser and enlarged confederation.

Eric Varley said, 'Stan, Peter and I are the only people in this room who voted against entry in 1967. We must now make a superhuman effort with the Executive before the next Election or we will wreck the Party. If we lose the Election the Party will split. Owen's paper is brave and realistic. On industrial policy the CPRS pointed out the dangers but the Common Market cannot deny member states the right to go for nationalisation.' He supported Owen.

Roy Hattersley said the UK had been less successful than the other member states for two reasons. First, the Labour Party was still opposed to membership, and this had tightened the pro-Marketeers together and made them less critical of the Common Market than they should have been; secondly, other members doubted whether we were serious and that had weakened our influence in the Market. A Europe of twelve was less likely to be federal.

'The Party is anti-Market,' Edmund Dell said, 'and David Owen's paper is the best line. The EEC is an alliance in which supranationality is inevitable.' He favoured direct elections, and unity could be achieved if the 'outs' withdrew from their position. Otherwise there would be a long period of fighting ahead.

Michael Foot reminded everyone that this issue had been a great danger to the Party in the past, and there was danger ahead on direct elections. We would also be in considerable difficulties if the National Executive document were passed. Jim's view on how to handle the Conference was the key.

At this point I looked at Jim and he was nodding vigorously, which confirmed my view that Jim's strategy is to get the trade union leaders to support him in defeating both National Executive documents – on the EEC and the Election campaign.

Jim spoke again and at this stage the whole debate took a completely new turn. I simply wasn't able to write precisely what happened, but it was something like this.

Jim suggested the Government publish a White Paper, before the Conference met, setting out its position over the next four or five years.

I said, 'I think it would be a very great mistake to issue a White Paper before Conference because it would be pre-empting the manifesto. The best thing would be to let Conference reach its view in the normal manner and then meet to consider which policies should go into the manifesto.

'If you go to the National Executive and ask them to change the policy statement before Conference, you will probably persuade them, because the NEC will be influenced by what the Leader of the Party says. You will almost certainly succeed in getting Conference to reject the NEC document for the same reasons, because the trade unions will support you. But it would be a most unwise thing to do because it would inflict the most terrible damage on the Party if it were done in that way.'

'And it would wreck the unity of the Cabinet,' Stan Orme added.

I went on, 'What I find incredible is that here we are meeting to consider David Owen's paper, yet we do not have before us the NEC documents which were cleared on Wednesday and on which they have worked for a year. We are not even considering what they said. Similarly, David Owen's paper has not been made available to the NEC.'

Jim said, 'Well, the Government must govern. I can't have Government papers put to the Executive.'

'But, PM,' I said, 'when the 1972 Industry Group of sympathetic industrialists prepared a report on industrial strategy, you set up a Cabinet committee to look at it. Never in my whole life do I remember the Cabinet ever taking NEC documents seriously or setting up committees to look at them. They just don't come to us.'

Jim, red-faced, pointed his finger at me. 'You are working against us.'

'That is a very serious thing to say. I have been in the Cabinet over many years and I don't remember a Prime Minister ever saying such a thing to a Cabinet colleague. If you believe that is the case, you have the remedy in your own hands.'

'Well, maybe I shall have to take the necessary action,' Jim replied.

I said, 'You have the power to decide who is in and out of your Cabinet and, I promise you, if I personally were your only problem, you wouldn't have a problem.'

'You are leading a faction against us,' Jim retorted.

'If you want my honest opinion, I am quite happy to go along with David Owen's general approach, but I want to see this country restored to itself, with the right to govern itself by its own legislation. That is what I think is important. You hear all this about our parliamentary democracy being undermined by Marxists or by extending the public sector, but the plain truth is that it has been undermined by Brussels. It may take twenty years to do it but I want to work to restore to the British people the power to govern themselves and then to work for others.'

The tension was electric. Bill Rodgers said, 'If others are going to speak on the Common Market question before Conference, then I am going to speak.'

'We don't want any more speeches,' said Denis, and David Ennals wanted an assurance that everybody would shut up.

I came in again. 'I remember well during the Referendum of 1975 that Shirley Williams said that if the vote went against the Market she would withdraw from public life.'

So Denis chimed in, 'You promised to abide by the Referendum and you have broken your word.'

All of a sudden a wave of hatred engulfed the room. It turned into a personal clash between Jim and me with odd interruptions. Stan Orme interjected, 'I won't have Tony Benn pilloried in this way; he is quite entitled to his view', and Michael Foot remarked, 'Tony reflects a very important element in the Party's thinking which has to be taken into account.' It was an amazing scene.

Jim finally said, 'I don't know what Tony Benn intends to do. We've had no clear answer from him as to what he intends to do.'

Harold Lever said, 'On the limitations of European legislation on the British Parliament, this situation is no different from the IMF or NATO or GATT.'

'But it *is* different,' I argued, 'because those bodies do not have the power to change the laws of this country. I sat at a committee the other day with John Silkin when we were told that the Ministers were behaving illegally and that is a complete change. My advice, PM, because I don't want a confrontation any more than you do, is to let the Party and the Government decide their respective views and then reach a compromise. If you force the NEC to climb down it will lead to a confrontation.'

Well, that was it, and the Cabinet adjourned. I had a word with Michael and Stan and John Silkin and they said, 'For God's sake, keep your mouth shut!' We walked back and I told Stan that I was surprised more than angry, genuinely surprised, because I thought it had been a constructive meeting up until the row. I was a bit shaken, and David Owen said, 'Well you did go a bit too far, when you held the press conference on the Common Market Safeguards Committee.'

*Saturday 30 July*
To Bristol for my surgery, which lasted five and a half hours. There were complaints about Hell's Angels; parents from a Catholic school whose headmaster had been suspended by the Avon Education Committee who thought he was mad and wanted him to see a psychiatrist; an old man of eighty-two who took down his trousers and made me examine the shrapnel wound in his hip from 1916, and so on.

The news tonight reported that Harold Wilson has demanded an inquiry into Chapman Pincher's statement that MI5 bugged Number 10. That means we are going to have a tremendous silly season debate about something of crucial importance.

*Sunday 31 July*
In the afternoon Caroline and I went for a lovely three-mile walk right round Shepherd's Bush and back.

*Monday 1 August*
The story of the Wilson bugging was still running in the press. Chapman Pincher had commented that the security services were perfectly entitled to bug even a Prime Minister if they thought he was engaged in a communist conspiracy.

Thus was revealed, for the first time, the reality of the power structure in Britain, where the security services, and no doubt the military, feel themselves to be above politicians. A most interesting admission. I think there will be some sort of an inquiry and it will at least open up the possibility for the National Executive Home Policy Committee to work on it next session.

Peter Hain came in the evening. It's hard to believe he's only twenty-seven, considering all he's done. He is South African and ran the 'Stop the Tour' campaign against the South African rugby team in the summer of 1970 so skilfully that the Cabinet on a number of occasions discussed it.

I have corresponded with him over the last six months and he sent me a book he'd written on radical politics. I would like to get him into the Labour Party, and clearly he's receptive to the idea of joining, but it's difficult for him as a former Chairman of the Young Liberals, which he left in April.

I gave him some material including the statement made by Dingle Foot and Lady Megan Lloyd George when they joined the Party in the 1950s. I also gave him the 1945 manifesto to look at.

I even went so far as to say that, if he were to join, he should do it on the eve of the Labour Party Conference and that I would lay on a welcome from a wide range of people. It would also add a completely new dimension of the Lib–Lab Pact because if David Steel thought that Liberals were joining the Labour Party it would be a great counter-balance to the formal, slightly shoddy parliamentary arrangements.

So I regarded that as a useful evening, and we agreed to meet later this week with four or five of his friends.

*Tuesday 2 August*
This morning Frances Morrell rang to say that the *Evening Standard* had asked her which of my children was having treatment in the private wing of the Radcliffe Infirmary in Oxford. It turned out that in today's first edition of *The Times* the diary column had contained a report to that effect and that we were using Caroline's maiden name. I must say I blew my top.

I rang *The Times*, made them read me the first edition, and wrote it down. Then I wrote a letter after about a dozen drafts. Arthur Davidson, the Parliamentary Secretary to the Law Officers, assured me the report was defamatory, so I sent the letter round to the editor and rang up to be sure it had arrived. Rees-Mogg came to the phone and said he would publish the letter and a retraction and apology tomorrow. I let it go at that, but, I must say, this really stirred me. It's the third absolutely blatant lie this year.

Frances was most helpful. She's at her best on these occasions and suggested I prepare a dossier and send it over to Stuart Weir, the deputy editor of *New Society*, who promised to do a piece on it. So this I did. It's not possible to convey my anger adequately.

The *Evening Standard* and the *Daily Express* rang up during the day to ask if the story was true. I mustn't get obsessive about the press, like Harold Wilson, or paranoid, saying Smear, Smear, because that's destructive. But I won't let them tell lies.

Anyway at 3.30 Dick Clements came over for a talk. He mentioned that the *Tribune* correspondent, on talking to one or two of the police at Grunwick, had received the impression that in arresting Scargill and Audrey Wise they were punishing the Labour Government for holding their pay back. That was an interesting story – quite a new dimension.

### Wednesday 3 August

Frances came and we had a bit of a talk about Harold and the security services. Frances said Harold was paranoid, and made the very shrewd point that Harold was afraid the security services would reveal that he himself had ordered the bugging of Denis Healey and Jim Callaghan and everybody else. It's a very amusing thought.

After that I went to say goodbye for the holidays to Jack Rampton. As a Permanent Secretary he is so remote from me that it's very difficult to do more than just nod at him; we're like ships passing in the night. He's completely given up trying to control me; he just pursues his own policy unless I stop him.

I dashed over to Number 10 to take part in the committee which handles Rhodesia – not a meeting I usually attend in full. David Owen described in detail his talks with Carter, who has reluctantly accepted that we will not send a Commonwealth force but is not ready for American military involvement. They have worked out a scheme which will all be publicised and tested long before this diary is ever typed and we shall see whether it works or not. In effect it is an Anglo-American initiative which we hope to sell to the UN, involving a UN force and a British administrator-general.

The crucial thing is that it constitutes Britain's formal disengagement from Rhodesia, which will mean Smith will have to face reality and the frontline presidents will also have to face the fact that we won't be reasserting British sovereignty. Once you internationalise something, you are no longer in control of it.

At 6 I went to see the PM. While I was waiting outside, Beaumarchais, the French Ambassador, scurried out. I spent about an hour with Jim. He was red-faced – with embarrassment, I thought. I said, 'It is very nice of you to see me. I felt somehow it had all gone wrong last Friday when we discussed the Common Market. I know you think of me as Dr Jekyll and Mr Hyde, but really I am Hyde, Hyde and Hyde again!'

'But looking like Jekyll.'

'Maybe,' I said. I told him I didn't think the Conference was going to be destructive; there was a way round.

So then he apologised. 'Do you know, to be perfectly honest, I was very rude to you, and I think I was unfair. I told Ken Stowe at the end of the day that I had overdone it, and I worried about it all weekend.'

'For Heaven's sake, don't apologise, you had a hell of a day. Anyway, I was a bit worried and I wanted to come along and have a word with you, motivated by the same spirit.'

So, like many rows with Jim, it blew up and blew over and blew out. And I am awfully glad I went to see him because he couldn't have been nicer. I wanted to make peace with him and retreat a bit.

He said, 'I thought you were really trying to wreck the whole Government and withdrawing as leader of the left in order to take over.'

'Look, it isn't like that. I am trying to persuade people, and I think if we get the framework of the Conference right then we can have a meaningful debate.'

'Of course,' said Jim, 'there are people on the Executive who just want to wreck the Government. I know there are.' He does have an obsession about this but I didn't pursue it.

I described the outline of what I would like to say about Europe. He said, 'Well, if you were to admit that the debate isn't an in–out debate, that would revolutionise the Conference.' I said I'd think about it.

He was very friendly and I told him I much preferred dealing with him than with Harold. He half repeated the apology and I felt embarrassed. I did tell him that I was glad that none of that sensational Cabinet had appeared in the Sunday papers. I had quivered as I opened them.

'Well, thanks for coming. I appreciate it very much.' And on that note I left.

*Tuesday 9 August*

Spent the morning working on the false private medical treatment story. Dick Clements had sent me a copy of a franked postcard conveying the inaccurate *Times* story which had been sent to the *Tribune* office, and we also discovered that *Labour Weekly* had received one as well.

I could just see the number of the frank so I rang up the Post Office and, believe it or not, it turned out to be the European Movement frank.* So it was from their office that these postcards had been sent,

---

* The European Movement was founded in 1948, with membership open to all organisations working for European unity. I concluded that this group was the source of the smear because of my opposition to the EEC, although the director denied that his office was responsible.

which may mean that they were the source of the story in the first place, though I can't prove that.

### Wednesday 10 August

Stansgate. Caroline went shopping. I had twelve hours in bed, which is my way of recovering. Later Caroline and I went for a jog in the lovely warm weather.

### Thursday 11 August

I worked on my letters. A carrier pigeon with a broken leg was found and Joshua took it to the vet.

### Friday 12 August

I planned a roof seat for the car. Whenever there is an Election I prepare equipment for the car, and this time I decided to do a really good job. There is a big roof rack on the car, which will be very useful.

### Sunday 14 August

Cycled to Southminster for the papers, which took an hour, and then worked on the roof seat. I have fixed a plank to the roof rack, sawn the legs off an old chair and bolted it on to the plank.

### Monday 15 August

Damp, misty and sunless but quite warm. Red box arrived. Melissa wrote from Italy. Joshua rescued an injured baby rabbit and has put it in a box until it recovers.

### Tuesday 16 August

Little bit of sunshine. Went shopping. The rabbit died.

### Wednesday 17 August

Thunderstorm, and a really wet day. Red box arrived. Elvis Presley died.

### Thursday 18 August

I should mention that over the last two weeks there have been clashes between the racialist National Front and the ultra-left in Lewisham and Birmingham, and the papers have been in a frenzy. The press is doing its best to put all the blame for the violence on the ultra-left and then use the National Front as an excuse for banning demonstrations.

### Sunday 21 August

Stephen's twenty-sixth birthday. He got a suit, albums and a cricket bat, and I gave him some camera equipment. Had a lovely birthday party with everybody except Melissa, who phoned.

Another injured baby rabbit was found. In the evening Stephen, Joshua and I went out and took some photographs with the polaroid.

### Thursday 25 August

Ron picked me up at 7 am and drove me back to London. I worked with Julie in the basement office, before leaving for Carlton House Terrace, the official home of the Foreign Secretary, for lunch with Kurt Waldheim, the UN Secretary-General.

I had never met Waldheim before. He is, of course, a career civil servant and as such has no real political background. Whether it is right to have such a man occupying that position is, I think, questionable. He had come to discuss southern Africa and also wanted a bit of support on energy questions.

It was agreed, despite my opposition, that the FO brief advising us not to take the lead on energy discussions would be accepted, but we carried it to the point that when Waldheim himself made a recommendation we didn't even respond to it. The fact is that the FO does not want us to take a lead on anything. They just want us to be tame members of the Common Market.

The extent to which the treachery of our senior officials in the FO has grown is astonishing. It prevents us in many ways from developing our potential and influence to the full. Just as we never wanted to upset the Americans during the days of the special relationship, now we never want to upset the Germans or the French.

In a curious way, we are led by a group of people who have a conception of Britain as a governed colony of some international organisation. The Treasury doesn't want to upset the IMF, and the FO doesn't want to upset the EEC, and the Ministry of Defence doesn't want to upset NATO. These are the organisations that govern affairs in Britain.

Anyway I did my best with Waldheim. There was a slight flicker of interest but, as far as he was concerned, the British view came from the Foreign Secretary, not from me; whatever the Energy Secretary had to say was only mildly interesting.

Back to Stansgate.

### Saturday 27 August

It was a sunny day, and Caroline and Stephen went to London in the afternoon to see *Don Giovanni* at Covent Garden. They found themselves sitting next to the Vaizeys, Lady Antonia Fraser and Harold Pinter.

*Thursday 1 September*
Today Frances Morrell's study, *From the Electors of Bristol*, analysing my
constituency correspondence from April 1972 to March 1973, was
published. It had tremendous coverage. The Bristol papers carried it,
*The Times, Guardian, New Society* and the *Economist* all had a piece, and
*Labour Weekly* had nearly a full page. Frances was interviewed on IRN,
BBC *World at One* and *Nationwide*. It was a tremendous success for her,
and she has been working on it for three or four years.

*Wednesday 7 September*
I spent the whole day at Bristol University chairing a seminar on the
Severn Barrage, which I had asked the Department to organise. The
Department had been very doubtful about this because Whitehall is
opposed to the Severn Barrage. They see it as another white elephant,
like Concorde, but they are also hostile to anything which might
challenge nuclear power's prime share of resources. If it could be
designed and built properly, this barrage would cost £4 million and
produce 10,000 megawatts of electricity, the equivalent of five or six
power stations currently operating.

*Thursday 8 September*
To Bristol in time for the GMC, which was absolutely crowded. I
distributed my programme of work for the constituency because there
had been some criticism of my neglect of the constituency, which was a
bit unfair.

At the end, Pete Hammond produced a motion calling on the GMC
to condemn those councillors and Members of Parliament who had
attended the Queen's visit to Bristol in connection with the Jubilee
celebrations on 8 August. He drew attention to the fact that on 14 July a
resolution had been carried at the GMC rejecting the monarchy and
calling on Avon and Bristol councillors not to attend the celebrations.
He said that those who had gone should account for themselves.

I had attended, and I quickly looked at the minute book and there
was no reference to Members of Parliament in July's resolution. I just
sat tight.

Herbert got up and said, 'At the risk of being reactionary, there are
many people who are glad that our councillors and MPs went.'

A vote was called and the resolution of condemnation was first
declared lost, but then a count was demanded and it was carried. So I
was officially rebuked for attending the Queen's Jubilee celebrations in
Bristol. I felt slightly ashamed of myself.

*Saturday 10 September*
Bristol again. Just after midnight I went to St John's Lane with a

Jim Callaghan's Economic Summit, 1977. From left: Guilio Andreotti of Italy, Takeo Fukuda of Japan, Giscard D'Estaing of France, Jimmy Carter of USA, Helmut Schmidt of West Germany, JC, Pierre Trudeau of Canada.

The Cabinet (1978): the first official photograph ever taken inside the Cabinet Room, Number 10. My earlier amateur efforts were frowned upon.

Jim Callaghan with Commonwealth leader Kenneth Kaunda *(above)*, one of the first and most distinguished of African premiers; and *(top)* A very special relationship: President Carter welcoming Jim Callaghan on the South Lawn of the White House.

David Owen, one of the founders of the ill-fated SDP, Foreign Secretary at 38.

The Callaghans visiting the Forties field.

## Ministers and Miners

Alex Eadie, MP, miner and 'Minister for Mines' 1974-9; highly respected throughout the coal industry.

(*Below*) One of several visits 'down the pit' at Betwys as Secretary of State for Energy.

*(Top)* Airborne with Bernard Ingham, my Chief Information Officer, to visit the Ekofisk blow-out April, 1977. *(Middle)* The legendary Armand Hammer, owner of Occidental Oil, at Flotta oil terminal, with (right) James Bretherton. *(Below)* Visiting Shetland's oil terminal Sullom Voe, March 1977.

Summit at Guadeloupe, Jan. 1979. Callaghan enjoying the sunshine with Carter, Schmidt and Giscard.

Callaghan with the General Secretaries who formed Trade Unionists for a Labour Victory. From left: Ray Buckton, Alf Allen, Bill Keys, David Basnett, JC, Moss Evans, Clive Jenkins, John Boyd.

## The Winter of Discontent – and the election that followed

Low paid workers at breaking point during the winter of 1978/9, show their disapproval of the Government's pay policy; rubbish piles up in central London and nurses and Health Service auxiliaries protest.

*(Above)* An uneasy partnership.

*(Left)* Dog-days: canvassing in Bristol in the May 1979 General Election.

Margaret Thatcher
arrives at Number 10,
May 1979.

Three Prime Ministers:
Thatcher, her hero,
Churchill, and her
predecessor, Callaghan.

councillor for Windmill Hill Ward and we stood for an hour and a half watching the comings and goings at a takeaway café which have caused anxiety among some of my constituents. Cars drew up, people urinated in the street, rubbish was thrown about, there was shouting and laughing and banging of doors, people parked on pedestrian crossings. It was completely unacceptable and I am going to take up the complaints. Got to bed at 2.30.

Woke up at 8 and heard the tragic news that Peter Shore's son, Piers, was found dead yesterday. He was a contemporary of Melissa's, and it is heartbreaking.

*Monday 12 September*

Jack Jones came to lunch at the office and we had a thorough talk. I asked him about the TUC Conference and said Jim seemed to have done well.

'Well, we warned him not to be provocative,' Jack said. 'Everything depends on the scale and timing of reflation, and we must try and get the £10 Christmas bonus through for pensioners.'

On pay, he said the Government would have a rough ride but it could be solved by productivity. He was in favour of local bargaining. Cash limits were a problem for the public sector, but of course Tory councils would support the Government. Then he said, 'I hope you're not going to come out in favour of a second chamber. We want total abolition of the House of Lords.' Of course, if he'd read the House of Lords statement he would know that was our position.

Later on he criticised the documents we had produced. Jack has a strong anti-intellectual strain in him.

I walked half way back to Transport House with him and asked him what he would do when he retired.

'I am going to do voluntary work,' he said.

*Tuesday 13 September*

My first appointment was with Sir John Hill, Chairman of the AEA, and we had about three-quarters of an hour's very interesting discussion. He said that if the Government didn't finance the glassification of nuclear waste BNFL would become uneconomic. It was a good example of the general assumption that the Government must pay all costs connected with the nuclear industry while the coal industry must pay for its own research.

He also wanted to authorise the signing of the contract to store Japanese nuclear waste before the Windscale Inquiry was completed. On the fast breeder reactor, I said we would have an inquiry next year before we reached a decision.

He mentioned that Marshall had been very upset at being moved but was getting over it and was working on the question of international fuel cycle safeguards.

Went to the NEC International Committee and got them to address the problem of the Namibian uranium contract first because I could only stay briefly. There is mounting pressure on me particularly. I described what had happened in 1968 and 1970, when I was misled about where our uranium was coming from. The Party was committed to cancelling the contract but the Government had decided in 1974 and again last year not to cancel it.

The position now – and I had checked it recently – was that, with Canadian uranium very hard to get, American uranium being used as a political weapon, Australian uranium being at the centre of a tremendous controversy between the labour movement and the Government, the Orkneys having stopped any uranium exploration and the Russians refusing to export natural uranium, we were in serious difficulties and more or less forced to depend on the Rossing mine in Namibia. Indeed, as Hill has said this morning, if *we* didn't use it, it would be snapped up by someone else.

Mik was helpful. 'Don't you think SWAPO would like to make it the source of their economic strength after independence?'

I said, 'I think that would be sensible but I can well understand them not wanting to say that until independence.'

Mik quite properly added that they would want to weaken the economy until they were free, and then build it up again after independence.

Went to see Jim on CEGB business and afterwards we talked alone in his room.

'What do you think about an Election date?' he asked.

'As late as possible.'

We talked about the scale and timing of reflation and I suggested we do a bit of secret reflation. 'We don't have to publicise it. You said you didn't want a pre-Election boom. Why can't we do it quietly earlier – raise pensions, a little easement on pay, and help the public sector, particularly health?'

Then he said, 'What do you think I should say in my speech to Conference? I want to put a bit of vision into it.'

'You are absolutely secure in saying that the partnership with the trade union movement is firm. I think the key to it is full employment.'

'Well, honestly,' said Jim, 'I don't know what to do. Does it matter very much? I remember the 1935 Election when there were 3 million unemployed but Labour still did badly.'

'In 1945 it was the heart of the whole Election.'

'The awful truth is', he said, 'that inflation affects everybody and unemployment comparatively few.'

'I think we might win the Election and Thatcher has overdone it.'

'Well,' said Jim, 'I see Paul Johnson thinks that you and Thatcher should lead the two parties.'

'Well, that doesn't help me very much.'

He concluded by saying, 'I would like to tell you personally how co-operative you have been about all this, and constructive and helpful.'

Came back to the office to discuss security matters with Jack Rampton. Clearly there have to be special measures for sensitive energy sites like Sullom Voe and Bacton, St Fergus and so on. We are pressing for a meeting of the Terrorism Committee; I have been a member for two years but was invited to attend only once.

### Friday 16 September

Brian Sedgemore's minority report of the Select Committee on the Civil Service is headline news today. Brian was himself a civil servant, at one time Private Secretary to Bob Mellish at the Ministry of Housing. He is also a barrister and he knows an awful lot about the subject. He has used extremely vivid language – talking about the 'Vichy mentality' of the Foreign Office, the obstruction and frustration imposed on Ministers by the Civil Service, and so on. He is absolutely right.

At 11 Caroline and I and the four children went to All Saints, Putney, for the memorial service for Piers Shore. It was a beautiful ceremony, conducted by Trevor Huddleston, but inexpressibly sad. All the Shores were there, Michael and Jill Foot, John and Rosalind Silkin and Judith and Tony Hart.

Huddleston said simply, 'We are gathered together to remember the life of Piers Shore – people of different attitudes to the church, some believers, some non-believers, some believers in other faiths, some who have never found help from institutionalised Christianity. We have all been close to Piers in some way. I didn't know him well but I am close to him through the fact that he was a believer.'

Then he described Piers: a very amusing boy, popular and well loved. He said, perceptively, that those who are loving and generous are also vulnerable. It was a most sensitive address.

We sang hymns, and Brian Abel-Smith read from Wordsworth and John Donne. It was a day for weeping, and along our family bench I could hear everyone in tears. Afterwards we talked a bit outside the church in the sunshine. Peter and Liz were so courageous.

### Sunday 18 September

Brian Sedgemore was bitterly attacked in today's papers for his criticism of the Civil Service. Lord Armstrong (formerly Sir William Armstrong) has attacked me and Crossman – 'Benn on the rampage', 'indecisive Crossman had caused all the trouble', and so on. The senior civil servants must be boiling with rage.

The Tory press are happy to attack bureaucracy except when the bureaucrats are obstructing Labour Ministers. Brian, to his credit, has opened up the whole question of bureaucracy and what it really means: bureaucracy meaning the establishment beating Labour Governments is fine, but bureaucracy meaning the development of the public sector is wrong.

*Monday 19 September*
To the South Bristol crematorium for the funeral of my former election agent, Ennis Harris. Maurice Rea, the Party chairman, was there, and his predecessor, Cyril Langham. Vyvyan-Jones conducted the service.

I must say it was very impressive, mainly because Vyvyan-Jones had known Ennis since he was nine, for forty-four years; he had married Ennis and his wife and buried his parents, so he spoke with real feeling.

As Vyvyan-Jones is himself a socialist, there was no pretence that politics was something you shouldn't mention at funerals. Everybody there was from the labour movement.

Afterwards we walked across in the cloudy weather to the new grave and saw the coffin lowered in. Mrs Harris stood there in black, a strong and determined figure. What agony to see your husband's body laid in a grave. She turned to me and said, 'Thank you so much for coming, I really appreciate it. The important thing is that Ennis's work should go on.'

In the evening I went to Liverpool Street to catch the train to Ilford, and a very interesting incident occurred there. I hadn't had a proper breakfast or lunch, so I went into the East End Buffet, bought two cups of tea, two apples and two sandwiches, and sat at a table near the door.

A drunk came in – a tough character – and spoke to the man at the next table, who brushed him aside. Then he came over to me and said, 'I want money for tea.' So I put my hand in my pocket and pulled out a 50p coin and gave it to him. He clenched his fist and said, 'I want that sandwich.'

'I have given you some money, go and buy one.' He said he was very strong and then began struggling with me. He was hungry and desperate, and he seized the sandwich. I just picked up my stuff and left; in a way I was modestly robbed.

*Tuesday 20 September*
I had Tom Jackson, General Secretary of the Union of Post Office Workers, to lunch, as part of a series of meetings I am having with the General Council of the TUC in the run-up to the Conference.

Tom is an old friend. I have known him for thirteen years since I was

Postmaster-General and he is an agreeable, cheerful man, though he is on the right of the Party without any doubt. He went to Newham to speak for Reg Prentice when he was in trouble, and he is a great supporter of Shirley Williams, a Gaitskellite and now a Callaghanite. But he is imaginative and he has got colour and vitality.

He asked about my future in the Labour Party.

'Well,' I said, 'I have a good job in the Government, and I hope we will win, as I believe we will.'

'Yes, but what about the leadership?'

I said there were an awful lot of candidates for the leadership – Denis Healey, Merlyn Rees, Shirley Williams, Peter Shore and so on – but he brushed them aside.

'Denis will not succeed unless he gets us back to full employment.'

'Well,' I said, 'I am thought to be ambitious and I would like to be Leader of the Labour Party; I stood last year in order to get my policy across but I am a sufficiently old hand at this not to wreck my life by ambition. I have seen too many people, like Herbert Morrison, ruined by it.'

Whether Tom was just having me on and flattering me I don't know; it is very flattering if a trade union leader asks you if you are going to stand for the leadership.

One of the comforting things about democratic politics, which you appreciate more as you get older, is that you don't have to take decisions alone. Decisions are taken collectively, by the Cabinet or the National Executive, by union executives or the General Council, by Conference, by a referendum, or by an Election.

Tom agreed – he said that funnily enough, on the nine or ten occasions when he had been beaten by his conference and been angry about it, on almost every occasion the rank and file had been right. A sort of wisdom from their own detached experience put them on the right tracks, which he couldn't see at the time. I found that touchingly humble, and it threw a new light on Tom Jackson.

He has just become a grandfather, and his daughter and son-in-law are both Militant supporters, so he is exposed to a degree of criticism from below. He is very proud of his grandson, and I envied him greatly.

At 5 o'clock, Lord Allen of Fallowfield, Alf Allen as was, the General Secretary of USDAW, came to see me. He is a funny chap, big but shy, and very right-wing. I have always felt that he thoroughly disapproves of me.

He was crabby at first. He looked at my trade union banners with a horrid fascination which is normally the prerogative of senior industrialists who feel they have come into a communist lair. Then he sat on the edge of the couch, not looking me in the eye, but frowning and fiddling with his briefcase, and a somewhat embarrassed discussion began.

When we got on to the problems of small businesses he began to warm up. He said how important they were and how the Wilson committee was looking into it, and then we came to Mrs Thatcher. She had once said to him, 'Lord Allen, the trade unions have too much power.' He had replied, 'If you ever become Prime Minister, which I very much hope you will not, you will get into trouble some time, and you will come to the trade unions and the CBI to help you. It will be no good then telling them they have too much power.' She had apparently replied, 'That is below the belt', and he had said, 'Not at all.'

Anyway, what I thought would be a fifteen-minute chat turned into a three-hour discussion about the TUC, about the power of the TGWU, about pay, about the moral strength that came from pay restraint, about the values of the labour movement, and about Bristol, his home town, of which he is proud. He told me he had actually been present, as a boy of sixteen, in January 1930 when Stafford Cripps was selected for the constituency. He was extremely warm.

### Wednesday 21 September
Next in my round of TUC leaders for lunch was Frank Chapple. He was disgusted with Jack Jones, and said Moss Evans was a big bully.

### Thursday 22 September
Mr Gillespie, the Canadian Minister of Energy, Mines and Natural Resources, came to see me with my dear old friend Paul Martin, and the High Commissioner. Gillespie is about three years older than me, and was in the Canadian Fleet Air Arm. He is a very bright guy, a Canadian Liberal, which is to say a progressive British Tory. He is Chairman of the IEA and was doing a tour in preparation for the IEA ministerial conference in Paris in a couple of weeks.

I discovered something my officials had not told me, namely that our supplies of uranium from Canada were stopped from 1 January because we are now a member of Euratom, and Euratom is regarded by Canada as a leaky and ineffective safeguard system. They are afraid that their uranium will get, through us, to the French, who are spreading technology abroad. It is scandalous that I wasn't told about this.

I suggested the problem could be put right with a bilateral arrangement, and Gillespie said he would agree to such an arrangement with us, but he could not agree to it within the framework of Euratom.

It was pointed out to me by my officials that the Euratom Treaty commits us to free trade in uranium, and therefore in fact we couldn't give the Canadians assurances. It is an absolute scandal, and it shows the extent to which all principles, even the national interest, have been thrown overboard by officials working within the Common Market.

*Wednesday 28 September*

David Basnett came to lunch, to complete my month of interviews with trade union leaders. We talked about Jim and he said, 'You know, I am a very close friend of Jim's.'

'So am I,' I said. 'I have known him for many years and I get on with him extremely well. I much prefer him to Harold. He is shrewd, and much closer to the movement than Harold ever was. He is a skilled political tactician.'

'You know,' David said, 'he is the first working-class Prime Minister the Labour Party has ever had.'

'Is that so? What about Ramsay MacDonald?'

'Well, he was a graduate.' I don't think he was actually, but David Basnett, who had come up from the bottom without the opportunity of a university education, obviously felt that Jim was somebody he could relate to. Of course, that is why Paul Johnson dislikes Jim so much – because he is not a graduate.

We went on to talk about the review of the Party's structure and he said, 'We want a commission on the Party with two general secretaries and other people from outside the Party.'

'Half a minute,' I said, 'you can't very well ask the Executive to declare its own incompetence. After all it is elected by Conference to organise the Party.'

'Well, we must have people from outside the Party.' Basnett wanted to clarify the role of the Party, the Government and the unions on this question. He is basically trying to get more outside influence on the Party as a counterweight to the constituencies, which he claims are élitist. I warned him that the trade unions themselves would come under scrutiny – particularly the block vote. But clearly he has made a deal with Jim.

I argued, 'It would be opening old wounds. It will look as if you are trying to punish the NEC for what Mikardo said about Jack Jones two years ago, or what happened at last year's Conference, or what Joan Maynard has been saying. That really would be awful.'

'That would not be the spirit in which I moved it.'

'Maybe not,' I said, 'but that is the way it would be seen and you should be very careful on this score.'

In the afternoon, I had a long talk with Frances and Francis and Brian Sedgemore. Brian showed me an article by Terry Ward which is appearing in *The Times* shortly and which argues that the Treasury has underspent substantially. Therefore we are much below the level of activity that even the IMF requires.

I asked Francis why the IMF had reversed its position on reflation. He said, 'They look at next year and they see deepening recession, so they are getting into a panic. Monetarism is dead.'

At 5 o'clock I went to the Terrorism Ministerial Committee (TRM) at the Cabinet Office – the first time I have attended it in two years. I had insisted on a meeting and we began by discussing the existing security arrangements for energy, and the SAS team based in Hereford which can be flown all over the country to deal with terrorism.

I urged that we have stronger defences. Our oil imports were worth £7 billion a year and any insurance premium to cover that sort of risk would be far higher than the cost of having the SAS on standby.

Fred Mulley very stupidly said, 'I welcome this support for increased defence expenditure.'

That was not the point. The point was whether current spending was being directed in a way that was really helpful.

Later Eric Heffer rang me at home. I alerted him to the threat of a resolution from Basnett for a commission on the structure of the Party which is really beginning to worry me. We must head that off.

*Thursday 29 September*
I asked Jim for a private word, after EY Committee this morning.

'Jim, I have done a lot of thinking and talking about Conference. I believe it is going to be all right, but there is one great problem looming out of the darkness and that is Basnett's motion on the Party structure. It would be a disaster if, just as we approached an Election, there was a committee set up to receive evidence which everybody could pump in, criticising every part of the Party. Let's look at the machine to tune it up, but let's leave the structure until later.'

'Well,' said Jim, 'there are all sorts of ideas about. You have got to be careful that a little coterie of left-wingers or right-wingers doesn't dominate the Party.'

'Well, I know that, but once you open Pandora's Box you will find Reg Prentice saying that we are all run by the Trots, Woodrow Wyatt that good Labour people should vote Tory, the left that the parliamentary leadership has got too much power, Paul Johnson that the block vote of the unions dominates the Party, and so on. This would be most unwise, and I wonder whether an initiative tomorrow would be sensible.'

Came home and packed, then went to Victoria Station to catch the train to Brighton. Sitting next to me was a quiet chap with long hair, spectacles and long sensitive fingers, reading a book of Marx's writings. He didn't say anything to me until we got to Brighton, where he offered to carry my bag, and it turned out he was a librarian at the Office of Manpower Economics and the Monopolies Commission. He whispered to me, 'I didn't want to embarrass you coming down, but you have got more friends than you think in the Civil Service.' It was an interesting episode, and to find that a librarian at the Department of Industry was a Marxist could be frightening to a right-winger.

*Friday 30 September*

Breakfast with Alex Kitson, who apparently spent a long time after the Conference Arrangements meeting last night talking to the other committee members. He told me that Jim has attempted to fix everything; that he called in all the general secretaries, has tried to fix automatic reselection for MPs and indeed the whole handling of the Conference.

Harry Urwin of the T&G came and joined us, and said much the same, but that the TGWU could hardly oppose reselection of MPs because they had introduced reselection of sponsored candidates some years ago when George Brown made a lot of trouble.

Went downstairs for the pre-Conference National Executive meeting at 11, and Joyce Gould came up and told me to be careful to ensure that the abortion debate did not have only one resolution demanding an end of the free vote for MPs, because that would wreck things.

Joan Lestor leaned over and said, 'I have some sensational news for you. I phoned and phoned the other day but couldn't get through, so I banged down the receiver. When I picked it up again I could hear you talking to Peter Hain – which shows your telephone is bugged.' Well, I didn't need to be told that.

We had a discussion about whether we should withhold credentials from the journalists of Westminster Press, who are in dispute with the NUJ in Northampton. We decided to defer that too.

Then a letter from Jim about the Common Market was put before us and we were given a moment to read it. Jim said, 'The document is my responsibility and, although it is based on an all-day Cabinet in July, the Cabinet has not yet seen it. My object is to marry some extreme views. I have put forward six criteria for judging the Community and I suggest we develop the policy along these lines, to be discussed at a meeting after Conference.' He added that it was a response to the NEC document, and that he was asking only for a discussion at this stage, and not for a decision.

After some discussion, Jim said, 'Well, I am only trying to get us together.' He is very clever, but it is at least a step in the right direction because now we have something to build on.

Then we came on to speakers. Michael would speak on 'The Next Three Years', I would address the campaign document on Monday, and Judith would speak on the economic strategy.

Mik thought Barbara should also speak, as she was chairman of the Financial and Economic Committee, so it was agreed that in the two major debates Barbara would speak on Monday morning and I would speak on Monday afternoon. Later, Michael was switched to the Common Market.

I had lunch with Barbara and we divided up the work. She will do a speech on economic strategy and prices in which she can be very critical of the Treasury, and I will do unemployment and industrial democracy.

From 4 till 5.30 I had tea with Julia Langdon of *Labour Weekly* and gave her all the material on the *Times* story about one of my children receiving private medical treatment. I told her that it had originated in the European Movement office. She took down the details. We moved on to the whole security business and what Wilson was up to.

The first twenty-four hours in Brighton have been great fun, but I do increasingly see Jim as the Godfather with his Mafia, and to beat him you have to play it absolutely square.

I feel more encouraged because I believe that the heart of the Party is beating strongly and that the leadership is what is defective. But then it always has been. The difference is that the trade unions and the rank and file are stronger than they ever have been and that is why the Tories have got to try to get us out; they can't be sure that, if we return to power, we won't do what we have always said we'd do. They know that it is only a thin veneer of right-wing leadership that protects them from the full weight and decency and radicalism of the labour movement.


# NOTES
*Chapter Two*


1.   (p. 98) Jet (Joint European Torus) was a European Community project to develop nuclear energy for western Europe through thermonuclear fusion. Although the research was done at Culham, near Oxford, the European Council could not decide where the reactor should be sited and this continually held up progress. The UK, France and West Germany all wanted it. The project was eventually sited at Culham.

2.   (p. 145) The *Daily Mail* of 19 May 1977 published a letter from Lord Ryder, Chairman of the National Enterprise Board, to British Leyland's Chief Executive, Alex Park, referring to a special account for securing contracts in the Middle East. The letter, dated October 1976, mentioned Eric Varley, Secretary of State for Industry.

The NEB denied that any such letter had been sent, and two days later the *Daily Mail* announced that a financial analyst with British Leyland, Graham Barton, had admitted forging the letter. An unreserved apology to Ryder, Park and Varley was published. Barton was subsequently charged with forgery.

3.   (p. 172) Grunwick Film Processing Laboratories in North London employed a mainly female Asian workforce at two factories. The factories were non-unionised in 1976 and pay was low. In August that year, a strike occurred in support of the refusal by one worker to do *compulsory* overtime and the strikers joined the clerical union, APEX, which made it an official dispute,

whereupon the company sacked 137 people involved. The strike thus became a dispute about union recognition, the company refusing to accept the workers' rights, and went on for over a year. It attracted enormous support and mass picketing from other unions and Labour MPs, and the attention of the right-wing National Association for Freedom, which backed the company.

Despite the support and the basic principle being fought under a Labour Government, the strike was a failure. The employer refused to co-operate with ACAS under the 1974 Trade Union and Labour Relations Act and nothing could be done under existing legislation to force the company to accept the workers' rights.

4. (p. 184) The white Government in Rhodesia declared independence (UDI) from Britain in 1965. Since then guerrilla warfare had been escalating. By the end of 1976 the Rhodesian Prime Minister Ian Smith had accepted black majority rule in principle but no settlement had been agreed with the leaders of the black nationalist movements – notably Robert Mugabe of ZANU and Joshua Nkomo of ZAPU. Together they had formed the Patriotic Front, which was committed to maintaining the guerrilla war until a real transfer of power from whites to blacks had been carried out.

After UDI, the British Labour Government had instituted a number of sanctions against the Smith regime. Included was the prohibition of oil exports, but this was repeatedly violated by subsidiaries of British oil companies operating through South Africa and Mozambique. In May 1977 the Bingham Inquiry was set up to look into 'sanctions busting', and a report published in 1978 was highly critical of the oil companies concerned (see chapter 4).

# 3
# The Calm before the Storm
## October 1977–August 1978

Denis Healey was interviewed by Brian Walden on *The World This Weekend*. Denis is radiating the approval of the world bankers (for a disastrous policy). He now says they have got such confidence in him that he is the one who is going to pull us all through.

National Executive at 2.30, and there was a tremendous discussion on abortion. The first composite motion required the Party to be clearly pro-abortion. Joyce Gould was terrified that we were going to go against abortion but the resolution in support of the status quo was carried by 31 to 3. We agreed unanimously not to impose a three-line whip on Members. The principle of automatic reselection of MPs was carried by 15 to 13. On nuclear weapons, there was a vote of 13 to 12 against the unilateralist resolution. I actually abstained on that one.

*Monday 3 October*
Conference opened. Denis was called in the economy debate and spoke for ten minutes, then Barbara wound up. She may not be at the next Conference and won't be in the next Parliament so it could be her last Conference speech. She was so keen and spoke skilfully, with passion and fire, but it didn't lift the Conference – I don't think anything could have done. Ted Castle is dying, I'm afraid – he looks terribly ill.

After lunch I dealt with the Chancellor's dilemma. He was in effect saying that under capitalism you couldn't do better than we had done. I argued that we needed structural change if we were to make progress.

But it didn't come over well. I must record that Hilary was shocked, Stephen didn't like it and Caroline was appalled, so I can't pretend it was a success. The fact that Jim came up and said, 'Congratulations, that was a real leadership speech', didn't exactly please me. I think the left were very disappointed.

*Tuesday 4 October*
NEC elections. Peter Shore did well and David Owen moved up. I came first, though with a drop of 26,000.

Jim made a long and clever speech. He attacked the Tories, came out in favour of racial equality, talked about Rhodesia. Then, having got a warm response, he gave us the same old economic nonsense that we had had from Denis, only in a rather more discreet form. He got a standing ovation.

*Wednesday 5 October*
Heard Dennis Skinner telling Frances and Francis and Brian Sedgemore what a lousy speech I had made. I said, 'Well, my family agree with you about that.' He was taken aback. They all thought it was an absolutely appalling speech.

Tribune meeting and I got on to the platform just as Mrs Desai, the woman leading the Grunwick strike, was getting a tremendous reception.

*Thursday 6 October*
*Labour Weekly* came out today with a marvellous account by Julia Langdon on the private medical treatment story, exposing all the lies.

I was just leaving the hotel to go to the Conference when I saw a huge crowd of police and photographers. I asked them what was happening and was told that Mitterrand was arriving. Then one of the French journalists came up and said, 'Who is meeting him?' I nipped into the hotel to find out and there was Jenny Little alone, so I stood with her.

Five minutes later his car drew up and I greeted Mitterrand, who was wearing a light fawn corduroy suit, and Robert Pontillon, the International Secretary of the French Socialist Party. I walked with him to the Conference chamber. He came on to the platform and, without notes, delivered a twenty-five-minute speech which was translated for the audience.

It was friendly and intimate: we don't like the French and I certainly don't like Mitterrand, but I must say it was a very clever speech. He is quite unlike Helmut Schmidt, who is breezy and speaks perfect English.

*Friday 7 October*
Last day of Conference. Apparently Edna Healey and Evelyn Jones had a discussion on Monday – which Caroline heard – over the fact that Jack Jones had criticised Labour Ministers for expensive living.

Although on the face of it Jim has got his way, in fact he has failed entirely to change the Executive. Radical motions were carried, and the vitality of the Party is phenomenal.

*Several potentially serious disputes involving the Government occurred in late 1977 and early 1978, foreshadowing the so-called 'Winter of Discontent' a year later. An unofficial stoppage in early November at power stations in the Midlands and Yorkshire brought the workforce into conflict both with their employer (the CEGB), which was responsible to me, and with the official union hierarchy. The power workers were eventually offered an average rise of 17 per cent.*

*This stoppage was followed by the first national strike of firemen (as firefighters were then invariably called), who were asking for a pay rise and a reduction of weekly working hours to forty-two. Army units were mobilised to maintain a fire service by a Government which saw its 10 per cent pay rise limit failing. A number of other pay settlements during the first six months of 1978 severely tested the credibility of the Government's pay policy.*

*The Government's policy was also conducted through a 'black list' of businesses and organisations which gave their workforces rises over the 10 per cent limit, by withholding contracts and/or financial assistance to them where it was possible. This strategy of 'pay sanctions' caused great tensions with the employers and unions and as in the case of Ford Motors was ineffective and untenable.*

### Sunday 9 October

There was an account in the papers of how Henry Ford agreed to Jim Callaghan's request to site Ford's engine plant at Bridgend, South Wales – which explains why the pay policy could not be applied to Ford.

Melissa and I went out for a two-hour walk and we had a lovely talk. She has terrific admiration for Caroline: Melissa is a serious feminist.

To the Harts' for dinner with the Foots and the Booths. Judith described her meeting with the Cabinet Secretary Sir John Hunt, held at Jim's request, about the security services' supposed confusion between her and Mrs J. Tudor Hart. Sir John Hunt confirmed that there had been a mix-up, and I said I didn't think that likely because the security services did a very thorough job.

Michael said, 'I sat with the Prime Minister when Judith was reappointed in March, and the security services did raise some objection.' He said Jim was good on security matters; an inquiry into the Wilson bugging story would not be helpful, but Jim was not against a general look at the problem at an appropriate time.

After dinner we discussed pay policy and I said I thought that the sanctions on firms to restrict wage rises were illegal, that they were acts of impropriety, that they were not effective or credible and would be politically dangerous.

Michael just blew his top and shouted, 'You just want us to go back to inflation. Face the real problems – you have got to help the lower paid.' He was red with anger.

Judith mentioned our industrial policy.

'I'm not against that,' said Michael. 'That's different.'

'It isn't different,' I said. 'If you want to get pay agreement and understanding about pay, you have got to implement the industrial policy.'

Jill rebuked Michael for being so excitable.

### Monday 10 October

Reg Prentice had wide coverage for his attack on the Labour Party and his decision to cross the floor to the Tories.

### Tuesday 11 October

Cabinet, to go through the Queen's Speech. We were told that devolution and the referendum and European direct elections were going to occupy most of the new session.

There was *nothing* about full employment in the draft speech, and I raised this. So a change was made, adding something about the Government regarding the return to full employment as being of great importance. But we don't think of full employment now. We have actually dropped it as an objective.

### Wednesday 12 October

At 4.30 to the Economic and Industrial Committee (EI) of Cabinet, which Eric Varley now chairs, after I had made an appeal for a non-Treasury chairman. We had to decide on the future of the KME co-operative at Kirkby. There was the usual Department of Industry argument from Alan Williams – it wasn't viable, it would cost money, and so on. He said he regretted this but it was a loss.

I was there to defend KME because I had set it up as Industry Minister, and I said we had been around the course before and Whitehall had always been against it.

Eric Varley remarked, 'We gave a pledge that our grant to KME was a once and for all payment', to which I replied that Cabinet had forced me to say that when I was Secretary of State, and they never say that to private companies.

Michael Foot was more sympathetic to my view, as was Harold Walker. But I was defeated. I must say, if we lose the devolution bill because the Merseyside MPs are so angry about KME, it would bloody well serve the Government right. Whitehall has been determined to kill KME off, and we are a most unsympathetic, unimaginative Government.

### Thursday 13 October

A most revealing Cabinet. First Jim told us that the balance of payments and the retail price index figures out tomorrow were good.

We then had a brief discussion about the Ford pay settlement. Jim thought it would be 14 per cent, while Denis estimated 12.5 per cent, but Jim said it was important not to admit that this was a defeat. Jim is not prepared to use sanctions against Ford, no doubt because of the deal he did with them on the Bridgend plant.

We came on to a long debate about the economic situation. Denis had prepared three scenarios in which he touched on the possibility of public expenditure increases, tax cuts, and various ways of handing out £1 billion this year, £1 billion in the spring and £1 billion next year. He said we were facing the problems of success.

I said I didn't share this wildly optimistic view. When it came to the IMF calling for reflation, it was a bit like Len Murray calling for wage cuts – the situation had to be pretty serious. The public expenditure cuts of last December had had no effect as yet, and our financial recovery was due to oil revenues and hot money coming in as a result of good housekeeping by the IMF. But the underlying position was still very serious and the reflation proposal was inadequate.

Eric Varley was vicious. 'Pay is the key. We can see the public sector being discriminated against under the arrangements. I cannot understand some people. Tony wanted a spring Election *this* year – now he talks about going on for eighteen months.' That was a reference to my opposing the Lib–Lab Pact.

'I didn't say that,' I replied.

Jim intervened. 'Anyone can change their minds. We must play it long. We don't have to decide today.' He said income tax cuts were probably helpful, but he had doubts about VAT. The thing that really worried him was whether higher public expenditure would affect confidence. 'There has been a tremendous attack on public expenditure and we must roll with the punch a bit' – by which he meant capitulate to Tory pressure. He said the Government's standing had increased enormously and that was the most important thing.

At 2.30 I had a meeting with some German bankers and industrialists, who wanted to talk about our energy policy. They asked about nuclear power, about coal, oil and the oil trade, and energy forecasting. One of them asked, 'Is there any likelihood of further nationalisation in Britain or are you going to maintain the market economy?'

I told them I couldn't say as yet but that the most successful sectors of industry were those where the investment was going in on public account.

I noticed that they were all older than me, so most of them were probably involved in some way in the Nazi war machine. They were absolutely hypnotised by my red banners which said, 'He who would be free must strike the blow' and 'Labour means unity and strength'. Seeing trade union banners hanging in a Minister's office was hairraising for them.

Rushed over to Number 10 for the GEN 12 Cabinet Committee on the South African and Rhodesian policy. I am only invited when oil is involved. The first question was on sanctions. A paper from the secretariat pointed out that we had enormous trading and investment interests in South Africa and concluded that the best way of influencing South Africa was not by sanctions but by a code of conduct for their industries agreed by the EEC.

David Owen favoured a code of conduct. Pressure was building up and we must stick with the nine, but the Americans were less anxious to pursue their policy on South Africa than when Carter was first elected.

'If the Americans are backing off, where will that leave us?' asked Edmund Dell.

Jim said, 'What are our objectives in South Africa? Do we want to end apartheid? Do we want one man one vote?'

Judith warned that we had better be ready for a crisis.

I pointed out the weakness and hypocrisy of the paper's argument. 'If we say we are so deeply involved that we can't do anything without damaging ourselves, then that has the merit of credibility. But if we say we want to remain involved in order to influence them from the inside, it isn't credible – people won't believe that that is our reason – and it is incompatible with saying that we should phase out our connections.'

*Friday 14 October*
To the office at 10.45, and Frances Morrell and James Bretherton had prepared a statement on the working document on energy policy for presentation to the press this morning.

It had become clear yesterday that the real issue was whether the Department had failed to inform me of the significance of the fall in fuel demand forecasts and were trying to put a pistol to my head on the decisions that would have to be taken, notably on the fast breeder reactor. So Frances and James, at my instigation, had prepared this alternative paper arguing that our position was easier and therefore we had more time to consider these important decisions.

At 11 the Department came in for the final briefing and we had a flaming row. They were extremely critical of the press statement and insisted that the figures were wrong. Philip Jones said that Hutber (from the statistics division) was a very valuable member of the staff but that his forecasts were only desk forecasts and were inaccurate because they related to quite different factors. Hutber just dug his toes in. 'These are correct: there will be a 10 per cent fall in demand and I stick to that figure.'

Then Jones attacked Frances Morrell, saying she had no right to talk to junior officials in the Department. It was the most amazing episode.

I said, 'Well, I'm awfully sorry, but I don't feel that the significance of this has been drawn sufficiently to my attention and I'm not prepared to shift from what I wish to say. This is a political decision.'

It was really open government beginning to bite, challenging the old idea that Ministers are there to give publicity to what officials say and not to question their assumptions. There are many forecasts and ranges of choices available, and open government is designed to bring them to light. For the first time I felt I had begun to get control of the core of policy-making in the Department of Energy.

After this unpleasant preliminary, I went down to the big conference room where all the energy correspondents had gathered to hear my statement. I was closely cross-examined.

*Saturday 15 October*
Mrs Thatcher's speech at the Tory Conference yesterday was reported in the papers. She had attacked me, and others, for having attended a public school and said that it was the direct grant schools that had given people of her class an opportunity which they would not otherwise have had. It was a very subtle argument. She did well and encouraged the Conference, though the reality is that the Tories are deeply worried that they might not win the next Election.

Caroline's birthday, and we had a lovely tea party at home.

Bing Crosby died today.

*Sunday 16 October*
I have found a new way of living with the problems that face me as a member of the Cabinet. So long as I don't criticise the Cabinet or Government policy, I am free to argue the socialist case – as if socialism were a hobby like ballet or cricket. So now I just put the Government entirely on one side and analyse the situation and argue for socialism.

*Monday 17 October*
At 7.45 Geoffrey Goodman came for the evening. Mike Molloy, editor of the *Daily Mirror,* is struggling to keep it a serious paper but the circulation battle is hotting up to the point where they just have to print any sort of trash: their circulation is indeed now increasing.

We talked about the Fleet Street Forum of Socialist Journalists in the Fifties, which Geoffrey, James Cameron, Kingsley Martin, Tom Hopkinson and others joined to provide an opportunity for the exchange of news that the newspapers wouldn't print. They invited speakers including Bertie Russell, who talked about the bomb. The Forum was eventually broken up after the journalists were threatened with dismissal. Geoffrey had received a phone call at the time from someone he understood to be a security man, who said, 'If you go on with the Forum, you are going to find it very hard to get work.'

Geoffrey told me he had had a third burglary in his house. They stole a portable television set and a brooch, but left money, and all his papers had been gone through. He is certain it was political. He thought they'd been in the house for about six hours and probably photographed some of his papers. They also stole a miner's lamp given to him by the South Wales miners.

We talked about the Tory Conference. He said that under Thatcher Toryism had a flavour of Nuremburg about it and he feared that the swing to the right would be terrifying.

I like Geoffrey very much; in many ways I find myself more in sympathy with him than with almost anyone else in Fleet Street – or in the Government.

### Wednesday 19 October
Eric Lubbock, now Liberal spokesman on energy in place of Jo Grimond, came to see me.* James Bretherton sat in and I went over my legislative programme. He seemed quite content.

Eric takes roughly my view on energy policy. He's not in favour of an all-out attack on nuclear power but he thinks it should make up a smaller part of our programme than my Department wants.

I asked James to leave and then questioned Eric privately about how he saw the Lib–Lab Pact. He felt it was going well and that we must keep Thatcher out. He hadn't really got many ideas about how things would develop. I gave him an outline of the fundamental reforms I felt were needed. He is an electrical engineer, a quiet, decent chap, one of those rare animals, an engineer with a social conscience; but he's not very political.

At 12.45 I went to the Penthouse Suite of the Dorchester Hotel where Rawleigh Warner, the Chairman of Mobil Oil – one of the largest oil companies in the world – was holding a lunch party.

Over lunch I talked to Warner, who is a cultivated man, and asked him about Carter. 'Carter's an enigma,' he said. 'Nobody understands him, and that's one of the reasons why American business is not investing.' He gave me an insight into how American business sees Carter, and he felt that Americans should be subjected to the same remedies as the IMF had imposed on us, namely cuts in public expenditure.

Came home. Caroline had been on a deputation today with Joan Lestor and others to see Ministers at the DES about Shirley Williams's new Education Bill. She has been co-opted on to the NEC Education and Science Subcommittee.

Caroline directed her critique at the folly of the new objectives in

* Eric Lubbock was Liberal MP for Orpington from 1962 to 1970. In 1971 he inherited the title Lord Avebury.

local authority allocations. She pointed out that local authorities were now busy developing an educational system at secondary level which was non-selective in character and interconnected various schools in order to maintain and develop a comprehensive system. She said that Shirley's Education Bill would make educational allocation subject to a number of factors, including the ability of the child. In short, the bill would bring selection back into education.

*Thursday 20 October*
Cabinet at 9.30.

The Education Bill issue was raised by Shirley. She said that every other bill that people wanted was included in the Queen's Speech except hers, which would be popular.

Since Caroline had said that it was contrary to the whole tradition of allocation and would create chaos in the local authorities, I decided to make a move. 'Prime Minister, I think this is going to be a very controversial bill as far as the Party is concerned.'

'Absolutely untrue,' said Shirley.

I went on, 'I am not arguing the case now but I think it ought to come to Cabinet.'

Shirley said that it had been to the Home Affairs Committee of the Cabinet and no one had raised any query – to which I replied that I wasn't a member of that committee.

'If Tony wants to raise it in Cabinet, he is entitled to do so,' said Jim.

So I stopped the bill from going into the Queen's Speech – not that I think it would have gone in anyway, but I may have helped to kill it. I wrote a note to Roy Hattersley suggesting we have a word about it and he nodded.

On defence expenditure, a rise of 3 per cent had been proposed which would contrast with an average 2.5 per cent for other increases in the coming year. Joel pointed out that it was against Party policy, and Jim suggested we discuss it fully at the Defence and Overseas Policy Committee and come back to Cabinet if need be.

At one stage I asked if we could have tea. 'We always have tea when we discuss public expenditure.'

'No,' said Jim, 'we only have tea when we discuss cuts.'

'I'm not sure there's much difference,' I replied. So we did have tea and I got my large blue and white mug.

We accepted Jim's final proposals – £100 million extra for construction, making £400 million in all; £20 million for aid; £10 million for education; and £20 million for the DHSS – with discussions to be resumed on Monday.

At 3.15 I had a visit from the Russian Minister for the Gas Industry, an Azerbaijani in his mid-sixties. He presented me with a beautiful tea set and I insisted that our tea be made with it. I drank from the large sugar basin rather than a cup and he laughed. It was very friendly and I am keen for my relations with Russia to be cordial. As I walked out with him, I told him they had a very good Ambassador in London. 'Anybody can be a good Ambassador,' he said, 'but he is also a good man.'

### Saturday 22 October
Apparently Ernest Wistrich of the European Movement is in an absolute panic about the discovery that the postcards spreading the false story about the private medical treatment came from his office. He had written to the *Guardian* to get hold of a copy of one of the cards.

### Monday 24 October
Cabinet at 3.

Denis introduced his measures on tax and increases in public expenditure.

Then we came on to pay policy. I was a bit sleepy and just dozing off, when I heard Eric Varley say something about the miners. Here was an ex-miner asking when Tony Benn was going to speak up in favour of the productivity scheme which is going to a miners' ballot. It was critical for the survival of the Government, he said; it would make him unpopular with McGahey and Scargill, but it had to be done. It was a violent speech full of alarmist rubbish.

After Roy Mason had spoken, I responded. 'Look, I have taken a lot of trouble to find out what is the right thing to do. I have consulted the miners' conference, discussed it with the Coal Board, with the NUM and Lawrence Daly, and the unanimous view is that it would be counter-productive for us to intervene. If there is a different view I shall look at it.'

'I take it that Tony wants this productivity scheme to go through,' said Eric Varley. Jim assumed that I did.

'Then you, Jim, had better consult Lawrence Daly,' said Eric – which Jim agreed to do.

Varley is like a bear with a sore head. I realised I was being set up to make a statement so I handed a note over to Roy Mason asking for his advice. He said, 'It depends on Lawrence Daly, but if the Government has to intervene it might be worth your considering a comment on the future of coal and investment, making clear that the miners are our friends, or the PM might say something and over-egg the pudding.'

I had to leave for Luxembourg and Number 10 wanted me to ring from Heathrow. When I rang, Jim had spoken to Lawrence Daly, who said it was absolutely right that I make a statement, and soon.

Alex Eadie, who was with me, said, 'They've set you up and it will do you a great deal of damage.' In the plane, with Alex's help, I drafted a statement which said that the productivity scheme would recommend itself to miners on three grounds: it avoided the evils of the past, it was against a background of expanding coal and it would provide cash; and I hoped and believed that the miners would give it a trial.

The statement was put out the following morning, after checking it with Lawrence Daly and Derek Ezra, and with Number 10, who grumbled that it wasn't strong enough. It was also made clear that I was available to do broadcasts. In fact, there wasn't the remotest bit of interest.

On arrival in Luxembourg I was taken to see Ray Vouel, the Luxembourg Commissioner for Competition Policy, and we again discussed the interest relief grant scheme, which the Commission is trying to stop. The scheme allows firms in Scotland to borrow money slightly below the going rate for equipment for the North Sea oil industry.

I went over the arguments, particularly in relation to the severe unemployment in Scotland, but he just went on about the Treaty being against discrimination, and so on. I felt again that we were a prisoner of all this Treaty theology.

In the end, I had to agree because I had been ordered to do so by the Cabinet committee, but I wanted a transitional period of one year.

'That's not good enough,' he said. 'There may be questions in the European Parliament.'

'Maybe,' I replied, 'but I have jobs in Scotland to consider.' Alex and Frances were boiling with rage, as I was. It was disgusting to see capitalist principles written into our constitution. I could hardly contain my anger.

We went back to the Holiday Inn and went over it all again.

*Tuesday 25 October*
The Research Council began at 10.15 and after long discussions Henri Simonet, the Belgian Foreign Minister, said, 'I ask you to take note of the fact that there is a 5 to 2 preference for siting Jet at Culham, with two abstentions, one of which will rally to the majority. Accordingly the Jet site will be in Culham.' So that was satisfying.

I loathe the Common Market. It's bureaucratic and centralised, there's no political discussion, officials control Ministers, and it just has a horrible flavour about it. But of course it is really dominated by Germany. All the Common Market countries except Britain have been occupied by Germany, and they have this mixed feeling of hatred and subservience towards the Germans. It is such a complex, psychological relationship. But our self-confidence is flowing back now.

*Thursday 27 October*

At 11.15 the Cabinet met. Jim referred to the mini-Budget, congratulated Denis, and reiterated that there would be no early Election.

We discussed South Africa. After the clampdown by Vorster, the Africans now want to go for a Chapter 7 Determination, which is a UN Charter provision allowing for mandatory sanctions to be imposed where there is a threat to world peace and security. The Americans are prepared to go along with this, if the mandatory sanctions are limited to military supplies.

Jim said, 'This is very serious indeed. We have a £2 billion investment in South Africa, £700 million worth of exports there every year, and about 100,000 jobs at stake here. Is there anyone in the Cabinet who would support the idea that we veto a Chapter 7 Determination alone?'

Nobody spoke.

He continued, 'The situation is not painless and we will have to act with others. If they pass the resolution, we will have to decide what to do in the light of what others do.'

David Owen feared a Chapter 7 Determination with full economic sanctions.

Peter Shore insisted, 'We really must define arms-related products, because jobs are involved; we have to be careful not to continue selling minor products and lie just the wrong side of the borderline as the world sees it. We don't want to lose jobs *and* get all the moral odium.'

I said, 'I take it there would be consultation before the United Kingdom contemplated any unilateral veto.'

Jim agreed.

Then David Owen referred to the Common Market business and the victory on Jet.

I thanked Jim for what he had done, and said I hoped Gerald Kaufman would be specially recognised for his fantastic job as Chairman of the Research Council last March, since Jet might otherwise have gone to Germany.

Then we came on to an extraordinary joint paper called 'The Wider Implications of the Industrial Strategy', which Denis Healey and Eric Varley had prepared for the NEDC. In effect it said the country was no good, and listed detailed points, most of which reflected Tory criticism of Labour policy.

Denis said, 'I hope we can settle this today because we have softened it as much as we can.'

Edmund Dell raised the British attitude to industry. 'The truth is that a whole generation of graduates have concluded that making profits is bad – we have got to get them to change that attitude.'

I said the paper provided a useful checklist but I was uneasy about the tone of its introductory remarks. It was just another public wringing of hands by the establishment, particularly the phrase 'the best of our national talent has been brought up to believe that it is not nice to dirty our hands at the workbench'. This was simply the establishment claiming that *it* was the best talent. It didn't ring true because it ignored our basic philosophy.

'After all,' I said, 'if graduates don't believe that profits are the beginning and end of life, it's because we as a Party have taught them that. We believe that an unequal and divided society is incapable of maintaining full employment. When I read in the paper that Britain is "effete and wrong-headed", I look at Germany or America and the state they are in, and it makes me wonder whether we shouldn't have a moratorium on masochism. It's like the Think Tank. First they suggest that the BBC Overseas Services are not worth having, then it's the boilermaking industry, and so on. We ought to have more self-confidence.'

In the end, the whole paper was sent back to be redrafted.

As I left the Cabinet, Fred Peart came up and said how much he agreed with my attack on parental choice in the Education Bill.

In the papers today, there was a report of a radio broadcast in Scotland by the Duke of Edinburgh in which he warned of a bureaucratic Britain in the year 2000 – an absolute party political on behalf of Mrs Thatcher, delivered with all the authority that comes from the Prince Consort. It was an interesting example of the way in which the royal family and the establishment have turned the Jubilee celebrations to good account; having established the royal family's popularity with the public, they are now trying to ensure that the royal family's view is thrown behind Mrs Thatcher.

*Saturday 29 October*
There are problems at the moment with Dick Mabon's visit to Australia. He is over there with Jack Rampton heading a delegation to discuss the possibility of Britain buying uranium for our nuclear programme. It is a very delicate mission and before he left I warned him not to get involved in Australian domestic politics because the Australian labour movement is against the mining and export of uranium. I also urged him, if an Election was called over there, as rumoured, to come back at once so as not to get tied up in it.

In the paper this morning, however, I read that he had made a statement at a press conference saying that the Labour Government wanted the uranium and that we hoped to persuade our Australian Labour colleagues to let us have it.

The Deputy Leader of the Australian Labour Party has complained bitterly that Dick Mabon is interfering in their domestic political affairs, and on the eve of a General Election that is a very serious matter.

I asked James Bretherton to get him to come home, but Bretherton said, 'He's gone to the Snowy Mountains for the weekend, and he's coming back through Singapore and Thailand.'

I feel really sickened by it because I don't want to damage the Australian Labour Party. I don't want to repudiate Dick, but nor can I be responsible for what he does.

*Sunday 30 October*
To the Foots' for dinner with the Shores and the Booths. We got talking about diaries, notably Dick Crossman's, volume 3 of which has just been published. The general view was that Dick had shown himself up in a bad light with all these criticisms of his colleagues.

The question came up whether it was immoral to write a diary and record what people said. I said I thought it was not a matter of whether it was published. It was the malice, not the leaking, that was unattractive, and having the record was valuable. I made one or two points about the lessons I had learned from 1968, which I could recall clearly with the help of my diary.

Jill said she had read Dick's diary twice, thought it was marvellous and would not wish for it not to have been written. Michael was ambivalent about it. I think they rather disapproved of me because, of course, they knew that I would come home and dictate what was said in my diary.

After dinner we went upstairs, and Michael, standing by the fireplace, said he wanted to tell us something. We sat round and listened. 'I've seen Jim a couple of times about the direct elections and he's absolutely determined that, *this* session, the Queen's Speech will commit members of the Cabinet to vote for direct elections. I've tried very hard but I'm afraid I haven't succeeded. I thought I ought to tell you.'

I said, 'Well, it's not on to ask Cabinet Ministers to destroy their credibility by voting against their own convictions – expressed so recently in July. It just isn't necessary, and we are talking about something which could replace our Parliament with a European Parliament. It is a gateway to federalism, and it's just not on. Jim will have to understand that.'

Peter hummed and hawed for a moment and then remarked, 'It's not possible.'

Albert was silent, so Jill turned to me. 'If you resign from the Government, you'll bring it down.'

'Who said anything about resigning?'

'If you won't vote for it,' said Michael, 'that's the equivalent of resignation.'

Peter and Liz drove me home and we went over it all again. Peter reiterated his view that Jim might think it was worth a few resignations – nobody was indispensable – and that I could very soon sink without any trace at all.

I told him I wouldn't plead with Jim for my job or my life, and if Jim were to tell me that Ministers were required to support the second reading of the bill I would refuse, on the grounds that it was contrary to the decision of Conference, which was opposed to direct elections, and contrary to the majority of the Parliamentary Labour Party, which had either abstained or voted against the bill; that the votes were not necessary because it would succeed anyway, that it would destroy the credibility of those who voted against their known convictions, and that for me, therefore, it was not a discussable proposition.

Maybe Jim will call for resignations over this. Since that could be as early as Tuesday, I could have only forty-eight hours left in the Government. It's going to be pretty rough. It might run to 17 November, when the second reading comes up, but if Jim does announce his position on Tuesday and say he'll leave us to think it over, then there will have to be massive canvassing of other Ministers who take this view, and we'll see where we are.

### Monday 31 October
Caroline came back from another meeting at the Department of Education. They don't really understand the bill she is promoting, and Caroline and her colleagues – Tyrrell Burgess of the ILEA, Chris Price [MP for Lewisham West] and Joan Lestor – understand it much better. At the meeting, Tyrrell Burgess summed it up by telling Margaret Jackson that twelve years' work on comprehensive education was being jeopardised in weeks by the legislation to return to selective education. I think the Education Bill has been killed off.

### Tuesday 1 November
America, France and Britain vetoed the proposal at the United Nations to impose full economic sanctions against South Africa. At least we weren't alone, but it's no good pretending our action is in the best interests of South Africa; it is purely that we have so many investments there.

My first meeting was the Cabinet committee considering nuclear proliferation, GEN 74. Sir Hermann Bondi reported on the studies that are taking place in Washington, where he is, very competently, representing the British Government. He recommended a study group under him, but Robert Press of the Cabinet Office said he hoped this wouldn't weaken the role of the interdepartmental official committee on nuclear policy.

'The more I think about this whole problem,' I said, 'the more it seems to me that safeguards are just a form of monitoring. There are no real safeguards, no real security, and the whole nuclear business makes proliferation easier. We ought to have a report from the Foreign Office on all potential customers for any nuclear technology so that we can assess both the political motives of these countries and their technical capability to produce nuclear weapons. This is the best way of maintaining a credible international position.'

I told the committee that I had recently refused to approve something going to South Africa on these grounds, and that it was really a political assessment.

Hermann Bondi said that the Germans, though prepared at the moment not to be a nuclear weapons state, might be uneasy if, for example, Zambia or Saudi Arabia acquired nuclear weapons. The Germans would not accept discrimination that made them second-class citizens.

I said that this problem had arisen over the Jet fusion project; the Germans wanted to be considered suitable for the Jet project because they were not prepared to be discriminated against, and Jet had no military potential.

Victor Macklen, acting chief scientist of the Ministry of Defence, disagreed. 'Some of the fusion work does have military potential.'

That was news to me. 'Well,' I said, 'I was never told, and I am afraid I have misinformed the Cabinet as a result.'

We came on to transport of nuclear material: inside this country we have armed guards, but internationally we send plutonium by air in freight planes or sometimes by ship, in containers welded to the deck, and there is the risk of hijacking. It was agreed that we should look again at the safety of international transport of nuclear materials.

What transpired from the meeting, apart from the revelation that there is a military potential in some fusion work, was that what we call safeguards are not safeguards at all. Very important.

At 11 Michael Meacher came in with Frances and we had a talk. He is anxious to influence people by having conferences and weekly meetings to get a different stream of analysis across.

While we were talking, the results of the NUM ballot came in, and it was 110,600 against the productivity scheme and 87,400 in favour, a substantial majority against. I heard later that it was much worse than Joe Gormley had expected.

At 2 Lord Aldington of the National Nuclear Corporation and Ned Franklin of the Nuclear Power Company came to discuss the proposals for a deal with Iran on the pressurised water reactor. The astonishing suggestion is that we set up a joint company from which the Iranians would order PWRs, provided that Britain adopted the PWR and ordered two. Thereafter the Iranians would own half of the NNC, producing fast breeders which would be available for export. Iran would order up to fifteen fast breeders if we also ordered fifteen. The more I listened, the more the idea of a lifelong partnership with Iran became unattractive.

In the middle of the discussion I was called out to have a quick word with Joe Gormley about the NUM ballot. He said, 'Just leave it at the moment. It will go back into negotiation and that is the beginning and end of it.' I decided not to make a statement.

I am now locked into an extremely difficult situation and there are many who will greatly enjoy the sight of me engaged in a fight with the miners; I am determined to avoid that. I can't run away at this stage, although it is tempting to do so. To be candid, it is tempting just to break with the Government because the policy is so awful, but I think I have to fight with an entirely different objective and spirit.

I said to Jim tonight that I thought the trade unions were our friends, to which he replied, 'Ah, I don't know about that. A lot of them are Tories.' He also has this idea that they are trying to bring down the Government. There is nothing whatever now between Jim Callaghan and Ted Heath except that Jim has a better working relationship with the trade union leadership.

### Wednesday 2 November

When I got in this morning, there was a letter from Jim Callaghan summarising the discussion I had with him last night on the power workers' strike. I had gone along with some suspensions of power workers taking unofficial action, and he put in the letter, 'as you and I agreed that this was right'. He added that he had spoken to Frank Chapple, who also supported suspensions, though Chapple would still represent those of his members who had been suspended. Chapple hoped that the electricity industry would consider the possibility of concentrating the power cuts in Yorkshire, where much of the strike action was based – an idea which appealed to Jim as a sort of punishment of Yorkshire both for supporting Arthur Scargill and for giving birth to the power station militants. A most extraordinary procedure.

Last week I had a message from Jim saying the power cuts had affected a hospital, and would I report to him on the matter. After a lot of enquiries, the incident was traced to Great Ormond Street Children's Hospital, where Audrey Callaghan works as a health visitor. Apparently she was there last week during a power blackout and had been shocked to see a child in an iron lung being kept alive by hand pumping. But it turned out that this particular power cut had been due to a fire at the local sub-station and had nothing to do with the industrial action.

I spoke to Albert, who was worried by the extent to which the Civil Contingencies Unit was pressing him to use troops. He gave as one example the West Drayton MoD Computer Centre last week. Albert had been told that it was necessary on the grounds of national security to use troops because the centre had to be kept going at all costs. In fact, as he later discovered, the MoD computer had been out of action for a fortnight during the summer holidays and this had not endangered national security. These are interesting lessons.

To the Cabinet Office for the committee which considers pay in public industries, and Jim had asked that only the power workers be discussed, not the miners.

'The first thing we have got to do', Denis announced, 'is to support the Prime Minister in his desire to encourage the Electricity Council to suspend the workers.'

I said my view had altered. 'I have thought about it more fully and I don't think it is sensible.'

'That's intolerable,' said Denis.

'It's not intolerable to give my considered judgement. My judgement to this committee is that we should concede the workers' demand for a travel-to-work allowance tomorrow, and defer the suspensions. That's a perfectly consistent position to occupy.' Denis broke in again and I told him to stop interrupting me. 'This is my advice. Frank Chapple even suggested to Jim that we punish Yorkshire for what they had done.'

'Leave management to decide,' Eric Varley chipped in, 'and if Frank Tombs [Chairman of the Electricity Council] wants to punish Yorkshire he should.'

I said, 'Eric, it is not Frank Tombs who wants to do it, it is Frank Chapple.'

Harry Ewing, very shrewdly, advised us all to keep out of it entirely.

I summed up. 'My advice to the committee is that we should indicate that we think it would be unwise to suspend people before tomorrow's negotiation, and that we hurry up with the concession.' They refused to defer the suspensions.

I left the room after a very bloody exchange. Varley is bullying and confrontational. Albert Booth is conciliatory but puzzled and slow. Michael Foot did think it would be wiser to adopt my advice, but he was turned down.

At 8.30 tonight there was a meeting of John Silkin, Stan Orme, Peter Shore, Michael Foot and others, and Michael asked me if I would agree to abstain instead of voting against the direct elections bill. He said there would be a three-line whip.

'They just can't do it,' I replied. 'It was a free vote before.' But I told him I could live with abstention. Michael is just a dogsbody dashing between Jim and me and trying to keep the left in order.

*Friday 4 November*

This morning the headlines were hysterical. The *Financial Times* had 'Callaghan Warns of Winter Strikes; Labour Ready to Fight Unions on Pay'. The *Guardian*: 'PM Appeals for Restraint through Hard Winter'. 'I'll Stand up to Miners Says Jim' from the *Sun* and 'Lights Stay Off; Blackout Threat to Kidney Patients' in the *Daily Mirror*. The *Morning Star*: 'Power Peace Hope Fades'. The *Daily Mail*: 'We'll Fight the Strikes'. *The Times*: 'Prime Minister Appeals to the Nation for Support in Winter of Dislocation'. I set these down as the background to one of the most remarkable days that I have experienced.

Denis Healey was in the chair at the committee to discuss the power workers. I said the message on suspension that the committee had instructed me to send to the CEGB had been conveyed: that 'Ministers have noted your decision to suspend from tomorrow and have made no comment on what must be regarded as a matter for management with which the Government is not directly involved.'

I reported that negotiations had begun at the National Joint Industrial Committee yesterday on travel allowances. I pointed out that the number of stations had fallen from 270 to 130, the large power stations, particularly nuclear ones, were in remote areas, and therefore the demand for availability twenty-four hours a day, seven days a week, meant workers had to have a car. The EETPU, the TGWU, the GMWU and AUEW had come together with the Electricity Council to urge a settlement of the travel allowance problem, so we were now dealing with the official unions and the employers in agreement. The union leaders had decided to defer the issue of concessionary electricity for power workers.

I said, 'I therefore want to recommend to colleagues that we accept the union leaders' view that the claim for increased allowances and concessionary fuel will be set aside; that we agree to the travel-to-work allowances on the basis proposed; and that we support the trade union view that unofficial action should cease.'

Well, to cut a long story short, I lost the battle. But it was agreed that I should make a statement that travel allowances were compatible with Government policy within an agreed framework, namely to remote power stations. It was also agreed that I should make a statement in the House.

I tried to get Frank Chapple to come and see me but he said he was going to Ireland and would see me next Tuesday. I later discovered that he was not going to Ireland until Sunday and would be at home tonight and tomorrow.

One thing – in the House of Commons yesterday the Education Bill was referred to and Norman St John Stevas said, 'It's bad enough having Macbeth in the Cabinet but having Lady Macbeth as well!

Who's running the Department of Education, Mrs Williams or Mrs Benn?'

*Saturday 5 November*
I watched Harold Wilson and David Frost – a couple of real old performers – in a Yorkshire TV series beginning tonight called *A Prime Minister on Prime Ministers* in which Wilson talks about his predecessors. He began with Macmillan and it was so insubstantial, just vague memories and gossip. There was nothing that I couldn't have said from the top of my head without research or preparation. At the end he said that Macmillan had once offered to come back into a National Government should that be necessary.

*Monday 7 November*
The papers are full of attacks on the firemen's strike and the power workers' strike. Yet the *Daily Mirror* carried a report that Princess Anne has spent £100,000 on new stables with a swimming pool to clean her horses and special lighting and heating in the stables so that they dry off immediately after a race. This is the Britain of Jubilee year.

To the ministerial committee of the Civil Contingencies Unit, with Merlyn Rees in the chair; Albert Booth, Bill Price of the Privy Council Office and myself were the only other Ministers present. Merlyn took me into a corner of the room and said, 'We are not discussing the politics or the pay here, we are just discussing the technicalities.' That suited me fine.

I reported on the operational position, and Merlyn described the Ministry of Defence contingency plans, which provided for 6000 servicemen to be made available to the power stations on condition that they could rely on the operating staff.

Afterwards he told me that the PM wanted to see me.

At 5 we heard that an eighty-four-year-old woman had died in hospital shortly after having an operation which had been interrupted by a power cut. In fact, she had had three heart attacks, one before, one during and one after the power cut. The operation had taken place in a high-risk warning period, the stand-by generator had failed, and she had been resuscitated and died after the power had been restored.

*Tuesday 8 November*
Over to Number 10 for EY Committee. Jim took me aside before the meeting. 'I hear you're saying this is not a problem for the Government. You're not suggesting the power workers be paid?'

'Well, it wouldn't present a problem for the Government,' I said.

'But this is unofficial action.'

'Jim, are you after winning the pay policy or grinding every shop steward's face into the mud? You must leave me with some discretion on how I handle this matter. I'm trying to improve the Government's position.'

I had a message from James Bretherton that John Lyons, General Secretary of the Engineers' and Managers' Association, had rung with regard to my favouring the unofficial strikers' demand that they shouldn't lose any pay. His men have been helping to cover the strikers' work. Lyons said that, if such payments were made, his members would withdraw their support. I must say his influence throughout this dispute has been entirely unhelpful and negative.

Ronny King Murray, the Lord Advocate, had some urgent news for me. 'You are shortly going to get a memorandum on a proposed change of policy on AEA guards. It will suggest that people holding plutonium should be shot on sight. I want you to know because this will be presented to you as the view of all the law officers, but it is not my view.' I was grateful for the information.

*Wednesday 9 November*
The papers reported that the NUT had come out against Shirley Williams's bill, and the *Daily Mail* said that the PM had stepped into the power workers' dispute and got himself into a head-on conflict with his Energy Secretary.

Frances and I had a talk and came to the conclusion that a Labour Government has seven stages from what it should be to what it might become. One was a Labour Government with a socialist philosophy and a socialist programme. Two, a socialist philosophy with no programme. Three, neither philosophy nor programme but still defending working-class interests. Four, simply surviving in power. Five, surviving in power with Tory policies. Six, positively anti-working class in its approach. Finally, a Labour Government which had embraced anti-working-class Tory philosophy to justify its anti-working-class programme.

In three and a half years of Government we had declined from one to five and were now half way between having Tory policies and being anti-working class.

At 12.30 I went over to Number 10. Tom McCaffrey was with the Prime Minister and he was rather nervous. I began by telling Jim that Bruce Millan and I believed that the power workers' strike would get worse because of the attitude of the local electricity boards and that we had agreed I should manage the matter as I thought best. I hoped Jim would back that.

I wanted assurances that we were not engaged in confrontation with the trade unions; I understood the pay policy but I made it clear that I didn't want to be in a Cabinet that wished to make war on the trade union movement. Finally, the press leaks were very damaging – not that I minded the information, but it was the malice that was unpardonable. I said I wondered whether some members of the Cabinet wanted to discredit me so that I wouldn't be of any use to Jim. I had never before spoken so bluntly to him.

'Of course I am not supporting confrontation,' he said, 'but I do believe we have to mobilise public opinion against sectional interests.'

I disagreed. 'What we are doing is dealing with people with real problems and asking them to forgo their reasonable claims in the interests of the whole. That is very different from unleashing the anger of the mass on the minority.'

He said, 'Perhaps we take a different view about "unofficials"?'

'God didn't make people into officials or unofficials,' I replied. 'All I'm trying to do is keep in contact with them. We must not think that all those who appear to oppose the unofficial strike share the same interests. The press just want to whip up feeling against the trade unions. Frank Chapple's interest is to discipline his members. I'm not sure what John Lyons's interest is but I know it isn't ours. I think he just wants to make trouble and hope he'll get credit for his wage claim. As for the civil servants in my Department, they are just amused to see a rerun of the 1973–4 confrontation.'

Jim stressed the need for discipline.

'But people have got the right to know,' I said. 'Joe Ashton* made contact on my behalf with these people, and found out what the problems are, otherwise we wouldn't have known *what* was going on.'

As to the leaks, Jim thought it was 'a bit of backbiting' and we had to discourage it.

I heard later that the Tories had put down a motion calling for me to be sacked, and that Joe Ashton's resignation as a whip had been announced, so I went up and sat on the Front Bench and heard Joe make a superb speech on the power workers – quiet, factual, excellent.

*Thursday 10 November*

At Cabinet Merlyn Rees reported that he was sticking to the 10 per cent limit for the fire services; that he was issuing emergency advice to the public, that troops were standing by, and that he was considering a broadcast to the nation on Sunday night. He had set up a headquarters in the Home Office to co-ordinate voluntary work and he said we didn't need a state of emergency.

Jim announced, 'One or two members of the Cabinet have been to see me and we must not give the impression that we are against the

---

* As MP for Bassetlaw, one of the areas affected by power strikes, Joe Ashton, a Government whip, met the strikers, provoking great opposition from both the Prime Minister and the union leaders.

firemen. We must not raise public opinion against these groups. The local authorities are having talks; there is a break in the cloud and our attitude now is very important.' He reported that a public opinion poll, which was being published at noon today, showed overwhelming support for the Government.

I raised the question of our attitude to these disputes. 'I don't get very much comfort out of the poll showing support for us because, looked at another way, it could be an indication of the extent to which the public have been whipped up against the trade union movement. The press just want a rerun of the Heath crisis, and no possible good for us can come out of that.' I pointed out that the media took no notice whatever of the problems of working people until there was a strike, and then they splashed it all over their front pages in order to whip up public hatred. If anyone wanted to have an issue discussed, all they had to do was throw a brick through somebody's window.

I had a message that Len Murray wanted to have a private word with me. Just before he arrived there was a power cut, so we had to sit by candlelight in my office. We had the most remarkable conversation.

'I want to tell you, Tony, that if Joe Ashton goes to the meeting of the unofficial shop stewards tomorrow in Doncaster I shall regard it as a hostile act as far as the trade unions are concerned, and the union leaders will denounce it, because he will be encouraging unofficial strikers at a time when they must deal through their official unions.'

The candle flickered, casting mysterious shadows across the big red trade union banner behind me.

'Len, can I talk to you absolutely confidentially?'

'Certainly.'

'Let me tell you something about my difficulties. Throughout the whole of this dispute Frank Chapple has absolutely refused to come and see me. He has made no contact with me. He himself favoured the suspension and non-payment of these people and suggested to the Prime Minister that, to punish them, Yorkshire should be blacked out. His role in this has been quite incredible and I, the responsible Minister, have been quite unable to talk to the responsible trade union leader. If Joe Ashton had not gone to see the power workers – and in fact I asked him not to – I wouldn't even know what the argument was about.'

'These are important but abstract matters,' said Len.

'They are not abstract. As the Minister responsible I must know what is happening and I don't.'

He agreed that the role of the shop stewards must be considered. 'But,' he said – and this did carry some weight – 'I've got the firemen's strike coming up and this power thing must be settled.'

I said, 'You mean if Joe doesn't go tomorrow they will be isolated and crushed, and they will simply feel they have got to give up.'

'Sometimes you have to be cruel to be kind.'

So here was the General Secretary of the TUC revealing explicitly the thinking of the top trade union bureaucracy towards the rank and file. I didn't want a row with Len because he has got enough on his plate, so I agreed to pass on his advice to Joe Ashton but stressed that he would have to make up his own mind. I said I was no more responsible for Joe Ashton than he was for Frank Chapple or John Lyons.

*Saturday 12 November*

Arrived at Bristol Temple Meads at about 1.45 and went to the Folk Centre, where I found five Pakistanis in a state of great agitation.

One of them, Mohammed Ramzan, is a shopkeeper in Eastville. On 11 September an Asian restaurant in Bristol had caught fire and a number of people had been killed, including Mr Ramzan's fifteen-year-old son. At the time it was believed to be a gas explosion, and I had been to discuss it with the Gas Board Deputy Chairman in Bristol. The police, however, suspected foul play and a possible insurance fraud. The man who owned the restaurant was subsequently arrested and charged with arson and manslaughter, and the boy's body has only just been released, the police having kept it for two months in order to carry out tests for the prosecution. The family have been desperately distressed by the whole incident.

Well, Mr Ramzan sent a cable to another of his sons in Pakistan to come to the funeral. This boy, Mohammed Aslam, arrived at Heathrow on Wednesday night requesting a two-month stay for the funeral and for the Muslim memorial service which takes place forty days after the funeral. The immigration officer refused, keeping him overnight at Heathrow and releasing him on Thursday to come to Bristol for the funeral on Friday. He was ordered to be at Terminal 3 with his baggage at 8 o'clock tonight ready to return to Pakistan.

Mr Ramzan had come to see me with various leaders of the Asian community and he wept when I arrived, having tried for two days to make contact with me while I was in Manchester.

I took down the details, went into the office at the Folk Centre, telephoned the Chief Immigration Officer at Heathrow Airport, described the circumstances of the case, asked for the boy to be given extra time and was told that, provided I applied to the Private Office of the Home Secretary, they would not insist on his returning to Pakistan tonight. So I had lifted the immediate fear of deportation.

I then wrote a letter for Mr Ramzan and gave it to him so that he would have proof that the matter was in the hands of the Secretary of State pending discussions with the Home Secretary. When I went out to tell Mr Ramzan he wept again.

The harshness with which the immigration service can deal with such circumstances is terrifying.

*Monday 14 November*
On my way to work this morning, it made me sad to see the firemen picketing outside the fire station just behind the Army and Navy store in Victoria. These men of such courage, who lose a man a fortnight in fires and are paid below the national average income, are now being put in the dock. But the ones who appeared on television today, the first day of the strike, came over very well. They were asked about their consciences and they replied, 'We have got consciences but a conscience can't pay the mortgage.'

Every time they show soldiers fighting fires, it draws attention to the tremendous dangers that face firemen. I don't think the Government is going to win on this.

John Hill of the AEA came to see me and I asked him what he thought about Roy Medvedev's story. Medvedev is a Russian writer – a friend of Ken Coates – and has written some stuff about the nuclear explosion in Russia in 1957. Nobody has taken it very seriously, despite Medvedev's assertion that there was massive radiation through the explosion of radioactive waste.

John was cagey. 'We don't know very much about it but American Intelligence knew that such an incident had occurred and apparently told our Intelligence officers that it was due to an explosion in an old Stanford-type military reactor which the Russians had copied off the Americans and of which there are none in this country. It was probably due to a coolant failure. It could all be true and I will try and find out, but it is very secret.'

I am going to try to discover from our Intelligence sources what they know. Of course the reason it hasn't been widely publicised is simple: they are happy to criticise the Russians over their technical incompetence but not when it damages the case for nuclear power – that is when the technical loyalty of scientists overrides political oneupmanship. Very interesting; I'll pursue it.

I told Hill, 'I don't want to publicise it. I would just like to know.'

*Tuesday 15 November*
At 10.15 I went to the Defence and Overseas Policy Committee [DOP] of Cabinet at which we were discussing the Falkland Islands. I am not a member of DOP as a whole and I am involved only with respect to the oil in the region. All the Chiefs of Staff were there. Before us was a secret Joint Intelligence Committee report marked 'Delicate Source – UK Eyes Only' which pointed out that the Argentinian forces were strong enough to take over the Falkland Islands, with their population of 1950,

without a shot being fired. David Owen reported that the Argentinians were likely to be very tough if the negotiations scheduled for December in New York fell through.

When I was called I said I appreciated the gravity of the situation but to divide the sovereignty of the islands with a three-mile limit from the sovereignty of the areas outside, where the oil is, could have tremendously damaging implications for us. It might be better to be defeated on this point than to concede it now. Going to UN arbitration was ruled out because world opinion was against us.

Jim, in a very John Bullish mood, said, 'World opinion may be against us, but they might feel differently if the Argentinians attack the Falklands.' So he asked the navy to send out two frigates and possibly a nuclear submarine *before* the negotiations began. A very tough line.

We were all sworn to secrecy about the military operations. I don't like secrets.

To the Friends of the Earth reception to celebrate the end of the Windscale Inquiry and had a long talk to Walt Patterson and Tom Burke, the director. They are a great crowd. They've done very well, and gradually their view is beginning to be taken seriously. I must get them into the Labour Party.

*Tuesday 22 November*
This evening I was handed a letter from Number 10 referring to a meeting I had arranged with colleagues to discuss the direct elections bill.

Dear Tony,

I am attaching a copy of a letter which was found by a Conservative on the top of the copying machine and handed to my office. You will see it says there is to be a meeting of Ministers in your room tonight and is signed by Michael Meacher, the Parliamentary Under-Secretary of the Department of Trade.

As you are aware, no meeting of Ministers should be called without my knowledge and agreement. I do not know whether you are aware of this letter but I am sure that now you know about it, you will cancel the proposed meeting.

Yours sincerely,
Jim Callaghan

The pressure is building up, and if this continues I am going to be in deep trouble. I don't believe for a moment that Michael left a copy on the copying machine. Anyway, it's out now, and I should think it will be all over the place. I decided to do nothing about it. Why should I cancel the meeting? I meet Michael and Peter and John every week – have done for years – without the Prime Minister's permission.

Later I went to see Michael Foot in his room, and Peter Shore and John Silkin were there. Michael was red and angry. 'What's this about this meeting you're having with the junior Ministers tonight?'

'I told you this morning.'

'Well,' he shouted, 'I think it's bloody crooked that you should hold it.'

'What do you mean?' I asked.

'We agreed we would do nothing and keep in touch and meet early this week,' said Michael.

'Fine, I've never said we wouldn't, I haven't made a statement, I'm just consulting people. I'm not going to be told I'm bloody crooked. The only other time that has ever been said to me was in this room by Dick Crossman, who called me a bloody twister, and I walked out. I won't be called bloody crooked. I am entitled to consult whom I like.'

'You've no business to do that,' said Michael. 'You know very well how it will be interpreted.'

'Michael, I am awfully sorry, but, if Ministers are not allowed to meet, who authorised *this* meeting?'

He withdrew his remark about my being 'bloody crooked' and I said we'd leave it at that.

Then we began arguing about how to vote in the direct elections bill. Michael started on me again. 'You just want the Tories in, and then we will be in the Common Market for life.' He says that every time, before every Election: do everything he tells you or the Tories will get in. 'You, with your halo of martyrdom,' he grunted. 'I've been anti-Market longer than you.'

The fact is, they are turning the flame-thrower on me, and I have no doubt whatever that if I did leave the Government and then we lost the Election the defeat would be attributed to me. I said surely there was room for one person in the Cabinet who actually believed in the Party's policies. Michael did at least apologise, but my links with him are severed completely.

Went back to my room and at 9 Brian Sedgemore, Michael Meacher and Margaret Jackson came for the meeting. I told them about Jim's letter and said, 'If you want to slip off, now's the moment to do it.' Michael Meacher was horrified by the story about finding his letter on the photocopier. Then Bob Cryer joined us and we talked for an hour.

It was quite clear that none of them wanted to go as far as voting *against* the bill so we left it at that.

*Wednesday 23 November*
As I was going into the Executive, Michael Foot handed me a letter in

which he apologised for what he had said last night. I can't quite bring myself to read it a second time but he ended with the old phrase on which we were both brought up, not to let the sun go down on your wrath.

After lunch I went back to the office and told Frances Morrell what was going on. She suggested that she and Francis Cripps take on the responsibility for commissioning my definitive paper on the thermal reactor to save me the strain.

Caught a train to Bournemouth for a packed meeting with about 200 people. Outside there were thirty firemen and a fire officer; I told them all to come into the meeting and I would have ten minutes with them afterwards.

I listened to their case. They asked if I would speak up for them in the Cabinet. Of course I shall, as I did last week. Jim Callaghan is at the EETPU Conference in Blackpool pledging himself to 10 per cent but in the Cabinet tomorrow I shall argue for more. The Government is going to lose this because it is obstinate and pig-headed, and it is not right that these guys should be victimised in this way.

### Thursday 24 November
A memorable day. I had pretty well decided to abstain on the vote on direct elections.

Derek Jameson, editor of the *Daily Express*, came to lunch. I don't like having the editors of Tory papers but he has an interesting background and he is a Labour sympathiser. He was born in an orphanage in East London and was looked after by an old lady in Winchester who had raised seventy children.

He worked for a while with Reuters but had difficulty because of his political opinions so he left to join the army. When he came out he was lying low – I suppose he hadn't really abandoned his basic socialist position. He worked for the *Express*, then joined the *Mirror* in Manchester. When he failed to get the editorship of the *Mirror*, he knew he would get the next editorship going, which was the *Express*.

Jameson told me that when he met Margaret Thatcher he had said to her, 'You make a great mistake to attack the left wing of the Labour Party because the British people are not a bit frightened of it.'

At 4.15 Tom Farmer came to see me. I knew him as a student at Oxford after the war. He became a Republican lawyer, and I saw him in Washington in spring after he had been appointed to a committee to review the operations of the security services. He told me on that occasion that he himself had been with the Joint Intelligence Services during the war. After Oxford he worked for Allen Dulles, former director of the CIA, and was one of Kennedy's Africa experts. I thought it would be nice to have a word with him while he's over here.

We talked about the review he's working on, and he said, 'Admiral

Stansfield Turner, director of the CIA, was a contemporary of ours at Oxford. He's a decent chap and we are trying to get it sorted out.'

Tom asked about the situation in Britain and I told him I didn't think anybody knew anything about it here. 'We don't know what they do. I was a Minister with some security responsibility at one time and never knew anything.'

He told me he was going to see Sir Leonard Hooper, the 'co-ordinator of British security services'. Well, I had never heard of him, and I said to Tom how absolutely typical it was that a Cabinet Minister had never heard of the head of the security services!

'Perhaps I shouldn't have told you,' said Tom. I indicated that I knew there were close links between British and American security.

Then he wanted to know what I thought about Carter. I said I liked him – he was small-town, principled, with a clear mind.

It was a useful talk; it is worthwhile having a direct line to a senior CIA man in the White House.

Heard the end of the debate on the second reading of the direct elections bill [European Elected Assembly Bill]. Douglas Hurd wound up for the Tories and was followed by Merlyn Rees. I must say it was with the greatest difficulty that I didn't go through the No Lobby. We abstained, and the PM failed to get anything like half the PLP voting for him. The bill got through with Tory and Liberal votes.

### Saturday 26 November
There was a friendly article by John Biffen in the *Spectator* saying he had underestimated Mr Benn, and that the policy I had put forward on national sovereignty and planning would be highly attractive to people. He said the Tories really had to produce a more relevant alternative than the one they had at present.

He has published a book entitled *The Politics of Office versus the Politics of Influence* and I found that interesting – he obviously thinks influence is more important than office and I think he's right. He's a thoughtful guy.

### Monday 28 November
I went straight to Riverwalk House at 9.30 for my first meeting of the Energy Commission, and I was very nervous. There were twenty-eight high-level people, including seven Ministers, seven chairmen of nationalised industries, Dr Tin Pearce, Chairman of Esso, members of the TUC General Council, and Sir Brian Flowers and Sir William Hawthorne representing environment and energy conservation. The general mockery about Benn having another talk-in made me uneasy. They are all bigwigs, but I suppose at my age I am a bit of a bigwig myself.

We sat in this room with a long narrow table and awful acoustics. No one could hear what was being said and I fully expected it to fold after about fifteen minutes. I began the discussion by pointing out that around the table were people who spent £3.75 billion a year, 16 per cent of our gross capital formation, and this meeting had been called to shape a co-ordinated and planned energy policy. I asked Frank Chapple and Denis Rooke, Chairman of British Gas, to say a word before we went through the working document. It turned out to be an absolutely thrilling day.

We discussed forecasts, economic growth, conservation and a range of other topics, and there was no doubt that people really enjoyed it. It was a mixture of a Cabinet committee, the top echelons of academic life and the trade union movement. I was immensely pleased.

Afterwards I chatted to Frank Chapple, and to Reg Birch of the AUEW, who is a most amusing and cultivated man. He said, 'Anthony, how are those children of yours?'

'They are all in the labour movement in one shape or form. Why do you call me Anthony?'

'In the Communist Party we used to call a chap "comrade" just before we tossed him over the edge of the cliff!' He got on to talking about the Crossman *Diaries* and he said Crossman was 'an unattractive Firbank'. I looked puzzled. 'Put it another way, he was a miserable piss-pot.' Everybody laughed. He is very amusing but way out politically – a Maoist.

Went back to the office and had a talk with Alex Eadie and my officials about the relative cost of coal and nuclear power. It emerged that the CEGB want to order thirty-five nuclear power stations because they don't think coal will be as available in the future and it will be more expensive. But if we went down this road we would be terribly dependent on nuclear energy. The *Financial Times* published a forecast of huge growth in nuclear, which probably emanated from Jack Rampton.

*Tuesday 29 November*
After lunch Brian Sedgemore and I went for a walk round St James's Park with Dennis Skinner. I have a lot of time for Dennis.

*Wednesday 30 November*
After lunch I began the campaign to defeat the guillotine which is being imposed on the European Elected Assembly Bill. Dennis Skinner said his contact was Norman Tebbit [Conservative MP for Chingford], who is very anti-Europe and trying to get more people to oppose the guillotine.

*Thursday 1 December*
Denis Healey made a speech yesterday which was interpreted as calling for a permanent statutory pay policy with a Minister for Pay to monitor the whole scheme. David Basnett attacked the proposal as 'lunatic' at this stage – two and a half years into a pay policy that is eroding rapidly.

Just before Cabinet, I asked Stan Orme what he intended to do about the vote on the direct elections bill and he told me he would abstain throughout. Mike Cocks had apparently said to him, 'We need you there to keep a House', and Stan replied, 'Keep a House when you've got such a huge majority for the bill? Go and get Ted Heath off a train on his publicity tour signing his books and records. Or get Harold Wilson out of the television studios doing a series on Prime Ministers. But don't ask us to keep a House for you.'

*Saturday 3 December*
Went over to see Mother, who has bugs infesting her larder. I spent four hours clearing it and scrubbing it out.

Two or three days ago, I had a note in my red box about an anti-terrorist exercise planned for 16 December at Winfrith to practise the defence of a nuclear establishment. It would involve the use of the AEA guards, the local police and the military, and I was simply told that it was all very secret. I wanted it discussed by Ministers before I agreed to it. I wanted to know exactly what was going to happen, and what impact it would have on our announcement about reactor policy and the publication of the Windscale report. They had no right to hold military exercises without the personal authority of the Minister most concerned.

So I had put all this in a note and I was then told I would have to write to Merlyn Rees.

This is one of those exercises where the military move into a derelict area in secrecy. They are never made public, never mentioned in the press, never admitted by the authorities, and they are entirely outside ministerial control. In the old days manoeuvres such as these were made public. Now there is this obsession with secrecy.

*Sunday 4 December*
At 1.55 *The Way to the Stars* was shown on television, the old Terence Rattigan tale about the RAF during the war. It was very nostalgic for me, as it was the period when my brother Michael died while serving in the air force, and I watched it with Melissa. Mother said she could hardly bear it, particularly as she had seen a programme this morning on the neutron bomb. She said she wondered whether the war was worthwhile – all those lives sacrificed, and now the risk of another World War.

In the evening Caroline and I went to the Savoy for a dinner given by the new Israeli Prime Minister, Menachem Begin. We got into the receiving line, and when we reached Begin he put an arm on each shoulder and said to me, 'Ah, yours is a famous and respected name in Israel.' He was probably thinking of Josiah Wedgwood.

We saw Armand Hammer there. The last time I met him was in Moscow at the Bolshoi Ballet, and I reminded him he had suggested then that Brezhnev should go to Israel.

'Ah,' he said, 'I am seeing Begin privately tomorrow and I am going to suggest to him that he goes to Moscow instead.'

Spoke to Arnold Weinstock briefly. 'We had better sit at separate tables!' he said.

The whole Jewish establishment was there. At the top table sat the two Rabbis (Ashkenazim and Sephardic), the Lord Chancellor, the Speaker of the House of Commons, the Prime Minister, the Israeli Ambassador in London, the British Ambassador in Jerusalem, Harold Wilson, Lord Weidenfeld, some Tory MPs including Julian Amery, John Davies and Keith Joseph.

### Monday 5 December
In the evening Melissa read her essay on Bismarck to Caroline and me; it was a good analytical piece of work. The three of us then went to the Windsor Castle, the local pub.

### Tuesday 6 December
I rang John Hill to find out his attitude to the proposed defence exercise at Winfrith. He had known about it for six weeks, as had my Permanent Secretary, yet I was only informed last week. He also told me that it was originally planned for Windscale but he had advised against that because of the sensitivity. He said he had wanted a deferment but it had not been agreed.

Over to the Legislation Committee, and I had a quick word with Merlyn beforehand. I asked him if he had received my note about the exercise.

'Yes,' he said, 'I only heard about it last night.' This was further confirmation that officials had not consulted Ministers and that these exercises were outside ministerial control.

### Wednesday 7 December
To Harrogate to address the NUM Conference in the Royal Hall.

I said this was an historic conference; it would pioneer the future of nationalisation and the mining industry. There were three possible ways forward: meaningless consultation, which didn't involve any serious transfer of power but was just window dressing and shouldn't be accepted; waiting for socialism and doing nothing until it was provided *for* us, instead of fighting for it; or a stage-by-stage transition to full workers' control, which I advocated. I got a reasonable response but I think some of the left in the NUM were angry that I had intervened in the ballot, and as far as the right was concerned my speech went too far.

One of the best speeches came from David Skinner, Dennis's brother, who in the usual Skinner way was whimsical but tough, saying he didn't think Parliament had much to offer.

### Thursday 8 December

Frances, Francis and my Assistant Secretary Richard Wilson are busy on the draft paper on reactor choice. I heard later today that the Cabinet Office thought it was an excellent paper. We have the basic case clear and they are now working on the attacking brief. They've dug out a document signed by Eric Varley as Energy Secretary allowing the NNC to negotiate with Westinghouse so that they could examine the safety of the PWR. Between the lines, it was in effect a conditional contract to order the PWR. The minute had been put to Eric the day before the Referendum of 4 June 1975 – four days before I was appointed – and I'm sure Eric didn't know what he was doing when he signed it.

### Friday 9 December

Economic Committee (EY) at Number 10 to discuss a paper stating that our balance of payments was now so strong that it was no longer possible to resist Common Market demands that we lift some of our exchange controls in order to move towards the free movement of capital. The paper only came to me last night and Sam Silkin, the Attorney-General, had attached a note with his advice on the legality of declining to assent to this under great pressure and at such short notice.

I had gone to the meeting determined to fight ferociously on this, not knowing at all what others would say. Denis supported some relaxation of exchange controls, as did Harold Lever, on the grounds that it would boost confidence abroad.

However, Peter Shore said this would be desperately damaging, and it was absurd that on the one hand we should be under the tutelage of the IMF because we had a *poor* balance of payments situation and on the other hand be told by the EEC to ease exchange control on the grounds that we had a *strong* balance of payments.

Of course it isn't the balance of payments that is strong, it's all the hot money that has flowed in over the last few years as a result of the cuts made in December 1976, plus the prospects of oil and the weakness of the dollar.

Peter also said we had an enormous debt repayment problem to consider, and high unemployment, which, under another article of the Treaty, allowed us special exemptions. He was good and clear.

I agreed absolutely with Peter and asked, 'Who would benefit from it? We are tightening control of pay to the point virtually of a statutory pay policy, but losing our control on capital. If the Commission want to take us to court, let them.'

*Saturday 10 December*
To the Commonwealth Society for a debate with Sir Keith Joseph about socialism and civil liberties. There were about 250 people there, including Patricia Hewitt from the National Council for Civil Liberties, Alan Watkins of the *Observer* and John Whale of the *Sunday Times*. The Professor of Jurisprudence at Oxford, Professor Ronald Dworkin, was in the chair.

I'm not sure it was worth doing. Joseph attacked socialism in a highly theoretical way and did not relate it to real experience at all. I identified Joseph with Burke and Cobden, speaking on behalf of the middle class, talking about capitalism without any reference to imperialism – for example, that the civil liberties of 600 million people had been taken away in order to provide a market for British goods. When he referred to an 'irreversible shift in the balance of power', I said that at Runnymede, in 1649, and at the time of the Reform Act, there had been irreversible shifts in the balance of power. There was a little bit of laughter.

*Monday 12 December*
Press conference in the Department, Bernard Ingham's last, as he is leaving to take over as head of the Energy Conservation Department, something I suggested to Jack Rampton when I was getting on badly with Bernard, but I'm sorry to see him go now.

Frances and Francis came in all excited because Kenneth Berrill has submitted his paper on nuclear reactor choice, on which the final decision is to be made next Friday, and he attacks the paper Bruce Millan and I have jointly submitted. Berrill says we should start series-ordering of PWRs. Astonishing! I asked to see the PM to discuss it.

Here is the head of the CPRS (the Think Tank – none of whom is an expert in nuclear matters) writing a paper flatly contradicting the two Secretaries of State responsible. This is a big constitutional point. The CPRS is now the Cabinet Office voice, with full membership of the Cabinet. It's the imposition of a sort of unelected European Commission on to the British system.

Frances decided not to come to Brussels tonight – she wanted to reply

to the CPRS paper – so I asked Brian Sedgemore and he was delighted.
As soon as it was known that he was coming, there was a hell of a row:
'You can't take a PPS to Brussels, it would make the European
Assembly angry', and so on. I said, 'Rubbish.' In the end it was cleared
that he could accompany me.

Had a meeting on petroleum revenue tax. The tax regime we have
makes Britain the most profitable oil province in the world, and
Tommy Balogh has been pushing for a reduction of the tax allowance.
At the moment, companies pay no tax at all on the first million tons of
oil, which is a scandal. Secondly, they get tax relief on a huge
percentage of their expenses in North Sea development – which is
outrageous. Tommy Balogh wanted PRT to be raised to 75 per cent.
Officials were doubtful, and Dick Mabon, who doesn't seem to think
these things out, supported the oil companies: 'We don't want to kill the
goose that lays the golden eggs.'

Flew to Brussels just after midnight. Bernard Ingham and others
from the Department were waiting for me in the VIP lounge. We talked
about Germany and how it now has a complete war psychology.
Bernard Ingham reminded us that many people clearly thought that
the Common Market was a way of containing Germany.

Talking to Brian Sedgemore later, he told me how he's working with
Frances, Francis, Michael Meacher, Neil Kinnock and Bernard Dix
[Assistant General Secretary of NUPE] in getting a little group together to
work on the renewal of the Labour Party. I must encourage them.

*Wednesday 14 December*
To EY Committee to discuss a response from Denis Healey to the IMF; Denis wants to suggest that we continue our relationship with them even though we don't really need to. He said they had sent him such a friendly letter that he had asked them if he could use it in his Election address. It was half a joke, but it is true that we are pursuing absolutely Tory policies and it is not surprising that the IMF like it or that the Labour movement should be getting restive.

In the evening Caroline and I went to meet the Friends of the Earth at their headquarters in Poland Street. The property is owned by the Rowntree Trust, and many dissenting groups work from there. One assumes that all the rooms are bugged. Even Tom Burke, the Director, assumed that the Special Branch kept an eye on them. There were about thirty-five young people and Tom Burke explained how the Friends are organised. They began seven years ago in America and operate in twenty countries, and the groups are autonomous and self-financing. They are concerned with energy, transport, resources, wildlife and food. Their strategy is preventive, that is to say to change policy-making, rather than to fight decisions once they have been made, and they are political only in the sense of wanting to influence events, not in seeking power.

They were an overwhelmingly middle-class group; they appeal to some radicals and dissenters, but I felt they could be drawn into the mainstream of establishment opinion without actually making any difference to the way in which society was run.

At the end I said to them, 'The influence you have will not be immediate, and don't be disappointed when you find more reactors announced, but the effect will be to broaden the choice for the middle-term future. You will have greater effect if you do turn your mind to the power structure.'

The PWR is a case in point. We have been fighting it very hard, and, if we do lose, it will be because Weinstock and Whitehall, with the support of the Prime Minister, will defeat the environmentalists and the trade unions and even the responsible Minister.

*Thursday 15 December*
To a meeting of the Campaign Committee, where Bob Worcester of MORI presented a most elaborate plan for the next Election, costing £50,000 to £100,000. He said MORI was the leading poll, the Party must provide details now, he was doing work on the marginals, and he wanted cash to put into Scotland.

After a discussion in which Joan Lestor, Mik and I expressed some doubts, Jim said, 'Worcester wants the work. The staff at Transport House want it and I would like it. It could be quite a close Election and we need to tackle the problem of Scotland and of women, so I think we should go ahead.'

So we agreed £50,000 in the first instance.

*Friday 16 December*
Prepared for the crucial EY Committee this morning to decide on the choice of nuclear reactor. Frances Morrell has done a marvellous job on this, and she told me that, although Roy Hattersley wouldn't be present, he had put in a letter of support. This letter, drafted by David Hill, Roy's political adviser, had apparently led to protests from officials that his was not the 'proper' briefing. Frances said Sir Kenneth Berrill had been ringing round Whitehall briefing people to support the CPRS paper against the Minister. An interesting piece of information.

I had asked to see Jim before the meeting and he seemed a bit restive. I said, 'I want you to appreciate that Bruce and I are resolute about this matter. I have been the Minister dealing with nuclear matters since 1966 and I have given more attention to this issue than any other – I know it absolutely backwards. It would be quite wrong for us to change to the PWR. The AGR is the only system for *now*, and we have time to review it later.'

'I don't take much interest in all this,' said Jim. 'I just keep an eye.'

'But you *have* taken a lot of interest. You have sent letters across to get information.' I thought he was slightly shifty about it, and, as I discovered later, he had reason to be. Anyway, I left him in no doubt that I was intending to fight hard on this – which might influence him marginally.

I went into the meeting feeling uneasy. Jim summed up the choice to be made. 'Do we order two more AGRs now, one for Scotland and one for England, and is there any alternative? Do we cancel the SGHWR? What do we do about the PWR? And I understand there is a problem of staffing.' There were two papers to consider, said Jim, one from Kenneth Berrill and a joint one from Tony Benn and Bruce Millan, which he then invited me to introduce.

'For my sins,' I began, 'I have been a nuclear Minister for eleven years and there is no subject I have studied in greater detail than this. Nuclear power has a key role to play in the future: 13 per cent of our electricity is now generated by nuclear power and that's likely to reach 20 per cent. These matters are difficult for Ministers because of the technical, industrial, safety, environmental and export interests involved. I want, therefore, to clarify the choices, narrow our differences and focus on the real issue, which is the proper timing of decisions. The background to our paper, on which Bruce and I have consulted and agreed, is that we now recommend cancellation of the SGHWR. £150 million has gone down the drain with that decision, because we spent £94 million before we ordered it, £40 million since, and £15 million in cancellation charges. But that is the cost of a decision that was not based on a design already cleared. We need new nuclear stations now because of demand and the needs of industry, and we believe that only the AGR can meet these needs.

'The forecast demand is based on a planning margin of 28 per cent on a retirement of 0.5 gigawatts of plant each year and a 2 per cent demand growth. Therefore we need an order in 1979, the CEGB and the South of Scotland Electricity Board both need a reactor, and only the AGR can meet that need. We have twenty-two years' experience of the AGR, it is publicly acceptable, it is licensed, and there is planning permission. But there *are* future uncertainties, and we have recommended that design studies on the PWR be carried out before our next ordering decision in 1982.'

I referred to the alternative proposal from the CEGB and the NNC for two AGRs now and a commitment to order one PWR in 1982. I argued that our critics would point out that the Government had shifted between three different reactors in as many years. The proposal would overstretch our resources, the design changes for the PWR were unknown, and it would mean coming to a decision now, four years earlier than was necessary.

I came on to the third alternative, advocated by GEC and the CPRS – that we have the PWR as the main system for series-ordering. The British problem, they believed, was that we had always had different types of reactors and by 1990 we would have Magnox stations, AGRs, the fast breeder and Jet. It was too much for a small country, but we would not end the uncertainty by ordering a PWR reactor which had not yet been approved.

The CPRS reckoned we would need to spend £15-20 billion on nuclear ordering in the Eighties. I said we should consider the CEGB forecast in 1974, after the oil price increase, that we would need eighteen PWRs by 1983. In fact none had been ordered since 1970 and only two to three were now contemplated. Therefore we could not commit money on that scale on the basis of unreliable forecasts.

I went on to say that the CPRS didn't think safety was a factor. It wasn't easy for Ministers to talk about nuclear safety, but certainly Sir Alan Cottrell, former Government Chief Scientist, believed that the PWR pressure vessel was inherently unsafe and that operator radiation doses were certainly much higher than with the AGR. It was for the Nuclear Inspectorate to decide on safety – not the CPRS – and the decision would have to be based on a design that had been approved. We would not know the answers to these questions before 1982.

Anticipating the argument that fifty PWRs were operational around the world with 200 years of accumulated experience, I pointed out that these were very small and that in fact there was only three years' experience of the size of PWR we would need. As for the CPRS claim that an argument against PWRs was an argument for de-industrialisation, on the contrary, each AGR would involve £1000 million of work compared with only £600 million for the PWR. The AGR had lower development costs, at £30 million against £40 million; a lower launching cost of £25 million against £30 million; and a much lower import cost of £1.5 million per reactor against £20 to £24 million per PWR.

On exports, we had been told that we would drop desperately behind America, France and Germany in the race to sell PWRs if we left the decision until 1982. They had already increased their capacity to build PWRs, whereas we would not be well enough established until at least 1994. Weinstock was not keen on the proposed deal with Iran. We might remember that, if exports failed, the world would only have the AGR to turn to.

However, I questioned the need to decide *now*. We were told that it would attract investment in Britain but Weinstock had advised me that, if we ordered the PWR, GEC would have to invest £15 million in new capacity and it would cost the Government £40 million to bring the work to fruition and to get exports. The idea that we would get exports by collaborating with France and Germany on PWRs, when they would be our bitterest competitors, was absurd. Was it right to decide now, five years before we could know, to commit £15–20 billion on a reactor system as yet uncleared and to cancel the AGR before it had been fully tested in practice?

I summed up the options: two AGRs but with the PWR as the main system, as suggested by Sir Kenneth Berrill and Arnold Weinstock; two AGRs and a commitment to one PWR in 1982, preferred by the CEGB and the NNC; and our proposal for two AGRs plus design studies for the PWR.

'My view,' I concluded, 'is supported by Bruce Millan, the Electricity Council, the South of Scotland Electricity Board, the TUC Fuel and Power Committee, Sir Brian Flowers, those who spoke at the Energy Commission and most of industry. The PWR is supported only by Weinstock and Kenneth Berrill. Therefore I think we should concentrate on AGRs today.'

Jim raised the point that nuclear power was a world system and a PWR order would end the uncertainty.

'We must order two AGRs now,' said Bruce, 'and the first task is to get them there on time. The PWR is residual and we can't allow it to become central. Industry can't sustain two systems at once and the fast breeder as well.'

Kenneth Berrill told us that the CPRS had been studying this for a long time and were worried that the power plant industry had no exports, the nuclear industry had had no orders since 1970, and construction delays on the AGR and the cancellation of the SGHWR had all caused trouble. The options were open now, but we wouldn't keep them open by opting for AGRs and only design work on the PWR. The AGR did not produce the cheapest electricity. We had experience of PWRs through Rolls Royce and so on. The PWR was seen by the world as cheap and safe; it was the cheapest option available, and without a commitment to it we would not get the necessary thrust. This was the view of GEC, Vickers and Rolls Royce. He therefore favoured building the two AGRs while concentrating on the development of the PWR.

Eric Varley said, 'I advocated the SGHWR, and Whitehall and the CPRS were bitterly opposed. I agreed we should have two AGRs from an industrial point of view, but the issue is whether design studies on the PWR are enough.' He didn't think they were and inclined to the view that we order one PWR.

Denis Healey agreed with Eric and the CPRS that we should commit ourselves to the PWR now, but not as the only system. He asked whether the work could be done successfully on both, obviously favouring one AGR and one PWR.

David Owen didn't want to close the PWR option; but he was suspicious of all the pressures and said we didn't have to decide now. His instinct was to support the two Ministers on one AGR for Scotland and one for England.

Shirley Williams supported David Owen on the grounds that we needed more time to look at the PWR. There would be ecological resistance to it in Britain, and she asked if we could leave the option open.

Merlyn supported Bruce and me. Peter believed we had missed out on the PWR already, we had twenty-two years of investment in the AGR and we should stick with it. The problem was the management of large stations and sites; therefore design studies should be carried out for the PWR but that was all – we shouldn't order it.

Edmund Dell said exports were a marginal factor but the world had chosen the PWR and history was ahead of us. It wasn't too late to change; the AGR magnified problems of cost and siting whereas the PWR was factory-made. We should change now and order two AGRs and one PWR.

'Common sense would have told us to go for the PWR earlier,' said Harold Lever. 'We should order a PWR as soon as possible.' He doubted the need for AGRs.

I came in again. 'If I were to be asked to make a statement in the House that we are committed to cancelling the AGR in 1982, what would the public reaction be? There would be confusion and opposition. My candid opinion is that the English disease may not just be poor performance but people at the top who chop and change between technologies they know nothing about. However, I realise there is anxiety , so let's push the PWR back until Easter, do a report on it, and just concentrate on the AGRs we need to order now.'

I offered to draw up a draft statement, and Jim said, 'Without commitment, yes, you can draft it and send it round if you like.'

I came away absolutely exhausted, commenting to Jim, 'This has got to look good in ten years' time, you know.'

'You may still be Secretary of State for Energy in ten years' time.' A strange thing to say.

I wasn't defeated because they didn't commit us to order a PWR and I did manage to put off a decision until the New Year, and to get one AGR agreed, so that was something.

When I got back to the office, James Bretherton showed me a letter from Arnold Weinstock to Number 10. Weinstock had been to see Jim last night and afterwards had written this letter which was circulated so late that it didn't arrive at my office until the EY had started. I was really shocked: Jim had said nothing about seeing Weinstock when I talked to him this morning and it was most improper. I was drained by the whole business because the Cabinet, with the help of Berrill, Walter Marshall and Weinstock, is being driven towards a fundamental decision. I shall pursue this with Eric Lubbock and Alan Cottrell.

Nor did Jim mention that he had seen Rampton, although James Bretherton had told me that Rampton had been there officially to discuss Anglo-French co-operation; I don't believe that.

To the Private Office Christmas party, where I had a talk with Philip Jones, one of my officials. He thought that if civil servants disagreed with the Minister they had the right to express their view.

'Yes,' I said, 'but not through the CPRS. You can't have a Think Tank which is in effect the voice of the Cabinet Office under a civil servant. That's outrageous.'

But that is Berrill's role. He simply presents the view of the Prime Minister or the Secretary of the Cabinet.

*Sunday 18 December*
Something I forgot to record. The other night Caroline came to dinner at the House, and we met Harold Wilson in the corridor. It was the first time I had spoken to him since his farewell dinner in 1976. It was clear that we couldn't avoid saying something to him, so as I passed I remarked, 'I saw your programme on Gladstone.' 'Yes,' he said, 'but they cut out a lot of what I said about his sex life.' He's a lonely, isolated figure now. Caroline has a theory that he stumbled on a security plot against himself and that those responsible were now trying to discredit

him in order to prevent him from ever speaking out about it – an interesting thought.

*Monday 19 December*
At 9 I had a meeting on the safety of oil rigs with Frank Kearton and John Archer of the Department's Marine Division. Frank warned that rigs were desperately dangerous installations because they compress gas at 6000 atmospheres in confined spaces, and that a leak would cause a massive explosion killing up to 200 people. The proposal was that I press ahead with an inquiry into the safety of the rigs using two engineers and two trade-unionists.

John Archer, who is chairman of the Marine Safety Committee – an interdepartmental committee – said there were uncompleted reports on fire, the safety of cranes, rigs and platforms under construction, and divers and standby vessels, and he hoped to have these reports in six months. He didn't want anything superimposed.

I reserved the right to take the matter to Cabinet colleagues.

*Wednesday 21 December*
Today I saw the minutes of the Prime Minister's talk with Giscard d'Estaing in which he had actually stated that Britain would be adopting the PWR, and David Owen had said that what was proposed would ease our transition to the PWR. So the Prime Minister and the Foreign Secretary have virtually announced a decision to the French.

Went to a few Christmas parties. At the *New Scientist* party I met a scientific adviser to the CPRS. He had been there a year and was very boastful. 'We are an institutionalised Watergate,' he said.

'What on earth do you mean by that?'

'Well, we tap what's going on in other Departments, we take information, which has perhaps been distorted on its way to the top, right back to the root and present it to Ministers in a new way. It's a sort of treasonable subversion of Departments: if ideas can't get from the bottom to the top, we extract them and put them forward.'

What he was *really* saying, as I know damn well, is that the CPRS permits civil servants to bypass their Ministers and go straight to Cabinet. I put this to him.

'Well,' he said, 'the Prime Minister is in charge.' He went on to tell me that political advisers were undesirable because nobody knew who they were or what they were doing. 'At least we are accountable.'

He, of course, has slipped in without either election or the severe test of a Civil Service career. He is a sort of chief scientific adviser to a civil servant, Berrill, who behaves like a Minister briefing Departments to support the CPRS against their own Minister. I found him shallow, arrogant and inadequate, and I really let fly.

Got home and Stephen looked in. He and Hilary have both been chosen as candidates in next May's council elections. Stephen is also the agent. I'm very proud.

*Thursday 22 December*
Cabinet at 9.30 on pay. Denis Healey introduced a paper, and said that public opinion supported the Government's pay policy and there was strong opposition to the idea of making a special case for the police or the firemen. TUC support for the policy was stronger too, the 'twelve-month rule' had held, and 93.2 per cent of CBI-monitored settlements were well within the earnings guidelines. It had turned out to be a less flexible policy than he had expected, but the only settlements above the limit were those at Ford and Vauxhall.

Jim said we had to consider the possibility of an Election in October, and he felt a lower figure would be necessary in the next pay round. Drawing attention to Frank Allaun's letter asking the Government to give up the pay freeze, Jim said, '10 per cent is not a pay freeze.'

We came on to my paper and I confined myself to the simple argument that pay must be seen in the context of economic policy generally, that the continued support of the TUC was an integral part of our policy and always must be, and that the General Council vote yesterday of only 20 to 17 in favour was a warning, particularly as Joe Gormley, Frank Chapple and Moss Evans, General Secretary of the TGWU, had all voted with the minority against.

I said that public opinion polls did not reflect the true position: Tories supported the restraints but not the Government; floating voters were being subjected to daily attacks on the trade unions, which couldn't help us; and Labour voters who supported the Government might not extend their support to the pay policy. The time had come for a fresh start and my paper could provide a basis for that.

Denis wanted a long-term policy, and Jim thought the analysis had been better than the synthesis, that the Government had done better than he could have expected, and that the power workers and the miners had presented a problem. He warned against any euphoria, thought 4–5 per cent next year would be all we could afford and emphasised that the 'twelve-month rule' must stick.

At 12.30 we broke for mince pies and a drink. Stan Orme and I were discussing the possibility of our writing a joint paper on incomes policy, when Jim came up and said, 'If you two are talking, I should be worried.'

I said, 'Jim, your credibility is better than Harold Wilson's, and I'll tell you why. Harold sounded like Nye Bevan at the Conference and Reg Prentice in the Cabinet, whereas wherever you speak you're an unregenerate old reactionary in everything you say. I try to say the same thing to every audience too.' He laughed.

Got to EY late, just as Shirley Williams was explaining her paper on industrial democracy, setting out our agreements and disagreements.

I said I thought we had gone as far as we could at the top level because industrial democracy really made its biggest impact on the trade union movement. 'We've had enough discussions about industrial democracy in the salons of power and we're just getting into a corporatist huddle. Now let it be discussed by the people who actually *do* the work.'

Well, the discussion dragged on and on until Jim said, 'I don't know where we are', and everyone just laughed. It was agreed he would talk to the CBI and the TUC.

This whole exercise has come to nothing. It is an extraordinary story because the scheme has just been completely frustrated. Why? Because the Civil Service know damn well how important industrial democracy is, and Peter Shore got it diverted into the Bullock Report, which was just corporatist and absolutely wrong. So nothing has happened, and now it has come back to Ministers. The CBI is divided, the TUC is divided, the Government is divided, and after four years in office we haven't even stimulated a discussion.

*Friday 23 December*
I heard today that the Prime Minister has vetoed my proposed consultative document on the thermal reactor strategy which I wanted to circulate to EEC Energy Commission members.

The papers yesterday reported that Friends of the Earth had written to the Prime Minister pointing out all the PWR's weaknesses. That motivated me to instruct my office to find out the estimated cost when ordered, actual cost on completion, operating experience and breakdown record of all operational PWRs.

Did some Christmas shopping and I'm beginning to relax now; I'm determined to enjoy Christmas with the family.

*Saturday 24 December*
Christmas Eve. Mark and Val Arnold-Forster came round, as they usually do at Christmas. Mark must be nearly sixty now and he looked very white and tired. Our talks are always interesting; now I know he is an Intelligence officer, I feel free to ask him things I wouldn't otherwise have done. He told me today that, according to the Danish Navy, there are Russian nuclear submarines in the Baltic hiding at depths that make it impossible for them to be located, and there are apparently Russian fleets in and around Greenland, hiding under the polar ice, that can destroy almost any American city – as well as those missiles in Russia targeted on America. He said this represented a serious shift in the balance of power.

Rearmament in western Europe is undoubtedly going to be one of the big issues of the 1980s.

### Sunday 25 December

Christmas Day. Although our eldest child is twenty-seven next year, they all turned up at home at 8 am to exchange presents and came into the bedroom to give us ours. The children love Christmas, and Caroline makes it such a marvellous occasion. Thirteen of us sat down to lunch.

Dave [Benn] told me some interesting stories. When the Colonels came to power in Greece, they organised their coup by basing it upon a NATO contingency plan so that nobody could suspect what was going on.

He told me that there was so much intelligence collection going on, and so many right-wing fringe organisations operating in Britain, that he wondered whether a coup was being prepared here. I said I didn't think there was much you could do about it. If there were a coup, a Government that came to power by force could only be removed by a general strike or something of that kind. When I talked to Caroline about it later, she said, 'It won't be like that. It'll be a coalition.'

### Wednesday 28 December

I rang the manager of The Clash, a political punk rock group, because there had been a suggestion from the BBC Television Community Programme Unit that I have a four-minute discussion with the group. I have grave doubts about a Cabinet Minister appearing with a punk rock group, given what the media would make of it, and he agreed with me that four minutes was not enough for a serious discussion. But what he said was interesting. The Clash are apparently very popular with working-class youngsters who don't find anything in our popular culture that meets their needs or reflects their feelings. He told me the group were not really concerned with being commercial and refused a lot of television because it put them into an artificial setting when they were really a live group. They are popular in Sweden, France and Yugoslavia. He said that to get any attention at all you had to be absolutely bizarre, but to understand what The Clash were trying to say you had to work really hard because the lyrics were in pidgin French.

### Saturday 31 December

In my heart of hearts I believe the country is moving sharply to the right. The trade union leaders are so enjoying their corporatist relationship with the Government that they don't want to hear anything about socialism. The real battle is within the labour movement now and it is a struggle for the soul of the movement. Jim

Callaghan is riding high. The press loves him because he's openly right-wing in the Cabinet, at public meetings and in the PLP. The Executive is hanging on to what remaining influence it has. It may be that one has to lengthen one's timescale – the whole of the 1980s may pass before we see a change.

Dictating this now, on the last day of the year, I feel depressed about it all, but I know that when we meet and start working on the General Election, which is likely to be in 1978, then the vitality will return.

The major issues of the 1980s will be the battle against federalism in the Common Market, the struggle to get back to full employment and to sustain the welfare state, and the question of civil liberties and the role of the security services.

### Friday 6 January 1978
Bristol, for a meeting at the Bristol South CLP headquarters to hear about the Boundary Commission inquiry which is being held on 9 and 10 February. The Commission will be challenged on the Tory scheme to redraw the constituency boundaries in Bristol. It would mean my seat would become marginal in the early Eighties.

### Monday 9 January
Chaired the NEC Home Policy Committee, where we passed a resolution condemning Judge Neil McKinnon. He had discharged Kingsley Read, a leader of the British National Party, in a case where Read had referred to 'coons, wogs and niggers'. McKinnon had actually wished him well, saying this had been a free country until the Race Relations Act had been introduced. He even ignored Read's comment on the death of an Asian – that it was 'one down and a million to go'.

### Tuesday 10 January
The *Mail* had a front-page spread drawing attention to my role in the unanimous resolution denouncing Judge McKinnon. The *Sun* had a headline, 'Wedgie in War on "Coon" Case Judge'.

Gladys Spearman-Cook, who runs a paper called the *Occult Gazette*, wrote to me saying I was a disaster, and God would strike me down. She was previously a great supporter and had described me as a reborn King Arthur, at the time of the Referendum!

### Wednesday 11 January
I had a meeting with Arnold Weinstock about the choice of reactors, and afterwards he told Frances Morrell to be careful not to report what had been said.

'I do not speak to the press,' Frances retorted.

He said, 'Jack Rampton thinks you're the one who's leaking it all.'

Went back to the House and watched Harold Wilson's programme on Ramsay MacDonald. It was most inadequate, but he did draw a comparison between 1931 and 1976 and made it clear that Jim Callaghan had survived by doing what Ramsay couldn't do. Very candid.

### Friday 13 January

John Dunster and Ronald Gausden, senior officials in the HSE, came to discuss the problems of nuclear energy. These are entirely independent people and they believe that the specifications required for two more AGRs would involve only relatively small changes from the present system. But if we were to go for a long-term programme of AGRs then we would need a mark two AGR, a new design. On the PWR again, if it were a one-off, they would accept fairly minor amendments to the basic design; Westinghouse would not want to make a lot of changes in case they appeared to be criticising existing systems.

Dunster favoured the AGR and an early fast breeder, but Gausden wanted us to go for the PWR and wait.

### Sunday 15 January

In the evening I reluctantly went to the Foots' house and I found it very depressing. For the first time I felt I had nothing in common with any of them. Tommy Balogh is a thoughtful, independent chap but Peter Shore has moved to the right in a really tough way that makes him another Callaghan. Michael is just lost.

The whole Labour leadership now is totally demoralised and all the growth on the left is going to come up from the outside and underneath. This is the death of the Labour Party. It believes in nothing any more, except staying in power.

### Monday 16 January

At 12 Derek Ezra and Frank Tombs came to discuss how to handle the power workers' claims. Joe Gormley, Frank Chapple and John Lyons will not accept the 10 per cent limit, and we have got to make it look more attractive. I am going to have great difficulties with my colleagues.

### Wednesday 18 January

At 10.30 I had my meeting on thermal reactor strategy with representatives from Westinghouse. Ned Franklin was also present. Discussing the merits of different systems, Mr Owen of Westinghouse said, 'I was converted from gas-cooled to pressurised water in 1955.' I found that comment revealing because the advocates of these different systems *are*

# What your boardroom needs is a few more like him.

like religious enthusiasts, converted from Catholicism to Lutheranism, or humanism to agnosticism. When I put this to them, they didn't really dissent; indeed they were proud of it.

### Thursday 19 January

I had a note today that Jack Rampton, my Permanent Secretary, wanted to see me. I asked James Bretherton what it was about, and he told me Rampton was worried about the security in my house and that I would have to return all Government papers except purely personal ones. I said I understood that but then later I got another note saying the Permanent Secretary thought the security services ought to check my house. I wrote back saying I didn't think that was necessary, present arrangements worked very well, and all Cabinet papers were returned overnight. I'll fight that one off but I see a slight threat there.

### Tuesday 24 January

At 9.45 to EY, to finalise the decision on the nuclear reactor, and we got almost everything we wanted. There is slightly more commitment to the PWR than I would like, but we achieved a great deal in getting one AGR for the CEGB and one for the SSEB. Apart from Richard Wilson, who has been most helpful, the Department have been utterly deceptive and have behaved disgracefully over this.

### Wednesday 25 January

To the House to make the statement on the reactor. Francis Cripps was not allowed into the civil servants' box at the back of the Chamber without a tie, so I told him to button up his shirt and put his sweater on back to front so no one would know.

The statement was received quite well, everyone seemed friendly, and I dealt with questions and comments for about forty minutes.

### Thursday 26 January

Cabinet, and Jim began by saying that things had been going wrong in a big way – a reference to the fact that last night we were defeated on two very important items in the Scotland Bill. First, an amendment by Jo Grimond to give Orkney and Shetland the right to vote separately and decide whether they wished to come under the Scottish Assembly had been passed. Secondly, George Cunningham [Labour MP for Islington South and Finsbury] had successfully moved a resolution requiring the 'Yes' vote to comprise at least 40 per cent of the electorate for the Act to be implemented.

Evidently there had been an attempt in the Lobby to prevent those votes we knew we would lose from going through, and this had infuriated people. Michael Foot said he would make an apology.

*Saturday 28 January*

At Temple Meads Station in Bristol waiting for the late train back to London, I went to the buffet on the platform and bought a sandwich, a Fry's chocolate bar, some Wrigley's spearmint gum and an apple. I was about to pay when an old man in a raincoat pushed forward and thrust a pound note at the girl. I thought he was trying to get ahead of me and I was going to say, 'Excuse me', but it turned out that he was paying for my food, which came to 54 pence. He turned to me and said, 'I know you, I know who you are', left the money and disappeared. I did not know what to do, but thought it was very touching.

*Monday 30 January*

This morning the *Daily Mirror* had the first extracts from *The Pencourt File* with a lot about Harold Wilson. The book is to be published in a few days.*

*Tuesday 31 January*

More from *The Pencourt File* in the *Mirror*, and Wilson was quoted on Marcia Williams's problems during the October 1974 Election – when her handbag was stolen and there was a possible sex orgy trap at Bickenhall Mansions in Marylebone Road. He had told me about this during the Election and I thought it was all very strange.

*Wednesday 1 February*

The third day of the extracts from *The Pencourt File* on Harold Wilson. Caroline and I talked about it, and came to the conclusion that though the two journalists might have started out wanting to expose Harold Wilson's fears about the security services they ended up being taken over by the Civil Service, and maybe by the security services themselves, and used to discredit Harold further. He is made to look utterly ridiculous. It is hard to make sense of it all.

After lunch my annual report, which I am calling 'Accountability in Labour Politics', arrived typed up. It's eighty-three pages – not long enough for a book but certainly enough for a good pamphlet. I'm delighted with it and I'm going to use it at a Nuffield College seminar next week.

*Thursday 2 February*

*The Times* carried a denunciation by Harold Wilson of the Pencourt book. This suggests that the journalists got to Harold by pretending they were looking into the South African connection, and then they tempted him to say things that he now regrets. They might well have

* Barrie Penrose and Roger Courtiour, *The Pencourt File* (1978).

been working for the security services all along. I must get the book.

Cabinet for the White Paper on the defence estimates. The scandal is that Fred Mulley has based his recommendations on charts from the NATO generals showing the growth of Soviet military expenditure and arms since 1968 – which was substantial – without including any comparable figures for NATO. He had also put in charts showing the balance of available forces for central Europe, but they left out entirely a quarter of a million French troops, thus giving the impression that the balance was heavily weighted towards the Russians. He also included battle tanks but not tactical nuclear weapons. The White Paper looked like a campaign document for higher military expenditure. This puts him in an impossible position, or would do if it were published that way. It would serve as a Tory propaganda sheet for rearmament. It was an outrage and was attacked by Elwyn Jones, Denis Healey, myself and others. Fred agreed to think about it again.

While I was sitting in the Cabinet I had a message from David Penhaligon [Liberal MP for Truro]. He had put my bill on re-organisation of the electricity supply industry to his colleagues, and they decided to reject it and will vote against it on second reading. I spoke to Eric Lubbock, who was furious that this had gone through without his being present, as he is the relevant Liberal spokesman, and Jo Grimond was peeved about it. The Liberals are disgusting.

In the Tea Room, Bob Cryer [Labour MP for Keighley], who is a junior Minister in the Department of Industry, told me that, when I was moved from the Industry and Eric Varley was appointed, the instruction went out to civil servants that it was to be treated as if there had been a change of administration. That is to say, Eric Varley was treated as an incoming Minister after a General Election and papers were submitted to him on the basis that there was no continuity from the previous Minister.

### Friday 3 February

The front page of the *Mirror* contained a reply by Penrose and Courtiour to Wilson's denials, saying they had fifteen hours of tape recordings and discussions with Marcia about the whole thing. In the back of my mind all sorts of thoughts are emerging. The help given to them by the police and the security services makes it seem they were in cahoots with the latter. The fact that Sir Martin Furnival Jones, the former head of MI5, was photographed and interviewed at his farm yesterday – something that has never happened before, to my knowledge – is an indication that the security services regard this book as helpful in so far as it discredits Wilson, and anything he says about the security services is therefore not going to be believed.

There was also a most interesting report in the *Mirror* today that

Geoffrey Goodman had advised Harold not to talk to journalists any more, in case he was brought into court to answer questions about what he knew of the alleged conspiracy to murder the former male model, Norman Scott. One cannot rule out the possibility that this could explode into an absolutely major scandal which would greatly damage the Labour Party at the time of the Election. The fact that Peter Bessell, the former Liberal MP, said he had worked for American Intelligence is also significant. I have seen Harold giving contradictory pledges to different people at different times and getting away with it – I used to wonder how long it could go on – and maybe he has been caught out in a horrifying and personal way after his retirement. It is sad, and I almost feel sorry for him, because he has got no friends left. He always managed to create such dissension among his personal staff and the people who worked with him that when he lost the magic power of patronage the whole ʋdifice crumbled.

### Sunday 5 February
Read some of Stephen's thesis on the American presidency and the White House staff. There is no doubt that it's going to be good and has the makings of a first-rate book.

### Monday 6 February
At lunch we discussed Thatcher's real campaign. Is she campaigning on British nationalism, on confrontation with the unions and with 'scroungers', on law and order and immigration? She will probably come out for the abolition of the rates, perhaps argue for the disenfranchisement of the Irish, and she will exploit unemployment and prices. The Labour Party has got to campaign on jobs and the need for a manufacturing base, on prices, on expanding public services, on defending our interests in the EEC, on having a society that works in harmony, on human values, hope and self-confidence.

There was a horrible article by Walter Terry in the *Sun*, 'Why Jim is Wild about Tony', calling for my sacking. The *Sun* campaign has really stepped up. It is most unpleasant to find yourself the recipient of such hatred. It is frightening because logicality and rationality fade from the picture.

### Wednesday 8 February
Lunch with Frances Morrell at the Stock Exchange on the invitation of John Wall, an old wartime friend of Harold Wilson's who is now a consultant to the stockbrokers Buckmaster and Moore. Also present were representatives of Hill Samuel, Lazard Brothers, Norwich Union Insurance, Guardian Royal Exchange, Kleinwort Benson, Barclays Bank and so on.

John Wall told me that Weinstock was the greatest demolition expert, never forgot a grievance and was always trying to knife people.

I had been asked to speak, and I developed the argument about de-industrialisation and the need for public investment.

Someone asked Frances what was so special about this country – if returns were higher abroad, better to invest there. Someone else enquired, 'Why do we need to manufacture? *Why* are you arguing for protection?'

'What do you think the Governor of the Bank of England was doing with his lifeboat operation to save the secondary banks?' I said. 'He was protecting them from the full consequences of market forces.'

'But that was to protect banks' – much more important than protecting jobs!

I said I assumed the City wanted the Labour Government to continue because they were afraid Mrs Thatcher would lead Britain to confrontation.

'We did believe that until yesterday!' said a representative from Barclays,* implying that the Government was being provocative.

To Cambridge to address the Tawney Group. I was met by Professor Raymond Williams, a quiet academic in his early sixties. There were about sixty people at the meeting and I was asked a lot of questions about the Common Market, import controls, protectionism and so on – good questions, but the audience was uneasy and didn't seem to know each other. Raymond Williams told me afterwards that Cambridge audiences were notoriously quiet and unresponsive.

*Thursday 9 February*
The *Daily Mail* had a picture of me getting into my car yesterday along with Michael Foot and Judith Hart, at a time when Ministers have been asked to economise on the use of petrol. The captions were: 'I have to get to work' for Michael; 'I would be happy to go by tube' for Judith; and, for me, 'I never go by public transport', which is quite untrue.

At Cabinet we discussed the question of a North Sea fund. The Cabinet Office has produced a paper outlining the case for and against a special fund for North Sea revenues. This is something I am very keen to get and we set up a little committee with Peter Shore, Bruce Millan, Harold Lever and Joel Barnett with an agreement to report after a week.

*Friday 10 February*
To Oxford with Stephen for the Nuffield College seminar, which David Butler had organised, on 'Accountability in Labour Politics'.

* On 7 February 1978 the Government was strongly attacked in the House of Commons for its policy of 'blacklisting' specific firms for contravening its 10 per cent limit on pay increases to workers, by withholding contracts and financial assistance.

I developed the argument about the various roles of a Member of Parliament, and afterwards I was cross-examined most sharply. David Butler asked, 'Is this typical of MPs or is it just you?' I said I could only describe it as I saw it.

I think British universities have lost their vitality; they have lost their cutting edge because they can't confront reality. I have come to the conclusion that middle-class intellectuals are not attaching themselves to Labour at all. They may not like Mrs Thatcher because she makes racialist speeches which frighten them, but a rap on the knuckles from the editor of the *Observer* or the *Guardian* doesn't worry her at all. She's going all out to get her people to vote. Raymond Williams said to me at Cambridge that the older intellectuals, even those who used to be Labour, were now frightened of the power of the trade unions.

At dinner I sat between the Warden, Sir Norman Chester, who will be seventy this year – an old friend of Herbert Morrison – and Philip Williams, who is a contemporary of Crosland, has just completed his *Life of Gaitskell* and is about to edit Gaitskell's diaries.

Upstairs for dessert and port. Stephen was amazed at the extravagance of the hospitality.

The Nuffield academics live somewhere in between big business, the mass media and the ivory towers of academe. They are cynical, detached and are only impressed when others are impressed – they respond to evidence of political power and strength but they themselves never really move.

*Sunday 12 February*

I caught the train to Oxford, where I was due to take part in a debate at St Aldate's Church. I was met by the Curate and we had a cup of coffee with the Rector, the Reverend Michael Green. They are both athletic, upper-class English evangelists, in a way muscular Christian types. I asked them if they went in for exorcism and they said, 'Oh certainly. There was a woman witch who came to us and we cleared her of witchcraft. We put oil on her brow and when she woke up she said it had burned her. And we have a patient who is dying of cancer, and after we had prayed with her the X-rays showed that the disease has been fought back.'

I must say I found it quite frightening. It was so absolutely medieval and my opinion of the two men fell.

There were about 800 people in the church and I spoke for twenty minutes from the pulpit. Michael Green followed with a most superficial and pessimistic speech attacking utopian ideas and saying man had put his confidence in reason, in science, in progress and in himself, and all of these had let him down. Christ offered instead an internal revolution. I thoroughly disliked it. It was preaching without reference to the practical experience of daily life. A warning on the dangers of professional preaching.

I attacked this pessimism on the grounds that it was being used to interpose priests between man and God – a marvellous way of carving out a place for yourself. He denied that.

There were some good questions about democracy and the class struggle. Somebody made the point that the labour movement was not looking for utopia – just a living wage, a job and better health facilities.

That the church is the opium of the people was entirely confirmed by the atmosphere there. On the other hand, there was a crowd of young people who were searching for something positive in the church. They are offered superficial doctrines of caring and concern, and it may be possible to win these groups for socialism.

Went back to the rectory with Michael Green and I met an American woman priest from the Episcopalian Church. I must say I preferred her to the two vicars.

It's been an interesting week, during which I have had the opportunity of trying out my arguments on a range of audiences.

*Tuesday 14 February*
Neil Kinnock came to lunch, and Caroline advised me to let him talk. Well, there was no problem there because he talked for an hour. He hadn't really thought deeply about the political situation and his conclusions were incredibly non-radical for a member of the Tribune Group. He believed that 'Emperor Jim with his quiet-life policy' was right for the Party and that this would be more comforting than Thatcher's divisiveness. We couldn't defeat right-wing populism, and his recommendations were so modest that they might have emerged from a latter-day Liberal. He often gave me the impression that he is not altogether serious. Not that he made jokes, but his arguments were just not convincing, and I found it rather depressing because I had looked to Neil for some sort of cutting edge.

Brian Sedgemore told me later that Neil was playing it long and didn't believe anything would happen until the late Eighties. But on his present performance I'm not sure he would have much to say even then.

*Wednesday 15 February*
The Liberals have now finally rejected my electricity reorganisation bill, and I went to see Mike Cocks and Michael Foot. Cocks is afraid that the Tories and the Liberals may vote against it. So I had to leave it at that.

What is so annoying about the Liberals is that they don't apply their minds to the issue. They have no ministerial experience, don't expect to form a Government, have no collective feeling in their own Shadow Cabinet or Parliamentary Party, and I think their attitude towards my bill was personal. They just don't want to be seen assisting me.

Hugh Jenkins told me he is thinking of giving up his seat in Putney as he will be seventy next birthday. He would like a job in the public sector but you can't be appointed after seventy.

*Thursday 16 February*
I had a strange minute asking my authority for the AEA to dispose of (I think) 540 kg of highly enriched uranium with a value of about £8 million. The AEA didn't need that amount and could sell it to the Americans in return for natural or low-enriched uranium, but this would upset the Common Market, which does need highly enriched uranium. The French would be able to get hold of it under the Euratom Treaty agreement, and if they enriched it further it would be weapons-grade material. The proposal was to blend it and sell it. It seemed to me *very* suspicious.

I raised a lot of questions with the Department: how and when the problem arose; why it was urgent; why the AEA had ordered it; what had changed that made it unnecessary now; whether there had been any pressure from the Common Market to buy uranium and if so when it had begun. In fact there *had* been pressure: the Common Market had written to say they would like to buy some uranium from us. I was told that the Euratom safeguard procedures meant that there had to be full disclosure on stocks of uranium.

I asked why we couldn't do a swap in this country – the military needed weapons-grade uranium and they could provide us with low-enriched uranium. But I was told we couldn't do that because the high-enriched uranium, when bought by the AEA, was subject to 'end-use' restrictions.

'Why not keep it?' I asked. 'It must be appreciating in value.' The Department just couldn't answer my questions, so I shall see Sir John Hill to get to the bottom of it. I have been caught so many times by half-truths and lies from the nuclear lobby.

Cabinet at 10.30, and we had a long discussion about the Scotland Bill. We had been defeated on a number of clauses, and Jim said that a defeat on the third reading would mean an Election.

I disagreed. It would damage the Government but there should not be an Election. People wouldn't understand it, and with Members voting much more freely now you couldn't regard every defeat as a vote of no confidence.

Joel Barnett took this up. 'Yes, you know there has been a change in the way MPs exercise their responsibilities now.'

Bill Rodgers said it wasn't a question of the Scotland Bill but of the

PM's authority. 'I think you should put your personal authority on the line.' He was rather implying that Jim should resign if we were defeated, and there was a sort of show of horror. Whether he actually meant it I don't know.

I asked how we would fight the Election. Would we say, 'Give us a big majority and we will introduce devolution', or what? You couldn't have an Election on this.

Jim was marginally influenced but he is basically an authoritarian. He said he wouldn't be able to carry on, he wasn't prepared to lead a rabble, and so on. He sees everything as a vote of confidence.

We came to the paper on North Sea oil, and I thanked Jim for giving Peter, Bruce and me a chance to present our case for a development fund.

I said there was a strong body of opinion in favour of the oil revenues being in a fund separate from other Treasury income. It was practicable and a matter of political will. 'We think it should be about £5 billion initially, rising gradually to absorb 50 per cent of the oil revenues. We would make an annual report and show how the money had been spent. It would account for only 2 per cent of public expenditure and it would answer Thatcher because it would show that we weren't going to fritter it away in tax cuts. It would give us a very strong electoral advantage.'

Joel Barnett thought the best way of frittering it away was to have a separate fund. 'It is not a problem of practicability; the question is, is it sensible?'

Peter Shore pointed out that Joel was really saying he didn't trust Ministers to spend the money wisely.

Lever was angry – you can tell because he goes red and his face becomes contorted. He said he was totally opposed to a fund. Of course Harold sees the possibility of tax cuts being removed, and it became increasingly obvious that this was yet another discussion about whether or not the Government was going to have an industrial policy.

Jim remarked, 'We have got very little in this paper to indicate how we would handle it.'

Denis Healey said, 'We would all *like* a fund but it would be at the expense of tax cuts or other programmes' – which was quite untrue.

Bill Rodgers was absolutely against it; John Morris was against because he thought it would raise expectations. David Ennals said it would distort priorities, and Roy Mason was opposed.

Michael Foot warned, 'There is a political danger, you know, that if you turn down the fund that will be the main news story.'

Eric Varley was opposed because private investment had a major role to play.

David Owen had been in favour of the fund, but wasn't any more, and thought we should explain the Government's conversion so that everyone would understand why we weren't having a fund.

Michael Foot suggested we discuss it with the Party first. Someone said you couldn't discuss it with the Party until you had a clear view. In the end it was agreed there would be a Party meeting to explain why there couldn't be a fund.

So that is the end of the saga of the oil revenues. They are now a part of the general public expenditure. Now that we have got money, we are doing a sort of IMF in reverse. We are not putting it into capital expenditure or public investment of one kind or another; we are going to give it away in tax cuts: that is the measure of the Labour Government.

### Friday 17 February

At 10 I went to the GEN 12 Cabinet committee on relations with South Africa. I have a feeling that Jim thinks it's convenient to have me there to tie me in. We had to consider how we should react to the mounting worldwide pressure to withdraw from our economic involvement in South Africa.

David Owen was in favour of a sort of disengagement policy. He said the US and France were now ready to move a little bit on withdrawing investment and the question was: should we do anything or just wait? He thought we should start working with the Common Market.

Jim Callaghan asked, 'What if we made concessions and there is no result? Why do it for political reasons? I won't be pushed. The Danes can do what they like, they've got nothing to lose, but jobs are at stake in this country.'

Denis Healey said, 'We must be ready to veto any UN move to push us towards mandatory sanctions. The question is how far we can drag our feet. I want to be carried kicking and screaming each millimetre of the way towards any interruption of our trade with South Africa. We might try and reduce our dependence on South Africa but we can't afford any overt actions.'

Michael Foot thought we should consider the Labour Conference.

'It seems to me', I said, 'that the basic argument is that we are too involved in South Africa economically to be free agents, rather than that sanctions would be counter-productive. However, the situation is rapidly deteriorating and the dangers will grow rather than diminish. Vorster will not move quickly enough to liberalise South Africa, to stave off fighting. Therefore it is in our interest to disengage as soon as possible to minimise the damage. I don't see the great gap now between the principle and our interests because even wise investors would get out.'

Jim said he didn't agree with that. He summed up, 'We agree that the situation will deteriorate, that it is in our interests to reduce our effort, that we should disengage, but it will take time, and we need international agreement.'

I must say, his summing up was totally different from the way in which he opened the discussion, so perhaps something was achieved.

*Sunday 19 February*

Caroline and I left for Chequers with Ron at about 9.45. It was a rather nice idea of Jim's that we should bring our wives, and Caroline had a swim in the heated pool.

We went up for the Cabinet at 11 and Jim said he would like to begin with a few items that weren't strictly related to the Budget and the pay situation. First he had some evidence that Margaret Thatcher was going to make a speech about law and order this weekend to try to influence the Ilford by-election, and Roy Hattersley had confirmed this because she had talked about nothing but muggings recently, no doubt to prepare the way. Jim said we would have to pre-empt that. Merlyn is going to make a statement this week.

Then he said he would like Ministers to make more speeches on Saturdays and Sundays. 'I know that Ministers don't usually make speeches over the weekend, not that I tap anyone's telephone' (which I thought was a strange comment), 'but we must now broaden the issues on which we speak beyond departmental interests.'

Jim went on to say that Thatcher was moving further and further to the right and it was something we hadn't seen before in a Tory leader, but that left us to occupy the centre ground.

'There are other factors here that we have got to take seriously,' Peter Shore argued. 'Mrs Thatcher is beginning to reflect a genuine English nationalist feeling, a deep feeling about the English and how they see themselves in terms of their own history.'

I said, 'What she is doing is long-range shelling deep behind our lines, attacking things we had assumed were already part of the consensus. There is a danger she will be political and we will be managerial, so I welcome what the Prime Minister has said about speeches being broader.'

Roy Mason commented, 'Thatcher is deliberately highlighting the security of the state, and stimulating fear, with talk of hooligans, rearmament, defence, and more money for law and order.'

From that little discussion I had a deep feeling of anxiety that we were being told we would have to move towards Mrs Thatcher on these issues.

We adjourned for lunch at 1, and as we left the room Sir John Hunt thanked me for sending my paper 'Accountability in Labour Politics'. 'I read it with great interest and I would like to talk to you about it.'

I said, 'Of course, it was written very much with you in mind because it's up your street.'

He gave me an impenetrable look. I'm glad I sent it to him. I don't want anyone to think I'm doing it under cover.

To sum up the day, there was a lot of goodwill but I feel isolated because I am in a minority. Jim is avuncular, calm, quiet, a Herbert Morrison type, always with an eye for what the man in the street will think and without much time for the rank and file of the Party.

### Monday 20 February

With Brian Sedgemore and Eric Huke, my Diary Secretary in the Private Office, I set off by car for the National Defence College in Cheshire, where I had been asked to speak. We had great difficulty getting there – no signposts, nothing.

As I went into the lecture hall with the commander, Major-General Bate, a bell was rung and everybody stood up. There was a scatter of uniforms, army, navy and marine, with one or two dark blue uniforms of police officers, and some civilians from the Foreign Office and the MoD, including a Professor Ian Wells from Newcastle University.

I spoke for forty minutes and then answered questions. Why had I accepted an open-cast coal scheme in Manchester against the advice of the inspector? Was the price of oil likely to fall? What about alternative sources of energy? One officer got up and asked about the power of the trade unions in relation to vulnerability of energy supplies. I said there were lots of powers in the land: the trade unions are powerful, the IMF are powerful, the media are powerful, the Civil Service and the military are very powerful. The art of politics is to try to govern by consent, to blend these powers into the common interest.

I came to the conclusion that the seven-month course there was more than just an academic exercise. I think they are really training up people for a military situation in Great Britain, no doubt drawing heavily on the experience of Northern Ireland. While we were having drinks before lunch, I asked them to what extent they were free to talk politically, but the truth is that uniforms and hierarchies of rank are absolutely inimical to the development of free thought. I daresay armies are like that all over the world.

At lunch I sat opposite General Bate, and the subject of a military coup here came up. Professor Wells mentioned Cecil King's coup plot and his approach to Mountbatten in 1968, and then General Bate said, 'There was a movement called PFP – Philip for President. The paras were supposed to be involved, and some movement of troops in Northern Ireland was contemplated.'

I said, 'I suppose in 1974 there must have been a theory that the incoming Government was a revolutionary one, that the General Strike had succeeded as it were, and Harold Wilson was going to introduce socialism – a laughable idea.' They all did laugh – rather nervously.

We went on to talk about military matters, and I said I was puzzled why guerrilla forces seemed to have done so well against highly armed, high-technology armies since the war.

They replied, 'Well, they're motivated. They can do things we can't do because we have to maintain civilised standards.'

General Bate said, 'Read Brigadier Kitson's book, *Low-Intensity Operations*. He is the great expert on methods of terrorisation.'[1]

I can't say that I got a clear indication that they were engaged in training of that kind but I would be very surprised if they were not. I was wearing my RAF tie and tweed suit and tried to look relaxed, but the whole visit was tense, and the General did most of the talking.

He said that the German Army, although intended as purely defensive, resembled precisely the old army that had been built up to attack Russia. He said that if you really wanted a defence from Russian attack in western Europe you would need *Volksstürmer*, ie just armed citizenry, but it would depend on motivation. The Russians could now advance into West Germany easily.

This provided an interesting insight, and I am absolutely persuaded that the hierarchy of a disciplined force is incompatible with intelligent thinking and intelligent operations. I have no doubt they are less silly than the old soldiers used to be, and no doubt more competent, but you cannot think and understand if you live in such complete isolation and are disciplined in such a hierarchical way.

After lunch we picked up Ron, who said he had been in the Sergeants' Mess having a meal: he said it was real 'eating by numbers'!

Eric Huke told me that he had to give notification of my movements every weekend to the Cabinet Office, and on one occasion when he rang them up with the details they said they wanted it in writing, because they have to send a copy to Special Branch.

Watched a *Panorama* special on Nazi Germany. In effect the denazification programme, the trials of prominent Nazis, had been completely blanked out by the Americans after the war as they built Germany up to be an anti-communist state under Adenauer. There was one German interviewed who said the Baader–Meinhof gang believe that Germany has not been properly denazified. It must be extremely difficult for German socialists; they must be worried that if they don't appear to be following a strong line they themselves will be gobbled up in a new Nazi movement in Germany.

*Tuesday 21 February*
Caught the plane to Washington with Frances Morrell, James Bretherton and David Jones, and we were taken to the residence in the

Ambassador's Daimler. Washington looked beautiful. It is the centre of the capitalist world, just as Moscow is the centre of the communist world, and when I come here I feel like a provincial. The Embassy, which was built by Lutyens in the Twenties, is lovely.

Lunch at the Georgetown University Center for Strategic and International Studies, where Schlesinger worked before he went into the White House. It is where top corporate lawyers and intellectuals rest between their administrative positions – a place where you are debriefed and rebriefed; we have no parallel for it. A guy called Frank Murray, I think, was my host. Murray worked in the CIA as an analyst. It is amazing to find people ready to talk openly of their connections with the CIA, which is still seen abroad as an evil influence, at least by the left.

I had a feeling that the place was full of agents trying to find out what British energy policy was. I simply listed all the problems that were unsolved.

Came back to the Embassy for a dinner which had been laid on by Peter and Margaret Jay. Jack O'Leary, the Deputy Secretary, was there. He was asked if he thought nuclear energy would grow, and he said, 'A hundred years from now, there won't be any nuclear. It will peak and fall.' His consistent opposition to nuclear power is remarkable.

*Thursday 23 February*
At 3.15 Frances, David, James and I were taken to the White House to see Schlesinger. He is an extraordinary man – like Dick Crossman in looks and intellect and Denis Healey in manner. He didn't ask me a single question, not even how I was getting on. He was quite cold and academic and simply answered my questions.

I asked how his energy policy was going and he said, 'We'll get it through.'

I said, 'What about an east–west energy conference?' He said that wasn't worth having; American and British Intelligence knew more about the Russians than the Russians would be prepared to tell us.

The phone rang and he answered, 'Give me ten minutes.' Then the phone rang again and he said, 'I have got to see the President', and left us.

*Friday 24 February*
Breakfast with Peter Jay and Senator Scoop Jackson, Chairman of an important Senate Committee, a tremendous hardliner on international affairs and violently anti-Russian, although he had a good reputation for fighting McCarthyism at home (so he said). He is quite liberal in domestic matters and in favour of a much bigger Government role in the energy field.

He has just been to China and I asked about Intelligence reports on China. He said, 'You see them as well as I do.' These top Americans talk about Intelligence reports as if they were newspapers that anyone can read.

Flew back in Concorde.

### Monday 27 February

Campaign Committee to consider the effect of women's votes on an Election. Joyce Gould introduced it and said there were more women working than in 1974, women had switched their vote to us in February 1974, but Thatcher was quite liked by working-class women; the Tories had produced a family policy, and married working women were more volatile and less conservative than women who were not at work. She said, 'We don't want special literature for women but we do want women's input in all our literature.'

Jim said women hated strikes and men who strike, and Labour was best able to deal with industrial relations; women like harmony and unity. He himself was going to speak for the Townswomen's Guilds and the WRVS as an indication of his desire to get out into non-Labour organisations.

According to Ron Hayward, studies done after the 1974 Election showed that we needed Labour activists to take over non-political organisations, and that unions on the whole were hostile to women.

Shirley Williams said, 'Women prefer Thatcher, but the consumer rights movement helps us because big businesses do exploit women.'

Eric Heffer thought young women were very selfish, particularly about the old.

'Well, we must watch Thatcher, and the broadcasting of Parliament would help us in that respect,' Jim concluded.

### Wednesday 1 March

Dashed over to the weekly PLP meeting and I'm glad I did because I heard about forty minutes of the debate on reselection of MPs.

Joe Ashton said he wanted to be practical; a local Party general management committee must be able to sack an MP – that was what democracy was about – but we must get it right, otherwise we could have twenty-five deselected Reg Prentices and it would be impossible for the Parliamentary Party to discipline them for the remainder of the Parliament.

Then came one of the most remarkable speeches I have ever heard in my twenty-eight years in Parliament. John Golding [MP for Newcastle-under-Lyme], who is a real tough cookie, got up and said, 'I was adopted as a candidate because I could organise the selection conference via the union. I got forty-six votes: it was a disappointment because fifty votes had been promised to me and I lost four votes in the course of the selection conference. I could hold that seat by organising the GMC any time I like, by packing the delegates in. I have organised more selection conferences, and seen how they are packed, than anyone in this room excepting Ron Hayward and Reg Underhill. The ideal method of selection under which people are chosen by the GMC is pure cotton wool. It doesn't happen like that at all.

'Now, if we choose to reselect MPs, it will be a traumatic experience because we shall start packing GMCs to see that our people get in. The Party would take two years to recover and it would be disastrous. The Parliamentary Party is already divided into factions and we must not translate that situation into the constituency parties.'

He added, 'I protect the trade union seats from the media men, from lecturers and lawyers, and if reselection is to take place it must be reselection by *all* the members of the Party.' Well, by this time people at the meeting were laughing at this extraordinary declaration of truth by a right-wing organiser. If it had been a left-winger who said this – Eric Heffer or Neil Kinnock or worst of all Andy Bevan – the place would have been in uproar. But the cynicism was such that the Party just took it. Michael Cocks said, 'He's right, you know, that's what actually happens.' I felt utterly sick.

Bob Cryer said, 'As a point of order, I hope that speech is not reported.'

Audrey Wise spoke next, and in a typically democratic way she said she very much regretted that Labour Party members *couldn't* hear that speech. It is indeed *because* you can pack one selection conference that reselection is necessary.

I had to leave then, but I am awfully glad I went. It was the talk of the day.

### Thursday 2 March
At 9.30 I had a talk with Derek Ezra about the Coal Board's financial forecasts. I had been asked to approve a letter to Ezra permitting the NCB, with Treasury support, to stock the mass of coal which is coming out of the pits as a result of the productivity scheme. I can see that the Treasury are going to get difficult, and there will be pit closures coming – as Arthur Scargill and Dennis Skinner have predicted.

Cabinet at 10.15, and for the first time ever official photographs were taken of the Cabinet. I don't know what made Jim do it. I had my camera and I took a couple of pictures in the Cabinet Room.

### Friday 3 March
We lost the Ilford by-election and there is no doubt that the Party is depressed at the apparent success of Thatcher's exploitation of the race issue.

*Monday 6 March*
At the Home Policy Committee, which wasn't terribly exciting, we agreed in principle that the Party should commit itself to opposing blood sports; we will also look at factory farming, the protection of the environment, vivisection and cruelty to animals.

*Tuesday 7 March*
Lord Aldington wrote to me recently saying he was confused about the PWR's role in our nuclear policy, so I saw him today and explained it clearly. I told him I had received a letter from Arnold Weinstock stating that he was not interested in the reorganisation of the nuclear construction industry. When I said I wanted to get on with it quickly, Aldington said, 'There's plenty of time.' I think the plain truth is that the PWR lobby, including Weinstock and Walter Marshall, are now trying to delay electricity reorganisation in the hope that the Government will lose office and they will be able to change the priorities back to the American PWR.

Caroline and I had lunch with the Soviet Ambassador, Lunkov, and his wife. We learned that this was a Russian festival with pancakes and other celebrations; it was the Shrove Tuesday of the Russian Orthodox Church. Lunkov told me he was a member of the Central Committee of the Soviet Communist Party – which I did not realise – and that Kosygin was extremely interested in the UK. He also said Mrs Thatcher had made a number of soundings about visiting the Soviet Union but Jim Callaghan was against her going at the moment.

*Wednesday 8 March*
Went with Brian Sedgemore to the *Sun* offices for lunch with Larry Lamb. I think he is a most unattractive individual. With him were Bernard Shrimsley, editor of the *News of the World*, and his brother Anthony, political correspondent of the *Sun*; and one or two others. We began rather awkwardly because the *Sun* is such a vicious paper. We got on to talking about moral responsibility, about journalists accepting responsibility for what they had done, about signing editorials and all that. Larry Lamb said, 'Your "lift operator" speech was marvellous' (this was when I stated at the 1972 Conference that trade-unionists in the media, including the lift operators at Thomson House, had a responsibility for what was said about the movement). 'The trouble was, you meant it.' 'I sure did,' I replied.

*Tuesday 14 March*
As I was sitting outside the Cabinet Room waiting for a meeting Jim came up. He was very agitated about something. He heard me cough and said, 'Nothing trivial I hope.'

Over lunch Frances gave me a great lecture and made a list of my strengths and weaknesses. My weaknesses, she said, were that I was thought to be fanatical and humourless, and that I was building on too narrow a base in the Party. She advised me, 'You must be more human and more relaxed. And you must go for more support in the PLP and TUC General Council.'

*Thursday 16 March*
To Acton Magistrates Court to act as a character witness for Audrey Wise on charges of obstructing the police at Grunwick last year. I was only in the box for a moment. She was found guilty of obstructing a policeman and fined.

*Friday 17 March*
To the new industrial archaeology museum in Bristol's Dockland. I got there early, and along came this old 1920s steam locomotive, built in Bristol, with a little van attached to the engine, to take us along the quayside past the SS *Great Britain*. It was just a four-minute journey, but thrilling. I wandered inside the museum and it was great fun. Industrial archaeology is now becoming popular; nostalgia is a powerful influence in life. There were fire engines, printing presses, a helicopter and a model of Concorde, and 'carriage and pairs' to take you along the front.

*Wednesday 22 March*
At 9 I had my first meeting with Ian Gillis, my new Chief Information Officer, who is replacing Bernard Ingham. I miss Bernard.

Picked up Mother at noon, and we went to the Harcourt Room of the House of Commons for this lovely lunch to celebrate the centenary of Jim Middleton's birth. Jim Middleton worked for Keir Hardie in 1902 as Assistant Secretary to the Labour Party. When Arthur Henderson gave up the secretaryship in the 1930s, Jim became General Secretary for ten years until Morgan Phillips took over in 1944. In the mid-Thirties he married his second wife, Lucy Cox, who was the MP for Plymouth Sutton from 1945 to 1951, so she and I overlapped in Parliament by a year.

The old brigade were all there. Mother sat between Malcolm and Alastair MacDonald, Ramsay's two sons. I'd never met Malcolm before; Alastair remembered my going to the Trooping of the Colour at Number 10 in 1930. There was Fenner Brockway, ninety this year, Will Henderson, who is almost eighty-six, son of Arthur, and Press Officer at Transport House till 1946, Ian Mikardo, Joan Lestor, Elwyn Jones and others.

*Saturday 25 March*

I'm reading E. P. Thompson's *William Morris*, which is a marvellous book. It gives me an insight into his relationship to the Romantic poets of the 1830s, influenced by the French Revolution. I found it a little difficult understanding the link between the Romantic movement and the Pre-Raphaelites, but I was more familiar with William Morris and the Social Democratic Federation. He opposed the parliamentary socialists in the first instance and was contemptuous of the Fabians.

*Saturday 1 April*

This afternoon the family watched *Mrs Miniver*, the 1942 film with Greer Garson and Walter Pidgeon about what was supposed to be an average English middle-class family facing the war. It was made in America but caught the spirit of England as well as American actors could. It showed with startling clarity the accepted class structure of the period, and I'd like to think it's all different now but I can't honestly say it is.

*Tuesday 4 April*

James Bretherton made the point yesterday that nobody takes the Government seriously. With an Election coming, civil servants are very leisurely and industrialists are busy preparing to get us out of office. So gradually we are moving from an administrative role to a campaigning one.

Shore said today that he felt more and more like a lame duck – I think the whole of Whitehall is getting that feeling.

I had a big success today. Some time ago Derek Ezra proposed selling coking coal to South Africa, and I said no because we didn't want to increase our economic entanglement there. I wrote round to Ministers informing them of this.

Predictably, Edmund Dell and Denis Healey thought we should sell, but David Owen put in a letter supporting me. Yesterday I received a note from Number 10 saying that the Prime Minister had seen the correspondence and agreed with David Owen (not with me, although it was my proposal). So the coking coal will not be sold to South Africa.

I had consulted Alex Eadie, saying our decision might cost jobs in the mining industry, but he felt the principle was such an important one that the NUM would support me, and yesterday he sent me a page from the *Yorkshire Miner* on South Africa, arguing that 'an injury to one is an injury to all'.

*Wednesday 5 April*

The first item at NEDC was the farewell to Jack Jones. Jack said he'd done his best and he hoped to work for the pensioners' campaign now.

John Methven, Director-General of the CBI, said, 'May I say something very personal. Jack Jones's contribution to the fight against inflation has made possible the tax cuts we all expect in the Budget.'

I thought that summed up, rather sadly, the end of Jack Jones's career – that by persuading workers to cut their wage claims he'd helped create a budget surplus that made it possible for rich directors to get tax cuts.

You can't but like Jack. He's done his work out of loyalty and affection for the labour movement – and patriotism, as he sees it.

After lunch I had to present the British Empire Medal to a man who had been a gas meter examiner for forty-seven years; there he was, very proud, with his two sons and his daughter-in-law.

Over to the PLP, which was delayed a bit, so I chatted to Joel Barnett and Denis about leaks.

I said to Denis, 'It must have been awful when you were Minister of Defence and Chapman Pincher was leaking everything.'

'Oh well, Chapman Pincher was extremely close to MI5,' said Denis. 'Don't tell anybody, but that, I know, was the position. There was a man at MI5, an extreme right-winger, feeding Pincher with stories until he retired or resigned – then that was the end of it.'

*Thursday 6 April*
At Cabinet I asked about the news item two nights ago, announcing that the British Government was supporting the neutron bomb. The news had showed Soviet tanks in action followed by American film demonstrating what the neutron bomb could do – ie kill people by intense radiation without damaging buildings. The neutron bomb is sometimes called the capitalist bomb because it protects property, which is what capitalists care about most.

I asked what the policy was, and Jim said he had spoken to Carter, who appeared to be coming out against it because of détente. Carter stated that American–Soviet relations were better than they looked. Jim didn't wish to take a strong line against the neutron bomb, as the Germans had, and he hoped that Carter would see the wisdom of holding back and thinking of the effect on SALT.

David Owen said the neutron bomb was less horrific than existing nuclear weapons, but he did think Carter was against it.

*Friday 7 April*
Bristol. I went to the Exclusive Brethren meeting hall in Wick Road. I have been looking into their dispute with the Charity Commission, which has denied them charitable status. The Commission had concluded that the doctrine of the 'pro-Taylorites' in the Exclusive Brethren – which states that one may not eat with, work with or be in

fellowship with those who commit adultery or business malpractice or whatever – is contrary to the public interest.

What I had taken to be a warehouse between the houses and factories turned out to be the most amazing circular auditorium with a gallery capable of holding 2500 people. As the lights came on slowly, I saw that each seat was fitted with a microphone so that anyone in the audience could speak. I was astonished.

### Monday 10 April

Organisational Sub-Committee at 3.30. There was a long discussion about the National Front. Frank Allaun believed they should be banned from TV and schools, and should be treated as pariahs. I said it wasn't their appearance on TV that gave them publicity so much as the press. You couldn't stop TV covering their meetings during the Election, and I thought it was better to argue it out.

Frank and I don't see eye to eye on this. I can understand his point. He thinks that, if Hitler had been crushed early on, the holocaust would never have happened.

I take a rather old-fashioned liberal view, but I didn't win. Advice is to be given to local candidates and I think I shall be able to justify whatever the Party decides.

Snow fell today. Unbelievable. It isn't quite frozen but it is very cold and the trees are bending with the lovely snow on their boughs. Caroline went out after midnight and I took a photograph of her with my polaroid against the white background.

### Tuesday 11 April

While we were waiting to go into GEN 12 Committee, Elwyn Jones, a

*'Horror upon horror! Someone else has defected to Capitalism!'*

great retailer of jokes, told me a story about a rather aristocratic and rhetorical Oxford professor of philosophy whose lectures drew huge audiences. Once, as he was making a point, the stucco fell from the wall and one of the students was heard to remark, 'I always doubted whether the premises would stand his conclusions!'

In GEN 12, the Cabinet committee on South Africa, David Owen put in a host of papers designed to bring about our disengagement from South Africa. He introduced the main paper on economic measures and said the principle was that we should stick with America, France, Germany and Canada and continue to veto the Chapter 7 Determination at the UN, although the US were less anxious to use their veto because they had fewer interests in South Africa.

Other specific proposals were withdrawal of export credit guarantees for insurance cover in South Africa; the end of Government promotion of trade, though there should still be chambers of commerce, which is the form of trade promotion that the Germans have adopted; withdrawal of our Service attachés; promulgation of the EEC code of conduct; and no new commitments by the nationalised industries.

Edmund Dell disagreed. 'Why should we take the lead? Export prospects are poor enough for Britain anyway because of political decisions, and we need raw materials from South Africa.'

Michael Foot said the choices would get harder later on if they weren't faced now. We couldn't afford a breach with America over African policy. Fred Mulley said it was all very abrupt, and, besides, the Service attachés were in the country for Intelligence purposes to find out what was going on there. Indeed, they were financed by the Intelligence Services.

The continuing argument was that because we were tied in so closely with South Africa we couldn't do very much. That, of course, is precisely why we *should* disengage.

### Thursday 13 April

Bryan Gould came to lunch with me. Douglas Jay thinks highly of him. He is an able guy, very much an establishment man, but anti-EEC. He was formerly an official on the European Co-operation desk at the Foreign Office, and was in Brussels for two and a half years before leaving to become a law don. He got into Parliament in 1974. We talked about the EEC and the drift to federalism – whether we should fight the direct elections and so on.

On economic policy he was a bit muddled. He did not agree with import controls, and he wanted exchange controls eased, on the grounds that the export of capital would bring the exchange rate down and make us more competitive.

Stephen looked in at home; he's going to be a candidate for

Queensgate Ward in the local elections, fighting Sir Malby Crofton, former Tory leader of the Kensington and Chelsea Council.

*Friday 14 April*
We won the Garscadden by-election, which represents a turning point in British politics because the Scot Nats were beginning to threaten Labour seats; an SNP victory could have meant losing twenty more seats in the General Election. One feels the tide of Scottish nationalism is beginning to turn.

Rang ACAS to try to find out more about the closure of the Spillers bakery in Brislington. The Bakers' Union is shocked at the Government's inactivity.

It is an awful story. On 7 April the workers at the bakery were told that it would close in a fortnight, and that they would get their basic ninety-day statutory redundancy pay. Within two hours of the announcement, people had turned up at the bakery and begun measuring up the trucks and equipment. The area secretary of the Bakers' Union, Serge Kuchavenny, told me that the workers wanted me to look into the possibility of setting up a workers' co-operative.

*Thursday 20 April*
Lunch with Harry Evans, editor of the *Sunday Times*. I keep in touch with him and have a certain respect for him. Publication of the paper has been severely disrupted by industrial disputes and he said the position could hardly be more serious. 'We have converted a £250,000 profit last year into a £200,000 loss this year, and although we stuck to the pay policy last year, because we believed in it, the *Daily Express* didn't and is now paying £200 a week for certain jobs, undermining the whole of Fleet Street.' He said there was absolute chaos and some of the shop stewards were communists and all that stuff. 'I've got very bad management, and I am trying to get a bit more participation.'

I asked him what he thought the Election would be about.

'Economic policy,' he replied, 'especially jobs, but it is also going to be about personal freedom.'

*Friday 21 April*
To Bristol, where I was met by Serge Kuchavenny and driven to the Spillers factory. I was taken into the canteen and about sixty people gave me a rather weak cheer. These were the bakery workers, half of them Asian, preparing to take on Spillers, a huge international corporation.

They told me they had done a complete study of how they could run the bakery with a small number of people and a few drivers to transport their products; they could operate it with 120 people out of the 564 employed there. The bakery itself was profitable but had been forced to carry a share of the heavy overheads of the London headquarters, and this was more than its profits could bear. They told me there were tons of administrators at the bakery now doing nothing but living off the workers.

The company had removed road tax discs from the lorries so they couldn't be used, and they had gone to -every conceivable length, including bringing in Securicor, to stop the bakery from continuing.

As I left, I noticed they had even welded the doors; under the Criminal Trespass Act, this can be used to keep out squatters. In 1974 I had asked Ministers if the Act could be used to prevent a work-in, and was told it had nothing to do with industrial disputes. But of course, as Serge said, if anyone breaks the weld they can be prosecuted for criminal damage and evicted.

So a Labour Government, Labour legislation and the monopoly situation have all conspired to increase the power of capital and diminish the power of labour. Outside I gave an impromptu press conference and said that we had seen the murder of 564 jobs.

*Thursday 27 April*
Alex Eadie and I had a meeting with Joe Gormley, Mick McGahey and the Nottinghamshire Area NUM, plus some NACODS people. They made an immensely powerful argument against the closure of the Teversal colliery on the grounds that it had always been profitable, that they could develop the Clowne seam and should be allowed to do so.

My brief was to tell them to settle it with the Coal Board: 'not a matter for me' and so on – the classic departmental line. But I had told Mick McGahey privately that I intended to inform the Coal Board that they could not close pits without the miners' consent. So I said I could not assess the geology but was absolutely determined not to repeat what happened in the 1960s when Alf Robens and the Government just passed the buck backwards and forwards on closures. It had to be settled between the Coal Board and the NUM, and the only way to achieve that was for me to instruct the Coal Board that closures must be agreed with the NUM. It would be a major change because, if the Coal Board felt they had a case, disclosure would be necessary to satisfy the NUM. I told them I would send a message to Derek Ezra not to give a final judgement tomorrow.

I am determined to leave a structure like this behind me to ensure that they can't start a closure programme after I have left without reopening the whole matter.

*Saturday 29 April*
Caught the 88 bus to Trafalgar Square for the Friends of the Earth

Windscale demonstration. There were about 10,000 people, mostly young, and it reminded me of the CND marches, with a combination of right-wing and rather prim ecological people and left-wing commune types with beards and babies.

I climbed up the steps of St Martin-in-the-Fields and sat on my portable seat facing the square. There was a group playing and then the speeches began. I couldn't hear very well so I went round and took a few pictures.

Friends of the Earth are not politically strong enough to stop nuclear power but they are hoping to check the mad rush towards the fast breeder, and I think that's an extremely powerful counter-pressure to have.

The 6 o'clock news reported Arthur Scargill's call for civil disobedience to stop Windscale, and Caroline remarked that he was really a general in the field – indeed, she had seen him recently in a television interview with General Clutterbuck talking about the army's role in civil disturbances, Clutterbuck having written on the subject.

Anyway Arthur came to dinner at 7 with his wife Anne, and some sympathetic journalists. Stephen looked in momentarily.

Arthur told me it was rumoured that I was there in the crowd, but I couldn't possibly have spoken because I am the Minister responsible for Windscale.

Throughout the evening, Arthur talked most of the time. He is about thirty-eight, a remarkable leader, tough, perky, amusing, with lots of personality, a marvellous mimic of all sorts of accents.

He said that coal production in Yorkshire had fallen in the first few months of this year; seven pits were now on strike as a result of arguments over the productivity scheme; accidents had increased substantially; and the only real increase in output had come about as a result of open-cast mining. I had figures prepared by the Coal Board in my red box and we went over them together. He gave me some good questions to ask.

It is desperately necessary to have new leadership in the NUM, and if there were a ballot for the President or General Secretary I have no doubt that Arthur would win. He suffers, as I do, from being seen as a public villain, and he's had to have police guards for a month at a time in the past. Somebody took a pot shot at him outside his house not long ago. Anne is very courageous and tries to see the funny side.

Arthur thought that, if we lost the Election, I would become Leader of the Party.

'I'm not so sure,' I said, 'because a lot of left-wing MPs would be defeated and the PLP could drift back to the right. Also the trade union leaders would have to work with the new Government and wouldn't want a critical left-wing Labour Party which might embarrass them in front of their own rank and file.'

'The miners would support you,' said Arthur.

### Monday 1 May
Air Chief Marshal Sir Neil Cameron, Chief of Defence Staff, who is in Peking at the moment, was quoted as saying he looked forward to close co-operation with the Chinese armed forces against their common enemy, Moscow. This has created a storm of protest – and rightly so.

### Tuesday 2 May
I wrote to the Prime Minister this morning expressing my hope that Sir Neil Cameron's speech in Peking would be raised at Cabinet on Thursday, on the grounds that it did not reflect Government policy and that statements on foreign policy should be made by Ministers and not generals.

Paul Routledge, industrial correspondent of *The Times*, telephoned to say that Terry Duffy had won a 4 to 3 victory over Bob Wright for the presidency of the AUEW, which confirmed my view that we would be facing a right-wing trade union leadership.

Hilary's wife, Rosalind, has got to go into hospital tomorrow because she has something on one of her lungs and they want to investigate it further.

### Wednesday 3 May
To GEN 119, a committee set up to consider a paper on public appointments written by Sir Douglas Allen before he left. Allen suggested that we issue nomination papers so that the appointments list could be broadened, but I wanted a system which included proper applications and selection boards. I recommended to Jim that where an appointment has been made – say, Chairman of the Coal Board – there ought to be a confirmation procedure, as in the American Congress, where the relevant committee could hear evidence. I said there was a much broader question to consider here and that was patronage.

Jim said, 'I just sign every name put through to me.'

'Well, that's not surprising,' I told him. 'As Prime Minister, you must be flattened by the burden of your patronage. Harold Wilson appointed 103 Cabinet Ministers, 403 Ministers of State and junior Ministers, 243 peers, 26 chairmen of nationalised industries, 16 Chairmen of Royal Commissions and all the bishops and judges.'

'I don't find it a burden at all,' Jim replied.

I said, 'That's not the point. There is too much patronage. Why shouldn't people be able to apply for jobs in the public service? It's honourable work.'

In the end, proposals for a new system were turned down – even Allen's limited proposal for nominations.

*Thursday 4 May*
Cabinet. At the end of foreign affairs, Jim asked if there were any other points.

I said, 'I want to make three points on the Neil Cameron business. First of all, it is not for a Service chief to define a common enemy. Secondly, the whole purpose of this is as a weapon against us; the Tories have taken it up in order to suggest that the Labour Party is pro-Soviet. Thirdly, I think it would be damaging to the Government if the impression was created that the military was out of control.'

David Owen said, 'Surely the right thing to do is to warm up our relations with China. What's wrong with defence sales? Maybe it was an error of wording by Cameron, but we do have to face the fact that the military *do* think of the Russians as the enemy.'

Then Jim chipped in. 'A part of our Party is pro-Soviet; but in this country most people are deeply suspicious of the Soviet Union.'

'It's a pity Tony never talks to ordinary people,' Denis Healey said.

I came back in. 'I hope we remember that the United Kingdom sent an expeditionary force to Russia to try and crush the revolution; the Soviet Union also lost 20 million people in the last World War. Apart from secret members of the Communist Party – if that is what the PM is referring to – we cannot assume that anyone who does not describe the USSR as an enemy, or does not want to be in an anti-Soviet alliance with China, is therefore pro-Soviet. After all, we are now trying to pursue détente policy while Thatcher is warmongering.'

Fred Mulley was asked to comment; he said that Cameron and the military were more under control than under his predecessors, and we must remember that it was a Marxist China that Mrs Thatcher was trying to get involved with.

Jim asked, 'Does anyone say we should have sacked Cameron?'

I recalled Truman's sacking of McArthur in similar circumstances, which won him a considerable reputation for firmness.

Jim said, 'I thought of making a statement, "I have every confidence in Aircraftsman Cameron", and downgrade him that way.'

The atmosphere was nasty but I'm glad I raised it.*

Worked at home on my red box and stayed up to hear the local election results. Hilary and Stephen both lost.

---

* The Cabinet minutes subsequently referred to the item as 'Relations with China and the Soviet Union – conclusions recorded separately', so the discussion obviously made some impact.

*Friday 5 May*
At 9.30 to the Economic and Industrial Committee of Cabinet for a decision on whether to give further help to KME, the co-operative in Kirkby which I set up as Secretary for Industry.

Edmund Dell just sounded like a right-wing Tory. 'The NEB are not interested in KME. They are there to finance viable enterprises, and the DHSS should deal with this case. When I have a closure in my constituency, people come to me and say, "You're a Cabinet Minister, can't you help?", and I have to say no. We must not encourage people to think they can get things just by asking Labour Ministers. It would be a public scandal to keep it going.'

Peter Shore came in; he really hasn't got the right feel. We had said we wouldn't give more support and he argued that if we did it would destroy our credibility. We couldn't single out Kirkby when there were other plants being closed, like the Leyland plant at Speke.

Eric Varley claimed that the Scots didn't want support given to Kirkby, and Mike Cocks said, 'Workers' co-operatives, as a last resort, are a bad thing. There is resentment among workers who don't get help. Kirkby is the worst area in Merseyside, with armoured grocery vans because of the vandalism. There are better uses for the money.'

Bob Sheldon, Financial Secretary to the Treasury, felt we couldn't have privileged sectors.

I called for the issue to go to Cabinet, and Eric Varley said he would minute the Prime Minister.

I must say, as I left, I couldn't bring myself even to speak to Peter, and I felt that the committee had nothing whatever to do with the Labour Party.

*Saturday 6 May*
Melissa is in bed with flu. Rosalind came out of hospital; she has a growth in her lung but it's not clear yet what it is.

*Sunday 7 May*
The *Sunday Telegraph* quoted from an article in the student magazine of the London Bible College in Northwood, in which Sir Neil Cameron had actually referred to communists as the Antichrist. With the Chief of Defence Staff declaring holy war on the Russians, it gives fresh impetus to the demand for proper political control over the military.

*Thursday 11 May*
The first meeting was Cabinet, and as I was waiting to go in I saw Fred Peart and asked him how the TV broadcasting from the Lords was going. Mike Cocks chipped in, 'People prefer the Lords broadcast to

the Commons radio broadcast. You'll find it impossible to abolish the Lords now.'

'Good heavens,' I said, 'we don't want the House of Lords; the country should be governed by the Queen. It should be an absolute monarchy. After all, she's much more popular than the Lords – she only makes one speech a year . . .' When he realised I was having him on, he got rather angry.

There was some discussion in Cabinet about the Finance Bill. Denis said, 'We've lost £340 million on the PSBR because of the 1p cut in taxation, and another £105 million because of the increased threshold – that's almost £450 million lost this week.' He didn't know what the effects on the markets would be. 'We should defer a decision on recouping, but a contingency plan is needed, and there are basically three ways of doing it.'

'Please don't mention them,' Jim interrupted, as if it were all terribly secret.

Well, as I left the Cabinet I heard the 1 o'clock news and the economics correspondent said, 'As the Treasury sees it, there are three ways of recouping this money. . .' So the Treasury brief had already gone to the BBC, while the Cabinet was denied the information on the grounds of secrecy.

We came on to KME, referred from the Cabinet committee, and it was a most unpleasant discussion. Jim interrupted every speaker, basically to deny that Merseyside was a disaster area.

I said it would cost as much to close KME, because of the subsequent unemployment, as it would to keep it going, but, if it were closed, imports would pour in. Unemployment in Kirkby was already 20 per cent – perhaps not a disaster area but still unacceptable. I told Jim I was glad he hadn't been appointed head of the IMF, because he would have been much harsher on us than the present one. The only criticism of Kirkby was that they had got their forecasts wrong, but, since this Cabinet had needed to have twelve Budgets in four years, we were not the people to criticise them.

Jim was furious. 'It's all very well you saying that, but I get the jeers and you get the cheers. It's clear that the Cabinet is against it, and now we must fight it politically – against the activists, who will be very angry about it.'

So that was the death of Kirkby – a story I have chronicled from beginning to end.

*Saturday 13 May*
Hilary and Rosalind came to tea. She doesn't look at all well but she's very courageous. Melissa argued violently against the Labour Party,

said it had betrayed everybody and she couldn't see the point of being in it. Hilary defended the Party.

*Sunday 14 May*
There was an 'Insight' article in the *Sunday Times* covering the fall in the pound which led up to the IMF cuts of November/December 1976. One or two references were made to my part in all of this; I had discussed it beforehand with Hugo Young. But what interested me most was that in the summer of 1976 the Americans – through a man called Edward Yeo – had forced us to agree to only six months' standby so we would be taken to the IMF and given the real treatment. This had never been brought to the Cabinet.

Rosalind went back into hospital for further examinations. It is a very worrying time.

This evening I went to the Foots' for dinner. I haven't had a meal with the usual crowd for about two months, although they obviously have been meeting. I have got quite separated from them now.

Michael thought October was the right date for an Election, but Peter asked about the Lib–Lab arrangement. Michael said David Steel would like it to continue but they would want a referendum on proportional representation.

'Presumably they would like a couple of Liberals in the Cabinet,' said Peter, 'and an electoral pact over which seats we contest against them.'

I had the feeling that Michael was testing the ground, because Jill kept looking at me for some reaction. I said they wouldn't get PR through the House.

I asked Michael what would be in the manifesto, and he said we had done very well, we had survived. I was sitting there biting my tongue and feeling more and more depressed when Jill asked what I thought. I didn't want to say anything really but I argued that we wouldn't get back on our feet unless we controlled imports of manufactured goods because our manufacturing industry was so weak. How were we going to explain to people what was happening? I wanted to see the analysis.

Then it all came out. Peter blew up, blaming the oil price increase for all the trouble. Judith, of all people, said British industry couldn't meet delivery dates and it was inefficient. Michael didn't want a return to inflation.

So even an attempt at a socialist analysis isn't on with them. Michael is white-faced and angry whenever he looks at me now. Peter just brushes everything aside, and Albert is a sort of clockwork teddy bear. Tommy Balogh, who has seen it all before, is much the shrewdest of the group. I came away feeling utterly depressed.

*Monday 15 May*
The papers are full of speculation about extending the Lib–Lab Pact.

Tonight was the debate on the Thorp reprocessing plant at Windscale, the culmination of all the consultations and the public inquiry, which has recommended it should go ahead. The debate was broadcast live on radio from 7 till 10 tonight – the first complete transmission of a debate. I think Windscale at the moment is much less about British energy needs than about getting the Japanese contract. I spoke at the end for about fifteen minutes, and, though I wasn't all that satisfied, knowing that it was going out to a huge radio audience took my mind off the House. We got an enormous majority – 220 to 80 – but the 80 were made up of Liberals, Scot Nats and a lot of Labour people.

*Tuesday 16 May*
The *Financial Times* had a big piece by Joe Rogaly called 'Humbug, Common Sense and Morality'; it said there were only four politicians who talked about politics in terms of human values – Thatcher, Keith Joseph, Eric Heffer and myself.

*Saturday 20 May*
The doctors opened up Rosalind yesterday and found that the growth had developed so much that they just closed her up again. Most of the morning was spent on the phone to Hilary, who has been fantastically courageous. Rosalind's parents, Peter and Lesley Retey, were obviously very distressed. I rang Liz Shore, who gave me some information, then Hilary arrived. As soon as he saw me his face crumpled in tears – he towers over me now – and I comforted him. I can hardly bear thinking about it.

*Sunday 21 May*
The second instalment of the revelations on the 1976 IMF loan appeared today in the *Sunday Times*. There was one passage in it about my role during this crisis, which I have never seen mentioned before.

William Rogers, a former US Secretary of State, was quoted as saying that it had become a choice between Britain's remaining in the western liberal financial system or pursuing radical change, and they had been concerned that Tony Benn was precipitating a policy decision by Britain to turn its back on the IMF. Rogers said, if that had happened, Italy and France might have followed suit and the whole system would have been in danger of collapse, with political as well as economic consequences.

Never did I imagine that the Cabinet paper drafted by Francis, Frances and me, outlining the alternative economic strategy, had been so amplified and exaggerated by the time it reached Washington. This was a political attack on our independence by people pretending to be bankers. It was political pressure by the American and German Governments and, when this comes up again, I shall speak out in the frankest terms in Cabinet because I am sure what I did then was right.

Hilary and Joshua went to see Rosalind in hospital. I tried to work this afternoon but I couldn't keep my mind off her. Rosalind was feeling better tonight. Joshua went to stay at Hilary's house.

*Monday 22 May*
At 10.15 I had a word about Rosalind with Dick Mabon, who was a physician. He said, 'You must get a second opinion, find out what the chances are, and how long she has. You must find out how much pain is involved because if she is going to have a long treatment she might not be able to take painkillers – that could be agony for her and it might be better not to try to prolong it.'

I did tell my driver, Ron Vaughan, about it and he said, 'It's turned summer into winter', which I thought was touching.

*Tuesday 23 May*
At 9 my literary agent Anne McDermid and David Machin and Graham Greene of Cape came to see me about publishing my speeches. They said exactly the same as Gollancz – that speeches don't make a good book unless they are substantially edited and reorganised. I haven't got time to do it so they suggested a man called Chris Mullin,* who works at the BBC Overseas Service and who might be prepared to knock it into shape.

Went over to see Jim, who had asked me about the pay of special advisers. Well, I had already minuted him in March when he agreed to pay increases for Frances and Francis, and the only reference he made to that subject was that he had heard rumours that Frances Morrell was doing too much work for the Party. I explained that she kept in touch with the trade union secretariats and research secretaries throughout Whitehall and how helpful that was to me in keeping the Party policy in line with Government policy.

'There may be nothing in it,' said Jim. 'There may be some disaffected person in the Department of Energy who is reporting these things.' I expect that's Jack Rampton.

We then came on to the real reason for the meeting. 'What I wanted to talk to you about is the timing of the Election. What do you think?'

I said, 'I incline to October.'

'That's a bit predictable.'

* Labour MP for Sunderland South since 1987; author of *A Very British Coup* (1982), *Last Man Out of Saigon* (1986) and *Error of Judgement* (1986).

'I know, but there is a risk that Civil Service departments will start abandoning Ministers if we don't make it clear how long we're staying. In fact, I hear it's already happening.'

Jim said, 'I have asked Sir John Hunt to discuss it with Permanent Secretaries and I warned him that I would take a very serious view if this were true. In any case, if the polls are going our way, the Civil Service will be frightened that we might be re-elected so they won't want to anger us too much.'

I told him we were doing marvellously in the Hamilton by-election, but Jim was afraid that our good showing in the polls might make our people complacent. 'Ron Hayward', he said, 'wants a very short Election period – three or four weeks – but, if we finish Party business at the end of July, everyone will know that October's the date. Should we hang on beyond that?'

I recognised the difficulties but my inclination was still for October, unless we were to go earlier. 'That would after all deprive the Tories of three months' sustained press advertising,' I said.

'Yes,' replied Jim, 'but I do want to get my devolution business through.'

I agreed, but advised him against having referenda in Scotland and Wales before the Election.

Jim was nervous about a long campaign, in case anything went wrong, and he asked me what I thought about the Liberals.

'My own view', I said, 'is that the Liberals should be released in order to play their historic role of splitting the right-wing vote by drawing votes away from the Tories.'

'David Steel would actually like to go on into the next session,' said Jim, 'but he will demand a referendum on proportional representation.'

'That would not work. The Party will not risk never holding office again for the sake of an extra six months now. Anyway Thatcher wouldn't support it.'

'Ah, yes,' said Jim, 'but it would please David Steel if Thatcher opposed it.'

'Maybe, but our attitude to referenda has been that they give the public a chance to ratify a constitutional change already agreed by Parliament – like the Common Market and the Scotland and Wales Bills. PR is by no means agreed in Parliament, so a referendum on the issue would be tantamount to a state-financed public opinion poll.'

Jim thought that was a good point and wrote it down. 'I have told David Steel that he would be better off on his own, and he feels that if the Lib–Lab Pact is to finish at the end of July I should announce it at Whitsun. That could create tremendous anxiety about an impending Election, it might affect the markets, and the whole thing might fall apart at the seams.'

I reminded him that the TUC Congress would be meeting shortly, and I said they really ought to know when there would be an Election because they wouldn't agree to a pay policy if they thought they were going to be manacled to Mrs Thatcher within a few months, whereas they might agree to some arrangement to see us through the Election and have a special congress afterwards.

He accepted that. 'But I am worried about one other thing, and you must keep this absolutely to yourself. There is a lot of funny business going on between the City of London and the Government over the gilt-edged market. The City are not buying gilts in an effort to force us to push up interest rates. What should I do?'

I replied, 'To an ex-Chancellor with your experience, there's nothing whatever I can say except that there might be a case for facing it out with them.'

'My experience with the City', said Jim, 'is that if they've got you by the knackers they'll squeeze you – even though they know they will have to give way eventually and then you can knock them out cold. They could do a lot of damage. I've already told them our interest rates are higher than in France, Germany and America but they say that's because confidence is higher in those economies. We could push up taxation.'

'Not before an Election.'

'Well, how about employers' National Insurance contributions, or VAT?'

I advised against that and suggested to Jim that he go for the City. I told him I didn't think the City wanted us to be defeated, and Jim agreed that they were only really concerned with their own gain.

We talked about the manifesto, and I said, 'I assume you don't want anything radical in it?'

He said he didn't want a wealth tax included because Mrs Thatcher would say we were just squeezing the rich, 'and I don't want the abolition of the Lords in either'.

'I assume you will include planning agreements and industrial democracy?'

'Yes.'

I said, 'What about the whole "machinery of government" theme? Open government, parliamentary control of the Executive, devolution, direct elections (perish the thought) – these are all changes in the way we govern ourselves. Then we could make the Lords redundant: with the European Assembly, the Scottish Assembly, the Welsh Assembly and a revamped House of Commons, you wouldn't need the Lords – we could call it overmanning!'

He was tickled by that. Then he said, 'You know they are going to try all this Marxist stuff against you. I suppose you aren't one!'

'Well, Jim, I wouldn't have mentioned it if you hadn't, but journalists often tell me that a lot of the briefing against me comes from colleagues. Harold used to do it and so did Denis Healey, so, if that stopped, it would be a great help.'

He went on, 'There'll probably also be a demand for a referendum on hanging on the eve of poll, and I expect the immigration issue will be raised again. It will be a very dirty Election and we'll have to fight hard.'

'Let's not cry foul before it all begins.'

'Well, think about it,' said Jim.

So that was how it stood. He is convinced that October is right, though he's worried about the long run-up, and what the City might do in the meantime. It was a candid discussion. I have no doubt he thought he had to keep me sweet, but I did manage to make some constructive contributions.

### Wednesday 24 May

By car to Charing Cross Hospital with Lesley and Peter Retey and Hilary to see the consultant in Rosalind's case. They are still waiting for the results of the biopsies from St Thomas's and the Royal Marsden. They think chemotherapy would be the best course of action but they can't start the treatment until the operation wound has healed. It might bring about a remission, driving the growth back into the lung, which could be removed, giving Rosalind two or more years.

It was a terrible thing to be told, but the Reteys stood up to it as best they could. Hilary said, 'What is so unbearable is that to look at her today you would think there was nothing wrong with her.'

### Thursday 25 May

Cabinet at 10.30. There were no officials present at the beginning; it was obviously going to be a political discussion.

Jim began by telling us he had been having talks with David Steel. If the Lib–Lab Pact was to continue, Steel would demand two things: that we reverse our stand on proportional representation for the Scottish and Welsh Assemblies (on a free vote the Commons had rejected it, but the Lords had reinserted it and Steel wanted another free vote in the Commons); secondly, that we agree to a referendum on a proportional representation voting system for the UK. Jim said that, after some consultation with members of the Cabinet, he had told Steel it wasn't on and he would be making a statement today. What Jim was anxious not to do was precipitate an immediate Election, and he expressed his concern about the rise in the money supply and the City's refusal to buy gilts. He thought it might be necessary to take some pre-emptive measures.

Harold Lever said the City were torn because they didn't want us to win but they didn't want Thatcher to win either.

I said, 'Looking at it politically, the Labour Party will be revitalised by the end of the Lib–Lab Pact because neither the Party nor the country ever really liked it.' I argued that Steel would be bound to attack us but it wouldn't be credible, since he had been supporting us for eighteen months. However, his attacks on Mrs Thatcher could well draw back people who have been unhappy about the extreme right position that she has occupied. 'We should take a very cheerful view of the whole thing.'

Jim half hinted that he would consider a deal with the Scot Nats or the Welsh Nats or even the Ulster Unionists, and that may be the way in which we survive into the next session.

*Sunday 28 May*
Read the final instalment of the *Sunday Times* review of the IMF controversy – 'The Day the Pound Nearly Died'. It was fascinating, and quite an accurate account of what happened in Cabinet. There was a lot about the Americans thinking I was Callaghan's most likely successor.

*Saturday 3 June*
Rosalind is not at all well and Caroline was distressed about it. Hilary is marvellous – in a way too strong. Joshua is staying with him, which is a great comfort.

I sat downstairs in my office trying to work and I found myself sobbing at the thought of that young couple being broken up by illness, and of all the agonies to come for her and Hilary.

*Monday 5 June*
We have the post of Deputy Chairman of BNOC to fill. Jack Rampton had told me that nobody of any merit had applied – except for one man from Shell whom he favoured – and that Lord Croham (Sir Douglas Allen as was) was still available.

I know he wants it, and Frank Kearton wants him, but I had said, 'Look, I can't just appoint the ex-head of the Civil Service Department; I am going to ask for applications, and, if Allen applies for it, fine.'

Well, he didn't apply for it; he just expected it to be given to him, and to apply with the possibility that he might not be appointed was too much for his pride.

Frank Kearton and I had a word about it today and went over the attacks on the BNOC from all quarters. He is always very encouraging, and he said, 'You know when Cliff Garvin, head of Exxon, first met you he thought you had horns and a tail but now he says, "If ever Tony

Benn leaves politics I would offer him a job on the Exxon board." '
Well, that worried me a bit!

I have known Frank for twelve years, and he is a most outstanding
industrialist and public servant. He said we would find that if we
defended British oil interests we would get strong support from the
British public.

*Wednesday 7 June*
My first meeting was with Joe Gormley, Mick McGahey, Lawrence
Daly, Alex Eadie and Brian Tucker.

Before officials came in I said, 'Look, I don't know what the outcome
of the Election is going to be, but I am going to leave some monuments
before I go which Mrs Thatcher won't be able to change. The three
monuments are a planning agreement signed, sealed and delivered this
month; a new policy under which we burn all the coal we dig; and a rule
giving the NUM Executive a veto on pit closures.'

After that I went over at 12.45 to the Department of the Environment
and had lunch with Brian Flowers. We had a long talk and I said he
must have had a terrible time after he published his report on
environmental pollution, because they must have seen him as a traitor
to his class – that is to say the class of nuclear scientists. 'Yes,' he said,
'it was the worst period of my life. The AEA have *never* discussed the
report.' They wouldn't face it.

The hatred of him by the Cabinet Office for putting a spanner in the
nuclear works was unbelievable; that chap clearly went through a
traumatic experience. Yet he was the agency through which environmental issues were brought into the arena of public discussion.

*Thursday 8 June*
We disposed of Cabinet business at 9.50 and then Jim said, 'There is
another item on the agenda – the economic situation.'

He argued that 8 per cent inflation was too high and it was necessary
to have a 5 per cent wage policy for the coming year. Inflation in
Germany and Japan was only 3 per cent and although American
inflation was high it would be brought down. It was our overriding
problem.

Now, by saying that, Jim was also saying that unemployment didn't
matter. That, of course, is the policy of the Government.

Denis said our basic position was good – output was rising,
unemployment was falling, job vacancies were increasing. Investment
in manufacturing industry was rising by about 13 per cent again this
year. Since the Budget, however, the financial situation had been
difficult. The £8.5 billion PSBR was the absolute limit the markets
would take and now another £465 million had been added to it. The

alternative would be to unify VAT, which would raise £800 million in a full year but would push up mortgage interest rates; or to increase employers' NI contributions by 2.5 per cent.

I said, 'Prime Minister, I am very much opposed to what is being proposed. It will take a very substantial bite out of our economy. While I have no doubt you can call upon the loyalty of the Labour Party, this is a very big decision. All this monetarist stuff is, in my view, absolute rubbish. When the history of the world comes to be written, the IMF will turn out to have been the major force for revolution. These measures are deflationary and will slow down our recovery, reduce the number of jobs and have an adverse effect on production.'

Stan Orme warned that the Party and the trade unions would see this as a conspiracy by the City to force a crisis on the Labour Government.

Jim said, 'We mustn't talk in those terms.'

Stan replied, 'I would not talk in those terms except in this Cabinet, but this is what the Party and the unions will say. Why can't we reverse the tax cuts? After all, the Finance Bill isn't through yet, and it will have a serious effect on jobs next year.'

'We dare not wait,' said Jim. Later in the discussion he added, 'On this question of the philosophy of monetarism, I am a Bennite.'

So I suggested, 'If we are going to capitulate to the banking influence, why don't we at least attack monetarism and admit we have been defeated? When Heath was defeated by the miners in 1972 he said, "I have been defeated." Why don't we tell the truth?'

'Look what happened to Ted Heath,' said Denis.

Anyway we were all sworn to secrecy. As I left I heard Joel Barnett remark, 'The trouble with Tony Benn is that he doesn't realise the City is the real world.' (I had said it had nothing to do with the real world.)

*Friday 9 June*
A visit to Windscale with Caroline.

Windscale was originally an army ordnance factory called Sellafield before the war, and after the war it was used to develop our nuclear weapons programme and its name was changed to Windscale. John Hill, who was present today, reminded me that he worked there in 1950, probably at the beginning of the civil programme. There is still a military operation there. They store spent fuel elements from nuclear-powered submarines and process the plutonium that's needed for the country's hydrogen bombs.

We were greeted by John Hill, Con Allday (Managing Director of BNFL) and others. We had coffee and then went round together.

We toured the oxide storage ponds, and I must say they are very mysterious, those deep indoor swimming pools with their dark green water. They are lit up underneath and you can dimly see these fuel elements that are used in nuclear power stations, vaguely threatening, though the water is apparently a complete shield against any radio-activity that gets out.

Then we went to the chemical separation plant, where they break the fuel elements down into depleted uranium, plutonium (which is the most deadly substance of all) and highly toxic waste. They showed us what they called the Harvest demonstration rig where they take these highly toxic wastes, which have been evaporated down to about a tenth of their volume, and mix them with ground glass, put them in a furnace and fuse them into a glass bottle which permits the heat but not the radioactivity to be released. This is placed in a metal flask and left to cool for twenty years, when they believe it will be ready to put in geological formations.

From a roof we had an immensely impressive view of the site. I remembered John Hill telling me last year that in the early days they didn't really understand what they were handling and the whole site was soaked in radioactive toxic wastes.

I comment on this because when you see this vast complex you are struck, on the one hand, by the skill and scientific knowledge of the people who run it and, on the other, by the exceptional vulnerability of such a complicated system. Nobody can truthfully say that this whole project can be handed over to future generations to look after safely when they've no idea whether future generations will be faced with invasion, earthquakes, floods, strikes or plagues. It is a tremendously risky thing to do, and the duration of the risk, 10,000 or 15,000 years, is enormous.

Caroline went off to see the medical department and the whole-body monitor group, while I went with James Bretherton and others to the plutonium store, which I had asked to see because security rotates almost entirely round the plutonium.

We went across the road into a high-security area and were given a badge with a 'criticality locket' which indicated when there was a likelihood of the rods getting critical. We were taken downstairs along a corridor, and it was something like the vaults of the Bank of England. There was a door about 2 feet thick and inside that another door with circular panels either side, each padlocked, through which the plutonium was placed and stored.

The whole thing is electronically monitored of course, and it would be impossible for terrorists to get through the door and into the safe and then remove the plutonium – although there's no question whatever that, if the country was invaded, a hostile scientific team could get the plutonium out in a jiffy.

Two years ago I had to introduce legislation to arm the AEA guards, but in fact I think there are military forces there, out of view, protecting the military establishment.

We went back and talked to the employee representatives – the staff and unions. They raised the Windscale planning inquiry and were in fact now persuaded that it had been well handled. The debate was broadcast in full last month from Parliament, and many of them had listened to it. It had given them the feeling that the work they do was explicitly endorsed by Parliament.

Lunch was a tremendous buffet with prawn cocktail and a decorated salmon, and turkey and strawberries and cream.

Drove to Newcastle across Cumbria and Northumberland. It's an area I'd never been to in my life, full of Roman forts and a bit of Hadrian's Wall. Arrived at the Park Hotel in Tynemouth for the NUM dinner.

At one point in the evening, George Grant, MP for Morpeth, took me aside. 'You come from an aristocratic background and I'm a working man, I've worked all my life, and I want to tell you that I think we'll be looking for a new Leader of the Party after Jim goes. We'll probably have Denis first, and then we'll be looking for a replacement. You're too radical and you'll have to be more practical and responsible instead of supporting the left wing in the NUM.'

I said, 'I know, George, but don't give me all that crap about my aristocratic background. My father was a Labour MP who was made a peer at the end of his life, like George Brown or Fenner Brockway. I am not particularly brilliant, and I didn't learn it out of a book. I have become a socialist because of the experience of seeing British industry decline, and jobs are the main question. I have seen lots of people ruin their lives by ambition.'

I was sharp with him. But of course he was trying to be friendly, and put a hand on my shoulder.

*Saturday 10 June*
Came back on the train. Caroline and Judith Hart went to dinner in the dining car, and Caroline told me afterwards that at their table was another diner who had been shooting a bit of a line about the wine, complaining and generally showing off to them.

At one point I walked up to the buffet, not seeing Caroline. As I went by, the man had apparently said, 'Who's let that bloody twit on the train?' (I hadn't heard this.)

Caroline had replied, 'That's my husband', and for the rest of the meal he hadn't said a word.

*Wednesday 14 June*
I got a message to ring the Prime Minister and he said we may be beaten tonight in the vote on Denis Healey's salary. Jim said he and Michael Foot and Mike Cocks were thinking of making it a vote of

confidence, and what did I think? I was doubtful, because if we were beaten we'd be precipitated into an Election. Could I think about it and ring him back?

I rang back later and I said I thought it would be better not to have a vote of confidence tonight. We had to preserve our right to choose the date of the Election. I asked for a special Cabinet to consider it.

Jim said he had to tell the Liberals, who were 'all over the shop'.

At 2 we had Cabinet in Jim's room at the House. Michael was in the chair because Jim was seeing President Ceaucescu of Romania who is here on a state visit.

Elwyn said we had no choice. I repeated my argument that we should not risk it.

Joel Barnett said we had to support the Chancellor. Roy Hattersley and John Morris agreed. Denis said he wouldn't be able to sell a billion pounds' worth of gilts tomorrow unless he got a vote of confidence.

The only people who supported me were Roy Mason (surprisingly), Albert Booth and Bruce Millan.

In the evening I went to hear Jim wind up the debate and he did quite well. We won the vote by 5, so that was a satisfactory end to the day.

*Friday 16 June*
Left at 9.50 for Bristol, where the Co-operative Wholesale Society has announced it is closing its clothing factory in Brislington. I was taken to the factory by Ann Richards, an USDAW shop steward there; I'd never met her before. She was a highly intelligent woman in her thirties.

I was greeted by a huge demonstration with Union Jacks and posters saying, 'Bye, Bye British'. Harlech TV and the local evening paper were there.

I had a very serious meeting with all the union representatives from USDAW and the Tailor and Garment Workers' Union.

The cause of many of the financial problems was the import of Korean-made trousers. It was pointed out by the unions that the cost of the Korean imports also included transport, duty and interest paid on money to buy the trousers up in bulk. About one-third of them were rejected and sent back by the retailers and then had to be sold off below purchase cost. So in reality they weren't cheaper than the items produced in the factory. I've heard this story so many times from private businesses, and now from the Co-op, and the more I listen the more I become absolutely persuaded that management's neglect of the views and experience of the workers is central to Britain's industrial problems.

Ann Richards was super, and when the General Manager of the menswear group came in he couldn't answer any of these questions.

I talked to Ann Richards afterwards, and she said, '*We* could produce cheap goods if we applied such low standards as those abroad, but we've never been allowed to produce to such standards.'

It turns out that she had got a plan for turning the factory into a co-operative – which is a touch of irony, since it is owned by the Co-operative Society.

### Sunday 18 June

Went to visit Rosalind. We hadn't seen her for a week and she looked paler and thinner. She had that slightly translucent skin tone which is the sign of a sick person. But her eyes were bright and she smiled.

I heard today that the Top Salaries Review Body chaired by Lord Boyle has come up with proposals for increases of 30 per cent for senior civil servants, chairmen of nationalised industries, senior forces officers and all the rest. That will mean another £8000 for Permanent Secretaries. It's unbelievable, and obviously causing a great deal of embarrassment.

### Tuesday 20 June

Had a meeting about Burmah shares. To recap, in December 1974 Burmah was on the point of collapse and the Bank of England, to help it through, bought its shares in BP at a very good price. Since then, Burmah have sold the Ninian and Thistle fields in the North Sea to BNOC and have staggered through the crisis, but the Burmah shareholders are still bringing an action against the Bank of England to get their BP shares returned. It was an absolutely fair deal and to reverse it would be outrageous, but if the shareholders win then the Government BP holding – via the Bank of England – would drop to 25 per cent.

Although some of the documents of the December 1974 meetings are confidential, the Bank of England made these available to the Burmah shareholders. It was claimed that the relevant confidential passages were blocked out from the photocopies, but in fact they were readable. The shareholders are likely to win their case and it is a public scandal.

### Wednesday 21 June

Brian Sedgemore, Frances and Francis and Michael Meacher came to lunch. To be perfectly candid it was a leadership planning meeting. Michael offered to draw up a list of people from the PLP who might be prepared to vote for me as Leader in the event of Jim leaving. He said we should start work on it now. Michael is very devoted and willing to do a lot of work on this. Obviously I found it encouraging.

In the evening Dick Mabon came in for a talk. I gave him a whisky and he went into a long account about how I was likely to be Leader of the Party if we lost the Election, and how the right would need to be reassured that I wouldn't crush them. If we won he thought Denis would be Leader for a short period, and he sort of pledged his support for me as Deputy Leader.

I said, 'You know what I'm like – I'm not a guy who crushes other views, I just want to live to see another 1945.'

With Michael Meacher on one side and Dick Mabon on the other, I feel the pressure is beginning to mount a bit.

*Thursday 22 June*

Cabinet, and the first item was the Official Secrets Act. When the Cabinet last discussed it about three weeks ago, Merlyn had claimed that only the middle class wanted open government and had launched into an attack on freedom of information. He was only prepared to relax the criminal sanctions on unnecessary secrecy, as represented by Section 2 of the Act. The Executive had asked to send a deputation to see him, so the issue had been postponed.

In the meantime, Eric Heffer had pressed Merlyn hard on the case for freedom of information, and Merlyn had included a new passage on open government for today's Cabinet. But in it he has simply stated that the Government already publishes a lot of information and he makes slighting references to legislation in America, Canada and Sweden, saying how expensive and ineffective it all is.

Michael Foot thought the proposal was better than nothing and favoured going ahead, but Jim was against legislation on freedom of information. He believed that those who had the responsibility for taking decisions were entitled to have their privacy respected.

I let this go on for a while before intervening. 'Look, there is an assumption that the security of the state rests upon secrecy, whereas actually it rests upon the maintenance of democracy, which in turn depends upon disclosure of what is going on. Dictatorships are extremely secretive but they're not a bit secure. The issue is not one of conflict between openness and security, but balance between democracy and security. Information gets out in a number of ways anyway – through press coverage etc – and it develops and strengthens democracy. But we are actually tightening up on the defence of international information.'

I raised the question of memoirs – Dick Crossman's *Diaries*, which had thrown so much light on the machinery of government, and the recent posthumous publication of Selwyn Lloyd's observations on Suez and foreign policy, which was in violation of the thirty-year rule. I really put the cat among the pigeons.

'Well,' Jim observed, 'I hope it's understood that all this publishing of information has been done by that old reactionary Jim Callaghan!'

'You'd better keep that secret,' I said.

I suggested a select committee on freedom of information with a report at the end. But Jim argued that parliamentary reports were always sloppy.

I said, 'Cabinets, by definition, don't want to disclose information because they are the Government, whereas Parliament represents the governed and takes a different view. They ought to be able to discuss it openly instead of having a secret commission on openness to be published at some later date.'

Michael got upset. 'I'm against all these select committees. We'd never get any Labour legislation through if we always had to go through select committees. They are just coalitions of Labour and Tory MPs.'

Stan Orme agreed, and I took the point, but argued that when Labour got into power Labour Ministers entered into a coalition with the Civil Service to keep the Party out. It was not a matter of Labour versus a coalition view, it was one coalition versus another, and we had to deal with that problem.

I was supported by Shirley, David Owen and Bill Rodgers – which was curious – but no agreement was reached.

On the Top Salaries Review Body report, recommending staged rises of 30 per cent on average, Denis advocated going ahead but Michael opposed, as did Fred Peart and Albert Booth. John Morris and Eric Varley supported it. David Owen said we ought to reduce the upper tax levels. That was David Owen trying to appear radical by opposing the TSRB's recommendation, while supporting effective rises for the wealthy through other means.

Denis reminded him that if you cut tax on higher salaries it wouldn't just benefit the relatively low-paid top-salaried people like the nationalised industry chairmen; it would also benefit people like David Steel, Chairman of BP, on £95,000. So Owen put a foot wrong there.

Elwyn Jones, the Lord Chancellor, said there were many people who didn't want to become judges on the present salaries and he couldn't man the bench properly.

Jim summed up. We had to accept the report; the movement would understand the Lord Chancellor's difficulty.

I said, 'I can see the difficulty because we have created an expectation that we will implement the report and, in the nationalised industries particularly, they feel they have been badly treated. But the impact on pay policy will be tremendous.'

I said the Top Salaries Review Body should be abolished because it had nothing to do with performance and operated without any sort of bargaining. It was Scargill's results without Scargill's militancy. I pointed out the added benefits for people at the top of the career scale – status, honours, perks and power. We weren't handing out confetti money, and they ought to be made to bargain like everybody else.

I made some impact, but we agreed that the 30 per cent would be staged over two years; 10 per cent this year with further reviews.

*Saturday 24 June*

The second day of a visit to Wales. To a meeting at Dinas Powys, where the papers rumoured that the National Front were going to send 600 people to demonstrate against me. The media have been building it up, so there were a lot of Labour people and Young Socialists there, and the Anti-Nazi League turned up to counter-picket.

Well, there were seventeen National Front supporters carrying Union Jacks and banners. So I walked towards them, feeling a bit like Gary Cooper in *High Noon*. They were silent. 'Well,' I said, 'what have you got to say?'

A man called Newman, apparently the leader, a tough-looking sixty-year-old, replied, 'We've come to get rid of the likes of you.'

'What's the point of that?'

'You don't stand up for the national interest. Take the Common Market.'

I told him I was opposed to the Common Market.

'Yes, but only because you want to break down the defences of the western world and make it easier for the Russians to come in – not because you want to put Britain first. Look at all these immigrants.'

I said, 'If you're talking about unemployment, there was mass unemployment before the war and very few immigrants here. Do you want every immigrant to leave – every Irishman, every Australian, every Rhodesian?'

'Why don't you stick up for the whites in Rhodesia?'

I explained, 'There are only a quarter of a million whites there, and they've only been there a short time, but there are six million Africans. It is their country.'

'Well, there you are – you don't know anything about it.'

'I do actually. I lived there for a year during the war when I was training as a pilot in the RAF.'

When he started to attack nationalisation, I reminded him that Winston Churchill had nationalised the Anglo-Persian Oil Company, to which he replied, 'Churchill was just the forerunner of you communist lot. He was a Zionist.'

That was a gift for the TV cameras. 'Look,' I said, 'you came here for a punch-up. Why don't you come to the meeting and listen?'

But they weren't interested in the meeting, only in a fight, and there wasn't one. I shall make this my practice from now on, and show that there is nothing to fear from the NF. They were pathetic.

It was a marvellous meeting.

*Monday 26 June*
To the Department, where I had an important talk with Chris Herzig, Richard Wilson and Alex Eadie about an AEA proposal to tranship plutonium nitrates from Scrabster Harbour near Dounreay to White-haven, to be reprocessed at Windscale. I received the proposal only a week ago and was told that, if I didn't agree, the prototype fast breeder at Dounreay would have to close down early next year. In short, they were putting a pistol to my head.

The AEA also wanted to build a plant at Dounreay for creating mixed oxides of plutonium and uranium at a cost of £8–10 million. I decided to leave that for now.

In the evening Geoff Bish, Norman Atkinson, Frances Morrell and I talked for nearly two hours about the manifesto in the event of an autumn Election. I jotted down some of the points we intend to fight for: Government control of BP; abolition of the House of Lords; a Ministry of Economic Planning; the amendment of Section 2 of the European Communities Act; nationalisation of the banks (a point on which we would concede); and defeating monetarism.

*Wednesday 28 June*
At the Home Policy Committee there was an argument on bloodsports. Eric Heffer, who is Vice-Chairman of the League Against Cruel Sports, spoke passionately against bloodsports. Fred Mulley was cautious and Shirley Williams wanted a compromise to give the Government more time.

I said we couldn't run away from the issue and I was personally very much against bloodsports. How we did it was the question. It had to go to Conference, and the Government should provide time for legislation, but it should be legislation against cruelty. I said I never understood why bloodsports weren't taken through the courts on grounds of cruelty.

*Thursday 29 June*
At Cabinet we came to an item deliberately not on the agenda, and that was top salaries. Jim said that Michael Foot had raised it with him and he was giving Michael the chance to talk about it.

Michael said he thought there would be an explosion in the Party –left, right and centre – if we approved the TSRB report in its entirety; it would raise the question of MPs' salaries, and trade union reaction would be sharp. He therefore proposed a major change – that we should award only 10 per cent, publish but not accept the report, and postpone staging the rises until we had dealt with Phase 4. There would be trouble from the top people but it would improve the chances of our White Paper on the Government's next phase of the pay policy, due in July.

Jim said there would be less reaction than Michael anticipated. Michael made it clear that if we were not about to have an Election he would resign on this issue.

After another long discussion we decided to go ahead with its implementation staged over two years. I think there will be a row; Jim said he would explain it to the Parliamentary Party at the meeting next Tuesday.

*Monday 3 July*

A full and fascinating day. I was picked up at 7.45 and flown by helicopter to Lydd, a tiny airport in Kent, to visit the Dungeness B power station.

Dungeness B was the first AGR station, ordered in 1965 and intended to come on stream in 1970; now it won't start up before 1980. The cost has escalated from £85 million to £191 million.

We were taken into the reactor itself and I found myself in an eerie world of pipes, welds, tubes and wires. I was beneath the top of the reactor and above the pressure vessel itself, and the roof was so low we had to crawl. There were 120 men working there and it was air-conditioned because they have to keep it free from humidity. Above was the machine which would be used to lift the fuel elements, and around the pressure vessel was what is called the annulus, a very thin ring, inside a great concrete jacket 22 feet thick at the base and 12 feet thick all the way up. Where I was standing, the $CO_2$ gas would be pouring up past the fuel elements at a temperature of 675°C, then be diverted down into the boiler tubes built into the annulus so that the water in the tubes could be converted into steam and carried to the turbine. The most thrilling moment was when we descended through a hole in the top of the pressure vessel where I actually saw the tops of the fuel channels. There were men working down there in the very dim light. It was really quite exhausting.

I went to look at the turbines – the 'sleeping giant' as one of the engineers called them – which had actually been in position since 1972. They had diverted some steam from Dungeness A to test them but they were rusting almost, before they had even been used. Seeing the complexity of it all – the tremendous operating difficulties and safety requirements – makes it almost impossible to justify, and I have to say my estimation of the value of nuclear power fell sharply. I have to be very careful not to go ahead with more nuclear power stations than are absolutely necessary.

We had a quick lunch and then I went to another canteen, where fifteen shop stewards had gathered at my request. The site manager and project manager were present.

I was told that the problems at Dungeness had been caused by the continual changes in design; they were constantly being asked to tear out completed work and start all over again. Secondly, they were being criticised for the delay, and non-union labour was being brought on site without their knowledge or approval.

But their main complaint was that the management wouldn't recognise the shop stewards and wouldn't allow them to meet except in their own time. I must say, my sympathies were entirely with the stewards. I told them I had seen the same problems in many other industries, and I agreed to let them have a note I would make of the discussion and then we could decide what action to take.

When it comes to efficiency, I think management in nationalised industries is better at getting investment and providing the jobs than in private industry – certainly that is true in the nuclear business. But in the nationalised industries the managers are much more arrogant than in the private sector. Because they are themselves often highly qualified engineers and technicians, they feel higher in the order of merit and they bully the workforce. They are as tough as old boots.

Came back to London, and in the afternoon I went to Number 10 for a garden party to celebrate the fiftieth anniversary of the granting of votes for women at the age of twenty-one. The actress Miriam Karlin was there, and an old lady of ninety-six who claimed she had been a *suffragist* and not a suffragette. 'They were the militants, we were the moderates,' she said. Harold and Mary Wilson were there, and it was a great party.

### Tuesday 4 July

Brian Sedgemore came in with news of the PLP meeting this morning at which Jim had announced that the Cabinet had agreed to the Top Salaries Review Body recommendations, with full implementation to be phased in up to April 1980. It had been a sensational meeting and apparently a rather right-wing Bradford Member had told Jim he was completely out of touch. Jim had banged the table and said, 'I'm not out of touch. I go round the country all the time and see as many members of the Labour Party and attend my GMC just as much as you do.'

Apart from Jeff Rooker, Arthur Palmer [MP for Bristol North East], Douglas Jay and George Park, who supported Jim, Brian said the meeting was universally critical. Jim was taken aback; his confidence in assessing the mood of the Party had been shaken.

Came over to the House and voted in favour of the televising of Parliament.

*Thursday 6 July*

At Cabinet Jim introduced a paper by Denis on public expenditure and stressed that this was most important, since it would take us into the next Parliament.

Then Denis said the picture was unwelcome. In 1977 we had anticipated an economic growth rate of 3.5 per cent but the figure had turned out to be optimistic. Import propensity was higher and there was less oil from the North Sea. Consequently the balance of payments surplus had been lower, the pound had fallen, pay rises had topped 14 per cent and the PSBR was higher this year than he had hoped. But he believed there was room for real tax cuts next year. He said inflation would stay around 8 per cent, but pay was critical, and we must avoid anything that damaged confidence or suggested any change of policy.

Jim Callaghan suggested we consider Mrs Thatcher's idea of making no increase in public expenditure (which she has forecast for her first Parliament). Of course defence spending would rise, and she would have to find contingency funds for that, but it would still allow her to contemplate cuts in taxation of about £5 billion. He went on to say that a Tory Cabinet could not finance the demographic changes that were taking place without imposing further charges in the Health Service. 'But don't underestimate its electoral appeal. Many people think they *should* pay for public services, and cuts in their tax bill would give them the choice.'

Joel Barnett pointed out that tax cuts *wouldn't* benefit the people who would be most affected by extra charges. But he was opposed to increases now in public expenditure because of the effect on confidence. 'A financial crisis between now and the Election will completely outweigh any popularity arising from such increases.'

Shirley said, 'Denis omitted to mention unemployment, and social resistance to unemployment is growing.' She favoured increases in public expenditure in line with the growth rate.

I said that it was a decision which would set the scene for the Eighties and it required discussion by the whole of Parliament. 'We need far more room to manoeuvre than this paper provides. The level of unemployment is unacceptable, and some polls are showing that the Tories have a lead over us on this issue. This morning's *Financial Times* quoted the Chairman of the CBI in Scotland saying that civil violence could come about if unemployment rises any higher. Low growth, more children leaving school, micro-processors and imports are all exacerbating unemployment.'

I opposed the curtailment of public expenditure, both in industry and in the public services. 'We simply can't answer the simple contradictions put to us about why construction workers are out of work while there are people whose homes are below standard or need insulation; why hospital wards are empty while nurses are unemployed; why schools are overcrowded while teachers are unemployed.'

Finally I pointed out that this document was in breach of the North Sea White Paper, in which we solemnly pledged that we would use the revenues for public investment and social infrastructure.

Stan Orme said, 'Mrs Thatcher's stand is public expenditure versus taxation and they are winning that argument. We should say we can't have tax cuts. As far as I am concerned, I would rather go down on high public expenditure than be re-elected on low.'

Roy Hattersley argued that Denis had moved our economy from catastrophe to steadiness but low public expenditure could not be the basis of future policy. That was Roy appearing in his democratic socialist outfit.

'We've all been wrong,' said Denis. 'I have often been wrong, but it is very difficult. We are in a hundred-year decline and our strength is very uncertain. We are not competitive, our performance is poor, and a decline is inevitable. Public expenditure won't help because it just harms competitiveness.'

Bruce Millan said cuts had produced unemployment and he could not accept the paper. Bruce is a chartered accountant, quiet and steady, and, though his instincts are mainly cautious, he has something of a radical streak.

Albert Booth remarked that it was costing us £3.5 billion to maintain 1.4 million people out of work. Public expenditure was labour-intensive, and we needed an employment Budget.

'Let's stick to the real world and not some dream world,' said Merlyn, who will say anything to get Jim out of a jam. 'Spending more money may be possible after four years, but we must get our priorities right. I was brought up in a poor home where unemployment was bad, but it is different now. We mustn't see things through the eyes of the past.'

Roy Mason agreed. 'We have taken the heartache out of unemployment. Male unemployment in Northern Ireland is almost 30 per cent, and there is no trouble there.' An astonishing statement.

Jim asked me how we would manage import ceilings, and I explained that I wasn't suggesting a trade war which would lead to retaliation. In any case, it was unlikely that countries who sold us more than we sold them would retaliate against us. 'All I am pleading for is that we examine the options. We are always told that import controls lead to a siege economy – eastern Europe and all that – but this is a serious option in the interests of this country.'

Harold Lever was very red-faced – which is always a sign that you're getting near the bone. 'Protection is a disaster,' he said. 'As to the contradictions Tony spoke of – unused resources, idle people, unmet needs – you simply have to create the wealth before you can deal with them.'

Jim observed, 'There have been worries, but we are facing reality. We can't afford the public services that we see abroad. It's not just a matter of wage restraint; we need to change the psychology of our people so that they realise that higher wages go hand in hand with higher productivity. Performance in this country has been deteriorating for thirty years and I've watched the streets get dirtier.'

He was particularly anxious that pay claims might be influenced by the higher settlement for the police, who were only catching up. He said that 2 per cent was the maximum increase in public expenditure we could contemplate, and our major ambition should be to reduce the PSBR.

I find Jim's deep conservatism thoroughly depressing. With all this talk about the psychology of the nation being wrong and how the streets get dirtier, I'm almost expecting him to say, like Mussolini, that *he* made the trains run on time! The grey vacuum that is Jim Callaghan will not be able to go on for ever because the Labour Party is bound to represent a basic class interest.

At 2 I saw Sir Brian Flowers about the proposal from the AEA to move plutonium nitrates by sea from Dounreay to Windscale. He was surprised that I had only recently heard of it, since he thought the AEA must have known this would happen for a long time, and indeed they had.

I am uneasy about it, mainly because there could be an accident at sea. On the other hand, if I don't approve, then I'm charged with sabotaging the fast breeder reactor. I agreed to ask the AEA to discuss it at their board meeting – Brian Flowers is a member of the board, and I shall ask the Nuclear Inspectorate to advise me. All this about being under pressure of time is rubbish.

*Friday 7 July*
James Bretherton and I had a meeting at my home with Commissioner Ray Vouel and two of his officials at 9.45. Vouel wanted to reduce our capacity to produce platforms and North Sea equipment, and he was not prepared to make any concession on EEC components. It all came out. Commissioner Etienne d'Avignon had complained that we were violating the free movement of goods, and Roy Jenkins had demanded an inquiry into our oil policy. This is clearly a major attack on our energy policy, but Vouel is taking care not to tell me too much before an Election here in case I decide to use it politically. It was a very tense meeting, but I can't say I am frightened of him.

At a summit in Bremen, Schmidt and Giscard have put forward a joint Franco-German plan for a European monetary system leading to European monetary union, which would deprive Britain of the right to vary the value of its currency. Jim has put in a lot of conditions about help for us to finance it before we go ahead, but there was no indication that they would agree to that.

*Saturday 8 July*

I got a paper through the post this morning that looked like *Labour Weekly* but turned out to be a major right-wing attack on the Labour Party entitled *The Hidden Face of the Labour Party*. It claimed that the Party had been taken over by communists, Marxists and Trotskyites and included an article about me.

I also received from Peter Hain a copy of a note he had sent to Audrey Wise, Tom Jackson and others about the Norman Scott investigation. He had managed to gain access to the police documents, which state that six people might have been involved in a conspiracy to murder Scott, including Jeremy Thorpe and David Holmes, the former Treasurer of the Liberal Party, and that several Labour Ministers apparently covered up for Jeremy over a long period. I don't really want to get involved but it is information that might bear upon the Election.

*Monday 10 July*

Today it was announced that the American Boeing aircraft would be bought for British Airways, which means that any hopes for the British Aircraft Corporation and workers in Bristol are dashed. The issue hadn't even been brought to Cabinet and it just breaks my heart. How we can talk about buying British and import controls and then do this, I don't know. Edmund Dell is behind it, of course.

*Tuesday 11 July*

First meeting was at Number 10, on trading links with South Africa. Eric Varley had put in a paper, written by his officials, showing our deep involvement in the country. He said some companies would suffer serious losses and possible collapse if they withdrew, and 80,000 jobs would be at risk. Britain brings in £250 million a year through dividends on shares in South Africa. ICI has exports of £26 million, and 10 per cent of its profits come from South Africa; 15 per cent of GEC's exports go there, and 7000 jobs would be at stake in GEC alone. BSC depended heavily on South African imports for manganese, chrome, vanadium and platinum. He warned that we could not extricate ourselves quickly and that we should not take the lead. Although we might be able to stockpile some of these minerals, diversification would take eight to ten years.

I questioned whether we were doing anything at all to reduce our involvement. Eric's paper made no study of South African vulnerability – only ours. We needed much tougher control of companies, particularly public-sector companies like BP.

'But why?' asked Jim. 'What's the point of doing it? Wouldn't it simply strengthen Germany, Japan, France and the USA?'

I answered that it would be to our advantage to disengage because there was going to be a bust-up there and we had to face that fact.

'But how do we disengage without damaging our economic interests?' said Edmund Dell. 'The objective is right but handling it is difficult. Companies have their own view of what will happen in South Africa – the long view.'

David Owen said he could imagine circumstances in which companies would get on well with a Steve Biko figure as Prime Minister of a liberated South Africa. But he could also envisage townships like Soweto suddenly exploding, no-go areas being declared and aerial bombardment by the South African Government. Tremendous world reaction would follow and we would be caught up in it.

'South Africa will survive,' said Jim, 'and in my opinion it will find an internal settlement. We shouldn't disinvest now because that's the South Africa we will have to deal with. We trade with Moscow and nobody complains about that.'

Michael Foot observed, 'A clash is coming and the labour movement will be riven by it. We should stockpile and disengage.'

Jim concluded, 'All right. We'll stockpile chrome, magnesium, platinum and vanadium.'

At 7 I met Guido Brunner at the office and was stuck with him for three hours. He said Bremen was a tremendous development. A year ago Schmidt had no time for a European monetary union and now he has swung round. Giscard, always a great interventionist, has agreed to abandon all subsidies and protectionism, and to open France's frontiers to foreign investment. 'Ultimately, we'll have a group of European Finance Ministers who will take all the big decisions and there will be no need for little interventions in domestic affairs, "European regulations to deal with cut flowers", as Schmidt calls them. The slump is leading inexorably to this situation and Britain will have to decide whether she wants to be in the top tier or in the bottom tier. She's too big for the bottom but maybe she's not strong enough for the top.'

He acknowledged that the British were misled during the Referendum. They were told it didn't make any difference and it wasn't true. 'European development will be strengthened when the European Assembly is elected because then the Assembly will appoint spokesmen on certain subjects, thus weakening the Council of Ministers. There will even be pressure to appoint the European Commission from the Assembly, and of course national Parliaments will be jealous.'

The scenario was one in which permanent ministerial chairmen would preside over each council representing specific subject areas – a German Minister dealing with agriculture, a British Minister with energy, and so on, making decisions for all of us in collaboration with Commissioners and parliamentary spokesmen on each subject.

I said, 'Maybe, but we are not all federalists. Jim isn't, and neither is Mrs Thatcher. In any case, our economy isn't strong enough to stand up to it.'

'But you'll earn your living in high technology, at which you are very good,' said Brunner, 'and in energy, which is your field. And of course we may have a movement of people – German fishermen to Hull, British workers to Germany.'

'As guestworkers?' I said.

'That's not a very nice word, but there is no reason why people shouldn't work in other people's factories. This is a confederal Europe.'

I told him it reminded me of what happened in Germany in the nineteenth century, to which he replied, 'Bismarck made a great mistake. He should have concentrated on the *Zollverein* or customs union instead of bowing to pressure and building up the German Confederation as an empire.'

So obviously he sees the whole thing as a rerun of German history, only this time Germany is putting on the pressure.

### Saturday 15 July

On the platform at the Durham Miners' Gala, Jim said to me, 'The Tories are going to try and create a lot of scandal before the Election. They are trying to dig up the story about Stonehouse and the Czechoslovak Government and hoping to drag Harold into it.'[2]

Hilary and Rosalind came over this evening. She has lost three stone and looks very weak, but she said she wanted to go out, so we walked to a pizza restaurant. She held her head up and I am sure it was a tremendous strain.

### Sunday 16 July

Chris Mullin came to see me. He is about thirty, fought North Devon in 1970, works for the BBC and writes for *Tribune*. Anne McDermid, my literary agent, has persuaded him to turn my speeches into a book. I liked him. He's just written a book called *The Manifesto of an Extremist* in which he discusses various themes – the press, the Cold War, and so on. It's an arresting title, but it may do him some damage.

*Thursday 20 July*

Cabinet, and we came to the very important White Paper on pay, *Winning the Battle against Inflation*. Jim began by indicating that the Liberals would not support us on the control of dividends, and Michael called for it to be published on Monday.

We dealt with percentages and what we should do about low pay.

Denis said, 'We should accept the 5 per cent limit recommended in the paper. The unions won't endorse any guidelines but they do accept that the Government has a responsibility in this field and are only really expecting 5 per cent. The CBI can't give a commitment but they like it very much.'

Albert Booth thought 5 per cent – and even 7 per cent – was too low. 'Some people will get more than 5 per cent, and that will leave less for the low-paid. The anticipated level of inflation for this year is 8 per cent.'

Michael Foot agreed that low pay should be emphasised.

'Inflation must be the key,' said Jim.

Peter Shore pointed out that 5 per cent would involve a cut in living standards.

'That's because we overshot last year,' said Denis. 'Don't forget that family benefits will reinforce the position of the low-paid. Differentials are the key.'

David Owen favoured the 5 per cent, as did Roy Hattersley, who said that 7 per cent would be too high and would mean higher inflation.

Stan Orme was absolutely opposed to a norm.

I suggested we put in an amendment, as we had last year, to the effect that the Government's intention was to retain the level of real incomes in the current pay year.

Jim said, '5 per cent it is, and I have told the unions that they have all the weapons. We are naked in their presence and we need their co-operation. I said that at Durham and got a warm response.'

*Monday 24 July*

A riveting meeting at 10.30 of the TUC–Labour Party Liaison Committee at Transport House. All the TUC barons were there – David Lea, Len Murray, David Basnett, Geoffrey Drain (General Secretary of NALGO), Alan Fisher (General Secretary of the GMWU), Hugh Scanlon and Moss Evans. Frank Allaun was in the chair, and Jim Callaghan, Eric Heffer, Barbara Castle, Michael Foot, Bryan Stanley and others were present.

We were gathered to consider our joint statement, *Into the Eighties*, and I moved amendments that had been agreed by the Home Policy Committee, beginning with the call for the expansion of public expenditure to relieve unemployment.

'I won't have it,' said Jim. 'We'll be tied to these words, and later on Tony Benn will say I have betrayed the manifesto. I know him.'

Scanlon, among others, opposed an increase, but we managed to get it through.

Next I called for £1 billion for the NEB. Jim and David Basnett, whom I appointed to the NEB, opposed. Jim was also violently against inclusion of the words 'the purpose of the NEB involves the acquisition of major companies and the creation of new jobs through investment'. 'We can't put that in,' he said. 'It will create a scare.'

After much argument, we got both the money and the statement included. I was, however, absolutely beaten when I tried to strengthen the planning agreements with statutory powers. Len Murray said, 'There would be a lot of anxiety if trade unions thought that Government money that would normally be available for their industries would be withheld unless planning agreements were signed.'

On public ownership in the building industry, we only wanted to take one company into public ownership, and Jim fought hard against it. Eric Heffer said it was Party policy, but Jim refused to defend it in an Election.

'Are we socialist or not?' asked Eric.

'If you don't like what I'm doing,' replied Jim, 'you know what you can do about it.' There was Jim's veto again.

Eric continued, 'Look, Jim, you're not God, you're just a member of the Labour Party', and threatened to walk out.

I stopped him from going as far as that but it was the first real clash over the manifesto, and very interesting to watch. People were unimpressed by Jim's arguments. We got an amendment saying, 'The public sector needs to create and extend its own capability to facilitate this.'

The wealth tax figure was raised from £100,000 to £150,000.

The amendment on the reform of the machinery of government went through but fell short of abolition of the Lords, mentioning only its 'undemocratic role'.

I said, 'You can't suddenly discover that it's undemocratic at this stage. Cut that out and say, "We look to the abolition of the House of Lords."'

'What?' said Jim. 'Do you want that?'

I reminded him that Jack Jones had moved it and that Conference had passed it unanimously. Moss Evans backed me up, so that went in too.

A thrilling meeting.

*Thursday 27 July*

I attended a briefing meeting with officials prior to signing a safeguards agreement later today with Doug Anthony, the Deputy Prime Minister of Australia, covering the purchase of uranium. When I got to the office, I discovered that Brunner and the Commission had decided that such an agreement would be contrary to the Euratom Treaty and had therefore forbidden it.

I was furious, and issued a statement of protest; Anthony, having already heard about it, had arranged a statement in Australia. So the whole nature of the Community's interference in our energy policy has been laid bare.

Had a word with John Hill about the plutonium nitrates transfer from Dounreay to Windscale. He assured me that in tests a flask had been dropped into the sea and successfully located. I mentioned to him that Hermann Bondi had told me the Americans had banned the movement of plutonium nitrates altogether. I shall put in a note about that to the committee concerned and the Nuclear Inspectorate.

At Cabinet I raised the issue of the ban on signing the nuclear safeguards treaty. Jim was angry and said he knew nothing about it.

To the Foreign Secretary's official residence to meet Doug Anthony. He is an absolute Tory, and the Frazer Government is most unattractive. He was scornful about people who objected to nuclear power on environmental grounds and said the French didn't seem to have much difficulty with them.

It was a jolly lunch, and Dick Mabon at one point said that the three most abused phrases in the English language were as follows: 'my cheque is in the post'; 'yes, darling, I will respect you just as much in the morning as I do tonight'; and 'I am from the Government and I am here to help you'.

Talked to Brian Sedgemore and Frank McElhone in the House. Frank, who is Under-Secretary of State for Scotland, was most amusing about his attempts to bring the various churches of Scotland together. He said he'd managed to get the Moderator of the Church of Scotland, the Wee Frees, the Catholics and the Episcopalians in his room for the first time ever, and he'd given instructions to his Private Secretary that, if he pressed the bell, coffee was to be brought in.

After the first exchange he felt the atmosphere was rather tense so he pressed the bell. In came the coffee, and just as the Moderator and Archbishop Winning of Glasgow were drinking and eating biscuits a growling voice from the Wee Frees said, 'Are you Christian gentlemen not going to ask the Lord's blessing before you break bread?' Frank said that Archbishop Winning's biscuit froze in his mouth and the Moderator quickly moved his coffee-cup away from his lips while the Lord's blessing was asked.

*Sunday 30 July*

The big news today is that the Attorney-General has announced that charges in the Jeremy Thorpe affair are imminent. The whole of British politics may now erupt over this. It will certainly affect the Liberal Party's Election prospects.

Since there is no certainty that the Liberals are going to put up a candidate against me, I may be fighting a much harder battle with the Tories. I shall appeal quite openly to all the radical Liberals in my constituency to vote Labour, and I'll just have to hope that enough of them do.

*Wednesday 2 August*

Caroline came to dinner at the House – the anniversary of the day we met thirty years ago. We went up to sit in my room for the last vote before the recess was called: maybe the last vote of this Parliament.

*Thursday 3 August*

My first appointment was with Joel Barnett at the Treasury to discuss funding for the fast breeder reactor. My Department and the AEA are anxious for me to have more money in order to extend the present six-monthly funding to two years, to carry them right through to the point when they can go ahead with the fast breeder on a commercial basis.

I'm doubtful about this, and I said to Joel that I had come to him to insist that we should fund only six months at a time. Normally, if a spending Minister requested not to be given too much money, the Treasury would be delighted. But Fred Jones, the Deputy Secretary at the Treasury, observed, 'Surely this will affect the morale of the people in the industry.'

I said, 'Wait a minute. Could I have money for the coal industry because morale requires it? You are forcing money down my throat only because this is the fast breeder.'

I got what I wanted – namely no extra expenditure in the current financial year – but they want me to put in a bid for a little bit more for next year. The Treasury will happily agree to fund nuclear energy, but getting money for coal is almost impossible.

To Number 10 for the Defence and Overseas Policy Committee [DOP]. I am not a member, and I was attending only for the item dealing with the defence of our economic key points.

I had asked for special studies on how to defend five key points: Sullom Voe, Flotta, Cruden Bay, Bacton and St Fergus – the latter two being gas terminals. The studies had shown that 5000 troops to defend these points would cost £100 million capital and £35 million a year running costs. A smaller force of 1400 men would cost £20 million now and £10 million a year. Just stocking spare parts and components, in case anything was blown up, would cost between £15 and £20 million. The Chiefs of Staff had concluded that it wasn't worth spending all that money, and had opted for financing research into various technological safeguards. I agreed, and Jim consulted with the Chief of Defence Staff, Neil Cameron, and he was content.

### Friday 4 August

Jeremy Thorpe was arrested today, along with three others, and taken to Minehead police station, where they were charged with conspiracy to murder Norman Scott. They were released on bail of £5000 each, put up by Eric Lubbock [Lord Avebury].

All the rumours that Thorpe is implicated have turned out to be correct. It is the most tragic story. Here is a well-connected, brilliant, amusing man who won North Devon from the Tories in 1959, became Leader of the Liberal Party when he was in his thirties after Jo Grimond retired, and who in February 1974 carried the Party to its greatest electoral achievement since the war. And he has had this terrible anxiety on his mind, being blackmailed by this male model. The man is completely broken. The charge of conspiring to murder is obviously very serious, and if he is convicted there can be little doubt that he will go to prison. Inexpressibly sad.

The question now will be how much did Harold Wilson try to cover it up to protect Thorpe for political purposes?

### Saturday 5 August

Tonight Thorpe went to see his local Party in North Devon and they asked him to stand again as a candidate. This has created a great stir.

### Sunday 6 August

Hilary and Rosalind arrived. She looks awfully sick. She's on a new drug and she has put on a little weight but she's started to cough and the fear now is whether her second lung is going.

We heard on the 10 o'clock news that Pope Paul has died after fifteen years in the Vatican. Not an attractive man – his attitude towards birth control was extremely blind – and, although he did travel and was supposed to be keen on the ecumenical movement, he didn't really make an impact, certainly not compared to Pope John, his predecessor.

### Tuesday 15 August

To Stansgate with the family for the summer holiday.

## NOTES
*Chapter Three*

1.   (p. 284) General Sir Frank Kitson, who had fought against the Mau Mau in Kenya, devised methods of terrorising terrorists which are described in his books *Gangs and Counter-Gangs* and *Low-Intensity Operations*. During his stay with the British army in Northern Ireland in 1970–2, he developed an effective system of undercover operations – including intelligence gathering, penetration of the IRA and use of black propaganda against terrorist organisations. Many believed that Northern Ireland was being used as a testing ground for counter-terror and also counter-insurgency techniques that would subsequently be employed in Great Britain and elsewhere.

2.   (p. 325) In 1969 a Czech Intelligence officer, Josef Frolik, defected to the USA, and gave names to the CIA of British Labour politicians suspected of espionage activity, or communist sympathies. Amongst these was John Stonehouse, allegedly the victim of a sexual trap in Czechoslovakia. MI5 was informed and Harold Wilson was given the information. Stonehouse, then Postmaster-General, was questioned by MI5 but Wilson was sceptical of the claim and Stonehouse remained in the Government until the defeat in 1970. David Leigh, in his book *The Wilson Plot* (1988), gives the full details of Frolik's 'revelations'.

# 4
## Stumbling into Crisis
### September–November 1978

*The first hint that the Government's pay policy might not hold came on 24 August, when the unions at Ford claimed a 25 per cent increase. Ford had made record profits in 1978 and were happy to negotiate a figure well above the 5 per cent which the Prime Minister had decided in the summer was to be the limit in the impending pay round. On 1 September at the TUC Congress the limit was rejected overwhelmingly by the delegates.*

*In addition to the rigidity of the imposed pay policy was the threat of sanctions by the Government against employers who accepted higher wage settlements, sanctions for which there was no statutory provision and which, had they come to the courts, might well have been held to be illegal. Ford settled for 17 per cent in late November and the Government attempted to impose sanctions against the company, only to be defeated by the House of Commons.*

*Some of the fierce challenges generated by the attempt to impose a rigid 5 per cent limit – leading to the 'Winter of Discontent' – are the background of these difficult months, while I was also preoccupied with the issues of security service accountability, growing doubts about nuclear energy and the arguments over Britain's proposed membership of the European Monetary System.*

### Friday 1 September
To Bristol, to go over the organisation for a possible Election. On the train a man who was slightly drunk came and sat opposite me. 'Mr Benn,' he said, 'I hate you.' I asked him why and he proceeded to tell me his life story. He was an orphan, illegitimate, sent to a Poor Law institution in Willesden and went to sea when he was fourteen. He served in the merchant navy and was now a middle-ranking executive for the Peninsula and Orient Shipping Company.

Jim Callaghan warned the TUC today of the consequences of breaching the 5 per cent pay guidelines, but the TUC rejected his warning.

### Saturday 2 September
I'm very torn on the timing of the Election. There's the Early School

who think we're all set and organised and want to get it over with now because they think we might be defeated in the winter. The Late School says hang on to power as long as you can and be defeated if necessary. I must admit, it is very difficult to give up power before you have to.

*Tuesday 5 September*
The BP sanctions-busting scandal has exploded and it's going to be a massive issue; someone is bound to get around to publicising the fact that I was Minister of Power in 1969–70 and that the Ministry of Power was deeply implicated in nodding and winking as the oil companies continued to supply oil to Rhodesia.

Brian Sedgemore and I take the view that this row will pinpoint the main issue, namely whether we were ever ready to have a quarrel with South Africa, which of course no British Government has actually been prepared to do.

Caroline and I went down to the TUC Conference in Brighton and Caroline's bag was searched at the entrance. The woman looked very carefully through a book to make sure there weren't any leaflets inside. Well, the fact that the wife of a Labour Cabinet Minister has her bag searched for leaflets as she goes into the Visitors' Gallery of the TUC reflects the extent to which the TUC has joined the establishment.

Looking at the trade union leaders on the platform, as Jim came on to address them, I felt how much power the *institutions* of labour had acquired, if not the ideas of labour. Labour is coming into its own, but since I am an old radical, and suspicious of power, it made me feel a bit uneasy.

Jim made a speech in which he attacked the media for their treatment of the unions. He hammered home the 5 per cent pay policy and sang a few lines of the old Marie Lloyd song, 'There I was, waiting at the church . . .', indicating that he wasn't letting on about the Election yet.

*Wednesday 6 September*
Joan Lestor rang and told me that, at Brighton yesterday, Jim Callaghan had asked her where she was going to be over the next few days. She's convinced an Election is imminent and thinks 28 September is a possibility, in which case the Election timetable would be very tight.

She doesn't think we'd get a weekend to discuss the manifesto but we might get a whole day. Of course, one of the reasons Jim may want an early Election is to *prevent* discussion of the manifesto and to disrupt the whole Tory campaign, which is geared up to reach its climax in the middle of October.

I was told last night that Bob Worcester of MORI had seen Jim

Callaghan on Monday night and said the date would definitely be 5 October. Well, I think it's most unlikely that Jim would divulge that, and most unwise of Bob Worcester to spread it around. I suppose, like most minor functionaries, he feels that his power and importance can be inflated by suggesting that he is in the know.

*Thursday 7 September*
Went into the office and found they were re-laying the carpet, which seemed very significant.

Cabinet at 10.30, and I was sure the Election was going to be announced. We met without officials present. Jim said that there had been much speculation and he had consulted his Ministers, especially Michael Foot and Denis Healey, but the responsibility was *his*, although it affected all our fates, and it was an enormous responsibility. He had considered other factors such as the devolution referendum, and the fact that according to most opinion polls Labour voters do not want an Election – though our activists do – and he announced that he'd written to the Queen last night to say that he did not propose to seek the the dissolution of Parliament.

I was most surprised, and indeed angry that the Cabinet had not discussed a decision of this magnitude. The letter to the Queen had been sent, and that was it. I later discovered that he had decided this course on 17 August, so when he asked for our opinions last week, as a result of which I wrote to him, it was already a *fait accompli*.

He thought we might get a majority in Parliament on the Queen's Speech debate and we would fight when we could see the prospect of outright victory. We could win now, but he said the position would be clearer once the improvement in the economy was felt more fully. He wanted to disprove the idea that Governments just go for an Election at the first sign of a blue sky and he intended to make that point in his broadcast tonight. There would be difficulties ahead in the winter, but he wanted the electorate to see the full picture and not just the first stage of our recovery, because the real question was whether an early Election would help with unemployment, pay, or any of the problems facing us, and the answer was no. He said he would prefer that there be no discussion of this matter because he could not unwrite the letter to the Queen.

So we came on to the Bingham Report on sanctions-busting in Rhodesia, and Jim said he thought we were right to publish it.* Then David Owen dropped a bombshell. He said that Bingham had seen the Cabinet papers for 1968–70, but that, of course, he hadn't referred to them in the report. That was quite an admission, and Denis Healey just

* See chapter 2, note 4, p. 223.

exploded. 'Are you telling us that Bingham saw the Cabinet papers of the Labour Government from 1968 to 1970 but not the Tory Cabinet papers from 1970 to 1974?'

David said he had let Bingham read the departmental files of the Foreign Office, and these *included* the Cabinet papers. He said that George Thomson (who was Secretary of State for Commonwealth Affairs in 1967 and 1968) had been interviewed by Bingham and, as Thomson disclosed publicly last night, had informed Wilson of a meeting he had had with the oil companies in February 1968. David preferred to avoid an inquiry arising from publication of the report and felt that Thomson's statement had made the situation worse.

David Ennals said there would have to be an inquiry and it would have to be announced when the report was published. Jim told us that Wilson was going to issue a statement tonight.

Denis asked again why Bingham had seen the papers, and Owen replied that at that time Cabinet papers were not returned by the Departments as a matter of course to the Cabinet Office.

I don't believe that the Civil Service would hand over Foreign Office files without looking at what was inside. The fact that the Tory Cabinet papers were not there was no accident. The FO officials wanted to shop *us* to Bingham but protect the Tories. I said an inquiry would be necessary.

Elwyn told us we would have to consult the Director of Public Prosecutions before deciding on an inquiry, in case it inhibited prosecution of the oil companies. Sam Silkin was seeking advice on that.

Harold Lever was against an inquiry. What could be learned? Everyone knew sanctions-busting was going on; we should focus on the reasons and the fact that we had no choice.

Michael Foot said there had to be an inquiry and a quick route must be found.

A fascinating discussion. Prosecutions are irrelevant because the Rhodesian situation might well be settled by the time the report gets out, if there is a counter-coup. What is important is the political implications – the fact that Cabinet papers were shown to a QC but might be denied to the House of Commons or the public; the relations between civil servants, Ministers and the oil companies, and so on. I don't think anyone around that table had any idea of the significance of what was happening.

I might add that I had asked whether any other Minister was involved, and I was told that Dick Marsh, who was Minister of Power in February 1968, had been informed about it but had not been told about the meeting between the oil companies and George Thomson.

That's important to me because it shows that ministerial involvement at the Ministry of Power stopped eight months before I got there. Marsh was against sanctions anyway, and when he was informed they were being broken he didn't want to know.

*Friday 8 September*
To Bath to give a lecture to the British Association for the Advancement of Science. Dorothy Hodgkin, the Chancellor of Bristol University, who I think used to be a good old radical, is this year's President of the British Association. Frank Kearton, who will take over from her, was also there, and lots of other distinguished people.

I delivered my lecture, 'Democracy in the Age of Science', which was in fact a very tough call for freedom of information and an attack on the arguments for secrecy.

*Saturday 9 September*
To my amazement and delight, *The Times*, the *Guardian* and the *Telegraph* had given tremendous coverage to my speech on freedom of information. *The Times* had a leader called 'Public ownership of knowledge', saying that Mr Benn was at his best when he was intervening directly on freedom of information 'with typical wit and ideological content'. Public ownership of knowledge, it said, is perhaps the one area where a collectivist aspiration is legitimate.

*Monday 11 September*
Stephen looked in at home and I told him I was considering writing to Merlyn about telephone tapping. 'You'll never do it,' he said, so I actually sat down and did it there and then.

12 September 1978

Dear Merlyn,

Can you please tell me whether telephone calls to my home, my Department or my room at the House of Commons are now or have ever been tapped by the security services or other public authorities and, if so, when, and who authorised it?

Yours, Tony

Stephen said, 'I don't believe you'll send it', but I told him I was quite serious. I showed it to Caroline and she said it was too harsh, so I added a cover note.

Dear Merlyn,

As you know, there is a revival of public interest in the extent of the accountability of the security services to Ministers. I know you share a deep concern for civil liberties and the need for them to be safeguarded.

In the United States citizens can now ask for information in relation to themselves to provide some sort of check on what goes on. I have therefore written the enclosed letter which I am sending you formally to test our response to a similar procedure and I now look forward to hearing your reply to it.

Yours, Tony

I do believe my phone is or has been tapped from time to time, when I speak to people like Ken Coates who would be tapped in their own right, but I have never dared to write and ask before. However, I took courage from the support for my speech on freedom of information. Secondly I thought of the courage of those dissidents in Moscow who are hounded by the KGB and really do have to stand up to a lot of pressure, and I decided it was the least I could do.

If Merlyn says, 'Yes you have been tapped', it will be sensational. If he says I haven't, and it comes to light later that I have, it will show that Ministers aren't in charge of the security services. He may say, 'I can't tell you', which is equally sensational. And of course if my request suddenly appears in an article by Chapman Pincher then it will show that the security services have leaked it. If I don't get a reply in writing, I shall ask to see Merlyn and record what is said.

*Tuesday 12 September*
I sent off the letter to Merlyn Rees.

International Committee at 10 o'clock, and we agreed to nominate Mik as President of the Socialist International, in place of Harold Wilson. Then we discussed the foreign policy statement to go into the manifesto.

Four points were agreed.

1. We live together or we die together – ie détente versus the Cold War. I pointed out the hypocrisy of the military here who were just using human rights issues in the USSR to get more defence expenditure.

2. We should develop friendlier relations with China, and I got added the point that we entirely reject the Chinese doctrine that war between China and Russia is inevitable.

3. The IMF should take human rights into consideration before allocating funds. I thought we should also state that peace and justice are important and that the IMF is a baleful influence, pressing for deflation. At the moment, it would give money to a reactionary regime pursuing deflationary policies, but not to a progressive regime opposed to monetarism.

4. We should reaffirm our 1974 manifesto commitment on defence expenditure rather than go for a cut of 25 per cent.

Tory Central Office was broken into last night, and the safe where they keep their manifesto was tampered with; documents may have been photocopied, and so on. It seems so improbable, but whoever it was also broke into Saatchi & Saatchi, the Tories' advertising agents, so it could be an ultra-left group or it could be the CIA wanting it to look like that, and to create a Watergate-type crisis.

*Wednesday 13 September*
At 10, Bert Williams, a messenger in my Department, presented me with two oil paintings of horses. He is a pensioner, and he told me that as a young man he was good at art so he took it up again in his old age. He started in oils only six months ago, and they are remarkable pictures.

*Thursday 14 September*
The PM has sent out a minute saying that as we were going on to another session he hoped colleagues would go to work with renewed vigour, and so on.

The first item at Cabinet was David Owen's report on Iran where the Shah has imposed martial law after fighting between the demonstrators and the army. His understanding was that the troops would remain loyal to the Shah and that the situation would stabilise. The Muslim-led coalition of reactionaries – the mullahs – and intellectuals on the centre and left was causing the Shah trouble. It was not in British interests for the Shah to fall because of our investments there, and he had been responsive to pressure for reform, encouraging moves towards a constitutional monarchy. The US and the UK should respond in the same way. There was the additional factor of hostility from Afghanistan, which was now communist, and from Pakistan, which was affronted at not being allowed a uranium enrichment plant and was therefore consolidating its links with China. Turkey was also unstable.

'Any questions?' said Jim.

I raised the human rights issue. 'I am strongly opposed to the repression of dissidents in Russia, but, if we are going to have human rights raised in some places, what about the rights of Muslims in Iran? It seems strange to me that the BBC can talk about Christian martyrs in Russia but Muslim extremists in Iran.'

I went on to say that these were difficult matters and the Cabinet should discuss them more fully to see what impact a human rights policy would have on our economic and political position.

'These Muslims are very reactionary,' said Fred Mulley.

David Owen said, 'The Americans share my view – that human rights should play some part in our economic policy. The RD Committee does discuss this.'

'What is RD?' David Ennals asked.

Well, RD is the Cabinet committee on relations with developing countries, but it was amusing because it proved that Cabinet members don't know what Cabinet committees there are. A handbook of how our committees work would be helpful. Open government is needed for *Ministers* to know what is going on, let alone anybody else.

'Look,' said Jim, 'the Shah wants to know our attitude towards his regime, and I take it that it is the view of the Cabinet that we must continue to support the Shah against the mad mullahs and the Soviet agents who are opposing him.'

Jim was obviously just going along with David Owen's oral report on Iran, and tonight there were copies of two telegrams in my red box which bear on this issue. Both were dated and sent yesterday, before the Cabinet discussion even took place. One, signed by David Owen, was a message from the PM to the Shah conveying the support of Her Majesty's Government. The other was a report by Peter Jay in Washington to David Owen of a talk with Zahedi, the Iranian Ambassador in Washington, in which Jay told Zahedi that the British Government was sympathetic and supported the Shah. The American and British establishments are fully behind the Shah at this moment: the primary reason is defence – to keep the Russians out of Iran – but our investments there are of course also a major factor.

Still on foreign affairs, we came on to Rhodesia, and David Owen said the Bingham Report would be published on Tuesday. The lawyers have advised that publication would not prevent prosecution, but Annexe 3, which contained the names of all the people involved, had been removed.

Jim said Cabinet would consider it on Thursday. He had written to Mrs Thatcher so that she could read it now, and he proposed to consult her.

David Owen stated that the *Sunday Times* had alleged that 'oil swapping' was still going on in the summer of 1977, when BP had increased its oil supplies to South Africa, and South Africa had, in turn, increased her supplies to Rhodesia. Of course, David Owen was already at the Foreign Office by that time.

Jim said, 'We all knew what was going on and we couldn't stop it. The question is, did we *try* to stop it?'

That was the beginning of the line that is going to be taken by the Government.

Then to the main business of the Cabinet, which was the forward look for the next few years.

Jim began by thanking Hattersley, Healey and others who had run the pay policy over last winter. He wanted to approach future problems objectively, was not a believer in masochism, and thought there was too much departmentalisation among Ministers. He said that detailed policies would not be as important as attitudes and themes, and we must not be afraid to bore each other with the same speeches.

The *Into the Eighties* document formed the basis, and employment was the key issue. We *could* win, and he hoped everyone would read the book on the Tory Party to be published on 28 September.

In effect Jim is a Heathite, and the difference in our Party between policy and practice is just like that between the Heathites and the Thatcherites.

Michael Foot said it would have been lunatic to have an early Election. The press weren't printing what we had to say; indeed, he had made a speech last night which wasn't reported.

'Yes it was,' Jim pointed out. 'In the *Daily Telegraph* – "Michael Foot attacks Mad Professor" ', which was a reference to Hayek, Margaret Thatcher's economist guru.

Denis said the only reason why unemployment had come to the top of the list was that prices were stable. If they began rising, inflation would go back into first place. Our control of pay and money supply had been the key. The CBI thought the current pay claims were not realisable. 'Let me give an example of our successes. Ferranti has now been sold off again by the NEB and that is a triumph.'

That appalls me: Ferranti went bust, the NEB saved it, and as soon as it is profitable again we sell it back to Ferranti Brothers, who will reap the benefit of investment put in by the NEB. It just makes my hair stand on end.

He went on, 'The Tories are vulnerable on education. Couldn't we consider some cheap gesture on the arts, for example, which would please middle-class people. A bit more on pollution would pay off.'

Jim Callaghan told us he had thousands of letters from Labour supporters in favour of delaying the Election.

David Ennals said, 'Now we have time over the winter, we shall have to go ahead with things I have been deferring. For example, I shall be closing the Elizabeth Garrett Anderson Women's Hospital.' He suggested keynote speeches on human rights, women's rights, seat belts and community action.

When it came to my turn, I said, 'Jim rebuked somebody a moment ago for talking about a spring Election. I am working on the assumption that there may not be an Election at all. If in a year's time the mad mullahs – Professor Hayek and his crowd – and the left extremists start to look dangerous, I take it Jim might well be asking the Shah to keep us in power!'

There was some slightly embarrassed laughter and I went on to say I welcomed the look forward. The events that would come up in the next twelve months would be pay problems, unemployment (where the polls were suggesting that the Tories would be better at dealing with it than us), and the strain on the public services, in particular the Health Service. I said we all knew of cases where people had been told by their doctors that you could have an operation sooner if you tipped the consultant – because that was what private practice involved – and it was a disgrace.

I recommended that each Minister should submit to the Cabinet on a single sheet of paper the future policy of his or her Department. The only time we ever discussed the policy of other Departments was when we had public expenditure exercises.

As a Government surely we could show a bit of imagination and have a planned policy of concessionary services. For example, it was mad that old people living alone in their London flats could not afford to visit their daughters or sons in Newcastle, when there were empty nationalised trains going backwards and forwards. And tons of coal were being stocked while people died of cold in the winter. I said this had a bearing on law and order too, if this was rightly seen in the context of social justice.

On industry, we should start discussions with the unions and companies on planning agreements and industrial democracy.

As I began on the question of public patronage, Jim said, 'I think I should remind members of the Cabinet that we haven't got an awful lot of time', which was a tactful indication that my speech had gone on too long.

David Owen thought educational standards were a problem, and people wanted to feel they were getting value for money. The family was a significant issue. As for vandalism, he wanted to see more Community Service orders made against young vandals so they could make restitution for what they had done. Couldn't we use unemployed teachers to organise teams of young offenders?

Behind the charming exterior and apparent liberalism of David Owen lies the hard thinking of a very right-wing person.

Shirley thought our philosophy was unclear; she wanted socialism with a human face. She talked about 'the citizen ten feet tall', meaning more participation, tenants' rights, planning inquiries against bureaucracy, and so on.

Jim said that the professionals – particularly the NUT – were against all concepts of self-help. We were up against the 'NUPE attitude'; voluntary effort was discouraged by the unions.

Stan Orme was in despair at the blocks of flats in the inner cities. 'Leaving it to the experts after the war was a mistake.' He felt that no one was spelling out the philosophy of the Party.

Jim told us that he had recently telephoned the Post Office accounts department about his telephone bill. 'I didn't say who I was, didn't give my name, and I was treated disgracefully. I was told they couldn't answer over the phone, I had better write in, and finally they just rang off.' Well, if Jim has only just discovered that it is not all plain sailing when you ring up about your phone bill, it shows how disconnected he is from reality.

Roy Mason said there were now a lot of dispirited prospective parliamentary candidates.

'It serves them right,' observed Jim. 'They had no right to believe there would be an Election.'

'Well, they did,' said Roy. 'On the 5 per cent limit and the black list, we are out on a limb. We bit deep in the last three years' pay policy and there will be anger from the rank and file.'

So here was a right-wing trade union member of the Cabinet warning Jim that he was ready to climb off the bandwagon on pay policy, which was very significant.

Elwyn Jones picked up the theme of law and order, which had been frequently raised. 'Crime rates are higher in the US, a capitalist country, and higher penalties are not the answer.'

Jim wound up. 'Thank you very much. I have noted all this down – but not for my memoirs. We all recognise the economic problems but our accent today has been on the rights and duties of citizens. Don't forget, Governments do well when people have money in their pockets. How do we do it? I like Shirley's point' (actually it was *my* point but Jim rarely refers with approval to my proposals) 'that Cabinet Ministers should put down their policies on one sheet of paper.' He would set up a little committee chaired by Michael Foot which would meet before the Conference, and would meet the NEC, and produce papers with a five-year look ahead.

Well, that was that, after almost an hour's discussion.

Peter Shore came over to my office in the afternoon to meet Arthur Scargill.

Arthur presented his arguments against the fast breeder awfully well, and I yearned for the day when Arthur is President of the NUM. He said the inquiry must first deal with the principle of the fast breeder, and then consider where to site it. He wanted financial support to help the anti-nuclear lobby present their views, and all the evidence to be published – both for and against.

Peter assured us that the inquiry would be broad-ranging and independent.

*Saturday 16 September*
At 10 to the University Settlement in Bristol, for the South West Region Women's Conference. Caroline spoke on equality and education – a

tremendously analytical, lucid, committed and factual speech much appreciated by the delegates.

*Wednesday 20 September*
To EY at Number 10. Eric Varley presented a paper in favour of the Peugeot takeover of Chrysler UK, which includes the old Rootes company. There was no alternative, he said.

Bruce Millan thought it was the best solution, and Jim asked if anyone disagreed.

I said I did. 'In 1976, in what was supposed to be a planning agreement, Chrysler gave us assurances, in exchange for funds, that they would stay in Britain. Now we're supposed to just hand the company over to Peugeot. I favoured public ownership then and I favour it now because their assurances are not worth the paper they are written on.

'The key phrase is on page 9 in Eric's paper: "the French Government would not allow us to take over Chrysler in France". Well, the difference between us and France is that *they* don't allow takeovers but we do. For years we have been told that ownership doesn't matter, only management. This proves that ownership does matter in the end.'

Jim said, 'Perhaps we are witnessing the end of the car assembly industry in Britain, and that may be a good thing. BL has been a continuing drain on our resources and the British motor car industry has done a great deal of damage to the reputation of this country.'

That was like Samson bringing the temple down around him. Jim is violently opposed to public ownership and committed to the market economy and to Europe, and he is actually hammering an industry which earns us probably over a billion pounds a year in exports.

I had to leave at this point to go to a meeting, and Jim said, 'Tony is about to throw himself out of a window', which I thought showed great disrespect.


*Thursday 21 September*
First meeting of the day was GEN 74, the Cabinet committee on non-proliferation chaired by David Owen. We considered a paper from me calling for a ban on the sale of invertors to Pakistan – devices that can be used in centrifuge uranium enrichment and which would have consequences for nuclear arms proliferation. David Owen had supported me in correspondence and Edmund Dell wanted it discussed.

I said the case seemed very strong; we all knew Pakistan wanted to build nuclear weapons but there was a broader question. We ought to have a proper Joint Intelligence Committee which concerned itself with countries engaged in proliferation. It should look at Israel, Pakistan, the possible nuclear link between Germany and South Africa (as a recent book suggested), Brazil and so on.

David Owen said we did have regular Intelligence reports on this and they were circulated to members of the Defence and Overseas Policy Committee; maybe we could also circulate them to members of the GEN 74 Committee.

Edmund Dell asked, 'How do we know these invertors will be used for centrifuges? A ban would harm our trade and it would be ineffective.'

David Owen suggested that perhaps the Foreign Office should discuss the issue with Pakistan and other allies, but Ken Berrill wondered if we could believe the Pakistanis. David Owen said the FO and the Department of Trade would talk about it; meanwhile the invertors would not be sold.

Over at 10.30 to the Cabinet, and Sir John Hunt opened the door between the Cabinet Office and Number 10. I said, 'My goodness, to have the Secretary of the Cabinet opening the door for one is most memorable.' Joel Barnett commented, 'I expect it will go into your memoirs.'

Jim began, 'I should tell you that I had a very emotional request from Kenneth Kaunda for me to see him at once. He wouldn't ask for this unless there were real anxieties in his mind, and I don't know what it is about, but I am concerned that Kaunda might be going to invite the Russians in, or the Cubans, or leave the Commonwealth or something awful like that.' So Jim had agreed to meet him in Kano in Nigeria on Saturday. He had agreed with Judith Hart an increase of £20 million in aid to Zambia on a loan basis.

There must be something significantly wrong for Jim to meet Kaunda on the spur of the moment.

The Bingham Report came up, and Michael Foot said we must have an inquiry, maybe a royal or special commission, but it shouldn't comprise only Privy Councillors, and the members should see Cabinet papers. We should consult with other parties to avoid an upset.

Jim Callaghan said, 'When the Monckton Commission on Central Africa was set up in 1959, people were offered Privy Councillorships in order to serve on it. I was offered one by Macmillan, but I said I couldn't accept it from him just for this purpose.'*

'The difficulty is that we're all interested parties,' I said. 'I was a Minister at the time, and a Foreign Office minute was sent to me in the autumn of 1969 which was frankly misleading. It did not tell me that the oil was getting through. I rather share the view that the Tories will

* In his autobiography *Time and Chance* (1987) Jim Callaghan recalls that 'to accept a Privy Councillorship from a Conservative Prime Minister would be as if a Welsh rugby forward had accepted an England cap (but times have since changed).'

vote to embarrass us. The inquiry would want to meet Ministers and former Ministers, officials and Government directors of BP, the boards of the oil companies and their executives. It would look at papers from 1965 to date. We know that George Brown had proposed that we take legislative powers to make the oil companies criminally responsible for the supply of oil by subsidiaries. And Dick Marsh was against sanctions altogether.' I didn't favour a Privy Councillors' committee, I wanted a Commons select committee, and it should have access to all the relevant Cabinet papers except those that the Government refused on grounds of national security, which they would have to justify.

Jim warned, 'We won't come out of it well.'

Peter Shore thought Rhodesia was no different from any other issue. If we were going to have an inquiry into this we might just as well have an inquiry into Suez, and Northern Ireland; it would completely change the relationship between the Cabinet and the Government, and between the Government and Parliament. He was against any sort of inquiry.

*Sunday 24 September*
Papers full of the Bingham Inquiry, and Kenneth Kaunda's meeting with Jim Callaghan. It makes me wonder whether there is some sort of a deal being fixed whereby Kaunda would ask us to send troops to Zambia in readiness for a counter-coup in Rhodesia. That could mean that we'd be involved in the end of the Rhodesian story – very dangerous.

To Hyde Park to address the Anti-Nazi League rally. There was a lorry with a steel band playing, and there were tens of thousands of young people. The average age was about twenty to twenty-five, and there were banners and badges and punk rockers, just a tremendous gathering of people. It was certainly the biggest meeting that I had ever attended in this country – bigger than the Upper Clyde Shipbuilders demos in Glasgow.

A speaker from the Socialist Workers' Party spoke from the platform first, followed by Arthur Scargill and me. Tom Robinson, a gay pop star and a committed socialist, sang. Bill Keys, General Secretary of SOGAT, and Dennis Skinner were there. As far as I know, Dennis and I were the only two Labour MPs. Multi-racial rock music has given the movement leadership and it is a tragedy that the Labour Party can't give a firmer lead, but it has never done so.

Arthur and I marched together down to the corner of Park Lane and Piccadilly. The youngsters were rushing along and pushing ahead – it made me feel like an old animal in a herd! By the time we got to Brixton there must have been a hundred thousand people gathered.

*Monday 25 September*

The *Morning Star* and the *Guardian* gave quite sympathetic accounts of the march. Every other paper emphasised the National Front march in the East End. According to the *Financial Times* there were 80,000 in Hyde Park.

This morning I wrote a Cabinet paper listing ten reasons why the 5 per cent pay policy wouldn't work, and calling for talks with the unions about the alternative strategy, including import controls and rejection of a European economic and monetary system.

Dashed to the Treasury with Alex Eadie, Francis Cripps and a clutch of my own officials to meet Joel Barnett and his officials about the assisted coal-burn scheme. I wanted £25 million from the Treasury to save the mining industry from loss or pit closures over the winter. Joel and I had a big tussle. He said if the money was given there would be less for health expenditure. I told him I thought that was rubbish.

'But you're increasing public expenditure,' Joel declared.

I said, 'You can't compare public expenditure and industrial investment of this kind with health expenditure. They're quite different.'

We really got to the heart of Treasury notions. In the past I have had in the back of my mind the idea that the Treasury has special intellectual powers and that the left's arguments are less developed. Of course the truth is that the Treasury obfuscate, complicate, mystify and deceive in order to conceal a completely old-fashioned way of keeping the nation's accounts.

Joel Barnett was prepared to shift some loans and make them grants. Well, that suited me fine. He asked me where I could make savings and I said, if I were forced to make savings, the nuclear industry would be the area I'd choose; I was not in a hurry for nuclear power, particularly the fast breeder. With that I left. It was very satisfactory.

Caroline has been working on a leaflet to be distributed at the Party Conference detailing Government subsidies to private education. The figure is £125 million, and includes the cost of paying for diplomats' and officers' sons to go to private schools.

It is a fortnight since I wrote to Merlyn Rees asking him if my telephone was tapped by the Intelligence Services or any other public authorities, and I still haven't had a reply. So I wrote again:

Dear Merlyn,

I wrote to you on 12 September with a covering letter to ask whether my telephone calls are or have ever been tapped by the security services. The letter went by hand in a Government car. I cannot trace any acknowledgement or reply and want to be sure that you received it personally.

I look forward to your reply.

*Tuesday 26 September*

I sent off the second letter to Merlyn Rees and a message came back in the afternoon from the Home Office. James Bretherton wrote me a note about it:

> Secretary of State,
>
> The Home Office rang about your two letters to the Home Secretary of 12 and 26 September. They wanted to assure you that these are in fact receiving attention and that a full reply will be sent to you in due course.
>
> James

I had a word with John Cunningham, who nearly died while on holiday in Italy recently. He told me he joined his nine-year-old daughter in the pool, but, not having eaten very much, he passed out in the water and just sank to the bottom. Some men pulled John out and his heart was beating but he had stopped breathing. He was sick, and that helped to clear the water from his lungs. It was the most shattering experience, and John said the thing that really worried him was that they insisted on carrying out tests on his brain and his heart. They told him that if he hadn't had reserves of oxygen, through playing a lot of squash, he would have been in a real jam.

At 5.30 I had an appointment with Moss Evans. I don't really know him very well but I suppose he's about my age and he's just taken on the biggest job in the British trade union movement, replacing Jack Jones as General Secretary of the TGWU.

We talked for an hour and a half; considering he has the Ford pay claim and a national Ford strike on his hands, it was amazing that he could come at all. I asked him how it was going. 'I notice Terry Beckett [Chairman of Ford] got an 80 per cent pay increase today,' I said.

'Oh,' he said, 'we've known that was coming for ages – profit-linked of course. It just isn't on; Ford have made great profits and our people have contributed to it. I cannot understand the Government, because in the summer of 1977, when Jack Jones failed to carry the T&G Biennial Conference behind a continuation of the Social Contract, it must have been obvious to everybody that it wasn't on for a fourth year. Alf Allen [General Secretary of USDAW], Len Murray and I have been trying to persuade Denis Healey, Albert Booth and Roy Hattersley that it isn't on. I just don't understand what the Government are doing.'

He said he'd seen Beckett yesterday and, for the first time, Beckett had actually issued a leaflet to Ford workers making it clear that it was the Government that was responsible for the 5 per cent limit. Beckett had specifically mentioned the Government's pay sanctions, and that had infuriated the Ford workers. Beckett had told Moss that it would be a three-month strike, so Moss had said, 'Oh well, we can take that; we've got £32 million in the bank.'

Moss told me it would cost the union a quarter of a million pounds a week to keep the Ford strike going, and they could borrow more money, interest free, from other unions.

He looked out of the corner of his eye to see my reaction to all this. I was quite impassive, and I said, 'I just want to know how we're going to get out of it without being painted into a corner like Ted Heath was. Jim feels that reducing expectations is the right thing to do.'

'Yes,' said Moss, 'when you talk to Jim he says, "The mass of the people are with us and will continue to support us", but, you know, the rank and file of our people are the public too. We have a million and a quarter T&G workers and we are just as much members of the public as those who don't want wage increases. You can't re-create the Social Contract, you just can't do it. You've got to have flexibility now, we've got to be able to renegotiate in industry.'

I put in my Cabinet paper on pay and economic policy, and when the Cabinet Office received it they rang and said they hoped it hadn't been circulated to all Ministers. James Bretherton told them it hadn't – only to Michael, Peter, Albert, John Silkin and Stan Orme. In April and July I put in papers which were never included in the Cabinet agenda, and this is a paper I am determined to have discussed.

It will make Jim hopping mad, because on the television tonight Denis Healey said there was to be no budging whatsoever on the pay guidelines.

*Wednesday 27 September*
I went to the committee of Ministers which Jim set up to 'look forward'. It comprised Michael Foot, Roy Mason, Shirley Williams, Merlyn Rees, Roy Hattersley, Peter Shore and myself. We had discussed papers from each Minister stating their Departments' plans for the years ahead, and they were an absolute ragbag. Some contained rubbishy civil servants' drafts saying things like 'the Department of Trade is mainly concerned with exports and wishes to assist firms who want help' and so on – no political content at all.

Michael had written a paper on three themes – full employment, democratic participation and the caring society – and put it forward today. Not to put too fine a point on it, it was absolute rootless liberal clap-trap – we would care about the young unemployed, we would adjust schools to industry, we would go in for training and retraining, we would press for world measures to deal with reflation, but we would also hold to our financial and monetary restraints and develop our industrial strategy. Under democratic participation, he referred to devolution, a more accountable broadcasting service, better information for parents about schools – all very vague. The 'caring society' was just overflowing with crocodile tears. It was a disgrace, to be candid: no content, weak, and where it had information it was a straight Treasury brief. I don't suppose Michael had written it at all.

Went back to the office and we had a little farewell party. James Bretherton is leaving, sadly, and we welcomed Bill Burroughs as my new Private Secretary.

*Thursday 28 September*
Packed for Conference and Caroline cut my hair.

One interesting story that I don't think I have mentioned in my diary yet: Anthony Tucker, science correspondent of the *Guardian*, came up to me at a meeting recently and told me he had been victimised by the Department of Energy and he wanted to make a complaint to me. I investigated this and received an astonishing minute referring to attacks made on Anthony Tucker by Bernard Ingham, sent to the Director of Information at the Central Office of Information. He said Tucker was completely unreliable, that he joined the anti-nuclear lobby and that his opinions 'weren't worth paying for in washers'. As a result, Anthony Tucker was taken off the list of journalists approved for COI work.

There are several questions arising from this. First of all, is it right for a Government Department to try to destroy the reputation of a journalist because he doesn't agree with the Government view? Secondly, is it right for a journalist to play for both sides – ie to be a journalist and to pick up money from the Government for writing official articles for the COI? Thirdly, isn't this an indication of the tremendous power of the nuclear lobby at the working level, pulverising an individual journalist? I have asked to see Tucker about it.

First appointment was at Cabinet, where we agreed to the televising of the opening of Parliament. Then we went through the Queen's Speech for the next session. There was a reference to the Queen looking forward to her visit to Iran, and Jim said, 'I was forced by the Foreign Office to write to the Shah and the letter is now being used widely in Iran. Our Ambassador in Tehran is over-enthusiastic in indicating my support for the Shah.'

That was interesting because it indicated that the Foreign Office was in a sense using Jim and he was trying to get off the hook.

We moved on to the reform of the Official Secrets Act. The draft stated, 'The Government will introduce legislation to reform Section 2 of the Official Secrets Act', and that in the meantime we would take action to improve the flow of information. Quite meaningless, I thought.

Fred Peart said, 'I'm absolutely against reform.'

'You won't get it through the House of Commons,' Merlyn Rees insisted. 'It is very provocative.'

Jim said, 'There are some interesting proposals as to how the Government could improve the flow of information, which would then be monitored by an outside body – perhaps the Ombudsman.'

I argued that that was very controversial and Jim asked why. 'Because the idea of freedom of information is to provide the statutory power to know via Members of Parliament; whereas this has been cooked up by the Civil Service and would be monitored by the Ombudsman, who has nothing directly to do with Parliament.'

Mike Cocks observed, 'If you did have a bill and it went to a standing committee, it would be very hard to pack the committee with enough time-servers to get the result you wanted.' An extremely candid remark!

'I think it would be better to do nothing,' said Michael Foot.

Merlyn reminded Jim that the issue would be bound to come up at Conference and Jim replied, 'At Conference, policy will be made by those who feel most keenly.'

That's how the Prime Minister dismisses the Party, by saying policy is made 'by those who feel most keenly about it'. I didn't say it, but, as far as the Cabinet is concerned, policy is administered by those who feel *least* keenly about it but who happen to be in power. Anyway, it was agreed that the GEN 29 Committee would be reconvened to discuss it. GEN 29 was set up by Jim when the Official Secrets Act was under discussion. Its proceedings were never disclosed to the Cabinet, and members of the Cabinet only found out what was going on when it was revealed subsequently in the *New Statesman*.

We came on to Zambia. 'This is absolutely secret,' Jim began. 'The paper is marked SECRET for both military and commercial reasons and because of the implications regarding Cuba and the Soviet Union.'

When he saw Kaunda in Kano last weekend, Kaunda was worried about Nkomo's ZAPU forces, which operate from near Lusaka, in Zambia. Kaunda said the guerrilla camps were growing, and he was afraid that if the attacks across the border against Rhodesia continued, Rhodesia would retaliate against Lusaka.

He had other problems. In 1977 the harvest in Zambia had failed and the country didn't have enough money even to buy the fertiliser for the 1978 crop. Jim went on to say that Kaunda was an old friend and a member of the Commonwealth and that unless he got some support he would feel he had to turn to Cuba or the Soviet Union.

The question had arisen whether British troops should be sent to Zambia and Kaunda had agreed there were difficulties in this but it was under consideration. Jim had discussed with him how Lusaka was to be defended from an air attack, and Kaunda had decided to impose conditions on Nkomo operating from Zambia – for example, that he stop attacking soft targets in Rhodesia.

Jim felt that after the Bingham Report it would be wrong to offer Kenneth Kaunda money because it would look like a bribe to keep him quiet. However, he had a plan to help Zambia out. A great deal of Zambia's copper couldn't be sold because of depressed world prices and so Jim thought we could buy up the copper for Britain's reserves. It would be a straight commercial transaction. There were forecasts of an eventual rise in copper prices so it would be a good bargain.

I asked a couple of questions. 'I have two fears. Since there is a potential conflict between Kaunda and Nkomo, notably on whether Nkomo's forces should be able to continue to operate from Zambia, is there a danger that our sending Phantoms to defend Lusaka might lead to their being drawn into that conflict? We might be asked by Kaunda to use them against Nkomo. Secondly, isn't there another risk that if the Phantoms are in Zambia, and particularly if British troops go with them, they will be so near the Rhodesian situation that it could amount to the first step towards a full-scale UK military involvement to save the whites in Rhodesia?'

These were severe warnings, and Jim said little in reply. 'It's possible, but not probable.'

He added, 'I notice that two Members of the Cabinet are writing notes' (one of whom was me) 'and this is so secret from a military point of view and so sensitive from a commercial point of view, because of the purchase of copper, that I must ask Members to treat this as if it were a Budget Cabinet and destroy their notes.'

I do not see why, on matters of this magnitude, there should be discussions all over the shop while Cabinet Ministers are not allowed to make notes. I did not destroy my notes but I didn't write any more on Zambia. Little more was said anyway.

Then we turned to the Bingham Inquiry. 'I have been talking to a number of people about this,' Jim announced. 'No new facts will emerge from any future inquiry. There will only be a judgement about what has happened, and it is important that we be fair. Tony Benn has put in a memorandum and so has Michael Foot.'

My memorandum called for a select committee, and I said I was not in favour of the prosecution of minnows, but, whatever inquiry we had, we should neither protect people from prosecution nor endanger them unfairly with prosecution. My select committee Cabinet paper was intended to guard against that. 'Rightly or wrongly,' I said, 'we did decide at a very early stage that we would not have a confrontation with South Africa, so there were certain things we couldn't do. But the conduct of those concerned causes me a great deal of alarm.

'I explained at the last Cabinet that I had looked through the papers carefully, and the role of those who had tried to frustrate George Brown's original proposal for criminal sanctions was very serious. *I* was certainly misled, and I feel strongly about it. The oil companies' conduct, notably that of BP, is also serious and there is bound to be a demand for the papers to be disclosed.'

I drew attention to the fact that Sir John Hunt had also circulated a paper to the Cabinet today pointing out that Cabinet papers were the property of Her Britannic Majesty's Government and that in law they belonged to the Government of the day. The doctrine that the documents of a previous administration belonged to that administration had now, for the first time, been challenged. We should agree now to accept an inquiry but leave the format to the House.

Jim Callaghan summed up. 'I think we should have a debate in the House without precluding an inquiry and the Cabinet Office should draft a summary of Bingham, a note on the various forms of inquiry, and a note on the legal background to the policy.'

To Euston for the train to Blackpool. I travelled second class, as I do when the Party or I am paying, and it was so crowded I had to sit in the buffet car. But one of the nice things about travelling second class is that a lot of people come up and talk. The black ticket collector said he hoped I would be the next Prime Minister. A man offered to carry my bag at Preston station and told me that the Government had let the working class down.

*Labour Party Conference, Blackpool*
*Friday 29 September*
Sir Fred Catherwood, Chairman of the Overseas Trade Board, Terence Beckett, and today Joe Gormley and Ray Buckton have all been attacking the rigidity of the 5 per cent pay limit. Jim is digging his heels in and Denis Healey had been in Washington saying the same thing to the IMF.

I had lunch with Lena Jeger, Judith Hart and Barbara Castle, who very much wants to speak at Conference on the EEC and the EMS.[1] We had a long talk about Rhodesia and I told them what I knew about Bingham. Barbara said, 'If there is an inquiry, I wonder whether my diary will be subpoenaed.' I hadn't realised diaries *could* be subpoenaed.

Had a word with Joan Lestor later and she said, 'Jim Callaghan has told me that if the vote is carried against the 5 per cent limit at tomorrow's National Executive he will resign at the Conference itself.'

It's really a great mistake for Jim to play that sort of card. I can see it is central to the Government, and if I were Leader and had a policy I believed in I would feel just as upset as he does, but it is a silly way to behave. On the other hand, the sooner he starts to threaten resignation, the weaker the threat will be when it comes to the manifesto.

*Saturday 30 September*
Pope John Paul died yesterday after only thirty-three days as Pope.

The *Economist* is carrying a story about the editor Andrew Knight's wife having had her phone tapped. Caroline thinks this may have something to do with my letter to the Home Secretary, in that the Intelligence Service may be trying to put out a lot of jokey stories about bugging so that any serious claim by a Cabinet Minister that he is being bugged would be dismissed as paranoia.

Had a word with Joan Maynard to try to persuade her that we should not vote on the motion on the 5 per cent policy at the NEC tomorrow when we go through the resolutions on the grounds that we didn't normally intervene in industrial disputes.

But then I saw Dennis Skinner, who was sitting with Ted Knight, the Labour Leader of Lambeth Council, and they both argued that it was crucial that we stand up and be counted on the 5 per cent policy at tomorrow's NEC. That made me even more determined to prevent it: when Jim, on the one hand, is threatening resignation if we don't follow his policy, and Dennis, on the other hand, is demanding a confront-ation so that the left gives a lead to the movement, then you are in a critical situation.

Barbara Castle is also extremely keen to have a vote tomorrow, though she herself intends to abstain. She is anxious to crucify the Executive over the very issue on which she was crucified in 1969, when she was forced to drop *In Place of Strife*.

*Sunday 1 October*
To the National Executive to consider the motions to Conference. Barbara Castle had an emergency resolution opposing the EMS but she took twenty minutes to speak on it. She quoted Harold, Jim, Roy Jenkins, the Party, the TUC and so on. She doesn't know when to stop.

Mik seconded the motion, and Shirley moved an amendment to delete the whole resolution after the opening phrase and add 'urges that the problems be further explored before any further decision is made'. She said there would be countervailing flows of finance; the inter-national monetary system could not survive the falling dollar; and the United States was giving guarded support for the EMS.

Eric Heffer said we had heard all this before and it was a disaster.

I argued, 'If we go for the EMS, it will be the greatest single leap into federalism because we shall lose control of our own currency. It's a pity Shirley wasn't more candid; at least in his speeches Roy Jenkins advocates joining the EMS as a step towards federalism. As to these "countervailing flows", what do they mean? They mean that, in return for giving up control of our economic future, we would become a development area within Europe asking the Germans to pay for our unemployment; they would no doubt give us social security payments on condition that we didn't subsidise our industry. But we *must* give subsidies through our economic and industrial policy in order to get our manufacturing going. This is the last chance Conference will have to decide it.'

'I don't share Tony's prejudices on this,' Jim said. 'The Government will meet the NEC to discuss it but of course we couldn't be bound by what the NEC or Conference says.'

Anyway, we voted, and Barbara's motion denouncing and rejecting the EMS was carried by 16 to 9 – a tremendous success.

Then we came to composite motion 28 on the alternative strategy, which Hilary Benn had drafted with a little help from his dad – that is to say planned import controls, compulsory planning agreements, reflation and the reversal of public expenditure cuts, and a programme to combat unemployment through earlier retirement, work-sharing and a shorter working week.

'It is an attack on the Government's economic policies,' said Jim.

I spoke up. 'Look, this policy was outlined in the 1974 manifesto and in the 1976 *Labour's Programme for Britain;* it is TUC policy, and it was carried on a card vote at Conference last year. It is not confrontational and we should support it.'

That was accepted by an overwhelming 21 votes to 3.

Composite motion 37 denounced the 5 per cent pay policy and called for a national campaign against wage restraint. This was clearly going to cause great problems, but Eric, though he had reservations, moved to accept this very hard-line resolution.

Norman Atkinson summed up the feeling about it. 'The 5 per cent issue will dominate the Conference. It will mean a reduction in living standards, though Ford and the AUEW will get rises well above the 5 per cent. We are on a collision course with the Government.'

Jim said, 'I want to redress the balance because Norman has left out the problem of inflation, which is uppermost in my mind. We agree on the objective of 8 per cent inflation, but what about the method? Inflation is the key problem. I don't want confrontation. I would like to get out of Government intervention in wages. But clearly we can't will the end without willing the means. I can't accept composite 37, and, if the NEC or Conference accept it, we cannot govern.'

The argument went back and forth and I intervened. 'I agree with Jim that this is a critical decision and I want to make a very unusual suggestion. Jim doesn't want confrontation and Norman Atkinson doesn't want inflation, therefore I suggest that we recommend remittance to a special meeting of the TUC–Labour Party Liaison Committee. We set up this Committee in 1972 to ensure that we would never again confront the unions.'

Jim said he was prepared to accept my suggestion. When it came to the vote, the motion to recommend Conference to remit composite 37 was carried by 15 to 11. I left it at that.

On independent schools, Shirley wanted us to oppose the Socialist Education Association's amendment to end their charitable status. I asked why, since this was Party policy, and I got it carried by 10 votes to 9. Shirley said that it would end charitable support for blind schools – which was rubbish.

I left the meeting at 6.45, quite exhausted. It was boiling hot in there, probably because there's a sauna next door.

There is great excitement and there is no doubt it is the left's Conference. Jim can't ignore that completely.

### Monday 2 October

Joan Lestor delivered her Chairman's address, ending with a quote from Tawney, and that was followed by an overwhelming vote against smoking at the Conference, so that was the end of my pipe.

In the afternoon Moss Evans made a most powerful speech on pay, economic policy and unemployment. Sid Weighell [General Secretary of the NUR] declared that, if the low-paid got more money, we all would, and then where would we be? It was vulgar, but at least it was shop-floor vulgarity.

Denis Healey breezed in and made an awful speech about how we must all support Jim and so on. After Michael had wound up with a call for loyalty, to everyone's amazement the motion against the 5 per cent was not remitted but carried by about 4 million to 1 million, and the alternative strategy motion was carried without a vote. The right tried to be clever by endorsing the Government's stand on economic and monetary policy and calling on the movement to support it, as part of a general vote of thanks to the Labour Government. They thought they'd get it through but it was actually defeated by 3 million to 2.8 million. The result was dazzling, and Jim's whole position now is endangered.

It's hard to know how to react because the IMF and the City of London may withdraw their support from the Government, and Heath and Steel might offer to back Jim up. The trade union leaders will be embarrassed by all this, but their rank and file had to be allowed to speak. We can't do anything without the support of the whole labour movement.

I refused all requests for interviews because it only makes trouble.

In the evening I went with Caroline and Stephen to Tiffany's Ballroom for the Labour Agents' Ball, where the big news was that Jim had decided not to attend – the first time in years that he'd missed it. The agents, who are mostly right-wing machine men, were utterly demoralised by the vote.

*Tuesday 3 October*

Yesterday's vote against the right's motion in support of the Government was significant because it prevented the Conference from facing both ways, as it did last year.

So Jim started the day with a handicap, though I must say he went on to make the best speech I had ever heard from a Party Leader at Conference. He was modest and fair, and he said that nowhere else could such an intelligent debate about pay policy be held. Yesterday's debate was outstanding for its relevance, and for the experience of those who argued the case.

'But the White Paper stands,' he said, 'and we have to prevent inflation from rising. Conference defeated the Government's pay policy yesterday and that was a dramatic moment.'

He went on to talk about the Government's achievements, about the caring society and participation and pressure groups. I sent him a little note, which I heard later was well received.

The NEC results were announced after two recounts. In the CLP section Ian Mikardo and Jack Ashley were knocked off and Barbara Castle dropped to the bottom. Dennis Skinner and Neil Kinnock came on, both having worked very hard. Neil Kinnock is more of a media man; he appears on television a lot and he is well known.

In the trade union section, Doug Hoyle of ASTMS replaced John Forrester, who died last month, and John Golding took Bryan Stanley's place – a disappointing result.

The NEC is probably two or three people further to the left. Joan Maynard was saved. My own vote dropped but I was still at the top.

After lunch we came on to consider changes to the election of the Leader. There were three choices of method: the status quo, election by the whole Conference or by an electoral college involving a pro rata combination of Labour MPs, constituency GMCs and trade unions.

All the resolutions favoured the collegiate system but the vote for the status quo – election by MPs only – was overwhelming. It was a good debate but there was no doubt that the trade unions had been kept in step by Jim.

On the resolution for mandatory reselection of MPs, though Victor Schonfield of the Campaign for Labour Party Democracy* had organised it beautifully, it was defeated and the NEC compromise was carried. It turned out subsequently that Hugh Scanlon, who claimed to have got into a muddle (which of course was untrue), had not cast the AUEW vote for mandatory reselection, and the difference between the

---

* The CLPD was founded in 1973 by a group of Labour MPs and Party activists with the aim of making MPs accountable to their constituency parties by reselection once in every Parliament. It also campaigned to increase the control of Conference over the PLP in policy-making.

two resolutions was less than his AUEW vote. What Hugh did was quite wrong. Of course, he's leaving the AUEW in a couple of weeks and he wants a job.

I saw Joan Lestor back at the hotel and I said I presumed there would be another vote on mandatory reselection tomorrow because of the Scanlon affair.

'Oh no,' she responded, 'we can't do that.'

'I did it when I was Chairman.'

'You're not the Chairman,' she replied.

I pressed her on it but she refused.

Hilary came down to our room. He read out the speech he is hoping to make tomorrow, and it was excellent.

### Wednesday 4 October

Joan Lestor asked me to tell Hugh Scanlon that, unless he explained from the platform how he made the mistake on the reselection vote, she would make a statement to the media. Joan is definitely feeling the strain. I did as she asked and he went up and had a word with her on the platform.

Hilary got up and asked whether the NEC's emergency resolution on the EMS was going to be put to a vote of Conference, and Derek Gladwin [Chairman of the Conference Arrangements Committee] said there wasn't time.

So I thought he wasn't going to be called, but Joan, bless her, let the mover and seconder of the composite resolution calling for us to leave the Common Market speak and then she called 'the delegate with the orange folder', who was Hilary. He made a super speech, absolutely to time, and got a tremendously warm round of applause. It was his initiation and he showed no sign of nerves. He has developed marvellously.

Dashed from there to the Claremont Hotel for the Civil Liberties fringe meeting with Tom Litterick, the MP for Selly Oak. No doubt all the security services in the country were there, because I was addressing the need for a select committee to look into the security services.

Dennis Skinner was fresh from his NEC victory and looked slightly manic and aggressive. Eric said, 'That man frightens me. Is he really democratic?' Dennis is a pyrotechnic; he isn't frightening at all. He's just pleased because it's another left-winger on the NEC.

### Thursday 5 October

There was a super picture in the *Daily Mail* of Hilary speaking and me listening to him. The *Mirror* had 'Little Benn Cracks 'Em'. The nicest of all was in the *Yorkshire Post*, which didn't link him to my name at all. It just said, 'the Conference was electrified by a young delegate from Acton.'

The energy debate was today. Peter Heathfield of the Derbyshire Miners and Gavin Laird both made helpful comments about me and I felt I had the trade unions behind me. The environmentalists made one or two points.

I paid tribute to the industries and their work, and to the need for an integrated policy. On the role of oil, I argued that BP must be brought under public control and I said I was not prepared to see control over our energy policy go to the EEC Commission. On revenues, we had to halt the decline of our manufacturing industry and rebuild it.

I lunched with Joe Ashton and Hilary and mentioned the possibility of moving ahead with the election of the Cabinet.

'Oh no,' Joe said, 'don't do that. Wait till the new blood comes in and then you'll get some support. Remember all the outgoing members are hoping to be in the Honours List, and with the power of patronage you'd never get anything through the PLP.'

'Maybe not,' I said, 'but at least the issue would be opened up.'

Of course the whole point of reselection of MPs and the election of Cabinet is to solve the problem of patronage. Joe told me that during the leadership campaign in 1976 Roy Jenkins, Jim, Denis and Michael got a total of 550 promises of support from only 325 MPs; they'd get jobs in the Government come what may. Joe is cynical.

As we spoke, Jim came over to Hilary, who didn't get up but just sat there very shyly. Jim shook his hand and was very friendly and grandfatherly. I was touched that Jim did that.

I was taken by taxi to do a Conference report with David Dimbleby, having been assured that the interview would only be about energy. A woman called Heather Scott, a middle-class sociology graduate, had arranged it with me and she took me into the studio. Dimbleby began by asking about North Sea oil and nuclear power and then he shifted on to the election of the Leader. Was I disappointed about the Conference vote on the leadership issue?

I answered him briefly and left without saying goodbye. I said to Heather Scott, 'You asked me to come and talk about energy, Windscale and oil, and it was mostly about the leadership. If I had known that I wouldn't have come.'

'I wasn't told,' she replied.

That's why the BBC is hated and distrusted – because it is a public service corporation and it doesn't deal squarely with people.

Paul and Lynn Routledge came to dinner with us. Paul said he was with David Basnett ten minutes before Jim announced in his TV broadcast on 7 September that there wasn't going to be an Election. David Basnett had got all his statements drafted and the champagne was literally being brought in. Minutes before the broadcast, Basnett had said it wasn't a question of if but when. He had recommended 28 September but he thought Jim seemed to favour 5 October. Then Jim announced that there wouldn't be one. Basnett was furious.

When Jim had declared that we would use monetary and financial measures to deal with excessive wage claims, Robin Day had said, 'Once you cut away the jargon of the Treasury, of which you were once the head, doesn't that mean more unemployment?'

'Yes,' Jim had replied, 'it does, and it will be unpleasant.'

*Friday 6 October*
To Conference for the last session, and I had a word with Bob Wright of the AUEW who is certain that Hugh Scanlon deliberately muddled the vote on mandatory reselection. There's a lot of bitterness over it. The abuse of the block vote by the trade union leaders is a very important development because it will in the long run lead to a clean-up.

I had a message to ring Frances urgently, and she had heard that David Owen is sending an official team to New York to discuss with officials from the other western UN Security Council members the next stage on sanctions against South Africa. David particularly wanted me to send a good person who would report back to me and support his line.

So I rang the office and they told me that the Assistant Secretary Ronnie Custis was going. Well, Custis is an absolute dyed-in-the-wool Tory and I don't want him to go.

In the end I decided to send James Bretherton instead. He knows my view – which is not only to toughen up on South Africa but also to watch that the European Commission don't get involved, and see what the oil companies are up to. For him it was a tremendously important appointment.

*Saturday 7 October*
Lissie came and we had a long talk. She has a place of her own now and she likes to come back to see us when she can. It's lovely to have her.

I heard from Frances Morrell that Mike Cocks had come up to Francis Cripps at Conference and said, 'Disgraceful letter you wrote to *The Times*.'

'What letter?' Francis had asked.

'The letter attacking Harold Wilson.'

Francis denied having written such a letter, at which point Cocks asked, 'Aren't you Stuart Holland?'

'No, I'm not,' said Francis.

Well, instead of apologising, Mike Cocks had said, 'Well, you can tell Stuart Holland that we're not having people in the House of Commons who attack Labour leaders. We expect obedience.' He was apparently most offensive and Francis was upset. Mike Cocks is a thug.

Frances Morrell also told me she had met the same Special Branch detective who had inadvertently told her two years ago that he was at Conference to see that the fascist groups got all the dirt on Wedgie Benn. She said to him, 'Are you still putting out stuff on Wedgie Benn?'

'No,' he replied. 'I'm just collating it.'

It occurs to me that I made quite a few new enemies at Conference this week: BP, for saying that we'd bring it into public ownership; the security services, for suggesting select committee supervision; the generals, for saying they were hired to work for elected Ministers and not the other way around. I wonder whether they might just try to polish me off. Sounds extreme, I know, but things may be very much worse than we think. I will be in an exposed position, but I can't do anything about it.

Still, the Conference did take the Party a stage further in its advance towards socialism and democracy. With that happy thought the diary ends for today.

*Sunday 8 October*

Caroline and I were reading the papers in the bedroom when a friend of ours rang and asked if I would see a chap called Trevor Brown, who worked at Aldermaston. So he arrived just after 11 and stayed for two hours.

He's in his late fifties and has had responsibility for the actual production of atomic weapons. But he didn't want to discuss weapons; he was very concerned about plutonium contamination at Aldermaston.

Brown was at Springfield and Capenhurst in the 1950s producing the basic material for the hydrogen bomb. He was moved to Risley and then to the Atomic Weapons Research Establishment (Aldermaston) where he was responsible for producing the plutonium oxide fuel for the fast breeder reactor. I had appointed him to the Process Plant Working Party when I was Minister of Technology in about 1967.

He thought it had been a great mistake to transfer Aldermaston to the MoD because the MoD was so parsimonious with its expenditure.

Anyway, the main point he made was that monitoring of the health of the people at Aldermaston was quite inadequate. He had asked for personal air samplers and alarm monitors and they had been rejected by the Ministry of Technology even before the MoD took over.

He explained that in the early Sixties and Seventies the plant managers had demanded full radiological training, but this had been rejected on the grounds that the safety officers could do all that was necessary. By 1974 the safety officers themselves had agreed that outside experts should be brought in; but neither the Department of Employment, nor the National Radiological Protection Board, nor the Health and Safety Executive, nor even the inspectorate of the AEA had provided any.

The basic methods of radioactivity monitoring were urine sampling, which registered the systemic burden of plutonium, and whole-body monitors. At first the whole-body monitor could not show levels of plutonium in the lungs, because as little as one centimetre of lung tissue had the effect of halving the gamma-ray emissions of plutonium. Work had been carried out to overcome this tissue blanketing effect and in 1971 the NRPB had developed lung monitoring to establish the true lung burden.

In 1971 Aldermaston had urine tests, surface-contamination measurement devices and general air samplers up in the roof, but they had no personal air samplers or alarm monitors, and no lung monitors.

Brown told me that in 1976 he had persuaded Aldermaston to send a delegation to Windscale and they had discovered that all six of the systems were in operation there; the BNFL health physicist had said that the Aldermaston methods were ineffective. Brown wrote a report but it was not acted upon.

Several health physicists at Aldermaston asked Brown to act for them in his capacity as a Liberal county councillor and raise the matter at the council, but Brown declined, preferring to deal directly with the MoD, who, after sending a team to inspect Aldermaston, concluded that the plant was overmanned and recommended reductions.

When personal air samplers were finally agreed in 1977, they revealed approximately 50 to 100 times more plutonium contamination than had been registered by the general air samplers. Some workers were ingesting more than the recommended maximum yearly dose of plutonium in a single week, measured by sampling the air by the side of a worker's face.

On 11 October 1977 senior management met to discuss the situation because of their concern. The Chief Medical Officer thought that there was no clinical risk, but that if Aldermaston were known to have these figures their standards might be criticised.

I interrupted Brown. 'Surely, if these figures are correct, many workers must have been receiving that amount over the last twenty years or more and are very seriously at risk.'

Brown concurred. He told me he had been put in touch with a Mr Holliday, the author of a standard work on monitoring, and chairman of an International Committee on Radiological Protection. Holliday was apparently responsible for advising on plutonium contamination and he told Brown that Windscale had gone through this ten years ago. Reliance on surface levels was quite unsatisfactory because it did not indicate the true levels of contamination. There had been a strong international recommendation that personal air samplers should always be used for monitoring, and the International Committee Board argued that the acceptable levels could be between one-hundredth and one-thousandth of current levels. Holliday had sent Brown a document produced by the ICRP in 1968, which set all this out with detailed figures.

So for about nine years Aldermaston had continued to disregard accepted international standards, and many people's lives had been put at risk.

Brown was slightly anxious – probably because he thought he was breaking the Official Secrets Act (which he wasn't), or perhaps because he was angry that his recommendations had been disregarded, or because people were dying of lung cancer. I assured him that I would not mention his name and that I had a perfectly legitimate interest in it.

This whole story has been told once before by Anthony Tucker in the *Guardian*, and it confirmed again that the nuclear lobby have conspired to cover up a safety scandal. It could be another Bingham if it comes out.

For my own part, the information demonstrates yet again that the AEA have lied to me. My confidence in the AEA and the nuclear industry is minimal. There is no doubt that the nuclear industry has produced a sort of managerial, trade union and scientific fascism, with a contempt for laymen.

*Monday 9 October*
It is a fortnight tomorrow since I last wrote to Merlyn Rees about whether my telephone had been intercepted, so I decided to write again.

Dear Merlyn,

I wrote to you on 12 September to ask you if my telephone calls are or ever were tapped by the security services. Having received no acknowledgement or reply I wrote again on 26 September and asked if you had received my earlier letters. Your Private Secretary telephoned my Private Office the same day. The message did not, however, confirm that you personally had received or even seen my letters.

I enclose copies of these letters and of your office message. Two more weeks have now elapsed without any word from you. The questions I put were quite straightforward. When may I expect your personal reply?

Tony Benn

I don't know why I have plucked up my courage so much, but I have no intention of being diverted from it now.

*Tuesday 10 October*
Anthony Tucker of the *Guardian* came to see me, and I told him that I believed he was right about being victimised. He said, 'It's not just me. Professor Lindop of Bart's Hospital, who is a member of the Flowers Commission and is a well-known expert on radiological protection, wrote an article for a paper in the East of England. She was violently attacked in a letter from Michael Michaels.' (Michael Michaels was my Under-Secretary at the Ministry of Technology.)

He also pointed out that there was a Euro-nuclear link, in that pro-Common Market people were also pro-nuclear, as I am well aware. He maintained that John Hill, Chairman of the AEA, had complained to the editor of the *Guardian* about what he, Tucker, had been writing. As a result, Tucker had been undermined. He gave me a copy of a memorandum that he had written to the editor and I drafted a minute saying that I would not have the Department penalising journalists because they were critical of our policy. When I showed it to James Bretherton afterwards, he advised me to consult Bernard Ingham, since it did imply a criticism of him.

At 4 Neil Marten [Conservative MP for Banbury] came to see me about a five-year-old boy in his constituency who was burned almost to death because he was able to climb over the wire fence surrounding an electricity transformer. I decided that I would ask the chairman of the local electricity board to make a £20,000 compensation offer for the boy, who was so badly burned that he will not be allowed out in sunlight until he is about twenty-five. After we had agreed that, I asked my officials to leave, and I then had a most interesting discussion with Neil about the EMS.

I said, 'I will be candid with you. I don't just regard the EMS as being contrary to the interest of the Labour Party, I regard it as being treachery to the country.'

He showed me the press release of a speech he is making tonight or tomorrow on the EMS at the Tory Party Conference, and said 'the unusual channels' – that's Marten himself, Enoch Powell, Douglas Jay and Bryan Gould – met every Monday to discuss the strategy on Europe. He also told me that Mrs Thatcher was really anti-Europe but that she was surrounded by a hostile, pro-European Shadow Cabinet.

'Surely the way to deal with that is that, if Jim tries to get the EMS through using the Tory vote and the pro-Market Labour minority of MPs, she must be persuaded not to help him.'

'That's what I will argue,' he replied, 'and I'll do my best.'

I must say I like Neil Marten.

*Wednesday 11 October*
As I was about to go to a press conference at 5, I saw a brown envelope

marked 'Personal' in my tray and, though I yearned to open it, I went to the press first.

Back upstairs I read the letter, which was from Merlyn Rees, and it was astonishing. He apologised for the delay, said that he thought the acknowledgement made it clear he *had* seen my letter, but that I could not be told whether or not my telephone was being intercepted. That had been the practice and he was not prepared to vary it in respect of a Member of Parliament. The fact that I am a Privy Councillor, a Cabinet colleague and a senior member of the Government made no difference to him.

He pointed out that, in respect of West German telephone tapping, the European Court of Human Rights had not ruled that this was an infringement of human rights, and he mentioned that the Machinery of Government Committee of the NEC had not suggested that these matters should be covered by a Freedom of Information Act.

I thought carefully about it and asked for advice from Francis Cripps, who is very shrewd about these matters.

'First of all,' he said, 'you must get the attention off yourself. There will be little sympathy for you. People will wonder why you're so anxious about it. Also they will ask why a Member of Parliament or a Cabinet Minister should be treated better than anybody else. Imagine you are the Archbishop of Canterbury asking in a quavering voice about the rights of defenceless people who might be the subject of unfair police activity. Why not just bypass the Government altogether and put it to the NEC Home Policy Committee?' He advised me to get the committee to set up a study group, to report in time to get something into the manifesto.

Francis pointed out, rightly, that Merlyn Rees had addressed me as if I were a complete outsider, and this gave me certain advantages. For a start, I had no internal knowledge of the matter. My letters to Merlyn were unclassified, as were his to me, so the whole exchange was perfectly publishable. 'You could say, jokingly, that even a Cabinet Minister can't find out if he's being tapped, so long as you make it a general point. It will be very popular and you would get a lot of support from liberal opinion.' I am sure Francis is right.

I should add that Merlyn mentioned that he had sent copies of the correspondence to the Prime Minister.

I came home and wrote an eight-page memorandum on the security services and the case for an inquiry.

Tonight, addressing the Tory Party Conference, Ted Heath pledged his full support to Jim Callaghan on pay. That can't be right.

*Thursday 12 October*
At 9.15 Sir John Hill came to see me, very anxious about the

reorganisation of the NNC. He suggested we replace three of the existing directors representing the AEA including Lord Aldington. He wants an independent chairman like Tin Pearce of Esso.

John Hill wants the NNC to be reorganised in order to speed up the fast breeder reactor programme, and one advantage of leaving the whole thing in a state of confusion (which is Weinstock's fault and not mine) is that the nuclear programme is being held back a little.

When we came to talk about the fast breeder, John Hill said they were looking at international collaboration for when President Carter's policy changes.

'Why will it change?' I asked.

'Because it is technically wrong.' That revealed the arrogance of the nuclear lobby.

Went over to the Cabinet, where Jim announced that he and John Silkin were going to Bonn at the weekend. 'As to the EMS,' he said, 'we'll continue to negotiate the matter when we return. We have to be very careful about the effect of all this on sterling. If it's thought we're going in, there will be speculation that we might devalue. If it's thought we're staying out, the speculation will be that sterling will weaken. We must be *very* careful and I don't want anyone to say anything about it.'

Peter Shore asked, 'Are we not going too far into the modalities of the EMS before we have really discussed the principle of joining?'

'I think that is right,' Jim replied, 'but it will be for the heads of Government to decide at the summit on 5–6 December.'

I asked Jim casually if we could see all the relevant papers.

'No, there's no need for that.'

So Cabinet Ministers are kept out of discussions on the EMS while the French and the Germans – and officials – consider it. It's a scandal. We must establish the right of MPs to choose the Prime Minister's advisers; that will be the next big battle.

Shirley Williams requested a note on the effect of staying out of the scheme and Jim agreed to that.

Then we had a discussion on the Christmas bonus for old-age pensioners. David Ennals suggested we raise it slightly to just over £10, which for 11 million people would cost £114 million. He said the Tories had already promised it.

Jim queried the increase, while Peter Shore opposed the bonus altogether. 'Better to subsidise television for old people, or put the money in the Health Service.' A typical Fabian view.

'We'll have to give the bonus,' said Stan Orme, 'because of the Election. We can always look at it again afterwards.'

Shirley Williams agreed with Peter. 'There is a danger of permanence, and I would prefer it to go into television licences or mobility allowances. We must make it clear that this is the last time we are going to do it.'

Denis was in favour of the bonus, and Jim said, 'You know, it's all very well putting it towards TV licences, but old people like to have the money, spend it on their grandchildren in toyshops and so on.'

Bill Rodgers favoured the bonus but he did think it might be better to have a national concessionary fares scheme.

'We are saddling ourselves with this permanently,' Harold Lever said.

Merlyn Rees thought we had to do it this year, 'but when television licences go up, I might keep them down a bit for old people.'

Roy Mason pointed out the anomaly on TV licences where the charge for old people living in wardens' homes was very low and it upset the others.

David Ennals warned that we would undershoot on our pledge to keep pensions abreast of prices, but Jim was firm and we didn't increase it. The announcement would be made next Tuesday prior to the Berwick and East Lothian by-election (caused by John Mackintosh's death).

The Bingham Report was next. Before us was a draft White Paper made up of three parts: a summary of Bingham's conclusions; a political background on relations with Rhodesia, taken from public sources; and a rehearsal of the types of inquiry we could initiate – royal commission, select committee, special commission, judicial tribunal, etc – giving the clear impression that all of them were impossible because they might interfere with the prosecutions of the oil companies.

Elwyn Jones said that the Cabinet Office had done the best they could to produce the draft, which would be useful for discussion, but if an inquiry were to be complete every document would have to be published, and that was unacceptable for reasons of Cabinet secrecy. He believed that the 1964–70 Government had been sincere in its efforts. There would be no public benefit in an inquiry; a debate was sufficient and there should be no White Paper.

We went round the table and at the end there was a vote on whether we should publish even the Bingham summary contained in the White Paper. There was a considerable majority against it: the biggest cover-up attempt I have ever come across.

We were just adjourning when Jim said, 'I should report that Michael and Denis and I met the TUC on Tuesday and they will produce a paper which will be discussed by the Neddy Six [the six union leaders on the NEDC] and six Government Ministers. The 5 per cent stays until we agree on a new line.'

David Ennals asked Jim if the Cabinet could see the TUC paper.

'No,' said Jim.

*Sunday 15 October*

Caroline and I read the papers in bed. There was a lot about the EMS suggesting that the Government is anxious to go in, though the Treasury has some doubts.

Jim has refused to allow me to see the documents. As a result of enquiries I made in my own Department about whether the EMS could be implemented under Common Market legislation, and what potential legal constraints there were, I had a note from one of my officials; the relevant points were:

(a) the negotiations are still proceeding and there is no certainty at the moment about any of the main parameters; (b) there will be provision for individual countries to change their exchange rates and this is likely to be 'by mutual consent'; (c) there is likely also to be provision for countries to leave the scheme 'on a temporary basis'; (d) although my informant at the Treasury thought it highly unlikely, there could be some form of ultimate reference to the European Court if some of the provisions of the scheme were not observed by individual participants.

No attempts are being made to lock people in indefinitely as under the provisions of the Treaty of Rome. It follows that if conditions become too onerous, a country which decided to terminate its membership could, by that act, cease to be legally liable.

It looks, then, as if the EMS would be at least as heavy a burden as the IMF or GATT, with the difference that, if Britain did try to get out, then the remaining member countries could bring pressure to bear on us by other methods.

I went to dinner at the Baloghs' with the Foots, the Booths and the Harts. It was a frightfully discouraging evening.

On the pay issue, I discovered that the TUC Neddy Six have come up with a scheme under which the TUC would use its influence to reduce inflationary pay schemes. In return, there would be a public-sector pay freeze, perhaps for six months. Michael thinks that if the deal could be settled on Friday night then there might be a special meeting of trade union executives to endorse it, and the TUC could then present it as an abandonment of the 5 per cent. That would greatly strengthen our position when Parliament met. He said, 'You know, Jim made clear to me before the Conference that he would consider resigning because he is not prepared to lead the country back into inflation.'

'What does he mean, resign?' I asked.

'Well,' said Michael, 'he's not prepared to go in for confrontation with the unions.'

'But if he resigns,' I continued, 'the Government would have to resign, and that would put the responsibility back to the Queen. Would she call Mrs Thatcher to form a Government or would she ask Jim Callaghan to carry on?'

Michael hadn't thought it out, because Jim's resigning is just a threat. It would mean a rerun of 1931, because the Queen would say, 'Oh, Mr Callaghan, do carry on', and Ted Heath and David Steel would then offer to support him and we would have a coalition Government. I think that is increasingly likely to happen.

Then I asked about Rhodesia. Were we going to send troops into Zambia? Judith got awfully angry and said, 'We must support Kenneth Kaunda and we've got our responsibilities if a race war begins in southern Africa.'

'Are we sending troops?' I repeated.

She replied, 'I don't know, but we are defending Kaunda. That's what Kano was all about.'

Michael Foot observed, 'We've got to be ready, you know. This is why the Election should be delayed. There is a plan to overthrow Smith and we've got to be ready. Surely the right thing is for us to support the UN.'

I told them I was all for supporting the UN, but I pressed them on troops to Zambia. They got so angry that I was convinced that some contingency plan was in hand for us to send troops, and the UN would then be invited into Rhodesia. But I am not sure the Africans would want British troops in Rhodesia.

We then launched into a row over steel subsidies and I was attacked on all sides on that too. I came home feeling thoroughly exhausted and isolated. I just don't know how this is going to last through the winter.

*Monday 16 October*
Bernard Ingham came to see me about Anthony Tucker. He was completely unrepentant. 'I don't see why we should pay people to write articles for the Central Office of Information who are critical of the Government, who don't come for a departmental briefing and who are not balanced and objective.'

I said, 'Well, Bernard, I agree that a lot of unfair things are said but if you believe in the free press – and you and I are both members of the NUJ – then it isn't whether they are fair or not that matters.'

But Bernard was rigid and dictatorial in his attitude. 'If you put out a minute, I won't object. I'll stand my corner so long as my minute goes out too.'

I accepted that. So I shall put out a minute with my judgement of the matter, which I hope will be a classic statement of the freedom of the press in a democracy, together with Tucker's letter of complaint and Bernard's reply, and see what happens.

'Tom McCaffrey at Number 10 does this sort of thing all the time,' Bernard said.

'Maybe, but a free press does not require anyone to be balanced or objective or to see Ministers. We should apply exactly the same principle to the COI as to the BBC Overseas Service, namely that people abroad hear a reflection of the domestic debate.'

I couldn't get him to see it, but he did tell me that Tucker had been criticised by officials in the Department of Energy, and I think that was part of the explanation.

I flew to Edinburgh to address a meeting with John Smith and John Home Robertson, the Labour candidate for Berwick and East Lothian. I was taken by car along Princes Street; in the light of the full moon, the illuminated Edinburgh Castle looked as if it was suspended in the air. It was quite lovely. We drove on out of the city through the beautiful countryside to Tranent Labour Club where a couple of hundred people were gathered. Then on to Prestonpans where I spoke again with the same team. It was excellent.

A new Pope was elected today – Cardinal Wojtyla from Cracow. He's taken the title of Pope John Paul II and he is the first non-Italian Pope since 1522, so it's quite an event. He was in a German POW camp or concentration camp. I think he's a good choice.

*Tuesday 17 October*
Got off the sleeper and had an hour at home before a meeting at 9.15 with Sir Ian Bancroft, the new head of the Civil Service Department. So secret was this that it had not been put on my programme, presumably to prevent the Permanent Secretary from knowing about it. Bancroft came in flushed and sweating – I've never seen a man look more uncomfortable.

'Do sit down,' I said. 'It's awfully nice of you to come and see me. I hate to bother you. It's a very simple point. About eighteen months ago, I asked Douglas' (that's Sir Douglas Allen, now Lord Croham) 'whether I could have a second Permanent Secretary. I have a lot of policy work on oil, gas, electricity, nuclear, the Middle East, OPEC, IEA, EEC, Environment and so on, and this Department really does need somebody at the top who can pull it all together.' I made no reference to Rampton, although it must have been obvious that I was describing his job specification.

Bancroft slowly recovered his self-assurance. 'I don't know,' he said. 'We're very tight on staffing.'

'Well, it's only a matter of promoting one of my Deputy Secretaries. David Jones would be first-rate. I have known him for twelve years and worked with him in four Departments.'

He didn't ask about my present Permanent Secretary and I was determined not to criticise Rampton. He agreed to think about it, and I said, 'As you know, I really wouldn't bother you unless it was urgent.' Then I completely changed the subject, asked him about his new job, and ushered him out.

The funny thing was that shortly afterwards Jack Rampton came to see me with Frank Kearton for the first time in weeks!

My paper for the NEC, which I am calling 'Civil Liberties and the Security Services', went out to David Owen, Jim Callaghan, Merlyn Rees, the Party officers and various MPs.

Cabinet at 10. After a word on Rhodesia, Jim said, 'One of the factors in considering the deferment of the Election was that we assumed there would be a majority for the Queen's Speech.'

Jim had obviously been assured that Michael Foot had fixed the minority parties.

He went on to say that he had talked to David Steel, who had promised to look at each bill on its merits and not to vote with the Tories if he could avoid it; we were to keep that quiet because, if it were known, Steel might be in trouble with Liberal MPs. 'But,' Jim said, 'this means Ministers must consult with all minority parties if they want legislation to go through.'

Michael Foot told us that on Monday we were meeting the NEC to discuss the Queen's Speech and we must be ready to consider amendments in the light of that meeting.

Well, it is absurd that there should be a discussion on the Queen's Speech as late as this – just weeks before it goes out. I believe the Palace has already seen it.

Jim referred to a problem with the NEC. 'One of the new members, Dennis Skinner, intends to make public everything that is said there – which will affect the character of the NEC.' Jim said that if that occurred he would have to give Ministers instructions to listen only and not speak.

Well, I have no intention whatever of doing that. The NEC will deal with Dennis Skinner in its own way, and Jim's just looking for an excuse to make NEC meetings meaningless.

Back to the office, and there was a great lunch in progress with Geoff Bish, Bryan Gould, Frances, Francis and Brian Sedgemore. They were discussing the paper opposing the EMS which Frances and Francis have written, and which Bryan Gould is going to distribute to all Labour MPs with a draft Early Day Motion. We will try to get a majority of the PLP to sign it; that would be a real bombshell. Hopefully we'll organise it rather better than we did the EEC Referendum.

### Wednesday 18 October

Colin Ambrose from my Private Office came to see me, looking very pale, and told me that Ken Stowe, Jim's Private Secretary, had asked if I had sent my paper 'Civil Liberties and the Security Services' to David Owen.

'Yes,' I said, 'and to the Home Secretary, and the Prime Minister of course.'

He announced that the PM wanted to see me about it when he got back from Bonn. That means that I have hooked the big fish, because no doubt Jim has interested himself in my correspondence with Merlyn. I think a talk with Jim about this will be rather fun, and I am quite looking forward to it.

*Thursday 19 October*

I had several evening engagements. The first, which was extremely interesting, was with Doug Grieve, the General Secretary of the Tobacco Workers' Union, who made a speech at the TUC Congress this year in support of a resolution on the Special Branch and the Special Patrol Group – a speech of exceptional perception and scholarship. It was carried unanimously, and the TUC is now committed to call for an inquiry into the role of these organisations. He was terribly pleased with my NEC paper and he wanted to take a copy and think about it.

Later, Terry Duffy, the new President of the AUEW, and his wife Joyce arrived for a drink. In the right-wing press, he is a brilliant, marvellous guy; in the left press, he is a man with horns. But in reality he is neither. He is just an American-type trade-unionist who is utterly cynical.

He began by saying, 'I am absolutely loyal to the Government. If Jim Callaghan asks for 4 per cent, I will recommend it to my membership and carry it through. After all, I skated in last year as President on a programme of moderation and support for the Labour Government.'

Loyalty was his favourite word. 'I was loyal to Gaitskell, loyal to Wilson, loyal to Callaghan, and if you are the Leader next year I'll be loyal to you.'

'That's not very likely,' I said.

'Well, I'm a man who supports the leadership. Isn't that right? Isn't that right?' He told me he hadn't liked Gaitskell very much when he first met him. 'He was born with a silver spoon in his mouth, and so were you. You've never had the rough end of the stick. I've lived in a council house all my life, still live in a council house.'

Then he came out with something very revealing. 'I could have gone into politics but it's such a dirty business. Trade-unionism is a dirty business too, otherwise how do you think I got where I got?'

He was totally non-political and terribly muddled. At one point he said, 'We must keep Thatcher out, but if she came to power I wouldn't pick a quarrel with her, no I wouldn't. Maybe she'd get the economy right, and then we'd pick up the benefit.'

*Saturday 21 October*
To Bristol with Caroline, and I went to the Party headquarters to talk to Herbert Rogers. I told him about my paper on the security services and he entirely agreed with it. But he said, 'They will get you for this. They will try and find some way of getting you.'

*Sunday 22 October*
In the evening Frank Allaun and Norman Atkinson came to have a bite to eat and a talk. It was the first time Frank had been to my house. They are both very decent people, and I have a lot of time for Frank, who is now Chairman of the Party. One of the great weaknesses of the Labour Government is that Ministers don't talk to other members of the Party. The constraints of the Official Secrets Act divide us from each other, and there are simple things that Members just don't know. For example, Frank and Norman had the idea that we would commit extra money to the Health Service, but the public expenditure survey went through Cabinet last July and the total has already been set. It certainly convinces me that our next great reform project must be to link the Labour Party much more closely with Labour Ministers.

We talked about the rumour in today's *News of the World* that there is going to be a reshuffle and I am to be made Minister of Labour. I asked their advice on that eventuality and their view was that I shouldn't accept it because I would be crucified by the 5 per cent. Of course I am crucified by it anyway as a member of the Cabinet.

*Monday 23 October*
To the National Executive for the special meeting on the Queen's Speech prior to the joint NEC/Cabinet this afternoon. Frank Allaun was in the chair, and Norman Atkinson was the first to speak. 'Isn't it too late to influence the Queen's Speech now, within a fortnight of it being delivered?'

Dennis Skinner said, 'I understand the speech has already gone to the printer's. I don't want to be involved in a fraudulent discussion', and Doug Hoyle, another new NEC member, asked how much influence we really had.

'No, no,' Michael Foot insisted, 'the options are still open. The press stories are wrong about this. No final decisions have been taken. I give you my word as a socialist' – which I thought was rather over-egging the pudding.

Eric Heffer spoke. 'What we want is a pre-Election shop-window display. We have got 1.5 million people out of work, and we must restore public expenditure cuts and put additional resources into the NEB, especially the construction industry.'

'Look,' said Dennis Skinner, 'is this a real meeting or is it just an exercise in PR? The alternative strategy isn't going to be accepted and I'd rather be telling the Cabinet what we want on jobs, reflation and redistribution of income. It must have electoral appeal – higher death grants, more money for the NHS, free travel for the elderly on a nationwide basis and concessions for schoolchildren, abolition of school meals charges, free TV licences for pensioners, earlier retirement and a thirty-five-hour working week to be phased in. If the Queen's Speech is defeated, our Election manifesto is ready, and without this sort of radical manifesto there is little chance of us winning. Where's the money? There's lots of money: look at oil for a start.'

I must say, I felt that Dennis was Blücher to my Wellington at the Battle of Waterloo, because I had been saying many of these things in my own way for a long time.

Michael Foot reassured the meeting. 'This is a genuine discussion. But we don't want to court defeat on the Queen's Speech. We can't write the manifesto into it.' He looked pale, ill and old, particularly when he heard Eric and Dennis.

Doug Hoyle wanted public expenditure increased, import controls introduced, and prices controlled. 'The NEB should have its guidelines changed and the unions should take control of occupational pensions. Nothing proposed so far would bring the Government down.'

Tony Saunois, the new Young Socialists' representative, spoke, and you could have been listening to Nick Bradley or Andy Bevan. The YS all sound as if they've come from the Ted Grant School of Public Speaking (Ted Grant being the Militant Tendency guru).

Neil Kinnock thought we needed priorities and consensus. 'If the Tories were in office, they would be buying victory with all sorts of popular measures. So should we. We shouldn't court defeat on the Queen's Speech. We should reflate, put money into health, go for the job-swap scheme, better housing, end stock relief for businesses, change the NEB guidelines and give it more money, restore the Regional Employment Premium, invest North Sea revenues and disengage from the 5 per cent policy. Labour Ministers must stop making the 5 per cent their only focus of attention.'

Barbara Castle was concerned about the EEC. 'We should make clear that the alternative strategy is incompatible with EEC requirements, and the EMS must be explicitly rejected. However, it is not possible simply to concentrate on spending without having a wealth-creating strategy, and we must say an awful lot about that. As for expenditure, money is needed to rescue the Health Service and to increase family support. We should help with animal welfare and with industrial democracy.'

I said this was one of the best meetings of the NEC I had attended. 'Over the next six to twelve months, it is crucial that the Government, which has the power, and the Party, which has the job of winning the Election, should work together for victory. There is a problem with the two timetables. For example, when it comes to public expenditure, the totals were set in July and it is a bit late to suggest new expenditure now. At the same time, the Queen's Speech is not the only instrument available to us – there is a lot that could be done administratively and in campaigning.

'As to the alternative strategy, if we adopted one-tenth of the spending programmes that have been discussed this morning, we would have to have an alternative strategy. Free collective bargaining, not only on wages but on investment, profits, prices and manpower, would mean planning agreements. But the specific proposal I want to make is that from now on the NEC and the Cabinet should meet every month – say, on the fourth Wednesday of each month. The Cabinet meets the PLP weekly and the TUC monthly, and the Neddy Six meet the Economic Ministers, but the Cabinet meets the NEC very infrequently. Elsewhere in Europe – Austria, Norway, Belgium and so on – they meet weekly. The NEC must have the opportunity to discuss current business, to help prepare the manifesto and to plan the campaign.'

There was a vote, and my proposal was unanimously agreed.

After other contributions, Ron Hayward read out the priorities emerging from the discussion: jobs and public expenditure; selective import controls; more cash for the NEB; more cash for the Health Service; earlier retirement; freedom of information; higher death grants; free travel for pensioners; opposition to the EMS and the CAP; and disengagement from the 5 per cent policy.

I leaned across to Mike Cocks at one point and asked if there was any truth in the reshuffle story.

'No, not a word.'

At 2 the NEC went on to Number 10 for the joint meeting with the Cabinet in the State Dining Room.

Frank Allaun opened for the NEC, welcoming the meeting but adding that in future he hoped such meetings could take place earlier. He then announced that the NEC had unanimously agreed on monthly joint meetings between the Cabinet and the NEC.

Jim, who by then was getting very red-faced, commented drily, 'Why not meet in continuous session?'

Frank went on to say that members of the Executive had picked out a number of vote-winners at this morning's meeting. He read through the list and Ron Hayward filled in on the details.

Jim Callaghan then came in, saying he had reminded Ministers of their duty to co-operate with the NEC, and that the joint working parties had worked well. But he didn't see the need for monthly

*'There'll be no mutiny on this Bounty!'*

meetings and he was not willing to let the NEC be either the co-Government or the alternative Government. 'Three joint meetings with the NEC in a year is sufficient and there would be no point in going further.'

He went on, 'Some of the points made this morning would involve a reversal of Government policy which I cannot accept. Ministers will go on making their 5 per cent speeches. We are seeing the TUC again tomorrow, and the policy is not losing us support – on the contrary, there is overwhelming support for it.' Adjustments to keep inflation in single figures were all he was prepared to consider.

On the EMS, he said it was not a theological matter; the question was would it benefit Britain? A policy of convergence could be achieved with the EMS but each nation could choose its own way.

Frank Allaun asked Denis Healey to give his views. Denis went over the current economic situation and concluded, '5 per cent is only a means to an end. Don't think that our policy is unpopular.'

Eric Heffer said that the Cabinet and the NEC should plan to win together because any Labour Government was better than a Tory Government. But we must get unemployment down and pump money back into public expenditure. He regretted that Ministers were expected to go on making speeches about the 5 per cent because both the TUC and the Party Conferences had rejected it. He couldn't understand why we were all behaving like King Canute.

I was looking at Jim and Denis as Eric spoke, and their faces were red with rage.

Dennis Skinner then stressed that this was a special period. The package he and Eric wanted might not be popular with the Stock Exchange but, if we wanted to win, we had got to remember workers.

Neil Kinnock doubted the popularity of the 5 per cent, and Doug Hoyle was disappointed that Jim continued to insist on it, despite the views of the NEC, because the 5 per cent policy was dead. It was inflationary to keep people out of work, public expenditure did not suck in imports, and selective import controls could deal with that problem. The NEC package would be popular.

Jim replied, 'I shall not ignore the NEC. But there is a fundamental difference on economic policy. Our policy is working, and I will not adopt policies if they are not in the national interest. Workers are accepting the 5 per cent. It is not a low norm – the German Ford workers settled for 5 per cent. If you don't agree with what I am saying, get rid of me.' Then he added, 'Anyway, all our public expenditure is committed until April 1979, and after that we'll have greater room for manoeuvre.'

What he didn't tell the meeting was that the Cabinet had already decided that there would be only a 2 per cent increase in public expenditure *after* April.

We had a brief exchange on international affairs. Then we came on to the EMS, which began with an immensely long attack by Barbara, followed by me.

I gave my economic arguments, and stressed that, above all, the EMS would make it impossible for us to implement Party policy. If ever there was a need for freedom of information, it was on this issue; we should publish all the working papers, and make it clear in the Queen's Speech that we oppose the EMS.

I had to leave for a longstanding engagement in Bristol, and Jim said, 'Tony has been giving his own individual view, but when the Cabinet decides on it there will be collective Cabinet responsibility imposed and anyone who defies it will have to take the consequences.'

I left, and by the time I arrived in Bristol the clash between Jim and me was the main item on the 6 o'clock news.

*Wednesday 25 October*
Lunch with Frances, Geoff Bish, Francis, Michael Meacher and Bryan Gould. Frances Morrell and Brian Sedgemore think I should be quiet now and just drift into the leadership of the Party by doing nothing.

That may be the right tactic, but I just feel we are fighting a battle and I am impatient to be in it. They don't understand my attitude on this. We analysed Jim's views on the EMS and drew some interesting conclusions as to what he must be thinking: that Britain was ungovernable and therefore we needed a federal European government; that there was great political value in being associated with Schmidt; that there would be a fear of a run on the pound before the Election. He didn't really have any faith in the pay policy, so international monetarist disciplines would be the best way of holding the unions in check.

At 5 I went to see Jim alone in the Cabinet Room about my security services paper, which I had put to the Home Policy Committee.

He said, 'I have asked you to come and see me because I feel you are peppering me with a lot of things at the moment. I don't know what you are up to, but you seem to be using the Home Policy Committee to get at the Government. I will give you an example – why did you raise the question of monthly joint NEC/Cabinet meetings without telling me?'

'I did tell you. Last summer, in this room, you asked some of us to stay behind after Cabinet and I raised it then. I suggested weekly meetings at the time, as in Norway, Belgium and Austria, and you said that those parties were very different from the Labour Party.'

Then he brought up the EMS. 'Why did you have to come out on it? It looked as if you were just trying to take a position before the Cabinet discussed it.'

I told Jim I hadn't come out with anything different from what I said at the NEC and Conference. I felt very strongly about it, in particular about not being allowed to see the papers.

'There are too many leaks,' he said, so I remarked, flippantly, that without leaks I wouldn't know what was going on. 'I read in the paper the other day that there was a committee of Ministers meeting on the EMS. I wouldn't have known otherwise. I depend on leaks.'

He pointed out that he had released that officially.

'So it wasn't a leak, but the point is that I have to read the newspapers to know what is happening.' I told him that Francis Cripps wanted to see the papers.

'Oh yes, that's right, let confidential papers get into the hands of these political advisers. The future of sterling may be at stake here – we may have to devalue.'

I said, 'Jim, that is a very important issue.'

'We'll discuss that at Thursday's Cabinet. Now on this business of the security services. Why did you ask whether you were tapped?'

I told him about the delay in Merlyn's reply to my note.

'That's because it came to me,' he said.

'It's a serious issue, Jim.'

'It is all under ministerial control,' he replied. 'We hardly bug anybody. Incidentally, your telephone isn't tapped.'

'I didn't say it was. But my son picked up my voice on the radio the other day, and my daughter made a call and heard a recording of what I had just said.'

'It's all under control,' he repeated.

'But how do we know that?'

'Look,' Jim replied, 'there must be an element of trust on this.'

I assured him I wasn't suggesting that I distrusted him, but you had no idea what the secret services were up to.

'Well,' he said, 'I have just changed the heads of MI5 and MI6, as a matter of fact. I have appointed Sir Howard Smith as head of MI5, and I have known him for years.'

'So have I.'

Jim told me that Howard Smith had just come back from our Embassy in Moscow, and Jim had informed him, 'Say goodbye to Gromyko – tell him you're coming back to take charge of MI5.'

'Well, if the Russians can know who the head of MI5 is, why can't it be published here?' I asked.

'He might be a target,' Jim said, 'an IRA target.'

'Lots of people are targets.'

He didn't tell me who the head of MI6 was, so I said, 'I heard from an American, who was on President Carter's Commission, that a man called Sir Leonard Hooper was head of MI6. These names ought to be known.'

'Just makes them targets for the IRA,' Jim muttered. 'The whole thing is under control.'

'Well, you say that, Jim, but I heard of a WEA course on William Morris in Wales where the police wanted to find out who had enrolled because they thought that Morris was a Marxist.'

'Well, let me give *you* an example,' Jim replied. 'Two MPs went to some Anti-Apartheid meetings and they complained to me that they had been followed by plainclothes men. I'll tell you why the men were there – to keep an eye on BOSS, the South African secret service, and to find out which meetings they were attending.'

I didn't say, but I found that hard to believe because Special Branch and MI5 work together with BOSS.

'Let me give you another example,' I said. 'Harold Wilson, in my presence, told the CBI at a dinner in March 1971 that the TUC were bugged. I didn't learn *that* as a Minister.'

'Oh, Harold is just a Walter Mitty. Once, in his study upstairs, he turned round the picture of Gladstone and there was a hole in the wall. He called Ken Stowe in and put his hands to his lips and said, "Shhh!", pointing to the hole. He's just a Walter Mitty.'

'Well, maybe, but the *Pencourt File* stated that he thought he was being bugged; and Chapman Pincher was certain Wilson was bugged.'

'Pincher's links with the services ended five years ago,' said Jim.

'Well, he has just published a book, *Inside Story*, saying that five members of the Cabinet are communists and one is in touch with Moscow. Presumably he thinks it's Michael Foot.'

'Oh, that's all stopped. Chapman Pincher has nothing to do with the security services now.'

I reminded Jim of my efforts to appoint Jack Jones to the NEB, and that I was told he was a security risk at a time when he was carrying the whole Government on his shoulders. I was told I couldn't have Hugh Scanlon on the British Gas Corporation because we needed somebody who was loyal to the country. How did we know security was under control?

'It is. And your telephone isn't tapped.'

'How many telephones *are* tapped?'

'139,' he replied, 'and each one has to be authorised by the Home Secretary on a warrant. Every three months the Permanent Secretary and the Home Secretary go over the list and discuss whether or not to continue tapping individual numbers. Not even all the foreign embassies are tapped.'

'Well, the POEU are of the opinion that between 1000 and 2000 phones in London alone are tapped.'

'That is not so,' said Jim. 'It has got to be a question of trust.'

'But a lot of people are worried, and I think we ought to have an inquiry.'

Jim said, 'I am not making available anything that is secret.'

'I didn't expect you would, but we should get some high-powered people to look at it and put some guidelines down. The Solicitor-General supports me on this.'

'He knows nothing about security.'

'Nobody does,' I said; 'that is the whole point.'

Jim continued, 'Now, on this freedom of information business. There's a committee looking at it – GEN 29.'

I replied, 'Yes, I read that in the papers too.'

'Would you like to be put on the committee?'

I said yes, so I was put on it.

I think Jim was sorry he'd blown up at me on Monday and I told him I understood; we were all under great strain. He admitted to having a very low boiling point.

I had the impression that he wanted to find out what I knew about the security services. I said I wasn't being paranoid; there was a big civil liberties issue here, and had been for many years. I was an old-fashioned radical liberal and I didn't believe in all this secrecy. He remarked that if I started inquiries I'd only drive the Intelligence Service underground. Well, that was rich, given that they were already underground.

*Thursday 26 October*
At Cabinet, Jim announced that we'd have a debate on the EMS next week and Denis Healey said it was turning into a religious war.

Shirley asked again for a report on the effect of staying out, particularly in view of the weakness of the dollar. Peter Shore thought we needed a wide-ranging paper, covering the difference between the Snake, relating to exchange rates, and the EMS, relating to monetary policy. We had to be clear about transfers and we needed the historical background.

I said, 'I don't see why papers that are available to the bankers should not be available to the Cabinet. Can we submit papers ourselves? Can we have an answer to the constitutional question? Would any restraints be placed upon our varying the value of our currency that might lead to our being taken to the European Court and being told that the Chancellor of the Exchequer is behaving illegally?'

'You can't believe all these press stories,' Jim replied. 'Don't put in papers yet. We can't circulate them because the Cabinet is too leaky, the information gets to political advisers, and the security of sterling is at stake. I had to tell Helmut Schmidt in Bonn that I was not anti-European, but that we were looking out for Britain's interests, that no decision had been taken and that the first priority was fighting inflation.'

We came on to pay, and Denis Healey told us that we were sticking to the 5 per cent until we found a better way; he'd seen the TUC, who would not accept intervention on pay, but the objective was a 7.8 per cent inflation rate and they wanted something on price controls and low pay. Two weeks would be necessary to sort it out. The CBI wanted to be in on the act and would be meeting Ministers this evening. It was difficult to reach an agreement but the polls showed that public support for the Government had increased since Conference.

Michael Foot doubted that the polls were true.

'Helmut says he always believes the polls when they're against him,' Jim commented. He keeps on quoting Schmidt – he's fixated with him. Three or four times each Cabinet it's, 'Helmut rang me up, Helmut said this, Helmut did that . . . '

*Monday 30 October*
To Luxembourg for a European Energy Council meeting. At 1.20 I had this little intimate lunch with Dick Mabon, Brian Sedgemore, Count Lambsdorff, the West German Economic Affairs Minister, and others.

Lambsdorff had just come back from Tehran, where he had spoken with the Shah. He found him hopelessly pessimistic and demoralised. Lambsdorff had asked about David Owen's support for him, and the Shah had answered, 'Yes, but the National Executive of the Labour Party criticise me. Everyone is against me – the BBC, everybody.'

Lambsdorff had apparently assured the Shah that the British Prime Minister took little notice of the National Executive on other matters, so why should he on this? Lambsdorff said there was a lot of emigration from Iran, and the demonstrations were largely motivated by the mullahs and Mossadeq's old supporters, the Nationalists.* He thought the technical class was very fearful and that there could well be a military government. The trouble was that there was no reforming middle class, and the religious opposition was divided because there was no Muslim leader. As a result, Mossadeq's National Front was re-emerging as the only viable opposition. What was needed was an urgent redistribution of wealth. But oil deliveries had been suspended because of the strikes and there were no shipments leaving Iran, so revenues were falling, and he didn't think OPEC were about to increase oil prices.

He said the military government, when it took over, would be right-wing, anti-communist and supported by the US, and it would come to power on the basis of attacking corruption, which had led to the total export of up to £500 million a year to foreign banks. He said the Russians were not really stirring the pot.

All this confirms the impending downfall of the Shah, and I was delighted to hear that the NEC had frightened him, because to know that he is actually affected by what the NEC says is marvellous.

Spent the rest of lunch talking to the Italian Energy Minister about the appointment of Pope John Paul II. He thought this would strengthen the church against Marxism, that there was an absolutely unbridgeable gap in Italy between the two, and that religion was necessary to keep the poor contented with their Government.

'That's just what Marx said,' I remarked, 'that religion was the opium of the people.'

'Well, the difference between Marxists and Christians is that Marxists believe in equality and Christians don't.' No wonder there is so much anti-clericalism in Italy.

*Tuesday 31 October*
The BBC rang to ask if I would review for Robert Robinson's programme a play called *The World Turned Upside Down* by Keith

---

* Mohammed Mossadeq, leader of the Iranian National Front party, and Prime Minister of Iran 1951–3, was responsible for the seizure and nationalisation of the Anglo–Iranian Oil Company installations in 1951.

Dewhurst, based on Christopher Hill's book about the Levellers in the English Revolution. I discovered later that the BBC would need to have my review in writing and approve it in advance; and apparently they told my office that they wanted to be sure that I wasn't going to use it as a political platform.

I rang up the producer, who confirmed this, so I said, 'The whole story of the Levellers was an attack on censorship and I'm not having my review censored.' He was very shirty about it.

When you think of the persistent right-wing propaganda from the BBC, it is intolerable that they should tell a Cabinet Minister that they intend to check what he says.

In the evening I went over to Number 10, where Jim read out the Queen's Speech and said, 'I am going to talk about inflation first, second and third, because this is what will win us the Election. This is where the public supports us.'

The news today carried the story of the Iranian financial crisis due to the strikes which had stopped deliveries of oil out of Iran. There could be a serious shortage if Iran is prevented from supplying oil, and BP could be in deep trouble. The Shah would of course fall.

It would help us with the North Sea and the sixth round of oil licences, but it would create very serious short-term problems for Britain, which is heavily dependent on Iranian oil.

### Wednesday 1 November

Today is the opening of Parliament, but, in the light of the strike in Iran, I thought I had better stay in the office and find out what was going on.

David Owen is of course acutely embarrassed because he came out for the Shah just at the moment when his regime was about to crumble. The office was reluctant for me to get involved; they were running it in their own low-key way and they'd tell Ministers when they thought it necessary for us to act.

I rang Sir David Steel of BP and asked for his assessment. Was it true that ex-pats – particularly British ex-pats – were coming under attack there? He said they were. Iran had cut back to 75 per cent of their oil trade. BP was still getting its full allocation. But I must keep that quiet, said Steel.

I agreed, and asked him to try not to cut back on oil supplies to the UK without consulting us. I told him I would be asking other oil companies to do the same. I gather Shell are already making cutbacks.

At 12.30 Harry Urwin [Assistant General Secretary of the TGWU] came and we had an extremely useful talk about security. He said that if a joint committee were convened to look at my NEC paper 'Civil Liberties and the Security Services' the TUC would probably

nominate him and Ken Graham of the TUC and possibly a General
Secretary to sit on it. The right thing would be to upgrade it to the
TUC–Labour Party Liaison Committee, so I agreed to do that through
David Lea and Len Murray on the TUC.

Harry was very critical of the corporate state, and of the top trade
union leaders, who were in the pocket of the Government. He said that
Heath, in his first two years, had offered the unions a degree of co-
operation they had never known before, and they had all fallen for it. If
the miners hadn't stuck it out, the union leaders would have gone along
with Heath's policy. I thought it was a shrewd comment. Harry is a
man of great integrity and toughness.

Had a word with Len Murray about my security services paper,
which I understand will be reported in *The Times* and the *Guardian*
tomorrow. I also sent a copy to Geoffrey Goodman.

*Thursday 2 November*
Peter Hennessy of *The Times* has done an absolutely straightforward,
excellent article. Richard Norton-Taylor has written an equally good
piece in the *Guardian*, headed 'Benn Demands Enquiry into Security
Services', and Geoffrey Goodman had a small item in the *Mirror* called
'Benn Watch'. I was very pleased, and it was all Frances's doing. She
pushed me into all these consultations and fed out the material. It is a
model example of what can be done if you are prepared to be patient.

Just before Cabinet, Merlyn Rees spoke to me, for the first time in
person, about our correspondence. He was sweating and looked
worried. 'About your paper,' he said, 'I want you to know that I am in
complete charge of the security services, twenty-four hours a day, and
nothing is done without my approval.'

Well, the fact that he felt it necessary to emphasise it was interesting
in itself. I said, 'Apart from anything else, there was a lot of concern at
the TUC about the Special Patrol Group.'

'The SPG only deals with traffic congestion. It was a great mistake to
call it the SPG.'

Of course the SPG were used at Grunwick as a battering ram to mow
down supporters of the strikers. To describe them as a group of
ordinary traffic police was laughable.

David Owen reported to the Cabinet on Iran. The Shah had told the
American and British Ambassadors recently that the old Government
couldn't continue, so he had appointed as the new Prime Minister a
man of eighty-five, by the name of Entizam. Elections would take place
as soon as possible, and the Shah was mounting an anti-corruption
drive. He was under heavy pressure from the military but he wanted to
stick to his policy of liberalisation. David Owen thought he would
become a constitutional monarch and he hoped the Cabinet would bear

in mind the UK's immense financial involvement in Iran. Owen's admission of the naked politics and economics of supporting the Shah was at any rate candid.

Jim said, 'If the Shah goes, he will be replaced by a much less attractive regime. David Owen is right to support the Shah.'

The last Cabinet item was the EMS. We had before us three papers – a bland background paper from the Treasury giving the history; a transcript of Jim Callaghan's press conference after his meeting with Schmidt in Bonn; and Denis Healey's paper for the Public Expenditure Select Committee tomorrow.

Denis argued that the EMS was dividing everyone, and even cutting across schools of thought: monetarist and Keynesian, Labour and Conservative. A view was developing in the United Kingdom that we shouldn't join unless the Germans changed their mind on certain key matters.

I asked a lot of questions, and said that the papers before us were not sufficient to allow the Cabinet to reach a collective decision.

Jim was furious. 'In my opinion, the papers before the Cabinet are adequate.'

Roy Mason asked, 'Are we strong enough to stay out? If we dither we will split the Party, and if we stay out and the Republic is in, the economic links between the Republic and Northern Ireland will be broken. It would mean exchange controls on the border; two-thirds of the firms in the Republic trade with the North and the banks are completely unified, North and South.'

I hadn't considered the Irish dimension.

Edmund Dell spoke. 'In the old days, the reason why the world economic system worked was that there was one dominating economy – Britain – with a stable currency. We can't expect that any more. The EMS will not be a substitute for the old pound sterling. Indeed, a full economic and monetary union would be better than an EMS.' He added, 'The divergence of the economies is the real problem. I would rather we dealt with the problems ourselves and not go in.'

Joel Barnett agreed with Edmund and spoke against it.

It came back to Jim for summing up. 'We are not reaching a final decision today and we probably should have a meeting with the PLP. Do we agree that there should be a zone of monetary stability?'

I frowned and Peter shook his head, so Jim said, 'I see people are frowning. Do we agree on the *desirability* of greater monetary stability?'

That we could accept, and the Cabinet ended. I do now feel we may not go in – particularly if Edmund and Joel don't want to. But we'll have to watch developments like hawks.

*Friday 3 November*

There was an interesting and revealing comment in *The Times* leader today. One sentence ran like this: 'If Mr Benn is worried about the bugging of trade leaders' (that was a misprint) 'or rebellious students, this should be dealt with by a royal commission and not by a select committee.'

I have said nothing about trade union leaders or rebellious students, except to Jim Callaghan. So he has obviously passed that on to the security services, who would much prefer a royal commission to a select committee, which would terrify them.

The Ford workers voted overwhelmingly today against the Ford pay offer. The BBC television coverage deliberately created the impression that motor-car workers are dangerous and violent, while the BBC is the voice of rationality. It is disgusting.

*Saturday 4 November*

I heard a funny story from Mother this afternoon. Recently she went to a meeting of the Council of Christians and Jews and shared a taxi with an old gentleman who was going in the same direction. He was a former army officer who had been in Rhodesia for a couple of years advising Ian Smith. 'I am here organising a campaign to stop the sanctions, and I've been having talks with the Tory Party. Mrs Thatcher is wonderful. We're working very hard and I am seeing every Member of Parliament I possibly can.'

'What do you think of Mr Heath?' asked Mother.

'Oh, he's no use at all.'

When they got to the Army and Navy Club, where he got out, Mother said, 'This will make you smile. I am Anthony Wedgwood Benn's mother.'

'Well!' he said. 'He is lucky to have such a nice relation.'

*Sunday 5 November*

Usual lovely Sunday morning reading the papers. There was an extraordinarily good extract from Arthur Schlesinger's biography of Robert Kennedy, in which he described how J. Edgar Hoover and the FBI bugged the hotel rooms where Martin Luther King stayed and discovered that King had a rather irregular sex life. They sent the tape to Mrs King, as a sort of veiled threat.

After lunch, an American friend of ours came to tea. He had once served in the US security services, and he told me he suspected that a completely new arm of security had been set up which doesn't even report to the President. 'We are afraid that all this publicity in the United States, due to the Freedom of Information law, has led British security to refuse to co-operate with American security. Your security service is the best in the world and we are losing out as a result of it.'

I asked him how he had coped with Hoover, and he said, 'He was a bit cranky, but there were many Congressmen who had to be put under surveillance because they weren't patriotic.'

The definition of patriotism to him – as a Republican – is whatever the FBI or the CIA or the National Security Agency determine it to be. It is not a matter of political definition.

*Monday 6 November*
Brian Sedgemore rang me at home this evening and said, 'Tony, I have seen the Chief Whip, and I have resigned as your PPS.'

I said he had better come round straight away and he turned up looking like a wounded elephant. I sat him down and gave him a cup of tea and this is the story he told.

Last Friday, at a sub-committee of the Select Committee on Public Expenditure, Brian had put a question to Denis Healey, who was giving evidence on the EMS. Brian had asked, 'What about the secret Treasury paper?', quoting the number and referring to the fact that the paper warned of the need for deflation.

Denis was completely taken aback. 'You seem to have seen the paper already.'

The paper, which was not sent to me, had got into Brian Sedgemore's hands. Brian had used the information in the committee but he may not have realised the gravity of what he was doing.

The newspapers at the weekend had carried the story.

I might add that in the last two weeks Mike Cocks has said to him on a couple of occasions, 'We would like to give you a job in the Government; what would you like?' So, having first tried to tempt Sedgemore into behaving more 'responsibly', Cocks has now changed tack. He said to Brian yesterday, 'I want to see you privately. Walk with me over to Number 11.'

They walked across Parliament Square, round the back of the Foreign Office, up the steps and into Number 11.

Mike Cocks said to Brian, 'Jim Callaghan is a very patient man. He steered the Government through the IMF, but he is extremely angry about this. I must now formally put three questions to you. One, did you receive the Treasury paper from a Minister, from an official or from someone else? Two, who was it? Three, will you co-operate in an inquiry?'

'I am not prepared to answer questions which might involve pressure from the executive in relation to the conduct of my duty as a member of the Expenditure Committee,' Brian replied.

Cocks was furious, apparently, and that interview came to an end, but Brian was later summoned again.

'The polls are going very well and it would be in the interests of the Party if you resigned,' said Cocks. Like a fool, Brian gave Cocks an assurance that he would and has written a letter of resignation.

'But you can't resign,' I said.

'I have given my word to Mike Cocks.'

'You can't do that. All this public school stuff about giving your word is nonsense. It would be damaging.'

I was anxious about it, so, in his presence, I wrote a letter in his defence. I pointed out that his work on the Public Expenditure Select Committee was very important; that it was a breach of privilege to threaten him; that it would imply that he had behaved wrongly; and also that I was being implicated as having passed him the document. I told him to tell Mike Cocks that he had discussed the matter with me and decided not to proceed with his resignation, and, if Cocks wanted to raise it with me, he could. Brian accepted that.

Then I spoke to Frances, and she thought it was ridiculous to write a letter. 'Just tell Brian to ring Mike Cocks and say he wants twenty-four hours to consider it.'

So Brian has been battered by Mike Cocks to resign, battered by me not to resign, and battered by Frances to defend himself. Anyway, he rang Mike Cocks and said he'd think about it and let him know tomorrow. Before he left, I said, 'Promise me you won't resign?' But for the first time he has got himself into big politics and the strain was tremendous.

*Tuesday 7 November*

I was on my way to a meeting when I saw Mike Cocks. He said, 'I have spoken to Brian Sedgemore on behalf of the Prime Minister, and the boss thinks he must go.'

I declared, 'There is one very grave aspect of this and that is the question of privilege. He is on a committee which has nothing whatever to do with me. Of course, I didn't give him the documents because, as you know, I don't have access to them myself.'

'Oh, there's no question of that,' he said.

I told Cocks I had advised Brian that, if he were sacked, he should consult the Speaker and take it to the Privileges Committee, and I would support him. This was a House of Commons matter and it was a serious error.

Mike looked white.

Saw Stan Orme in the Tea Room and he told me he had heard that Jim Callaghan had leapt with anger at what had happened. I said, 'It may come up in the Cabinet on Thursday and if so perhaps you could help me out.' He was sympathetic but non-committal.

Len Murray rang, very angry about a report in *The Times* that there was to be a joint inquiry by the NEC Home Policy Committee and the TUC about security. 'Your terms of reference go much wider than the ones that came up at the Congress. It's quite inaccurate to say we have agreed to a joint committee.'

'I didn't say that,' I told him. 'I said we were going to ask the TUC if they would like to nominate anybody.'

He said, 'Well, it will have to go to the whole General Council.' He has been getting a lot of press enquiries and I think he felt I was using him as a way of challenging Jim Callaghan. So that's going wrong, but I'll let it ride for a while.

Later that evening my office rang to say a minute had arrived from the Prime Minister: 'I regret to tell you that Brian Sedgemore no longer enjoys my confidence.'

Frances's instinct was that Brian had made a muck-up of it and that I should cut adrift. I won't sack Brian, but the Prime Minister might.

The BBC rang tonight for a comment and I refused to make one. *The Times* called me on my private number and I just put down the phone.

### Wednesday 8 November

At 8.45 Mike Cocks came to see me. 'I have come at my own wish', he said (though I don't know whether the Prime Minister had told him to defuse the situation), 'simply to see how we can handle this matter without damaging the Party.'

'From my understanding of the papers this morning,' I observed, 'Brian Sedgemore has been sacked by Jim Callaghan.'

'Yes.'

'Well, in that case, it doesn't concern me any more.'

'Look,' he said, 'dismissal doesn't necessarily destroy a political career. People bite the bullet and then they get appointed later. He's a very able chap.'

I repeated, 'It doesn't concern me any more.' I think he was surprised.

I added, 'Of course there are matters that Brian may raise. I think he has a strong case on privilege.' I established clearly that I had not sacked and did not intend to sack Brian Sedgemore.

Brian came into the office and told me the press had been at his house this morning. He said they had photographed him just after his bath, and, sure enough, in the afternoon papers there was Brian looking like Mohammed Ali after a fight.

### Thursday 9 November

Cabinet at 10.30. Denis reported on his talks with the TUC, which he said had occupied four to six hours, twice a week, for some weeks. The Government were not prepared to move on the 5 per cent and the TUC were committed to free collective bargaining. Provided pay increases did not lead to higher prices, the Government might ease up on sanctions against companies. The Government had agreed with the TUC and the CBI on the strengthening of the Price Commission and to lengthen the time interval between price increases.

'If all goes well,' said Denis, 'both sides will agree a statement tomorrow and the TUC would then be in a position to give guidance to negotiators. This would restore the TUC to a position of helpful neutrality, such as they occupied during the pay year 1977/8.' In Denis's judgement, there were risks, because it might be interpreted as a sell-out to the unions, but if we agreed tomorrow it would help us all.

Jim thanked Denis, Albert, Michael, Eric and Roy Hattersley for their work. He added, 'My fear is not that we shall sell out to the unions, because they are our political colleagues, but that it will have a serious effect on the market. Our enemies might misconstrue the joint statement.'

'The situation in the markets at the moment is difficult,' Denis said. He then turned to Jim and asked, 'Would you like me to mention it?'

'Yes, please do,' Jim replied.

So Denis, turning to us, said, 'I think I ought to tell you that the minimum lending rate is going up by 2.5 per cent to 12.5 per cent at noon today, and the 8–12 per cent monetary targets are going to be reaffirmed. This will mean a tightening of the money supply, and mortgage rates will rise by 1 per cent. The uncertainty about pay and the impending negotiations on the EMS require us to be tougher.'

Jim added, 'This is very secret until 12.30, and if any members of the Cabinet wish to go to the lavatory they will be escorted there by a man with a revolver.'

Thus a major change of economic policy was simply announced to the Cabinet with no preparatory work, no discussion, no consideration of alternatives, and no time to comment. The decision had already been reached. So the Cabinet now is not even a rubber stamp, but a mere spectator of decisions made by the Prime Minister and a tiny group of Ministers, including Denis Healey and Michael Foot.

On foreign affairs, David Owen announced, 'I must warn the Cabinet that there is a risk that in the next couple of days we may have to veto a UN resolution which would force us to impose sanctions against South Africa. I hope we shall not have to use the veto alone but we can't tie the United States down; we aren't sure what they are going to do. We cannot be pushed and pushed and we must abide by the agreement reached by the five Foreign Ministers in Pretoria. France is being most unhelpful at this stage.'

I said, 'I take it that we will not use our veto until the Cabinet has been given an opportunity to discuss it', thus indicating, as modestly as possible, that I was opposed to a veto.

'I cannot give that assurance,' David replied.

Jim said, rather testily, 'It might happen in the middle of the night. You might be telephoned at 2.30 in the night and be told the vote was coming at 2.45.'

On Iran, David reported that the situation was a mess. 'The Shah is trying to forget that he has been Shah over the last twenty years. He had insisted that under no circumstances would he arrest the former Prime Minister Hoveyda, but now Hoveyda and the police chief have been taken.'

Jim said, 'He does seem ready to lay down his friends for his life.'

Then we came on to the question of Rhodesia and the oil sanctions. David Owen reported that the PLP were demanding a parliamentary inquiry, as were some sections of the Opposition. Enoch Powell was against it, the Tory Front Bench were uncommitted and would play it politically, and Heath thought an inquiry was unnecessary.

Jim said, 'The Tories are really letting us stew in our own juice over this and they don't really want an inquiry. But if we recommend against it the House of Commons would certainly defeat us.'

I restated my preference for a select committee inquiry. 'It is the duty of a select committee to interrogate the executive, and it should have very wide terms of reference. Its composition should be confined to senior Members of Parliament, but the idea that only Privy Councillors could sit on it is absurd. To take a responsible backbencher whom you wanted to have on the inquiry and wheel him off to the Palace to swear the Privy Councillor's oath of secrecy so that he can help Parliament to open up what has hitherto been a closed area of Government activity is ridiculous. The Cabinet papers should be available, since Bingham himself was allowed to see them, as well as the oil company papers.'

At the end of my contribution, Jim said, 'Thank you for that very helpful intervention' – heavy with sarcasm, no doubt because he was still angry about the Brian Sedgemore affair.

Michael warned that members of the PLP might not protect Labour Ministers in the same way that Tory MPs protected Tory Ministers, for example, during the Poulson inquiry.

'That is the nature of our Party,' Jim commented. 'Its lovable quality is related to its motivation to do the right thing rather than protect its own people.'

Michael Foot made the point that the availability of Cabinet papers was absolutely essential; Harold Wilson couldn't defend himself without access to Cabinet papers.

Of course, the real motivation of Jim and Michael and others is to have an inquiry to allow Labour Ministers to clear themselves, and they can't be absolutely sure that Labour MPs would go along with that.

I went back to the office, and Bryan Gould, Brian Sedgemore, Michael Meacher and Frances Morrell came to lunch. Bryan now has 114 MPs' signatures on the resolution against the EMS – more than half the backbenchers. He put out a statement today.

*Saturday 11 November*
Vanessa and Corin Redgrave have effectively lost their libel case against the *Observer*; the jury ruled that the information in the *Observer* article in 1975 that the Redgraves and other members of the Workers' Revolutionary Party were violent and unlawful was false and libellous, but they made no award as to damages on the grounds that the plaintiffs' reputations were not injured. The Redgraves have to pay £70,000 in costs. An absolute scandal. If the media can destroy your reputation and then a jury can conclude that you have no reputation to save, the libel laws are no protection at all.

Mind you, it did confirm me in my view that libel action is not the answer. The proper way to deal with libel is through the trade unions and journalists on the paper concerned. Any remaining feeling I had about the decency of the *Observer* has completely gone.

I heard on the news that Edmund Dell has resigned to become Chairman of Guinness Peat, the merchant bank. The fact that a Cabinet Minister can leave his post for this purpose at this moment is a scandalous betrayal of duty to the labour movement – although I am delighted, of course, that Dell is going, because he is actually more right-wing than the Tory Party.

I also heard that because the Mayor of Wolverhampton (who is a woman) has allowed gay ex-servicemen to attend the Armistice Day celebrations the British Legion are refusing to participate. And the ordination of women ministers has been defeated by the Church of England by an even bigger majority than last time. Such stories reflect a combination of tribalism and trade-unionism in society – as Father used to say.

*Tuesday 14 November*
Very significant news tonight: the TUC General Council has rejected a unanimous recommendation from its Economic Committee that the joint statement on pay policy by the Government and the TUC be agreed. I am sure it was the secrecy around it that led to it being rejected. Nobody was told. It's a real kick in the teeth for the corporate state.

*Wednesday 15 November*

Caught the 8.20 to Bristol to attend the hearing of the Local Government Boundary Commission, which has proposed major changes in the ward boundaries in Bristol. If these are extended to the constituency boundaries, Bristol South East would become a Tory seat.

*Thursday 16 November*

Jim Callaghan had some of his grandchildren in the Cabinet Room before Cabinet began and some photographs were taken. I must say the Cabinet gets more and more like the royal family.

John Silkin was congratulated on his recovery after being knocked down by a moped, and John Smith was welcomed as the new Secretary of State for Trade in Edmund Dell's place.

Dennis Healey announced, 'I am aiming to publish the Green Paper on the EMS just after the meeting of European Finance Ministers on Monday, so that will appear on Tuesday. On Thursday, the Cabinet will meet and there will then be a Party meeting on the following Tuesday followed on Wednesday the 29th by a debate in the House of Commons. The PM will then go to the summit on 5 December. We should take a decision after the debate.'

I asked for clarification and argued, 'A lot of the steam would be taken out of this if the Prime Minister came back from the summit, put the scheme before us and then let the Cabinet and Parliament decide whether to accept it.'

Jim said, 'No, I want a decision *before* I go and we agreed in the summer that we would decide it in December.' He was very angry at what I had said.

On pay limits, Denis said he was extremely disappointed that the TUC General Council had split; the reasons for their vote had varied. Ministers must now observe the 5 per cent guidelines, in the absence of an agreement with the TUC.

*Friday 17 November*

To Bristol to present the Stafford Cripps–Wedgwood Benn Sports Shield at St Patrick's School, a Catholic primary school which I first visited twenty-eight years ago this month. The headmaster, Peter Begley, is a really radical socialist who had been removed from the school for his views, and subsequently reinstated. It was a lovely occasion. The children were lined up and the former head, Bill Mitchell, made a speech reminding us that in 1935 Lady Cripps had presented the original sports shield. I had asked Peter Begley to have the shield remounted on a new carved board with my name added. I played the children a short extract of a recording in 1935 of Stafford Cripps.

*Sunday 19 November*
Flew to Paris and was met by the Ambassador, Nico Henderson, and driven to his residence prior to meeting Michel Rocard for dinner tonight. In the car he told me Rocard had moved from left to right. 'Just like George Brown and Dick Marsh and Edmund Dell,' I added. Henderson asked, 'Was Edmund Dell on the left?' He was surprised when I told him Dell had been in the Communist Party – he didn't know, although he was at Oxford with Healey before the war and knew Healey was in the CP. He himself had been on the right wing of the Labour Club.

We were taken to dinner with Rocard and his second wife, Michèle, in their very glamorous and fashionable apartment: the homes of British socialist leaders are much scruffier than that. She is a sociologist studying the sociology of business enterprises. Rocard described Mitterrand as an elected monarch; Mitterrand appoints all the candidates for constituencies in France, and the French Government is extremely centralised. He told me that, although everyone calls each other 'tu' in the Parti Socialiste, Mitterrand always insists on being called Monsieur Mitterrand. Rocard was much amused when I said I had called him François when I met him. 'Good heavens,' he said, 'that was a bit like addressing the Queen as Elizabeth!'

*Monday 20 November*
Heard on the morning news that proceedings against Jeremy Thorpe begin in Minehead Magistrates' Court today.

Went downstairs at 8.30 to have breakfast with Robert Pontillon, International Secretary of the Parti Socialiste. We had the sort of grand English breakfast you only now see in English domestic comedies or Hollywood films about the British aristocracy.

We talked about the direct elections. Pontillon thought there might be a low turnout and he understood that British candidates would be of poorer quality than the French and German socialists who would be contesting. He believed there was no such thing as a Eurocommunist, because the French, Italian and Spanish communists were entirely different from each other.

At 11.30 I went to see André Giraud, the Minister for Industry. He asked about fast breeder reactors and I told him I was in no great hurry to go ahead with the fast breeder; we had led on Concorde and there was something to be said for not being first in all these fields.

Then we got on to nuclear policy generally. He thought it was quite inappropriate to inform the general public about the technical details of nuclear power. Information just stimulated opposition and made people difficult.

Flew back frightfully tired and found a letter waiting for me from

Howard Smith. After Jim told me he had appointed him head of MI5, I had dropped him a note inviting him to lunch. I hadn't made any reference whatever to my own campaign or recent paper, but the reply said:

> Dear Tony,
>
> Your letter of 2 November reached me only this weekend. It had been forwarded by mistake to Moscow. Thank you so much for suggesting we should have a talk over lunch. I should have been delighted to accept but with me in my new job, and the Home Policy Committee of the NEC setting up a study group as reported in *The Times* on 2 November, a meeting between us at this time could very easily be misunderstood and that is a risk I have no right to take. I feel sure you will understand.
> With best wishes to you both.
>
> Ever, Howard.

So I have an admission from him that he is head of MI5 – not that I needed to after the PM had told me. But I am now cut off from MI5. I think his refusal to come and see me is amazing, really.

*Tuesday 21 November*
The papers are full of the Jeremy Thorpe case. On the face of it, it would appear that he had a homosexual relationship with Scott – though that is no longer a crime – and that there was a plot to incite people to murder Scott. It's tragic for Jeremy.

I wrote today to the Redgraves, enclosing £20 towards their libel costs against the *Observer*. I composed the letter with care to make it clear I wasn't supporting the Workers' Revolutionary Party, to which they belong.

*Thursday 23 November*
At 9.45 Charles Clarke,* the son of my former Permanent Secretary, Otto Clarke, came to see me and we had a pleasant talk. He had just returned from Cuba, where he was the British representative on the Preparatory Committee of the World Youth Congress. He said Cuba was most impressive, although as a student he had little direct contact with the Cuban people. There was apparently enormous Soviet influence and the only other Party with any power was the German SPD, which he was sure was backed by German capital, much as it is in Namibia and Greece. Fidel Castro was very much an authoritarian but a most impressive man. Cuba had historical links with Angola and Algeria, and in Clarke's view these were pivotal countries today, with

---

* Chief adviser to Neil Kinnock (Leader of the Labour Party) since 1983.

considerable influence on world development. Clarke was critical of the British Labour Party, which he thought was inactive and without influence. When he had applied to work in the International Department at Transport House, he hadn't even been shortlisted.

Brian Sedgemore told me, just prior to the PLP meeting at 6, that Jim Callaghan had remarked to him, 'Nothing personal, you know, Brian.'

At the PLP, Frank Hooley [MP for Sheffield Heeley] said, 'I know we are going to gallop round the course on Wednesday, but I take it there will be no commitment on the EMS without a clear vote after next month's summit.'

Douglas Jay and Barbara Castle also argued that there should be a vote *after* the summit.

Jim responded, 'I'll have to answer all that at next Tuesday's PLP, but the Government has the right to vote at the summit. Do you want us to block the EMS or just not to join? There won't be a vote next Wednesday in the House of Commons. As Prime Minister, I shall go ready to make a decision and that will be that.'

Hugh Jenkins said, 'There are two decisions: do we want an EMS, and should we join it?'

'On 4 or 5 December or whenever it is,' said Jim (as if he didn't know), 'we are expected to reach a decision.'

Barbara pointed out, 'But then the only role left to us would be to repudiate what is done at the summit. Surely we must consult before we enter into any commitment.'

'I cannot undertake to do that,' said Jim, reflecting the combined power of the European legislation on Britain and his own dictatorial manner. 'I can't defer a decision just to get PLP and parliamentary approval.'

'But do we have a vote before we join?' asked Barbara. 'That's the key question.'

Dennis Skinner said, 'The Prime Minister is saying that he will decide even though the PLP is opposed.'

Jim replied, 'The House of Commons will just have to register its view in the debate next week, but I won't promise I won't join.'

Of course, what Jim is doing is exactly what Heath did when he signed the Treaty of Rome before Parliament had even seen it and then said it was a matter of prerogative.

In the Tea Room I had a talk to Gerry Fitt, the Northern Ireland SDLP Leader, an awfully nice guy. I really like him. He told me things were difficult at the moment. 'I am sure Michael Foot doesn't want to do it, but has had to offer more Ulster Unionist representation in return for Powell's support for the Government over the winter. My people say to me, "Well, what are you getting out of supporting the Government? It just appears to be capitulating to the Ulster Unionists." Next

Tuesday there is a debate on the voting system for Northern Ireland and if I can't get at least 100 Labour MPs to vote for proportional representation, when the Tories are voting with the Government, my people will say it's not worth supporting the Labour Government.' He said he could understand the Ulster Unionist position, but they couldn't understand his.

I sympathise with Gerry. He is under tremendous pressure all the time. But politics does put people under pressure, and if you crack that's the end of it.

*Saturday 25 November*
The big news today is that Jim has been in Paris ahead of the summit and has agreed with Giscard to vote for setting up an EMS which Britain will join at a later date. I was so angry and frustrated, I felt like resigning, but Caroline and Frances Morrell urged me to take it slowly. I remembered that there is a joint meeting of the Home Policy Committee and the International Committee on Monday, which I shall chair, and a number of questions will be put to Denis Healey. We shall urge that a decision be made by Parliament with a free vote for Ministers.

In the afternoon I caught the train to Newport, where I was met by an AUEW shop steward at the British Leyland plant at Cardiff, and he drove me to Neil Kinnock's house in Bedwelty. Neil has a council house where he spends the weekends. Then over to a rally where over 300 people had gathered to celebrate the Chartists' march on Newport. The first speaker, a young woman, made a real Militant speech. That little crowd of sectarian socialists who make up the Militant Tendency are so hardworking and dedicated. They are working within the Labour Party to get their message and interpretation across.

Neil Kinnock made a speech which alternated between serious radical comment and light-hearted humour and which was very attractive to the audience. Neil generates the impression that he is saying it for them. His speech ranged from attacks on the multinational companies through to the Shah of Iran and Princess Anne being taken to a dinner by helicopter this week at a cost of £800. It was good stuff, but it made me feel slightly uneasy.

*Sunday 26 November*
The Thorpe trial still dominates the newspapers, and this has been a week of sensational allegations. It is alleged that Liberal Party funds were diverted to Thorpe so that he could bribe someone to kill Norman Scott. The whole case is riveting and is as much about the activities of the Liberal Party as it is about Thorpe's homosexual affair.

I did get a chance yesterday to discuss with Neil Kinnock a

resolution for the joint meeting of the Home Policy and International Committees tomorrow, affirming our opposition to the EMS and calling for a vote in the House of Commons with a free vote for Ministers. If I can get that carried through I shall be well satisfied.

Picked up Mother and brought her home for a birthday tea for Hilary. We watched a remarkable film about Paul Robeson. I had thought they would describe him as a great singer and dismiss his political activities as a sort of aberration, but in fact they dealt with it fully. They showed his campaign for civil rights, his visits to Russia, his persecution by the press and how he used the chapels to sing his message to the black community. They showed his visit to London, when he came to the House of Lords with Father and sang 'Ol' Man River', in the Tea Room. Then there were the last eleven terrible years when he was ill and suffered from acute melancholia. It was a most moving film and I sat there with tears rolling down my cheeks.

*Monday 27 November*
Went over to the House of Commons for the joint meeting of the Home Policy and International Committees . Denis Healey had been invited there to present the Government's Green Paper, 'The European Monetary System'. I got there early and slipped to Frank Allaun, Neil Kinnock and Eric Heffer the resolution that I had drafted last night.

Denis Healey opened the meeting, and he was bored and lackadaisical, as if he were addressing a group of children. 'We want the maximum stability of exchange rates. There is a case for a high exchange rate and, provided there is an opportunity for change, this should lead to greater growth and higher employment. No decision will be taken until the summit but the basic position is clear.'

Eric Heffer said, 'The NEC has rejected the EMS because Conference rejected any encroachment on the powers of a Labour Government. The Paris meeting has left me confused because it appears that the Government has already accepted the EMS in principle.'

Denis Healey denied this.

'Well,' Eric continued, 'Roy Jenkins said the EMS would lay the foundation for the EMU, and where are we now?'

Denis replied, 'The proposals made at Copenhagen for an EMS lay down certain principles and the Government did not agree – even in principle – to these principles, but we did call for greater monetary stability. Since Copenhagen, the Finance Ministers have been meeting to discuss it.' He said that Schmidt was against the strong economies carrying the weaker ones.

Les Huckfield, a new member of the NEC, commented, 'I can see what Schmidt gets out of all this because he has locked us into a system where we can't depreciate against his greater strength. As for Giscard, he gets support for his monetary policy at home. But what do we get out of it?'

'We would benefit from the stability,' Denis replied. 'The Germans and the French are divided, indeed we are all divided – the monetarists, the Keynesians, the left and the right.'

Dennis Skinner said, 'My concern is whether or not it advances our class interest and the Chancellor ought to bear this in mind. Giscard is a Tory, and the question is will it do anything for the real creators of wealth in this country?' At the end of his speech he added, 'I'm telling you, you are only where you are because the labour movement worked to put you there.'

Healey replied that national and class interests were the same in this case. The Italian Socialists and Communists solidly supported the British view and all this 'mouthing of ideological claptrap' got you nowhere. 'Dennis,' he said, 'you don't carry a certificate authorising you to speak on behalf of the working class. The EMS *as proposed* would not be in our interest, but we have *all* worked in the labour movement to get where we are.'

Neil Kinnock spoke. 'We were told we would be frozen out if we didn't join the EEC, but what is in it for us? What is happening is that the strong are getting stronger and the UK weaknesses are being compounded. There is nothing for us in the EMS except deeper enmeshment in the EEC, and it will not guarantee stability or growth.'

In response to a number of other interventions on this theme, Denis said, 'Since 1976 we have reduced unemployment a bit and inflation has been cut by half. Living standards were up 7 per cent this year and our popularity is growing . . .'

'Rubbish, rubbish, rubbish!' Eric interrupted, so I told him to let Denis finish.

Denis continued, 'Interest rates were 5 per cent and are now 12.5 per cent, which I regret intensely, but the alternative was a possible run on sterling. Now we have large areas of agreement in the Party. The Government will not join the EMS where it is unhelpful. I hope we will remember the impending Election and stress the things we agree upon.'

Denis actually stayed longer than he had intended, I suspect because he didn't want us to pass a resolution. So I said, 'Well, Denis, we will have to consider it. Thank you very much for coming.' There was reasonable goodwill despite the harsh words.

After he had gone, Frank Allaun moved a slightly amended version of my resolution on the EMS. It read: 'We oppose the proposed EMS and, at the appropriate stage, we will veto it if it becomes an EEC regulation.' After some discussion, it was agreed by the remaining people – Dennis Skinner, Eric Heffer, Neil Kinnock, Doug Hoyle, Joan Maynard, Frank Allaun, Norman Atkinson, Alan Hadden and myself

– without a dissenting vote. I must say it was remarkable. I said I wouldn't give a press conference about it but it was made available to the press later.

I should report that Stan Orme told me that, according to Eric Varley, Harold Wilson had confided to him on his retirement that he believed the Party would recall him within six months to take charge of a great crisis. I am sure Harold believed he would be called back one day, but whether he thought it would be as soon as that I don't know.

*Tuesday 28 November*
At 10.30 I went over to EY Committee. The Cabinet Secretary, Sir John Hunt, came up to me and said, 'The Prime Minister thinks you ought to see the reports he is getting from Sigint about the situation in Iran. In order to explain them to you, he would like Sir Brooks Richards, the head of Sigint, to come and see you.'

I asked about Sigint and he explained, 'It intercepts radio messages in and out of Tehran, including, no doubt, messages from refineries to the managers of the oil companies and so on.'

I thanked him, but when I thought about it I began to get suspicious. After all my recent campaigning on Intelligence, it seemed most improbable that Sir John Hunt should offer me this opportunity. I began to think that he was trying to involve me in the activities of Sigint, and to get me into a commitment to Iran, perhaps by giving me information about Russian interests there. Perhaps he was giving me information which would then be monitored to see whether it had leaked so that action could be taken against me. Or maybe Brooks Richards was really coming to see me about something quite different. He may also be the head of MI6, I don't know. All these things went through my head and I record them today before I actually see the man and discover the truth.

I had to go to a small dinner at Number 10 given by Jim for the Prime Minister of Luxembourg, Gaston Thorn. Also present were the Luxembourg Ambassador, Shirley Williams, John Morris, Joel Barnett, Michael Palliser [head of the Diplomatic Service], Tom McNally, Bryan Cartledge [Callaghan's Private Secretary (Overseas Affairs)] and our Ambassador in Luxembourg, Patrick Wright. I scribbled a few notes on the menu.

At the end of the dinner, Jim asked Thorn, 'Will you tell us how you now see the Common Market?'

Thorn told us that Robert Schuman, the founder of the Common Market, was born in Luxembourg, which, because of its position between France and Germany, had been crushed many times. Luxembourg didn't want another war. He had wanted Britain to join the Common Market more than thirty years ago, and the important point was to anchor Germany to Europe. He was afraid it wouldn't be long before Germany looked towards East Germany and asked, 'Aren't we friends? Aren't we cousins?' Then unification would follow and that could be dangerous because he didn't think Germany was sufficiently anchored to the west. Then he said, 'We want to know, is Britain in or out?'

So Jim replied, 'I think I will ask Tony Benn to answer that.'

I said, 'Well, I would put it like this. I find your presentation, Prime Minister, most moving and intelligible. We *have* had a very different history. When I sit round the table in Brussels and look at all the other Ministers, except for the Irish we are the only country that hasn't been occupied or conquered by Germany, so we don't have that same combination of fear and respect for them. I think the problem with the idea of a federal Europe is that the federalism is concealed. I don't think there is any serious pressure to withdraw, but the effect of our membership of the EEC has been to produce a radical transfer of power from the British Parliament to the British Government, from the British Government to Europe, and from Ministers to officials, and it has even brought in the courts. The Treaty of Rome is hostile to what the Labour Party believes in, and we will be chewing over these issues, like a dog with a bone, for a hundred years.'

Joel Barnett added, 'The British people are not interested in Europe but there is no serious pressure to withdraw.'

Jim referred to the press in Brussels. 'Every time we criticise, it is said that we are not good Europeans.'

Thorn replied, 'I am inclined to say to you very frankly what the Continent says to you, and that is if you don't like it you should get out. We don't really care very much.' Actually he put it more politely than that, but that was what he meant.

Michael Palliser commented, 'The United Kingdom joined the EEC when growth had dropped, and, though the Danes and the Irish have done very well indeed in the Community, the UK has fared badly. De Gaulle got the CAP and it has strengthened France, but the Community has got to change its economic policy. I disagree with Tony because I think we have only got twenty years to chew things over before Germany reunites. Germany is beginning to question the EEC and France is beginning to question its relations with the USSR.'

There was a division, and when I returned I just had time to say, 'You mustn't underestimate this question of invasion, Prime Minister: we haven't been invaded for a thousand years and we haven't had a revolution for 300 years, and democracy in Britain means a deep hatred of centralised power. We see the Common Market in that context.'

Patrick Wright said, 'I don't think the people hate power.'

Went back to the House. John Silkin came into my room for a talk, and we got on to the subject of Jim's leadership. I had heard that Silkin fancied himself as Leader, so I said, 'Well, if you became Leader, I would be very happy to serve under you.'

'And I under you.'

Of course it was a ridiculous discussion because neither of us is going to become Leader.

### Wednesday 29 November

Had a meeting with Jim Schlesinger, the US Energy Secretary, who is over here. He was once Secretary of State for Defence and was sacked by Ford because of a disagreement he had with Kissinger, and he has also headed the CIA. He is a tough Republican intellectual, lives an austere life, in line with the Presbyterian faith to which he was converted from Judaism, and is a very dour man. He doesn't believe in publicity or any of that stuff, and is not gregarious at all. When I took him upstairs to my room, where a huge crowd of people had gathered, he just sat down and stared at everyone. He doesn't suffer fools gladly.

Anyway, I welcomed him and said I'd been looking forward to his visit. 'I hope it's OK if we do our business in this order: your energy policy/our energy policy; the world energy scene; Iran, Mexico; OPEC and oil prices; UN international energy; coal policy; fast breeder reactors; and anything else you might like to raise.'

'Fine.'

'How would you like to start?'

'Up to you.'

Tea was brought in at that point and he said, 'Is that your mug? If it were any bigger you wouldn't be able to lift it!' I told him I had a two-pint mug at home but I didn't bring it to the office. It was a sign of friendliness on his part after a slightly tense beginning.

'Tell us first how your energy policy in America is going,' I said.

'Well,' he replied, 'politics is like ju-jitsu. We asked for more powers than we got, but we got more than they realised, and we are now going to use them.' He went on to give a very tough presentation of their policy.

I said, 'My assessment is that we have to think long-term and that is beyond the range of market forces. I don't worship market forces, though I am not being completely ideological about it. You've got these great big companies and you've got to keep an eye on them.'

What followed was a very informed discussion between two experienced people – he with far more power and experience, but it did range over everything and I must say I enjoyed it.

He looked at my Workers' Union banner and said it was beautiful. I said, 'You see the religious themes depicted in it – trade-unionism grew out of the chapels in this country.'

'It could have come from the Soviet Union, with those realistic figures,' he said, to which I replied, 'Socialist realism is very much the same as capitalist realism.'

'What do you mean?'

I said, 'Developing societies with a lot of self-confidence and thrust go for realistic art. It's only in decaying societies that you get all this decadent stuff like the Impressionists. That's why Khrushchev and Eisenhower agreed about chocolate box art.' He laughed.

I asked him if he knew where the hammer and sickle were to be found in London and he didn't, so I promised to show him.

We walked out to my car to go to lunch at the Dorchester Hotel; he had no security guards with him, and when I asked he told me that he never allows them.

I got the driver to pass by St James's Park because Schlesinger is a great birdwatcher. I asked him about the CIA and he said, 'I was there for five months at a difficult time, right in the middle of Watergate when we had done some terrible things.' He said the CIA got up to some funny things but at least they tried to maintain some standards and co-operate up to a point with the White House. But Nixon had just expected them to do anything he wanted and that wasn't on.

'I am puzzled about Nixon's departure,' I said. 'I never could quite understand it.'

'Nixon lied to the American people and they wouldn't have that. If he had said, "Yes, there was some funny business for which I take full responsibility", his popularity would have risen enormously, but he looked the American people in the eye and he lied to them.' Schlesinger thought Nixon had behaved stupidly and could otherwise have survived. Also he thought a Democrat could have got away with it because of their majority in Congress but, as a Republican, Nixon had miscalculated.

As we passed the imposing Victoria Memorial in the middle of Buckingham Palace roundabout, I said, 'There's the hammer and sickle.' There were the two lions, and a man holding a hammer aloft and a girl carrying a sickle. He laughed.

I told him I admired Carter and that he struck me as a sensitive guy. 'Do you know that Jim Callaghan is very attached to him, and when the dollar was in difficulties I think Jim called in the American Ambassador just to express his support for Carter.'

'Yes, the President knew that and was pleased.'

At lunch were Frank Kearton, Derek Ezra, Moss Evans, John Hill, Dick Mabon and others.

After lunch I said to Schlesinger, 'I am not going to make a big fuss so I am going to ask you just to say a word.'

Schlesinger replied, 'I have enjoyed today very much but I never thought I would be taken by a British Secretary of State for Energy to see the hammer and sickle outside Buckingham Palace!'

So Dick Mabon turned to Frank Judd sitting beside him. 'Tony's done it again!'

'My God,' I said to Schlesinger, 'if you go round telling that story, I'll be in trouble with the CIA.'

I think he took me literally. 'Oh, don't bother about that,' he said. Everyone laughed and it was fun.

*Thursday 30 November*
Before Cabinet, Merlyn Rees came up to me and said, 'By the way, Tony, I want to make the point again that I control all the security services personally. I check and review everybody whose phone is tapped and I assure you it is completely under my control.'

'Well,' I replied, 'Chapman Pincher's recent book claimed that you weren't told anything.'

'That's absolute rubbish,' he said.

Cabinet. After David Owen had gone through foreign affairs, Jim announced, 'I should say a word about Germany. It is possible that there is some change taking place there. I don't quite know how to describe it but there is some anxiety and a lot of gossip that the Russians are offering the Germans a rather better deal than was previously thought possible.' He said it could be that the Germans were moving away from the Common Market and closer to Russia, possibly in return for German reunification. 'Schmidt is entirely reliable, but if Strauss becomes Chancellor the situation could look quite different. I just mention this because I think people should know but it is very confidential and I don't want anyone to mention it.'

I must say it immediately flashed through my mind that, with the dictatorial methods of the Common Market and with German arrogance, the Germans are beginning to flex their muscles again, thirty-five years after the war. The possibility occurred to me that the Russians might offer Germany reunification as a way of getting her out of NATO and into a more neutral position, to safeguard Russia's western flank while she copes with China. If that were to happen, the Common Market would no longer be able to control Europe. This is all over the horizon but I have thought for some time that this would be the great issue of the Eighties.

Afterwards I walked over to the Foreign Office with David Owen for lunch which Frances and Owen's political adviser attended. He had replaced the picture of Palmerston with a huge oil painting of the thirty-two-year-old King of Nepal. Extraordinary. At least Palmerston was a British Foreign Secretary.

We chatted over lunch and after a while he said, 'Let's get down to business. First of all, your inquiry into the security services.'

I was amazed; it had never occurred to me that he would raise that. He is officially in charge of MI6, but still I was staggered – the second Minister within four hours to raise it. I sat quietly and he continued, 'I can see a case for a periodic review but I don't think much can come out. I took complete control of security, just like Merlyn, but it wouldn't be a bad idea if we had some collective discussion, maybe in the Cabinet.'

I said, 'There is the Security Commission, I believe.'

'I'd have to have a word with Jim about that,' he answered. But he did say, 'Whatever you do, don't recommend the centralisation of security under the Prime Minister; it is much better to have the power diffused in the hands of the Foreign Secretary and the Home Secretary, with the Prime Minister keeping an eye on it.'

The idea that either Merlyn or David Owen could stand up in any way against the Prime Minister on security matters, particularly as Jim has himself been Foreign Secretary and Home Secretary – not to mention Chancellor – seemed to me inconceivable.

'Of course,' said David, 'there is anxiety about security being in the hands of unsuitable people. For example, the Tory MP for Wycombe, Ray Whitney, who is terribly right-wing, was the head of the FO's Information Research Department before it was wound up.'

The IRD was the Intelligence organisation which a Colonel Sheridan asked me to join in 1946, and from which Jenny Little came. I looked out of the corner of my eye and saw Owen's political adviser taking a keen interest in this discussion and I wondered why.

I said, 'Well, I've taken a lot of trouble over this problem of accountability. Peter Archer [Solicitor-General] is in favour of it, and I have spoken to Len Murray and Harry Urwin. I think we should look at what would be a sensible scheme for *running* the security services rather than try to find out what's going on now. Then we can consider how we can bring it into line and publish more information.'

Frances Morrell said, 'This must be an area of policy on which the Labour Party is entitled to have a view.'

David Owen did behave as if he was God's gift to civil liberties. Later he observed, 'There is disgraceful disloyalty in the Foreign Office and the first one to make a slip is out. They pass minutes across to other people and so on.'

At 2.45 Sir Brooks Richards came to see me. He is officially a Deputy Secretary in the Cabinet Office and co-ordinates the security services under Sir John Hunt. The office knew little else about him and just described him as 'The Man from UNCLE'. He is a weak, aristocratic and rather wet ex-diplomat – they are all paper tigers of course.

He began by saying that Sir John Hunt had suggested I might like to see the information on Iran; this information was considered by an Intelligence Committee in the Cabinet Office, and a Department of Energy representative saw all these telegrams. There was also a secret network known as Comint, which intercepted Iranian military intelligence and could tell us a bit about what was happening to the monarchy there. It shared common intelligence with the Americans and was therefore beneficial to us. 'In order to have access to this,' he said, 'you will have to sign this form.' He opened his briefcase and produced two A4 pages.

'That's very kind of you,' I replied, 'but I don't know whether I do really need to know. Nobody has asked my opinion on Iran. I read the telegrams from Tehran, I read the newspapers, and I am told the oil figures. But my interest is only really in oil. I have never heard of this form.'

'It's for people on the Defence and Overseas Policy Committee.'

'Well, I was on DOP in 1969 and 1970 and I was never asked to fill in a form. How long has the form been in existence?'

'Certainly since the end of the war,' he said. 'Baldwin accidentally gave away some secret interception details and we lost control of the Soviet ciphers. A former Tsarist cryptographer who had defected to the west had been helping us, but after Baldwin's mistake we lost control.'

The form was all filled out with my name on it, asking me to recognise that I would be getting very secret information and to swear that I would not disclose it to anybody, and stating that I would be liable to prosecution under the Official Secrets Act unless any information I disclosed was authorised by the Department of Energy.

I realised what the visit was all about. It was to get me to sign a Top Security form which would enable the security services to proceed against me if they wished to do so, or commit me in a way that was quite unnecessary. In my judgement it was obviously to do with my inquiry into the security services.

'What's the position between me and people in the Cabinet who haven't signed the form?' I asked. 'Can I talk about Iran?'

'You'd have to be very discreet. You would of course know who else had signed – other DOP members.'

I told him I wouldn't like to be in a position where I couldn't talk candidly to members of the Cabinet. 'I have been very discreet in my time. I have handled a great deal of high-security classified stuff – "Top Secret Atomic UK Eyes Only" – but I have never filled in such a form. I wouldn't dream of disclosing anything I shouldn't. But this procedure seems strange to me; I don't understand it.'

In the end I said, 'Thank you very much for coming but I don't really think I do need to know. If you have any problems over particular information, can't you let me have it in an informal way without divulging the source of your information? And if I have any problems and I need information I will ask about it.'

His face absolutely fell. As we walked out towards the lift, he remarked, 'Isn't that an RNVR tie you're wearing?' I said, 'It certainly is. I was a pilot in the Fleet Air Arm.' When I looked him up in *Who's Who* afterwards, I found he was a lieutenant-commander in the navy with a DSC and bar.

# NOTES
*Chapter Four*

1. (p. 352) At the Bremen summit meeting in July 1978 of the Common Market Heads of Government (the European Council) a scheme for a European Monetary System was proposed and on 18 September the finance Ministers of the EEC agreed the details of the operation of the system, although the UK expressed reservations. Barbara Castle and other senior members of the Labour Party, including me, who opposed the EMS were keen to try to prevent the agreement of the Government to it at the next meeting of the European Council in December 1978.

# 5
# The Winter of Discontent
## December 1978–May 1979

*The 'Winter of Discontent' was a phrase borrowed from Shakespeare's* Richard
III *by the unlikely person of Larry Lamb, then editor of the* Sun, *to describe the
mood of Britain in the early months of 1979, when at one point one and a half
million workers were on strike against Government pay policy. The Conservatives
used images of uncollected rubbish covered in snow piled high in the streets, of health
workers withdrawing their labour from hospitals, of the 'dead left unburied', to
great effect in their May General Election campaign; and perpetuated the myth that
the Labour Government was defeated because it was too left-wing, that it was
controlled by the trade union movement, and was ultimately destroyed by the unions.*

*The Government's policy had been seriously breached by the workers at Ford in
November 1978, and after that the Cabinet was engaged in a damage-limitation
exercise followed by virtual abandonment of a pay policy as different groups of
workers refused to accept a fall in living standards. In December 1978 I was
directly involved with an overtime ban and possible total strike by oil-tanker drivers,
employed by BP, Esso, Texaco, Mobil and Shell. Fears of a serious national crisis
in oil and petrol supplies triggered off pressure within the Government for a
proclamation of an energy emergency. I argued – successfully – against such a
decision and my diary for December is inevitably preoccupied with the day-to-day
development of this drama.*

*The drivers succeeded in getting 12–15 per cent rises, settling with the individual
oil companies in January, but their dispute was compounded by a strike of lorry
drivers in the road haulage industry which was made official by the Transport and
General Workers' Union on 11 January 1979 and for which regional emergency
committees were activated by the Government, under the control of Bill Rodgers,
Secretary of State for Transport. This dispute was much more disrupting than
either the Government or the Road Haulage Association expected, demonstrating
the extent to which the country had come to depend on the movement of relatively
small supplies of crucial items by road.*

*Although concerned in my capacity as a Cabinet Minister with the general
situation during the first three months of 1979, day-to-day developments and
decisions on other stoppages were not my responsibility and details of individual
strikes are not recorded in my diary.*

*The Conservatives concentrated their attacks on local authority and Health Service workers belonging to the TGWU, GMWU, COHSE and NUPE. These unions included among their members low-paid water and sewerage workers, gravediggers, hospital ancillary workers and ambulance personnel, and their stoppages, working-to-rule and overtime bans to win pay increases were emotively exploited by the Opposition; in fact there was only one one-day stoppage, in which 125,000 manual workers took part on 22 January. Between 16 January and 5 February five parliamentary debates were concerned with the economic and industrial situation.*

*There were four one-day stoppages by 20,000 train drivers in January, which coincided with severe snow blizzards, causing chaotic conditions for travellers. Action by the Association of Broadcasting Staffs blacked out BBC television before Christmas, and between February and April clerical and executive civil servants carried out widespread action affecting even the staff at Number 10.*

### Friday 1 December

Lunch with George Williams of the United Kingdom Offshore Oil Operators Association – a nice man of about fifty-seven who had served with my brother Mike in the North African Coastal Air Force in Algiers. He was a wing commander and Mike was a flight lieutenant. Williams also knew Father. He'd been a station commander in Suffolk at the end of the war and he'd been told that Air Commodore Lord Stansgate was coming to visit. Father had said to him, 'We are just about to win the war; how are we going to win the peace?'

Had an appointment with Guido Brunner, the Commissioner from Brussels, to consider Euratom arrangements, which are hair-raisingly federalist.

Brunner said, 'Let us tell you first of all what the Supply Agency set up under the Euratom Treaty will do in normal conditions, then how it will handle the oil crisis and what it will do about investment.'

There was a German and a British lawyer present. The German explained that the Agency would have a common supply policy, and a monopoly of all trade in nuclear materials, would monitor and control all fissile material, would impose safeguard clauses and would ensure that competition was preserved. It would be up to market forces to fix the price of natural uranium and intervention would be limited. It would conclude contracts for the purchase and sale of nuclear materials and give its seal of approval for all uranium contracts. The public utilities might not have the strength to bargain and this would help to beat the cartels.

A man from the AEA provided more information. After thanking them I asked how we would be affected. 'For example, if we discovered uranium in Britain and wanted to use it, would that be all right?'

'You would have to ask permission from the Supply Agency to use your own uranium, and if the Commission didn't permit it you could take the matter to the Court. But if the Commission took it over it would pay a negotiated price.'

'And if we buy foreign uranium what would happen?'

'The Supply Agency would be a monopoly purchaser. It would have to guarantee that the purchase of uranium did not affect the free market or upset the international obligations of the EEC or use safeguards language that was unacceptable.'

Then I asked, 'Would the Agency have their own stocks of uranium?'

'Yes, they would have the right to stockpile.'

On weapons and weapons-grade materials, I said, 'Would we be allowed to sell high-enriched uranium to a research reactor in France but not to a research reactor, say, in Italy?'

They got terribly embarrassed with all these questions and began arguing amongst themselves. But they said the Court could rule that there would be no restriction on the supply of fissile materials within the Community because it would interfere with the nuclear Common Market, which would mean that the Euratom Treaty would be used almost to encourage the proliferation of nuclear weapons. All high-enrichment uranium had to be offered to the Agency, and the Agency would acquire ownership of all plutonium from reprocessing.

I said, 'If BNFL reprocesses CEGB fuel elements and then wants to sell the recovered uranium to the fast breeder reactor in Scotland, what would happen?'

'Oh,' they said, 'the Supply Agency would have to do it; the contract between the CEGB and the AEA would have to go through the Agency.'

'How realistic is all this?' I asked.

Brunner, who is a stupid bureaucrat and who, I think, took my questions to be quite innocent, said that the procedures were being devised.

'What happens if you don't get the procedures agreed?' I asked. 'If you don't confirm the revision of the Treaty? Surely you are deadlocked by vetoes.'

'We can't put the clock back,' said Brunner.

It was, dare I say it, a devastating cross-examination without giving them grounds for complaint, and I think, when they left, they realised how ludicrous the whole thing was. This is a complete Common Market takeover of our nuclear policy and it is wholly unacceptable. My blood pressure must have been very high at the end of the meeting because it took me a few minutes to calm down. I doubt if we will get support unless the nuclear lobby splits off from the European lobby. They are normally the same, but they might be divided on this issue, and I might get British nuclear lobby support.

*Saturday 2 December*

Caroline and I had dinner with Geoffrey Goodman and his wife and Dick Clements and his wife Biddy, who is Ramsay MacDonald's granddaughter. Biddy's mother and her elder sister Ishbel moved into Number 10 in 1924 and, because their mother had died when they were young, Ishbel became the hostess at the age of sixteen. Biddy said that Ishbel had written her memoirs and had sent them seven years ago to a publisher but they never arrived. Ishbel had been completely relaxed about the loss but to me it sounded like one of the great literary tragedies of our time.

*Monday 4 December*

My first appointment was with Tom Farmer, an old American colleague who was with me at Oxford. He is now one of the three presidential advisers on the security services.

After a preliminary chat, he said to me, 'By the way, I saw in the *Guardian* that you're working on something to do with security.'

'Do you mean the report I wrote on security? I think I have got a copy.' I gave it him and then I said, 'Remind me what your interest in this is.'

He described his job, which is to monitor the American security services and their guidelines. 'I look at individual projects that come up and put to the President those that might have political implications.' Then he added, 'Of course, in this country the Prime Minister doesn't really seem to know what's going on.'

I said, 'Broadly, the only thing that could be studied here seems to be our guidelines. You can't deal with individual projects and security operations but the guidelines ought to be clear. As far as I remember, when I last saw you, you had come across to talk to people here because the British security services were worried about what was happening in America.'

'Yes,' he said, 'they were afraid there might be a leakage at the American end that would interfere with the very close links we have with British Intelligence.'

I shouldn't have done but I asked, 'I suppose you have seen everything relating to my report?' He didn't blink an eyelid and was trying to be friendly. I added, 'In general, you know, we are trying to model ourselves on American practice because we are now experiencing the ripples of Watergate in Britain.'

At the Organisation Sub-Committee of the NEC, we came to Eric Heffer's paper calling for a committee or working party on collective Cabinet responsibility, and, since he was in the chair, I moved it. 'Collective responsibility of Cabinet began in order to protect the Cabinet against the King,' I pointed out. 'Nobody can be bound by what they say when they are discussing a future Parliament and I hope we will go ahead with this.'

Michael Foot said this was a far-reaching constitutional question. He had no objection to a working party looking at the issue but not just before a General Election. 'Neither side can push its rights to extremes. We all have many loyalties.'

By 8 votes to 4, we agreed to set up a sub-committee or working party.

### Tuesday 5 December

The press made much of the decision to set up a working party on collective Cabinet responsibility, and it was presented as a direct attack by me on Jim.

Frances and Francis were upset and angry, and said I was getting too exposed again, what with the security inquiry, this and various other issues.

### Thursday 7 December

Cabinet, and on the EMS summit Jim had little to say. Sterling was firm and the final decision of both the Irish and the Italians on the EMS had been deferred. At Brussels Jim had stated our unwillingness to join the exchange rate mechanism to be set up on 1 January 1979, while being prepared to participate in other aspects of the system.

He then said that a proposal had come up that there should be an informal summit meeting between Schmidt, Giscard, himself and President Carter on the island of Guadeloupe to discuss political and security developments.

'Where is Guadeloupe?' asked Peter.

'It's a French island in the Caribbean,' said Jim, obviously pleased that he had been included, because it showed he was still part of the big league. 'But keep it very quiet because the French don't want it to get out.'

A few minutes later someone came in and handed Jim a note. He then announced, 'I can tell you that the *New York Times* have published the news so we can now refer to it.'

Jim's psychology is quite extraordinary.

We came to the main item on the agenda, which was pay, in the light of tonight's adjournment debate forced by the Tories on 'the unjust and arbitrary use of sanctions on industry'. The discussion gave a good indication of how the Cabinet is thinking at this moment.

Denis introduced it. 'Half a million people have now settled within the guidelines and only two companies – Ford and British Oxygen – have exceeded them. We must get across how well the policy is working. The *Financial Times* has shown that the sanctions are frightening quite a number of firms and the polls indicate support for our policy.'

He wanted more Cabinet Ministers to speak out on pay policy. The TUC General Council did not want confrontation, not even Clive Jenkins wanted it, and the TUC Economic Committee was meeting with a group of Ministers.

Jim then took up the issue. 'The purpose of this Cabinet is a morale-building exercise because the public and the trade union and Party rank and file all support the policy.'

David Ennals was afraid the public services might unite against the Government, and Fred Peart warned that the public-service unions were now very militant.

'Yes,' said Jim, 'it's in the public sector that we shall have the most trouble.'

Harold Lever said, 'Sanctions are not intended to hurt, only to help create a climate for pay restraint. No doubt some solo pianists with the London Philharmonic Orchestra could earn more money working in a brothel, but they don't do it. It is a moral question.'

Roy Hattersley thought that CBI anxiety over the sanctions was based on the fear that they might be extended to cover other areas, such as planning agreements. He believed legislation was the only answer on pay limits.

Jim said, 'I dislike not having a statutory cover and in the next Parliament we had better start with a clean sheet.'

I took this to mean Jim was in favour of going over to a statutory pay policy in the next session, or at least statutory sanctions – this was the first indication of Jim's real thinking on this.

He added, 'The use of powers without parliamentary authority is weighing on my conscience a little.'

'What about tonight's vote?' Merlyn asked. 'MPs are very worried.'

Jim said, 'It is going to be difficult and I shall be interested to see what happens.'

'What do you think you are going to do?' asked Stan.

Jim replied, tight-lipped, 'I have no intention of enlightening you now.'

Then we discussed the issue of low-paid workers, and Albert Booth said it was a real problem. 'I would like a £3 minimum rise, that's to say nobody who is low-paid should get less than £3 as a result of the 5 per cent. Some of the lowest-paid will get only £2.15 or £2.25 on the present guidelines. The poorest people in the community are no better off now than they were in 1949; indeed, the lowest quarter of all are worse off.'

Michael Foot supported Albert, and Jim said, 'It's just a moral issue.'

Denis intervened, 'Child benefit and other assistance of that kind have helped the low-paid. Employers in the private sector couldn't afford to pay £3.'

In the end, the Cabinet agreed to resume discussions, especially in the light of the TUC Economic Committee's meeting with Ministers.

At the PLP meeting, Jim made a speech about the crucial vote tonight. He was on his way to meet Premier Trudeau of Canada and came in only for a moment. 'This motion tonight on the adjournment debate is not a technical motion but a political one. If we lose it will be a body blow to the Government. The Tories expect to win, and Saatchi & Saatchi would very quickly exploit it. The political initiative would pass to the Tories. Personally I don't like sanctions, but the private sector must be checked to help with the public sector. I would be happy to have further meetings with the trade unions and I appeal to trade union members to recognise the Tories' hatred for them, and the necessity of winning this evening.'

I must say, it was a very effective statement. None of the Wilson-type bullying or thuggery; it was quiet and absolutely serious.

While we were sitting there, the annunciator – the television screen that tells you what's happening in the Chamber – was flashing up confusing information. Points of order were coming up, then 'Sitting suspended for ten minutes.' The House met again at 8 pm and the regular adjournment debate was getting under way when someone in the Strangers' Gallery threw a pot of paint into the Chamber. The debate was postponed and I came home.

### Saturday 9 December
To Newcastle for an NUM dinner. Arthur Scargill told me there was a rumour that Joe Gormley was going to go in July, so Arthur is busy campaigning all over the place for the presidency of the NUM. He told me a story about one of his NUM officials in Yorkshire who suspected that his phone was being tapped, so the official rang up a friend by prearrangement and told him there was going to be a huge picket at a particular power station (which wasn't true). He then drove past the station and found lots of police cars there.

### Monday 11 December
I had a report from my Under-Secretary, Robert Priddle, about the oil-tanker drivers' dispute, for which the Civil Contingencies Unit had produced Operation Drumstick. There are two options: to mobilise troops before Christmas, which would of course be very provocative to the unions; or wait till after Christmas, which might be too late to prevent a serious oil shortage. I decided to go for the slower option and try to get the guidelines slightly fudged – which the Prime Minister would endorse. If an emergency arose, we would then ask the unions

themselves to maintain essential services, thus avoiding the use of troops.

## Tuesday 12 December

The press attacks go on. The *Daily Mail* wrote an article implying that when the House of Lords was abolished we would have no more elections in Britain – a scandalous comment.

EY began at 10.10 with Gerald Kaufman reporting on a recommendation from a study group that we accept BSC's proposed closure of Shotton steelworks. This would be a direct breach of a clear pledge given by the Chairman, Charles Villiers, and by Eric Varley last year that Shotton would not be closed until 1982–3.

Kaufman said there was substantial over-capacity in the steel industry and the situation would deteriorate further with the coming on stream of the new integrated steel plants at Ravenscraig and Redcar. 'BSC now proposes major closures at Corby and Shotton in 1979–80. These are the best closures to choose if we are going to follow this course. It would involve 5000 redundancies at Shotton in North Wales, affecting Merseyside, and 5500 at Corby. Male unemployment in Shotton would double, and at Corby it would increase from 20 per cent to 28 per cent. But the failure to close Shotton would cost £29 million and defer the viability target for BSC beyond 1980 to 1981.' He said the Foreign Office and the Department of Trade feared that keeping the plants open would give rise to American and Common Market objections.

Eric Varley said it would be very difficult for him because in Merseyside Dunlop were about to announce another 3000 redundancies.

Jim asked, 'Why, with all these redundancy announcements, are the figures for unemployment going down?'

'Because the service industries are picking up redundant workers,' said Denis.

Albert Booth said, 'It's also because of a tremendous mobility in labour – last year something like 8 million job changes took place.'

Jim Callaghan pointed out that, as far as Cardiff was concerned, half the redundant steelworkers had found jobs and at Corby and Shotton it would surely be the same; therefore we should consider it.

Michael Foot believed that the unions had to be brought in. 'We should seek union comments before we make a decision because we did make a pledge on Shotton.'

'That just shows the unwisdom of giving pledges,' said Jim gruffly.

John Morris reminded us of the electoral consequences next year and urged that the pledge be respected. There could be a national strike and that would be a disaster.

Jim said, 'In Cardiff I had to face the problems of a broken pledge, and I can tell you that I am having more trouble with the steelworkers who had to *continue* working than with the ones who took their redundancy money. Indeed, it's the ones who stayed on and didn't get the money who won't be voting for me.'

I asked, 'What would be the estimated cost of the closures in terms of the Assisted Area Status we would have to give, providing redundancy and unemployment pay, tax losses, the rate and rent losses, and the possible consequences for coal? The North Sea oil is keeping our payments in balance, but behind that we are de-industrialising motor car assembly, shipbuilding, now steel and possibly coal. We must talk to the unions before we decide.'

'That means you are in favour of doing nothing,' said Jim.

'No, I am in favour of operating, as we always said we would, on a tripartite basis through some sort of a planning agreement.'

Eric Varley said, 'We have talked to the unions, and, as far as BSC is concerned, the six elected steelworkers on the BSC board support Villiers.'

Of course, this is exactly what workers opposed to having representatives on company boards really fear – that they join the management intellectually and cease to represent their men. That is why, in my view, workers on a board are such a disaster.

Jim said, 'We can't prevent the board from going ahead.'

Michael Foot argued, 'You can't let BSC loose on the unions – the Government must be involved.'

'Why?' asked Jim.

'To hear the trade union view,' Michael replied.

Jim said, 'Can Eric talk it over with Bill Sirs, the General Secretary of the iron and steel unions?'

'I already have talked to the unions,' Eric replied.

Denis Healey observed, 'Bill Sirs is in a very difficult mood. I don't mind Eric seeing him to get his views but you can't take the decision out of the hands of BSC.'

'Summing up,' said Jim, 'Eric will see Sirs, the Government should support BSC, and there could be a tripartite committee to consider the consequences of the closures.'

So now the purpose of tripartitism is to deal with decisions *after* they have been made!

At the end Jim thanked Kaufman, and Kaufman left – the butcher, on behalf of the Government, of another great industry. I don't know what to do. I say my piece and nobody takes any notice. I can tell that Jim is angry with me at the moment and there is nothing more I can do.

*Wednesday 13 December*
Did my box and then watched *Edward and Mrs Simpson*, a marvellous programme about how to get rid of the King, with Baldwin, Monckton, Attlee and Churchill.

At 10 we had a division on the debate – suspended last week – in which Mrs Thatcher had tabled an amendment condemning the use of sanctions on firms to restrict pay rises. It was carried by 6 votes – owing to five Labour abstentions.

So Jim got up immediately and announced that the Government was going to ask for a vote of confidence tomorrow. There were wild cheers and counter-cheers.

I saw Dick Mabon later and gave him a drink in my room. He told me that Jim was going to resign tomorrow.

'Really?'

'Oh yes,' said Dick, 'absolutely. That's the word. He has this idea that he is God – he is so dictatorial. He's got to go, got to go. But not now. He no longer talks to any of his friends, only Tom McCaffrey. It would be better if he stayed until after the Election, but if we lose the vote of confidence tomorrow his leadership of the Party will be contested. Denis will get it.'

It emerged that Dick Mabon knew all this because he had been appointed campaign manager to Denis Healey, and Denis had offered him a job in his Cabinet. Dick told me that Denis had said he would get on with Tony Benn, and he would give me a top job. Michael Foot would have to give way so that I could be Deputy Leader. 'Top job for Tony, no problem about that,' said Dick. 'You will have to stand. I expect Peter Shore will try to get ahead of you, and John Silkin might stand; but Denis will win and, in a few years' time, it will be your turn.'

I said, 'Well, Dick, I'm afraid I couldn't offer you a seat in my Government because I would go for the *election* of the Cabinet.'

Came home, exhausted.

*Thursday 14 December*
Cabinet had been deferred by half an hour and there were a million photographers outside Number 10.

I noticed there was no hostility over last night's vote. Jim was cheerful and there was no reproaching the left, as on past occasions.

Mike Cocks declared, 'The prospects for tonight are not bad.' He told us that the five Labour defectors yesterday were Ron Thomas, Syd Bidwell, Eddie Loyden, Roy Hughes and Arthur Latham.

'Sam Silkin's view', said Denis, 'is that we should now drop the sanctions on employers, and I agree. Though sanctions have been valuable as a deterrent, we think that the cost to the private sector will be about 1 per cent on the wage bill.'

Peter Shore followed. 'There is an immediate issue in the public services and, as far as last night is concerned, our moral authority on pay policy has been stripped from us. We need a reassertion of our authority. If not, we should go to the country.' So he is hawkish too, throwing down the gauntlet. To whom? To the trade unions?

Jim said, 'Well, a "Who Governs Britain" Election was tried in 1974 and wasn't very successful. I wish we didn't have all this Election talk. It's an invitation to the Tories to prepare.'

Hattersley thought we couldn't ignore the House of Commons and act in a totalitarian way.

I was going to speak but I didn't.

Jim had said something about how he was really going to fight and Denis replied, 'Who would have thought the old man to have had so much blood in him?' – a quotation from *Macbeth*.

We won the vote of confidence this evening by 10.

### Friday 15 December

My first appointment was at EY(P), the Cabinet committee that handles pay matters, and the first item was an oral report on the oil-tanker drivers' overtime ban.

Last week we had approved putting the troops on standby for after Christmas and Jim had sent a minute saying he wanted the whole thing quietened down; he didn't want troops on standby or anything of that kind until much later.

I said that, now the sanctions were over, the unions would be rallying round the Government, and the oil companies could settle.

Denis kept interrupting me, 'There's no question of the pay policy going.'

'Denis, will you please let me finish. You never let anybody finish and you don't listen to what they say.' So he shut up and I got my point across. It was agreed that Albert Booth and I should see Len Murray on Monday.

Later today the Government was defeated in the Commons over the use of economic sanctions against Ford, following their settlement of 17 per cent with their workers last month.

### Sunday 17 December

Worked at home this morning, and in the afternoon Lissie and I sat and watched the end of *The Railway Children* and I had a good weep.

I must say, the more I think about the political situation, the more it looks as if the whole atmosphere is clouding over. I can see a series of disputes starting in the early part of the year. The oil-tanker drivers' dispute could drag on, and then we go into the spring with a deepening world recession as a result of the impending oil price rises.

*Monday 18 December*

Went over to the Department of Employment to meet Len Murray, Albert Booth and Merlyn Rees, to discuss how to handle the oil-tanker drivers' dispute.

Then at 4.30 I had what turned out to be a very useful meeting on the dispute with Albert, Moss Evans and Jack Ashwell, national officer of the TGWU. I explained the problems if the strike started on 3 January and we had to call the troops in. We would have to put people on alert immediately. I told them I would like to get the goodwill of the T&G.

Jack said, 'That's OK.'

Moss Evans asked Jack Ashwell if the strike could be deferred and Jack said no.

'Of course,' said Moss, 'we don't want the troops used.'

'Neither do we,' I told him, 'but if I need to use them I will have to declare a state of emergency.'

We agreed that I would see Moss again and discuss how we would handle the emergency arrangements in the event of a strike. It is very exciting because, if you call in the trade unions to help you allocate oil, then you are getting to a situation of joint government.

Albert and I went straight to EY(P), the committee on pay, where Albert reported on our meeting.

I said, 'Moss will help us to avoid the use of troops, but if we have to use them we would need a state of emergency.'

Sir Clive Rose pointed out that under the 1976 Energy Act there would have to be four emergency orders: to release the oil companies from their legal requirement to supply; to restrict the hours of petrol stations; to arrange for the closure of some petrol stations; and to prohibit cans being filled at petrol stations.

Denis said, 'This will have to come to Cabinet tomorrow.'

'Not until I have discussed it with Moss,' I said. 'I hope we won't decide anything except upon a contingency basis.' It was agreed I would see Moss in the morning.

'I want to draw the threads together,' said Healey. 'On pay, there will be no move. On the strike, we must give the unions a description of the essential supplies and services required, and explain the implications for deliveries. If there is a strike, we will have to recall Parliament early in January.'

I said I wanted the unions involved in the meeting of the Four Wise Men – the military commander, the Chief Constable, the Regional Commissioner and the head of the Oil Committee in each region.

It was left that I would report at Cabinet tomorrow.

We adjourned at 7.30 and I went over to McDonald's and whom should I see there but Ralph Gibson and his son; I thought it was a sign of the times that a High Court judge and the Secretary of State for

Energy should be queuing up for hamburgers next to Westminster Cathedral!

Came home and brought my diary up to date. When you get trade union leaders and Labour Ministers together, there is no hostility or difficulty; it's just a question of finding a way through. Gradually Ministers and the unions could get together and run the country in the same way that the Tory Party and the business community have. The trouble is that our civil servants are uneasy with the trade unions. In any case I am not in favour of a corporate arrangement. But the dispute is an interesting example.

*Tuesday 19 December*

Moss Evans came at 9.30 and I had a few officials with me. I gave Moss a paper called 'Essential Services' outlining the measures the Government has drawn up for use in the event of an oil emergency. They would mean in effect that 4000 out of the 33,000 petrol stations would be kept open for motor users; and there would be a list of essential services that would have to be met. I also offered Moss close consultations at national level between him and me, and between Jack Ashwell and Dick Mabon, whom I had put in charge of an Oil Industry Emergency Committee. I asked him for a list of all the union's regional officers with whom I should maintain contact.

The final point of the paper appealed to the TGWU to maintain the oil deliveries to the extent necessary to keep essential services going. He said he would take it away and think about it. Then I dismissed the officials and said, 'Look, Moss, we are in a hell of a jam because the timetable for the use of troops is such that I will have to make a move this week if I can't get the TGWU's agreement. We have got to find a way through, particularly now pay sanctions are over. I can't give a nod and wink to the oil companies: the Government can't now push the companies to settle – that's asking too much.'

Moss appreciates the terrible political damage of using troops and I am hopeful.

To Cabinet, and Jim was in a frightfully cheerful mood and joked, and the atmosphere was very jolly. The first item was the tanker drivers' dispute, and I had to give a report. 'Prime Minister, I shall have to carry the can – the only one with petrol in it! On the strictest interpretation of an emergency, we would have to notify the instructors and the troops today. The instructors would begin training drivers on Boxing Day; on 29 December we would go to Sandringham for the Privy Council to declare a state of emergency; on the 30th and 31st we would requisition 4000 tankers; on 3 January the strike would begin and we would recall Parliament; on 5 January Parliament would be asked to approve the state of emergency, and by then we would have about 15 per cent of our normal petrol supplies. By 6 January we would be able to supply 30 per cent of the nation's oil needs.'

It was a pretty difficult scenario, and so we had looked at an alternative, namely whether we could get a contingency agreement with the unions to guarantee 30 per cent of supplies without the troops. 'Yesterday Albert and Merlyn and I saw Len Murray, who steered us to Moss. We saw Moss in the afternoon and he and Jack Ashwell gave a clear undertaking that the union would help with emergency supplies. This morning I saw Moss again and gave him the list of essential services.'

Jim asked, 'Should we take advantage of the T&G offer? Industry without oil would be in real trouble. Secondly, do we advise the companies to settle? And, thirdly, when do we proclaim a state of emergency?'

Bruce Millan and Stan Orme thought the TGWU should be brought fully into the emergency arrangements. Fred Mulley said it would be feasible to get the troops in within four or five days, but it would create real problems in deployment, on picket lines and with the police; he hoped it could be avoided.

'The way this has all been described,' said Jim, 'I can see an enormous Thatcher victory. I wonder whether life in these islands will break down.' After further discussion Jim concluded that Albert and I should be supported in our efforts to postpone the strike.

Merlyn said that we had better activate the Four Wise Men to start preparing in every region today.

'OK, and please keep secrecy,' agreed Jim. So that was how it was left.

Cabinet ended at about 12.20, and I had a drink with Peter Shore and Stan Orme. Jim came up to us and said, 'Do you know, I just feel that 1979 is going to be my year. I think everything is going to come right.' I thought for a moment he was joking, but I am sure he was serious. I nearly asked, 'Have you tried walking on water, and will you rise on the third day?', but thought it irreverent.

I was due to have a meeting with Moss Evans, Alex Kitson who is a TGWU official and Albert at 6.45, but at 6.15 I had a message from Moss, saying, 'They've turned me down, there is no point in seeing you. They won't accept the essential supplies.' I said, 'You must come; I have to make a report tonight.'

So Moss, Alex and Jack Ashwell turned up at 6.45, and told us what had happened. 'We gave the Texaco shop stewards the list of supplies. Jack Ashwell argued for emergencies, but the only emergencies they will accept are fire, ambulance, police, hospitals, old people, British Oxygen gases and livestock. Beyond that any discussion about who should get what would be a matter for local decision.'

The men had turned it down because they thought the emergency supplies defined on our list would prolong the dispute and they were determined not to supply any oil to power stations or for gas and electricity operations. They said there was no prospect of deferring the date of the strike beyond 3 January. Indeed, the men had increased the overtime ban to bring forward the crunch.

Moss said, 'The plain truth is, we can't deliver.'

I then reported on the exact emergency arrangements that would be needed. 'Now I must tell you that today we should alert the troops.' I went through the timetable and said the situation was awful. 'Let's look at the prospects for a settlement. The pay offer of 13.7 per cent could be acceptable if the conditions were removed.'

Alex Kitson said to me, 'We are sticking up for TUC and Labour Party policy, and the official policy is a return to free collective bargaining. I can't bargain with you.'

'I'm not bargaining. I am just trying to find out what the position is. If the Government withdraws completely from the battlefield, what will happen?'

Alex replied, 'We will get the money by strike action.'

I said, 'Then I will have to use troops to protect people in the meanwhile.'

I agreed to see Moss tomorrow at 1 o'clock after his meeting with his General Council and my meeting with the NEC.

From there I went with Albert to EY(P) at 8 and reported what had happened.

Denis said, 'There will have to be advance warning to the troops on Thursday at the latest, and Moss's ability and will to help us are both limited.'

I suggested, 'Let's defer it for a couple of days if we can', and Clive Rose said that the Four Wise Men were not actually meeting until Thursday.

Someone remarked that the Cabinet had agreed they should meet today.

'Well, we thought it inadvisable.'

So officials simply changed the Cabinet decision.

Mabon said, 'Give Moss a chance on Thursday.'

It was agreed we would meet again tomorrow at 2.

Went up to the Press Office Christmas party. Nobody asked about the tanker drivers, thank God. The key thing now is that the story shouldn't break.

*Wednesday 20 December*
At 1 o'clock I went to the meeting that had been arranged with Moss Evans, Jack Ashwell, Alex, Dick Mabon and Albert.

The first thing I did was to hand around copies of the quarterly report of the Price Commission, showing it couldn't be used to enforce pay policy, and the draft statement that had been before EY(P) which proved that the Government really had abandoned pay sanctions completely.

I pointed out, 'We are therefore back in a situation of free collective bargaining, but the Government can't press the companies to pay more; that would be absurd.' Did they want me to attend the shop stewards' national negotiating meeting tomorrow?

Alex Kitson didn't think it would be right for me to go to it.

Jack and Moss told me that the lads would not defer the strike without a new offer and that nothing would be moving over Christmas.

This meeting ended just before 2, and I went straight from there to the Cabinet Office for the EY(P). I gave the latest news; Albert reported that Esso meet tomorrow, Mobil meet on 27 December, and Shell and Texaco had no date fixed. BP won't meet the TGWU until they withdraw their ban on contractors. Moss will try to get the full 30 per cent cover.

Denis Healey asked about petrol supplies. Clive Rose said that the Contingencies Unit thought there were seven to fourteen days' supplies in the refineries.

Denis summed up, 'There has been no real change and there is likely to be a strike on 3 January; the overtime ban is beginning to bite; we should decide on giving the orders to troops tonight; training should commence on Boxing Day, and a proclamation should be made on 29 December.'

I went over to Transport House and looked into Moss Evans's room. He was sitting reading a book about Frank Cousins, having a rest. I said, 'Just to let you know, Moss, that the troops are being alerted today and we may have to have emergency orders under the Energy Act on Friday.'

He replied, 'Fine, fine.'

At 5.30 I went over to the new Home Office at Queen Anne's Gate. Merlyn reported that the Prime Minister had agreed on the warning being given to the troops tonight. A draft press statement by Clive Rose, announcing that 15,000 troops would be deployed, was read out.

I asked about the command structure, and it is quite clear we must set up a Department of Energy information centre tonight. The PM wants an emergency committee made up of Merlyn Rees, Fred Mulley, myself, Bill Rodgers, Denis Healey or Joel Barnett, Dick Mabon and Albert Booth. There will be an operations centre and something called the OSG – Operational Sub-Group – housed in the Cabinet Office. We shall all meet on a daily basis in Conference Room F. Technical enquiries will go to the Department of Energy, operational enquiries to the Cabinet Office.

The draft press briefing is being sent over to Moss. I am determined to run this emergency on the basis of open government. I said, 'We must make it clear what our objectives are and not run this like a military operation against an enemy. Dick will liaise with the companies. I will liaise with the Transport and General Workers' Union and I will stay at the centre of this.'

I think the authorities are determined to do it in a way that is hostile to labour whereas I am doing it in a way that is friendly to labour. It may be that it will all be settled because I think both the oil companies and the unions are only now beginning to realise that there will be absolute chaos if this strike takes place.

*Thursday 21 December*

At EY(P) Dick, Albert and I briefly described what was happening. We agreed to tell the press that, owing to local shortages of petrol, motorists on long journeys were advised to take account of the position in making their plans, and we decided not to make an emergency proclamation yet.

Denis said that the BBC was being bloody awful and that on the 1 o'clock news Peter Hennessy had referred to the Civil Contingencies Unit and this 'sinister' figure who ran it called Sir Clive Rose. There is a part of me that tells me that I am just being sucked into this terrible military operation. I know I have to protect emergency supplies, but there is no doubt I am compromised up to the hilt by remaining in this awful Government.

*Friday 22 December*

Radio 4 news this morning reported that troops were being prepared to be brought into the dispute. The *Guardian* quoted a senior army officer as saying, 'We will bloody well do the job properly, and in our funny military way we will be ready for everything.' The *Morning Star*'s headline was 'Troops in Germany Train to be Scabs for Healey'. I was extremely anxious and Caroline was very agitated.

At 8 Moss Evans called me to say that all the union negotiators working on the Esso offer had recommended acceptance. He asked that we didn't publish it because he wanted the men to hear directly from their negotiators, not on the news. So I went from one traumatic extreme to another in the course of one hour.

At 11 I went over to GEN 158, the Christmas emergency committee set up by the Prime Minister. Albert Booth reported on the Esso situation. Voting would not be completed until next Wednesday. The overtime ban was likely to be lifted immediately, and if the offer was accepted by the Esso drivers, this would provide a basis for all companies. Esso are offering to pay a combined rate of £78 for overtime and basic. The company had told Albert that this amounted to 12.8 per cent, 5.8 per cent of it being related to productivity, leaving a straight 7 per cent without strings.

Fred Mulley said, 'The soldiers have now all been told. All the notifications are out – but we could use the press to communicate any cancellation.'

'We have got to continue with the contingency planning,' Merlyn warned. 'The press coverage could affect both the public and the unions and we should try to dampen it.'

Bill Rodgers was worried that if the total settlement became known it would have implications for the Road Haulage Association, which is moving towards a 'bad' settlement for its drivers (ie a settlement whereby the men get too much money). He suggested that Albert could indicate publicly that the Esso offer is only 7 per cent.

We left it until Thursday, by which time more drivers' meetings would be over. It is now quite clear that, once you do begin bringing in the troops, the whole machine starts to move.

I went back to the office, and Albert and I met Moss Evans. We agreed on a statement along the lines that 'The Government understands that, in view of the progress made in the negotiations, some return to normal working is expected, but that some local shortages may persist.' He was content with that.

Then I came home and I went out shopping with Lissie.

### Saturday 23 December

I set myself the objective today of trying to stop the 160 army instructors from being brought back from leave on Boxing Day to prepare for a possible emergency on Friday.

At 12 we had another GEN 158 meeting, and I suggested that we stand down the instructors, first of all to give them a Christmas holiday and secondly to avoid provocation.

Merlyn Rees said, 'On the military side, we must go ahead with the preparations.'

'Can't we let it slip for three days, now that the situation is totally different?'

'You can't suddenly change instructions at this stage,' Merlyn replied.

Bill Rodgers said that the vehicles had to be got ready anyway. 'If it all goes wrong, we will have a proclamation on Friday the 29th. Arrangements will be made for a Privy Council at Sandringham at 5 o'clock on Friday. Who is to go?' There was no real answer to that.

I asked, 'Have any other preparations or decisions been taken that this committee should know about?'

Sir Clive Rose said, 'The Operational Sub-Group met yesterday, and it has set up a high-level airport co-ordinating group, because only nine airports would be allowed fuel. On filling stations, instructions have already been sent in bulk to the oil companies, but they will not be issued to filling stations on a regional basis until the end of next week.'

I remarked, 'Now I expect the Transport and General Workers' Union, both nationally and regionally, to get all the regulations at the same time as everyone else. That's very important.'

Sir Clive Rose continued, 'We have got an order which will come into force at 0001 hours on Saturday to close all pumps until midday Saturday. After that only 6000 stations will open with fuel supplies on the most restricted basis.'

*Monday 25 December*
The children arrived at 8 am and all came to the bedroom to give us their presents.

*Wednesday 27 December*
The news from the tanker drivers is not good. At Stanlow and Southampton the Esso offer has been rejected by the men, and tomorrow we have to make the big decision whether to mobilise the troops. Rang Moss Evans and he was hopeful.

*Thursday 28 December*
The situation in Iran is getting critical. Oil supply has dropped from 6 million to about half a million barrels of oil a day. The troops are shooting demonstrators; there is petrol rationing and there are rumours of importation of petrol. It looks as if the days of the Shah are numbered. So far I haven't felt in any way handicapped by the lack of secret signals.

GEN 158 was held at 11. Albert Booth was first to report. The Esso vote was very close and we wouldn't know about the other depots until noon tomorrow, or possibly 2 January. Twenty hours of negotiations with Shell had taken place already, with more to go. BP and Texaco were the most difficult.

Clive Rose raised the question of 'Save It' press advertisements which had been booked for 30 December and 2 and 3 January at a cost of £90,000 a day. He said we must decide today.

I should add that we had before us a whole range of options for handling the problem. I favoured Option C, which involved not doing anything until 2 January. Albert agreed.

Summing up, Merlyn Rees said, 'Option C is right. We will meet tomorrow. As to public information, we should say that essential services will be minimal. The decision on troops should be deferred day by day.'

The danger that I foresaw was that we would be driven, by the requirements for advertising and by the army arrangements, to advancing the emergency ahead of what was really necessary.

*Friday 29 December*
At 2.45 I went to the office to discuss whether the Department of Energy or the Cabinet Office should be the headquarters in the event of an emergency. I am clear that we don't want to take the lead in this. After all, the real news will be coming from the military, who will be moving the petrol, and from the Home Office, who will be responsible for any law and order problems that arise. We will be a low-level information centre.

*On 30 November 1978, after disagreements with its unions over the introduction of new technological equipment,* The Times *had locked out its employees and the paper ceased production.* The Times *and the* Sunday Times *were owned by the Thomson Organisation, and this confrontation – which foreshadowed the much more violent dispute with the Murdoch media empire (News International) seven years later – was to last for a year, during which neither newspaper appeared. In early December, I had written a paper for consideration by the TUC–Labour Party Liaison Committee in which I argued that, in the public interest,* The Times *could be acquired and run by the BBC, whose independence was guaranteed by its Royal Charter. The BBC had successfully adopted new technology with the agreement of its unions, and its operations were already highly diversified. Taking over the* Times *presses would also enable small publishing ventures to develop and flourish. In the short term I proposed a small working group of trade union leaders representing the* Times *and BBC staffs together with Ministers and Labour Party representatives, to examine the idea. Needless to say it was not popular with certain sections of the press, nor indeed with the leadership of the Labour Party.*

Caught the train to Bristol and on it was Kenneth Harris of the *Observer*, on his way to see his eighty-eight-year-old mother in Wiltshire. I asked, 'What's going on at *The Times*?'

He said, 'Well, it's like betting on a race in which you don't know any of the horses. Lord Goodman, who is pretty knowledgeable about Fleet Street, was absolutely certain that there would be no strike. But others have said that it will go on for three weeks or even two months.'

'What will happen if *The Times* really goes wrong? Will people want to buy it? What about the owner of the *Observer*, Robert Anderson?'

He said, 'It's a delicate matter, but Anderson is interested in acquiring a daily newspaper. He bought the *Observer* as a public service; he's a very serious man.'

'Could you print *The Times* on your own presses?' I asked.

'Yes, because the *Observer* printing press is only used on Saturday night.' Incredible! 'We could certainly print *The Times*. But then, of course, if we bought *The Times*, we would have the *Times* presses.'

I went on to ask Kenneth about his recent interview with Jim Callaghan for the *Observer*. He said he had recorded it all, and Jim only wanted one sentence cut. It was a remark he had made relating to *In Place of Strife*: 'Looking back on it, it is hard when your view of what should be done to the trade union movement conflicts with your desire to run the country.'

Kenneth Harris said this indicated that Jim had really believed in *In Place of Strife* but if he were to be Leader of the Labour Party it was impossible for him to vote against the trade unions. Kenneth said what a pity it was that Jim had removed the sentence. 'Only you, Jim Callaghan and the girl who typed it know that he deleted that sentence.'

I was surprised, because in the Cabinet Jim had been consistently opposed to *In Place of Strife*, and I thought that it accorded with his general view.

### Saturday 30 December

Got the train to Stansgate and joined Lissie, Caroline, Stephen and June.

I sat down and wrote a memorandum called 'The Maintenance of Essential Services during Industrial Disputes', urging that the trade unions take on responsibility by agreement with the Government. If I write it as a Cabinet paper, it becomes classified, and nobody will ever know about it. However, I think I will send it to Len Murray, and if the TUC is favourable put it to the TUC–Labour Party Liaison Committee.

### Sunday 31 December

Jim Callaghan was interviewed at Chequers for *The World at One* by the presenter Gordon Clough. It was an interesting broadcast, and I recorded the whole thing. Much of it was taken up with the Government's pay policy, but Clough also asked Jim about the leadership: 'Haven't you had to use the weight of the Party Leader and the Prime Ministerial hand rather heavily to slap down some of your left-wing colleagues?'

Jim replied, 'No, I don't think so. I have just reasserted the traditional position in relation to such matters as collective responsibility in case anybody had overlooked it. But, you know, there is always this attempt to try to write off the left as being some great animal that is waiting to spring on the British public. The truth about the left wing of the Party is that they are an essential element: they are like the yeast when you bake a loaf; they are an essential activating element that makes the bread rise, works on the flour. You couldn't make a loaf out of yeast alone. If you had a party that was made of the left wing alone, it wouldn't represent the British people, whereas the Labour Party does represent the British people.'

Towards the end Clough asked, 'Would you expect to see yourself here in Chequers in January 1980?'

Jim said, 'Would I expect to see myself in Chequers in January 1980, Mr Clough? I don't want to boast; that's for the British people to say. And if they wish me to continue then I pledge now that I will try to govern even better with the aid of the whole of the British people on the basis of the Labour Party and the labour movement as a whole; I will try to govern even better during the next five years than I have managed to do during the last three. It depends on the support of the people. So I am not going to be so bold as to make forecasts of that sort. I am ready to try because I believe Britain has got a great opportunity in the 1980s if we take it.'

### Monday 1 January 1979
Snowed in at Stansgate. Melissa is writing something called 'Fight Sexism in the Benn Family' in which she denounces the men for leaving all the work to Caroline.

### Tuesday 2 January
The 1948 Cabinet papers, which have just been released, were referred to on the 7 o'clock news. Churchill apparently wrote a private letter to Attlee in that year advocating the use of nuclear weapons to break the Berlin blockade.

A snow plough cleared the snow this afternoon sufficiently for us to get to the village to buy some food.

### Wednesday 3 January
Left early for GEN 158 Committee for a report on the latest news. Shell have made an offer to its drivers, with no productivity strings, which is being considered, and the strike has been put back to 10 January.

In Northern Ireland, BP drivers are already on strike, but there is no need for a proclamation because Northern Ireland is handled under different legislation.

Bill Rodgers said, 'I don't understand all this chatting with Moss Evans. Why don't we just tell him to settle? What is the sticking point? Are we going to see our whole pay policy disappear?'

### Thursday 4 January
At 8.30 this morning I had a phone call from Bill Burroughs, my Private Secretary, to say that Texaco drivers had gone on all-out strike.

Frances Morrell has been invited to a nomination meeting at Birkenhead, Edmund Dell's constituency. It would be lovely if she could get selected there; she has certainly earned it.

*Friday 5 January*
The Texaco strike is worse, and Manchester, the north-east and parts of Scotland are running out of oil.

*Saturday 6 January*
In my red box was a telegram from Sir Anthony Parsons, our Ambassador in Tehran, who has consistently misinformed us throughout this whole crisis. I was so angry, I wrote to the Prime Minister saying we ought to learn some lessons from all this.

To Oxford to attend the Study of Parliament Group at Exeter College, where I had been invited to talk about parliamentary reform. The only other MP was Kenneth Baker. Otherwise there were Tony Barker from Essex University, David Butler from Nuffield, Norman Chester, the recently retired Warden of Nuffield, Professor Max Beloff, Vice-Chancellor of the new privately owned university at Buckingham, and Sam Brittan of the *Financial Times,* who is on a sabbatical at Nuffield.

When I first went to Oxford it was a new world. Today it was like going back to kindergarten. We sat at a long oak table with little lamps while the college scouts served soup, fish, meat, dessert and various wines. These dons feed very well.

Sam Brittan, though a monetarist, is a gentle and courteous man. Kenneth Baker used to be rather bombastic and pompous, but today he was quite agreeable.

We went into the senior common room where a fire was burning. I was asked to speak, and the crux of my argument was that we had created in Britain a new corporate state around a rotting consensus, pursuing policies that had manifestly failed.

This did have a somewhat electrifying effect because, of course, the right-wing academics, who also see this corporate state developing and don't like it, have attached themselves to Mrs Thatcher.

My argument was that monetarism was not the answer; we needed a fresh infusion of democratic accountability. I argued for several essential reforms: the abolition of the Lords; the reform of the Commons; a Freedom of Information Act; select committees; and a review of patronage. The last seven Prime Ministers had, between them, made 2634 major appointments. I advocated the televising of Parliament and more research facilities for MPs. I concluded that the problems of Britain were mainly political and not economic.

They cross-examined me closely about proportional representation and devolution.

I came back on the train with Kenneth Baker and we had a long talk. He said he was pro-European but he had been influenced by some of my arguments about the impact on Parliament of our membership of the Common Market. He remarked that he was a Heathite and therefore, along with Heath and Peter Walker, simply not acceptable to Mrs Thatcher. He thought that if she had any sense she would offer Heath a place in the Shadow Cabinet before the Election. I agreed it would be a boost for the Tories.

He said there was a great deal of difficulty with Jim Prior and Keith Joseph, and Joseph should be put in charge of the Ministry of Defence. In his view the Labour Party had better discussions than the Conservative Party, which hadn't really learned to debate policy at all. Anyone who spoke out against the leadership now was classed as a traitor. He said he would like to be Secretary of State for Industry.

It was an enjoyable talk. I don't often get the chance to talk to Tory MPs.

### Sunday 7 January
As a result of Melissa's campaign, I cleaned the house from 10.30 till 7 and did five loads of washing. In the *Observer* there was a complete account of the paper I am presenting to a Cabinet committee tomorrow on miners' pay.

There was a most interesting radio phone-in programme about Iran. That terrible Tory, Michael Charlton, was the presenter and he interviewed a close colleague of Khomeini, the Muslim leader who lives in Paris. It was extremely good; an Iranian woman caller asked if women would have rights in an Islamic republic. He said, 'Yes, absolute full voting rights, but we are not prepared to have women turned into sex symbols.'

On *The World at One* Mrs Thatcher was reported calling for a state of emergency and saying she would take away social security payments from strikers.

### Monday 8 January
At 1.30 I went with Robert Priddle to Shellmex House to the emergency committee which Dick Mabon has been chairing. As I entered the room, I couldn't but remember that these were the biggest companies in the world and any common interest that a Labour Government might have with them at this moment is strictly temporary. John Greenborough, the President of the CBI and Chairman of Shell, was present.

In effect, about half the oil company plants are closed either by strikes, like Texaco, or by picketing. Oil supplies are down to 50 per cent; a quarter of all filling stations are closed; in Northern Ireland there are no deliveries, as in the north-west, where supplies are down to 5 per cent. The situation is really very serious.

Esso are expecting a favourable settlement today but they may take disciplinary action if Esso drivers are turned back by pickets. Shell said the same.

I enquired, 'Could you give me notice of when you intend to implement disciplinary action? I would be grateful if you would not do it until I have consulted my colleagues.'

We had a brief discussion about the interaction between this and the Road Haulage Association dispute.

To the Cabinet Office at 2.45 for GEN 158. Albert reported that Moss expected the road haulage strike to become official, and Merlyn Rees suggested Albert and I talk to him this evening.

When we discussed picketing, Merlyn Rees asked, 'What is the legal position as far as the police are concerned?'

'Unofficial picketing is exactly the same legally as official picketing,' Albert replied, 'but the trade union leaders, of course, may disapprove of it.'

I said we ought to see Moss about picketing and emergency supplies. 'I want confirmation that the companies will be told not to take disciplinary action against workers.' That was agreed.

Michael Foot was then asked by Merlyn whether he, as acting Prime Minister while Jim is in Guadeloupe meeting Carter, Schmidt and Giscard, wished to comment.

'No!' said Michael. 'The picture is gloomy enough without my commenting.' He just sat there like a stuffed dummy. He contributes nothing now.

Merlyn gave the latest on the military involvement. The troops are on thirty-six-hour notice. After a long discussion about when we could reduce this period of notice, we agreed to leave any decision until the morning.

Then we agreed to reserve advertising space for 'Save It' energy ads for Friday.

Straight from there to EY(P) chaired by Denis, who said, 'The Prime Minister will be seeking legislation to use the Price Commission to enforce pay policy, despite the risk of defeat in the House.' He said the four economic Ministers and Michael Foot were seeing the TUC on Thursday, and the Prime Minister wanted a new statement with the TUC to cover the period of the next Government.

I had to leave to see Moss Evans and Jack Ashwell. When I arrived, I heard that workers at Esso had voted in favour of the settlement, as had those at Shell, but with a smaller majority. We should know the result of the BP vote tomorrow.

EY(P) again at 5.45 and I reported on the meeting. We came on to the miners' pay and I said, 'Never in my whole life have I seen such an explicit leak of a Cabinet paper as that which appeared in the *Observer*. It was a detailed account both of my paper and of the Whitehall reaction.'

'Well, you had better put that right in your Department,' Denis remarked.

I said it wasn't the responsibility of my Department. I made my point but didn't pursue it.

I continued, 'The miners are making a very large and comprehensive claim, and the Coal Board response will be that they can't afford to pay.' I was seeing the chairman, Derek Ezra, and suggested the PM might see the NUM. What was proposed was a twenty-month settlement at 9.5 per cent which would allow 12 per cent for face workers; rises for surface workers would be kept down. Our objective was to play it long to avoid confrontation; to reach an acceptable settlement with minimum repercussions; and to consider productivity and cost cutting.

Denis commented, 'The financial position of the mining industry is so awful that Ezra is in a strong position to say he can't afford to pay anything.' The NCB would have to play for time, and he didn't like the idea of a twenty-month settlement.

It was agreed that there should be a tripartite meeting of the NUM, the NCB and the Government.

Well, the new year has begun with a vengeance. I would like to believe that, if a left-wing policy were being pursued, we wouldn't be having all this trouble with the unions. But the truth is that our society is so vulnerable through its centralisation and interdependence that whatever policies you pursue you can't avoid problems like this. Having said that, the situation is made worse by the Government's philosophy, which is still basically anti-trade union. There will have to be a fresh deal with the trade unions to involve them more closely with the business of government because, frankly, they have got too much power to be excluded – thank God. That's what the planning agreements and industrial democracy were all about, and we've done nothing about implementing them.

*Tuesday 9 January*
The first item on the NEC's International Committee was Iran, and there were a large number of resolutions condemning David Owen for his support for the Shah. We agreed to accept all of them without discussion.

Frank Allaun introduced a resolution criticising the proposed sale of Harrier jet aircraft to China, and Joan Maynard seconded it. Both argued that it might damage the chances of successful disarmament talks with the Russians.

'We can't let the Russians dictate our policy,' said Eric Heffer.

Alan Hadden thought we needed to know more about it because a big new market was opening up in China and we ought to be in on it.

Neil Kinnock said, 'Peace must be the overriding consideration. There are masses of potential customers for arms and we had better be careful who we supply.'

I proposed that we ask the Government for a clear statement on arms supplies because we didn't really know what the position was.

In the end, without a vote, we agreed to send the resolution to the Prime Minister for his comments and ask for a statement on the Government's arms policy, deferring our decision in the meantime.

*Thursday 11 January*
At 10.40 Jack Cunningham came to report on the emergency situation. The oil-tanker drivers' dispute is resolved, and there is no point in having a state of emergency for the road haulage drivers because the troops couldn't provide emergency coverage of that magnitude.

Cabinet, and there were Jim and Sir John Hunt, all bronzed.

Jim said Mrs Thatcher had written to him asking for a debate and she wanted a state of emergency declared. He would make a statement on Guadeloupe on Monday and if necessary have a debate on the industrial situation next week.

We discussed the emergency itself, and Roy Mason reported on Northern Ireland, which he said was bleeding to death. He might have to declare a state of emergency there tonight. A vote against settlement by the Ulster tanker drivers was down to 'right-wing, hard-line, working-class Protestants' – not a bad description of himself, in fact! He said they had decided not to accept Moss Evans's advice because Moss was in the pocket of the Labour Government – at which the Cabinet burst out laughing. John Freeman, the Northern Ireland Regional Secretary of the TGWU, had tried to solve the strike but failed. Fortunately, Roy said, as Northern Ireland Secretary he himself didn't have to report to Parliament or get parliamentary authority for a state of emergency there.

'Couldn't you take over England as well?' said Shirley, under her breath, and Denis Healey added, 'Perhaps that is a pattern we could follow here.' In a way they were half serious, because Northern Ireland is the testing ground for repression in Britain. With Shirley Williams's deep pessimism about the unions and Denis Healey's strong-arm tactics, that's what they secretly think we might have to do.

Jim reported on Guadeloupe. On the SALT talks, Schmidt and Carter had drawn attention to the fear of Russian domination in the grey areas of strategic arms limitation. Carter was annoyed that the western countries were concentrating on the neutron bomb and made no reference to the SS20, a Soviet nuclear missile with a range of 4600 kilometres enabling Bonn, Lille and Birmingham to be destroyed from Russian bases just over the central European border. Schmidt would not accept the siting of neutron bombs in Germany and thought we might have to build a new counterpart to the SS20. He said Giscard would not allow French nuclear weapons to be included in any talks. Schmidt was extremely anxious about German security, and Jim feared that a future German Government, say under the Christian Socialist Franz Josef Strauss, might be nationalistic. It was important that the west should take sufficient military measures to allay German fears. Jim was in effect calling for a rearmament programme.

Elwyn Jones said, 'I wish the importance of these Guadeloupe discussions could be understood and explained to the public because you, Jim, had a very bad press when you were away.'

'I expected that. I tried to explain that I didn't think there was a crisis when I got back but I got kicked on the shins for it.'*

The next item was pay. Jim began by saying, 'I had feared that the tanker drivers' dispute would lead to a state of emergency but I see now that it's the road haulage drivers who are the problem. An official strike may be declared today and I have spoken to Moss Evans. He was fatalistic but optimistic about a settlement which would be in the order of 18–20 per cent. The period of chaos would be short because the employers would give way. He is to suggest a meeting with me today at the Finance and General Purposes Committee of the TGWU.

'On the local authority workers, we can't do much because of the defeat of our sanctions policy. The 5 per cent is not working and it now looks as if we are getting 15–20 per cent settlements. A high local authorities settlement would mean higher taxes and perhaps a 20 per cent rates increase, as well as cuts in public expenditure. Moss takes the view that he is working for the best deal for his members and it's up to the Government to govern. The TUC simply can't help us at the moment and we can no longer rely on them. I must tell colleagues to prepare for an Election in the near future. We must go to the public, and I don't know whether the unions will come with us because they have not helped us over the last two years.'

It was a patently false statement and very threatening in tone.

I said, 'PM, before we plan an Election campaign based on the idea that if we can't get trade union support we'll go it alone, shouldn't we have deeper discussions? A pay policy has never yet lasted for four years and it is far too rigid. It is misleading to think that the unions' rank and file are moderate while their leaders are militant. I have seen Moss

---

* On his return from the meeting of French, German, British and American premiers, Callaghan was greeted by a barrage of journalists and photographers asking him to comment on the industrial situation. The *Sun* invented his reply, 'Crisis, what crisis?'

Evans every day in recent weeks and what had really burned into his soul was seeing Jack Jones overturned by delegates to the TGWU Conference.'

'Well,' said Jim, 'he should forget all these past experiences and stand up and take control, as Jack would have done.'

I continued, 'We must recognise that there is a mass-media attack now on the trade unions of a kind I have never seen before. Every newspaper, every programme attacks them. Compare it with *The Times* lock-out. If the employees there had been out on strike since 30 November, they would be screaming about the freedom of the press. But because the employers have taken action they ignore it . . .'

Harold Lever broke in, 'The trade unions are responsible', and Jim said, 'I am the only one who is allowed to interrupt Tony!'

'Finally,' I said, 'quite plainly there is no future for a Labour Government without an understanding with the TUC. This is a political problem, not an economic problem. We have got to institutionalise the power of labour by bringing it into government. I don't personally believe that wage militancy has got much to do with socialism, but, if we retain an economic system which denies the trade unions the right to influence profits, investment and dividends, then inevitably their huge power will be used on wage claims. We also know that Tory policy won't work. Indeed, from the experience of the past few days, the troops cannot replace labour. The trade unions have got to be given real power, and we can start by asking them to deal with emergency supplies.'

Jim declared, 'What you are discussing is what sort of a Labour Party we should be, and I'll tell you this: if you go that way, there will be a split in the Party.'

'You know,' I said, 'there are other powers in the land besides the trade unions: there's the IMF, which had the power to cut our expenditure by £4 billion and called it "facing the harsh reality"; but when the trade unions make their demands we don't look at it that way at all. Anyway, the Labour Party will never split. It might be defeated but it will never split.'

Denis asked if we could persuade the TUC to support the objectives of our policy against inflation. 'Can't we get back to our old statement and explain that we can't reflate without increased productivity? The road haulage strike has already led to 100,000 people being laid off and it will be a million by next week. We can't stop firms laying people off and we should tell the TUC Economic Committee that they are putting their fellow trade-unionists out of work. As to secondary picketing, this is the latest form of action and we should suggest a code of conduct. The Government can only use fiscal and monetary solutions if this is the way they carry on.'

Jim said, 'We should put it to the TUC that we want their co-operation, but if they won't give it we will have to go it alone.'

Denis added, 'The TUC don't believe that Thatcher could win this either.'

Jim concluded, 'We are heading for an Election. We should all go on television and speak our minds – although we recognise that Tony has a different slant.'

I realise that Jim felt guilty about being in Guadeloupe. He had had a bad press and had done poorly on television, and he was worried about the situation. But at the same time it was a historic Cabinet at which we were warned of a higher level of defence expenditure and of a possible break with the TUC. A Cabinet to remember.

### Saturday 13 January

Went to the Civil Contingencies Unit to consider the emergency. GEN 158 has now disappeared and the Contingencies Unit meets at ministerial level.

Sir Clive Rose, back from the Caribbean with the Prime Minister, said, 'The Prime Minister wants reports every three hours on transport, industry, food and Northern Ireland. Starting on Monday, five Departments must make daily reports: Industry, Transport, Food, Northern Ireland and the Scottish Office.' A standard format for circulation to all members of the unions concerned would be undertaken. Number 10 would be briefing the press.

Denis Howell began, 'As President of APEX . . .'

'You had better explain what APEX is,' said Merlyn, 'because there are people here who don't know.' I am sure that's true – the officials and the army officers and so on. So the Association of Professional, Executive and Clerical Staff was explained and Denis continued his point.

With Bill Rodgers having negotiated emergency supplies with the TGWU, Huckfield describing his experience as a lorry driver, and Denis Howell as a trade union leader of considerable authority addressing us, I began to feel that we had control of the Contingencies Unit. The other representatives, the officials and the army couldn't offer anything like that amount of knowledge or ability.

Then a Treasury man told us, 'The pay of the water authority workers is on the agenda for Monday.'

Clive Rose said, 'The army locally must know what is required and the water authorities must keep in touch with them. They can allow absolute confidentiality.'

Denis Howell made a plea for no publicity, but I asked, 'Couldn't secrecy destroy our credibility if we are not making clear what we are doing?'

Susan, widow of Tony Crosland, with daughters, at his memorial service, March 1977.

*(Below)* Jeremy Thorpe, Liberal MP for North Devon 1959-79, and former leader of his Party.

*(Far left)* Larry Lamb, erstwhile editor of the *Sun*, knighted 1980.

The 'Fourth Man': Sir Anthony Blunt, Adviser for the Queen's Pictures and Drawings.

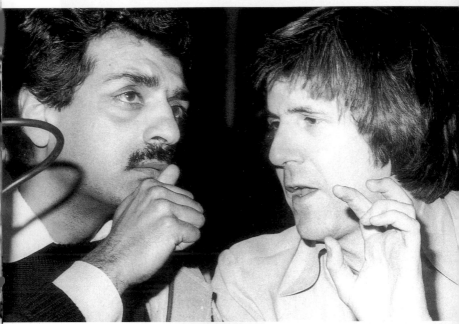

Paul Foot makes a
point to Tariq Ali.

Rosalind Retey Benn,
born 1953, died 1979.

**Colleagues of the Left**

*(Left)* Michael Meacher and Les Huckfield (bearded) in post-electoral mood.

*(Inset)* Tony Banks, later to become last Chairman of the GLC (1985-6).

*(Below)* Frances Morrell with Geoff Bish.

Fundamentalism of east and west. Ayatollah Khomeini of Iran, 1979; President Reagan of America, 1980.

Came home and heard on the radio that the strike in Northern Ireland was off. We are getting over the hump, but the pay policy is finished.

### Sunday 14 January

In the evening we had a party with about thirty people, including Chris Mullin, Eric and Doris Heffer, Frances Morrell, Michael and Molly Meacher, Albert and Joan Booth, Bryan and Gill Gould and others. It was the first party we had ever given where everyone was on the left. It was a great liberation really.

### Monday 15 January

At Cabinet Jim asked what was the case against having a state of emergency. Clearly that was what Jim wanted, but Merlyn said the Tories were only demanding a state of emergency for cosmetic purposes. Denis Healey said we would only need it if we required extra powers, which we didn't at present.

'Well, is there a case for having a cosmetic state of emergency?' asked Jim.

'It's too early,' muttered Shirley, and Roy Mason said, 'No, because it raises false expectations that we can solve the problem when we can't.'

'When should we have it, then?' asked Jim.

Elwyn Jones advised us to consider very carefully whether the Prime Minister wasn't in fact right, but John Morris thought it would do us damage.

Joel Barnett was against it. 'The tanker drivers' dispute proved that we can get out of difficulty without a state of emergency.'

Bruce Millan remarked, 'The TGWU could do a better job than the troops, and the General Officer Commanding Scotland thinks that the use of troops would worsen the situation.'

Jim said, in a very threatening way, 'The key to all this is trade union power. They have got us and themselves into a real difficulty. Thatcher, trade union power, secondary picketing: these are the real issues. The trade union solution of their moving emergency supplies doesn't help. It is having a very strong effect on the middle classes and many of our own people. This is a setback but we must not desert our policy now.'

He went on, 'How should we cope with the matter? I would like a new deal with the TUC but they must face their responsibilities or the Tories will mangle them. The 5 per cent policy was right; Methven, the Director-General of the CBI, said so last night. We should advise those who are working not to tolerate secondary picketing. This calls for a code of conduct and Len Murray accepts the need for such a code.

Picket lines are not inviolable. We must take powers through the Price Commission to control prices, and this would check wage demands. A high settlement for local government workers would have a tremendous effect on the rates, and we shouldn't finance it out of taxation. We need a tight money policy and I shall spell all this out in the House tomorrow. It won't be popular and it won't help us electorally.'

Denis said, 'The TUC leaders are punch-drunk and shell-shocked. Instead of Hugh Scanlon and Jack Jones, we have Moss Evans, who is widely disliked, and Terry Duffy, who is of limited ability. Do we want raging inflation before we act? Appeasing Moss Evans is no good. We must redress the balance of power. It is cheaper to strike in Britain than it is in other countries because we give strikers unemployment pay and social benefits.' Denis sounded just like Mrs Thatcher – which of course he is. He said, 'I don't want to move in this direction but the Opposition will push it.'

Jim asked, 'Would it be right to take away the right to strike from all those who perform essential services?'

Peter reminded us that the police were in that position and they got better pay without industrial power.

Michael Foot said, 'There are the rights of the community to consider but we also have a duty to apply our minds to each case. Workers think they have a just cause. We can't escape when people think they have a case.'

It was a good contribution actually. He went on, 'We have not persuaded people and we must have the unions on our side. The breakdown of cohesion between the Labour Party and trade unions could be very serious. Trade union power is not wicked. Don't just lump everybody together and look for devils.'

John Smith said he had been looking at secondary picketing and thought Thatcher would ask for a legal change.

'Secondary picketing was allowed in 1906,' said Michael, 'and we can't stop it.'

A debate on secondary picketing ensued in which Roy Mason put it all down to 'comms and Trots'.

I tried to make a speech but was cut short by Jim. 'I don't want to hear all that,' he said. 'Shall I tell the House of Commons or shall I tell the TUC about low pay?'

On price safeguards, ie strengthening the Price Commission to ensure pay rises aren't passed on to prices, Roy Hattersley preferred to leave it until Thursday and Michael Foot agreed.

Jim said, 'Let me set out what I plan to say in the House tomorrow. I believe in an incomes policy, and price control as a safeguard will be helpful. On secondary picketing, we must have a code of conduct. On low pay, we'll make a change. We'll offer something on comparability and the machinery for ensuring it.'

Roy Hattersley feared that Mrs Thatcher would pre-empt all this.

It was an exhausting Cabinet.

### Tuesday 16 January

Today I began a regime which will probably last for twenty-four hours. I jogged in the bedroom for about twenty-five minutes and did some exercises. Resolved not to eat any bread, potatoes or sugar, and to stop smoking. It's terrifying the extent to which one is dependent on drugs. If I tried to give up tea as well, I think I would go mad!

Heard Mrs Thatcher in the debate called for by the Opposition on the industrial situation. She launched into an attack on the trade union movement, and Jim then paid a warm tribute to her speech. He offered a few sops to the trade unions on low pay and comparability but basically he stuck to the pay policy and tightening the rules on picketing.

It's 10.45 pm and I still haven't smoked.

### Wednesday 17 January

Did my jogging while the bath filled.

Now that the Iranian oil has stopped, South Africa and Israel are in difficulty. The South Africans are trying to get North Sea oil but I have refused to supply it. I don't know how we will handle Israel; we have agreed that any oil exports will go to the countries of the International Energy Agency or the EEC, which excludes both Israel and South Africa.

I am so pleased that the Shah has gone. He left Iran yesterday, officially on a state visit to Egypt, but that's just to keep up the pretence. He is an ex-Shah now and I shouldn't think he will ever go back.

I had Philip Jones, Francis Cripps and others in to consider the energy forecasts. I am not at all sure that these forecasts are right. Common sense tells me we should let the nuclear programme slip, particularly the fast breeder, and concentrate on coal.

We are at this moment debating this wretched bill to give Northern Ireland more seats in Parliament.* In fact it would only give more seats to the Unionists just to buy a bit of extra support for the Labour Government. Didn't get home till about 4 am.

---

* The House of Commons (Redistribution of Seats) Bill increased the parliamentary constituencies in Northern Ireland from twelve to seventeen, as recommended by the Speaker's Conference in February 1978. The bill was passed but did not become effective until after the 1979 Election.

*Thursday 18 January*
Up at 7. My third day without smoking.

There was a rail strike today. The industrial situation is getting worse.

Cabinet at 10.30, and we had a discussion about unemployment measures. Shirley Williams came forward with a package – £200 million, which had already been provided, and £30 million from the contingency fund – to help with unemployment.

Albert warned that an increase of 80,000 unemployed would be announced next week.

'We had better be careful,' said Denis, 'because cash limits are going to be squeezed as a result of all these wage claims. We may not be able to afford to pay even what we have agreed, let alone go into the contingency.'

Harold Lever told us that the stock market and the money markets were on a knife edge.

Shirley Williams said, 'I think we might even discontinue our work on industrial democracy, since that is at risk. Indeed, our relations with the trade union movement are at risk. If there is no prospect of co-operation with the trade union movement, then what is the point of going ahead with these plans?'

'Look,' I argued, 'before we write off the trade union link – without which there isn't a Labour Party – we had better just examine our own policy. We appear to have found a perfect scapegoat – the trade unions are responsible for everything. We should go to Chequers and consider very carefully whether we ought to re-examine our policy.'

'There's no time for that,' said Jim.

'Well, if there's no time, I had better say this now,' I replied. 'We are accepting more and more the Tory view of the trade union movement, and that will be very damaging to us electorally. Their view is totally unjustified.' I regretted speaking so harshly but I thought it would be the last chance to say it.

Then Jim reported on pay. 'Following Tony Benn's point, I have talked to Len Murray and we have agreed that we need a common front. In a month's time we must agree on the role of the unions in a modern society, and have a really long campaign leading up to the Election.'

On the road haulage dispute, he said there was no support among colleagues for a state of emergency, and Len and Moss had agreed to a code of practice prepared by Albert. Moss wanted two to three days to let it start working and he thought things were improving.

Merlyn Rees said, 'Alex Kitson and the TGWU are now in the Cabinet Office dealing with practical problems.'

So we have reached the point I always wanted – the TUC is now involved in the Contingencies Unit itself; a tremendous advance.

Bill Rodgers, who is a great hawk, argued that the situation had deteriorated.

'What about declaring an emergency now, using the armed forces?' Denis suggested. 'We must have an emergency for reasons of public understanding.' Another hawk!

Jim asked, 'Do we tip a wink to the road haulage employers to settle?'

Roy Hattersley said, 'I think we should make an order to control the road haulage employers' capacity to settle by restricting their capability to increase prices.'

'Moss fears that that would prolong the strike and you'd have an emergency,' Albert pointed out. 'There would be a loss of control, and he can't respond to the Road Haulage Association offer while this threat is hanging over his head.'

Denis said, 'An order on prices would be ineffective anyway because it would only affect a few firms in the road haulage industry.'

Fred Mulley reported on the situation with the army. 'The troops can be ready at short notice, but let's be clear: there are half a million vehicles normally operating in Britain, and I could lay on only 10,000 army drivers. We'd get a good press for a day, and then we'd be proved to be impotent.' Not for the first time, Fred brought common sense to the discussion. It was a very important point, and I think that killed the state of emergency.

Fred Peart argued, 'If you do have a prices order against the Road Haulage Executive, it probably won't get through the Lords.' That's the power of the Lords being used at a critical juncture (not that I'm in favour of the order).

'We had better decide on the state of emergency,' said Roy Mason, 'but you can't declare it until you are absolutely ready, to avoid a hiatus between the declaration and something happening.'

'Right,' Jim summed up, 'are we agreed on no prices order?'

Clearly Jim was prepared to accept an end to the road haulage dispute on the drivers' terms. He proposed to put out a statement today that there would be no prices order so as to achieve an early settlement.

'If anyone is to do it, I should do it,' said Roy Hattersley. 'I don't see why you should be exposed.'

Bill Rodgers refused to go along with a statement of that kind today. He was extremely determined and I think it was an implicit threat of resignation. It was finally agreed to make the statement on Monday.

So the strike will continue over the weekend with the possibility that we might use the prices order, which we will announce next week that we have rejected.

We moved on to the water workers. Jim said, 'We may be forced to pay 16 per cent. People appear to prefer inflation to the cost of the strike.'

'That means the end of the pay policy,' said Shirley, and Denis Healey warned that such a settlement would mean a wage freeze in less than four months.

'But a million people are without water in the north-west,' said Jim.

'Two thousand,' Peter corrected him. 'Many people are getting water that hasn't been purified but only two thousand are without supplies and they have standpipes.'

'We must use troops tomorrow,' Jim declared.

Peter wanted to wait and see how the negotiations went. 'On the local authority manuals, the Local Authorities Conditions of Service Advisory Board think that an 8.5 per cent settlement plus comparability would work if we phased it in over the next two years. It would mean increasing the cash limits by £50 million.'

'I think that's the best thing we can do,' Jim concluded. So he jumped over the pay policy at that stage. You have got to watch everybody in these discussions because, under the guise of being very tough, Jim and Denis were jettisoning the 5 per cent.

### Friday 19 January
Caught the train to Bristol for a meeting at the boardmill factory at St Anne's to consider the management's proposed redundancies of 650 out of 1700 workers. I have now got enough information to write to the Chairman of the Imperial Tobacco Group (the parent company), Sir John Partridge. It is such a tragedy that the Government simply hasn't got its industrial policy in position. This should have been subject to a planning agreement, because that firm, on its own admission, has had £750,000 of Government money. But there is no public accountability at all; the money is just handed over to the firm to spend as they think best.

Did my surgery, and I had a call from Dawn Primarolo saying she was standing against Herbert Rogers for the secretaryship of the Party, which will cause trouble.

It was dark and wet with snow, and it was impossible to get a taxi, so I trudged with my two suitcases over to the hotel.

### Saturday 20 January
Caught the train back to London.

I am finding it extremely difficult not smoking and trying to cut down on my food at the same time. Not smoking makes me want to eat, and not being able to eat makes me jumpy. I doubt I'll be able to keep it up.

### Sunday 21 January
Had my first pipe for about five or six days. Somehow the pressure of not smoking made me think of nothing but my pipe.

*Monday 22 January*

Today was the Day of Action for local government employees and 1.25 million workers took the day off. The press is just full of crises, anarchy, chaos, disruption – bitterly hostile to the trade union movement. I have never seen anything like it in my life.

To Congress House for a most important gathering of the TUC–Labour Party Liaison Committee. Len Murray looked poorly: he is powerless now; he's lost all his vitality by going along with policies that were not in the interests of the trade union movement. The union leaders simply have no strength left. David Basnett, one of the great architects of the pay policy, is now absolutely outflanked by his rank and file. Moss Evans was there, and Terry Duffy, who didn't say a word. It was an extraordinary meeting really, reflecting the powerlessness of the TUC and the vitality of the Party.

We had before us the TUC's Economic Review for inclusion in its annual report. Jim said that all these studies about the future would be academic unless the framework was right. He hoped there would be urgent talks as a basis of co-operation between the Government and the TUC over the next vital months. 'The Government's room for manoeuvre is narrowing rapidly and I would tremble if we went over the edge. It would be a tragedy if the labour movement was swept aside by the electors at this moment.'

After Denis Healey had complained about the current strikes, Moss Evans commented, 'I hope that Ministers will be careful what they say. For example, if we take Ford, the pay costs per car in 1977–8 went up by 5 per cent while the profits per car went up by 80 per cent. The company indicated that they were prepared to increase wages without passing on the costs to the consumer, but that was not acceptable within the pay policy. Ford are now actually *advertising* for labour because low wages have caused a shortage. On the tanker drivers' dispute, Texaco's offer meant only a 4 per cent increase because the drivers' hours had been kept down – that was what caused the trouble.'

David Basnett said, 'We shouldn't be discussing wages, we should be talking about policy – you can leave wages to the TUC and the Government.'

So I felt absolutely free to argue my case for a change of Government policy in the presence of the Prime Minister and Denis Healey. I advocated a hard-core agreement between the TUC, the Party and the Government upon which we could build our manifesto. It had to be a tripartite arrangement: it was not enough for Ministers to see the TUC because the Party had to be involved. With the hostile press campaign at its peak, we had to have an early agreement as a basis for our public campaign.

Barbara agreed with me. 'I think we should issue a statement today, emphasising the advances made and showing our determination to work together to improve growth, contain costs and deal with imports. We are prisoners of the media.'

After much discussion, Jim said, 'I'm afraid I have to leave. There is a great will and desire to find common ground, and the Government must share its anxieties with the rest of the movement, but we must face the practical concerns. No single policy, if we changed it tomorrow, would solve our problems.' He would be addressing the issue at Congress House tomorrow.

On imports, he said, 'We have discussed it time after time but there is no clear consensus. You have to look at imports case by case. Edmund Dell and John Smith are waiting for evidence and import controls are not the easy solution.' On pay policy, he said, 'However wrong the Government was, we would have succeeded if the 5 per cent had stuck. Government policy has been defeated and the TUC must help us.'

Went over to the House of Commons, and outside St Stephen's entrance there were 70,000 local government demonstrators who had come to protest against low pay. It was biting cold. There were grave-diggers, dinner ladies, caretakers, ambulance drivers – in short, our constituency – appealing for more money to keep the public services going. They were very friendly to me. 'Tony, how are you? . . . Keep at it . . .'

To Number 10 for the Defence and Overseas Policy meeting. Fred Mulley had proposed that depleted uranium from American nuclear reactors be used for ammunition against Soviet tanks. Apparently these tanks have thick armour-plating which the shells fired from the Chieftain tanks won't penetrate. We are already putting tungsten alloy in the shells to aid penetration, but if we could use depleted uranium cores they would turn into fireballs inside the tanks and completely destroy them. Fred wanted approval for us to allow the Americans to store this depleted-uranium ammunition in Britain, and also proposed that we develop it ourselves and test-fire it at Shoeburyness in Cumbria and Kirkcudbright in Scotland.

I opposed it – the only one who did. David Owen put in a qualifying paper saying we shouldn't sell the stuff abroad. The Germans already have it but have not been prepared to admit it to their own people.

Jim said, 'We will bring it to colleagues if Tony will give his reasons.'

'The public won't understand it,' I said. 'They will think we are moving across the frontier from conventional into nuclear warfare – which we would be. It will also increase anxiety about nuclear power because, as I understand Fred Mulley's paper, the depleted uranium is coming from civil power reactors and people will see nuclear power no longer as "atoms for peace"; each nuclear reactor will also be seen as an armaments-manufacturing unit. Test-firing the depleted uranium will create tremendous opposition. The Germans are very impatient with critics of nuclear power, describing them as chaotics, and they won't even admit that they have the stuff. We shouldn't do it. I am absolutely opposed to it.'

Fred Mulley responded. 'The American depleted-uranium ammunition is arriving this week, and I would be unhappy to refuse the Americans now. Depleted uranium is used widely, in helicopter blades and a whole range of other things. It's no more dangerous than the radiation from a luminous wristwatch.'

Jim said, 'Tony has a point about the psychology of it, but the main thing is to reassure the Germans.' This is the new theme – spend more money and build up the Cold War to reassure the Germans.

'The alternative is to build more tanks,' David Owen argued, and Peter Shore added, 'If the Russians are doing it and the Americans are doing it, we should do it.'

Then Bruce Millan said, 'I am not against it in principle but we can't have test-firing in Scotland. I am already having trouble with the Torness power station. There is criticism in the Orkney Islands of the idea of even *mining* uranium.'

I protested, 'There is no penetration advantage in this ammunition – its advantage is only that it creates a fireball.'

'Well,' said Jim, 'there's general agreement. We've decided.'

So I lost it.

*Tuesday 23 January*

Heavy snow, very cold. Another rail strike today led by ASLEF.

At the office, Don Dunstan, the Labour Prime Minister of South Australia, arrived with two colleagues to tell me that, although he had played a large part in opposing the development of uranium mining, the uranium in South Australia was reckoned to be about 250,000 tons with a current market value of £1.25 billion. I talked to him for forty minutes and told him we were in the market for uranium, but that generally speaking I discouraged nuclear power. I think he thought I would pat him on the head and say how marvellous it was of the Australians to sell us uranium.

Jumped in my car and drove to the Cabinet Office for GEN 29, the Committee on Official Information which Jim Callaghan put me on in October when he was trying to be friendly. It was fascinating.

Clement Freud won the Private Members ballot and has introduced an Official Information Bill giving public access to Government papers and repealing Section 2 of the Official Secrets Act. Because of our manifesto commitment to repeal the OSA, we couldn't oppose the bill, so it got through a second reading. But it has galvanised the whole of Whitehall against it.

The Government and GEN 29 don't want to court unpopularity but they don't want the bill either. So officials are panicking and have written masses of papers for the committee stage, attacking the proposals and listing all the difficulties. I must say I was amused.

In the evening, Caroline, Melissa, Stephen and I went to dinner at Khan's Indian restaurant in Westbourne Grove, and who should we meet but Julie Stonehouse, John's daughter. She said, 'You haven't seen me since I was a little girl', which is probably true because Caroline and I had dinner with the Stonehouses in 1967. I asked about her father, and she said he had had a serious heart operation. He was better now but still anxious and he felt he was innocent. I will have a word with Merlyn about his chances of parole, but I don't think Merlyn would want that before an Election.

On the midnight news I heard that Jim Callaghan has said in the House that there is no legal or moral obligation on anyone not to cross a picket line and that he would have no hesitation in doing so. It is a most disgraceful statement. He said the same thing in the Cabinet but it was never agreed. If I am asked I shall say that, if supplies were for emergency use, I would expect the picket to let me through, but otherwise I would not cross a picket line.

*Tuesday 30 January*
Cabinet, and Jim began by saying that the road haulage drivers' settlement of between 15 and 20 per cent reminded him of Munich, that's to say he felt relief and disquiet in equal proportions.

Reporting on his talks with the TUC, he told us that two working parties had been set up, one on employment policy and the other on economic policy; they would meet on Wednesday and Thursday and have to agree by the end of next week. The objectives would be to fight inflation and unemployment and to get productivity up. 'I have asked for industrial calm, and the TUC will use their influence to achieve it. But they did refer to current pay problems. It was agreed that both sides would aim to reduce the rate of inflation to 5 per cent by 1982. A Treasury paper is being prepared, and Number 10 is co-ordinating.'

Peter Shore was against tackling the current pay demands on a case-by-case basis because it would mean a defeat-by-defeat situation; we should put a new counter-inflation White Paper to the Commons and seek their approval, and then go to the country on it. 'We should mobilise the heart of our Party which is not in favour of free collective bargaining and we should isolate Mrs Thatcher as the architect of the free-for-all.'

Joel Barnett agreed with Peter that we had to go to the country on an incomes policy, but a new White Paper wouldn't help. We couldn't print more money or raise the cash limits, and the low-paid were irrational in wanting more money. As to the Election, we should use the incomes policy to our advantage and get the TUC to support us, but in the manifesto, not in a White Paper.

Bill Rodgers said we couldn't influence the present pay round. We had to recognise that 8–10 per cent was the new norm, and we should have a statutory pay policy with a pay and price freeze.

David Ennals was pessimistic. He saw no hope of standing firm against the nurses and the ambulance workers because it would be so unpopular, and, if we settled high, we'd have to have public expenditure cuts or tax increases.

Jim said if NHS pay went up the workers would have cut the service themselves through their pay claims.

I said I was glad we were having this broad political talk because it was long overdue. 'As to the present pay round, we have to settle case by case because we have no option. The low-paid have a lot of public support and it's no good talking to them about confetti money. We have to face the fact that people must pay for what they get in the NHS and in the local authorities.

'Nor is it credible to talk about greedy people, because the nationalised industry board members have had a £65–70 a week rise this year. These comments by highly paid editors about greedy workers earning £70 a week are incredible. We have to defuse the present anxiety, and that can be done using codes of conduct and essential supplies, and that will defeat the Tories who are calling for panic measures.

'We have to have a common stand for the Election, but a statutory pay policy wouldn't work. It is not free collective bargaining but Government policy that has failed, only we can't admit it to ourselves.

'On the Election campaign, Peter Shore, Bill Rodgers, Joel and Shirley are putting forward pure Edward Heath policies,' I said.

'Well, they're not Thatcher policies,' Shirley interrupted.

'No, but they are Heath policies and he failed in 1974, as we would fail now. We have to be a little bit careful about assuming that public opinion is on our side because the media can create a demand and then produce a poll to confirm it. I think we'll win the Election because the choice will be Heath or Thatcher or the manifesto, and I think our policy is right.'

Jim was cross about that.

Roy Hattersley argued that we had to go case by case on our established policy and the 5 per cent was the best we could hope for. Public support for the low-paid was real, and we had adjusted the policy on low pay, but it had to be economically realistic.

Jim said it was clear that the Cabinet was divided between the 'case-by-case school' and the 'cataclysmic school', and I said we mustn't forget the cataclysm-by-cataclysm school!

Stan Orme favoured a case-by-case basis. A going rate was developing, and why were we so sure that the twenty-two of us around this table were right and everyone else was wrong? We had not convinced people outside and we had to ask why. It was partly because in the north-west, where the feeling was strongest, people were earning £40–60 a week. We were not in a strife-torn society for ever, and after this pay round we'd sit down and talk to the TUC. The TUC wanted a Labour Government.

A very good speech, and I heard later that he had been put on the group of economic Ministers to meet the TUC.

Eric Varley thought a case-by-case approach was unfair. We had to stand firm on British Aerospace and Rolls Royce and stick to the 5 per cent. 'Tony Benn talks about nationalised industry board members' salaries, but he himself asked for special moneys for BNOC salaries not long ago. There is wide public support for our counter-inflation policy and we should put it to the test, not in an Election but in a referendum.'

So Varley is explicitly suggesting that Thatcher's monetarist policy be reinforced by a plebiscite. Incredible!

Albert Booth said the unions had helped us more than any trade union movement had helped any Government around the world. A case-by-case approach with a public-sector norm was the best we could do.

Denis Healey argued that every pay policy breaks down and so does all free collective bargaining. But history was no help to us at all. We had to mess and muddle through. He refused to finance any excess above 8 per cent by printing money. We might have a week or two of aggro but a new limit now would soon become a floor. As for Shirley's idea of an agreement with the TUC to bring settlements down into single figures, there would be some leapfrogging but an agreement might be reached, plus a commitment on unit costs, comparability in the public services and a restriction on strikes.

Once again, Thatcher's policy.

'Meantime,' said Denis, 'we should think about future policies with a statutory element.'

Jim wanted to leave it there. He feared winning and then not knowing what to do about it.

Elwyn Jones asked about the reports that in the north dead bodies weren't being buried because of the local authority workers' action.

Jim said we couldn't use the troops for that purpose.

'Let the dead bury their dead,' Harold Lever said.

## Wednesday 31 January

Brian Sedgemore came up to me in the Lobby and told me that John Biffen had warned him that someone from the BBC was spreading a story that I had two children in nursing homes in London. It was decent of Biffen to tell Sedgemore, and it indicates that the scandal factory is beginning to go into full production again.

*Thursday 1 February*
The local authority workers and the Health Service unions are out on strike and the manual workers in the water industry are engaged in spasmodic disputes. There is a general sense of unease all over the country. We are in an atmosphere of siege and crisis which the media are continuing to play up.

Cabinet at 10.30, and it was one of the best discussions we've had in a long time.

School caretakers and maintenance workers are out on strike now, and Shirley Williams said there were picket lines outside many schools, in some cases supported by the teachers. The unions were saying that children and teachers could cross the picket lines but that no effort must be made to carry out the caretakers' work. The strike of the maintenance men meant that temperatures in schools were falling below the 60 degree legal minimum, making it impossible to keep the schools open.

'That is fantastic,' said Jim. 'When I was at school there were days when you couldn't put your pen in the inkwell because the ink was frozen. What nonsense.'

Shirley pointed out that the Health and Safety regulations required it.

Jim asked how the Cabinet was going to survive. We had got to the point where indiscipline was threatening the life of the community and the Government must have a clear line. The situation was extremely grave and the Tories could win, giving Mrs Thatcher a mandate for the most violent anti-trade union policy. But at least the trains would run on time, he said.

He praised Peter for his speech in the Commons yesterday when he urged us to spell it out that what was happening in this country was a threat to democratic society.

I didn't believe that. 'I have always worked on the principle that, where large numbers of people behave irrationally, something else is usually wrong. People feel a deep sense of injustice and they don't feel properly represented. We have to be careful not to fall for this idea that everybody has just gone mad. David Owen says that what is happening is pure thuggery, but I doubt that. It can't be easy for people to go on strike. They lose their income and they have a deep feeling of anxiety. When I was in Newcastle recently, I heard an NUJ man deliver the most violent attack on the management of his paper and he swore that he would die in the last ditch with the printers. I discovered that he was a Tory candidate for a north-east constituency.'

I talked about picketing and the reasons for not crossing picket lines, and Jim said, 'What about intimidation? Strikers are intimidating people.'

'The people of Grunwick were intimidated,' I replied, 'and, if I may say so, some Cabinet Ministers give the impression that they really support what Mrs Thatcher is saying. The trade unions have no interest in penalising the public – they just want to be in a position to develop their arguments in an effective way.'

It was a bitter exchange but at least they listened.

'Tony is right,' said Michael. 'The TV mobilises the public against the unions and we need to have sympathy with some of the reasons behind the disputes. We have to keep our nerve. Mrs Thatcher has now put the trade union movement in the front line and we must go for a case-by-case solution. We don't want any scapegoats.'

Denis said, 'Lectures based upon the little flowers of St Francis or an article in the *New Statesman* are just not enough. There are serious problems of burials and hospital services, and voluntary work, described as blacklegging and strike breaking, is right.'

Jim said he was more depressed as a trade-unionist now about the future of this country than he had been for fifty years. He never believed it would come to this.

Denis remarked that we had sympathy with the low-paid, but it was the unions themselves who insisted on maintaining differentials. NUPE was not in control of its members, and all this support rested on middle-class guilt.

Jim then reported on his latest talks with the TUC. They had produced a paper on economic policy, '95 per cent of which was guff'. The TUC showed no signs of urgency to win the Election or to save themselves.

Joel Barnett wanted to consider the options for a settlement in the NHS. 'We must spell out the consequences,' he said. 'The NHS auxiliaries are well-paid unskilled people and the trade union leaders have raised the expectations of people on £60 a week, who do not starve, and anyway 50 per cent of their wives are at work.'

Jim immediately latched on to this hard-line Treasury argument. 'I want to thank Joel for putting it so clearly. If the destruction mounts because of NUPE, if the hospitals close and the press reports of low pay continue, public opinion will demand a settlement. If we don't get what we want, we shall have to have an Election.'

Another Election threat from Jim, who was looking so red-faced that I wondered whether he was ill. A little later, when he asked for the Cabinet's view, he said, 'I will give up the leadership if we don't stick to single figures.'

Denis said the water workers resisted 14 per cent. Michael thought we should negotiate case by case – 16 per cent for the water workers, 10 per cent for the local authority workers, comparability for the Health Service. We should make an offer and show some flexibility. We could finance it by taxation. An Election was not the solution.

'It is a solution,' said Jim, 'in the sense that we would be relieved of office.' He said he felt totally disillusioned.

Michael Foot pointed out the similarity with 1931 – quite rightly – and Jim replied that Ramsay had carried on as Leader of the Party for five years after giving up the Labour premiership, something Jim would not do.

I said, 'Look, PM, before we go any further, you have made many references to an Election but we're not being asked as we go round this table to agree to an Election if this policy fails. That raises quite separate considerations.'

'Well,' Jim replied, 'I am not ready to carry on. I am fed up with the NEC and a defeat this way would at least be an honourable end to this Cabinet. I'll tell the TUC that I've had enough because when I read their document that really filled my cup of disillusionment to over-flowing. Someone else can take up the leadership because I am not going on.'

Denis Healey said, 'We all understand the strain you're under as the "youngest" member of the Cabinet.'

'All I can say,' Jim replied, 'is that if we have an Election we are likely to be defeated.'

I said, 'I very much hope the minutes won't record that', and Sir John Hunt shook his head.

As we left the Cabinet, I was so annoyed with what Denis had said earlier about middle-class guilt and so on that I said, 'Speaking as a peer of the realm, I hope nothing I have said will be attributed to middle-class guilt.'

### Sunday 4 February
Chris Mullin came and we tackled the section of the book dealing with foreign affairs but it wasn't very good. I hadn't thought it out enough. But he is working away on the book and he is conscientious and serious.

Hilary rang to say that Rosalind had got three secondary cancers. She is just living from month to month; she is a most remarkable woman.

### Monday 5 February
Picked up Mother at 12 to take her to lunch at the House of Commons. She hasn't been during this Parliament, though she has seen every one of the eighteen Parliaments in session since Edward VII's last in 1910. She is such fun to be with. I put her in the Gallery to hear my answers to

the energy questions. I got in a couple of cracks at the Tories, saying their only advice to the nation had been to brush their teeth in the dark!

*Tuesday 6 February*
A poll this morning was showing a 19 per cent Tory lead and Mrs Thatcher more popular than Jim Callaghan.

*Wednesday 7 February*
Driving over to the House, Ron Vaughan told me that Herbert Rogers was on the lunchtime news. Yesterday NUPE announced that as part of their campaign for local authority workers they are going to dump rubbish in the constituencies of Cabinet members. So the BBC went to Peter Shore's constituency and interviewed a number of people who said they would never vote for him again. Then they went to talk to Herbert, the secretary of my Bristol Party, and he told them, 'Oh, we all support Tony here because Tony supports us, he doesn't agree with the Cabinet, he's a good chap. We all understand that he can't do much in the Cabinet.'

He shouldn't have said it but I can't say it did me any harm.

At 7 I had a fascinating meeting with the five general secretaries of the print unions: Bill Keys of SOGAT, Joe Wade of the NGA, Owen O'Brien of NATSOPA, Ken Ashton of the NUJ and John Jackson of SLADE. Someone from the TUC was also present. They had come about my recommendation that the BBC acquire *The Times*.

Bill Keys found the rescue idea interesting but thought it was most unlikely that Lord Thomson would sell. Joe Wade doubted whether there would be any resumption of publication. The technology issue was irrelevant because this was a union-bashing exercise. Somebody would be producing a new *Times* and *Sunday Times*, the BBC was worth exploration, and he liked the idea of a national printing corporation.

Bill said a void was likely. The press had prostituted itself and the movement needed an independent paper, a downmarket version of *Le Monde*. He said we should buy time on a new press for a Labour paper and we could start with a circulation of 400,000 and bump it up to 600,000.

Ken Ashton wanted to leave industrial relations on one side. Journalists would work for anyone and in that sense they *were* prostitutes. There was a vacuum but it could be filled. He wasn't against a national printing corporation but was it practical? Where would the money come from? There had been various Labour and Liberal failures in the past.

Joe Wade said, 'Let's exploit Tony's initiative.' They suggested that I formally put out my document on the BBC acquisition of *The Times* in time for Monday's papers. I was delighted.

*Thursday 8 February*
Cabinet met at 10.30. On foreign affairs David Owen said there was a serious possibility that following the Vietnamese invasion of Cambodia we might have to take some action. The UK couldn't stop aid to Vietnam because contracts were already signed. The Chinese were likely to invade Vietnam, though it would be a limited and selective invasion, and the Soviet Union might well retaliate. So already the issue has arisen as to whether, having decided to send Harriers to China, we aren't actually arming an aggressor. I didn't say anything.

To Bristol for the constituency Party AGM, which was sensational. Maurice Rea read the apologies and Bob Glendinning said he hoped we'd have no smoking for an hour. Bob was then elected chairman and Pete Hammond vice-chairman. Joyce Perham was elected minutes secretary and David Tatlow got the treasurership, which is a great advance.

Then came a motion that the job of secretary and property secretary should be *divided*, which was obviously an attempt to allow Herbert to continue as property secretary while having a new political secretary. It was defeated by 25 to 17.

So then Dawn Primarolo, who was standing against Herbert, won the secretaryship by 26 to 24, and Herbert got up, thanked the meeting, handed over the instructions for the secretaryship of the Party and went to sit in the front row.

People were shocked, though they had half expected the result. Cyril Langham, who has argued with Herbert for years – both men are in their eighties – made the great mistake of paying a tribute to Herbert. Herbert stood up, said it was a lot of humbug and stormed out. Joyce Perham then resigned as minutes secretary and walked out after him.

I then told the meeting that I thought we should set up a committee to find out how we could properly recognise Herbert's role. I offered to give up the presidency of the Party for him, and that was agreed; it was also decided that we would put out a tribute to him for his work for the Party.

Herbert had gone into the club and I saw him after the meeting. He said, 'I've just come to tell you that I'll never come back again.' It was tragic that after sixty-one years as secretary he had been defeated, and understandably he was very bitter. 'They all wanted to get rid of me,' he said.

'No, they didn't. They just wanted a new secretary. It's a relay race; they just want to hand it on.'

*Friday 9 February*
At the Cabinet committee GEN 74, the Foreign Office presented a paper showing that Pakistan is working as fast as it can to produce

nuclear weapons. It was a turning point really in my thoughts about nuclear power because I came to the conclusion that when it came to the crunch the British Government was not serious about the Non-Proliferation Treaty.

David Owen said it was very secret and we didn't want it to be revealed that we knew. There had been an argument between those who believed, as India did, that Pakistan could explode some nuclear device very soon, and our officials, who had apparently said it couldn't be done till 1982.

Robert Press of the Cabinet Office Scientific Staff reported that the Intelligence Service and the technical people had not been consulted about the timing of when they might test the device.

David Owen said we should consider the goods we could still supply and look at the order for invertors again.

This was really a test case about whether people had the political will to stop proliferation. I said, 'A couple of years ago, a presentation was made on the full fuel cycle and the experts concluded that there were so many points in the cycle, from the mining of uranium through enrichment to the handling of plutonium and reprocessing, which might lead to proliferation that the only possibility of stopping it was a very powerful political response. Are we content simply to hinder Pakistan in its development of nuclear weapons, or do we want to prevent them?'

Goronwy Roberts thought it would help to bring India in on the NPT but Peter Shore said that was absurd. India was democratic and Pakistan was not. You couldn't compare the two.

Bondi believed India had a very sound nuclear energy programme and the weapons side was really not as big as it was in Pakistan, where it absorbed all their nuclear resources.

I commented that I shared Peter's love for India; but were we developing a new non-proliferation policy based on the principle that democratic countries could have the bomb but not undemocratic countries? A sort of people's bomb? We couldn't possibly justify such a policy.

Goronwy Roberts argued that Pakistan was motivated by fear of India, and Bhutto, the former Prime Minister, who is now in the death cell waiting to be hanged, was publicly in favour of the bomb for Pakistan.

Dr Press remarked on how the Indians had developed theirs in secret, and I said, 'We talk about these things being done in secret, but so was the H-bomb in Britain. And when Truman became US President in 1945 he discovered for the first time that the Americans had a nuclear capacity. Can democracy control nuclear power? That's the real question.'

Fred Mulley asked if pressure could really help, and said it had to be collective; we didn't want to be 'a lot of boy scouts' out on our own.

That was Fred's way of criticising me for my stiff line on non-proliferation, involving possibly a ban on trade. Evidently, our policy now is merely to hinder the spread of nuclear weapons.

We moved on to China's request for Magnox reactors. They don't want the AGR or the PWR, they want Magnox, because Magnox produces more plutonium for the bomb.

### Sunday 11 February

Gordon Clough from *The World This Weekend* came to interview me about my *Times* proposal. When the programme was put out later, William Rees-Mogg was on, and he was violent and unpleasant.

The main news today is the revolution in Iran; Prime Minister Bakhtiar, appointed by the Shah, has resigned and handed over power to Ayatollah Khomeini's choice. So the country is now moving towards the construction of an Islamic socialist republic.

### Monday 12 February

EY(P) met to discuss nationalised industry pay claims. Denis began by saying that, after we'd dealt with these claims, a small group of Ministers – Peter Shore, David Ennals, Albert Booth, Bruce Millan, Shirley Williams and Denis himself – would meet to discuss local authority workers, water manuals and Health Service workers. He reported that they had previously met from 3 pm on Friday till 2 am the following day and appeared to be reaching some sort of solution.

So a very limited group of Ministers has been secretly negotiating to find an answer to the pay problems. Roy Hattersley was clearly furious that as vice-chairman of EY(P) he's been left off this little committee.

Denis reported on the Government's talks to get an agreement on future settlements. He made some very disloyal comments with regard to Jim, like 'I'll see the Shah when he gets back from his winter palace', Jim being up in Glasgow today.

I took my camera to two Cabinet committees today. No one ever sees what a Cabinet committee looks like, so I decided to photograph them.

When I opened my red box tonight, I found this note from my Private Secretary:

> Number 10 tells me that the Prime Minister understands you have been taking snapshots in recent GEN meetings. I have been asked to pass on the message that the PM assumes you will not be taking any pictures at EY tomorrow.
>
> Bill
>
> PS. I have since learned from the Cabinet Office that the Prince of Wales will be sitting in on tomorrow's EY.

*Tuesday 13 February*

A watershed day. To Room 13 at the House for the NEC International Committee. The only resolution was Frank Allaun's, deferred from the previous meeting, on the sale of jets to China: 'that the International Committee, whilst welcoming non-military trade and contacts with China, opposes the supply of Harrier jets, since, notwithstanding facile and overconfident denials, this supply would undermine the prospects for east–west peace and détente, halting the arms race and SALT agreements. The IC therefore asks the Government to reconsider the Harrier deal.'

I added an amendment asking the Government to make clear its policy on arms supply, and that was how it stood for the discussion.

In the end it was carried by 7 to 4; the four were Fred Mulley, Neville Hough of the GMWU, Alan Hadden of the Boilermakers and Russell Tuck of the NUR.

Into EY, and the Prince of Wales appeared, well groomed, with his hair neatly swept back and wearing a blue suit and a signet ring on his left hand. He sat on Jim's left, and Jim welcomed him. 'We can't find any account in the records of when the Prince of Wales last attended the Cabinet. I suppose you won't be able to come when you're sovereign and I suppose the last sovereign who chaired the Cabinet was George III.'

'And he lost us the American colonies!' Denis Healey said.

Jim referred to an article in today's *Guardian* outlining the agenda for this Cabinet and asked who put it out. The Prince of Wales said, 'Not me', which made us laugh.

We then had a typically complacent Board of Trade paper on imports. John Smith introduced it, saying we were exporting twice as much as Japan and there was an underlying trend of rising imports. There had been a decline in our share of world trade. On motor vehicles, iron and steel, we were performing poorly and we had been selective in our import controls.

Jim said this was just a progress report, and had we not in fact stiffened our import controls over the last two years? John replied that to protect our industry on the scale needed we'd have to leave the Common Market.

I raised the question of oil. 'I don't know what the oil earnings are on the balance of payments this year but they are probably £5 billion.' (Jim put them at nearer £2 billion.) 'We are living off oil, and our trade balance, including the flood of import manufactures, has been financed by oil. Then there's outward investment – nine times as much is invested by Britain in the Common Market as there is coming into Britain from the Common Market. I think we shall have a serious balance-of-payments problem and we need systematic protection.'

Peter Shore pointed out that, after five years of effort, our level of world trade was still only half that of the Germans and a quarter of that of the French and the Benelux countries. Our revival required import controls because free trade was not sufficient.

The Prince of Wales told us that he'd recently been in Africa, where there was a huge demand for Range Rovers and Jaguars, and he had got fed up with making excuses for lack of supply. On a recent visit to the Coventry factory, he found that there were too many models. It was a question of morale.

Jim hoped there would be no pressure on the Government for panic measures because, with the Budget coming up, demand for panic measures would already be building up.

Back to the office at 2.30, and there was a message from Number 10.

Secretary of State,

I have been asked by Number 10 to pass on a message from the PM. He has requested that you do or say nothing re: *The Times* until further notice. If you wish to circulate a paper on the subject it should be by way of the Home Affairs Cabinet Committee.

Well, my proposal has already been launched through the Home Policy Committee and will be coming to the Executive; so that's that.

I went over to the House of Commons and saw Chris Moncrieff, political correspondent of the Press Association, who asked, 'What happened at the International Committee this morning? I gather there was a motion on Harriers for China.'

'I can't say anything about it to you,' I replied. He asked me if I had voted for the resolution. I said, 'I won't answer that.'

On the way to the Treasury later, Ron Vaughan told me that there was a stop press item in the evening papers saying, 'Benn Defies Callaghan on Jets for China'. When I arrived, I was summoned to Number 10 immediately, so my meeting had to be cancelled.

I waited downstairs and at 6.10 I was invited up to the Prime Minister's study. It was an amazing dialogue lasting over an hour.

Jim began, 'I was told by my Press Office twenty minutes ago that the press are asking what happened at the International Committee this morning on Harrier jets.'

So I said, 'Well, last month I got a resolution opposing the sale deferred in the hope that the Government would make a statement about its arms sales policy. It came back to the committee, and was amended so as not to criticise the sale but to ask the Government to reconsider it and to issue a statement on arms supply. I voted for that amendment. You may argue that I should not have done, but it was not a motion of censure, it was only asking the Government to reconsider. As you know, I was very steamed up about the sale of these Harriers.'

'Well,' Jim replied, 'reading from the Cabinet minutes, the Cabinet decided to approve. You have no right to do it. What about collective Cabinet responsibility?'

'It did not censure the Government; it only asked for reconsideration of the matter.'

'Do you really want to be in the Cabinet?' asked Jim.

'Of course, and if I left the Cabinet I would be voting for it in the House, and if Labour were defeated in the House I would be trying to get a Callaghan Government re-elected. Of course I want to be in the Cabinet, and my local Party wants it too – they had a vote on it.'

'That was two years ago,' said Jim. 'If we were in calmer waters I would sack you, but I have got such a lot on my plate I don't think I will.'

'Well, I now know exactly where I would stand after an Election if you win with a majority of a hundred, which I hope you do, a working majority.'

'I didn't mean that . . .'

'Well, you have made it absolutely clear.'

'It was not necessary to vote that way. I have spoken to Harold Wilson about all this.' He flourished a letter Harold wrote to the *Telegraph* about collective Cabinet responsibility. 'I must seek from you a reaffirmation of your commitment to Harold on collective Cabinet responsibility.'

'I wrote to Harold in my own hand, accepting collective Cabinet responsibility with all the consequences that flow from it, and I cannot withdraw from that, but I think that, if you're going to do anything, it would be better just to rebuke me. Even you admitted that collective Cabinet responsibility only applies when you say it does.'

'Look,' said Jim, 'I don't want to rebuke you but you do cause trouble.'

'I'm not having that, Jim. Bill Rodgers makes a speech about a statutory pay policy, a pay and incomes freeze. That isn't Cabinet policy. Joel Barnett goes in a boiled shirt to talk to the bankers and attack the unions. Denis Healey talks about public expenditure cuts. Shirley makes her speeches. Edmund Dell leaves the Government in the middle of a difficult wage round.'

'You give the impression of being very calculating,' he said.

'That's not the case. I didn't even know it was on the agenda this morning. The press are just blowing it up. You think I'm calculating? Well, let me tell you, I control myself very well but I boil and fume at what goes on. Your speech on picketing, for example. I heard questions about that everywhere and I absolutely disagree with it.'

'That's what I thought,' he said. 'But what about collective Cabinet responsibility?'

'How much of it is there really? Last Thursday a rise in the minimum lending rate was announced and when the Cabinet met that morning we were never told. I am a member of the Cabinet and I wasn't told. I heard it on the 6 o'clock news in my constituency.'

'I forgot to tell you,' said Jim.

'Take my paper in September on pay policy, which anticipated everything that has happened – you wouldn't even circulate it to the Cabinet. The Cabinet is not like it used to be. There is no discussion. I feel like a backbencher.'

'What are you trying to do?' he asked.

'Well, Jim, I am trying to be a little modest beacon so that the Party realise they haven't been deserted.'

'That's so self-righteous.'

'No, Jim, I say the same everywhere, just like you, and I admire you for it. If you bug my telephone, or get someone to report on my meetings or listen to me in the NEC or the Cabinet, you will hear the same thing. I am going to make a speech about the Common Market shortly.'

'Are you going to let me see it in advance?'

'No, because if I do it will be struck. Everything I do is checked – I don't know if you even see it yourself. Tom McCaffrey stops things, and if I protest I am appealing over Tom McCaffrey to you personally.'

'Why do you write all these notes in the Cabinet?'

'I am a diarist, Jim, as you know. I do not leak and I do not talk to the press, as you also know. We get so little in the way of paperwork at Cabinet that if I didn't make notes I wouldn't know what was going on.'

'Why is it always you who's in trouble? First it was Harold and you, now it's me and you.'

'Well, before that, Jim, it was Harold and you!'

'Only once, in 1969.'

'In 1966 in this very room Harold Wilson told me you were plotting against him and I told you, though I never believed it. In 1972, when we were in Vienna together at the Socialist International – when you weren't well after your prostate operation – you said, "I see Harold is getting on to you; it used to be me he got on to." Harold also got on to Roy Jenkins. Maybe it's just what PMs do.'

I'm glad I got it off my chest. We were both very angry. Actually I expected him to sack me, and I said that to him.

### Wednesday 14 February

I wrote to Jim asking if I could go on a television programme about referenda, as he had said he would prefer me not to.

Alex Eadie came for lunch and we talked about my row with Jim. He is so supportive.

To the House to hear Jim's statement on the agreement reached with the TUC on future pay policy.

*Thursday 15 February*
The Gallup Poll puts the Tories 20 per cent ahead.

Incidentally, GEN 74, the committee on nuclear proliferation, received a letter from the Prime Minister saying that the Pakistan nuclear issue is to be taken out of the committee forthwith and to go into the Defence and Overseas Policy Committee, of which I am not a member. A further indication that the Government is not serious about non-proliferation.

Just before Cabinet at 10.30, Jim called me to his study. I thought, 'This is it, he has decided after all that he is strong enough, following the TUC pact, to get rid of me.' When I got there, there was Tom McCaffrey with the letter I had written to Jim about appearing on the referenda programme.

'I didn't know you'd accepted this,' said Jim. 'Do the rules permit it?'

I said it had nothing whatever to do with the Government, it was a programme about the constitutional role of referenda.

He said I should have asked him first, as I should have asked about the BBC/*Times* proposal. 'We don't want to give the impression that you're running the whole Government. Besides, Merlyn Rees deals with referenda.'

'I should tell you, then, that tomorrow I'm giving a big lecture to the Bristol Baptists on the demise of the Nonconformist conscience.'

'Oh, that has nothing to do with the Government,' he snapped. 'I don't mind if you do this programme but you should let us know in advance.'

'Well, I won't do it if you don't want me to.'

'I don't mind,' he said.

To Cabinet, and Jim reported on the current disputes. On Thursday Len Murray had come to see him at 11.30, then that night Moss Evans, the head of COHSE Albert Spanswick, David Basnett and Alan Fisher had gone to talk with him. Then on the Friday the small group of Ministers had negotiated a settlement of the local authorities' and related disputes, sticking to the 8.8 per cent plus comparability and productivity, which the unions were asked to keep secret. The water workers' dispute was over.

Denis said a 9 per cent settlement would have repercussions on the low-paid but comparability would be repercussive too. We'd have to watch this like hawks.

We went through the settlements individually, and Jim said he would give his not very considerable personal fortune to anyone who could get us out of this annual torment.

I said, 'A norm, a norm, my kingdom for a norm.' That didn't go down very well. I argued that there was a difference of philosophy between whether we were operating on the basis of a norm which would go across all the industries, or whether we were working on the ability of the industry to pay – something quite different. Coal couldn't afford it, gas could, but if the one repercussed on the other then we would be in trouble.

Denis said comparability was the curse and the whole thing was an intellectual muddle as always. We couldn't finance excessive settlements and we had had to tighten fiscal and monetary policy. At the moment the markets believed us, and the MLR increase last week had done the trick. The increased water charges had financed the water workers' rise, and the NHS was agreed. Some 30 per cent of private-sector wages had been settled at an average of 11 per cent, but only 2.5 per cent of public-sector workers had settled. He hoped at least that it would be below 13 per cent; 11 per cent would mean £10 billion on the PSBR.

Jim said there would be a run on sterling if we didn't stick to an £8.5 billion PSBR. He warned that any leaks about a disagreement in the Cabinet on the need for cuts would be fatal.

It was left there, but of course we're right back where we were in 1976. Having cut public expenditure and restored faith in sterling, we have now lost the battle with the unions, and sterling will be under attack again.

As we were leaving, a note was handed to Jim and he said, 'I've just had a letter from Len Murray, who wants to come and see me. The public-service unions are no longer prepared to recommend to their members the settlement we agreed last week. I am fed up with this. I shall see Len Murray but I'm going to my constituency and I am not going to see the general secretaries.'

So the whole meeting ended in an atmosphere of disaster.

*Tuesday 20 February*
Lunch with Peter Jenkins of the *Guardian*. I talked about the bankruptcy of the social democrats, which he didn't dispute. He thought Healey would become Leader in the summer after an Election defeat, and Shirley would push the Labour Party towards the German SPD position. I thought that was a complete illusion. The PLP might move to the right after the Election but you couldn't remove the interests that the left represented. There was no grassroots support for the right wing.

He was obsessed with a split and I said there wouldn't be one. We might lose the Election, but the Party wouldn't split; it would simply lose more voters to the Tories. He was so insistent that it made me think discussions *may* be going on.

*Wednesday 21 February*

I had some trouble with Mike Robinson, my diary secretary. On 9 March he had arranged my programme as follows: London to Bristol to address the trade union industrial strategy conference; back to London; plane to Perth for the Scottish Labour Party Conference; then to Bristol that night for a day school on the Sunday on the history of the Labour Party!

At 12.20 David Owen and Denis Healey arrived for an extremely serious meeting with BP. Since we last met, I have read in the *Financial Times* that BP gave an assurance to the German Government that if BP were allowed to acquire the German oil company, VEBA, they would guarantee supplies of oil to Germany – which was never cleared with me. Secondly, BP are swapping Conoco North Sea oil for Indonesian oil, which they are proposing to supply to South Africa. Thirdly, there is a rumour that BP and Lonrho have set up a subsidiary company to supply oil from the Middle East to South Africa. I heard from Frank Kearton that they are using all their influence in the International Energy Agency to get production restrictions lifted from oil producers in the western world; that is absolutely contrary to our policy.

There were masses of officials, and I went through these issues. They wanted to talk about Iran; they thought production might rise to 4 million barrels a day by autumn. They said they had improved the allocation of imported oil and they denied any deal with Lonrho. They tried to explain away the VEBA assurance as not relevant for the current year.

Sir David Steel sounded extremely nervous and there was certainly no love lost between us. Denis Healey had been shown a brief written by my Department which said we should approve flaring in the North Sea. Dick Mabon was furious about it but I had discovered that they had disregarded flaring restrictions since January and therefore, to keep flaring down to the quarterly total approved, they would now have to shut down the Forties field for a month. That would be inconceivable, so they have us over a barrel – literally!

I approved a paper saying that we'd move to monthly or even weekly approvals of flaring to get some control of BP. I must say it made me totally sick. They have no loyalty to this country at all.

Stayed for GEN 29, the committee on official information, with Merlyn Rees in the chair. A draft Green Paper had been produced by Kenneth Berrill and it reflected the fact that the Government, while making all the right noises about open government, was justifying why you couldn't have it.

The issue of whether ministerial memoirs should be agreed by the Cabinet Secretary was raised. I pointed out that Harold Wilson himself had not signed a declaration to that effect until after he had ceased to be

Prime Minister – so he and Barbara Castle and others were exempted from it. I didn't say I hadn't signed it. Michael nodded approval and that was dropped.

*Thursday 22 February*
The Terrorism Committee met at 9.15. Just beforehand, Merlyn Rees told me that as chairman of the committee of the Contingencies Unit he was considering whether we could have steam trains running up and down the country for emergency purposes, in the event that we ran out of electricity or diesel fuel.

Several papers were before us – all marked 'Secret'. The first concerned the safeguarding of nuclear materials from terrorists. The paper was introduced by the Permanent Secretary at the Home Office, Sir Robert Armstrong, formerly one of Harold Wilson's Private Secretaries. The risk of terrorists getting hold of plutonium or nuclear material was low, but it was recommended that we spend £1.5 million on detection and disablement equipment, mainly from the Americans, to be able to deal with the situation. We should also keep in touch with the French and Germans.

I asked what would happen if there were a hoax, or a yacht turning up at Southampton claiming to have a bomb or plutonium on board, stolen from a British nuclear site. That would require a bigger response than 'Shall we call in the Yard?' They agreed to study that. As for the cost, it should be allocated between the MoD and the Department of Energy, particularly as the paper said it would cost hundreds of millions of pounds per kilometre to decontaminate an area in which there had been a nuclear explosion. That is an awful lot of money – a huge extra expense that is simply not included in our nuclear costings.

Another paper was a report of an official committee which claimed that the activities of the Provisional IRA and the Arab states were hotting up in Britain. An intense police and Intelligence operation was in progress and it might be necessary among other things to extend the Prevention of Terrorism Act from the Irish to other groups. It was an excuse for giving authority to the police and the Intelligence Services to expand their activities.

So, after Merlyn had hinted that he knew lots of things that he couldn't refer to, I raised a point. 'I am very concerned with the question of civil liberties. What are the guidelines?'

'Oh,' replied Merlyn, 'don't worry about that, it's all under tight ministerial control.'

I said, 'Well, I don't want to know the details but I think we should know what the guidelines are.' That was for them, he said. I went on, 'I want to register the view that you could accidentally back into a police state as a result of all this.' So that's on the record.

Cabinet at 10. Jim read out a statement on tomorrow's Civil Service strike which will affect 75 per cent of the staff from the two unions, the Society of Public and Civil Servants and the Civil and Public Services Association. It was a firm denunciation and David Ennals said the Prime Minister was absolutely right to do this.

On foreign affairs, Jim said he was cabling Varley in China to tell him only to sign a framework agreement; there was to be no specific arms deal with China. So my warning on the Harriers was timely.

*Friday 23 February*
To EY, and as I expected there was a civil servants' strike and CPSA pickets were standing at the end of Downing Street. One picket looked through my car window and asked if he could speak to me. The driver went on but I stopped him and got out. I assured him I was not going in to do their job or replace their work, and I went in.

I sat down at the table outside the Cabinet Room and worked on my papers while other Ministers arrived, and I overheard David Owen talking and Jim laughing, making a huge joke out of the whole situation. I thought I heard David saying that nothing had given him greater pleasure, then Jim said, 'Now Tony, don't pretend you're not listening', so I just continued to read the papers and didn't look up.

I presented my two papers, arguing that oil flaring was wasteful, national control was vital, and I intended to introduce much tougher limits to control it. Jim agreed on restraint of 45 per cent.

On Iran, David Owen reported that the new Prime Minister was more helpful, but Kenneth Berrill thought that Marxists in the southern oilfields of Iran might not allow development. (Such a silly comment, given that Marxists in China are buying our Harriers!)

I got everything I wanted.

*Wednesday 28 February*
Bert Williams, one of the Department's messengers, who is retiring today, came to say goodbye with his wife and daughter and grand-daughter.

In the afternoon Caroline and I drove to the Yamanis' home at Windlesham for dinner. We drove through two security gates, and outside the house there were about six armed men. It looked like something from a James Bond film. Yamani greeted us and took us inside. His wife was there and a son (by another wife), who is studying law at Pembroke College, Oxford.

Yamani, Bill Burroughs and I retired into his room for a talk. On Iran, he was most interesting. He said that Khomeini may not last but we wouldn't know for a few months. Khomeini may be able to make rhetorical and religious speeches but he wouldn't be able to cope. He didn't know what the young officers in the army really thought. What he would like would be for the young technocrats, socialists and officers to come together in a Mossadeq-type government.

He said the Russians needed the gas so they wanted a new government that would work in Iran. China was more interested and active in the area.

I should add that for the whole discussion the radio was on, presumably because he thought he was being bugged.

After about ten courses at dinner, we went to another part of the house – past the air-conditioned swimming pool and the new barbeque room – to hear a blind Egyptian musician who played a synthesiser and then an old-fashioned lute. He is about thirty-five and apparently lives in the house. At one stage Yamani said something to his wife in Arabic and she laughed, and he explained, 'I asked her if she would like to sing, and she said, "Why, do you want the Benns to leave?"'

### Thursday 1 March

Cabinet at 10.30 and the first item concerned the devolution referenda in Scotland and Wales which are taking place today. Jim suggested we react slowly to tomorrow's press stories. We had given people the choice and the Government must not rush to a decision.

Then Jim went on to the claim by nurses in NUPE, COHSE and the Royal College of Nursing, saying they were the 'heroines of the hour'. But Denis felt it would be difficult to give the nurses more money even on the basis of the RCN commitment to no strike action.

At this stage Jim and Denis got engaged in a nasty exchange, with Jim pressing for more money for the nurses and Denis resisting. What would be the repercussions on the Health Service and the Civil Service?

'Denis is trying to put me in the dock,' said Jim. 'I spend 80 per cent of my time on pay and I shall decide how to handle this.'

On foreign affairs, David Owen reported that the US were sending observers to the Rhodesian elections;[1] a UK delegation might go but he warned the Cabinet that if British observers went there was a serious danger that they would be physically attacked. So Jim said he would choose which member of the Cabinet to send.

'I might not be free, Jim,' I said.

### Friday 2 March

To Manchester for a meeting at the university and I saw Michael Meacher on the train. He told me his life story. His grandfather was a farmer and his father went into the City of London on some venture or other and lost all his money. Michael's mother was a much stronger personality, and Michael went to the local school in Berkhamstead and got a scholarship, reserved for people who wanted to take holy orders, to New College, Oxford. At that time he was completely non-political and went on to LSE to do social work, having decided that the church was not for him. There he came under the influence of the sociologist Professor Titmuss and was converted to socialism almost overnight.

He was selected for the Oldham seat because he was a well-spoken young man with an Oxford education, articulate and nice – the very opposite to the reasons for which he wanted to be selected. When you look at Michael you could easily think he is a young bishop or a keen vicar.

Today the results of the referenda were announced. The Welsh voted about 4 to 1 against devolution, and the Scots 32 per cent in favour of the Assembly and 30.8 per cent against. So the Yes vote was well below the requirement of 40 per cent of the electorate. Now the Government's life is at risk.

### Sunday 4 March
Referenda results in the papers – lots of speculation. Will it bring the Government down? etc, etc. I rang Jim at about 11.45 and offered to go in if he wanted to have a chat.

We talked over the phone about how to win the Election, about the women's vote, and so on. He was sure we could win, and we couldn't just walk away from the devolution issue. We would discuss it with the PLP. He thanked me for ringing and I said I didn't want him to think his old friends were deserting him in his moment of need.

### Monday 5 March
The *Guardian* had coverage of *Labour Activist*, the new paper issued by the Labour Co-ordinating Committee, which is run by Frances Morrell, Francis Cripps, Bob Cryer, Michael Meacher and others. The LCC has replaced the Tribune Group in a way, because it's much broader but includes people on the left.

At 2 I attended an EY(P) with the Prime Minister in the chair. I've never known the PM to chair a Cabinet sub-committee before. He thanked us for coming and he told us he had an idea. So far, we had dealt with pay problems case by case. Denis, who usually chaired EY(P), was busy with the Budget and a trip to Washington; so he decided Roy Hattersley should be in charge of pay policy and attend all the negotiations. This would be no derogation from other Ministers' responsibilities.

Albert Booth was disappointed not to be put in charge; he had looked after pay policy all this time. Jim agreed that he had a lot of experience and EY(P) would continue to have responsibility but Roy Hattersley would carry the load.

The plain truth is that, in the presence of all of us, Roy Hattersley was put up as Deputy Chancellor, and Albert Booth was demoted and humiliated. Shirley was jealous because it looked as if Roy was being moved into line for the Treasury when Denis goes.

Spoke to Tam Dalyell and Frank McElhone in the Tea Room about the referendum in Scotland and what was to be done next. The truth is that Tam is cockahoop, even though Scotland lost and the Party is obviously divided on it.

*Tuesday 6 March*
Peter Jay came to the office for a talk. America is in serious economic difficulties, and Carter, he said, was taking a terrible risk in trying to settle the Arab–Israeli conflict singlehandedly – but that was the sort of man he was. Peter greatly admires Carter; he is a tough character and Peter responds to tough characters in the way that many intellectuals, such as Paul Johnson, gather round Mrs Thatcher.

We talked about when the Election might be. I had inclined to late May, which was the view of a lot of people, but others wanted to hang on till the last possible moment.

John Hill, Chairman of the AEA, came to see me. He had written me a letter querying some of the things I had said in a lecture on science, technology and democracy about controlling nuclear power. So I thought we should talk it over.

He asked why nuclear power differed from anything else in terms of control; I mentioned the unique aspects of proliferation, waste and so on. Then he implied that the AEA didn't know anything about the nuclear accident in Russia in 1957. There were no satellites at that time, and besides he wasn't Chairman then. I knew that, but I said it turned out that a U2 aircraft was flying over at the time and took photographs, which John Hill had seen. He then said the accident was in fact at a military reactor, probably based on the American one at Los Alamos during the war, producing plutonium for weapons. So I learned a great deal; I had thought the incident was at a reprocessing plant.

He asked what it had to do with us anyway. I said it was very important when a reactor blew up anywhere in the world and I didn't like to hear about such things from TV. He argued that this was a Russian defence matter and did not concern us. It got worse and worse.

On the disappearance of 200 tons of uranium from Euratom, he said the uranium had been bought. Well, I didn't know that either. He added that there were no safeguards then, so I mentioned the IAEA.

I felt I had him on the run, and I went on to raise a few other issues and said I would send him a note indicating the areas of my interest. I wanted to think broadly about proliferation, terrorism, civil liberties, safety and so on.

To the House to vote in support of the bill by Maureen Colquhoun [Labour MP for Northampton] to abolish the status of the common prostitute, which was carried overwhelmingly. It was funny because the prostitutes' lobby had threatened to name any Member of Parliament known to have patronised a prostitute who voted against the bill. Those of us who voted for the bill were described as being in 'the red light lobby'.

To the Manifesto Committee. The manifesto entry on abortion said the Labour Government would improve and extend the NHS facilities. I thought we should put in something about conscience and I drafted a sentence: 'The Labour Party has always believed that the question of abortion is one for the individual conscience; however, for those women who require this treatment on the NHS the Labour Party will improve provision under the NHS to avoid an increase in private abortions.' That was accepted.

### Wednesday 7 March

With Alex Eadie to see Varley at the Department of Industry for what turned into a most dramatic meeting. Derek Ezra and Charles Villiers, Chairman of the British Steel Corporation, were there, and the issue was very simple. BSC want to sign long-term contracts for imported coking coal, which will mean a loss of 10,000 jobs in South Wales and massive losses for the Coal Board. BSC claim that only imported coking coal is good enough because the NCB can't supply the quality. It was very tense, and in the end Eric Varley realised that, if he agreed to this, he'd be responsible for major closures in Durham and South Wales. So he asked Villiers to think again; Villiers said that was unbusinesslike and constituted political interference.

Of course it was nothing of the kind. These public-sector barons have to be brought to account, but we're too weak to do very much.

### Thursday 8 March

Last night I had a letter from Harold Evans, editor of the *Sunday Times*, asking me to talk to him tonight before I met the *Times* employees. So I rang him as a courtesy and he agreed that the press had behaved badly over the winter.

I had a message from the Prime Minister saying he wanted to see me before the Cabinet. Albert, who is currently engaged in talks with the *Times* workers and managers, was there when I arrived. Well, Jim was extremely frosty. Albert reported on the talks, and then Jim said I shouldn't go to the meeting this evening. I told him I had seen the general secretaries and I had never given any impression that I was involved in the dispute itself, which had nothing whatever to do with me as a Minister. I wanted to go tonight to talk about the press, its future and the lessons learned.

'You have an EY(P) at 6 and you can't go,' said Jim.

'That's pure Cabinet Office skulduggery,' I replied, 'because that meeting was fixed for 7.30. They've shifted it back to prevent me going tonight.'

Jim said he'd look into that but the Cabinet Office didn't work for him, it worked for the Cabinet as a whole.

Albert said, '6 o'clock isn't convenient for me either because I'll be speaking in the House. I want to say, Jim, that Tony is absolutely meticulous about consulting me on all these matters.'

'Well, you're an embarrassment to me,' said Jim, turning to me. He said he kept getting all these questions about my speeches – yet another one today.

'What about Bill Rodgers and the others?' I asked.

In the end, Jim actually referred to it during the Cabinet meeting so the minutes will record that it was agreed I couldn't go.

Item 3 at Cabinet was the defeat of devolution in the referenda. The Government is legislatively committed to repealing the devolution Acts. The Liberals would not support repeal, nor would they support a vote of confidence in us, though the SNP's view was less clear. Jim said he would be sorry to see the Acts repealed without anything to go in their place. The Scottish Executive of the Labour Party was meeting tonight and they had already reaffirmed their commitment to devolution and hoped the Government would agree.

John Morris favoured a transfer of more responsibility to the Welsh Office now that a Welsh Assembly had been defeated. Michael Foot agreed. On Scotland we couldn't implement but we shouldn't ditch the Act, and we might face a vote of confidence the week after next.

I said we had to be ready for a possible spring Election. There was a deepening crisis and we needed a strategy.

'I only want to talk about devolution,' Jim interrupted, so I said I'd shut up. I was rather crabby.

Jim pointed out that the Thorpe trial would start on 13 April and the Liberals wanted an early Election to avoid all the embarrassment. We should lay the order for repeal of the legislation and offer all-party talks with the Liberals and the Tories on the future of devolution.

At 12.35 Jim sent the officials out and we had a talk on the timing of the Election.

Jim said, 'Mrs Thatcher – and don't ask me how I know this – wants May because she thinks she will be able to exploit pay problems in the local government elections campaign that month. She's going to campaign against bureaucracy, for the restoration of freedom, the reduction of direct taxation and an increase in indirect taxation. And she's going to ask for power to clip the wings of the unions.'

Back home, I turned on the 9 o'clock news and there was my picture with the news item that the *Times* workers had accused the PM of preventing the Energy Secretary from attending a meeting. (Brian Sedgemore had gone in my place.) That won't please Jim but it's his own bloody fault.

### Sunday 11 March

I had a note in my box that the Prime Minister wants to talk to me about Frances's work on *Labour Activist*, saying that she is in breach of her status as political adviser.

### Monday 12 March

Jasper Cross and Bryan Emmett, Assistant Secretary, came in about the vetting of personnel working on offshore installations.

From the beginning I have taken a strong line about the protection of our offshore establishments and we have told the oil companies that they must take precautions. We ourselves have arranged for various defensive preparations to be made in the event of an attack. Now the oil companies tell us they want the Government to use the Criminal Records Office and Special Branch – with its links with Northern Ireland – to check people employed on oil rigs. The companies would give us the names, and *we* would be expected to check them out and blacklist them if necessary for previous convictions or political reasons.

It would mean moving towards a police state as a by-product of having oil. I put this bluntly to Jasper Cross, who said that, if we refused to help out, the Government would get the blame if anything went wrong. I said I'd like to see all the correspondence with the oil companies and discover how the AEA handle security. They told me this was an innovation because up to now security had been about secret information and not about the nature of sensitive work.

After that Hermann Bondi and Philip Jones came to discuss a proposal to fund the study of alternative energy sources. I told them I also wanted to help channel money to groups contesting us at public inquiries. Hermann argued that recipients would have to be academically qualified. I asked why, and said that what was important was that the research be relevant and the people be competent. That wasn't the same as being qualified. They also wanted to give £25,000 to Bristol University for energy research. Since I didn't accept that there should just be more money for the university gravy train, I suggested that Hermann set up a committee under his own chairmanship in which Friends of the Earth and other environmental groups could be represented.

Home Policy Committee at 5.30, and I was given authority to suggest names for the inquiry into civil liberties. Then we considered a resolution from a constituency Party denouncing the PM for his statement in January in the House that he would happily cross a picket line. Normally resolutions criticising Ministers are referred to the person concerned for comment first, but Dennis Skinner suggested we go ahead and support it. I said it was our normal practice to give the Minister a chance to respond. By 9 to 1 we decided to send it to the PM.

We were warned of the emergence of the Ecology Party and advised that we had to be better organised to deal with it.

Neil Kinnock thought these environmental issues were political: we couldn't sympathise with 'the bourgeoisie' and their ecological preoccupations. These fights were against big business.

Eric Heffer said pollution and nuclear waste were key issues. Joan Maynard agreed it was a political question and favoured tougher measures against nuclear waste and factory farming.

Norman Atkinson made his usual pro-nuclear speech and supported the fast breeder.

We agreed that the environment group of the NEC would look at these areas and produce a statement for the manifesto.

### Tuesday 13 March
François Mitterrand's press officer came to see me, acompanied by someone from Transport House, to discuss future meetings being hosted by the French Socialist Party in preparation for the direct elections.

She told me about this fantastic spectacular being planned in Paris to which leaders from all over Europe will be invited to read poems in their national language, to reflect the culture of Europe. It will all be paid for by the Common Market – fireworks, orchestras, triumphal marches and demonstrations. No political speeches: it has nothing whatever to do with socialism or democracy. Meanwhile the Labour Party here is starved of money. It is one of the most revolting aspects of the whole direct elections exercise.

### Wednesday 14 March
EY Committee at Number 10. Jim warned us to expect another vote of confidence in about two weeks' time. If the worst came to the worst, said Jim, we had better leave Thatcher to inherit the situation. If prices rip the Tories will have to cope with it and then we'll get back in again because of their inability to cope.

The officials left and we discussed what to do about the orders to repeal the Scotland and Wales Acts. Jim was strongly in favour of delaying and forcing the Tories to table a motion of no confidence. If we went ahead with the repeal he thought the Party would split, but if we resisted the Tories in a vote of confidence the Party would stick together. I asked if the legislation should stand on the statute book until the next Parliament. Jim said that was difficult.

In the end Jim concluded that we couldn't hang on till the summer and that we'd win or lose a vote of confidence at the end of the month by one or two votes. Surviving on a day-to-day basis was just too much. Election dates in May or June should be considered.

Shirley Williams and David Owen wanted 7 June – a week after would be disastrous and a week before would be difficult.

It was clear that we were on the brink of an Election. I think May is the best if we can't last till October. Jim gave the impression that we had to go soon. At least we were talking about it.

Spoke to Frances before my meeting with the PM at 4.45 about her role on *Labour Activist*. She said that, as the breadwinner in the family, if she lost her job she might be forced to take the Government to an industrial tribunal. I kept that in the back of my mind but I have a feeling that, with the Election coming, things won't get that far.

Jim was sitting with *Labour Activist* in his hand. He said Frances was described as its secretary and Tory Central Office were questioning Number 10's Press Office about it. If he got a question about it in the House he'd like to be able to say she'd resigned as secretary. I said I'd speak to her.

Then we discussed the Election and he is still talking about May.

Later Frances told me her name was mentioned on the back page in connection with a directory of organisations which the Labour Co-ordinating Committee was compiling.

### Thursday 15 March

Cabinet, and on foreign affairs David Owen talked about the Arab–Israeli situation. Jim said the Labour Party had a long historic association with Israel and a desire that Israel should survive. Since the war we had always supported the US lead on these matters, especially when a Democratic President was in power. But the Queen's recent visit to the Gulf States showed how important were our relations with the Arab world too. David Owen said, incidentally, that Schmidt hates Carter.

We came on to open Government, and Jim said he found the subject unutterably boring. The active and articulate people wanted it but they were a vociferous minority and the rest didn't care. Merlyn Rees described the parliamentary situation and criticised the make-up of the committee looking at Clement Freud's Official Information Bill.

Michael Foot said this 'vociferous minority' in favour of the Freud Bill included the Labour Party and the Conference. He had opposed the Freud Bill in the Commons but we should support repeal of Section 2 of the OSA.

Peter Shore said he had no compunction whatever in opposing the bill. He spoke with great passion and force. This was a charter for paranoids, it showed a lack of faith in Parliament, it suggested Ministers were incompetent. He thought a select committee was the best means of dealing with disclosure of information. MPs considering the bill in committee were totally unrepresentative. He, for one, was not at all 'bored' with the subject. A most powerful speech.

David Owen said we had to kill the bill but the question of repeal of Section 2 of the Official Secrets Act was serious. David Ennals remarked that Clement Freud was punishing us now for treating the matter as boring.

So then Jim Callaghan said, 'I stand rebuked for saying it was boring.'

I said I supported the Freud Bill and it was nice to hear from Jim that anyone who supported it was active and articulate. We lived in a time when the Government was drowned by a flood of leaks. There were the memoirs of Wilson, and the diaries of Crossman and Castle. Civil servants were interviewed on television. For my own part I was dependent on these sources because of lack of information from the Cabinet. I thought the best thing was to have a select committee to look at the whole question of open government. Jim agreed to the select committee, and I said he should announce it early.

*Friday 16 March*

To Greenwich for the annual reception of the Greenwich Labour Women's Council. While I was there I was introduced to a woman who told me a most tragic story. In 1944 she had three boys of thirteen, eight and four, and one afternoon a friend of her boys came over for tea, so she went round to the Co-op to get some things for them and at that moment a flying bomb landed and threw her to the ground. She got up and rushed back to her house and it had disappeared. Two of her boys, and their friend, had been killed, and the thirteen-year-old had a fractured skull. She just told the story as if it had happened that afternoon, every detail. She had a house built near the original house so that she could be near her babies. She subsequently had two more children. Then in came a man of nearly fifty and it was her son. An amazing story.

*Sunday 18 March*

Had a call from Bill Burroughs to say there had been a terrible mining disaster in the Golborne Colliery near Wigan. He arranged for an RAF plane to fly me and Colin Ambrose to Manchester, and we drove over to the colliery.

We waited with the Mining Inspectorate people and rescuc teams and others till Sid Vincent, the Regional Executive member of the coalfield, arrived. Three men had been killed and eight badly burned. It was really very distressing. I asked if I should go to the hospital but I was told the relatives were too upset. That's the third big colliery disaster that I have been to, one in 1975 and then Bentley Colliery last year.

Came back in a raging blizzard about 9.30 pm.

### Monday 19 March
I have a filthy cold.

Learned at the office that the St Anne's Boardmills protest had ended because the men had accepted redundancy pay. Redundancy pay is an absolutely necessary lubricant to de-industrialisation. People accept it and don't fight for their jobs.

### Tuesday 20 March
To the Treasury to see Joel Barnett. Joel wants the nationalised industries to keep within their own broad cash limits and is asking for £80 million from me. In the end I said, 'Look, all this rubbish about cash limits is nonsense. If British Gas were denationalised, it wouldn't count in your bloody cash limits.' So he said he'd note for his memoirs that I favoured the denationalisation of gas.

'Not at all,' I replied. 'The PSBR is rubbish; that's what I'm saying.'

'Well the PSBR *is* rubbish,' he said, and I told him I'd note that in *my* memoirs. Anyway I agreed to try to find the £80 million, though God knows how.

Back to the office, and Bill Burroughs said he wanted to raise a rather embarrassing matter with me. He handed over to me five or six manuscript pages by Frances, in response to an article in the *New Statesman* attacking *Labour Activist*, which she had asked to be typed out. Bill remarked that in view of the PM's minute it was inappropriate for it to be typed in the office. I told him to get it typed in another typing pool.

### Wednesday 21 March
Clive Jenkins came first thing in the morning and gave me his acceptance of my invitation to him to join the board of BNOC.

He gave me photocopies of all the Treasury and TUC papers which had been distributed during the TUC–Government talks.

Clive is trying to be friendly. He thinks he's telling me things I don't know and I don't disabuse him of that idea.

EY Committee started with an assessment on Iran. Eric Varley estimated that 50,000 jobs were at risk because of the cancellation of a number of defence contracts. We did have an awful lot of trade with Iran.

I gave a report on the oil situation and went on to say that we had paid a high price for poor intelligence and we would have done better reading *Tribune* or listening to Iranian students over here. We ought to study Islam more carefully: we didn't know the difference between Shi'ites and Sunnis and it was like trying to understand Northern Ireland without knowing the difference between Catholics and Protestants. We'd had some near misses over Iran – the Shah wanted to buy BP shares and buy into our nuclear industry.

The committee was stunned, and when I finished Jim said, 'You were given an opportunity of seeing Intelligence telegrams and you turned them down.'

'Only because I was told to sign a piece of paper which put me under the instructions of a junior official in my Department, and I wasn't prepared to do that.'

Denis said Tony Benn was in favour of cutting off hands in public – that was what open government was. The atmosphere got quite nasty. Shirley supported me a little, saying that very rapid change did produce a conservative reaction. Jim thought conservative reaction here would be felt in relation to the House of Lords; people didn't want it abolished.

I said I thought people in a slump go back to their roots – the Archbishop of Canterbury to the Ten Commandments, Mrs Thatcher to Adam Smith and socialists to Clause 4. In truth, anything I say annoys my colleagues now. I am an irritant.

Later Rampton told me that Derek Ezra wanted to be a board member of Solway Chemicals, an international chemical company, and that it should be cleared before I confirmed Ezra's reappointment as Chairman of the Coal Board. I had never heard this before: I think Rampton is trying to delay Ezra's appointment until after an Election, in the belief the Tories will win.

Francis and I had a chat in the evening. He said if we lost the Election we had five years to convert the Labour Party to planned trade. I don't think that goes far enough, but Francis is a liberal economist working to produce a new form of economics for managing capitalism.

### Thursday 22 March

Cabinet at 10.30, and Jim told us that Richard Sykes, our Ambassador in the Hague, had been shot dead along with his footman. Nobody knew why.

Jim handed round the table his statement on devolution, which we discussed at great length. It is clear that we might buy a month of support but, when we come to the end of the talks with the Tories, Liberals and Nationalists, we'll be voting on the orders to repeal the Scotland and Wales Acts, and on that we can't survive. So the Election will have to be in May, though Transport House and Jim and all the pro-Europeans want it on 7 June.

Talked to Barbara Castle later about direct elections to Europe. I think she's just realising that the European Parliament is not all the fun she thought it would be. I must say, I have no sympathy with anyone who is a European candidate, but I know it's awful.

Everyone is talking about an Election. Mrs Thatcher has put down a motion of censure for Wednesday and it looks to me as if it's hopeless. I spoke to Michael, who feels we should have been more positive and asked the House to endorse our approach to devolution. I think control is slipping through our fingers and, quite frankly, it's better to have the Election now. Thatcher would not have tabled a motion of censure unless she knew that she'd get people into the Lobby. So this time next week we may be tidying up and polling day will be imminent.

### Friday 23 March

Spent the evening in Bristol discussing the Election campaign. At this moment I am not optimistic. Merlyn Rees doesn't think we'll win Wednesday's motion of confidence and said on TV tonight that if we didn't there'd be an immediate Election. I shall fight it very much on my own beliefs as set out in the Party programme.

### Saturday 24 March

Frances has several nominations for the Blackley constituency in Manchester. I desperately hope she pulls it off.

### Sunday 25 March

Hilary told me that Rosalind had asked her doctor how long she had to live if she took no further treatment. She was told between three and six months – maybe longer. She doesn't want any more treatment. She is on a grape diet and looks frail but is active. She's spending a lot of time at Stansgate now, alone, thinking and walking. A most courageous girl.

### Monday 26 March

David Butler turned up at home in the morning. He thinks the Election is quite open. His guess is that, if Thatcher loses, Francis Pym will be Leader of the Conservative Party and he will favour PR. David could see the whole of British politics being reshaped.

To the Commons for the meeting of the TUC–Labour Party Liaison Committee. David Lea, Geoff Bish and Derek Scott, Denis Healey's political adviser, had prepared a paper on employment and technology which sounded as weak as water.

Barbara Castle made a good contribution. She observed, 'This is a most monotonous discussion. Denis always gives the same old answers and he always passes the buck to working people. If you squeeze the economy you won't keep production down. You're using deflation to deal with inflation. Our only hope of winning an Election is to have a policy for growth, and we shall have to finance the borrowing requirement without pandering to the profit demands of the City of London.'

Norman Atkinson said, 'Don't blame the Chancellor. This room is full of experienced socialists and there are no remedial solutions by fiscal or monetary means.' Manufacturing employment had fallen by nearly half a million since 1968; we were now importing unemployment and if we expanded it would get worse.

I pointed out, 'We are doing the thing that we said we'd never do. We are in effect allowing the balance of payments gains from the oil to finance imported manufactures and strengthen the pound. We are importing manufactures we could produce and therefore losing jobs.'

I gave examples. BSC had totally ignored a request by Eric Varley and myself not to import coking coal from Australia which would put the Durham and South Wales coalfields at risk. Burmah went ahead and ordered ships from Japan against the requests of three ministers. I was afraid we were going to be the Merseyside of the EEC.

Jim Callaghan spoke. 'My contact with international leaders shows that they have the same problem. We mustn't be insular. This is a world problem and not just a free world problem – Poland and the Soviet Union are facing the same difficulties. We need international discussions. Tony Benn says Britain could become the Merseyside of Europe and I share his fears but the state can't do much to stop it. Nobody knows the answer. I cannot offer a plan. It does not exist.'

This is Jim abandoning his role as a British Prime Minister, let alone as the Leader of the Labour Party.

*Wednesday 28 March*
National Executive at 10. Having been tipped off by Barbara on Monday night that the manifesto for the European election candidates in the UK had already been printed, I had obtained a copy. It is a sort of orange-red with the symbol of the European Socialists instead of the Labour Party symbol; 24 million of these have been printed at a cost of £175,000 without a single elected member of the NEC being consulted. Norman Atkinson moved that in future all European elections material should be checked before publication with the Publicity Committee, and that was carried by 23 votes to 3.

This episode reveals how Transport House treats the Party with contempt and works hand in glove with the Government. It is just like the Conference Arrangements Committee, which pretends to defend the delegates against the Executive and actually defends the Govern-

ment against the delegates. The whole business of Party democracy has
got to be dealt with.

In the House in the evening, I heard the end of Willie Whitelaw's
speech in the motion of censure and then Michael Foot. It was very
much like an Oxford Union debate with a lot of joking. It didn't address
itself to the main issues at all. Thatcher apparently made a rather dull
speech.

To the vote. Roy Hattersley, it was said, tried to get a couple of
Scottish Nationalists to support us by promising an inquiry into prices
in Scotland and Wales, and had given Frank Maguire, the Independent Member for Fermanagh and South Tyrone, three bottles of
whisky and offered an inquiry into food prices in Northern Ireland, to
try to gain support. I sat on the Front Bench next to David Owen and
Roy, and it looked as if we might have won at first because one Member
came from the Aye Lobby and put his thumb up. He apparently
thought we'd won by one vote – 312 to 311 – but actually we had only
had 310 votes. As the tellers came in, Spencer Le Marchant, the Tory,
took his place at the right of the table facing the Speaker and we knew
that they had won.

So at that moment the Labour Government ended. Jim and
Thatcher made short statements and as we walked out Labour
Members sang the Red Flag.

That's the end of a memorable day in British politics, the first time
for fifty-four years that any Government has been defeated on a vote of
confidence.

### Thursday 29 March

I heard today that KME had finally gone into liquidation on Tuesday –
symbolically, the day before the Government was defeated.

Cabinet was advanced by half an hour because of our defeat.
Downing Street was jammed with photographers behind the crush
barriers. Jim announced the date as 3 May. Parliament would end next
Wednesday. The new Parliament would meet on 9 May for swearing in
and it would be officially opened on the 15th. We were then given a long
list of bills that the Tories agreed should complete their passage,
because after losing the vote of confidence we can only legislate with
their consent. It didn't include the Education Bill.

On procedure, Jim said Ministers would receive word about the use
of official cars, writing articles for the press and so on, which he was
sure we'd treat 'with our usual regard for instructions'.

On the manifesto, Jim emphasised, 'I want to make it absolutely
clear I am not prepared to be worn to a frazzle by an argument with the
NEC, and I hope other members of the Cabinet will take up the battle
and not leave it entirely to me. The Cabinet will have a meeting with

the NEC later, but I am not prepared to see the NEC give instructions to Ministers in a future Labour Government because the purpose of the manifesto, if it has one, is to appeal to the public and to give the general direction of policy. The NEC wants detailed commitments and I shall resist that.'

I said, 'I hope very much that we are not going to be given a new draft, as rumoured in the *Guardian* a few days ago, quite different from the one we've been working on. For example, there will be pressure to put abolition of the Lords in because that was agreed at Conference. We will need plenty of time for the Clause 5 [manifesto drafting] meeting.'

Jim replied, 'I am only prepared to have one Clause 5 meeting, and, as far as the House of Lords is concerned, let's leave that issue out. We've had enough of constitutional change with devolution and all that and we need to look forward. I shall submit a draft and I shall insist that a decision is taken the same day. Ron Hayward can convey the gist of it to the press that afternoon and it can be printed and released the next day.'

That was the worst news I'd heard, but it didn't surprise me. It just means there's a real tussle ahead.

Got to Bristol at 8 for the campaign committee meeting. I have to finalise my Election address tomorrow. Left at 8.45 and caught the train back to London.

*Friday 30 March*
Ron Vaughan picked me up from home at 3.30 to take me to Paddington and told me that a car had been blown up at 3 o'clock in the House of Commons car park. We later heard that the car belonged to Airey Neave, Conservative MP for Abingdon and shadow spokesman on Northern Ireland. It exploded as he drove out of the car park, causing the most terrible injuries. He died later in Westminster Hospital, after being cut out of the car with an oxyacetylene lamp.

He was a very courageous man who had been a prisoner of war at Colditz, but he took a hard line on Ulster and that presumably was why he was killed – by the Provisional IRA or another splinter group.\* But this does introduce the possibility of tremendous police protection and pressure for a toughening up of security measures. I am sad and sorry at what has happened but it confirms my belief that we must have a new look at Northern Ireland.

*Sunday 1 April*
Hilary gave me for my birthday (on Tuesday) a long stick with a mirror and torch attached so that I could look under my car for bombs. Joshua had given me exactly the same. So touching.

---

\* Both the Provisional IRA and the Irish National Liberation Army claimed responsibility for the killing of Airey Neave; the police at the time believed the INLA planted the bomb. The murder has never been solved.

*Monday 2 April*

Half a million civil servants are on strike.

To the National Executive at 11 in the boardroom to discuss the Election manifesto drawn up by Geoff Bish. Jim Callaghan said it was well rehearsed and we'd had more democracy than before, but the Tory manifesto would be very general with a few major themes: to reduce taxes, to cut the power of the unions, and to assert law and order. We should do something similar – to focus on cutting unemployment, getting lower inflation and dealing with union unrest by negotiation. We couldn't have two manifestos. He asked, 'Am I to be committed to this? I have drawn up a document that is about one-third of the length of Geoff Bish's and I would regret it if we had two documents.'

He continued, 'On a quite different matter I must warn you that with the political assassinations that have taken place, particularly Airey Neave's, there is a risk to NEC members. Therefore on the issue of Northern Ireland and terrorism we should have as little difference as possible between ourselves and the Tories. I think there should be talks with both Parties to discuss it.'

Joan Maynard pointed out that we lost the vote of confidence because Gerry Fitt and Frank Maguire didn't vote for us in view of our policy on Northern Ireland.

We stood for a moment in Airey Neave's memory and Shirley Williams suggested sending a letter of condolence, which was agreed.

Joan Lestor asked what was meant by an agreed response to terrorism. Did it mean capital punishment?

Jim said no.

Michael Foot thought whatever we did we must avoid adverse press comment and have one manifesto and not two. Today we should just agree to the themes. So Barbara Castle said that was an attempt to reduce discussion of the manifesto. It had to include specific commitments.

Jim said that was true to a point, but he couldn't accept that everything that went in tied Ministers' hands.

After some argument, Eric suggested that a small group should be established now to reduce the manifesto to the right length, and Jim then asked, 'What about my document?'

So by 17 to 6 it was agreed that a sub-committee be set up to consider the documents. A long discussion then ensued about who should be on it. In the end it was agreed that the members would be Jim Callaghan, Frank Allaun, Eric Heffer, Denis Healey, Tony Benn, Michael Foot, Lena Jeger and Russell Tuck, to meet at 6.15 tonight at Number 10 and no doubt work through the night on it.

As we were leaving, I told Jim that I had been asked to do an interview on the Harrisburg nuclear accident,[2] and he said that was all right so long as I was at the manifesto meeting tonight.

*Right Reverend host: 'I'm afraid I've got a bad egg!'*
*The curate: 'Oh no, my lord, I assure you! Parts of it are excellent.'*

Over to the House through the civil servants' picket lines. There was a lot of security at the House, as you'd expect.

At the office I got the basic information on Harrisburg – the reactor was a PWR of Babcock & Wilcox design and there had been a coolant loss. I spoke to Bondi about it.

At the Campaign Committee I learned that our theme is going to be 'The Labour Way is the Better Way'. We agreed to spend £25,000 on opinion polls, which Jim wants.

Then the drafting group which had been set up this morning met at Number 10 for the manifesto discussion. It was a dramatic evening.

Jim Callaghan took the chair in the Cabinet Room, which was overawing for people who hadn't been there before. Apart from the members agreed this morning, there were David Lipsey, Reg Underhill, Ron Hayward, Joyce Gould, Jennie Little, Geoff Bish and Tom McNally. Because of the strike of civil servants there were no Number 10 staff but a Private Secretary brought in a plate of sandwiches and drinks at 8. I had about four ginger ales but there was no tea. At midnight the messengers appeared and brought refreshments, so the old 'family retainers' formally made their protest and came back on duty.

Anyway we had two drafts – a shortened version of the original one by Geoff Bish; and Jim's, drafted by Tom McNally and David Lipsey, a meaningless document of half the original's length.

After a tussle we took Jim's draft as the basic manifesto and I raised every single point from our original draft.

The toughest battle came on economic policy, since Jim had left out full employment and concentrated on inflation. But of course if you go for inflation targets it is just a green light for the Treasury to go on with its monetarism. Denis and I had some sharp exchanges; in the end we included something on employment, but it was pretty meaningless.

We got commitments to increase public expenditure and then discussed industrial policy – whether planning agreements should be statutory, and whether the NEC would include investment in profitable manufacturing industry.

We kept jumping from text to text, from past manifestos to the TUC–Government *Into the Eighties* document and so on. It was really a very tiring meeting. One thing became clear: we should have got a set of points solemnly agreed between the Government and the Party, even if they weren't published; the detail may not matter to the reading public but it does matter as far as the agreement between the Party and the Government are concerned. It was also clear that the whole thing was about Party democracy, because in effect Jim was purporting to speak on behalf of the Government, yet none of Jim's proposals had ever been before the Cabinet and he was just speaking for the whole ministerial team without consultation. He felt that he had the final word.

We came to the House of Lords, and I said that the Party had believed for a long time, and it was unanimously accepted at Conference, that the Lords held back our legislation, there was too much patronage and we should state that.

Jim said, 'I won't have it, I won't have it.'

Eric lost his temper and banged the table. 'What do you mean you won't have it? Who are you to dictate? Who do you think you are? You are just a member of the Party.' He banged the table again.

'Well,' said Jim, 'I won't have it.'

I said, 'You can't do that.'

'I can.'

'No, you can't. What are we to say to people who joined the Labour Party to have some influence on our parliamentary system? They will say, "We joined the Party, we got this through, we've elected a Labour MP and we want him to implement our policy."'

Jim said, 'You'll have to change the Leader.'

I said, 'That's making it into a personality issue, not a political issue at all.'

'Well, I won't do it. I am the Leader of the Party and I have to decide what is right. I have responsibilities that I have to take and I won't do it.'

So in the end we decided to put the House of Lords on one side. That will be one of the big issues that come up on Friday at the Cabinet–NEC meeting.

On the Civil Service, Jim said he wouldn't have an inquiry into it, and Denis said any Minister who was any good could control his Department. I said that wasn't the point.

We came on to open government. Jim didn't want all this 'statutory access' put in. Denis chimed in, 'The truth is, the people who write this stuff about freedom of information know nothing about the Government whatever.'

I said, 'That's the whole point, Denis', and that really deflated him.

On Europe, I thought we should look at the European manifesto; Jim said he hadn't read it (which I don't believe). There is definitely going to be a fight on Europe. Jim said he wished somebody could say something good about the Common Market; was there no good in it? Eric answered, 'No.'

When foreign policy and defence came up we had an extraordinary discussion. Frank Allaun drew our attention to three commitments in our last manifesto: that we'd keep our defence expenditure in line with the GNP of other countries, so that would mean a substantial percentage cut; that we would end the American nuclear bases in Britain; and that we would not go for a new generation of nuclear weapons.

Jim said, 'This is a very difficult problem. I'm the only one who understands this. I carry a heavy burden of responsibility; we haven't started a new generation of weapons, but within a few years the Polaris submarines will be phased out, and therefore in a year or maybe eighteen months we *will* have to decide whether to go ahead with a new generation. Denis as Chancellor will probably be against it on grounds of cost; but I can only tell you – and I am saying this absolutely openly, I don't want to deceive anyone – that if we go out of the nuclear arms business others will enter, and that means Germany. I have talked to Giscard and Helmut about this, and Jimmy Carter. I could say we are not going ahead, but it wouldn't be altogether true.'

Well, all this 'if you knew what I knew' stuff was having a tremendous effect on Frank Allaun. He reiterated, 'Well, PM, I am against it.'

'I understand that completely, and I fully respect your position,' said Jim.

'And I respect yours,' returned Frank.

I just left it because there was no point in joining in at this point, but I shall definitely express my view on Friday. It was revolting really.

At one stage Denis leaned over and said, 'You're being very helpful. Why are you so cheerful?' I said it was my birthday in half an hour, so, as midnight struck, Denis announced, 'It's Tony's birthday', and Jim started singing, and then everybody joined in: 'Happy birthday to you, happy birthday to you. Happy birthday, dear Tony, happy birthday to you.' I said thank you very much and that I wished I had my tape on to record it! The whole evening was a funny mixture of table banging, shouting at each other and slightly nostalgic sentimentality. There was a lot of conning and overawing going on.

I shall have to think very carefully about future manifestos. Of course the real answer is for the Government and the NEC to meet regularly instead of once every five years.

At 3.15 am, as we left, Geoff said we'd given away a lot tonight.

I had a terrible aching headache that went right down to the base of my skull. I'm not feeling too well at the moment; I'm puffy, my ears need syringing, I have the most ghastly piles, and my eyes are burning. Generally speaking I feel absolutely whacked.

To bed at 3.45 am and Caroline, bless her heart, wished me happy birthday, my fifty-fourth.

### Tuesday 3 April

Heard from Frances how she was kept off the short list of nominations at Blackley. It was an absolute scandal but she was fairly relaxed about it.

Francis Cripps came in and we talked about the next five years if we lost. I said I'd try hard to get some money for Frances to be my political research assistant. Francis Cripps, of course, is all right, as he can go back to Cambridge University.

They both thought that I would not be the Leader when Callaghan goes. I asked them whether they thought I should stand against Callaghan immediately after the Election, but they reckoned it would alienate the unions and the new PLP. Frances wanted us to go for Peter Shore in order to keep Denis Healey out. Of course Peter would be the Leader for a very long time.

I have to recognise that my chances are actually nil because I haven't worked at it, and because the views I hold are unacceptable to the majority of the PLP. Jim will probably go in July, and Denis is all set to take over and he'll campaign ruthlessly. It is very important that he doesn't become Leader because he's not a socialist; he's not reliable or trustworthy.

The police rang up to check my movements over Easter, because of the IRA campaign and the death of Neave.

### Wednesday 4 April

Jim held a party at Number 10 for the end of Parliament. He and Audrey received us and we all went upstairs possibly for the last time as a Labour Government. Jim made a speech standing on a chair.

'It's three years tomorrow since I became Leader and I want to thank you all and I hope you all enjoy the campaign. We went through the manifesto the other night, and because it was Tony's birthday he was very nice to me!' (Actually *he* was a little bit nicer to me because it was my birthday.) He thought we'd win. Mrs Thatcher was worried and he said he was going to enjoy the fight. Whatever the outcome, we'd meet again in a month.

### Thursday 5 April
Farewell party with the Private Office and Press Office. Bill Burroughs made a little speech and they gave me a Wedgwood mug. I thanked them all and said this was my third farewell party – the first was when I thought Jim was going to get rid of me, and the second when I thought there was going to be an Election last year!

### Friday 6 April
To Number 10 for the joint NEC–Cabinet manifesto meeting in the Dining Room.

Jim opened the meeting, though Frank Allaun as Chairman of the Party was in the chair. After the Election, Jim said, all Ministers would be told to get their Departments to take up the points in the manifesto and those items that were not included would go to Ministers for consideration.

Ron Hayward said we had to have an agreed copy by 4 o'clock because there was a press conference tonight, and 'Please leave your copies behind after you go', which I had no intention of doing.

The meeting went on for eight hours. First we agreed on the title, 'The Labour Way is the Better Way'.

Norman Atkinson got us to amend the description of our policy as 'Fair Deal Free Bargaining' to 'Fair Deal Collective Wage Bargaining'.

I moved to include a big chunk about statutory powers of intervention and planning agreements, taken straight from *Labour's Programme 1973*. I said this was the only way to give credibility to our industrial policy.

Jim said we had to proceed by agreement and John Golding wouldn't accept it. Norman Atkinson said this was the most important issue of all.

Judith suggested a shortened draft, so I worked on one and passed it round. Eric Heffer supported it and said the powers existed in Italy and France. Neil Kinnock said the powers were comparable to the powers of the banks and there was a growing sense of disquiet about handouts to industry. Dennis Skinner said planning agreements were a halfway house to public ownership and they needed to be spelled out. The Bank of England bailed out the secondary banks with huge chunks of money that could only be described as planning agreements.

Peter Shore sympathised with Dennis Skinner, but thought the problem was not *having* the powers but knowing how to *use* them. John Smith supported Peter Shore – 'Why have this albatross around our neck?'

Jim said he had decided to include the planning agreements, but why spell out the powers? The political effect would be to double the hostility and he thought there was no agreement on this.

That was the Prime Minister's veto being used. He went on, 'We have a mixed economy and unless we move towards a centralised economy we can't have all this central planning. It would sour the atmosphere and kill investment. No doubt Tony would like to take over all companies but it's not on. The Tories tried statutory powers with the Industrial Relations Act and failed, as we would. We have won the confidence of business. Acquiescence is vital, and I must tell this committee there is no agreement on this.' There was the veto again.

There was further disagreement, so Eric Heffer suggested repeating what we said in the 1974 manifesto, namely that we'd reserve the right to take a public stake for all money we put into industry, and all aid to major companies would be channelled through planning agreements. The NEC trade-unionist members agreed.

Then David Owen suggested leaving out the reference to public ownership, and Jim said we'd be a target for the Tories. In the end, at Joan Lestor's suggestion, Jim agreed to the words 'We reaffirm the policy we have pursued that . . .' – and that was it.

On imports, we agreed to allow 'imports to acceptable limits'.

On banking, Tony Saunois tried to get a nationalisation commitment and Tom Bradley said that wasn't what the working party proposed.

Joan Maynard made a valiant attempt to get agricultural workers' low wages dealt with, but it couldn't really be done without our appearing to adopt a policy of statutory pay control.

On energy, I managed to strengthen a reference to 'parliamentary control' against the Common Market powers. I got in additions on safety, the fast breeder and alternative energy.

Jim repeated that he wouldn't have an inquiry into the Civil Service, so I wrote out an amendment saying 'We will be putting forward proposals to reform the machinery of government and the structure of public administration to bring it into line with modern conditions.' Jim accepted that.

On the Lords, I tried my hand at another draft, put in the most attractive way I could: 'We will reform and strengthen the procedures of the House of Commons to enable it to undertake all the work of the House of Lords and we shall introduce a bill to bring to an end the role of the House of Lords as a legislative assembly.'

Well, I may have compromised too early but I had in mind that Jim had said he would resign the leadership rather than have a statement on abolition of the House of Lords. I moved it, and a tremendous debate ensued.

I said the Lords had the power to delay legislation, patronage was an abuse, power in our society was too centralised, and it had to be dealt with.

On my side were Eric Heffer, Neil Kinnock, Dennis Skinner, Norman Atkinson, Stan Orme, Doug Hoyle, Barbara Castle, John Silkin (who had a weakening amendment), John Smith, Michael Foot (who had an even weaker amendment) and Alan Hadden. Against me were Peter Shore, who made a passionate speech saying that no one knew what to put in its place, Jim Callaghan, John Golding and Mike Cocks.

But the reality was that Jim wouldn't have it. After a lot of discussion, Michael Foot came up with a phrase that 'the power and influence of the House of Lords is indefensible in a democratic society and we will abolish their power to delay or veto our legislation'. Eric Heffer wanted to add 'as a first step towards abolition', but Jim wouldn't accept that. I tried to add 'the *existence* of the House of Lords was indefensible', but he wouldn't have that either.

In the end the words that will be printed in the manifesto are 'that the House of Lords is indefensible with its power and influence'. That was the best I could get.

Opposition to fox-hunting was excluded from the manifesto but we put in deer-hunting.

On the Common Market, there was a passage which was most confusing. I said the Party hadn't been consulted on the policy for Europe. It was no good stating in the manifesto that we'd strengthen the power of the Commons to amend or repeal European legislation at the time of the enlargement of the Community, because there was no power to do it. It hadn't even been raised as an amendment to the Treaty of Rome. That was a Cabinet secret.

After a long argument in which David Owen got furious and Bill Rodgers got angry, we retained our commitment to strengthen the House of Commons against European legislation. I must have spoken ten times on that one.

We agreed to reaffirm our commitment to bring our defence spending in line with the GNP of other countries. Jim had cleverly reaffirmed our position on Polaris and added that there would have to be a national debate about nuclear weapons.

At about 6 we agreed that my phrase, the 'fundamental shift in the balance of wealth and power in favour of working people and their families', should be put in. I had to forgo the words 'and irreversible' after 'fundamental'.

At that we finished. It wasn't too bad really. I thought we'd done rather well.

Back to the office, where a Granada TV unit was waiting, apparently to interview me about Harrisburg. The reporter told me he wanted two and a half minutes so I sat down with my tape recorder and he proceeded to fire about twenty questions at me, filling up ten minutes. I said, 'What are you doing?', and I asked if he planned to edit the interview. He said yes.

'That's not the basis on which you invited me,' I pointed out. 'You told me you wanted two and a half minutes and I'll give you two and a half minutes.'

He insisted on using the interview, so I threatened to ring up the IBA and left my recorder on, so I had everything that was said. He rang his producer, I rang the IBA, and we came to an agreement and he interviewed me again.

Frances was furious that we hadn't got the abolition of the Lords in and I said we did our best. She thought it was worse than nothing but I disagree.

### Saturday 7 April
Bristol all day. The papers today described the manifesto meeting as a triumph for Jim over the left and me. If we do lose the Election, no one can say we lost it by forcing through a more radical manifesto than Jim wanted. But the battle to democratise the Party has to start now.

*From 7 April 1979 the General Election campaign began in earnest. Apart from the work of canvassing and holding public meetings in my own constituency, in which I had a majority of 9373, I, along with other Cabinet Ministers, campaigned all over the country – in Penzance, Greenock, Birmingham, Newcastle, Liverpool and other towns and cities. I have been able to do little more here than give the main events of that hectic month and provide a flavour of the general political assessment and speculation.*

### Wednesday 11 April
To Bristol by car, with all my Election gear. I drove like the wind and arrived for lunch with John Tinsley, the Bishop of Bristol. Then canvassed all day.

### Saturday 14 April
The *Mirror*'s poll showed Labour ahead by 3 per cent in the marginals. But I heard later that the *Observer* was showing a 16 per cent Tory lead. Can't make head nor tail of it.

*Wednesday 18 April*

Canvassing in Eastwood Crescent, which is pretty marginal, turned up twenty-six supporters and twenty-two against. We didn't get the warmth of reception we did elsewhere and I began to think, for the first time, that the polls giving a Tory lead might be right.

Canvassing all day, and in the evening I went to the BBC Bristol studios to discuss 'the power of the unions' on the news. For a start, describing this as a major factor in the Election was prejudging the issue. The *media* have the *power* to discuss what they like. Before I came on there was a news item about teachers voting to strike, and Robin Day tried to take me to task over the strike. I said it wasn't for me to comment, but, I said, 'You earn £25,000 a year on television, and I earn £13,000 a year as a Cabinet Minister . . .' I learned later that he was furious.

*Friday 20 April*

My solemn assessment now is that Mrs Thatcher will win this Election with an overall majority. We have been betrayed by the Labour Government and the manifesto doesn't say anything.

I was taken to the Sikh temple in St Paul's, Bristol, and I sat on the floor with a cloth round my head and listened to the prayers and the singing. The head of the Sikh community welcomed me and wished me success, and he told all the Sikhs there that under no circumstances were they to vote for anybody but me!

At 3.30 I met up with the other Bristol candidates, Arthur Palmer, Mike Cocks and Ron Thomas, and we drafted a joint statement to electors. We outlined the achievements of the Labour Government and Bristol Council and described what would happen if the Tories won.

*Monday 23 April*

At the Campaign Committee Bob Worcester of MORI produced figures to show that on every issue the Tories had a lead on us – except for the Health Service, and for Jim as leader.

To Merseyside for several Election meetings, and in the evening I met Dr Thackrah, the superintending nuclear inspector, and Mr Helsby, the nuclear inspector for Windscale.*

They explained exactly what had happened at Windscale: 2200 gallons of unconcentrated high-toxic liquor had escaped over the years and was in the ground 10 feet below the soil with only the clay separating it from the water table. When you hear all the warnings

---

* At the end of 1978, soil samples taken at Windscale, which were not analysed until 1979, revealed a very high degree of radioactive contamination. I was not informed, as I should have been under my standing instructions, until March 1979. While in Liverpool I met the senior Health and Safety Executive inspectors for the area.

about how dangerous nuclear waste is going to be – with its 30 years of half-life, 500 years of danger and for centuries beyond – it is horrifying to think that this was just 10 feet below the soil.

They said that you'd have to build a new plant to process and clean the soil. My impression of Windscale is that it is a very dangerous site indeed. John Hill had said nothing about the leak. I discovered that the evidence which had been analysed in March had come from borings taken in November. So it was three months before anyone knew about it. Of course, BNFL are absurdly reassuring. Once again my confidence has been shaken by the behaviour of the nuclear industry.

I asked if we should close the plant, and they thought not, because there was no danger on the surface. I'm sure we'd come across some very surprising revelations if this incident were examined independently.

### Thursday 26 April

Bristol. Caroline went to meet twenty-two disabled miners from Betws Colliery who had come to canvas in St George's West.

I did five meetings – in shopping centres, at dock gates and in housing estates. I saw the last Concorde (number 16), which had its first flight a few days ago, flying over Bristol. It was really thrilling to think I was there to see 001 rolled out in Toulouse eleven years ago. It will still be flying in the next century.

### Saturday 28 April

Up early and prepared for a visit at home by John Hill and Dr John Dunster, Deputy Director-General of the HSE. John Arnott from my Private Office was present, and Frances Morrell also came at my request. I'm glad she did because it was one of the most remarkable meetings I think I have ever experienced.

Hill was embarrassed and Dunster was uneasy. I said, 'Thank you for the report on Windscale. I have arranged for it to be published today.'

Earlier John Arnott, who is one of my Private Secretaries, had told me that it wasn't possible to publish anything on a Saturday. I said it was, and he said the Press Office advised that it wouldn't get much coverage. I then said I didn't care what they advised, I wanted it out as soon as possible, and then he told me they couldn't do it in the afternoon. I had to be sharp with Arnott. 'Type out a note saying that I am releasing the report from Sir John Hill, that the HSE will report later, and send it round to all the newspapers, the BBC and ITV and the Press Association.'

We began the meeting and Sir John Hill argued there was nothing in this leakage.

I said, 'This is the most deadly toxic waste there has ever been.'

Dr Dunster asked, 'What about these chemical factories where the soil is absolutely sodden with toxic waste?'

In effect the Nuclear Inspectorate, which should be an independent watchdog, is in cahoots with the AEA and this is the great problem. The nuclear fraternity feel they know each other very well, they trust each other as being united in disliking a Minister, particularly a lame-duck Minister who they think will be out of office in four days and to whom they therefore have no further obligation.

I went over what I'd been told by the inspector in Liverpool.

That was how we left it, and I insisted I'd put out the reports and that there would be a public inquiry. They were horrified by that; they just didn't think it was serious.

Then towards the end I looked at the note I had sent to Hill instructing him to stop work on the PWR pending the Harrisburg report, and I found the original was in my file. I said to John Hill, 'Why is that here? Have you seen it, John?'

'Yes,' replied John.

Then I realised that the letter had already been folded, and when I get letters for signature they are always flat. I asked, 'Why have *I* got it?'

He said the Department of Energy office had asked him to return it.

I turned to John Arnott. 'On Monday I want the names of the people who recalled this letter – which was done without my authority – and the reason why they recalled it.'

On this note we closed the meeting.

John Arnott asked to use the telephone and then he came back into the room and announced, 'I think I should tell you that I recalled your letter.'

I said, 'Thank you very much indeed; that is the end of the matter.' He left.

I talked to Frances. This was an act of open defiance and I am absolutely determined that I will not leave office until I have got across to the public that there must be a public inquiry. I will not be prevented from doing my job on nuclear safety just because there is an Election.

The real anxiety about nuclear power, of course, is the bomb – civil power is only a cover for that. Windscale is a military as well as a civil establishment, and that is what frightens the Civil Service, the Cabinet Office, the military and so on.

At 4.45 I had a message to ring Bill Burroughs. He said the PM had seen the text of my release and thought it was alarmist. There should be an investigation, not an inquiry, and there was to be no reference whatever to the military aspect. As far as the Atomic Weapons Research Establishment (Aldermaston) was concerned, if asked I was to say that Sir Edward Pochin of the NRPB had settled the matter – a reference to the information I had received from the scientist at Aldermaston about health and safety hazards. I had asked some questions about this and received factual answers from Fred Mulley, but every month Fred has prevented me from publishing them on the grounds that it would lead to difficulty in getting a pay settlement at Aldermaston.

I told Bill that I couldn't accept that an investigation was the same as an inquiry. But the Cabinet Office had obviously advised the PM on what he should say and they'd concentrated mainly on the military aspects; this confirms my view that the main anxiety is military. The fact that the PM was wheeled into play in the middle of the Election on what was a fairly harmless press release I thought was very interesting.

I decided I'd write to Jim.

### Sunday 29 April

Wrote three important letters and kept copies. One was in my own hand to the PM saying there were three nuclear matters causing me concern: (1) the serious leak at Windscale which demanded an inquiry; (2) the Harrisburg accident, which had made it necessary to hold up the PWR work; (3) the questions and answers on Aldermaston, which went back to the time I was at Mintech, and on which I hoped he would intervene to help me publish.

Next I wrote to Jack Rampton. I said I wanted to know who recalled my letter to Sir John Hill and for what reason, and I wanted an immediate reply on that. Thirdly, I wrote to Bill Burroughs and asked for a copy of the questions and answers for dealing with Aldermaston and the correspondence with Fred Mulley, as I intended to raise it with the PM.

### Tuesday 1 May

Bristol all day. Some polls show a 0.7 per cent lead for Labour and others a Tory lead of 17 per cent.

### Wednesday 2 May

Without any doubt the Tories are going to win. I'm not sure about the majority but my guess is that our own campaign ran out of steam because Jim didn't make use of the Party at all. He ran a one-man band because the polls put him ahead of Mrs Thatcher and therefore he felt free to ignore the Party, never mentioned the manifesto at all. Mrs Thatcher has come through remarkably and it proves, as Caroline says, that you don't have to be popular – just capable of getting the message across.

Jim will try to blame the loss on militants or hecklers or the Young

*Cummings*

'You can let me in, dear! I'm not a mugger –
I'm only your dear old Uncle Jim!'

Socialists or the unions, but the reality is that we've had a right-wing Leader, a right-wing policy, a right-wing Cabinet, a right-wing manifesto and a right-wing campaign. Even the date of the Election was fixed without consultation. If we win, we then have to say that the real debate is within the Party. The Party and the unions have to be free to represent their interests and to campaign for socialist policies – without which we'll never deal with the slump.

### Thursday 3 May

For eleven hours Caroline and I drove around the constituency, in cold weather which turned to hail and snow. I sat on the roof of the car in a blanket with rubber overtrousers, wearing a woolly cap and anorak. It was freezing. We went round every single ward and it was terribly exhausting.

The first result was from Glasgow Central, where there was a Labour swing, as expected in Scotland. In the north-west we didn't do too badly but it became clear that in London and the Home Counties and the Midlands we were going to lose heavily.

At midnight we went to my count. The result was finally announced at 5 – scandalously inefficient. I was fed up and our Party workers were a bit depressed. To cut a long story short, the Returning Officer gave the result without inviting the candidates on to the platform. My majority went down from over 9000 to 1890; the Liberal vote slumped and the Tories picked up the extra votes. I felt mortified, although I'm in for five more years. I made a speech outside, as dawn broke, to a crowd of supporters. I declined steadfastly to go on any of the Election post-mortem programmes. The media were utterly corrupt in this Election, trying to make it a media event.

Tragically Ron Thomas was defeated in Bristol North East. David Owen held his seat at Devonport but the West Country as a whole was disastrous for us.

### Friday 4 May
It was a warm day and we got home totally punch drunk.

Shirley Williams was beaten, and the media treated it as if it were a state funeral – this remarkable, able, brilliant girl – whereas for me it was 'Benn beaten back by poll'. The difference in treatment between the right and left of the Party was unbelievable.

Watched all the rituals on television – Jim going to Number 10 and to the Palace, and Mrs Thatcher at Tory Central Office, then at the Palace and to Number 10, surrounded by great crowds.

We lost Audrey Wise, Tom Litterick, Doug Hoyle – such excellent people. John Pardoe was beaten; that gave me a lot of pleasure, I confess. Thorpe was beaten in North Devon and was interviewed in the most cruel way, looking absolutely ashen.

Stephen looked in. We lost Kensington, for which he was agent, by 5000, but he did a grand job.

Bill Burroughs and Ron Vaughan came over from the office with my possessions. I gave Bill the key to my red boxes and my pass and seals of office. Ron was near to tears. I gave him the oil painting of autumn which was a gift to me from the Russians.

Julie Clements was there doing champion service. I don't think I'll have any of the withdrawal symptoms I had in 1970. It's almost unbelievable that there are no more red boxes.

A dramatic day in British politics. The most right-wing Conservative Government and Leader for fifty years; the first woman Prime Minister. I cannot absorb it all.

I have the freedom now to speak my mind, and this is probably the beginning of the most creative period of my life. I am one of the few ex-Ministers who enjoys opposition and I intend to take full advantage of it.

# NOTES
*Chapter Five*

1.   (p. 465) Rhodesia's first multi-racial elections were due to be held in April 1979 until which time a transitional government under Ian Smith's premiership ruled the country. However, between the announcement of an 'internal settlement' in March 1978 and March 1979 some 5000 people were killed in the civil war, and elections, and progress towards an independent democratic Zimbabwe, were delayed until after the Labour Government's period of office.

2.   (p. 480) On 28 March 1979 cooling water pumps and the emergency back-up system at the nuclear power station on Three Mile Island, Harrisburg, Pennsylvania, failed. The temperature of nuclear fuel rods rose dramatically, and a hydrogen bubble developed in the reactor, posing the possibility of a devastating nuclear explosion. Because of radioactivity leaks in the surrounding area children and pregnant women within a 5-mile radius were advised to leave. The reactor was similar to the PWR being considered for adoption in nuclear power stations in Britain. The full story of 'an unbelievable chronicle of confusion, misinformation and contradictory advice' is given in *Nuclear Power* by Walter Patterson (1980).

# 6
# Beginning Again
## May 1979–May 1980

*After Labour's defeat in the General Election, three constitutional issues became of pressing importance within the Labour Party, and reflected the discontent at constituency level about the condition of the Party in Parliament.*

*The first was the election of the Leader of the Party by Conference or some kind of electoral college, in place of the traditional arrangement under which he had been chosen by secret ballot of Labour MPs (the PLP) alone.*

*Second was the reselection of Labour parliamentary candidates once in each Parliament, a change intended to ensure that no sitting MP could assume that he or she was in the House of Commons for life.*

*Third was the proposal that the General Election manifesto of the Party be drawn up by the NEC alone. Clause 5 of the Labour Party Constitution provided for the manifesto to be drafted by a joint meeting between the NEC and the Cabinet or Shadow Cabinet, known as the Clause 5 meeting, at which the Leader claimed a veto on policy to be included.*

*These constitutional amendments were partly inspired and fuelled by the way in which the 1979 manifesto had been drawn up and by the more general complaint that Labour MPs and Labour Governments often ignored policy agreed at Conference.*

*Of these three proposals, which were fought for over the next two years and became the focus of division between right and left, two came to fruition. Mandatory reselection was adopted by the 1980 Conference, and an electoral college system for electing the Leader was established at a Special Conference in January 1981. The third proposal – the drafting of the manifesto by the NEC – has never been accepted.*

*A subsidiary but related issue arose immediately after the Election: how Government funding for opposition parties should be employed.*

*Edward Short (now Lord Glenamara) had, as Leader of the House of Commons, 1975–6, introduced a scheme for state funding of opposition parties based on the number of votes each had received at the previous General Election. The funds, which became known as 'Short money', were intended solely for financing the parliamentary work of the parties in opposition. As Leader of the Opposition, Margaret Thatcher had handed this money to Conservative Central Office for work by the Conservative Party in Parliament. Jim Callaghan, after May 1979, channelled it directly to the PLP, where it was used to recruit researchers for the Shadow Cabinet, bypassing the national Party.*

*In this way, with its own funds, the PLP inevitably became more independent of the national Party; while the NEC was having to lay off staff to make economies, the PLP was taking on staff who had no legal contracts and not necessarily any connection with the staff of the Party. They were based in the House of Commons and were seen to be working for the Shadow Cabinet and not the Party.*

*The possibility of a widening gap between the PLP and the national Party led a number of members of the NEC, including me, to argue that the Short money should be paid direct to the NEC, which would then appoint people who could be seconded to the PLP, but who would be employees of the Party like the General Secretary and other officers at Transport House (subsequently Walworth Road).*

*In this respect we were urging that the method adopted by Mrs Thatcher should be followed by us.*

*The financial argument was never put to Conference because it was claimed that this was an entirely internal matter for the Party Leader to handle. Jim Callaghan, like subsequent Leaders, retained control of the money, supervised by some trustees appointed by the PLP.*

*In some ways the Opposition in Parliament has become a part of the Civil Service, less dependent on funds from, and therefore less accountable to, the Party nationally including the constituencies and affiliated trade unions.*

*All these proposals for change produced a strong response from the trade union leaders, who historically had always provided the praetorian guard of the parliamentary leadership and had traditionally enabled the Leader to keep the left at bay. The TULV – Trade Unionists for a Labour Victory – comprising all the most powerful general secretaries, was set up before the 1979 Election, ostensibly to channel trade union funding to the Party in a more organised way and avoid the individual appeals for trade union finance that had hitherto been the norm. It became immensely influential because the general secretaries held the purse strings and could therefore choose which political research and campaigning they favoured.*

*After May 1979 the general secretaries decided among themselves that the time had come to institute a thorough inquiry into the organisation, structure and activities of the Party, strengthened in their determination by the fact that members of the NEC's narrow and precarious left-wing majority were pursuing these constitutional reforms. In this way, and through their overwhelming voting power at the Conferences, they hoped to nip these reforms in the bud and delay the democratising process.*

*The Commission of Inquiry with trade union and Labour Party representation was duly set up and its deliberations are recorded in the following chapter, which ends as the progress towards reform of the Party is in full swing.*

### Saturday 5 May

Thirteen hours in bed and woke up at midday. My first concern was to get advice about what I should do. I had decided I wouldn't sit on the Opposition Front Bench and that when a leadership election comes I shall stand.

## Sunday 6 May
Worked on my speech for tomorrow's May Day rally in Birmingham and in the evening Joshua and I drove round to drop copies off to the BBC, ITN, the daily papers and Transport House.

## Tuesday 8 May
Dick Mabon rang. He is involved in a campaign to run Denis Healey for Leader, and I asked him how it was progressing.

He said, 'Oh, we don't want Jim to go yet, and of course when Denis does become Leader he'd like you to be his Deputy.'

'So you're still his campaign manager?' I enquired.

'Yes, but he doesn't fully realise it yet!' he replied.

I went off to Buckingham Palace. What amuses me about ex-Ministers is that they behave as if they are God's gift to the British nation, temporarily in retirement, and when the British people discover what a terrible mistake they've made they'll beg them to come back. That's the great illusion of all ex-Governments.

What I did notice was a complete detachment among them. Of course, for most it is shattering, but for me it is exciting.

I said to Peter Shore, 'I take it you're going to be Shadow Chancellor', and he replied, 'I don't think there'll be a change.' He was being very quiet and statesmanlike. I think he believes great things are about to happen to him.

I went in and shook the Queen by the hand, and she said, 'Mrs Williams was saying how troublesome politics was, with so many changes.'

I replied, 'Oh, I don't know about that. A change of Government is useful because it gives you a new snapshot view of the country; you get so tied up in office. Whereas twenty-five years ago we were an empire, now we are a colony with the IMF running our financial affairs and the Common Market Commission running our legislation and NATO running our armed forces, and to get a view of that is valuable.'

She said, 'Well, what will you do now?'

'I'm a parliamentarian, I like my work, and I shall write about my experiences. Both my grandfather and my father were Members of Parliament, and my wife and children are involved in political activity. In my family, politics is like a hereditary disease, rather like the monarchy!'

She gave a rather slow smile. 'How interesting. In some families people diverge and take other interests.'

'Not in my family.' I added, 'I only see you every five years – on my way in and out of government – but you've read so many papers over a long period, it must be interesting.'

'Oh, I don't read them all. Some of these FO telegrams I find hard to read.' I agreed with her on that. She said, 'Of course, as a result of the strike at the GCHQ* telegrams can't come in, so I don't have to read so many and I must say it is a great blessing.'

I remarked that, assuming the Ambassadors hadn't written them and the Foreign Secretaries didn't read them, I wondered who did look at them. She said she just 'dipped about'. I thanked her for sparing the time to see me; I knew she had lots of people to see. As I got up to go, she said hesitantly, 'Thank you for what you have done', and I left.

At 4 Joe Ashton came to see me at my request. He is very shrewd. He said incomes policy had been the cause of Labour's trouble and by October this will be a key question again. Joe thought I was right not to stand for the Shadow Cabinet but I felt I should delay announcing it because Jim would be re-elected tomorrow with goodwill and it would add a sour note.

### Wednesday 9 May
Went into the Commons for the meeting with the ex-Cabinet at 10, and there were four policemen checking each car. The meeting was in the Leader of the Opposition's suite overlooking New Palace Yard.

The first item was the leadership. Michael Foot suggested Jim be elected unanimously and that was agreed. Michael said all the other officers within the PLP would have to be elected and we settled dates for that.

I asked when we were going to talk about what had happened in the Election.

Jim said, 'I'll tell you what happened. We lost the Election because people didn't get their dustbins emptied, because commuters were angry about train disruption and because of too much union power. That's all there is to it.'

I insisted, 'I think we ought to go back over what has happened.'

Jim said, 'No inquests', echoed by Roy Hattersley. 'We must maintain collective Cabinet responsibility, and I don't want anyone to table a motion in the PLP without first clearing it with the Chief Whip, and I don't want any member of the Shadow Cabinet to speak without consulting the appropriate spokesman.'

That was just amazing – collective Cabinet responsibility in opposition!

* Between February 1979 and April 1981, members of Civil Service trade unions at GCHQ were involved in selective action to improve pay and conditions. The Conservative Government ultimately withdrew union rights there for reasons of 'national security'.

Went and had coffee with Ron Hayward, who was all steamed up. He said Jim had his own kitchen Cabinet and they were planning to expel the left, Jim thought he was God, and so on.

Up to the PLP meeting at 11.30. Michael moved Jim as Leader, and that was carried unanimously. Jim thanked us and said he was going to carry on. 'There is no vacancy for my job.'

At 12.15 I left and wandered round and chatted. In the Tea Room I talked to Michael Meacher and David Stoddart [Labour MP for Swindon], Mik, Dennis Skinner, Alex Lyon and others. It was a show of goodwill really.

Into the House at 2.30 and sat at the end of the Opposition Front Bench, perhaps for the last time. The House was summoned to the Lords. Then we trooped back and George Thomas was duly re-elected as Speaker.

### Thursday 10 May

I put out my press statement that I wasn't going to stand for the Shadow Cabinet and, as a courtesy, I rang Jim immediately afterwards to let him know. I think I woke him because he sounded very gruff.

The calls started to come in. ITN wanted to interview me and I said no. If the media people won't behave responsibly, I shan't speak to them. *World at One* rang and I turned them down.

Jim rang me later and he said, 'I was taken a bit by surprise by your statement. Would you come and have a talk today?'

I replied, 'Of course, but it isn't negotiable. I've decided.'

Julian Haviland phoned from ITN and tried to persuade me to talk to them; as a matter of fact, he wasn't too bad.

IRN rang and said they wanted to do an interview and I refused, so they asked if they could tape-record my statement. I agreed to that and they said they were sending someone round. Before he arrived, on the 12 o'clock IRN bulletin, the same chap reported, 'The most left-wing member of the last Cabinet has resigned from the Shadow Cabinet in a bid for the leadership. . . . He wants more socialism and more democracy and a leadership change. Enter stage left Mr Benn.'

So when he arrived I made him listen to this, and I said, 'Why do you put labels like "most left-wing" on me? Why do you say things I haven't said? Why "Enter stage left"? You could have said, "Mr Benn has been in Parliament for thirty years, has held office in five Governments, introduced the Referendum, fought a peerage case to stay in the House of Commons," etc.'

He replied, 'Listeners would have switched off.' In fact he did give me a chance to tape my statement.

At 1.45 I went to see Jim in his room. He said, 'If I'd known you were not going to stand for the Shadow Cabinet, my decision might have been different.' I presumed he meant his decision to stand again. When I asked why, he said, 'I'd like to go back to my farm.'

I told him, 'I think you're right to stay in, and I am pleased you've said there isn't a vacancy because we can debate the issues without the leadership question interfering. There has to be a debate because some very important themes will arise. You've had me in the Cabinet a long time, you know what I think and what I'm going to say.'

He said, 'You talk about the Party but there are two communists on the NEC.'

'Who?' I asked.

He named them.

'Are you saying that they are members of the CP?'

'No,' said Jim, 'but they are in continual touch with King Street.'

'Well, all that tells me is that MI5 bug their telephones, and that worries me much more. When I asked whether my phone was bugged, I didn't get an answer.' I said I honestly didn't think he knew what went on, and that was worrying too.

I went on, 'Look, Jim, we have a broad-ranging Party. Anyway, I had decided that I wouldn't serve even if we won.'

He remarked, 'I hope nothing I have said to you in anger influenced you.' That was a reference to my interview in March when he said he'd sack me if we were in calmer waters.

I said no but I wanted the debate on future policy to take place without rocking the boat or making it harder for us to win the next Election, because there had to be a debate.

He said, 'What about?'

'About the relationship between the Government and the Party and the NEC and Conference. If the Government were a bit more responsive to Conference, Conference wouldn't pass such extreme resolutions. There has to be confidence in the Party. No Leader has ever taken charge of it and the left won't take charge of it. What worries me is that if you'd won the Election you would have tried to "clean up" the Party.'

'What are these great issues that have to be debated?' asked Jim.

'One of them is the question of the leadership, not the Leader. It is much too autocratic and there's too much patronage.'

'I don't take that view,' he said.

'Then, when we're in opposition, the Shadow Cabinet should make recommendations to the PLP and the PLP should vote on them each week at the Thursday meeting.' That really riled him. I went on, 'We don't want any more honours. Labour peers appointed by Harold Wilson attack us now.'

Jim asked, 'What about my resignation honours list?'

'That's just the point. We don't want it.' I added, 'This debate has to take place with goodwill, and I hope I can see you from time to time. I have enjoyed working with you, and you have restored integrity to the leadership of the Labour Party, which is very important. We haven't agreed on everything but it has been a friendly relationship.'

I took him completely by surprise.

At 2.20 I went into the House and sat two rows behind the Front Bench, just like a new Member, and I realised that for years I had paid no attention to Parliament whatsoever.

Mrs Thatcher came in. MPs were being sworn in, and I joined the queue to affirm, after all the Ministers had been through.

At tea I saw Michael Foot and Stan Orme looking at the newspaper headlines – 'Benn in Showdown with Jim', 'Benn Out for Jim's Job', and so on. Michael said, 'I see the press are representing your motives in the finest manner', and I laughed.

Tea with Adam Raphael of the *Observer* and I told him my usual complaints about the media and said the only place my speeches were printed in full was Hansard. He said the popular press was appalling, and I said it wasn't the popular press I was talking about. Conor Cruise O'Brien in the *Observer* had said I was a Marxist and wanted to take away people's liberties, and the *Observer* is far more serious as an opinion-former than the popular press. He wrote it all down.

Came home to a flood of requests to do broadcasts, which I ignored. Spoke to Frances, who is very depressed because she failed to get into Parliament.

### Friday 11 May

The papers this morning had huge coverage of my decision to return to the back benches and every single one of them attributed it to a bid for the leadership of the Party.

The worse of all was the *Sun*: 'Tony Benn yesterday made a desperate bid for the leadership of the Labour Party . . . his message is that he is fed up with Jim Callaghan, wants Labour to swing to the left', etc.

It was so outrageous that I wrote a letter to the father of the NUJ chapel at the *Sun* with a copy of an article and the NUJ code of conduct, which says that conjecture should not be presented as fact. I said I'd be grateful if I could attend a meeting of the chapel. I don't believe that the Press Council or the libel courts are the right bodies to go to. There is no solution other than driving responsibility back to the journalists themselves.

I had an invitation to appear on *Panorama*. I was tempted. I'd like to get across to people what I'm doing, but on the other hand I am frightened of the BBC's power. They get you in the studio and simply put questions to you that have nothing whatever to do with what you want to talk about and you can never recover from it.

So I had a word with the producer of *Panorama* and explained this to him. In the end I decided not to do it. But I did let my hair down in talking to the BBC and to Fred Emery, the presenter of *Panorama*. I told them my character was being assassinated. I think they were surprised at the depth of feeling they provoked.

Frances Morrell said on the telephone that I ought to behave as if I were the Leader of the Party, brooding over the nation's problems. Interesting. It will take me a long time to work out what my role is.

I had a letter from Richard Gott of the *Guardian* inviting me to write a weekly column. Caroline thought I shouldn't. On balance I think not. I see myself withdrawing and playing a larger role within the Party in the country. A lot of people are pleased at what I've done, and on the Executive I will be much better able, out of the Shadow Cabinet, to speak openly.

To Bristol. At the GMC I commented on the Election and explained why I hadn't stood for the Shadow Cabinet. I was asked why I hadn't consulted the Party. I should have done of course, and I lost a certain amount of support which I would otherwise have had.

The left in the House of Commons are hesitant about what I've done. Neil Kinnock and Eric Heffer, who are going for the Shadow Cabinet, are afraid that it will look as if they've sold out while I am still free on the back benches. Dennis Skinner is doubtful too. The right-wing on the back benches are seeing this as a leadership bid and are saying all sorts of cynical things. It's an interesting situation.

*Sunday 13 May*

The *Observer* had quite a reasonable article as a result of my talk with Adam Raphael, who wrote that Benn's struggle for the soul of the Labour Party had begun. He was absolutely straightforward and I was pleased at that.

To the Harts' house. Judith's husband Tony is standing for the European elections. The Baloghs, the Shores, the Silkins and the Foots were there.

Michael asked me, 'Why did you decide not to run for the Shadow Cabinet?'

'You know my position, Michael. I wasn't in sympathy with the last Government, though I stuck it out till the Election. We worked very hard. I was threatened with the sack in March for voting against the Harriers and I decided during the Election that I would not stand again, even if we won. When Jim said there would be collective Shadow Cabinet responsibility, that was the final straw. I want to be on the back benches.'

Michael absolutely turned on me. 'What are you going to say on the back benches?'

'I want to talk about democratising the Party, getting rid of patronage, putting the PLP back into a clearer position of control over its own affairs and into a more creative relationship with the NEC, and so on.'

He blew his top. 'We don't want to put the PLP back in charge. That was the trouble during the Bevanite period. We can't have that.'

I went on, 'I'm also in favour of the election of the whole Shadow Cabinet and Cabinet when we're in office.'

'That's a recipe for keeping the Party in the wilderness for twenty years.' He was so angry.

I said I thought the situation was serious and that we were moving sharply to the right; that was my honest opinion.

He said, 'Oh, all these fascistic ideas that you believe are taking hold in Britain . . .' He was furious.

Of course, if Jim goes, as Deputy Leader Michael will then take over the leadership and keep the seat warm for Peter.

I cannot avoid getting into these terribly combative discussions. I don't think these people have any idea of what the Labour Party is about any more. It has gone much further than I thought. When you get the so-called left of the Party so far to the right, then does it mean there is no support in the country for radical views?

### Monday 14 May

Fantastic amount of coverage today about the latest issue of *Labour Activist*, which is run by the Labour Co-ordinating Committee, the organisation set up by Frances and Francis, Brian Sedgemore, Geoff Bish, Chris Mullin, Bob Cryer and others at last year's Conference. The broadsheet contained a bitter denunciation of the NEC and the Cabinet for failing to include in the manifesto a pledge to abolish the Lords and many other points that had been contained in the last Labour programme approved by Conference. The press used it to continue their campaign against me. The *Daily Telegraph* led on it with 'Benn's Men Draw Up Charter: Radical Proposals to Swing Party Left', the *Daily Mail* said, 'Benn Plans to Censure Jim', and so on. *World at One* wanted me on the air but I have decided to refuse all media invitations for the time being.

*Labour Activist* is seen as an instrument to make me Leader of the Party. In fact they have never shown me anything they have written because they don't want to be seen merely as my leadership campaign group. I didn't even know it was coming out today or what was in it, but nobody will believe that.

Walked through St James's Park, the most beautiful sunny day, hot and balmy. The winter has melted away.

*Tuesday 15 May*

Opening of Parliament. Seeing the Lords and Ladies in their finery made me realise how little we did in power to make the country look more democratic. We are such a disappointment in office.

Jim looked old and bent and sad and tired. Mrs Thatcher made a most impassioned speech, from notes, except for one passage about Rhodesia which had been typed out no doubt on the insistence of the FO – the most rumbustious, rampaging, right-wing speech that I've heard from the Government Front Bench in the whole of my life.

Afterwards I saw Ted Heath and told him, 'I've never heard a speech like that in all my years in Parliament.'

He said, 'Neither have I.'

'I suppose this really was what Selsdon* was all about.'

'Oh, there never was a Selsdon policy,' Heath replied. 'It was invented by Harold Wilson. Look at our 1970 manifesto; it wasn't there at all.'

I went on, 'Well, Keith Joseph, when he was Shadow Minister of Technology in 1969–70, made a lot of similar speeches.'

'Quite different,' he responded.

I said I had some sympathy with Thatcher – with her dislike of the wishy-washy centre of British politics. He gave me such a frosty look that I daresay I had touched a raw nerve.

*Wednesday 16 May*

Caroline, Hilary and Rosalind went to America today. Their visit is tinged with enormous sadness because Rosalind is critically ill. Caroline decided to take her to America for a holiday; Hilary hasn't been there for eight years.

To the PLP meeting, for the first discussion since the Election. A lot of MPs wanted to speak.

Giles Radice [MP for Chester-le-Street] said, 'We have suffered a decisive defeat but Jim saved us from worse. We might have won in October, but as it turned out the winter destroyed us in the short term. In the longer term, there is a shift from Labour which marks the desertion of the skilled working class.'

David Winnick, who regained Walsall North for us in the Election, argued, 'We lost because of right-wing policies and a negative campaign. We shouldn't blame the unions – the yellow press do that. We are a working-class party and activists are our best people.'

Gavin Strang [MP for Edinburgh East] believed we needed to reform Parliament and abolish the House of Lords. He was shocked

* Edward Heath held what *The Times* called a council of war at Selsdon Park Hotel, Surrey, in February 1970 with his Shadow Cabinet. The radical programme outlined became known as 'Selsdon policy' and Heath as 'Selsdon man'.

that American students – cheap labour – should be helping MPs with their research and said we wanted MPs out in the country campaigning.

I agreed, as Alex Lyon had said, that there was no future for a Party which repudiated its past. It would be silly to do that because within a few weeks people would be looking back and saying what a wonderful Government we were. I said I thought we should make the PLP the main forum for discussion, Front Bench proposals should be put to the PLP for endorsement, there should be an end to all patronage in the PLP, and all Front Bench spokesmen should be elected. We should stop nominating people for peerages because patronage was the curse of the Palace of Westminster and some of it had rubbed off on us. We had the power to end it. Finally, I said we had to study our past but we didn't want any scapegoats or personal bitterness, as happened between 1951 and 1961.

Neil Kinnock observed that opposition was easy; the problem would be what to do when we got back. For the third time, he said, the Labour Party had saved capitalism, and lost, and his concern was with the next Government. We were a marvellous party of opposition but we had to be better. When in Government, he said, we should stick to our guns; we were the party of production and we had to plan it.

Eric Heffer echoed what Neil had said. There had been no mass desertion of working-class votes, there had been a loss of Liberal votes, and we were all there because the working class didn't desert us. He hoped there would be no tearing ourselves to pieces.

Jim Callaghan wound up, saying that this was only the beginning; he had always thought we should let the PLP decide policy. As to the 5 per cent limit, which Members had attacked, he took responsibility and said we should consider the dilemma we had faced. Our credibility hinged upon our record in reducing inflation last summer and we would have destroyed our credibility by returning to higher levels of inflation. We would win the next Election, but what would we do then? Wages were the central problem for future Labour Governments and, he said, he didn't know what to do. He wouldn't stay if the Party split. We had great maturity and we could win people over if we went back to our radical tradition. Socialism, he said, came from practical experience and he quoted Ernie Bevin, 'A fish rots from the head'; we needed to keep together.

### Monday 21 May

Sat in the Chamber from 1.50 with no one about. Spoke in the first major debate on the Government's industrial policy after Keith Joseph on the Conservative side. The speech wasn't a brilliant success but it was effective. Thatcher listened throughout. I referred to her speech on

15 May about individual selfishness and said, 'No doubt it was the language that ultimately drove Christ out of the temple in Jerusalem when he tried to get rid of the money changers.'

I do realise that I have got to win back the confidence of the PLP.

*Tuesday 22 May*
The *Guardian* devoted its 'Parliamentary Sketch' to yesterday's debate. I like the simplicity of making Parliament my main forum and allowing the press to cover it or not as they think best – to save the artificiality of media debates in which one is pitched against Robin Day or the Dimblebys.

The debate in the House on the Government's industrial policy and philosophy resumed. Norman St John Stevas, the Leader of the House of Commons, made a brilliant Cambridge Union speech and devoted a big chunk of it to me. He ignored Callaghan, Healey and Varley, mentioned Foot, and then said, 'Now I turn to the Right Honourable Gentleman, the Member for Bristol South East . . .'

His motives were interesting. There is no doubt that my quoting from the scriptures yesterday to attack Tory philosophy made Norman St John Stevas feel some sort of answer was required. He was frightfully funny.

He said it was the money lenders and not Christ who were thrown out of the temple and he preferred St Matthew's account to mine because St Matthew had had the marginal advantage of having been present at the time.

Well, yesterday, in the debate, Keith Joseph had stated that his object was to galvanise the entrepreneurs in society. So I rose just before the vote, when the House was absolutely crowded, and said to St John Stevas, 'On spiritual matters, I yield to the Right Honourable Gentleman, but is he really telling the House that in his view the carpenter of Nazareth went to the temple in order to galvanise the entrepreneurs?' There was a pause, and then the House dissolved in laughter.

*Wednesday 23 May*
In the *Guardian* Peter Jenkins commented on the Joseph/Benn ideological debate, saying that we were both parochial – neither socialism nor capitalism was possible in one country. The idea of a political debate without personal malice, dealing with the ultimate verities of life, is immensely attractive. I enjoy it.

NEC at 10 for a review of the Election loss. Frank Allaun, Chairman of the NEC, said we didn't want recriminations but we had failed to keep close to the Conference. He observed that all socialism grew from defending people in real situations. And, he said, there should be no compensation when we renationalise.

Joan Maynard said, 'We have lost our crusading spirit.'

Jim Callaghan thought there was some organisational weakness. 'We need mass membership. We have to deal with Trotskyite influence, the people who go round carrying Party cards and shouting "Troops out of Ireland". We are a progressive party and you can call it socialist if you want to.'

Neil Kinnock agreed, and he didn't want to compensate when we renationalised.

I said that, considering all the bitterness after the 1959 Election, it was nice to see a different spirit. The Tories would keep us united, since they were not, like Macmillan, riding on a wave of rising prosperity. We must restore the legitimacy in the public mind of democratic socialism because the press were actually engaged in outlawing any argument to the left of the centre of British politics. They were identifying and hounding and persecuting people and assassinating their characters. I said I took this seriously because in the Election, when I visited one council estate which I had represented for thirty years, someone told me, 'I am not voting for you, Mr Benn, because if I do it will be the last Election ever held in this country.' We must make the Labour Party reintegrate with other activists with whom we sympathised, such as the women's movement and the Friends of the Earth.

*Thursday 24 May*
At 10 to Great Peter Street for the press conference on Labour's manifesto for the Euro-elections. The final version contained a paragraph inserted at the NEC's insistence stating that Britain would withdraw from the Common Market unless 'fundamental reforms' were carried out.

Into a little messy back room with Barbara, Jim, Eric Heffer and Ron Hayward. Jim got as near as he could to repudiating the manifesto by saying he gave it general support. Under his breath he said, 'It is not my manifesto.'

*Friday 25 May*
Great deal of coverage on the manifesto, with a nasty article by George Brown. He is a fallen angel. He was one of the high-flying leaders of the Party and now earns his living attacking it.

*Saturday 26 May*
The *Guardian* today suggested that John Silkin intends to run as Leader of the Party. If Healey, Silkin, Shore, Hattersley and Rodgers are all being promoted as candidates, then behind the cover of their contest I can advance the argument about the nature and powers of the leadership. Until the idea of ambition and personal contest are

extracted from it, people won't listen. The press are determined to keep it personal. The reality is that it doesn't matter who is Leader if the structure of accountability and the policies are right.

*Friday 1 June*
Arrived at Transport House at 9 and had about forty minutes' chat with Moss Evans. He said Labour policy was a bit sickening. 'When the Tories were in power, my union paid £1 million in fines for breaches of the Industrial Relations Act, but under Labour our funds were depleted by £6 million in strike pay to members in official protests against the pay policy.' He felt very strongly about it.

Later I dropped in a couple of resolutions to Ron Hayward's office: one, that the Leader of the Party should not appoint any more peers (which will come before the NEC Home Policy Committee); the other, that sums of money paid out of public funds to finance the PLP should be paid not to the Leader but to Transport House, which would then channel the same amount to the PLP. It is not the amount which matters but the control of it.

*Saturday 2 June*
The press had an extremely interesting story about Sir Nicholas Henderson, our Ambassador in Paris, who retired from the Foreign Service on 31 March and has been reappointed as Ambassador to Washington by the new Government. He sent a farewell dispatch to David Owen which was leaked to the *Economist*, and the *Daily Telegraph* had a full account of it on its front and back pages. I have always suspected Henderson was a most unattractive Conservative and it proved to be so. I didn't see the telegram itself, but it clearly gives the Tory view on everything – on Britain, on the unions, on our inefficiency, even on our moral standards. It is a sensation, but of course the main story will be how it was leaked, when really it should be looked at quite differently. Why can't all the telegrams from Ambassadors be read by the public so that we learn what advice is reaching the Foreign Secretary and other Ministers? Then the labour movement would learn the true nature of the diplomatic service, which, like the higher ranks of the Civil Service, takes an aristocratic Tory view of life. I certainly intend to make use of the dispatch in a lecture on the Civil Service.

To Hull for a Euro-election meeting with John Prescott, who told me that the security services had deeply penetrated the trade union movement. Once when he was in the National Union of Seamen's office talking to the former General Secretary, William Hogarth, two policemen in plain clothes came in and asked Hogarth to identify people in photos of NUS demonstrations. The union, for its part, was kept informed by the police about what the militants were doing so it could keep an eye on its own dissidents. This police penetration of the NUS was apparently so complete in 1966 that, during the strike, one of the NUS's committees consisted entirely of the Special Branch! This police activity is becoming a direct infringement of civil liberties in many areas of society.

## Tuesday 5 June

To St Martin-in-the-Fields for the memorial service for Lady Cripps, Stafford's widow, who died in April. I'm glad I went. John Cripps, who is her son and the father of Francis Cripps, greeted me. The Labour establishment was well represented – Mervyn Stockwood, Woodrow Wyatt, Geoffrey de Freitas, Lord Listowel and Michael Foot.

## Thursday 7 June

European direct elections today.

Mrs Thatcher is apparently much impressed by the French nuclear programme and in my opinion will almost certainly now drop the AGR and adopt the PWR, which is what Sir Kenneth Berrill, Sir Jack Rampton and Sir Arnold Weinstock want. That would mean foregoing our safer system and adopting the same American system which broke down at Harrisburg. It would be a grave error of judgement. She'll also press ahead with the fast breeder reactor.

In the evening I did a little work locally to persuade people to vote Labour in the direct elections. Then I went to the polling station in Portobello Road. I have never voted with such a deep sense of hostility, but I had no choice.

## Friday 8 June

The turnout in the Euro-elections was around 31 per cent. I was delighted. We had bust a gut to run the best possible campaign for the Labour Party in a fundamentally unsatisfactory situation but the British people had just seen through it.

Rosalind is very much worse. I don't know how to contemplate her death. She's been so courageous and so determined and I just hope the girl is spared pain and suffering when she goes.

## Sunday 10 June

Watched the Euro-election results coming in and I must say it turns my stomach. Labour has about seventeen out of eighty-one seats.

## Monday 11 June

To the Intercontinental Hotel to participate in this great International Monetary Conference attended by bankers from all over the world, absolutely top level. The President, Walter Wriston, delivered an arrogant but brilliant speech saying that, with the capacity to transmit information worldwide by electronics, all markets were now international, and this introduced a discipline greater than the gold standard. In effect, he was saying that all national governments were obsolete. The banking priesthood's assumption that politicians and Governments and hence democracy are entirely irrelevant to the world was breathtaking. It put me in mind of my own thinking as Minister of Technology nearly ten years ago – since when, of course, I have reappraised everything carefully. In the end, the multinational oil companies, who thought they ran the world ten years ago, were quickly brought to their senses by OPEC. What is needed is a strong reassertion of the role of Governments.

My session was called 'Two Views of the World: Free Market versus Intervention', and it was a debate between William Simon, former Secretary of the US Treasury, and myself. Simon delivered a real right-wing American politician's speech. I responded by saying that the argument against intervention was largely phoney because everyone intervened and there was no shred of evidence that intervention had anything whatever to do with freedom. I depicted the problem of a capitalist system deadlocked more by democracy than by socialism and then made the case for import controls. I went over the three courses open to us: monetarism, corporatism and democratic socialism. It went down very well.

Among the British participants were Lord Armstrong of the Midland Bank, Sir Jasper Hollom of the Bank of England and Lord Barber, former Chancellor of the Exchequer. Most of the questions came to me and they were rather fun. I greatly enjoyed it.

Organisation Committee of the NEC, and before I arrived they had voted 8 to 4 to reopen the question of the election of the Party Leader, so that issue is a live one again. They also decided this year to support mandatory reselection of MPs, so that will go back to Conference.

Then Home Policy Committee. We took my resolution inviting the Leader of the Party not to make recommendations for peerages and requesting members not to accept peerages.

Judith said, 'We should exempt Jim's resignation honours list because it's just coming out.'

Neil Kinnock was against the resolution on the grounds that we had to tackle the real problem by abolishing the House of Lords.

The resolution was carried unanimously. Another defeat for Jim. So both issues will now go to the NEC.

## Tuesday 12 June
Went to the Commons to hear the Budget speech and fell asleep. It was

a very short Tory Budget – gave to the richest and took away from the poorest.

Awful *Daily Mirror* leader on Jim's resignation honours announced yesterday. Lena Jeger is now in the House of Lords, with George Strauss, the former MP for Vauxhall who founded the Tribune Group; Judith Hart, a violent anti-colonialist, is now Dame Grand Commander of the British Empire.

### Wednesday 13 June

Went by taxi to Mile End station, where 5000 people had gathered for the funeral procession of Blair Peach, who was in all likelihood killed by a member of the police Special Patrol Group and probably with an illegal cosh made of rubber and lead. Peach was a member of the Anti-Nazi League; he had been in Southall opposing a National Front meeting in April and was hit during clashes with the Front. Many Labour MPs – Joan Maynard, Ron Brown, Stanley Clinton Davies, Dennis Skinner, Neil Kinnock and lots of others – were in the funeral procession and we walked for an hour and a half through the East End of London behind the hearse.

Talked to Frank McElhone later, and he told me that Roger Stott, Callaghan's PPS, with whom Frank shares a flat in London, had informed him that Jim was terrified that I would become Leader. Frank also told me that I should abandon my campaign on reselection because that's what really frightens MPs.

### Thursday 14 June

The Shadow Cabinet results were announced at the PLP meeting. Denis Healey came first, John Silkin second and Peter Shore third. David Owen dropped heavily. Eric Heffer was the runner-up and Judith Hart came very low down. So the Shadow Cabinet is predominantly right-wing. The only people in it you could conceivably call left-wing are Stan Orme and Albert Booth, and they are the captive left nestling in the embrace of the right. I am so glad I'm not in it. The most important change is that Peter Shore is taking over the Foreign Office. David Owen has been given Energy, and John Silkin has Industry.

After the meeting, Stan Newens [MP for Harlow] came up and asked me to join the Tribune Group. I told him I'd been asked by Nye in 1951 and I'd always felt sympathetic but I didn't want to be in a group unless it was a single-issue group – on peace or anti-colonialism, etc. – though I would welcome Tribune meetings within the Party where the discussions are open to everyone. I wanted the Tribune Group to become a leaven in the Party.

Caroline and I went to see Rosalind's parents, Lesley and Peter Retey, for an hour and a half.

'There was an Old Man of the West,
Who never could get any rest,
    So they set him to spin, on his nose and his chin . . .'

Came home and prepared another draft of the paper Eric Heffer and I are writing on the future work of the PLP. Eric said he'd also sign the resolution on the amendment to Clause 5 of the Party Constitution relating to the drawing up of the Election manifesto.

*The Benn–Heffer proposals, as they became known, advocated a number of measures intended to strengthen the PLP but to give it closer links with the labour movement outside Parliament, whether the Labour Party was in power or in opposition. These included:*

*1.   The Shadow Cabinet and principal Front Bench spokesmen and women should be elected by the PLP for each session, and allocation of portfolios should be approved by the PLP meeting.*
*2.   There should be regular meetings between the Shadow Cabinet and the NEC, with reports to the PLP.*
*3.   Staff engaged on work for members of the Opposition should be employees of the Party.*
*4.   No more nominations for peerages should be made on behalf of the Party.*

*The amendment to Clause 5 of the Party's Constitution was a small but significant change of wording. Paragraph 2 of the clause stated:*

*The National Executive Committee and the Parliamentary Committee of the PLP [Shadow Cabinet] shall decide which items from the Party programme shall be included in the manifesto which shall be issued by the NEC prior to every General Election. The joint meeting of the two committees shall also define the attitude of the Party to . . .*

*The wording was changed to 'The National Executive* after consultation with the Parliamentary Committee . . .' *and the words 'The joint meeting of the two committees' were replaced with* 'and the NEC'. *The effect was to make the NEC the overriding authority on the Party programme.*

### Friday 15 June

Caught the 3.55 from King's Cross to Huddersfield. Read E. P. Thompson's *The Making of the English Working Class* and looked up all the references to Huddersfield, which gave me a very clear picture of trade union agitation and poverty in the area in the early nineteenth century.

I was met at the station and taken to the Trades Club, which was originally the Mechanics' Institute, where much of the early Luddite agitation had been organised. It was a marvellous meeting. One man shouted at me for attending Blair Peach's funeral, complaining that I had been a member of a racist Government which had effectively killed Blair Peach. It was very stimulating.

### Sunday 17 June

Our thirtieth wedding anniversary, and a marvellous thirty years we've had together. If the next thirty years are as happy, I will be richly blessed.

Took breakfast to Caroline and read the papers. The *Express* had a piece about the great struggle for the future of the Labour Party between Callaghan and Benn, Heffer and Atkinson. It is right in a way. The *Daily Telegraph* had a most vitriolic editorial yesterday about my attending the Blair Peach service. I must say, compared to the tributes paid to Airey Neave when he was murdered and all the speeches made then about violence in Northern Ireland, the bitter hostility to Peach is very revealing. The *Telegraph* described my attendance as a 'depraved act'.

### Thursday 21 June

Looked in to see Ron Hayward, who told me about yesterday's Shadow Cabinet. He said that the 'Short money' issue had been raised, and Jim had said that if the money went to the NEC we would have a Marxist Party. So Jim believes that the NEC is Marxist while the PLP, under his leadership, is socialist or democratic. A sub-committee is being set up to look into this question.

At the PLP meeting, Jim said the Shadow Cabinet had insisted he allocate further appointments of Front Bench spokesmen for this session, and Frank Allaun protested, 'We were assured that we'd discuss these.' Dennis Skinner said it was absolutely wrong to go ahead, this was a key issue, and we must make progress on electing all our Front Bench spokesmen.

Jim replied, 'Well, I am not against election in principle but we shouldn't rush a conclusion. I am sure no one would deny that the appointment of our new Shadow education spokesman, Neil Kinnock, was a brilliant one.'

There is Neil Kinnock accepting an appointment from the Leader of the Party and totally undermining the left's position.

*Friday 22 June*

My old driver, Ron Vaughan, turned up with a picture I had left in the office. He is now driver to Lord Trenchard, son of the First Marshal of the RAF, who, he said, had read my speech on 21 May in the Commons attacking Tory industrial policy and had said to Ron, 'His analysis is absolutely right.' Ron was amazed! He said Trenchard and Keith Joseph had discussed it.

Caught the 11.30 to Exeter for the ASLEF Annual Conference. I made a speech and they gave me a standing ovation – which was very agreeable.

Eric Doody, the ASLEF organiser for Bristol, drove me back to Bristol. He told me the most heartbreaking story about his family. I record it exactly as Eric recounted it to me. He was born in 1918, the youngest of eleven children. His father was gassed in France a month after Eric's birth and remained in hospital for years. Eric only got to see him in 1924 when his mother took him to the hospital on Christmas Eve, and his father's face was half covered because of the mustard gas burns. His mother just managed by taking in washing.

When his father died shortly afterwards, a man from the British Legion came and said they were going to give him a military funeral with a gun carriage. A few months later there was a knock at the door and a big man came in demanding 35 shillings for the hire of a gun carriage for the funeral. Eric's mother told the bailiff she had no money and was just managing to keep the children by taking in washing; she thought the British Legion were taking care of the funeral costs. He told her it was her responsibility so she sent Eric to fetch the pawnbroker, 'our only friend'. The pawnbroker came in, looked around and said he would take the mangle which she used for wringing out the washing. He took a few other things and gave the bailiff 35 shillings. But the bailiff wouldn't leave and asked for 1s 8d, 'my wages for the time I waited'.

His mother died a few years ago. Eric said he would never forget what had happened. 'We wheeled her round for the last twelve years of her life because of the rheumatism and arthritis she had from doing laundry work for so long. She was beaten down and couldn't imagine a different way of life. All my brothers and sisters went the other way from me. They just became wide boys, making a quick buck wherever they could in order to get back at a society which had treated them so poorly.'

Eric Doody is a man I shan't forget.

Jeremy Thorpe got off today, acquitted on all charges. That poor man has suffered.

## Monday 25 June

I was late for the TUC–Labour Party Liaison Committee. When I got there Len Murray was speaking about the confidential talks taking place with the Government this afternoon. The TUC was going to press on jobs and the CAP and they were anxious about energy, particularly the sale of BP shares. He said the TUC did not want confrontation.

Jim said Government–TUC relations would be different now, and the TUC would obviously be driven to stick to pay and conditions. Disillusionment had set in, and the labour movement must agree to TUC involvement in Government policy.

Denis Healey spoke, very red-faced indeed. He said, 'Let us look back. After 1970 we had an estrangement with the TUC. This time our relations at the top have remained good. We were defeated because the trade unions were unable to pass the message down the line. The large trade-unionist vote for the Conservatives was a warning to us.'

He said elections didn't change the laws of arithmetic and we had to be careful not to have high pay claims which would be as damaging under the Tories as under Labour. He said this Government was not, in fact, more inegalitarian than Heath's Government, the tax changes only took us back to the 1974 position, and Thatcher was in the same position as Heath had been in 1970. Would there be a U-turn now as in 1972?

Michael Foot thought the new situation would lead to a recession and Tory policy this time was more dangerous. The Labour Party reaction had to be swift, and by early autumn we must put ourselves at the head of a campaign.

I said we all recognised there was a new role for the TUC in relation to the Tory Government, but Heath, to whom I had talked recently, denied that what was being proposed was a new Selsdon Park policy; indeed he denied that Selsdon Park was a policy at all! The situation was much more serious than was thought, and we must get an explanation over to people about what is really happening. We also needed to educate the public not only about socialism but about the legitimacy of trade unions, the public services and full employment. If private investment didn't occur, and public investment was scaled down, law-and-order issues would predominate.

Hattersley said we had to face realities and a wages policy had to be considered.

## Wednesday 27 June

Just after midnight (of 26 June), the phone rang and it was Hilary. He said he thought Rosalind was dead. We took a taxi to his home in West London.

Caroline felt Rosalind's pulse. Hilary rang the doctor and he came and declared her dead. Lesley and Peter Retey arrived. Gradually our whole family arrived and sat in the bedroom and talked and talked. It was all very painful.

## Thursday 28 June

Condolences came in from Dennis Skinner, Frank McElhone, Dick Douglas [the Labour MP for Dunfermline], from a Tory MP and many others. The Labour Party staff sent a telegram to Hilary, and that sort of sympathy and support is a tremendous comfort.

## Friday 29 June

Caught the end of the ITN news and there were several items involving the royal family. The Queen was at Aldermaston making a speech about how important nuclear weapons were for the maintenance of peace, and how we had to preserve the new technology – that is produce a new generation of nuclear weapons. Prince Charles was in champagne country in France to consolidate Britain's relations with the Common Market. It was the most crude use of the royal family by the Tories for political purposes.

## Monday 2 July

Tonight on *Panorama* there was a massive propaganda effort for the PWR. Leonard Rotherham, the former CEGB man and Vice-Chancellor of Bath University, said what a disaster it was to have gone for the AGR. Frank Tombs of the Electricity Council and Glyn England of the CEGB were attacked for their opposition to the PWR. Arnold Weinstock was shown at the Derby, and was interviewed without it being mentioned that he had a huge commercial interest in the PWR.

## Wednesday 4 July

To the NEC for what turned out to be a thrilling meeting.

I reported on the resolution from the Home Policy Committee that the Leader of the Party should not make any further nominations for peerages and that Members shouldn't accept peerages. Fred Mulley moved the reference back. Judith Hart supported the resolution and

Shirley said she had no time whatever for the House of Lords and would like to abolish it, but they had a job of work to do.

Jim argued that it was a political issue. We needed more Labour peers; we tried to abolish the Lords in 1967 (which is quite untrue), and the time had come to stop this Constitution-mongering. 'We've had far too many changes in the Constitution.'

When I summed up I said, 'This is no reflection on those who have accepted peerages. My father accepted one and worked very hard. It is about patronage. Harold Wilson made 243 peers, and if there were three people hoping for peerages for every person who got one that meant a thousand people were in his power. We must eliminate patronage within the Party.'

In the end, the motion to refer back was defeated by 14 to 10, so that was a tremendous achievement.

Jim said, 'Well, now we have a problem. The Executive will have to consider how I am going to man the Labour benches in the Lords.'

'That is for the PLP to discuss, not for us,' I replied.

Next was the question whether the method of choosing the Party Leader should be considered by Conference, despite the fact that last year there was an overwhelming vote in favour of the PLP electing the Leader. John Golding moved the reference back and Fred Mulley seconded. Dennis Skinner said that this was an issue that wouldn't go away, Eric Heffer agreed, and the reference back was defeated by 14 to 11. So the leadership issue will go to Conference this year. That was a triumph.

*Thursday 5 July*

Rosalind's funeral. The family have rallied round wonderfully. Hilary's front garden was covered in wreaths; the one that touched me most was from Dave, the milkman. Hilary's workmates at ASTMS had sent white roses. There were masses of flowers. It was a boiling hot day.

At precisely 10.45 the hearse came. On top of the coffin was a lovely wreath of red roses from Hilary.

When we got to Chiswick cemetery the chapel doors were open and the organ was being played by the head of the music department of Holland Park (Rosalind and Hilary's old school). Mother read from the Bible, and Peter Retey read a poem by Hartley Coleridge called 'Early Death'. Ann Morrish read the sonnet 'Shall I compare thee to a summer's day'. Stephen played a piece he had composed on the organ. Then Hilary got up and, a few feet from his beloved Rosalind, delivered his beautiful address, without a tremor in his voice. It was perceptive, sensitive, tender and amusing but at no stage was it sentimental.

Six men including Joshua, Stephen and Hilary and Rosalind's two brothers carried the coffin to the grave. Mother said, 'Ashes to ashes, dust to dust', Hilary tossed some soil in, and we all threw in red roses. It was terribly, terribly sad.

*Wednesday 11 July*
The PLP meeting was held in the Grand Committee Room. Fred Willey, the MP for Sunderland North and new Chairman of the PLP, reminded us that our main job was to attack the Tories. The labour movement was made up of three entities – the trade unions, the NEC and the PLP – which were difficult to co-ordinate and there must be a limit to what we could do. The PLP should have better co-operation and dialogue with the NEC.

I presented the Benn–Heffer proposals and said there was a wide measure of agreement between ourselves and other parts of the Party. I spelled out the paragraphs dealing with the money for the PLP staff and the election by the PLP of Front Bench spokesmen, and generally tried to be conciliatory, but I pointed out that this problem of patronage was real. We all wanted a more democratic structure.

Willie Hamilton [MP for Fife Central] said he might 'lack the finesse of Tony Benn'; he was a blunt man. He himself had no ambitions left, therefore he could speak brutally: patronage must be reduced. It hadn't been well used, there was still too much deadwood on the Front Bench, and Jim should sharpen his hatchet because the time for assassination was now. If Jim failed, he should use the hatchet on himself. No one was indispensable. We wanted the complete elimination of patronage by the Leader and by the whips, perhaps with a transitional period to be approved by the Party. Young and untried blood was needed – spokesmen must be free of the last Government's record. We should have a finance committee and a treasurer of the PLP to handle Government funding of the Opposition and we should stop the whole honours system.

Eric Deakins [MP for Waltham Forest] made a terribly disappointing speech. 'I want to make a point relating to the PLP and the status of Conference decisions. The PLP is the most important group in the Labour Party, and the Party Conference cannot take precedence over us because we have experience in translating policy into action. Conference decisions are not sacrosanct. Do Tony and Eric think they are in the 1950s? There is a mutual suspicion between the PLP and Conference. The PLP thinks that many Conference resolutions are unrealistic and that Conference wants miracles. The PLP is not the poodle of Conference or the Leader of the Opposition or the Prime Minister. We are important and we have to regain our self-confidence.'

Phillip Whitehead [MP for Derby North] said that reform was necessary for the Party as a whole. We couldn't attack Conference and not look at ourselves. We could start with the PLP because that was seen as crucial to the whole Party. If the PLP didn't exercise its judgement then we were in difficulties. Our constituents were not worried about the extremists but about the pressures from outside. We should elect the Shadow Cabinet, all the spokesmen and the Leader. But we couldn't end the election of the Leader by the PLP unless we democratised the PLP.

Jim Callaghan spoke – which was a surprise, because he wasn't expected to. It was a rambling and tetchy speech. If the Conference discussed these esoteric issues and not politics, he said, it would be a great mistake. This was a valuable discussion but we were opening Pandora's Box, as Gaitskell had done in the 1950s. There would be great embarrassment if every member of the Government was elected. (This presumably meant that MI5 might raise security objections against elected people.)

As to new blood, said Jim, there were twenty ex-Ministers now on the back benches and he'd brought new people on to the Front Bench. The average age was forty. If we wanted to increase the size of the Shadow Cabinet, OK, but nineteen was quite enough in opposition.

He said he'd never thought of what he was doing as patronage. It was a heavy responsibility and he hoped no one thought he'd abused it. He didn't appoint according to taste but according to ability.

Jim went on like this for about half an hour, blanking out Eric Heffer and Michael Meacher, so it was agreed that the PLP would meet again next Wednesday.

*Thursday 12 July*
Boris Ford, Professor of Education at Bristol, has banned my forthcoming lecture at the university. I had already released the text of it to the *Guardian* under the title 'The Constitutional Premiership'. When I spoke to Ford on the phone he said, 'You were asked to talk about education and democracy.'

'Not at all,' I told him. 'I said I would talk about democracy.' He was embarrassed but insisted he couldn't unban it.

*Sunday 15 July*
Knowle Ward had organised a picnic in the Forest of Dean next to the Speech House. In 1017 Canute had established the first Court of Verdurers to resolve forest matters, and they met in the Speech House from 1676, when it was built. Trust House Forte have now bought it.

It was lovely, sitting under the trees – none of this rushing around in the car making speeches.

*Monday 16 July*
NEC Home Policy Committee, which I chaired. We had a marvellous

paper from Geoff Bish revealing how the last Election manifesto had come to be drafted. Eric Heffer moved our resolution on Clause 5: that the manifesto be decided by the NEC and that a constitutional amendment be drafted and put before Conference. Neil Kinnock seconded it. John Golding disagreed. He thought the Cabinet and the PLP were respected and credible in the country but the NEC was not. Dennis Skinner got very angry with Golding and in the end he left the room to calm down. John concluded that the NEC was not fit to decide the manifesto. Eventually the resolution was carried 8–2.

Jim, of course, is confident that he'll be able to get the trade union leaders to defeat the NEC on this but he may be wrong, because the rank and file of the Party want this change. Come September, I will have to work hard on the union leaders.

### Wednesday 18 July

The PLP met to continue last week's discussion on Party democracy. Eric Heffer summed up the general agreement on some issues. There was a need for a working party, the PLP should have more say, there should be greater democracy in the PLP, and there should be a reduction, if not elimination, of patronage. All appointments of staff to work for the PLP should be cleared with the Party, and the peerage system should come to an end. Eric went on to say that in the past the Labour Government had not consulted the PLP; it made everything a vote of confidence.

Nigel Spearing [MP for Newham South] believed the debate was between supporters of the system of monarchies, hierarchies and spoils (patronage) and the democratic view. The monarchical view was 'I am paid, you are rewarded, he is bribed.' He said the court of King Harold had done a lot of harm in this respect. Everyone recognised that the Leader needed freedom, but there must be a balance between freedom and accountability.

Joe Ashton said that the last time we elected the Leader there were 550 promises from 300 MPs! He argued against reselection; he believed MPs had the right to be consulted on the terms of their unemployment. Joe was down to earth and cynical, but he does see himself as the MPs' shop steward and someone has to say it.

There is no doubt at all that mandatory reselection is the greatest fear in the minds of many MPs. Until it's settled they won't relax. But it is an important issue.

### Thursday 19 July

Heard that Melissa got a First Class degree from LSE. As soon as the House had voted against hanging – by a majority of 120 – I dashed home and gave her a hug. She was told that she was the first woman for twenty years to get a First in history at LSE, and there had not been a First Class in history there for seven years. She was so excited, we stayed up till 3 in the morning talking.

### Sunday 22 July
Stuart Holland, MP for Vauxhall, had a party this evening for the Meachers and Mik and others. I met Pierre Joxe, of the French Socialist Party. He said they didn't understand the Labour Party, which governed Britain with all the grandeur of the Conservatives. He and Stuart Holland are thinking of starting a journal called *Socialist Economics* on a Europe-wide basis. I strongly favoured that, though I thought it would be helpful if we could have a broader range than economics alone.

Stuart is certainly one of the brightest recruits we've had to the PLP.

### Monday 23 July
Had a brief word with Bernard Braine, MP for Billericay, who is a decent Tory. There must be a lot like him who are unhappy about Thatcher's savagery on public expenditure. The whole situation is so serious, there is a real danger that the Government is going to drive us deeper into slump and depression.

### Tuesday 24 July
Eric Heffer, Joan Maynard, Dennis Skinner, Tony Saunois and Frank Allaun came to my room and went over tomorrow's NEC agenda, to work out what we should do.

There is no doubt that although I have made no attacks on anybody I have touched a raw nerve in the PLP about the role of the NEC, partly because the two never meet. Stan Orme is angry at what I am doing. But, if all these matters are brought into the open, people like Michael Foot and John Silkin and Peter Shore, who have been nestling in the embrace of the right, have to choose between sticking with the right or fighting for the left. Also, of course, the PLP think I am making life difficult for them and they are being hostile; I may have blown my chances of doing well in the PLP in a future leadership election. They'll go for a leader like Silkin or Shore, acceptable to both sides. Still, that's better than Healey.

### Wednesday 25 July
A very important NEC at 10 at Transport House.

Under emergency resolutions, there was one attacking the treatment of dissidents in Czechoslovakia which was carried unanimously. A demand for an inquiry into Blair Peach's death was agreed; Tony Saunois proposed an amendment calling for the disbanding of the SPG, and that was carried by 11 to 10. Alan Hadden's resolution calling on the Government to allow greater numbers of Vietnamese boat people into Britain was carried by 22 votes.

We had a resolution from the Organisation Committee that the 'Short money' be paid direct to the Party. Jim regretted that this had been raised, but the motion to refer back was defeated on Frank Allaun's casting vote.

Then on to the big discussion arising out of the Home Policy meeting, on the amendment to Clause 5 – whether the manifesto should be written by the NEC alone.

Michael Foot moved the reference back, saying there had been no consultation with the PLP, and Shirley echoed this feeling. Eric Heffer said the reality was that the PLP was never consulted by the leadership, and Tony Saunois argued that Conference should decide the issue. Alan Hadden said there was ungainly haste in dealing with it. I pointed out that the MPs who were on the NEC had never objected in the past to the PLP not being consulted on the drafting of the manifesto. Why? Because they knew the Prime Minister had a veto. At the last minute on the night of 2 April Number 10 had produced a new manifesto draft which the PLP had never seen, and we had been told that the Party Leader would resign if he didn't get his way. We couldn't go on like this. The Party had to be able to reflect the needs and anxieties of the rank and file.

The motion to refer it back was defeated by 9 to 8. So it will go forward, but I don't think we're going to get it agreed at this year's Conference.

Quite a meeting, lasting six hours.

*Thursday 26 July*

To Transport House at 10 for a joint meeting of the Shadow Cabinet and the NEC. Frank Allaun was in the chair and said this meeting had been called by the Shadow Cabinet to discuss the problem of the manifesto and the funding of the PLP.

Jim Callaghan began by saying the BBC had described this as the beginning of a confrontation and in order to get today's meeting properly reported he had written out a statement and proposed to read it – a technique that Harold Wilson used to employ.

'This meeting takes place when the unity of the Party is endangered. Its purpose is to overcome the problems and . . . to consult and maximise our efforts against the Tories. The Tories are so strong that nothing but a united Party can dislodge them. We do not exclude a calm review of our structure – we have a low individual membership, a problem of organisation, and funding which is inadequate, and both bodies have been considering these problems. The PLP have been having a lot of useful discussions and are an effective Opposition.'

Jim went on, 'These proposals are the most fundamental change ever in the Party and are not acceptable to the PLP. On the question of funds for the PLP, my signature is required to get the money and the Shadow Cabinet does not agree that the National Executive should control it.'

Stan Orme declared that there was no bitterness at the PLP meetings over these proposals, and that the Benn–Heffer paper was about democracy.

The Party didn't belong to us, Dennis Skinner said. The argument would never end because it reflected the rank and file's desire for more power, which was right.

I emphasised six points of agreement that we could put across to the press after this meeting. The Tory Government was the most dangerous we'd had and was a threat to Britain and to parliamentary democracy; this situation required the closest co-operation between the unions, the CLPs, Conference, the NEC and the PLP; the trade unions elected eighteen out of twenty-eight members of the NEC, and twenty-one out of those twenty-eight were Labour MPs, so there could be no division between the unions, the PLP and the NEC; we were determined not to repeat the divisions of 1951 to 1964 and we would not allow the press to create them; we needed to review our structure of organisation and finance as soon as possible; we agreed there should be regular monthly meetings between the Shadow Cabinet and the NEC.

'There is one division,' I said, 'and that is about whether we are one party or two parties; the question of the money and the manifesto is absolutely central to this. In my opinion the manifesto should be subject to the widest consultation, should go to Conference *every* year, and the NEC should simply publish its contents when there is an Election.'

Denis Healey believed the NEC/Shadow Cabinet relationship was the key. The NEC had been uncomradely in recent months, there had been a stream of NEC discussions, resolutions passed ahead of this meeting and attacks on the Leader. We had only just elected a new Shadow Cabinet, and if changes were made it would alter parliamentary democracy as it had existed in Britain for 200 years.

That was a very important and dangerous statement by Denis. Parliamentary democracy in 1779? Female suffrage in 1779?

On the Clause 5 question, Denis went on to say that if Conference accepted this change lots of Labour MPs would not continue to serve. The PLP would be united against the NEC if it went on with this. He had been on the NEC both as an official and as an MP over some twenty-five years, and Labour MPs had wider responsibilities than to their GMCs. They were responsible to all Labour voters and all constituents and couldn't run things like a bear garden, even if certain bears had sore heads. Those who believed in brotherhood had better preach it.

That was Denis the thug, absolutely true to form.

David Owen then spoke, and this was very amusing. He said this meeting should have been held earlier and he was sorry that Conference had been devalued. The restoration of the importance of Conference decisions was top priority. How could we re-establish this trust? We ought to have an inquiry as a way of coming together. But the PLP was worried about reselection of MPs and he personally was doubtful about a change in the election of the Leader.

Michael Foot was dubious about constitutional change because of the attempt to change Clause 4 after 1959. Tony Benn wanted one party. You couldn't get a decision at the fag-end of a meeting by 9 votes to 8 and then put it to Conference.

Eric objected, 'Look, Michael, I moved the resolution, not Tony Benn.'

Michael said he would plead at the September NEC that we didn't put it forward. It would take much longer and we didn't want a clash between the NEC and the PLP.

Joan Lestor welcomed the idea of an inquiry into the Party and of meetings between the Shadow Cabinet and the NEC, but we were talking about how to respond to the clamour of grassroots opinion for greater say in the decisions in the Party. We had to respond. On reselection, there was real feeling. We needed inspiration and ideas and Jim had to recognise the danger.

That was a good speech by Joan, and Neil Kinnock followed with one of his best. On the funding for the Leader of the Opposition's office, he thought the money should be given to the national Party. He was in favour of the Clause 5 amendment because of the experience when the manifesto was drawn up in April. He said he'd expect the Leader to defend his position but not to be able to veto policy. There was a groundswell of opinion in the Party that Labour in office had not shown sufficient fidelity to Conference decisions, and that led to distrust and bloody-mindedness, and this was coming out at regional and union conferences and in the CLPs. This was a demand for fidelity to Conference decisions and not an attack on the leadership. The demand for change was part of a historical process, part of a sincere purpose, and not a challenge to the wisdom or the prerogative of the Leader.

In response to Kinnock, Jim said that he was the elected Leader and that Neil was effective and sincere but he could be wrong. He begged Neil to accept that it should be more widely discussed, not rammed through Conference. 'We didn't lose the last Election because of the manifesto. Read the Conference proceedings from 1932 and 1951. The Labour Government and the Party never gel together easily.' If Clause 5 were changed, the Party would be split. The PLP under the control of the NEC would produce an East European-style Government.

That was the end, and we left as millions of journalists gathered outside. I said nothing except that the meeting had been a good one.

### Tuesday 31 July

After a meeting of the Fabian Society Executive, Michael Meacher, Larry Whitty of the GMWU, Brian Sedgemore and I went and bought hamburgers at McDonald's and sat in the piazza outside Westminster Cathedral. Dusk was just falling, the cathedral was beautifully illuminated and a half-moon rose above it. One felt one was in Istanbul.

Larry Whitty described the trade union leaders' attitude. The general line was going to be that all these constitutional questions should be postponed at this year's Conference and referred to an inquiry.

I think we *should* perhaps postpone the constitutional amendments but get the Conference to vote on the *principle* of the manifesto being written by the Executive, an electoral college to elect the Leader and mandatory reselection. Eric agrees that there should be no compromise – if we're beaten that's fine, but no compromise.

### Wednesday 1 August

Phoned Ray Buckton, the General Secretary of ASLEF, who told me he recently had dinner with Michael Foot, Ron Hayward and Jim Callaghan. He said Jim was still pushing the line that the NEC has to be controlled. Having lost the Election, killed the manifesto and lost all his powers of patronage, Jim's a man without a future now.

### Wednesday 8 August

Invited Alan Fisher, the General Secretary of NUPE, for a chat in the early evening, and he stayed three hours. I have always found him a bit strange. He appears to say wild things but has developed the strength of NUPE remarkably: it now has 750,000 members and is the fourth largest union in the country. Last winter it showed the tremendous muscle of public employees who hitherto had been regarded as a rather pathetic group of workers who could be safely sat on.

We talked about Trade Unionists for a Labour Victory, which, he said, didn't quite know what to do with itself now, having helped with the Election and with buying the Party's new premises in Walworth Road. We also discussed reselection of MPs and the election of the Leader and the manifesto, and at the end I think I made some progress in persuading him to my view.

### Monday 20 August

A week ago Frank Barlow, the Secretary of the PLP since 1959, died, and today I went to his funeral in Leatherhead. I travelled down from

London, and found a huge crowd of ex-Cabinet Ministers there, though Jim wasn't present.

The service was prefabricated, the organ music sounded taped although I think it was being played live, there was no address or anything; it was very mechanical.

On the way back to London, sharing a car with Ron Hayward, I remarked, 'Probably we are going to be defeated on these changes to the Party, but these issues must be faced without bitterness.'

'If you win,' he said, 'Jim will prepare to give up the leadership and that will make it a vote of confidence.' That means in fact Jim will have a pyrrhic victory for a year and then we will win.

*Thursday 23 August*

Eighteen copies of the book Chris Mullin has been working on with me, called *Arguments for Socialism*, arrived today. It is a great moment seeing for the first time a book one has written.

The *Economist* had their cover story on me: the article inside said that the Labour Party was bankrupt and that I was filling the vacuum with new ideas (dangerous ideas, of course).

*Sunday 26 August*

Stansgate. Hilary and I had a day out. First we drove to Hatfield to see Ray Buckton, who lives in a delightful 400-year-old thatched cotttage which he has renovated.

Ray told me about the threats to his life during the 1972 and 1974 miners' strikes (when ASLEF was providing industrial support), and inevitably we went on to talk about the security services. He said that as a result of the threats a chap from Special Branch was attached to him, and he turned out to be the son of a Welsh miner and got to know Ray quite well. He more or less told Ray that some of his telephone calls were being bugged. Ray wondered whether some of the death threats hadn't been engineered to provide an excuse for his being under surveillance during the dispute.

He told me the ASLEF motion to the TUC Conference in September, calling for implementation of the manifesto, might be deferred pending the Commission of Inquiry into the Labour Party. He also said there was a right-wing group – including Bill Sirs and Sid Weighell – working hard to gain control of TULV.

On to Harlow, to Clive Jenkins's house, where we had arranged to meet Caroline and Stephen. Clive was wearing an apron saying 'YOU CAN'T BE TOO THIN OR TOO RICH'.

His house consists of four cottages knocked into one, in which forty-one people lived before the war. Now it is just he and his wife Moira, and his two children.

There were guns on display, two wagon wheels at the front and a commemorative plaque of John Milton that he had bought. He was barbecueing sausages; we sat down at 2 and got up at 4.30 after a fantastic lunch of five courses.

He told me that David Basnett wants Jim to give up the leadership, and in conversation David had asked Clive, 'Who do you want?' Clive had replied, 'Tony Benn.' On David's list of candidates are Owen, Healey, Shore and Merlyn Rees. Clive said, 'David is nervous of you because you are serious', and implied that David was offering me support for the electoral college if I drop everything else. But what I really care about is the manifesto and accountability: the Party Leader issue won't make any difference.

He told me *en passant* that Tom Jackson had once been in the CP. Clive is full of lots of little stories – he loves exchanging gossip.

He has been offered a year's scholarship in Washington, which he can't take, but he has accepted a six-week stay and they have laid on facilities for him. His attitude is: if it is going, take it.

*Monday 27 August*
Drove to Southend to see Bill Keys of SOGAT. Bill is a nice guy: I don't know him well but he is passionately in favour of racial equality; he said his experience in the East End of London as a kid had really converted him to that view.

He gave me a copy of David Basnett's paper proposing the establishment of a trade union advisory committee responsible for watching the Party from outside. There is no doubt that this is a potential threat to the NEC's sovereignty. Bill said it wasn't meant to be; it was there to provide support for the Party.

He was afraid I'd get a bloody nose over the manifesto, and he wanted an inquiry.

'Maybe,' I said, 'but these issues won't go away.'

He told me not to lobby David Basnett – he doesn't like it.

Bill was terribly friendly. There is no doubt whatever that the trade union leaders, even those who don't like me very much, see me as a factor in the situation that they have to take seriously.

Drove home. On the news we heard that Lord Mountbatten and his grandson had been killed in an explosion on a boat off the Sligo coast, close to the border with Northern Ireland.[1] It may have the most tremendous repercussions: the murder of an international figure, the Supreme Allied Commander in South-East Asia during the war, a Viceroy of India, a member of the royal family, is going to make people think again about Northern Ireland. The whole world will discuss this particular event and I think it may be a turning point.

*Tuesday 28 August*
Eighteen soldiers were also killed in Northern Ireland yesterday, and two British Army bandsmen in Brussels were injured by a bomb explosion. There is of course no political solution other than the unification and independence of Ireland.

Hilary was adopted as the Labour candidate for the Walpole Ward of Ealing Council. A Labour gain in London on the eve of Conference by Hilary Benn would be a tremendous boost. I am so thrilled for him.

*Monday 3 September*
To Blackpool to speak at a fringe meeting of the Campaign for Press and Broadcasting Freedom at the TUC Conference. On the train I met Louis Heren, deputy editor of *The Times*, a terrible right-winger, who told me that the strike at *The Times* had cost £1.7 million a month for nearly a year; half of that would be paid for by *The Times*, the other half by tax adjustments for the losses. That means the Treasury would have lost £10 million in tax revenues, equivalent to £10 million from North Sea oil profits. While I was at the Conference I saw Clive Jenkins who thinks that we'll get reselection considered at the Party Conference but the electoral college and the question of the manifesto will have to be referred to the inquiry.

*Wednesday 5 September*
Mountbatten's funeral. Waited in the bright sunshine at Westminster for the armoured cars and the Land-Rovers and the gun carriage.

State occasions are always interesting because it is then that Britain presents itself in the way that the establishment thinks is proper. Discipline, authority and order are all part of the ritual.

I talked to David Crouch, the Tory MP for Canterbury, and he told me he had served as an RAF officer in Mountbatten's staff during the war. The Tories had been very suspicious of Mountbatten after the war: Churchill didn't like him and sent him off to be Commander-in-Chief of the Mediterranean. Now I come to think of it, when Churchill was First Lord of the Admiralty in 1914 he sacked Mountbatten's father, Prince Louis of Battenburg, as First Sea Lord, so he probably felt embarrassed having Mountbatten around. Other Tories thought he was too popular and too Labour inclined. Then Michael English, the Labour MP for Nottingham West, told me a story about a parliamentary candidate who had gone down to Mountbatten's home, Broadlands, to canvass, and Mountbatten had opened the door and said, 'I'm afraid you can't rely on our support but I believe the butler votes Tory.'

*Thursday 6 September*
Huge number of requests coming in at the moment for interviews or broadcasts: the Michael Parkinson chat show, 'Thought for the Day' on Radio 4's *Today*, a review in the *New Statesman* by Bruce Page of *Arguments for Socialism*, and so on.

Had a word with Frances, who is very excited about the way things are going. Also a very long, kind letter from Jack Jones.

*Sunday 9 September*
Denis Healey launched a great attack yesterday on the trade unions for losing Labour the Election. He came out with proposals for tight monetary control and a permanent incomes policy, and stated that 'those who had attacked the powers of the Prime Minister sounded like dogs without tails who wanted everybody else's tail cut off'.

Had a party at home with about forty people on the left: Clive Jenkins, Eric Heffer, Norman Atkinson, Neil Kinnock, Joan Maynard, Joan Lestor, Ian Mikardo, the Meachers, Frances Morrell, Tony Banks, Ken Coates, Chris Mullin, the Sedgemores, Dick Clements and so on. Those of us who were members of the NEC gathered after dinner and discussed tomorrow's meeting of the NEC Organisation Committee, to which the general secretaries of the trade unions have been invited to discuss how the inquiry into the Party should be conducted.

Clive said we hadn't got a cat in hell's chance of getting the resolutions through the Conference. The votes just weren't there. Clive is always for playing your cards carefully, for fixing in your own favour, and actually that's not the way we want to do it.

The people here tonight are my real political allies. The leadership of the Party must come from the group we had tonight. I feel more cheerful now. We may lose the battle but we are going to win the war.

*Monday 10 September*
Caroline went up to the cemetery to plant some shrubs on Rosalind's grave.

The NEC Organisation Committee meeting with the general secretaries was held in the boardroom of Transport House and Eric Heffer was in the chair. At 11.30 in trooped this tremendous delegation – David Basnett, Moss Evans, Bill Keys, Alan Fisher, Clive Jenkins, Lawrence Daly, Joe Gormley – a huge and powerful group of people.

Eric Heffer welcomed David Basnett as Chairman of the TULV, inviting him to explain their position. So David Basnett began a long speech in which he summarised the history of the trade unions in coming together to help us buy the Party's new premises in Walworth Road. He described the work of the TULV in the Election. Then he came out with a number of propositions.

First, he listed the matters which the trade-unionists thought should be the subject of an inquiry: organisation and structure, finance, the funding of agents, membership, the development of membership in the trade union movement, the structure and constitution of the NEC, and policy making generally.

He went on to say that he hoped the NEC would not press any changes at this year's Conference. Reselection might possibly be handled this year, but he hoped the NEC would agree not to put the electoral college issue and the drafting of the manifesto to a vote at this Conference. He thought a special conference dealing with these three matters should take place before the next annual Conference.

It was a speech of great moderation and absolutely as I expected: he claimed that this was the unanimous view of all the trade union leaders, not only those present but all those associated with TULV.

The enormity of that statement just took my breath away. Not one of these individuals had consulted their trade union conferences or delegations. They were demanding that we neuter the Conference so that delegates would have no opportunity to vote on the matters on which they'd been mandated.

That Jim Callaghan should wheel out the unions to crush the NEC was a grave warning of what could happen, a repeat of the events of the 1930s when the praetorian guard of the unions supported the PLP not only against the NEC but also against the rank and file of the Conference and unions.

The membership of the Commission of Inquiry is to be five trade union leaders, members of the National Executive, and possibly the Leader, Deputy Leader and Chief Whip of the Party.

I said nothing at this stage.

Jim Callaghan observed that this was an important discussion and that the Chief Whip should be on the inquiry (trying to stack it against the NEC and the CLPs).

Moss intervened to say this was not an attempt to take over the Party or the functions of the NEC.

Alan Fisher was wooden and silent and Bill Keys sat quiet; but it was a démarche really. These men had come in to tell us what they expected the Party to do. When you think the NEC had been defending the interests of TUC policy against the Labour Government throughout our term in office, it was an amazing experience.

We broke off for lunch and had sandwiches and chatted till about 1.15 in the boardroom.

At 2.30 the Organisation Committee reconvened and Fred Mulley moved that we accept all the recommendations put by Basnett. Alex Kitson said that as a trade union representative on the National Executive he thought we should also vote on the issues at Conference.

He moved an amendment that 'the three main items . . . should be discussed, debated and voted upon at this Conference and that the rest of the items should go to the Special Commission of Inquiry.' Alex is of course the Assistant General Secretary of the TGWU and is taking a different view from Moss. He said that Neil Kinnock and Les Huckfield, both T&G-sponsored MPs, were able to support him.

Neil Kinnock moved a further amendment that the whole object of the inquiry would be to produce an open, democratic and accountable Party at every level, which I seconded.

Michael Foot said it would be madness not to accept an inquiry. It would take time, but reselection should go ahead and the election of the Leader and the manifesto should be deferred.

Alex's amendment – an inquiry without precluding votes at Conference – was put to the vote and carried by 11 to 6. Michael Foot, Fred Mulley, Tom Bradley, John Golding, Alan Hadden and Russell Tuck voted against having votes on the issues at Conference.

The whole package – the inquiry and the decision to proceed with votes at Conference – was then carried by 18 to 0.

Then we came to the paper Eric and I had put in on closer links between the unions and the Party. Russell Tuck attempted to refer it to the inquiry committee and I said that was an attempt to stop it being discussed. Anyway, Alex Kitson supported me, and eventually the proposals were carried by 10 to 4.

At 5.45 we went on to Home Policy Committee and the main item of the afternoon was a paper in which I set out the concept of a 'rolling manifesto' for the Party based on four principles:

1. The manifesto should be firmly based on policies decided by Conference, and should be approved each year by Conference.
2. A draft manifesto should always be available in readiness for an Election and as the basis for the Party's campaigns in the period between Elections.
3. This draft should be widely circulated throughout the movement for discussion each year, including discussion at properly constituted meetings of the full PLP at which all Labour MPs are present.
4. The Leader and Deputy Leader should play their part, as full members of the NEC, in the final stages just before a General Election but neither should have a veto.

Michael Foot opposed this, saying the PLP had not been consulted and Members had a vital interest in Clause 5. We couldn't have votes all the time – it wasn't practical.

Eric Heffer argued that the PLP was never involved in the manifesto. We were told that those who took our view were trying to establish an Eastern European state. He was really reminded of an Eastern

European state when the manifesto was drawn up in April at Jim Callaghan's demand. He was amazed at Michael's attitude.

Neil Kinnock said that the manifesto was crucial and the last one was useless. On 2 April the Party's Constitution had actually been amended by the use of the veto.

Golding maintained that in reality Elections were fought between two sets of Party Leaders, and if Leaders were thought to be against the manifesto it would be difficult to contest an Election credibly (that is to say the Labour Party is a fan club for its Leader). He went on to argue that a rolling manifesto was impossible in practice. You could get resolutions passed but there'd be no money for them.

Barbara said she opposed the paper because the Conference was a jamboree. There was no costing and we had to revive the role of the PLP. The manifesto in February 1974 was the best. She came out for an electoral college and reselection, and thought Clause 5 should be revitalised by electing PLP representatives to draft the manifesto.

When it was put to the vote, the paper was carried by 9 votes to 2 – with Michael Foot and John Golding voting against it. What a combination! Barbara abstained. A tremendously important decision.

Went downstairs and met the press with Eric Heffer, Ron Hayward and Geoff Bish.

*Tuesday 11 September*
Robin Blackburn, deputy editor of *New Left Review*, came to interview me about my book, *Arguments for Socialism*. He is a great intellectual and he put to me a lot of questions from the left. 'Aren't your remedies very modest considering the magnitude of the crisis?' I agreed.

Went up to Corby by train for a demonstration by steelworkers. Before the war, Stewart and Lloyd, the private steel owners, discovered low-grade iron ore in Northamptonshire and built Corby up over twenty years into the biggest steel plant in Europe attracting people from all over the world; 72 per cent of the workers were from Scotland. The workforce lived in camps until about ten years ago when they started building up the new town. But Corby was always a one-industry town. Now the plant, at least the iron- and steel-making part, is under threat of closure.

I couldn't tell them, but the Labour Cabinet had decided in February this year to support the closure of Corby. These guys are now faced with the possibility of 30 per cent male unemployment, and they have called in the Labour Party to help them fight. An awful irony; I felt tremendously guilty.

*Wednesday 12 September*
At 3.30 I went to see Jim Callaghan; I had suggested we had a word

before Conference. He's in his new room, in the Serjeant-at-Arms's old flat.

I tried to be friendly and said I hoped he would be safe when he goes to Ireland because I had read that he might be in danger after the Mountbatten business. He wasn't too concerned but he said, 'Poor old Roy Mason is deeply worried; he has absolutely maximum security but still he's afraid of what they'll do to him.' I sympathise with him.

I had decided that I would talk about how we could make Conference the launching pad for the Party's winter campaign against the Tories. We had to have a really good programme with the TUC for economic and social advance and jobs. I didn't want him to think I was concerned only with the internal Party democracy issues.

'Well,' said Jim, 'we have to be realistic about public expenditure; we do need more productivity in British industry.' He just gave the old Thatcher/Healey view.

We came to the question of Conference's power over policy, and he said the Party would split over it. I declared, 'Jim, you've had more experience of this than I have but the situation is nothing like 1951 or 1959.'

'For the first time in my life,' he said, 'the trade unions are openly talking about disaffiliating from the Party. And take this Militant group. I am very worried. If you saw the reports I am getting' (presumably security reports) 'you'd realise what a danger it is.'

I remarked, 'Is it any different from the Bevanites, or the Tribune Group, Victory for Socialism or CND? I don't think so. No one group has ever got hold of the Labour Party.' I was more concerned with the Reg Prentices and Dick Tavernes.

'It is very regrettable what they've done.'

Jim is obsessed with the left. On the Conference, he agreed that reselection could be discussed. He had an open mind on the question of the electoral college – of course Healey wouldn't become Leader if there was a college. On the drafting of the manifesto, he would not accept the proposed changes. 'I must warn you I have a quote here on the subject from Keir Hardie that I shall use. If you press this today you'll be in real trouble.'

'You know my view, Jim. Conference must be free to decide.'

'Maybe I didn't handle the NEC very well on the manifesto issue but I will not allow this to happen. I may have been obstinate but the Lords issue was absolutely wrong.'

He told me he had seen my picture on the front of the *Economist* and had thought to himself: There's a man who has really got a great section of the Party behind him; why doesn't he use his influence? and so on. He accepted that I didn't want to be Leader, and I said, 'If I did, I'd be a bloody fool to be saying what I'm saying now because it's alienating a lot of people.'

There was one amusing exchange. Jim said I was more devious than I admitted. I reminded him that he had once told me he wasn't as nice as he looked, and I said I wasn't as nice as I looked either.

I left at about 4 and jumped into my taxi. The driver had kindly waited for half an hour so that I didn't miss my train to Bristol. He talked non-stop about how awful the Tory Government was, what a betrayal to the Labour Party George Brown had been, and how he wanted me to be the next Prime Minister. 'But you must break with the extremists,' he said, 'and you mustn't smoke your pipe on television because people don't like that, and you really must smile more'!

*Thursday 13 September*
Walked to the Lord Mayor of Bristol's Chapel at 12 for the memorial service for Martin McLaren, the Tory MP for Bristol North West in 1959–66 and then 1970–4.

Incidentally, before the First World War, my dad proposed to Martin McLaren's mother, Lady Furness, but she turned him down. He was a young MP of about thirty, and Mother told me Lady Furness had turned him down because she didn't think he was sufficiently well connected socially.

Mike Cocks was also there and afterwards we had a drink together. We talked about the NEC, and he said he hated it and thought Frank Allaun, this year's chairman, was awful. He believed the south-west was a complete write-off and there was no hope whatever in our lifetime of changing it. He was against any Government money going to the south-west, as a punishment for the way they voted. He just went on in his pessimistic and cynical way.

Coming back I looked into St Mary Redcliffe Church, the first time for thirty years. It is a lovely church and I saw that great quotation from John Donne:

No man is an island entire of itself; every man is a piece of the continent, a part of the main; . . . any man's death diminishes me, because I am involved in mankind; and therefore never send to know for whom the bell tolls; it tolls for thee.

*Friday 14 September*
Worked in my hotel room and the woman came in to make my bed. I asked her where she was from and she said, 'A country you will never have heard of – Lithuania.'

I asked her how she came to England.

'I was taken by the Germans in 1939 when I was thirteen and sent to work on a farm in Germany, and I escaped to England and have lived here ever since. I married an Englishman and I have four children.'

I enquired about her family in Lithuania.

'Well, we tried to contact them through the Red Cross but I've never found out. My father died before the war and I know nothing of my mother, my brother or my sister.'

'Do your children speak Lithuanian?'

'Oh no, and I haven't spoken it for twenty-five years.'

I was suddenly aware of the things that most of us in this country take absolutely for granted: knowing where our families are and having food and shelter. All that is taken from millions and millions of people in World Wars and famines and earthquakes. I count my blessings.

Went to see Dawn Primarolo, the Bristol South East constituency secretary. Dawn is under very heavy fire but I think she'll pull through. I must say the Party is in a worse state now in terms of personal division than I remember in the thirty years I've been the Member. The Labour club takes up all the time and causes great bitterness. The people north of the river want the club, the people south of the river dislike the decay north of the river, and the Militants and the moderates are at each other's throats.

There is a flaming row in progress because on Tuesday night six Labour councillors voted against the cuts in Bristol and six others abstained. The Labour Party in Bristol is divided and doesn't know how to handle it. I shan't get involved but it is sickening.

*Sunday 16 September*

'Jim Losing Out to Benn' said the front page of the *Observer*. I was sorry it was a personal reference; but I felt the argument was getting across.

*Monday 17 September*

Up at 5.30 for a train to Newport to go to Bedwas Lodge, of which I am an honorary member. Went underground to see the new face, B101, which they were opening up.

We were about 2000 feet underground and there by the side of the new roadway was a perfectly fossilised tree – 250 million years old. The crew had actually excavated the trunk, which extended from the bottom of the roadway to the top and was about 20 inches thick. It was a tropical fern of some kind, South Wales apparently having had tropical weather in former times. Fantastic.

Every time you go down a pit you're struck by the appalling conditions in which miners work – these blackened men who have to use the roadways and the corners for lavatories. They were sitting eating their sandwiches and Mars bars and drinking from thermos flasks. It is really just a prison sentence. Will people go on doing it I wonder?

Got home and spoke to Eric Heffer, who pushed me to write a joint broadsheet for distribution at Conference. So I sat down and wrote 1200 words.

*Tuesday 18 September*

Ian Aitken interviewed me for a piece in Thursday's *Guardian*. His tape recorder wouldn't work so I lent him mine – which discomfited him.

He referred in an idle way to *Arguments for Socialism*. Then he hinted that Jim might resign if he were defeated over policies at the Conference. I said I couldn't believe that. He asked what would happen if Mrs Thatcher failed. Might the Tories not get rid of her, offer PR and try to get a national government?

'The Labour Party would never consider it,' I replied.

Undoubtedly the right in the Labour Party are considering a breakaway, which is what Jim hinted at when he talked about the unions disaffiliating. I don't rule out the possibility that we might lose a chunk of the right, but they wouldn't have a future. Aitken probed it. He is so cynical, not a bit interested in ideas, mainly in gossip and scandal.

My literary agent Anne McDermid phoned to tell me Michael Parkinson wants me on his programme next week. Rang Frances, with whom I had a long discussion about the strategy for both defeat and victory at Conference. If we're defeated, then the whole argument will go on in the inquiry. If we win, then it's possible Jim may go and a leadership election would follow. Would Michael Foot continue as Deputy Leader? If the Conference had just voted for a new system for electing the Leader it would have to be set up, and that would take time, so everything really does depend on Michael's being able to carry on.

There might be a breakaway of some Labour MPs. All sorts of things could happen. That's assuming we win, and I must admit I don't think it's likely.

*Thursday 20 September*

*Arguments for Socialism* was published today by Jonathan Cape.

There is a great row going on between *Nationwide* and *The Parkinson Show* as to who should have me on. Parkinson insisted I cancel a *Nationwide* interview I had agreed to.

The NEC has been attacked for its constitutional proposals by Bill Rodgers, David Owen, Roy Mason, Shirley Williams and Roy Hattersley.

*Friday 21 September*

The TGWU is worried that the electoral college would not give the trade union movement sufficient weight in choosing the Leader. All we have to do is get an electoral college accepted in principle at Conference and then go from there. It is a very thrilling period and I'm getting more optimistic, even though the campaign of the right is gathering force.

### Saturday 22 September

Listened to *Talking Politics* this morning, introduced by Tony King. He interviewed Brian Crozier, who said that all politicians should be subject to a college examination and put forward ludicrous right-wing arguments about the state.

Tony King then went on to talk to David Marquand. David said that there were twenty or so Marxists in the House of Commons, and probably more who sympathised with Marxism, some in favour of a revolutionary takeover of the state. He went on to say that the Labour Party was in danger of being infiltrated and had a discussion on this basis with Tony King without referring to Reg Prentice's defection. Then I watched Bill Grundy's programme, Grundy being a journalist for whom I have no time; he was attacking the trade unions in violent language.

I think we're going to be engaged in the most bitter struggle over the next ten years, and if this philosophy gains hold in the public mind then not only might we not win the next Election but socialism could be in retreat in Britain until absolutely vigorous campaigns for democracy are mounted again.

### Monday 24 September

To Selfridges for a book-signing session. I was nervous because I heard there had been a scene when George Brown was there, and Sophia Loren had been mobbed. I was put at a desk, and fifteen or so photographers and cameramen gathered round. I signed 160 books in an hour. There were many people from abroad, and a lot of women and young people.

### Tuesday 25 September

To Wilshaw's bookshop in Manchester where a great crowd of people had arrived for another book-signing session. It was a pleasant little bookshop. In one hour I signed ninety copies and the people were extremely friendly.

By the way, yesterday I referred to the *Daily Mirror* as being hostile to the Labour Party and today it had a stinging reply. They printed all the front pages since the war which had recommended their readers to vote Labour. I shall come back to that theme because their writers Woodrow Wyatt and Terence Lancaster are very anti-working-class. It is now an anti-working-class paper, which is a pity.

The Plumb-pudding in danger! Jensen a long way after Gillray.

*Wednesday 26 September*

Julie and I are absolutely swamped by letters – they are just pouring in. I don't know how to cope with it all.

Tonight is *The Parkinson Show*, and Caroline and the children gave me lots of advice about how to handle it.

I was picked up at 5 by Anne McDermid and Chris Mullin and we went to the studio. I had never met Michael Parkinson before and I liked him immediately. He's a very agreeable and intelligent guy. The actor Stewart Granger and the showjumping commentator Dorian Williams were the other guests.

We did a runthrough and then I was interviewed alone for half an hour. It was a delight; Michael was so friendly. He asked how it felt to be the bogeyman, and I said it had nothing to do with me. He asked about the Conference amendments and resolutions and I explained them. Would there be a split? No. Then he asked about Father and the peerage case and I dealt with that. He finally came back to the Conference and asked if I thought we'd win. I said yes, I thought this view would prevail.

In fact it was the best TV interview I have done. About 8 million people watch it, I believe.

Eric Heffer, Frances, Mother and Dave all rang later to say how good the programme was.

*Thursday 27 September*
Caroline and I went to canvass for Hilary in Walpole Ward for today's council by-election. Last time there was a Tory majority of about 350.

In the afternoon I packed for Conference and travelled down to Brighton.

I rang Caroline at home late and she told me that Hilary had won the council seat. He had a majority of 250 – about a 10 per cent swing. I am absolutely over the moon to have a son who is a Labour councillor.

*Labour Party Conference, Brighton*
*Friday 28 September*
The NEC met at 11 in a terribly hot room in the Grand Hotel.

We had a statement on South Africa drafted by Jenny Little, calling for comprehensive mandatory sanctions against South Africa by the UN. There was a vote in favour of leaving out 'comprehensive'; Jim failed to get 'mandatory sanctions' removed.

We had a long discussion on the resolution about PLP funding. Jim said, 'I've done the best I can with the money. It all went to the PLP', and so on.

'It is a matter of fundamental principle,' I emphasised. 'Never in the history of the Party has the PLP ever been an employing body. If the PLP employs research people, policy will shift from the NEC to the PLP. We are one party, not two.'

I spoke on the subject with some passion, and I think it made an impact. In the end, we agreed with a slight modification to stick to our position but decided we would not put it to the Conference.

Michael Foot said it was important not to wash our dirty linen in public. Of course, if the PLP got a lot of money and the national Party went bankrupt, it would be tragic.

We came to the drafting of the manifesto, and on that I was log-jammed. Members argued that it couldn't be discussed till Sunday, when the NEC considers the statements and resolutions to Conference, so rather than risk being defeated today on a sort of procedural technicality, I agreed that it could be deferred for final endorsement on Sunday.

We adjourned just before 6, and at 7 Eric and I held a press conference to launch a pamphlet we had produced containing our papers to the NEC and briefing material on the manifesto procedure.

Alex Kitson brought the TGWU Assistant General Secretary Harry Urwin over to talk to me, and Harry will support us on mandatory reselection and an electoral college, but not on the manifesto change.

I asked him about Moss Evans, and he said Moss was not a very deep person, he wanted to keep in with Jim and Basnett, and he would be pulled in several directions. So I'm now clear we're going to lose the manifesto issue because if the TGWU don't accept it we're sunk.

### Saturday 29 September

At 6.15 there was a special meeting of the Conference Arrangements Committee. I went through the whole reselection question with Derek Gladwin, the chairman of the committee, with absolute clarity: what order the CLP resolutions were to be put in, and how they were to be grouped. Those who wanted reselection to begin now would vote for composite resolution 33 and then would vote for the constitutional amendment. Those who wanted reselection to start next year would vote against composite 33 and for composite 32. Those who wanted the status quo would vote against both composites. They accepted that.

Then I took them similarly through the leadership question and the manifesto, step by step – so that nothing could go wrong.

### Sunday 30 September

Press coverage very hostile to me. Hilary arrived from London and I gave him a big kiss.

At lunch, who should Barbara Castle bring along but Janet Brown, who does the brilliant impersonation of Mrs Thatcher. She was all dressed up like Mrs Thatcher, and a lot of photos were taken, including one with me.

Mik said today, 'I expect a thousand people have told you but you were brilliant on Parkinson.' I felt that programme was a turning point.

Hilary went off to the Common Market Safeguards Committee AGM. He was introduced as a councillor and got a tremendous reception. Afterwards I was told by Jack Watson, who clutched me by both arms, that Hilary had made a great impression, and Ron Leighton [Labour MP for Newham North East] told me that he eclipsed me. I was so proud.

At 2.30 I went to the NEC meeting to consider our position on the resolutions to Conference.

After some attempts to muddle the issues, I won the vote 15 to 11 recommending Conference to take the constitutional amendments.

I then moved the Coventry South West resolution from Victor Schonfield and the Campaign for Labour Party Democracy on mandatory reselection of MPs.

Shirley said, 'This removes all safeguards for Members – an MP isn't even given notice if he or she is removed.'

'Shirley is absolutely wrong,' I insisted. 'She doesn't understand it. If you have a selection conference you are not removing any safeguards because there are none.'

Jim said, 'I can only tell you it won't stand up, it won't last. MPs do a job of work. What about the militants who are taking over the GMCs in the small inner-city CLPs?'

A vote to accept the resolution from Coventry South West was carried by 15 to 9.

On the manifesto there was a long and complicated discussion, but in the end the constitutional amendment to Clause 5 that I had drafted and moved (and that had gone through the July Executive by 9 to 8) was defeated by 14 to 12 because Alex Kitson voted against it on behalf of the TGWU, and Doug Hoyle voted against it on behalf of ASTMS. So two important unions defeated us. Even if they had voted for it in the NEC, their unions would have voted against it in Conference because they were clearly mandated. So we lost a point, but we can try again next year.

The composite resolution calling for an electoral college in principle was carried by 20 votes to 3.

We won six votes out of nine. A marvellous success for us.

The NEC considered the rest of the composite resolutions, and then I caught a taxi to the Institute for Workers' Control fringe meeting on accountability versus patronage.

### Monday 1 October

Woke up to find Stephen and Hilary in their sleeping bags on the floor.

This afternoon we had a debate on cuts in public expenditure, and Tom Litterick made a courageous speech attacking the last manifesto and Jim's role in the Election; Michael Foot made a contemptible one in which he said that those who didn't agree with the Cabinet should have got out (having pleaded with me not to resign). In a way that's the final break with Michael, and I think he feels guilty about it.

Jim led the applause for Michael and went on clapping and clapping and clapping.

During the day I received a telephone message from Colin Semper, head of religious broadcasting at the BBC, announcing that they were not going to put out my three 'Thought for the Day' pieces this week on Radio 4 because it was deemed an inappropriate time. I got through to the duty officer at the BBC and then on to Monica Sims, the Controller of Radio 4, who told me, 'Colin Semper has used his editorial discretion to postpone them.'

I said, 'You're senior to him. Why not use your editorial discretion to put them back?'

'I can't,' she replied, 'because he discussed it with the Director-General.'

I asked her, 'Will you please get on to the DG?'

She said she was having dinner with him tonight at Television Centre, and I said I'd call back.

'It's only a postponement,' she added.

'Look, when I was asked to do this, the date was given to me. I asked if it was all right, knowing it was the week of the Party Conference, and was told it was. I worked on them very hard and have made changes to the script. I recorded them in advance and there were many queries raised which I dealt with. You have had John Selwyn Gummer recently. You talk about dissidents in other countries but the BBC is just as bad. Do you imagine they would have been cancelled if it had been Shirley Williams presenting them?'

I think that registered. I told her there would be a hell of a row if they were taken off.

With Caroline, Stephen and Hilary to the Agents' Ball. Jim gave Caroline a watery smile; he couldn't look at me, he is so angry.

It is a tremendously tense situation. If we lose tomorrow it will reveal the pattern of power in the Labour Party – that many of the unions are instruments of the PLP. David Basnett will vote against all the changes, because he thinks everything should go to the inquiry.

*Tuesday 2 October*
'Callaghan's Day of Agony', 'Get Off Jim's Back', etc., were the headlines today, after some bitter speeches yesterday.

The first 'Thought for the Day' *was* postponed, so I sent a note with a copy of the text to the Press Association, the *Morning Star* and other papers. I am told that all three will be broadcast in a fortnight, but the BBC may now cancel them altogether. That's fine with me.

The first item of Conference was the NEC election results. I was top of the CLP section. Jo Richardson replaced Barbara Castle. Shirley came top of the women's section with full trade union backing, and Renée Short and Joan Maynard were saved.

It was Jim's speech today, and he was quieter than I expected, amusing and light-hearted. It was effective, to be candid. He robustly defended the Government's achievements and attacked those who had attacked him. He warned against the constitutional changes, and talked about internationalism and compassion. No socialist content whatever, of course.

But it was warmly received, and I did get up for the standing ovation at the end. Joan Lestor turned to me and said, 'What a scandalous thing to do', and I said, 'Not in the slightest. I served in his Government and I respect him.' I am rather fond of Jim anyway.

In the afternoon Conference debated the constitutional resolutions. On the election of the Party Leader through an electoral college, the AUEW had split and voted against. It made all the difference, because with the AUEW vote we would have passed the resolution. But the fixers won't win. We'll come back next year and put it right. I went out while the result was being read out; I didn't want to hear.

I came back in for the debate on the mandatory reselection of MPs. Mik made a good speech, and Eric Heffer wound up, with quite a lot of barracking from the floor. It was an angry Conference, with the PLP

'I do believe you're right — normally it is the ship which is set alight!'

and trade union sections pitched against the constituency Labour parties. When the vote was taken it was 4 million to 3 million for composite 33, which instructed the Conference Arrangements Committee to put immediately to the Conference the amendment to the Party Constitution. This amendment provided for reselection of MPs once in every Parliament and this was carried by a majority of 2 million.

So the efforts of the right have failed. It has been the most amazing campaign, and after five years of hard work we've carried it through. The MPs will just have to accept it. It means there are 635 vacancies for candidates in the next Parliament. MPs will have to take notice of their GMCs.

I'm not aiming for a great victory tomorrow on the manifesto. I just want to set the scene for the Party over the next decade.

The right are furious about their defeat. Even if the election of the Leader is left to the PLP, mandatory reselection changes the whole balance of power in the Party.

I don't see why we should be bullied any more by the union leaders. They got it wrong and they have to accept that the Party is entrusted to the NEC. We desperately need their money but they desperately need the Party.

*Wednesday 3 October*
Frances and Francis and I went over my speech to Conference for this afternoon. It didn't look very good on paper, but then they never do.

To the conference hall, and the first debate was on the manifesto – the composite resolution calling for constitutional amendments to be put before the 1980 Conference to give control of the manifesto to the NEC alone. It was proposed by Stuart Weir of Hackney South and Shoreditch CLP, and we won by almost a million votes. Amazing when you think the matter was first raised by me only in June at the NEC's Home Policy Committee. Although we didn't get the constitutional change itself through, we got a clear statement of how it was to be organised.

Fenner made a marvellous speech on a resolution from Brighton Kemptown – tremendously inspiring. Then I wound up the debate on behalf of the NEC. I was terribly nervous, so much so that my hand shook visibly. I had to steady it by holding on to the lectern, but it was, I think, my best Conference speech.

Walked across to the Tribune meeting. Among those on the platform were Jo Richardson, Eric Heffer, Barbara Castle, Neil Kinnock, Michael Foot and me. The Tribune Group has in a sense become the Labour Party, in so far as the rank and file support it, but at the same time it has moved towards the right. There is no rebellion in Michael Foot any more; he is entirely an establishment figure.

Barbara made an unpopular speech saying that socialists must fight in the Common Market. The audience didn't like the Common Market, so she was in a difficult position. Caroline thought my speech went on for too long.

Michael just spread gloom about the future and said we should do nothing, but sit tight.

*Thursday 4 October*
Refused all BBC interviews – which made them hopping mad.

The whole Conference has been really friendly, and not only is it a turning point for the Party but I felt I had been taken to its heart.

*Friday 5 October*
In the debate on Northern Ireland, Michael wound up for the NEC. He looked so angry about terrorism, and you felt he didn't understand at all what was going on.

I should add that Michael apologised to me yesterday for a piece in the *Guardian* suggesting that when he said at the Tribune meeting that some people never grow up he was referring to me. I brushed it aside.

Caroline and I came back to the hotel and packed, then went back to hear Frank Allaun's winding-up speech before we drove home.

A month ago I never expected we'd achieve any of these things. The PLP is absolutely furious. There will now be a major attempt by the right to oust Jim Callaghan, partly because they'll say he wasn't strong enough to beat the left, but also because they only have a year to get Denis Healey elected by the PLP before any rule changes occur.

*Saturday 6 October*
Frances told me on the phone that she had heard that David Basnett genuinely feared there might be plots to get rid of MPs as a result of mandatory reselection. I also spoke to Eric Heffer, who said his constituency agent, who is on the executive of the GMWU, had dinner with Basnett and Callaghan, and they were determined to restore the proscribed list of organisations and get rid of Militant.

*Tuesday 9 October*
The *Morning Star* carried the text of my first 'Thought for the Day'.

To the Reform Club in the evening where I had been invited to speak. It was an unbelievable experience. It was quite an intimate gathering: Lord Amulree – a nice old Liberal peer – was in the chair and there were two professors, four ex-civil servants, three bankers, two publishers and a former Ambassador. I was told quite openly by my host that one of the audience was in the Intelligence Services. It was like a board meeting of the *Daily Telegraph*.

I was questioned by a very angry banker, who asked me about the Labour Party's plans to renationalise without compensation. I said, 'The view we take is that it is daylight robbery to sell public assets that have been bought with public money, and we're not prepared to compensate people that have bought assets in this way. It would be morally wrong.'

'You're not answering the question,' he shouted.

I said I was giving him the answer he didn't want to hear, and he stormed out.

The members of the Reform Club were proud of the fact that the press never heard of these meetings and there were never leaks.

I felt like a political archaeologist – digging through layers and finding all these men (no women), still powerful, with international contacts. I planted in their minds the idea that capitalism and democracy were incompatible: democracy gives the poor and the disinherited the political power to demand hospitals and schools which capitalism can't pay for. Of course the origin of their mistrust is the spectre of communism which has haunted capitalism since the publication of the *Communist Manifesto* in 1848.

### Wednesday 10 October

I rang up the religious broadcasts department at the BBC about the postponement of my three 'Thoughts for the Day'. I assured the producer that I realised it had nothing to do with him, and he confirmed it was out of his hands but said it was a salutary lesson to him and he wondered how long he could go on compromising like this. They are to be broadcast next week, and of course the BBC has attracted a larger audience to them as a result of the publicity last week. It is ironic that the *Morning Star*, which is publishing them, is giving access to Christian ideas that the British establishment was embarrassed to broadcast. It is a further stage in my thoughts about the links between Christian ideas and socialism.

Rang Michael Parkinson to say how much I had enjoyed doing the show. He said the news and current affairs department were a bit angry because he'd scooped them.

### Friday 12 October

Went to the Greenwood Theatre, where the live chat show *Friday Night Saturday Morning* was being broadcast. It was hosted by Harold Wilson, and the other guests were Pat Phoenix (Elsie Tanner of *Coronation Street*) and the Yorkshire cricketer Freddie Trueman.

Harold tried to needle me. He asked me things like 'What do you think about Karl Marx? Do you want to be Prime Minister? Why did you have a map of Britain upside down in your office?' – a reference to my days as Energy Secretary when I wanted to emphasise the importance of Scotland in the economy.

He asked me quite a lot about workers' control, and I said I believed workers should hire capital and that workers' skills in this country were greatly wasted.

Referring to my radicalism, he said that in the Soviet Union I would have been sent to run a power station in Siberia, and I replied that he had sent me to the Department of Energy, which was the same thing. I mentioned his boast that he had never got further than page 2 of *Das Kapital*, and said I was *ashamed* that I hadn't read it because Marx was one of the four greatest philosophers of the past hundred years, with Einstein, Darwin and Freud. It was actually like having a private discussion with Harold in public.

### Saturday 13 October

Arrived in Glasgow at 7 am for the first conference of the Labour Co-ordinating Committee. I was met by George Galloway, secretary of the Dundee Labour Party, a first-rate man. He took me to the City Hall, where 250 people from the Institute for Workers' Control, Independent Labour Publications, the Campaign for Labour Party Democracy, Tribune and a few MPs – Robin Cook, Michael Meacher, Ernie Ross of Dundee West and so on – were gathered. A tremendous day.

Caught the plane back to London for Hilary's victory party, held in a little hut in Ealing. Hilary proposed a toast to Rosalind; he is such a popular figure and I was filled with affection for him.

### Monday 15 October

Caught the tube to Heathrow for a three-day lecture trip to the United States. It is the first time for many years that I have travelled non-VIP, entirely on my own: being a Minister with chauffeur-driven cars and helicopters and police escorts makes you out of touch.

### Thursday 18 October

One thing that struck me in America was that if you haven't got money you're finished. That's probably true of any country, but here money is worshipped; it completely dominates society.

But I've noticed the decline of America as a world power since Watergate and Vietnam, and now Carter is a head of state, on a par with Schmidt and Giscard. The presidency is up against the power of the Pentagon, Wall Street and the media.

Being free from the legacy of an ancient history, the USA is able to move more quickly than most countries, and it did occur to me that if America went socialist it would happen quickly. There would be none of the endless debate by liberal intellectuals which took the steam out of the reform movement here. Some of the big campaigns like Jane Fonda's economic democracy and Ralph Nader's attacks on the big corporations have a socialist flavour about them.

*Friday 19 October*
Prepared for *Any Questions* in Bristol tonight. Struggled with a backlog of letters. Julie and I have to turn around about a hundred letters a day.

Haven't done *Any Questions* since 1974 because the PM would never allow Ministers to appear on it. The other participants were Donald Stokes, President of BL, whom of course I know and like, Teddy Taylor, a more interesting Tory MP than most, who resigned from the Government over the Common Market, and the novelist Susan Hill, who turned out to be a real fan of Mrs Thatcher.

The questions covered homosexuality, prostitution and Brezhnev. It was the first time I had really commented on sexual matters and I defended homosexuals and prostitutes 100 per cent. I managed to survive without any particular problems.

*Saturday 20 October*
The Eastern Region of the Labour Party held its conference in Cambridge chaired by Stan Newens. I spoke with Roy Hattersley and others. Roy took a tough line, saying we must not repudiate the last Labour Government; we needed an incomes policy, we had to rediscover the Tawney/Crosland socialist tradition – I must say it went down like a lead balloon. After the fall of Labour there is a lot of disenchantment, and people want a message of hope and inspiration.

*Tuesday 23 October*
Question Time in the House was devoted to education. Listening to the Tories demanding the dismantling of the state education system, of free school meals provisions, of the transport service, was quite frightening.

The next Labour Government, locked as it will be into the Common Market, NATO, the IMF, without exchange controls, is going to be extremely vulnerable. To that extent international capitalism has defeated democracy and it is going to require a very great change to reverse it. People may not of course see the consequences of this defeat, but the achievements of 150 years will be severely set back.

During PM's Questions Mrs Thatcher qualified her statement to the European Council in June that Britain would not pay her full EEC contribution. She said that she would obey the law of the UK, which of course requires us to obey Common Market law. So her bold words were worthless.

The PLP meeting at 5 was most unpleasant. There was a backlash against the Conference.

Jim described various discussions he had had about the Commission of Inquiry. The NEC was to meet tomorrow and he hoped no final decision would be taken then about the composition of the Commission. Jim said he was going to serve on it as Leader of the Party; the PLP had a particular role in the Party's Constitution and merited special representation.

Gerald Kaufman made a most aggressive speech. The inquiry would change the relationship between the PLP and the NEC. The PLP had a duty to carry out Party policy; Conference policy-making was inadequate and had to be improved. He said Herbert Morrison had invented the device of composite resolutions to defeat proposals he didn't want. There was a lot of laughter at this – it was an amazing admission of the reality of Conference fixing.

There was a lot of bitterness and hostility throughout the discussion, which raged mainly around what representation the PLP should have on the Commission of Inquiry. They got off their chests what they thought about Conference and the NEC, but it bodes ill for the future. The PLP has strayed far from the grassroots and that is the problem. Jim sees the PLP as a separate party.

*Wednesday 24 October*
NEC, which was clearly going to be a very difficult one.

After going through the agenda, we came to the composition of the Commission of Inquiry into the Party and Lena Jeger supported the view that the Commission should elect its own chairman.

Jim Callaghan said he feared confrontation and he wanted discussion of the PLP representation to be deferred to a later meeting.

So Eric Heffer jumped in and said the representation of the PLP could be solved by having the Leader and the Deputy Leader on the Commission, and we must decide it today.

'Oh no,' said Jim. 'I intend to serve as Leader of the whole Party, not just as a representative of the PLP.'

Neville Hough of the GMWU thought we should decide the composition today – five NEC members, five general secretaries, and three PLP representatives including the Leader.

I said, if we were to have five general secretaries, the five representatives from the NEC should come from the constituency section; the constituencies after all put up half the Party's money.

'This argument is about power,' Dennis Skinner said. 'MPs are not a separate party and we should have five general secretaries, five from the constituency section of the NEC, plus the Party Treasurer Norman Atkinson, the Vice-Chairman of the Party Alex Kitson, and the Leader.'

After a great deal more heated discussion Eric Heffer formally moved that the composition should be five trade-unionists, five NEC representatives and the Leader. Then lots of amendments were added and I moved that it should be five plus five, plus the Leader, Deputy Leader, Alex and Norman, and this was carried by 13 to 8 – fantastically satisfactory.

So then nominations were made for the five from the NEC, and Eric, Joan Lestor, Frank Allaun, Jo Richardson and myself were elected. Shirley Williams, Lena Jeger, Alan Hadden and Les Huckfield were runners-up.

I reckon that the left–right balance is potentially 10 to 4 in our favour – a great victory.

### Thursday 25 October

In the papers there was tremendous coverage of yesterday's NEC meeting, and cries of outrage from Labour MPs. It became clear during the course of the day that there would be a backlash.

Of course, you can't change the balance of power without a battle. One of the things that came out of tonight's PLP meeting was how chaotic it is – it is not equipped to have votes or decisions, it has no minutes, no agenda, nothing. Allan Roberts, the new MP for Bootle, got up and said he'd never seen anything like it.

The truth is that the PLP has been a cosy little club for years, and the Party Leaders have provided jobs for Labour MPs, and we are now lifting the lid on all of it. It is a great shambles, and we will have to inject some proper democracy into the PLP.

Yesterday morning when I was getting out of bed I had a pain in my elbow, and today in the Tea Room I felt a pain in my left hand and it had gone pale, and I immediately thought it was a heart attack. I was going to go to Westminster Hospital but I swung my left arm so the blood circulated and I felt a bit better. Perhaps I've been overdoing it a bit.

### Friday 26 October

Last night I dreamt that I visited KME in Kirkby and found that all the equipment had been taken out, and there were wires hanging from the ceiling and gaps in the floor where all the basic machine tools had been torn out. There was just one candle, and by this candlelight fifty workers were trying to turn the rubbish, the old pieces of wood and stuff, into little objects to sell. It was too much for me, and in my dream I burst into tears and put my hands over my eyes and wept uncontrollably before speaking to them.

Anyway, the papers this morning are full of the developments in the Party. Callaghan is rumoured to be thinking of resigning.

To Bristol, and I asked the regional organiser, Alan Mason, about the proposed redistribution of boundaries. My seat may become unwinnable. That of course depends partly on the political situation at the next General Election, but I'll have to watch this. I do want to stay in Parliament but I am devoted to Bristol South East and I don't want to give it up.

### Sunday 28 October

I marched in a huge demonstration organised by the TUC against the Tory MP John Corrie's bill, which would restrict a woman's right to have an abortion. About 40,000 people joined in, but the BBC gave most of its coverage over to Lord Longford and other anti-abortion campaigners going to 10 Downing Street with a wreath.

### Monday 29 October

Had a drink tonight with Chris Moncrieff of the Press Association, a nice man. He told me that Peter Walker and Ian Gilmour were extremely worried about the public expenditure cuts and felt that they couldn't go on. The liberal wing of the Tory Party is obviously getting restive.

### Tuesday 30 October

I asked Jack Dormand in the Whips' Office if I could be paired next week so that I could give a sermon in Mansfield, and he asked me if I was a Christian. I thought for a moment that he was a Christian and was rebuking me for some reason, so I said, 'Well, I am a follower of Jesus, but I am not an active member of the church.' It turned out he was a rather militant humanist and we had a useful argument, which helped to clear my thoughts a bit.

I dictated my diary. I'm terribly tired. Of course a lot of my day is easy – just drifting about, chatting in the House. I don't really work in the way that a manual worker or a busy office worker does.

I saw Merlyn Rees tonight; he'd just been to Bristol University debating with Tariq Ali on a motion declaring that the police were repressive. 'Tariq Ali made a marvellous speech,' he said. 'He is a very intelligent guy. I had dinner with him beforehand and asked him if he ever went back to Pakistan and he said, "Certainly not."'

That Merlyn had been impressed by Tariq Ali was really something, because you may be absolutely sure that, when he was Home Secretary, the security services would have persuaded him that Tariq Ali was a danger to society.

### Wednesday 31 October

The PLP to consider the inquiry was held at 11, and a long and bitter meeting it turned out to be. There was one resolution from the Shadow Cabinet and five amendments.

The meeting started with a row about whether or not the votes should be recorded.

Then Fred Willey, in the chair, moved the motion that the PLP should be represented on the Commission independently of NEC MPs and Norman Buchan moved my amendment, proposing the formula agreed at the NEC. Norman said the inquiry must deal with the problems of the Party as a whole, and the PLP must not seek special prerogatives for itself.

Gavin Strang spoke in support of another amendment – that one PLP member should sit on the Commission. Nigel Spearing and Robert Maclennan moved further amendments. Bob Maclennan said MPs owed their position to the votes of Labour voters and not the NEC or the activists.

Bob Mellish made a very strange speech. He said he wanted to refer to rumours in the press that he was going to be made a peer and appointed Chairman of the London Docks Development Corporation.* He said he was all for it, but no one had offered him this. He got very emotional!

After everyone had spoken Jim Callaghan summed up. He agreed with Eric Heffer that the idea of the inquiry had started with the intention of looking at finance and membership and had now been extended, but the NEC had not safeguarded the rights and responsibilities of MPs and he wanted to safeguard the PLP. Eric Heffer tried to interrupt him. Jim went on, 'Let me warn you that entryism in the Party is a big problem which the NEC will not face. With reselection of MPs you will get the bedsitter brigade coming into the constituency parties – and left as well as right MPs will be under attack.

'There is not a unanimous view on the NEC, and as the NEC have chosen an unbalanced group for the Commission of Inquiry then the PLP should correct it. There was a 9 to 8 vote on the NEC in favour of changing Clause 5 in the summer. Now, Eric Heffer is not a communist, but what about the others? One member of the NEC told me he wanted victory, not peace. That is not good enough and the NEC must reconsider its attitude.'

Jim spoke very passionately, arguing that he wasn't for the right against the left but was the peacemaker between the two sides. There was a lot of applause – the right banging the tables very hard; they always applaud louder than we do.

Four amendments were then voted on; mine lost by 50 to 137. Finally the main motion was carried by 133 to 61.

Jim was interviewed on television by Shirley Williams, who has a series now that she is out of Parliament. He came over most

* Appointed Deputy Chairman of the London Docks Development Corporation 1981, created a life peer 1985. Mellish later left the Labour Party.

charmingly. He said the Party had forgotten fraternity and 'Tony Benn has a lot of good ideas but he is wrong about freedom of information'. So I rang him up and told him I thought he was very good. He was taken aback, and I'm sure he thought: What's that bugger up to? But it was genuine – I did think he was good, and it isn't a bad thing to emphasise that these arguments aren't personal.

### Saturday 3 November

Took the train to Manchester for a weekend conference of the Labour Co-ordinating Committee. Got a cheap weekend return for £16.10, and prepared my speech on the way. I met up with Colin Barnett, secretary of the north-west region of the TUC, a radical Christian socialist. His wife has a theological degree and they met when they were working for Donald Soper at the Methodist Conference. Now they are both Anglicans. During the winter, as a full-time NUPE official, he really organised the public service workers in the north-west, and he has now been turfed off the North-West Labour Party Executive as a result. He thought the unions should disaffiliate from the Party if the Labour Government couldn't do better for the low-paid workers.

There were 600 people jammed into the meeting. Jack Spriggs from KME made a marvellous speech, followed by Arthur Scargill and Michael Meacher. Chris Moncrieff of the Press Association was there, and there was a lot of news interest.

Afterwards I signed copies of my book. Saw Tony Banks, Frances and Francis, Stuart Weir, and many others. A great gathering of the clans.

Colin Barnett had heard a rumour that Prince Philip had intervened to prevent my 'Thought for the Day' being broadcast during the Labour Party Conference. He said Prince Philip was a close friend of the Director-General of the BBC, Ian Trethowan. Interesting.

### Sunday 4 November

Got home and I was just too exhausted to go to a firework party with the children. I spoke to Frances, and she told me Audrey Wise had defeated her as vice-chairman of the LCC. She is critical of some of the people in the LCC. So there are troubles ahead.

### Tuesday 6 November

The *Daily Mirror* had a savage piece on me, saying that I was a 'cool, calculating and deliberate liar'. It was the most violent attack yet, I think.

Sir Keith Joseph introduced his Industry Bill. John Silkin made a very boring and trivial reply, and I waded in and said that after denationalisation the Special Patrol Group would be brought in, because industrial policy would end up as a question of law and order. Millions of people were worried about their jobs, and Government policy had nothing to say about dealing with this. I think I was too strong even for the PLP.

*Wednesday 7 November*
*World at One* rang repeatedly to ask if I would be interviewed about my point in the House regarding the Special Patrol Group. I was busy, so they sent Robin Day round with a sound recordist. He sat there looking like a commissioner from the Vatican come to try me for heresy. As he left he said he 'couldn't make a habit' of coming to see me.

On the programme, after my interview with Robin was played, Assistant Chief Constable Booth of Northamptonshire came on to deny that the SPG had been used in Corby during demonstrations against the closure. Well, that wasn't the issue.

After lunch I collected Mother and drove to Mansfield Theological College in Oxford, to give my sermon in the chapel there. I spoke for about twenty minutes, and afterwards was invited to the senior common room for discussion. Mother was marvellous: she'd been on the council of Mansfield College for a long time. I was asked whether I called myself a Christian and I said that the older I got the less I found the mysteries of Christianity interesting – the Virgin Birth, the Assumption, the Blessed Virgin Mary, the Resurrection, the Trinity and so on. I had been to the anti-religious museum in Leningrad and had seen all those layers stripped away and what was left was much stronger. I called myself no more than a student of the teachings of the historical Jesus. Charles Brock, the chaplain, said, 'You'd qualify to be a Minister and take orders in the United Reformed Church, because they have no creed. All you have to say is you are a follower of Christ our Lord.' That's interesting: it has always been on my conscience that I didn't feel a Christian, but more that I was interested in Christian ideas.

*Friday 9 November*
Dashed for the train to Bristol. Opened my letters of which some were a delight. A man wrote from Corby saying that Assistant Chief Constable Booth had been wrong – there were buses of police with riot shields and visors and it had thoroughly upset the town. That was interesting. It's like having my own intelligence service.

*Sunday 11 November*
To Bristol Council House for the Cenotaph service. All the bigwigs were there as usual. Now that Thatcher is in Government the power of the establishment seems to have been restored. They look much stronger than they did.

To the station, and a man approached me and said, 'I work at a local printer's, and despite the attacks on you in the press I want you to know that everybody here supports you.' I thanked him for his encouragement – that sort of thing is happening a lot at the moment.

*Tuesday 13 November*
*The Times* was published today – the first issue for eleven and a half months.

*Wednesday 14 November*
To the Labour Party Commission of Inquiry meeting. Ron Hayward reported on progress and we discussed whether we should yield to the PLP's continuing pressure for a member. We also had an inconclusive talk about the chairmanship. Norman Atkinson wanted the trade-unionists to have it, and he and Eric argued bitterly. They don't like each other.

*Thursday 15 November*
The American Government have frozen all the Iranian assets in the US, reported to be about £5 billion dollars, in response to the Iranian Government's intention to withdraw all their money from America – reported to be about £12 billion dollars. I must say, if we'd done the same in 1976 to fight off the encroachment of the IMF we'd have been in a very much stronger position, but the British Labour Party has no guts.

To Bristol and in the hotel I heard the most sensational news bulletin. Sir Anthony Blunt, the Adviser for the Queen's Pictures, knighted in the 1970s, was revealed as the 'fourth man' in the Burgess/Maclean/Philby spy ring. He confessed in 1964 to having been a Russian spy and was protected, and knighted *after* that. Now he's been stripped of his knighthood and he's left the country.

All this came out in the Commons in a written answer from Mrs Thatcher, but that means it was known to the 1964–70 Labour Government, the Heath Government and the 1974–9 Labour Government. If Andrew Boyle had not given this away in his book *The Climate of Treason* it would have never been revealed. Amazing. It shows again that the British establishment trusts the upper class to be reliable without vetting, whereas Philip Agee or Aubrey, Berry and Campbell are outlaws, hounded and treated quite differently.[2] Incidentally, had the Official Secrets Act been amended as is now proposed, Andrew Boyle would be liable to prosecution for publishing this.

The minimum lending rate has gone up to 17 per cent; this will lead to bankruptcies on a large scale and unemployment.

*Friday 16 November*
It appears that Prime Ministers from Home onwards were *not* told by the security services about Blunt, and therefore the key question is whether there was a secret state within a state which was not under democratic control.

*Sunday 18 November*
The *Sunday Times* is back on sale and there was a lot about Anthony Blunt.

There was also a most interesting article by Hugo Young suggesting that, when Roy Jenkins delivers the Dimbleby Lecture this week, he may indicate his return to politics and that he and Bill Rodgers will try to set up a democratic party that will pick up the Liberals and drive the Labour Party into a minority position. I don't actually think it would succeed. The class interests and the class orientation of a society like ours are too strong for the Labour Party to be crushed.

It is possible, however, that a coalition democratic–conservative Government might be elected in the 1980s, particularly if Healey becomes Leader of the Party. An absolutely clear alternative to Thatcher has to be staked out.

I went out with Caroline to Rosalind's grave; we planted some bulbs and walked around the graveyard.

*Monday 19 November*
Had tea in the Tea Room with Frank McElhone and Joe Ashton, and I asked their opinion of this new democratic party forecast in the *Sunday Times*. Frank was absolutely certain it would happen. He thought Roy might pick up twenty-five people from the PLP. Joe Ashton was more scornful, but he does believe that the reselection procedures will create terrible trouble in the PLP. He thought Shirley Williams, Tom Bradley, Bill Rodgers, Ian Wrigglesworth, John Horam, Mike Thomas and Neville Sandelson might go with Roy, and that was about it.*

'The media will be behind them,' said Frank, 'and there will be money behind them too.'

I can't say I would weep if we did get rid of that crew.

*Tuesday 20 November*
Blunt is to give a press conference today. When you consider that his 'offence' ended in 1945 it is hard to see him dragged through the mire.

On the 1 o'clock news Blunt was shown being cross-examined by a small group of journalists on behalf of the BBC and ITV. He came over with some distinction really. He said he'd put conscience above the law

---

* Joe Ashton's prediction was remarkably accurate: the Labour MPs mentioned defected from the Labour Party to join the SDP in 1981.

and his loyalty to his country, and he regretted it, but that was his explanation. Nothing had happened since the war, he claimed, and all he'd done was to hand over military intelligence about the Germans to the Russians – nothing that put our own security at risk. It's a very interesting story and I asked the Speaker this morning if I could speak in the debate tomorrow. Mrs Thatcher announced that business would be postponed to debate the Blunt affair.

## Wednesday 21 November

Worked all morning on my speech for the debate on Blunt.

Thatcher opened with a carefully prepared speech which she had obviously had written for her by her civil servants.

Merlyn Rees followed with a totally inadequate speech in which he said everything was all right and the best thing was for there to be close inter-party talks between the Ministers of the day and the Opposition spokesmen. Altogether muddled.

Willie Hamilton made a crude speech, about it being the upper-class people who betrayed their country, not working-class people. Ted Heath summarised the situation as he remembered it and said there should not be a witch-hunt.

I described the freedoms we were trying to defend, and argued for accountability of the security services. I concluded, 'We cannot entrust our liberties to a state within a state, with its own policies, its own prejudices, its own funds, its own enemies.'

Sat through to the end of the debate. Jim said he wasn't told about Blunt, but he did agree there should be some sort of an inquiry.

## Thursday 22 November

Went to see the doctor because I have a very bloodshot infected eye and horrible red spots on my face. He gave me some penicillin, and checked me over.

Roy gave the Dimbleby Lecture tonight and I watched it at home; there was this pompous man, so self-important, describing British history without any reference to economics, and indicating that it was the failure of Government that had caused the decline of Britain. We needed PR and a radical centre which could break away from the Labour Party. The invited audience clapped him enthusiastically. Of course there *always* has been a centre party in British politics in the twentieth century; it is made up of Butskellites, including Macmillan, Callaghan, Wilson and Heath at one stage. It is that grouping that has presided over our decline. This is clearly what Roy wants to see happen.

*Tuesday 27 November*

To Transport House at 10.30 for a joint meeting of the NEC and Shadow Cabinet, Lena Jeger in the chair. Fred Willey, in his capacity as Chairman of the PLP, said the principle of the inquiry had been established, and his objective was to remove the sense of unfairness felt by the PLP which might prejudice the inquiry. The PLP had a special part in the movement, and anything agreed by the NEC affected MPs. They wanted strong representation on the Commission.

Jim Callaghan reinforced this view, and he hoped that the NEC would reconsider their decision.

Denis Healey welcomed the inquiry. Individual membership was poor, we had too few full-time agents, local parties had been taken over by a handful of extremists, the NEC had refused to publish the National Agent's report on entryism: the Commission of Inquiry must look at everything. The NEC members were from a single tendency. They were elected by delegates who were 90 per cent middle class, and he was worried about the credibility of the NEC composition on the Commission. They had excluded the Chairman of the Party and put on the Vice-Chairman. The findings would not enjoy the confidence of the Party unless there was a better balance. He hoped that in a wise and comradely spirit the NEC would reconsider the composition.

Peter Shore agreed that the present balance would not carry weight and he asked the NEC to think again.

Dennis Skinner pointed out that the inquiry was not the brainchild of the NEC, it came from 'right-wing trade union leaders like Basnett'.

David Owen said there was a dangerous political vacuum that was waiting to be filled. He himself had been against the constitutional changes because of the memories of Clause 4 in 1959. The manifesto was the key issue. He feared that, if the NEC controlled the manifesto, this vacuum would be filled by the Liberals. We must begin fighting the General Election now. How could we shut out the PLP?

Norman Atkinson argued that the PLP hadn't been frozen out, and as far as the manifesto was concerned the trade-unionists dominated the Conference.

Neville Hough said we should all be loyal to Jim. He hoped that Tony and Eric would agree to one more representative.

The argument then revolved around what the Commission should consider – organisation and finance alone or constitutional changes. Ron Hayward said that, since the inquiry had to conclude by next year, not everything could be included by June, so we had to have priorities.

Joan Lestor raised Denis Healey's point about middle-class delegates and said they were also white, male and elderly.

Jim concluded the meeting. At the end of his speech he mentioned the Militant Tendency – he didn't know whether the inquiry would deal with them, but they frightened Labour MPs, who thought they were being undermined.

As we left, the media were gathering outside like a lot of vultures.

Sat in at the end of the NEC sub-committee set up to consider the security services and civil liberties. Jo Richardson, the historian Edward (E.P.) Thompson, Peter Archer, Pat Hewitt of the NCCL and journalist Duncan Campbell were there.

Frank McElhone told me later that Hattersley's campaign for the leadership was going like the wind. Hattersley's strategy is to push Healey into attacking me, saying, 'If you really want support from us you have to take on Tony Benn', in the hope that Healey will destroy himself. Frank said that Peter Shore was hoping to get his campaign launched, and Eric Heffer had told him that he was not a Bennite and that he intended to stand in his own right.

### Wednesday 28 November
Caroline and I had dinner with Arthur and Anne Scargill in the House. Anne had never been before and Arthur had only ever been to committees. I took them into the Lords, to the Royal Gallery, and into the Commons to hear a few moments of the debate.

We talked about the leadership. Arthur thought that, if there was an election in July and Denis was elected, there would be an opportunity to dislodge him after an electoral college had been established. That may be the best strategy.

### Friday 30 November
At 2.30 a guy called Dr Kim Howells, senior research writer in the Welsh Coal Field History project, financed by the Social Science Research Council, came to see me to talk about the mining industry. He's an interesting guy; he's Welsh, and has worked in the pits. He said he was a communist as a young man. Then he went ultra-left and joined the Socialist Labour League. He says the Communist Party is moving to the right again and is more Stalinist, and he's now sympathetic to the Labour Party. I gave him a candid interview, including details of my role in the productivity deal, against my wishes, in 1977.

At the Dublin meeting of European heads of state, Thatcher has failed to get a reduction of our contribution to the Community Budget, so I am going to launch a campaign for withdrawal from the Common Market. I shall introduce the idea at the Home Policy Committee on Monday. I'll get Geoff Bish to write a paper on how we could abrogate the Treaty, repeal the Act and make transitional arrangements. There has to be an effective break. This will have the secondary effect of winning support in the Party and isolating the right-wing pro-Marketeers.

What is happening at the moment in the Common Market is scandalous. Some Labour Party organisers went to Brussels recently, and one of them told me that it was odious and corrupt in its hospitality and that I was personally loathed.

*Saturday 1 December*
Bill Rodgers made a speech in Abertillery last night, in effect giving the Labour Party one year before it split – thus supporting the Jenkins view.

*Monday 3 December*
Went in to hear Mrs Thatcher answer questions on the Dublin summit. She looked frightened – the first time I have seen her look like that. She had talked big about getting a billion back from the Common Market and it has backfired.

I got up and said, 'As the Prime Minister has now raised expectations, what the people of Britain want to know is what is she going to do? Is she going to boycott the Assembly? Is she going to amend Section 2 of the European Communities Act and restore power to Parliament? Is she going to consider the possibility of withdrawal? If she doesn't offer something, all her speeches will be sound and fury, signifying nothing. Instead of being the Iron Maiden, she will be the Paper Tigress.'

That last point I thought rather good and it was quoted on the news.

At Home Policy Committee a resolution from Doug Hoyle was amended, so that it read: 'In view of the lack of progress to meet British demands at the Dublin summit, Britain should immediately cease paying all the EEC taxes, stop Ministers attending EEC meetings, and decide to undertake a study of the options open to us including the amendment of Section 2 of the European Communities Act and withdrawal from the EEC, and to prepare alternative policies for Britain.' It was carried unanimously, and Geoff was commissioned to draw up a paper for the spring for discussion at the PLP and Conference.

*Tuesday 4 December*
At 12.10 I was taken to the Cartoonist pub in Shoe Lane to receive the Golden Joker Award. I was uneasy about going but the atmosphere was jolly – all the cartoonists were there. I mustn't impute to everyone who works in the media the hostility that one gets from the proprietors and editors. I was presented with a gold tie-pin and I made a speech about the important role of the cartoonist in society.

Appearing in a human guise from time to time is quite useful – Mrs Thatcher and Enoch Powell have both received the award. Vic

Gibbons told me he was a socialist; his grandfather, John Burgess, was a founder of the ILP. He gave me two original cartoons. Mac, the *Daily Mail* cartoonist, presented me with a cartoon showing me walking along the street smoking my pipe and a lot of flies buzzing round my head, while round the corner Jim Callaghan, David Owen and Denis Healey were wielding great clubs, one of them saying, 'Remember, if we're asked, we were just swatting the greenfly!'

I received a pamphlet called *The Banning of Tony Benn at Bristol University and Sir Keith Joseph at the London School of Economics* published by the Council for Academic Freedom and Democracy, so I sent a copy to the Bristol media and to the Vice-Chancellor at Bristol, for when the university court meets to discuss the case.

*Thursday 6 December*
At the PLP meeting I raised the leak in the *Guardian* this morning that the Government is going for the PWR. The *Guardian* said that a small Cabinet committee had decided this but was worried about the public reaction and was therefore playing it low key. I said that as a Party we had gained the confidence of the environmentalists and it was important to keep it. The formation now of a green party would damage us. Jim agreed warmly, and said he had told the press as much this morning. That was funny, considering he had once told Giscard we favoured the PWR.

*Wednesday 12 December*
To TUC headquarters for their Economic Committee. My general impression of the TUC is that it is a fake – like the Labour Party leadership – appearing to be fighting publicly but privately working with the people it is supposed to be opposing.

We came on to a draft statement on the steel industry. Bill Sirs pointed out that the rundown would have effects on the whole economy: the entire industrial base of the country would shrink if this went on. He said the comparative productivity figures issued by the BSC were most misleading, because for Germany they did not include the number of people in training or research, whereas in Britain they did. Also, interest payments were phased over a longer period in Germany than in Britain. The adjusted figures showed that the average German steelworker produced 200 tons a year and the British 292 tons.

I've long suspected the BSC figures were completely fraudulent but you never can prove it.

In the evening Dora Gaitskell, Hugh's widow, came up to me in the House; I've always admired her – she's a real little fireball.

'Why are you so unfair to Labour peers?' she asked.

'I've never said a word against them.'

'You're always attacking them,' she said.

'No. I'm just in favour of the abolition of the House of Lords.'

'Why?'

'That's been Labour Party policy since Keir Hardie,' I replied.

'Yes, but it's never been done.'

'Was Hugh in favour of the abolition of the Lords?' I asked.

'That's nothing to do with it. Eric Heffer wrote an article in *The Times* called "Who wants the Lords?" and I'm going to write back, "Who wants Eric Heffer?"'

I said the electors of Liverpool Walton want Eric Heffer, and off she stomped. When Labour people get to the Lords they love it: they don't want to move or change it; they can't see any problems with it. I did have a chance to slip into the conversation how much I was enjoying Philip Williams's biography of Hugh.

### Thursday 13 December

First engagement was the joint meeting between the NEC and the Shadow Cabinet at Transport House to discuss the Tories' cuts in public expenditure. The attendance of the NEC was very poor, and Eric Heffer and Neil Kinnock had to leave before the end.

Jim called Roy Hattersley to speak on the advice being given to local authorities.[3]

Roy launched into a speech which I'm sure he must have released to the press. He described the success of our campaign for higher levels of public expenditure. There was a problem in the sale of council houses and local authority spending because Michael Heseltine, the Environment Secretary, had brought forward a bill to punish local authorities that didn't co-operate. The councils didn't want to be forced to behave illegally but the pressure was building up for illegal action.

Norman Atkinson said, 'If you support the law you simply become the agents of the Tories; therefore we have to explore alternatives.'

Neil Kinnock said he'd had some experience of defiance of the law in Bedwas and that led to a commissioner being brought in. We couldn't make people break the law, just as we couldn't make people obey the law. Our writ didn't run in that area. We wouldn't win the next Election unless we had an alternative. He thought resignation was open to councillors expected to implement unfair policies.

Tony Saunois argued, 'The question is how best to defend our people, and if councils are faced with the choice of being an agent of the Tories or opposing the law then they should oppose the law. The sanctity of the law is very limited. George Lansbury gave a lead in 1921 when he refused to levy a rate in Poplar, and he won. If we have to go outside the law so be it.'

Stan Orme said, 'Our object is not to damage the movement. Money to the local authorities will be stopped if councillors refuse to co-operate, and then where will they get the funds? As to the trade unions, the "Pentonville Five" and so on, that is different. I will certainly support the unions defending jobs, but it's easy to shout from the sidelines, "Labour councillors should resign." Do MPs resign if we lose in the Commons? Of course not. We could use the courts. We mustn't turn in on ourselves.'

Denis reminded the meeting that there were two Party Conference decisions making it clear that we should obey the law. The Government had all the cards in their hand. The Tories would deflect anger towards the lawbreakers, and if we destroyed respect for the law then when we won the next Election the lawbreaking would be used against us.

Jim Callaghan regretted that only nine members of the NEC were present now. It wasn't worth carrying on the discussion. He said he didn't base himself on Conference decisions, he only regarded them as important declarations of opinion. Although the NEC should give support to those under pressure, we would not support the law-breakers. The NEC had to give guidance because the Government were committing a moral crime and taking us back to the 1930s. In the case of industrial problems, however, the TUC–Labour Party Liaison Committee was the proper place to discuss them.

Next May we could win 2000 council seats, Ron Hayward said, and we shouldn't poke our noses into industrial matters. We should simply issue a statement of what was discussed at this meeting.

'That's not good enough,' said Jim. 'Militant are putting pressure on us through the reselection decision.'

I said we had a huge crisis, and the damage being done by Mrs Thatcher to our industries was as great as that done by Hitler's bombers. Instead of 2 million demobbed people we'd have 2 million unemployed. I believed we should consult at local level between the Party and the councillors. On the resignation of councillors, the comparison with MPs was wrong because councillors had to carry out the Tory law, MPs didn't. A closer parallel was the NEB, from which trade-unionists have resigned. But the key to it all was future policy. People want to know what a Labour Government would do. Then the question of the law would fade into insignificance because it wasn't the major issue.

Jim summarised: we should say we encouraged the maximum resistance and would act with maximum vigour, within the law.

It was a pointless meeting, really.

To the House to hear the Defence Secretary, Francis Pym, announce the NATO decision yesterday to install new nuclear weapons in western Europe – that is, to site 160 Cruise missiles in Britain. Jim didn't press him because he agrees with him. But the question is: does the British Government have a veto on the use of American nuclear weapons from British bases? I've always assumed there was a veto. When Pym was asked he said the consultative arrangements were the same as before. Have the American Government got the power to use these missiles from our bases without the explicit consent of the British Prime Minister? That is what I want to know. It may be that Jim had agreed in the past that they could use existing missiles without consent. I'm going to write to Mrs Thatcher about this and try to get it on the record.

*Friday 14 December*
To Bristol for my surgery. Surgeries do bring MPs up against the harshest and saddest aspects of life. One woman who came to see me was a widow of about seventy living on a pension. A year ago she took into her house an elderly disabled man whom she had befriended, a bachelor. So the local DHSS had stopped her widow's pension on the grounds that they were cohabiting and would have to be treated as a single unit and receive social security as a married couple. The man would otherwise have to go into a home (at a great cost to the ratepayers). She had appealed to the tribunal for the restoration of her pension and she said that the head of the tribunal had asked her whether they were having sexual intercourse – she broke down and wept because of the shame of it. Having met them together, I knew it was an absurd idea. They have separate rooms. But even if they were cohabiting what does that have to do with her entitlement to a widow's pension? I promised to write to the DHSS and get the matter reviewed, but I know I won't win.

Walked in the pouring rain to the hotel and got soaked to the skin. Had a hot bath, dried my trousers on the radiator and slept until the Party GMC at Unity House.

The GMC went on for three hours and was entirely dominated by Bryan Beckingham, Pete Hammond and others from the Militant Tendency. They moved endless resolutions. Their arguments are sensible and they make perfectly good radical points but they do go on interminably in their speeches. They have a certain pleading manner which just infuriates the others. 'Comrades, surely we must understand that the neo-colonialism in Zimbabwe is a threat to the very standards to which the movement belongs', and so on.

But the top of the Party is so rotten and the danger of alienation of the young is so great that if you don't have a bridge like the Militant which brings young people in contact with an analytical view of society then you end up with a sort of squashy Young Fabian movement without backbone. They may well split the Party and leave the right to fend for itself, but to expel them would be a disaster. My strategy is to try to make the Party what I want it to be and hope that the right will stay.

### Tuesday 18 December

Tony Saunois is upset about a story in the *Sunday Times* that Militant has a fund of £180,000 – probably a security services story. He felt it was part of the witch-hunt against Militant.

I told him that – witch-hunting apart – the Party was entitled to know about the finances of organisations inside it. Militant would have to come to terms with the fact that there would be pressure for this. I said people thought Militant was a piggy-back operation, riding on the back of the Party and building up its own organisation – which is true.

### Wednesday 19 December

At the end of the NEC we had a discussion about the new Labour Song Book and someone pointed out that 'Jerusalem' was going to be omitted. Eric Heffer objected strongly; he said it was sung at his wedding. So Michael Foot remarked, 'You know, "Jerusalem" is a hymn in favour of free love – "Give me my bow of burning gold, give me my arrows of desire."' There was a lot of laughter at this and the meeting ended with a rendering of 'Jerusalem' – slightly fake camaraderie.

We adjourned at 12.20 and I had a talk with Ron Hayward and Tom Bradley. They told me that Roy Jenkins would never have gone to Brussels if he had been offered the Foreign Secretaryship, and that he does intend to come back into British politics. I said I had listened to the Dimbleby Lecture carefully, and Tom commented, 'You should have seen the bits he left out.'

At 4 we had the Commission of Inquiry meeting: Jo Richardson, Frank Allaun, Eric Heffer, Joan Lestor, Jim Callaghan, Michael Foot and me from the Labour Party side. Alex was absent. From the TULV were David Basnett, John Boyd, Clive Jenkins, Sid Weighell, Bill Keys and Bill Whatley, the new General Secretary of USDAW. Before the meeting I had looked up Sid Weighell's article in the *News of the World* on 9 December, in which he wrote of Eric and me, 'I say these men must go; they couldn't run a fish and chip shop.'

It was a historic meeting.

I moved that Eric should take the chair, and that was agreed.

Basnett opened for the trade-unionists and said he spoke for the whole TULV. They were anxious for the Commission report to be acceptable in its findings and that it should not be challenged. They had accepted the five plus five plus Jim formula. But the NEC had added two more – the Treasurer and the Vice-Chairman of the Party. Since the Vice-Chairman might be Chairman next year, and was therefore unsuitable, he hoped he would withdraw. The Treasurer should be on it but without a vote. They would then accept the Commission and recommend that the PLP do the same.

Eric said many groups had argued for representation – the constituencies, the Euro-MPs, the Co-op Party, the Young Socialists, the Party staff, and so on. The problem was that if you added one group you had to add them all. The press attacks on the NEC were terrible. 'Sid Weighell – and I say it to his face – made an unforgivable attack upon members of the NEC as "left-wing extremists", and I think that's disgraceful.'

David Basnett was red in the face with anger. 'Stick to the point,' he shouted and added, 'We'll take you on if you want.' Eric let it go, but the temperature was raised enormously.

Clive Jenkins asked if they could have an answer to their question about NEC representation, and Eric said he couldn't respond. Moss said they were trying to be helpful. They regretted the NEC additions.

I said I had hoped that today would be the first proper meeting of the Commission. It had been set up on the basis that the NEC would be entitled to 50 per cent representation and at present we had seven members from the NEC, five trade-unionists and two members from the PLP. Of the NEC, two were elected by the trade union section – Alex Kitson and Norman Atkinson – so half the Commission were trade-unionists and the other half were MPs. The political balance was exactly equal: seven were in favour of Conference decisions, seven were doubtful about them. I appealed to the trade unions to accept it.

David Basnett kept interrupting but I held my ground. I said we'd done it in good faith, and as for this question of it being rigged . . .

'I didn't say that.'

'Maybe not, but others have said so. We have picked the best people we could – a most distinguished group – and I hope it will be accepted.'

John Boyd said he thought we'd covered the argument and asked the NEC members to retire to consider the TULV request. So we moved to another room and had a discussion there. We decided we couldn't agree to their proposals – though Michael and Jim urged that we did – and we would have to refer it back to the Executive. We trooped back into Room 12 and told them.

David Basnett said, 'Thank you for taking it back to the NEC. We all want to get this going.'

### Friday 21 December

To Bristol, and on the train were a lot of slightly drunk business executives in their late thirties singing in the buffet car. One was wearing a paper hat.

I queued up to get my tea and bacon and egg and they were saying, 'There's that f . . . . . g extremist, Mr Benn', and they sang bits of the Red Flag, and kept up an absolute barrage of insulting remarks.

As I went by carrying my tray they opened the door with elaborate and false courtesy and bowed and said, 'Happy Christmas to you, sir', and I said, 'Thank you' and went on.

I think that was the first experience of real whipping up of feeling by the press against the Labour Party. After the victory of Mrs Thatcher, the old establishment is now wildly self-confident – the Civil Service, the military, business, bankers and so on.

*Sunday 23 December*

I shall have to think carefully over Christmas about my political strategy. We are being driven into a defensive position by the arrogant right. The people at the bottom lack champions – I was going to say leadership, but it's champions they lack. It may be that I will have to ratchet myself down to be less interested in getting to the top and more interested in championing people – that is what is needed most.

I have decided that if there is a leadership election in 1980 I'd better make basic preparations. I have already photocopied the *Guide to the House of Commons*, cut out all the Labour MPs' names and photos and stuck them on a sheet of paper with their biographical details – 278 of them.

*Monday 24 December*

I don't think I have a chance of being elected by the PLP if the election takes place before the establishment of an electoral college, which the Commission of Inquiry is likely to recommend. Jim will be pressed to retire by those whose hopes rest on PLP support, but who would not be elected by a college.

I think the strategy is this: get a body of opinion organised so that if Jim retires in the summer it should be left to the Deputy Leader to carry on till Conference has endorsed an electoral college; then have a leadership election after that.

If there is a leadership contest before the Conference, despite that advice, I should get the NEC to ask all constituency Party GMCs to vote on their preferences and publish them, so that MPs will at least know the views of CLPs; also to get MPs to publish who they voted for, so that reselection could influence the leadership elections to a small degree.

Next year I have to turn my mind more to PLP support. I don't want to be knocked out in the first ballot, and I would do much better in a final contest against Healey than against Silkin or whoever.

I started work on my annual report to the Bristol South East Party.

At 8 Mark and Val Arnold-Forster arrived for our traditional Christmas Eve drink. Mark looks terribly ill. He suffered a stroke some years ago and it has made it hard for him to speak. His voice is almost inaudible.

I felt I could ask him to tell me about the Blunt affair, because last year he confirmed that he had worked for MI6. Did he think that Andrew Boyle had been tipped off by American Intelligence or by someone in British Intelligence who was chewed up at the establishment cover-up?

He thought that was unlikely. He said the information would have come mainly from the Library of Congress files, which had referred to the fact that the 'fourth man' had a name beginning with B, which is why *The Times* eighteen months ago wrongly said it was a Donald Bevis, whereas actually it was Anthony Blunt. A historian, Janet Adam Smith, who worked on the *New Statesman* in the 1950s, had known about this, and Boyle had got on to it and so on.

Every year Mark tells me a little bit more. He is clearly angry at the cover-ups that go on and at the risk to his own life in the past. He told me an amazing story about how he was almost captured by the Russians during a mission in 1954, presumably so that he could be traded for a Russian spy in Britain. He conjectured who might have betrayed his mission – George Blake? Or was it just MI6 incompetence in employing someone on the mission who turned out to be KGB?

*Tuesday 25 December*
The children arrived – just as excited as they were when they were kids. Thirteen of us for lunch. A lovely day.

*Monday 31 December*
Stansgate. In the evening, after the meal, Mother sat and talked; she is fascinating. She is eighty-three next year, and first came to London in 1910 when Edward VII was on the throne. She knew Asquith, Lloyd George, Ramsay MacDonald, Arthur Henderson, and so on. She has a wide theological knowledge, and to hear her describing the various meanings of the immaculate conception, the physical ascension of Jesus and all that is so interesting. She reads the Old Testament in Hebrew and the New Testament in Greek and so she knows the nuances of translation.

Looking at the Thatcher Government, it has begun implementing its reactionary policies with great vigour. Of course, it is a unifying force for the labour movement at a time when our debates are inevitably internal and divisive.

I don't know whether we'll win the next Election. That will depend on whether Thatcher goes too far and on whether the media and the establishment succeed in building up a Liberal/Tory/Labour alliance under Jenkins, Heath and Steel. But certainly by the end of the Eighties there will be a great move forward towards reform, and I think we have to work towards that. It's going to come ten to fifteen years later than I thought in 1974.

*Monday 7 January 1980*

Granada's *World in Action* programme called 'Mr Benn's Secret Service' goes out today. I have been helping them make this on and off; it is about the Civil Service and nuclear power. I saw a preview, and I must say they had made it beautifully.

E. P. Thompson has written to me about Cruise missiles; he is concerned about the civil liberties aspect. He fears that spying and counter-espionage will follow the missiles wherever they move around the country, and anyone who reports them or says anything about them will be liable to police surveillance. It is another example of how our liberties are being removed, and it is a fundamental problem.

*Tuesday 8 January*

Sir Brandon Rhys Williams, the Conservative MP for Kensington, said to me in the House of Commons, 'I don't agree with much that you say, but I certainly agreed with you in last night's programme about nuclear energy.' So I think it has made an impact. I have a feeling it has upset Whitehall considerably.

*'As some day it may happen that a victim must be found,*
*I've got a little list – I've got a little list*
*Of society offenders who might well be underground,*
*And who never would be missed – who never would be missed!'*

(The Mikado)

*Thursday 10 January*

By train to Gloucester, and on the train was a scientist from the Royal Military School of Science, who said there had been a great deal of discussion there this week about the role of the Civil Service: 'Of course the Civil Service runs the country' had been their response. They were rather surprised at my emphasis on it.

*Friday 11 January*

Went to Hartcliffe School, where fifty teachers are refusing to work the new timetables prepared by the headmaster to allow for the cut of five teaching posts imposed by Avon Council. The headmaster is planning a referendum among parents, and in the staffroom later a couple of parents were organising a petition of support for the teachers.

*Saturday 12 January*

There was an article in the *New Statesman* which had the interesting statistic that 48 per cent of all the delegates to the 1978 Labour Party Conference, when asked whom they wanted to be the next Leader, answered Tony Benn, compared to 15 per cent for Denis Healey, 11 per cent for Shirley Williams, and 7 per cent for Michael Foot, John Silkin and Peter Shore.

*Tuesday 15 January*

Appeared on *Question Time* with General Sir John Hackett, who is supposed to be an intellectual soldier, Germaine Greer and Norman St John Stevas. Greer I quite liked; Stevas is odious. The questions were about Afghanistan, women, Militant, and then at the end one on British Leyland, and Hackett maintained that the Institute for Workers' Control wanted to set up a communist dictatorship in Britain.

After the programme I said, 'I was very disappointed with your answer. The IWC have run tremendous campaigns in support of Soviet dissidents and you were disgraceful to them. Saying that about them is like saying in Northern Ireland that Ian Paisley supports the Pope because they are both Christians.' He said, 'If I am wrong, I will recant.' I observed, 'It's a bit late, but I did think you would be intelligent and try and understand what is going on.'

*Wednesday 16 January*

To the PLP meeting at 11 to discuss defence matters. Bill Rodgers opened, saying it was a great mistake that there had been no debate before Christmas on Cruise missiles. He mentioned the Soviet invasion of Afghanistan, which had changed the perspective. He hoped for a defence debate soon and, he added, public opinion polls showed people favoured an increase in defence spending, including more on nuclear weapons.

He went on to say that there was no moral issue involved in modernising our weapons system in Europe. 'The Soviets have modernised and the control of the Cruise missiles remains as before', but he didn't say what that was.

Tam Dalyell said we must get our troops out of Northern Ireland. Tam makes good points, but he always raises them at the wrong time. People listen courteously.

Referring to the invasion of Afghanistan, I said, 'What Russia is doing is what every superpower has done. We did it in Suez and the Americans did it in Vietnam; that is simply using power when you have it.' On public opinion polls, I urged that we should not be influenced by them. There were aspects of military expenditure that people didn't talk about, namely the use of the armed forces for internal purposes, as in Northern Ireland. Our job was to shape opinion, not to follow it.

Then Dick Douglas talked about creating more jobs through an expansion of weapons programmes. He said, 'What am I to do if at a reselection conference I am asked if I am in favour of more jobs in my shipyards through building warships?'

Bob Cryer welcomed the debate we were having. 'The Labour manifesto of 1974 was quite clear. Nuclear weapons are a moral issue; they destroy democracy by the very fact of a country having them. You can't control them.'

Douglas Jay said that Afghanistan was a faraway country of which we knew little. He suggested that we keep the shipbuilding and steel industries going by defence subsidies and have a bigger naval building programme to compete with the Soviet submarine fleet. 'An increase in the defence budget is inescapable, and it would help to create jobs.'

Stan Newens said, 'I am not a pacifist but I am a unilateralist. There is overwhelming western superiority in strategic weapons.' He was against the Cruise missile.

Jim Callaghan wound up; his speech did reveal the extraordinary degree of unanimity between him and Mrs Thatcher and his evasion of the key question of how the Cruise missiles were controlled. I think it is quite clear there is no British veto, just an agreement to consult.

'The nuclear deterrent is a secure base for peace. The situation in the Middle East is dangerous. There are at least four countries with a nuclear capacity – Libya, Iraq, Pakistan, Israel – and it is our duty to revise the Non-Proliferation Treaty. Polaris missiles will be needed if there is any decoupling of the US from Europe, because the UK will have to provide nuclear cover for Germany. If we don't, there are fears that Germany might acquire nuclear weapons herself.' He went on, 'The US forces in the UK are controlled by the US Government, and the situation works. There are close consultations between the two Governments and, unless we wish this country to be under Soviet control, the United States must control their missiles in the United Kingdom.'

In a way he did answer my question by justifying the absence of a British veto.

I saw Dick Mabon later, and he said there was a terrible battle going on in the right-wing Manifesto Group of MPs between those who wanted to split from the Party and follow Jenkins and those like himself who wanted to stay and fight. He thought seventy MPs would follow Roy Jenkins. I think the splitters are trying to use the threat of leaving the Party to get us to abandon reselection.

### Thursday 17 January

I saw David Steel and said, 'Congratulations on coming top of the poll in *The Times* for the leadership of a new third party. I was amused that Roy Jenkins came low down, and I must warn you, if you think of what he has done to the Labour Party, don't have him in yours because he will wreck it!' I added, 'All decent Liberals join the Labour Party – like my dad – and end up on the left, because the right wing of the Party is so bureaucratic and authoritarian.' He laughed.

### Monday 21 January

Went with Eric Heffer and Joan Lestor to the Russian Embassy and met Ambassador Lunkov and his aides to discuss Afghanistan. I took the lead and told him the NEC had passed a resolution condemning the invasion. It was seen by the world as being a massive military intervention, and as with Suez and Vietnam we opposed it. I said it would also do damage: Pakistan would rearm, it would have a serious effect on China and India, and it could destabilise the whole Middle East.

Lunkov gave the official explanation: that the Democratic Afghanistan Republic had come to power, it was threatened by exiles who had been armed by the Chinese, the Egyptians, the Americans and ourselves, and the Government had asked the UN to help, in vain, so the Russians had gone in reluctantly.

Eric made some more points. At least we registered our view.

### Wednesday 23 January

NEC at 10, and the first item of importance was Eric's report on December's meeting with the TULV. He moved that the Executive should confirm the existing membership, and oppose the removal of Kitson and Atkinson, which is what the trade union leaders wanted. We confirmed it by 12 votes to 11, with Neil Kinnock, Judith Hart and, I believe, Renée Short abstaining. So it was tight.

Had lunch at the House. There is open talk now of the early formation of a third opposition party; Roy Jenkins has stated it will be this month or next.

## Monday 28 January

Delivered my lecture on 'Mandarins and Manifestos' to the Royal Institute of Public Administration at Chatham House. It was a very grand event, chaired by Sir Richard Way, a former Permanent Secretary at the Ministry of Aviation.

In the audience were Lord Croham, formerly Sir Douglas Allen, who is now Deputy Chairman of BNOC; Sir Leo Pliatzky, who has just retired as Permanent Secretary at the Department of Trade; Sir Kenneth Berrill; John Liverman, Deputy Secretary at the Department of Energy; and Bruce Williams, who was my economic adviser at the Ministry of Technology years ago.

It took me an hour to deliver the lecture and there was three-quarters of an hour for questions. I think the *World in Action* programme had slightly paralysed them and they expected me to make some terrible revelations, but I was analytical, cool and fair. When I gave examples of Civil Service tricks to defeat Ministers, they actually laughed. I thoroughly enjoyed it.

## Wednesday 30 January

I rang E. P. Thompson, who has been lobbying me about an initiative declaring a nuclear-free zone in Europe.

To a joint meeting this morning of the NEC and Shadow Cabinet on defence. Frank Allaun spoke strongly against the Shadow Cabinet, and Bill Rodgers in particular, for their stand in last week's Commons debate on Cruise. He said there was no difference between the Tory and Labour Front Benches and referred to the last Labour Government's secret plans to prepare for Cruise.

Bill Rodgers said, 'We have always had differences on defence. We are a party seeking power and we want proper defence. The public opinion polls show Thatcher is 2 to 1 in the lead on this.'

Eric Heffer said that Party members deserved an explanation of Jim's admission that Fred Mulley had prepared for Cruise missiles to be introduced to this country. Had there been a secret committee of the Cabinet preparing for the next generation of nuclear weapons? He thought a nuclear-free zone in Europe was a good idea. 'After all, public opinion was not very friendly to the Party at the time of the Boer War or the First World War, but it came round.'

Denis Healey then said, 'Well, when you look back on the tizzy that defence caused in the 1950s' (a typical Denis comment dismissing the whole controversy over nuclear weapons then as a tizzy) 'we've had thirty-five years of peace because of nuclear weapons. When there is no nuclear threat the Soviet Union uses force. The Chevaline programme, which hardened the Polaris missiles, did not constitute a "new generation of weapons"; it had been announced anyway when we were in power, but, as we don't announce new weapons until they are ready, we haven't said much about it. The Tories started the project and we carried on with it. So there is no issue of socialist principle at stake.'

David Owen agreed that the Chevaline refurbishment was not a new weapons system. No other Government, he said, had taken more interest in disarmament than the last Labour Government, and 'we can't be tied to a few words hashed up in a manifesto.'

Kitson had a letter from Fred Mulley dated 25 November 1977 in which Fred had stated that there were no plans for new nuclear weapons.

Peter Shore said, 'We are not masters of the situation. Afghanistan has changed things. NATO has had to respond to the Soviet SS20s. Nothing will happen for three or five years anyway.'

I said we must recognise that there had been a return of the hawks in all the major capitals. Brezhnev's invasion of Afghanistan had marked the victory of the hawks in the Soviet Union; in Britain we had a very hawkish Prime Minister and in America Carter was trying to be hawkish to win the election.

'There has been a huge world escalation of arms spending – 25 million people in uniform and another 75 million making weapons for them – and this is encouraged by arms sales. The growth of arms expenditure in real terms has been well above world economic growth. The real question is: who makes the policy we have talked about? The manifesto and policy can't be made by the Shadow Cabinet. Our policy was very good – no Cruise, no Pershing and no successor to Polaris – and we have to accept that. There is no point in having consultations if we don't know how we are going to decide policy.'

Jo Richardson couldn't understand why we should take more notice of what the SPD in Germany thinks than of the Labour Party Conference. She said, 'The missiles are not under our control, and I for one am in favour of us leaving NATO. I am for no nuclear weapons at all – and we need a campaign to get this across.'

Jim concluded the meeting by saying, 'Britain should be properly defended; on that Bill Rodgers and Eric Heffer agree. Fred Mulley had done preliminary work on the hardening of the Polaris missiles, and had admitted it quite openly, and had also done some study on the next generation. No decisions had been taken, no Cabinet committee had been set up, he was the man who had this awesome responsibility. Nuclear terror has kept the peace. Tony is absolutely wrong in saying we have abandoned the Non-Proliferation Treaty: Carter is upholding it. The danger now is the third powers – Iraq and all those other countries that are getting nuclear weapons. We are united on a great deal – NPT, SALT, the Comprehensive Test Ban Treaty, and reductions in the mutual balance of force. Our major differences are on the Polaris replacement and the Cruise missiles. Cruise is basically the same as the F111, and if we want two keys for the Cruise missile we had better ask for two keys for the F111.'

At 1.30 I met a group of people campaigning in favour of Corrie's abortion bill. There were two key leaders – a Catholic nurse in her fifties and an Irishwoman. Their argument was that abortions were killing children who could survive at twenty-four weeks of pregnancy. People wanted to adopt, but abortion made fewer children available for adoption. They wanted to limit abortion to cases where there was substantial risk to a mother's health. One woman, all of whose children are adopted, objected to abortion on demand and said the conscience clause for doctors should be tightened so that they didn't have to abort.

I put my view as best I could. 'I respect that this is a matter of conscience. I feel strongly about preserving life, and I am opposed to capital punishment and euthanasia. But, after all, any abortion is killing, so if you are in favour of any abortion at all it is still an act of killing. On the practical side, we must avoid any encouragement of back-street abortions. And people with money can always get abortions.'

*Thursday 31 January*

There was a tremendous story in the *New Statesman* this morning about the phone-tapping headquarters at Ebury Bridge Road from where the Intelligence Services can now tap 1000 calls simultaneously. They operate under the title Post Office Research Department. I can't say it surprises me in any way. Bruce Page of the *New Statesman* has done a good job.

At 11 Eric, Joan Lestor, Ron Hayward and I went to Jim Callaghan's room where he, Michael Foot, Mike Cocks and Bryan Davies, the new Secretary of the PLP, were gathered to discuss state aid for political parties.

I went over our argument. The Short money was given to the Labour Party for parliamentary purposes. The money belonged to the Party, and nobody doubted that it should be used to finance the PLP's activities, but not directly from the Leader. I referred to the rundown of our Research Department at Transport House while the Front Bench was being built up. The Leader of the Party was the Leader of the *whole* Party, not just the PLP, and if he got money he should hand it over to the whole Party. I must say, by the end of my speech Jim was hopping mad.

Eric Heffer and Joan Lestor supported me. There is no doubt we made an impact, and in the end Jim asked me what we would do. So I committed myself to write a paper. I think Jim was surprised to hear the full argument. Eric said to him, 'It's not personal to you, Jim. We might get a Leader who takes the money – like Ramsay MacDonald.'

### Monday 4 February
There's a funny cartoon in the *Evening Standard*. I am signalling with semaphore flags on the top of the House of Commons, and Eric Heffer is sitting by me interpreting the flags: 'Is your phone still being tapped?'

### Tuesday 5 February
20,000 people, mainly young women, crammed into Central Hall for a rally against the Corrie bill. I spoke briefly to offer my support, and said there should be no restriction of a woman's right to decide within the provisions of the present law. This was one of many attacks on women's rights – the Employment Bill, the sexist and racist immigration laws, child benefit cuts, the tax laws – and women must organise; it was the only way to win. In calling for the right to choose and the freedom to control their own bodies, these women are rediscovering what the whole trade union movement has been fighting for – the right to choose, the right to decide how our own bodies are going to be used.

### Wednesday 6 February
I had an incredible message from the BBC asking if I would join in a discussion on monetarism and Government intervention, following the showing of a series of six half-hour talks by Milton Friedman, the American monetarist economist, called *The Right to Choose*. I would be in discussion with the Deputy Governor of the Bank of England and Roy Jenkins, under the chairmanship of Peter Jay.

I rang up the producer and said that six programmes of Milton Friedman was more than all the party politicals put together during an Election. I had never known the BBC give so much time to this particular religion. The woman I spoke to said, 'Well, we are going to balance the discussion.'

I told her I was prepared to do half an hour with Friedman, but I would not be a token left-winger with three monetarists. She went off saying they would rethink it.

### Thursday 7 February
The PLP was interesting. Mik asked, 'Could I please have a clear account of the Front Bench attitude towards repeal of the Tories' Employment Bill and Education Bill.'

Eric Varley made a short statement saying we would repeal the former, but might reintroduce passages about ballots. He was a bit evasive.

Then Neil Kinnock got up to speak. 'Well, I can't give an assurance we will repeal the Education Bill. We are committed to ending the assisted places scheme, but we cannot pledge reinstatement of school meals and milk because of the economic situation we shall inherit.' He sounded just like a Minister, indeed like the Chief Secretary to the Treasury, and it went down very badly.

Reg Race, the MP for Wood Green, and Kevin McNamara, the MP for Hull Central, were alarmed at Neil's statement. Other Members spoke, and it was clear from the shouting that Neil had dropped a clanger.

Up jumped Neil again and made it worse. 'It could cost many millions to restore cheap school meals and school transport.'

People were aghast at his second attempt.

Someone brought up the defence vote, but then Jack Ashley got to his feet – being deaf he had only just been informed in writing of Neil's comments – and said it was the most staggering statement that he had heard at a PLP meeting.

Afterwards the right was laughing itself sick that a left-wing Front Bench spokesman should have made such a statement and the left was saying, 'That is what happens when you become a Shadow Minister.' Poor old Neil has taken a knocking.

*Friday 8 February*
First thing was the Commission of Inquiry. Two letters were brought to our attention – the first that Terry Duffy would replace John Boyd, who was ill; the second from Bill Keys, asking that his proxy vote be given for the election of Basnett as chairman.

Jim said, 'Well, we have got three representative parts on this Commission, and I therefore move that Michael Foot, Eric Heffer and David Basnett alternate the chair, in alphabetical order, which means David Basnett today.'

In the circumstances, that was the best we could get; at least we had prevented David Basnett having a casting vote, since he was only a rotating chairman.

After some discussion about the priorities of the Commission, we elected the panels that will consider individual aspects – organisation, finance and political education.

Jim Callaghan proposed a special two-day conference in the spring of 1981. 'We must look at the composition of the NEC, at the Women's Section and at local authority representation.' He added, 'By the way, we must consider Militant, particularly as the Executive is not publishing the Underhill Report on entryism.'

Michael Foot said, 'We wish to exclude it.'

I said, 'I am against it because there are nine tendencies within the Party, including the Social Democratic Alliance – we just don't want to look at them all.'

Terry Duffy argued, 'We can't sweep it under the table. The AUEW are worried about Militant.'

It was a fairly peaceful meeting.

*Monday 11 February*

Organisation Committee in the afternoon, and we came to the key debate on entryism. It was long and at times sharp. To cut a long story short, I put forward my resolution that 'The NEC reaffirms its view that it is not its wish to set up an inquisition into the activities of groups within the Party. However, it invites all such groups made up of Labour Party members to make available details of their own organisation's membership and finance and to release their own working documents, on the same basis as is now done by the NEC, to permit a wider discussion of socialism within the movement.' My motion was carried by 8 votes to 2.

Then we had a motion from Neil Kinnock that a committee be set up to examine Reg Underhill's latest reports. An amendment was moved by Tony Saunois: 'to consider not only the latest reports on entryism but to include reports from all enemies of the working class including business, industry, the CIA, etc.' That vote tied 6 to 6 and was carried on Eric's casting vote.

Then a motion to set up a committee of five to look at all these various matters was carried by 11 to 0. The committee will comprise Eric Heffer, Lena Jeger, Tom Bradley, Michael Foot, David Hughes and myself.

We went straight on to the Home Policy Committee. We had a report calling for the Party to set up a study group whose terms of reference would be to examine the possibility of establishing a policy for the labour movement on the unity and independence of Ireland.

Alex Kitson, who had come specially to the meeting to stop my terms of reference, said, 'We should start from square one and not focus our attention on a particular solution.'

Michael Foot agreed with Alex. A lot of people spoke up against it and it was clear that I wouldn't win.

I said, 'I was brought up to believe that the independence of Ireland was the right of the Irish and that partition was a crime against the Irish people, and I still hold that view.'

We amended the motion in a very unsatisfactory way, so that it recommended to the NEC the establishment of a study group to examine, after full consultation, all possible solutions to the bloodshed in Northern Ireland. That was carried by 11 to 0.

Following Neil Kinnock's conduct at last Thursday's PLP meeting, John Golding proposed that the next Labour Government be invited by the Executive now to commit itself immediately to restore school meals, milk and school transport. His motion was carried unanimously and will now go to the NEC.

*Tuesday 12 February*

Had lunch with Clive Jenkins, who told me that a while ago someone in the security services had written to Len Murray saying he was a Labour man and wanted to warn him that there was a bug at the TUC. The TUC had been examined, and a bugging device had been found there and at Labour Party headquarters. I said, 'I think the security services are completely out of control.'

Clive wants Militant out of the Party. Clive is halfway between being a challenger of authoritarianism and an absolute authoritarian leader himself. He told me ASTMS was investigating Militant. I think the trade union leaders will go back to the old disciplinarianism if they can get away with it.

*Saturday 16 February*

Came back with David Owen from a regional Party conference in Taunton; David said he was thinking of writing about his years in the Foreign Office. He went over and over whether it was right to appoint Peter Jay, and it obviously rankles with him. We talked a bit about democracy and the Party, and he claimed he was a supporter of greater democracy. I find him an arrogant and rather shallow man, very self-important.

Caroline has been making a programme for *Open Door* called *Carry on Comprehensives*, and it was shown tonight, so I took a portable television set with me on the Underground all the way to Upminster (where I had a dinner) in the hope I would see it.

What I managed to see was marvellous and will encourage all those people who have their children at comprehensive schools, and those who are fighting for them or working in them. The programme cost only about £1200. Caroline wrote the script and went round filming, asked the questions and then edited herself out of the final version. That is Caroline all over – tremendously modest and yet determined.

*Wednesday 20 February*

Melissa's twenty-third birthday.

A joint meeting between the Shadow Cabinet and the NEC to discuss the paper that Eric Heffer and I submitted to the Home Policy Committee in September on the concept of a rolling manifesto.

I introduced it, and started by saying that the Commission of

Inquiry might want to include this in its deliberations. 'The manifesto is the link between the Party in the country and the PLP, between the PLP and the Government, between the electors and Parliament, and is the basis of Civil Service attitudes to politics and Government. Clause 5 of the Constitution provides for it to be produced by a joint meeting between the whole PLP and the Executive Committee, but the practice has varied. In 1945 the NEC drew up the manifesto alone. In 1966 it was written by Harold Wilson's office, as was reported in Dick Crossman's diary. In 1973 Harold Wilson produced the idea of a Leader's veto. In 1974 we agreed it as a campaign document before the Election. In 1979 a draft was considered at Number 10 Downing Street on the night of 2/3 April and key policy commitments were excluded – for example, the construction industry and the House of Lords.'

I believed that the problem was wider than that; sometimes Conference pushed policy further than it really should in order to force the PLP to take note, and the parliamentary leadership didn't bother to argue with the Conference because it thought: We've got a veto in the end.

I concluded, 'The recommendations we make are that the manifesto should be based on the policy agreed at Conference, that it should be available in advance, and that it should be widely circulated annually for discussion – that is to say a rolling manifesto. As the Leader and the Deputy Leader are on the Executive, this would guarantee that the parliamentary Party view was clearly represented.'

Michael Foot didn't agree with my account of past events. He thought the most important thing now was the attack on the Tories and he said we should be discussing the present situation, not dealing with these matters.

This is always Michael Foot's view: don't discuss anything important because we have got to attack the Tories, get into power, stay in power. He has absolutely abandoned, and did at least ten years ago and probably longer, any idea that you are in power for any particular reason or that democracy within the Party, or socialism, matter.

He said, 'Conference is not the best body to choose between priorities, especially in the field of expenditure. Conference will go on producing resolutions and it will not add up the bill. The language of priorities is the religion of socialism, as Nye Bevan said.' He was against a rolling manifesto; indeed, he thought the Commission should reintroduce the rule that no Conference decision could be reconsidered within three years.

Denis Healey believed the present system had not worked badly. He went on to talk about the role of the Party Leader and, considering Denis's aspirations in that direction, what he said was interesting. 'The role of the Party Leader is unique in an Election. His personality and authority are of immense importance. Jim Callaghan was 15 per cent ahead of the Party in popularity. He was always ahead of Mrs Thatcher, and was trusted, respected and liked. It would be absurd to commit the Leader to a policy he doesn't like. Leaders have a key role.'

John Smith said it was difficult to understand what was being proposed. Was the Shadow Cabinet going to be excluded?

Jim spoke out. 'I hope the Executive will be influenced by this discussion; we can't carry it much further now. People are fed up with all this argument about the Constitution.'

He added, 'There were 178 pledges in the manifesto – on the Common Market, on the Open Broadcasting Authority, on the Joint Representation Committees, on phasing out television licences, on ending fee-paying schools, on child benefit, on open government, on compulsory planning agreements, on the wealth tax. What are we arguing about? It is simply about the House of Lords and the construction industry. If we had won the Election and had abolished the House of Lords, people would have thought it was a completely irrelevant act. We can't be accused of ignoring Party policy.'

It was left there; it was clear that there would be no progress.

*Thursday 21 February*
Caught the 3.20 to Bristol, and who should be sitting opposite me but Sir Leo Pliatzky, who has just retired as Permanent Secretary at the Department of Trade. He was on his way to give a lecture at Bristol University.

Leo was a friend of Tony Crosland and Roy Jenkins in Oxford after the war and, although he is actually five years older than me, he is part of that telescoped generation. He's the son of an immigrant family, got a scholarship, was a Marxist as a young man, joined the Civil Service and ended up as a Permanent Secretary. He said that in his lecture at Bristol he was going to refer frequently to my lecture at the Royal Institute of Public Administration. He didn't believe in the conspiracy theory of the Civil Service; civil servants were just trying to do a good job.

Apparently, when Leo was due to retire last summer, Mrs Thatcher called him in and asked him to do a study for her on quangos – which she was committed to cut back – and to recommend which should go. He told her, 'If I am asked to do it, I will have to do it myself and be free to recommend, and I will have to get Ministers to agree because I am not going to do something that Ministers won't implement.' He said she was very friendly, and he thought that she would bend, that her strict monetarist policy would shift. He supported her in her tough line on the Common Market and hoped the Foreign Office would not soft-soap her.

Leo believed that the UK had rather more influence within the Common Market than we would have outside it; the various Ministers who were responsible for negotiating with America in their capacity as European Council presidents found they had much greater impact because the Common Market was on a par with the United States in terms of power. He thought that had influenced Denis Healey and others.

He told me that in September 1976 he was asked to negotiate with the IMF team. He said to the Treasury, 'I must have a completely free hand to do what I think is necessary.' There was a great argument and in the end he was sent in under those conditions.

When the negotiations were in progress, the IMF told him they wanted more in cuts than he had proposed and he said, 'I must tell you, that will bring down the Labour Government.' They were absolutely horrified when he said that. He told me, '1931 was very much in my mind. They only got away with £1400 million plus the sale of BP shares, and anyway how would we have financed the deficit?'

### Saturday 23 February

To Bristol, and I visited the picket line at Woodbury Chilcott, where fifty Welsh steelworkers were picketing a steel stockholder. They were cold and fed up. They said the police had pushed people in the chest and arrested them; they felt the police were being provocative and that the limit of twenty-five pickets the police had imposed was just arbitrary. I talked to them for about an hour.

### Sunday 24 February

The *Sunday Times* had an astonishing headline, 'Benn Toppled by Left-Wing Revolt', and an article saying that an informal gathering of moderate lefts on the National Executive, that is Judith Hart, Neil Kinnock, Renée Short and Doug Hoyle, were fed up with my leadership and the NEC was no longer under hard-left control. There's enough of a grain of truth in it to be damaging.

### Wednesday 27 February

To the Executive, and as we were moving out of Transport House to Walworth Road I proposed that we expressed our thanks to the TGWU for the hospitality they had given to the Party over the many years it had been housed there. Somebody said, 'We ought to have a plaque put up.' Russell Tuck remarked, 'So long as we don't have to pay for it' – a typical Labour Party comment! Then we had a report on the financing of the move.

Walked over to the House with Neil Kinnock, who was very embarrassed by the account that had appeared in the *Sunday Times*. But the *Sunday Times* is right about Kinnock; he has departed from the left group on the Executive. However, I thought I would be friendly because I wouldn't want bad relations with him. I said, 'Don't worry about all the attacks on you. It's all just jealousy.' He was friendly, but he kept coming back to that particular story.

*Friday 29 February*
Leap Year. Went into the House early for the Corrie bill debate.

Jo Richardson and Joyce Gould, the National Women's Officer, who was sitting under the Gallery, are really masterminding the campaign in the House. Joyce had written to every Labour MP who had voted against Corrie last time to thank them and to guide them through the next stage of the debate. For the first time I thought the PLP was doing its proper job. Why don't we have Labour Party officials sitting under the Gallery in the civil servants' boxes when the Labour Government is in power?

It looks as if we have defeated the bill by talking it out.

*Saturday 1 March*
To a steelworkers' rally in Scunthorpe. I went first to the Duke of Edinburgh's Award Centre, which, ironically, is where the strike committee is based. Upstairs in a tiny room the men were organising pickets all over the country. I was driven to the beginning of the march; about 5000 people with a Scots band at the head marched through the shopping centre to the swimming baths. John Ellis was there, on strike. He had been MP for Bristol North West and for Scunthorpe, and was defeated last May.

*Tuesday 4 March*
Robert Mugabe has won the Rhodesian elections outright. It's a fantastic victory and I can't remember anything that has given me so much pleasure for a long time. When I think of the systematic distortion by the British press of Mugabe's position, it's an absolute disgrace. The Tories must be furious.

*Saturday 15 March*
The South-West Regional Labour Party Conference was being held in Exeter, and I decided to go to the fringe meeting organised by the Campaign for Labour Victory. My presence greatly embarrassed those speaking. David Owen and Betty Boothroyd [Labour MP for West Bromwich] were on the platform.

Betty made an awful speech about how we need a radical policy but we can't be too far ahead of public opinion; that there is great attraction to private investment in public industry and perhaps we should consider giving people a share, a 'divvy' in the nationalised industries, and so on. She said, 'We want to create a society on the basis of a consumer democracy. We have got to strike the right balance between individual and collective rights.' She was critical of the NEC for presiding over a declining membership.

Bill Rodgers talked about the origins of the Campaign for Labour Victory, and how it was set up in 1976–7 to rally support for the Government. 'People don't want extreme positions, and if the Labour Party becomes a party of the left or the far left it will be suicide for us.' He said the NEC should have initiated a review of the Party using universities and academics; resolutions wouldn't help us. He wanted to see the Party as a broad coalition from the legitimate left to the right. He wasn't afraid of being called a member of the right. He said, 'We all believe in parliamentary democracy, but the last nine months have been divisive, and I appeal to Tony: let's be tolerant and work together.'

### Sunday 16 March
One interesting item in the papers – that the Shah of Iran had offered money to fund a third opposition party in Britain.

### Monday 17 March
Worked all day at home and prepared my speech for the so-called Debate of the Decade in Central Hall sponsored by the LCC. Peter Hain was in the chair; on the platform were Paul Foot of the Socialist Workers' Party, Hilary Wainwright, Tariq Ali, Audrey Wise, Stuart Holland and myself. Peter Hain opened by saying the left was in crisis, though the left of the Labour Party was stronger than it had been.

When I began to speak all hell broke loose. I think the first six minutes were interrupted by barracking by the revolutionary communist groups and anarchists and a group of people stood up displaying a huge big sign: 'Are you with Benn or the H-Block Men?'* I said, 'Well, if you want to know my view on Ireland, it is that the partition of Ireland was a crime, and I want to see the unity and independence of Ireland.' That obviously didn't quell them, but to avoid trouble I said to Peter Hain, 'Let the thing settle down.' I was interrupted a lot but I got across a bit of my speech.

Tony Saunois was shouted down by the ultra-left. Tariq Ali made a mellow and charismatic speech about socialism not being all about state power and so on. Audrey Wise was extremely strong and said that socialism is about reason and love.

---

* The protesters were drawing attention to conditions in the Maze prison, Northern Ireland, where Republican prisoners were kept.

*Friday 21 March*

To the Commission of Inquiry first thing. Afterwards Bill Keys asked for a word, so we went into the cafeteria and had a chat. He told me the funniest thing. During the last Government, he was in the Reform Club for lunch and Reg Prentice was at the next table with Michael Heseltine. Bill (whom Reg doesn't know) heard them discuss the date when Reg should announce his membership of the Tory Party – while he was still in the Labour Cabinet!

I went to Bristol for a dramatic meeting of the council's Labour Group, which decided to withdraw the whip from eight councillors who had either abstained or voted against the Labour Group resolution endorsing the council budget, which included a lot of cuts.

The atmosphere was horrible. But the eight were impressive: they just read their statement and left it at that. However, it did reveal the conflict between those who use socialism as a ladder into the municipal corridors of power versus those who regard socialism as a campaign.

What the expelled councillors now have to do is use the council chamber to expose what is happening, to launch a tremendous attack against the Tories and ignore the Labour leadership entirely.

*Tuesday 25 March*

Joan Lestor told me that Neil Kinnock is now canvassing for Michael Foot as Leader. I am terribly torn because I don't actually know whether my prospects are at all good.

The position on the leadership at the moment is like this. Healey is obviously the front runner, and he has Barry Jones of East Flint, John Smith and Dick Mabon all competing for the privilege of being campaign managers, with Joel Barnett really doing the work.

Then to the right of Denis you have Roy Hattersley. I suppose he is a serious candidate of a kind – he does lots of meetings around the country and projects an impressive image and has a group working for him in the PLP.

Then other possible candidates on the right are David Owen, Eric Varley and maybe Merlyn Rees.

Then there is Peter Shore, a right-wing, anti-European figure; and John Silkin, who allegedly has received £10,000 from the TGWU to run his leadership campaign.

Eric Heffer I know has been going round seeking support.

Finally Michael Foot, on whom there is heavy pressure to keep Denis out.

*Wednesday 26 March*

Went over to the House and listened to the Budget – tremendously boring, though Geoffrey Howe rattled it off at such a speed that it made one slightly less sleepy than usual. But it began with this awful monetarist philosophy, which is nonsense, because it will deepen the depression and create mass unemployment and involve cuts in the public services. The most vicious of the measures was the £1 per item prescription charge; it has multiplied fivefold since we left office. Also they are cutting back on education, and the only expenditure that is increasing is on defence and law and order.

*Sunday 30 March*
Hugo Young had an article in the *Sunday Times* about the complete failure of the Labour Opposition Front Bench to put up an effective criticism of Thatcher.

*Tuesday 1 April*
Went into the Chamber at 3.30, and Willie Whitelaw made a statement on telephone tapping. I did not believe him and when asked about surveillance – bugging as distinct from interception – he said that was left to Chief Constables to decide. Totally misleading. Merlyn Rees got up and mumbled on about how he had discharged his obligations and he was sure Willie Whitelaw did the same. This club of ex-Home Secretaries is, in my view, one of the worst features of British public life; they all compliment each other on their brilliant protection of civil liberties and for being in command of their departments, but nobody believes that Home Secretaries are really kept informed by the security services.

*Wednesday 2 April*
At lunch I talked to Merlyn Rees about telephone tapping. I asked him about the difference between a warrant to intercept and bugging, and got no clear answer, although it *was* clear that a lot of surveillance goes on that isn't subject to warrant. I asked him whether foreign embassies were included in the official figures. He said, 'Oh yes, yes.' I said, 'There are 120 embassies and yet there are only supposed to be a total of 120 bugs.' He seemed unwilling to deal with the subject. He declared, 'We have got to protect against crime, against terrorism and against subversion.' I said, 'We all agree about serious crime and we all agree about terrorism but what is the definition of subversion? Is Paul Foot a subversive? Is Tariq Ali?' He said, 'No, no, no!' But I know quite well that they are tapped, and I know Ken Coates is too – Harold Wilson had hinted as much to me. I said I thought Parliament ought to consider the criterion for subversion. He did agree with that.

During the evening Caroline came into the basement office and said the news bulletins were full of rioting going on in the St Paul's area of Bristol. Apparently the police had decided to make a major drugs raid on the Black and White Café in Grosvenor Road and had arrived in force, with dogs. A tremendous confrontation developed between police and young blacks and young whites, many of them unemployed. To cut a long story short, the police were not there in sufficient force, so they withdrew from the area for four hours, during which looting and burning occurred. By about midnight it was over.

*Thursday 3 April*
Went to the House at 9.30, spoke on the phone to David Lane of the Commission on Racial Equality, rang William Waldegrave [Conservative MP for Bristol West] and Dawn Primarolo.

Went to Bristol, and as I arrived the station master handed me a file from the Bristol Resource Centre which Dawn had given him for me, setting out the facts of youth unemployment in St Paul's. Marvellous service! I attended the press conference at which David Lane, the Chief Constable of Bristol and others were gathered. As the rioting was in Arthur Palmer's constituency of Bristol North East, however, I felt I must be careful not to tread on his toes.

Got back to London in time for a tea party for my fifty-fifth birthday.

*Thursday 10 April*
NEC at 2.30, to consider plans for a special conference we had agreed to hold in May. The decision had been made at an NEC meeting on 26 March, after we had discussed a letter from Moss Evans asking for a recall conference to deal with Labour's policy, particularly industrial aspects.

Ron reported that it would be held on 31 May at Wembley. I said Geoff Bish had prepared a short draft statement putting forward an alternative to the Tories' programme, and, subject to approval, this should be put before the conference.

There then followed an argument about whether amendments from CLPs to the statement should be allowed. Ron got very angry at this suggestion, given the time it would take to organise the constituencies. Finally we moved unanimously to put a statement of overall Party policy to the conference, as the sole agenda item, and agreed that all points made in the course of debate would be noted.

*Friday 11 April*
Chris Mullin came to see me; he has just come back from Vietnam and Cambodia. He described how the Chinese had invaded Vietnam on a punitive mission, dynamiting all the schools, hospitals and factories in the towns they occupied. They removed all the equipment from factories and sent it to China, leaving the Vietnamese nothing. An astonishing story of brutality.

*Saturday 12 April*
To Bristol for the day. Bryan Beckingham, the Militant supporter in Bristol South East, told me he used to be a Christian, until the church told him he should have attended church over Easter instead of going on a CND march. He was a great admirer of Michael Foot. He is really a local guru, who organises and encourages young people. I wouldn't have them thrown out of the Party for anything in the world.

I got rather sentimental looking at my Party; I feel warmly disposed to all of them.

*Thursday 17 April*
Had lunch with Clive Jenkins at ASTMS. He and David Basnett had been to see Jim about the leadership, and Jim had told them he would consider the matter in November, but Clive thought he would carry on. Clive has an idea for an electoral college: it should be 150 strong, 50 from the PLP, 50 from the trade unions and 50 from the constituency parties.

To the House, and Mother arrived at 3.45 for a celebration in the Pugin Room of her first visit to the House of Commons seventy years ago. The Speaker, George Thomas, received us, and he was enchanting to Mother. He gave us a conducted tour and told us about the various Speakers. Mother loved it.

In the evening Michael Meacher, Chris Mullin and I talked about the Commission of Inquiry, the election of the Leader, reselection and the manifesto. We considered how we could put some life back into the PLP. We thought that after the 31 May gathering we might put to the PLP the statement that had been approved there and invite them to endorse it. If they did endorse it, that would commit them. If they didn't, then the difference between the PLP and the grass-roots would become acutely clear.

*Friday 18 April*
At 11 we began the long meeting on the statement for the special conference. Jim was in the chair, and Eric, Norman Atkinson, Michael Foot and I were present. We went through Geoff Bish's draft and there was a lot of goodwill. Jim realised he had to concede a lot but he wanted to make a stand on a couple of things. One was defence, and we had a long discussion on what we would say about Cruise missiles and the Polaris replacement. What we got was a reaffirmation that the Party was opposed to the deployment of Cruise missiles; we were opposed to the next generation of nuclear weapons, but we were in favour of multilateral disarmament. It wasn't perfect, but it was the best that Eric, Norman and I could get.

I got about 99 per cent of what I wanted, and I am now persuaded that we must get rid of the American missile sites because we don't control them – but that's a very big change of policy. The statement will include a reference to amending the European Communities Act, import controls, a large section on economic and industrial policy, a pledge on full employment, and the abolition of the House of Lords. It really is quite a good draft rolling manifesto; it's the one we should have published last year.

*Tuesday 22 April*
At 7 I met the Glasgow University Media Group, who gave me a copy of their latest book, *More Bad News*, in which they analysed press coverage of labour movement affairs. The points made are first-rate. They thought all broadcast material should be deposited for study in the British Museum or a national archive. They talked about editorialisation; in three months of the Glasgow dustmen's strike, not one striker had been interviewed by the media. They described their studies of language; for example, 'industrial news' always meant strikes, and the vocabulary was systematically weighted against labour. Management always 'offers' whereas the trade unions 'demand'; management never 'demands' and the trade unions never 'offer'; management always 'pleads' and the trade unions always 'threaten'. They said, 'Television news has a credibility not given to the newspapers', but the content and coverage by BBC and ITN were similar; they had a standard format. There was an incestuous relationship between television and the establishment. It was a fascinating talk.

*Wednesday 23 April*
I saw Mrs Thatcher this evening and apologised for calling her a Right Honourable Gentleman yesterday during Prime Minister's Questions. The whole House had begun shouting at me, but I had continued without taking any notice – 'Is the Right Honourable Gentleman aware that if she doesn't . . .' – and I never noticed my mistake until the Hansard editors asked me to correct the words. So I said to her tonight as I passed, 'I am awfully sorry, I didn't realise I had said it.' She remarked, 'Well, I knew you weren't thinking very hard and hadn't meant it.' I said, 'I meant to write you a note but I assure you it wasn't a cheap smear on you.' She laughed.

*Friday 25 April*
Heard on the news this morning of the Americans' abortive attempt to release their hostages in Iran. Three helicopters failed to operate, a plane struck the sea, and eight men were killed. It was a dramatic and sensational item of news.[4]

Went over to the House at 9.30 and immediately raised the matter with the Speaker, who said I could put down a Private Notice Question at 10. Ian Gilmour, Lord Privy Seal, made a short statement. Peter Shore was cautious but firm. I was called next, and I asked if the Government had known, advised or approved of the attempt. I didn't get a clear answer, though in fact the SAS did assist the Americans. I asked if the Government could make clear to the Americans that there was no question of British bases being used for any military action including rescue operations.

### Saturday 26 April
Willie Whitelaw wants to see me on Monday before he makes his statement about the Bristol riots. He is apparently going to announce that there will be an internal police inquiry into the activities of the police, that the Chairmen of Avon and Bristol District Councils will get together to consider further resources for St Paul's, and that the Home Affairs Sub-Committee at the House of Commons will visit Bristol to take evidence on the cause of the riots. Mike Cocks was keen that I should support the measures. I told Mike that they were sensible but they didn't allow for a full expression of the feelings of the communities themselves, through the labour movement or their own organisations, and I hope they will have their own inquiry. Secondly, there was an attempt to depoliticise the whole incident, but it is all to do with highly political matters like deprivation, unemployment, bad housing and so on.

### Monday 28 April
Cyrus Vance, the American Secretary of State, resigned today in protest at the military rescue operation in Tehran. It is an indication that the military are in charge now in Washington.

At 11 I went into the House to launch the international campaign for a European nuclear-free zone; it is being simultaneously launched in Lisbon, Oslo, Paris and Berlin. On the platform were Mary Kaldor, Eric Heffer, Monsignor Bruce Kent, Edward [E. P.] Thompson and Zhores Medvedev, and in the audience were Michael Meacher, Stuart Holland and a lot of journalists.

Willie Whitelaw made a statement at 3.30 about the inquiries into the Bristol disturbances. I got up and asked, 'Is the Right Honourable Gentleman aware that there is a demand for a public inquiry and that there are real problems here that are political and economic and cannot be dealt with by strengthening the Special Patrol Group? If there is an inquiry organised by Bristol Trades Council or the local ethnic communities, will the Government give assistance to it?' It was the best I could do, but mine was the only dissenting voice.

At 5.30 the NEC Home Policy Committee went through the draft rolling manifesto and made some improvements. It was a good meeting.

Melissa passed her driving test today.

### Tuesday 29 April

I had a letter from a woman called Selma James, of the English Collective of Prostitutes. To explain the background, about ten days ago there was a trial of a madam who ran a brothel in a house in Streatham, South London. According to the police who raided the place, one peer, one Irish MP, and various judges, magistrates, barristers and business people used the brothel. Cynthia Payne, who ran it, was sentenced to eighteen months in prison, but none of the girls or clients were jailed. Robert Kilroy-Silk, Labour MP for Ormskirk, asked me to sign a motion condemning the sentencing of Cynthia Payne, and the letter I received today thanked me for signing the motion and enclosed a memorandum on the prostitution laws explaining how they oppress women. I replied, wishing them success in their campaign.

### Thursday 1 May

May Day, but not celebrated as such in Britain because the Labour Government agreed to make the holiday the nearest Monday to the 1st, so, alone among countries, we usually have our public holiday on a day that is not May Day. One of the most absurd decisions perpetrated by a Labour Government, under pressure from the Civil Service and conceded by Michael Foot – and, I suppose, by the rest of us, who should have made more fuss about it.

Victor Schonfield of the Campaign for Labour Party Democracy rang to confirm arrangements for the CLPD fringe meeting at the conference on 31 May. He said he was getting reports from people on the left in the trade unions that Eric Heffer and I are seen as being anti-trade-unionist and are being attacked by John Boyd.

I'm fed up with this, so I said, 'First of all, I haven't attacked the trade unions at all and I don't control Eric. Secondly, what the bloody hell are the left-wing trade unions doing? Of course John Boyd attacks Eric and me, because what we are arguing for is democracy, and that would take power out of the hands of the trade union bosses and give it to the rank and file.'

This is the ageing ex-communist left who are terrified of political initiatives. As a result of a lifetime of struggle, they have got themselves near the seats of power, but have lost their grassroots support now, and are afraid that if you stir it up they will be defeated either by an angry right-wing backlash or by a new real left. If you go along with that crowd, you are committing yourself to decay of a very serious kind.

*Friday 2 May*
To the House for the Private Notice Question about the appointment of Ian MacGregor, the sixty-seven-year-old, Scots-born, Canadian industrialist who, at the cost of nearly £2 million compensation to Lazard Frères, has been appointed Chairman of the British Steel Corporation. Michael Foot raised the matter in the House and said there should be a debate. I asked if the Leader of the House, Norman St John Stevas, appreciated that people who cared for the steel industry saw this decision as a grave error of judgement which would undermine the morale of both management and unions in the industry, and that there were those who thought that this was a most improper transaction. I said that all the correspondence involved should be published because there were those who thought it bordered on bribery and corruption. This was very strong language, and Norman St John Stevas said I would regret having used that phrase. But I remembered that this was a phrase that Keith Joseph had used on 1 February 1968 when I was introducing the Industrial Expansion Bill.

*Sunday 4 May*
Worked solidly on my speech for the Granada Guildhall Lecture on the role of the trade unions.

It was the most beautiful day.

President Tito died today. He had been in intensive care for such a long time that his death had in a sense been forgotten about, but it was a great event, and a man of his magnitude in world history will not easily be replaced. He is the last of the great war leaders, the only one left being Hirohito, the Emperor of Japan.

*Friday 9 May*
Chaired the Political Education Panel of the Commission of Inquiry. Before us was a good report written by the NUJ chapel at Walworth Road. It is a statement of how we could make the Party's political education more effective, and an amended version will go to the Commission next Friday.

*Monday 12 May*
Home Policy Committee at 5.30, with lots of resolutions. The most serious one was an attack upon the Government for contemplating the break-up of the ILEA. We agreed to propose its reinstatement if that happened, but Neil Kinnock as Shadow education spokesman didn't want to commit himself. He really is behaving like a Minister already, without ever having held ministerial office. Eric Heffer attacked him and said, 'You really worry me, Neil.' But Neil believes this demonstrates that he is responsible.

We went over the draft rolling manifesto, and again Neil opposed our commitment to restore the school meals, school milk and school transport services. It is a gross misjudgement of the mood of the Party at the moment. Neil's argument is that if you pledge to do something in an immediate response to a situation, and then you fail to keep that pledge, people are disappointed.

### Tuesday 13 May
I watched television and listened to some of the news bulletins about the TUC Day of Action tomorrow. What is interesting is that the coverage doesn't give any information about the union view. It doesn't tell people where the rallies are, doesn't say what the demonstrations are about, doesn't describe the reasons. It is simply presented as a row between two partners at the top – the TUC leadership and Ministers – and the idea that it is about the closure of schools and hospitals and unemployment in the steel industry is not mentioned at all.

I really do think the BBC is a disgrace: it has betrayed its own charter.

### Wednesday 14 May
Went down to Plymouth for the Day of Action. It was the biggest political meeting there has been in the West Country within living memory.

As far as I was concerned, it was a tremendous success, but the press described it as a flop, a fiasco. However, the press attacks on the TUC actually have the effect of solidifying the loyalty of activists.

### Thursday 15 May
At 6.15 pm I was picked up by a fancy chauffeur in a peaked cap with a sleek green Jaguar and driven to the Guildhall for dinner and to give the annual Granada Lecture. It was a tremendously distinguished audience – the Guildhall is absolutely the centre of Tory power. It's where the Lord Mayor's Banquet is held every year, when the Chancellor of the Exchequer tells workers to work harder.

After dinner I walked into the hall with Monty Finniston, former Chairman of BSC, who was the chairman for the evening, and we stood behind our chairs while the National Anthem was played. Then Monty introduced me and I went to the rostrum. The occasion was so overawing that either nobody felt able to express their feelings or I didn't do it very well, but the response was wooden. I think I rattled off the lecture, called 'Trade Unions and the Future', quite rapidly.

Looking round, I saw a lot of sympathetic people – Ken Gill, Jack Jones and his wife, Jack Dromey of the TGWU, George Guy from the Sheet Metalworkers, Frances Morrell, Eric Heffer, Frank Allaun,

Audrey Wise, Ken Coates, Dick Marsh, Tom Litterick, plus a lot of shop stewards and a couple of Tory MPs. Tom Litterick actually sat and smoked a cigarette during the National Anthem – which I thought was courageous of him.

When I had delivered my lecture, Monty Finniston got up and opened the discussion and, in what was meant to be a little vote of thanks, attacked me. So Frances Morrell shouted, 'Boo', and Jack Jones at the back got up and raised his hand on a point of order, and the whole thing started to come alive.

*Friday 16 May*
Went to the Commission of Inquiry this morning.

David Basnett said, 'We should be doing more about women.'

So I raised the question whether we should consider opening up affiliation to organisations again. Why not have the women's movement, or the black movement, affiliated to the Party?

David Basnett, to my surprise, said, 'That is quite a constructive suggestion; we ought to look at it.'

So we shall, and I think I shall move that we open up affiliation to any organisation that wishes to affiliate – that would enormously strengthen the Party.

*Sunday 18 May*
I had a phone call from the London Labour Party a couple of days ago asking if I would deliver the Herbert Morrison Memorial Lecture, and I've accepted. It will give me the opportunity of turning the issue of collective leadership into a proper manifesto for the leadership election.

I chose the title 'The Case for the Collective Leadership of the Labour Party'. I have now got to do a really good job on it. I shall make it clear that I am only interested in a Labour Party that is collectively led; in that case it wouldn't matter who was Leader, but I would be one of the candidates. This may all sound very egocentric; that is the trouble with writing a diary.

Another beautiful day: for the last ten days it has been absolutely cloudless, temperatures high. I can't remember such a period of perfect weather during May.

*Tuesday 20 May*
Went into the House. Martin Jacques, the editor of *Marxism Today*, the Communist Party magazine, came to see me at 5. He would like me to write for *Marxism Today* but I told him I couldn't. He also asked if Eric Hobsbawm, the Marxist historian, could interview me and I agreed to that.

Then Gus MacDonald arrived and we had dinner together. Gus is a most interesting guy. He began as a shipyard worker on the Clyde, came to London, wrote for *Tribune* for a while and got taken on by Granada Television. He is now head of documentaries at Granada. We talked about Granada's battles. The courts are trying to force them to disclose the name of the person in their organisation who got hold of a document from the British Steel Corporation and used it against Sir Charles Villiers during the steel strike. Lord Denning gave a judgement against Granada. When Labour was in power, no doubt Denning would have found for the individual against the big nationalised industry, but now the Tories are in power and the state corporation is supporting Mrs Thatcher he finds for the state against the individual. A significant judgement, in my opinion. Granada may well be fined £20,000 a day unless they give the information.

After Gus went, Dan Jones, the seventy-two-year-old Labour MP for Burnley, came up to me (he does frequently). 'Now look, dear Tony, the Party has got to be united, and we must have evolutionary socialism and not revolutionary socialism.'

I slightly blew my top. 'Dan, I wouldn't worry about revolutionary socialism. I don't suppose there are half a dozen revolutionaries in London. There isn't a Labour Party – it's dead – and nobody has thought about socialism in this House for years. Actually we have got a very long hard job to do to try and convert people to any sort of socialism, and I wouldn't worry about revolution, I would worry much more about how we can prevent fascism.'

*Wednesday 21 May*
Martin Jacques rang and said Eric Hobsbawm had agreed to interview me in the framework of a seminar at Birkbeck College (of which he is Master), for reproduction in *Marxism Today*.

I am looking forward to that very much indeed: to be taken through one's paces by a distinguished Marxist philosopher will be an extremely interesting and demanding experience.

*Sunday 25 May*
At 9.30 I went to LBC radio to do an hour-long phone-in about the special conference taking place next Saturday. I had a real bash at the press and at BBC and ITN on bias in handling industrial affairs, particularly the *Daily Mail*. A woman from the *Daily Mail* later tried to contact me but I have no intention of speaking to the *Mail*.

Went for a long walk with Melissa.

Later I switched on the television and *Hamlet* was on. I have never seen it before – what a thing to admit at fifty-five! But like many people I was forced to read it at school and that put me off for a long time. A remarkable play.

*Tuesday 27 May*

Left home at about 7.45 to catch a plane to the Isle of Man. On the Underground to Heathrow, which was quite busy, there was a great thump and I looked up and saw a tall man of about twenty-five had collapsed. An old man sitting opposite just looked at him and nobody else moved, so I got up and pulled him flat across the floor. He was absolutely white and I thought he had died, but I felt his pulse, and gradually he opened his eyes. I said, 'You're OK, you just fainted. Where are you going?' He said, 'Hatton Cross.' Fortunately, the old man had got out at the next station and found a guard, and I helped him up and he was able to walk with his arm around the guard. But it really was quite amazing – nobody moved! There were men and women and young people in the compartment. I found it quite shocking.

Caught the plane to Douglas for the Co-op Union Conference. The Co-op Union is made up mainly of the trading members of the co-operative movement, worthy middle-aged, lay-preacher types with no particular commitment, I would have thought, to the democracy or vitality of the co-operative movement. The trading role of the Co-op combined with this philosophy of consumerism has led the co-operative movement into terrible byways.

Harry Bailey, the President, had made quite a radical speech yesterday, reported in the *Guardian*, saying we must get back faith, idealism, compassion and so on. So I took up this theme and it went down well. Afterwards several old ladies came up to me and they all said the same thing – 'My grandson is a great fan of yours' or 'My grandson agrees with what you say but I have always had my doubts until now.'

I had arranged to meet the Manx Labour Party, so after lunch I was taken into this empty nightclub, with coloured lightbulbs and black walls, and I sat and talked with about a dozen members of the Isle of Man Party. They told me the Isle of Man is run by a mafia; it is a tax haven, and rich people retire there. The Budget that had been announced today in the Tynwald (the Manx Parliament) had cut income tax top rate to 20 per cent. Wages were low, housing expensive, social services inadequate. They said it was illegal to distribute leaflets in the streets, and a couple of their members had been sentenced to a week in prison for failing to pay a £1 fine for delivering leaflets without authority. They still have corporal punishment in the Isle of Man. Amazing.

Got on the plane, and who should I find on my left but the former Chairman of GKN, Sir Raymond Brookes, now Lord Brookes. I couldn't remember who he was for a moment. He told me one interesting thing which I shall pass on to the unions: before the steel strike the GKN works in Llanwern were making a 30 per cent profit. I took the opportunity to ask him what he thought of Mrs Thatcher's monetarism. He said, 'She's a very bright woman and the country needed somebody like that, but the situation has been oversimplified and she is going too far. Every politician should leave themselves a line of retreat, and she hasn't.'

### Wednesday 28 May
Willy Brandt was giving a lecture at Chatham House, and had asked if while he was in London he could visit me. I must say I was very honoured. He came to see me at home, after he had seen Jim, accompanied by Jenny Little and his own private secretary and stayed for an hour and a half. I have known him since 1957, though I don't suppose he remembers that I met him when he was Deputy Mayor of Berlin. Then I met him again in Bonn in 1975. When he is thoughtful and relaxed, as he was today, he couldn't be nicer.

He thought Schmidt would win the elections in Germany, and that the SPD should open up to absorb the Green Movement in Germany. He talked about his famous North–South report and said Olof Palme was initiating a disarmament report similar to his.

The thing he really wanted to discuss was the Common Market. He wondered if an initiative by the German SPD would help the Labour Party.

I said, 'For many years our socialist friends in the Community thought that Roy Jenkins spoke for the Labour Party – which he didn't – and we have had to fight to get across our view that there has to be some constitutional change. But we are not behind Mrs Thatcher with her nationalism and the Budget and the CAP. Our concern is a broader one, and I think the way to deal with it is to recognise that the Treaty of Rome has caused a log-jam, and that we have to get round it by initiatives on east–west relations, on disarmament, on the Third World and on energy.'

Then we talked about east–west relations. He thinks the Russians are not planning an advance into western Europe but a strong military directorate is growing up in the Soviet Union. He said that low-level détente in Germany means that families who couldn't meet when the Berlin Wall was put up can meet now.

I said I welcomed the fact that Giscard had gone to see Brezhnev.

'Yes, so did we, but Giscard did insult Schmidt.'

I asked, 'What do you mean?'

He said, 'Well, he advised Schmidt not to go, and then he went himself!'

We laughed; that was typically French.

I told him he mustn't think that the Labour Party was inward-looking about Europe; we were struggling to fight off the most right-wing Government we have had, and it will take us a decade to put it right. I think he understood that.

Altogether, Brandt is a wise man, and what I like about him is that he is past the management stage and is now the father of his tribe, in a way.

*Friday 30 May*
Frances Morrell rang to tell me about the Rank and File Mobilising Committee, which is working to get together the CLPD, LCC, Institute for Workers' Control, Independent Labour Publications and the Socialist Campaign for a Labour Victory, to agree on a programme of Party democracy.

In the evening we had a party, a sort of new left gathering, with Frances, Ken Livingstone of the GLC, Victor Schonfield, Audrey Wise, Tom Litterick, Chris Mullin, James Curran, a lecturer at PCL, his wife Margaret, George Osgerby, one of James's students, Dick Clements and Biddy, Geoff Bish, Dawn Primarolo, Jon Lansman of CLPD, Peter Hain and others. These are the people who have formed this Rank and File Mobilising Committee and, when the time comes, they will be the people who organise the Benn election campaign.

*Saturday 31 May*
Caroline and I picked up Stephen and June at 9 and drove to Wembley for the special conference. Caroline and Hilary sat in the gallery; Stephen was the delegate for the North Kensington Labour Party. I wandered round to the room where the Executive were meeting. Jim and Audrey Callaghan came in but we didn't speak to each other all day. I am afraid the hostility is quite strong on his part, although I would like to have talked to him.

We went into the conference at 10. The conference hall didn't look crowded because it was much bigger than we needed and the central block, where the trade unions usually sit at Party Conferences, was pretty empty. Moss Evans, Clive Jenkins and David Basnett were there on and off, and the constituencies were represented in large numbers.

Jim opened with a lame speech that lasted forty-five minutes. He barely mentioned the National Executive's statement called 'Peace, Jobs, Freedom'. The only thing he really cared about was wages policy, which he wants, and that went down like a lead balloon. I thought it was a very poor speech: he got polite applause.

When David Basnett spoke he said, 'There are three questions. How can we be sure the Tories get the blame for what is happening now? Secondly, what alternatives are there? Thirdly, how do we defeat the Government? The Party must understand and reflect the radical change in trade union policies.'

David Owen made a speech in which he said we wanted fresh

policies. He remarked that he was against unilateral disarmament – at which there was shouting. He went on, 'If you knew what I knew, we must have nuclear weapons to be at the top table on SALT.' It was such an unwise thing to say and he got more booing. He looked angry when it was shown on television later.

There were no motions or amendments; people just came to the rostrum to make particular points and pleas.

After lunch Denis Healey took the rostrum and there was a shout of 'Out, out', and he said, 'Well, comrades, including those who shouted "Out". . .'

He looked sort of jolly and friendly, and started off in a pleasant way, talking about the need for using the revenues from North Sea oil – the very opposite of what he had insisted on as Chancellor. But he couldn't resist attacking the Executive. 'We can't go on these ideological ego trips, saying that if every dot and comma of what the Executive want isn't carried we don't want to go into office.'

He finished up by saying, 'And we must get rid of the Toytown Trots in the Young Socialists and the Militant Tendency.' There was an enormous boo at that, and he looked angry and a bit stupid.

After the rest of the speeches I wound up, and by then the trade union section was pretty empty. I spoke for fifteen minutes and it was quite hard – no rhetorical flourishes. I got the biggest cheer when I quoted from the Glasgow University Media Group's report on the anti-working-class language of the broadcasters. At the end of my speech I had a standing ovation from the constituency delegates, but not from the platform or the trade unions. The document[5] was then carried by over 5 million votes to 6000.

# NOTES
*Chapter Six*

1. (p. 582) Earl Mountbatten was 'executed' by the IRA when a bomb exploded in the boat he and members of his family were taking out for a fishing trip in waters near his Irish home in County Sligo. His 14-year-old grandson Nicholas, a local boy called Paul Maxwell, and the Dowager Lady Brabourne were also killed by the explosion. The following day eighteen soldiers were killed at Warrenpoint when a haycart, concealing some explosives, blew up an army convoy as it passed. In October 1979, Margaret Thatcher appointed Sir Maurice Oldfield, former head of MI5, as 'security co-ordinator' for Northern Ireland.

2. (p. 556) In February 1977 three men – Crispin Aubrey, John Berry and Duncan Campbell – were arrested and ultimately charged under the rarely used Section 1, and Section 2, of the Official Secrets Act. Their 21-month trial

became known as the ABC Trial and included accusations of endangering the nation's safety. Campbell and Aubrey were journalists, Berry was an ex-corporal in Signals Intelligence who had agreed to talk to them about his experiences. The arrests took place against the background of the Agee and Hosenball deportation and the trial at the Old Bailey revealed the methods and paranoia, bordering on farce, of the secret world of intelligence and security.

The prosecution, endorsed by the Labour Government's Attorney-General and Home Secretary, was a disreputable one, and the trial ended in ignominy when the Attorney-General, Sam Silkin, instructed the court to drop the important charges. Berry received a six-month suspended sentence, Aubrey and Campbell conditional discharges.

3.   (p. 563) In December 1979 the NEC produced a paper 'The Tories' Spending Cuts' to help Labour local authorities resist by legal means the Conservative Government's cutbacks in public expenditure on housing and social services, and their restriction of local authority rate support grants. The legislation particularly affected metropolitan Labour councils and ultimately led to the surcharging and disqualifications from service of individual councillors. The arguments in the early 1980s revolved around whether councils and individuals would be justified in refusing to implement legislation: an argument which has returned in 1990 with the introduction of the Poll Tax to replace the rates sytstem.

4.   (p. 590) In November 1979 student supporters of Ayatollah Khomeini seized nearly 100 civilian and military staff from the US Embassy and Iran used the hostages to demand the return of the ex-Shah from the United States to face trial. On 25 April 1980 the American Government attempted to rescue the hostages in Tehran, but 'Operation Eagle Claw' ended in disaster when one of the helicopters involved crashed 200 miles from Tehran, in the desert, exploding a refuelling aircraft on the ground. Eight men died and their bodies were left in the scramble. In fact, the mission had already been aborted by Washington as a result of mechanical failures in the helicopters launching the rescue. President Carter took complete responsibility for the attempt and subsequent cancellation, and the fiasco contributed to his defeat in the presidential election of November 1980.

5.   (p. 601) 'Peace, Jobs, Freedom' contained most, though not all, of the policies for which I had been campaigning throughout the 1970s. By its overwhelming acceptance at the special conference in May 1980 the Party endorsed a genuine and comprehensive alternative to present to the British public. Key passages from it are included in Appendix III.

# Principal Persons

## (I) Political and Official

*Each person is named according to his or her status as the Diaries open. A complete list of Labour Government members as at January 1977 and Conservative Cabinet members as at May 1979 is given in Appendix I. Appendix II lists members of the National Executive Committee in 1977 and 1980.*

ALDINGTON, Lord (Toby Low). Chairman of National Nuclear Corporation, 1973–80. Deputy Chairman of GEC, 1968–84, and Chairman of Westland Aircraft, 1977–85. Conservative MP for Blackpool North, 1945–62. Created a hereditary peer in 1962.

ALI, Tariq. Socialist author and journalist. Editor of *Black Dwarf* and *Red Mole* in the 1960s and 1970s.

ALLAUN, Frank. Chairman of the Labour Party, 1978/9, and Labour MP for Salford East, 1955–83. Vice-President of CND and President of Labour Action for Peace.

ALLEN, Sir Douglas. Permanent Secretary of the Civil Service Department (Head of the Home Civil Service), 1974–7. Permanent Secretary to the Treasury, 1968–74. Deputy Chairman, then Chairman of British National Oil Corporation, 1978–85. Created a life peer, Lord Croham, in 1978.

ARMSTRONG, Robert. Home Office Deputy Under-Secretary, 1975–7, and Permanent Under-Secretary, 1977–9. Secretary of the Cabinet, 1979–87, and Head of the Home Civil Service, 1983–7. Treasury official 1950–70; Principal Private Secretary to Chancellor of the Exchequer, Roy Jenkins, 1968. Principal Private Secretary to Edward Heath and Harold Wilson, 1970–75. Created a life peer in 1988.

ARNOLD-FORSTER, Mark (1920–1981). Senior journalist and

political commentator on the *Guardian*, the *Observer* and ITN, 1946–81. Distinguished service with the Royal Navy while engaged on secret missions during the Second World War. Married to Val Arnold-Forster, journalist. Family friends.

ASHTON, Joe. Principal Private Secretary to Tony Benn, 1975–6. Labour MP for Bassetlaw since 1968.

ATKINSON, Norman. Treasurer of the Labour Party, 1976–81. Labour MP for Tottenham, 1964–87.

BALOGH, Lord (Thomas Balogh) (1905–1985). Oxford economist of Hungarian birth. Deputy Chairman, British National Oil Company, 1976 8. Close adviser to Harold Wilson in the 1950s and early 1960s and Economic Adviser to the Cabinet, 1964–8. Minister of State at the Department of Energy, 1974–5. Created a life peer in 1968.

BANKS, Tony. Assistant General Secretary, Association of Broadcasting and Allied Staffs, 1976–83 and Head of Research, Amalgamated Union of Engineering Workers, 1968–75. Last Chairman of Greater London Council, 1985–6. Labour MP for Newham North West since 1983.

BARNETT, Joel. Chief Secretary to the Treasury, 1974–9. Labour MP for Heywood and Royton, 1964–83. Created a life peer in 1983.

BASNETT, David (1924–1989). General Secretary of General and Municipal Workers' Union (later General, Municipal, Boilermakers and Allied Trades Union), 1973–86. Chairman, TUC General Council, 1977–8, and of Trade Unionists for a Labour Victory, 1979–85. Created a life peer in 1987.

BERRILL, Sir Kenneth. Economist. Director-General of the Central Policy Review Staff ('Think Tank'), 1974–80. Special Adviser and subsequently Chief Economic Adviser to the Treasury between 1967 and 1974.

BIFFEN, John. Opposition spokesman on Energy, 1976–7. Chief Secretary to the Treasury, 1979–81, Secretary of State for Trade, 1981–2, and Lord President of the Council, 1982–3. Leader of the House of Commons, 1982–7. Conservative MP for Oswestry, subsequently Shropshire North, since 1961.

BISH, Geoff. Head of Research, subsequently Policy Director, of the Labour Party since 1974. Research Assistant at Labour Party Research Department, 1968–74.

BONDI, Sir Hermann. Chief Scientific Adviser to Ministry of Defence, 1971–7. Chief Scientist, Department of Energy, 1977–80.

BOOTH, Albert. Secretary of State for Employment, 1976–9. From 1966 to 1983 he was Labour MP for Barrow-in-Furness, a shipbuilding constituency which he lost after his principled stand against the construction of nuclear submarines there.

BRETHERTON, James. Principal Private Secretary at the Department of Energy, 1976–8. Head of Oil Industry Division, International Energy Agency, 1980–82. Assistant Secretary, Department of Energy, 1982–6. Since 1986, a senior official, subsequently Secretary and Commercial Planning Director, of Atomic Energy Authority Technology.

BUTLER, David. Political scientist and broadcaster, whose special subject is the study of elections; the first person to coin the term 'psephology'. Co-author of *British Political Facts 1900–79*. Life-long friend.

CALLAGHAN, James. Prime Minister, 1976–9, and Leader of the Labour Party 1976–80. Held junior posts in the 1945–51 Labour Government, was Chancellor of the Exchequer, 1964–7, and Home Secretary, 1967–70. Foreign Secretary, 1974–6. Chairman of the Labour Party 1973/4 and Labour MP for South, South-East and again South Cardiff, 1945–87. Father of the House, 1983–7. Made a Knight of the Garter and a life peer in 1987. Married to Audrey Callaghan.

CASTLE, Barbara. Secretary of State for Social Services, 1974–6, dismissed by James Callaghan when he formed his Government in 1976. Minister of Overseas Development, 1964–5. Minister of Transport, 1965–8, First Secretary of State at the Department of Employment and Productivity, 1968–70. Chairman of the Labour Party, 1958/9. Labour MP for Blackburn, 1945–79. Leader of the British Labour Group in the European Parliament, 1979–85. Her late husband, Ted Castle, was created a life peer in 1974, Barbara in 1990.

CHAPPLE, Frank. General Secretary of the Electrical, Electronic Telecommunications and Plumbing Trade Union, 1966–84. Member of the National Economic Development Council, 1979–83. Created a life peer in 1985.

CLEMENTS-ELLIOTT, Julie. Private secretary to Tony Benn, 1976–84. Labour councillor since 1971. Chair of Southall College of Technology Governing Body since 1986. Currently working as political assistant. Married Michael Elliott, MEP, in 1979.

COATES, Ken. One of the founders of the Institute for Workers' Control and a director of the Bertrand Russell Foundation. Senior

Tutor, subsequently Reader, in the Adult Education Department, Nottingham University. Author of numerous works on socialism and industrial democracy. Elected to the European Parliament, 1989.

COCKS, Michael. Government Chief Whip, 1976–9, Opposition Chief Whip, 1979–85. Labour MP for Bristol South, 1970–87. Created a life peer in 1987.

CRAIGIE, Jill. Author and journalist, married to Michael Foot.

CRIPPS, Francis. Economic adviser to Tony Benn, 1974–9. Founder member of the Cambridge Economic Policy Group.

CROSLAND, Anthony (1918–1977). Foreign Secretary from 1976 up to his sudden death in February 1977. In the 1964–70 Government he was successively Minister of State for Economic Affairs, Secretary of State for Education and Science, President of the Board of Trade, finally Secretary of State for Local Government. Secretary of State for the Environment, 1974–76. Labour MP for South Gloucester, 1950–55, and Grimsby, 1959–77. Married journalist Susan Barnes in 1964. A personal friend from the war years.

CROSSMAN, Richard (1907–1974). Labour MP for Coventry, 1945–74, and senior Cabinet Minister in the 1964–70 Wilson Governments; his *Diaries of a Cabinet Minister* were published posthumously.

CUNNINGHAM, John (Jack). Parliamentary Under-Secretary of State, Department of Energy, 1976–9. PPS to Jim Callaghan, 1972–6. Labour MP for Whitehaven, 1970–83, Copeland since 1983.

DALY, Lawrence. General Secretary of the National Union of Mineworkers, 1968–84, previously General Secretary of Scottish NUM. Member of the TUC General Council, 1978–81.

DALYELL, Tam. PPS to Richard Crossman, 1964–70. Labour MP for West Lothian, 1962–83, and Linlithgow since 1983.

DELL, Edmund. Secretary of State for Trade, 1976–8. Joint Parliamentary Secretary at the Ministry of Technology, 1966–7, Joint Under-Secretary of State at the Department of Economic Affairs, 1967–8, Minister of State at the Board of Trade, 1968–9, and at Employment and Productivity, 1969–70. Resigned 1978 to be Deputy Chairman of Guiness Mahon; later joined the SDP. Labour MP for Birkenhead, 1964–79.

DONOUGHUE, Bernard. Senior policy adviser to the Prime Minister and head of the Policy Unit at Number 10, 1974–9. Member of staff at the London School of Economics, 1963–74. Created life peer in 1985.

EADIE, Alex. Parliamentary Under-Secretary of State at the Department of Energy, 1974–9. A former miner, Labour MP for Midlothian since 1966.

ELWYN-JONES, Lord (Sir Elwyn Jones) (1909–1989). Lord Chancellor, 1974–9. Attorney-General, 1964–70. Labour MP for Plaistow, 1945–50, for West Ham South, 1950–74 and for Newham South, February to May 1974, when he was created a life peer.

ENGLAND, Glyn. Chairman of the Central Electricity Generating Board, 1977–82, previously CEGB engineer. Chairman, Council for Environmental Conservation since 1983.

ENNALS, David. Secretary of State for Social Services, 1976–9. Secretary of the Labour Party's International Department, 1958–64. Under-Secretary of State at Defence, 1966, and at the Home Office, 1967. Minister of State at the Department of Health and Social Security, 1968–70. Minister of State at the Foreign and Commonwealth Office, 1974–6. Labour MP for Dover, 1964–70, and Norwich North, 1974–83. Created a life peer in 1983.

EVANS, Moss. National Officer of the Transport and General Workers' Union, 1969–78. General Secretary of the TGWU, 1978–85. Member of the NEDC, 1978–84. Member of the General Council of the TUC, 1977–85.

FALKENDER, Lady (Marcia Williams). Personal and Political Secretary to Harold Wilson since 1956. Created a life peer, Lady Falkender, in 1976.

FITT, Gerard (Gerry). Founder and leader of the Social Democratic and Labour Party, 1970–9. Represented Belfast West as Republican Labour MP, 1966–70, as SDLP MP, 1970–9, and as Socialist MP, 1979–83. Also MP in the Northern Ireland Parliament (Stormont) and the Assembly, 1962–75. Created a life peer in 1983.

FLOWERS, Sir Brian. Chairman of the Royal Commission on Environmental Pollution, 1973–6, and of the Standing Commission on Energy and the Environment, 1978–81. Nuclear physicist, Atomic Energy Research Establishment, 1946–58. Rector of Imperial College, 1973–85, Vice-Chancellor of London University since 1985. Created a life peer in 1979.

FOOT, Michael. Lord President of the Council and Leader of the House of Commons, 1976–9. Backbencher during the 1964–70 Labour Government. Secretary of State for Employment, 1974–6. Deputy Leader of the Labour Party, 1979–80, and Leader, 1980–83. Member of the National Executive, 1971–83. Labour MP for

Devonport, 1945–55. Ebbw Vale, 1960–83, and Blaenau Gwent since 1983. Author and journalist; close friend and biographer of Aneurin Bevan. Married to Jill Craigie.

FRANKLIN, Ned. Chairman and Managing Director, Nuclear Power Company, 1975–8. Chief Executive, British Nuclear Fuels Ltd, 1971–5. Chemist with Atomic Energy Authority, 1955–71, and consultant since 1968. Vice-Chancellor, City University since 1978.

GOODMAN, Geoffrey. Industrial Editor of the *Daily Mirror*, 1969–86, and Head of the Counter-Inflation Publicity Unit, 1975–6. Former journalist on the *Daily Herald* and the *Sun* and member of the Labour Party Committee on Industrial Democracy, 1966–7.

GORMLEY, Joe. President of the National Union of Mineworkers, 1971–82. Member of the National Executive, 1963–73. Created a life peer in 1982.

GOULD, Bryan. Labour MP for Southampton Test, October 1974–9, and for Dagenham since 1983. Served in the Diplomatic Service, 1964–8.

HAINES, Joe. Chief Press Secretary to Harold Wilson, 1969–76, previously political correspondent of the *Sun*. Since 1977, a journalist on the *Daily Mirror*, subsequently Political Editor of the Mirror Group.

HART, Judith. Minister for Overseas Development 1974–5, sacked by Harold Wilson after the Referendum, and reinstated 1977–9. In the 1964–70 Government she was successively Joint Under-Secretary for Scotland, Minister of State for Commonwealth Affairs, Minister of Social Security, Paymaster-General and Minister for Overseas Development. Chairman of the Labour Party, 1981/2. Labour MP for Lanark, 1959–83. Clydesdale, 1983–7. Married to Tony Hart, a scientist and leading anti-nuclear campaigner.

HATTERSLEY, Roy. Secretary of State for Prices and Consumer Protection, 1976–9. Joint Parliamentary Secretary at the Department of Employment and Productivity, 1967–9, and Minister of Defence for Administration, 1969–70. Minister of State at the Foreign and Commonwealth Office, 1974–6. Deputy Leader of the Labour Party since 1983. Labour MP for Birmingham Sparkbrook since 1964.

HAWKINS, Sir Arthur. Chairman of the Central Electricity Generating Board, 1972–7. Joined CEGB as planning engineer, 1957.

HAYWARD, Ron. General Secretary of the Labour Party, 1972–82;

National Agent, 1969–72, previously a regional organiser of the Party.

HEALEY, Denis. Chancellor of the Exchequer, 1974–9, Secretary of State for Defence, 1964–70. Deputy Leader of the Labour Party, 1980–83. Labour MP for Leeds South East, 1952–5, and Leeds East since 1955.

HEATH, Edward. Backbencher since 1975. Leader of the Conservative Party, 1965–75. Prime Minister, 1970–74. Minister of Labour, 1959–60, Lord Privy Seal, 1960–63, and Secretary of State for Industry and Trade and President of the Board of Trade, 1963–4. Conservative MP for Bexley, subsequently Old Bexley and Sidcup, since 1950.

HEFFER, Eric. Minister of State at the Department of Industry, 1974–5, sacked by Harold Wilson over the Common Market. Chairman of the Labour Party, 1983/4. Carpenter/joiner by trade and Labour MP for Walton, Liverpool, since 1964. Married to Doris Heffer.

HESELTINE, Michael. Shadow Spokeman on Environment, 1977–9. Parliamentary Under-Secretary at Department of Environment, 1970–72, Minister for Aerospace and Shipping at Department of Trade and Industry, 1972–4. Secretary of State for Environment, 1979–83, and for Defence until his resignation in 1986. Conservative MP for Tavistock, 1966–74, and Henley since 1974.

HILL, Sir John. Chairman of the UK Atomic Energy Authority, 1967–81, and of British Nuclear Fuels, 1971–83. Member of the Advisory Council on Technology, 1968–70. President of the British Nuclear Forum since 1984.

HUGHES, Cledwyn. Chairman of the Parliamentary Labour Party, Oct 1974–9. Minister of State for Commonwealth Relations, 1964–6, and Minister of Agriculture, Fisheries and Food, 1968–70. Labour MP for Anglesey, 1951–79. Created a life peer, Lord Cledwyn of Penrhos, in 1979.

HUNT, Sir John. Secretary of the Cabinet, 1973–9. Second Permanent Secretary in the Cabinet Office, 1972–3. Deputy Secretary, Civil Service Department, 1968–71. Created a life peer, Lord Hunt of Tanworth, in 1980.

INGHAM, Bernard. Director of Information at the Department of Energy, 1974–8, Chief Information Officer at the Department of Employment and Productivity, 1968–73. Reporter on the *Yorkshire Post* and the *Guardian*, 1952–67. Chief Press Secretary to the Prime Minister since 1979.

JACKSON, Margaret, (Margaret Beckett since 1979). PPS to Judith Hart at the Ministry for Overseas Development, 1974–5. Secretary of the Labour Party Study group into the National Enterprise Board. Labour MP for Lincoln, Oct 1974–9, and for Derby South since 1983.

JAY, Douglas. Leading anti-Common Marketeer. President of the Board of Trade, 1964–7. 'Resigned' in the reshuffle of August 1967 and returned to the back benches. Labour MP for North Battersea 1946–83. Created a life peer in 1987.

JEGER, Lena. Labour MP for St Pancras and Holborn South, 1953–9 and 1964–74, and for Camden, Holborn and St Pancras South, 1974–9. Chairman of the Labour Party, 1979/80. Created a life peer in 1979.

JENKINS, Clive. General Secretary of the Association of Scientific Technical and Managerial Staffs, 1970–88. Member of the General Council of the TUC, 1974–8.

JENKINS, Roy. President of the European Commission, 1977–81. Minister of Aviation, 1964–5, Home Secretary, 1965–7. Chancellor of the Exchequer, 1967–70. Home Secretary, 1974–6. Deputy Leader of the Labour Party, 1970–72, in which capacity he sat on the National Executive. Labour MP for Central Southwark, 1948–50, for Stechford, 1950–76. Leader of the SDP, 1981–3, and SDP MP for Glasgow Hillhead, 1982–7. Created a life peer, Lord Jenkins of Hillhead, in 1987.

JONES, Jack. Assistant General Secretary of the Transport and General Workers' Union, 1963–9, General Secretary, 1969–78. Member of the Labour Party National Executive, 1964–7, and of the TUC General Council, 1968–78. Vice-President of Age Concern since 1978.

JOSEPH, Sir Keith. Secretary of State for Social Services, 1970–74, for Industry, 1979–81, and Education and Science, 1981–6. Junior Minister from 1959–64. Conservative MP for Leeds North East, 1956–87. Created a life peer in 1987.

KAUFMAN, Gerald. Minister of State, Department of Industry, 1975–9. Labour Party press officer, 1965–70. Previously journalist on *Daily Mirror* and *New Stateman*. Labour MP for Manchester Ardwick, 1970–83, and Manchester Gorton since 1983.

KEARTON, Lord (Frank Kearton). Chairman and Chief Executive of the British National Oil Corporation, 1975–9. Chairman of Courtaulds, 1964–75, and served on the Atomic Energy Authority, and the

Central Electricity Generating Board, 1955–81. First Chairman of the Industrial Reorganisation Corporation, 1966–8. Member of the Advisory Council on Technology. Created a life peer in 1970.

KINNOCK, Neil. Leader of the Labour Party since 1983, Chair, 1987/8. Labour MP for Bedwelty, 1970–83, Islwyn since 1983.

KITSON, Alex. Executive Officer of the Transport and General Workers' Union, 1971–80, and Deputy General Secretary, 1980–86. Chairman of the Labour Party, 1980/81.

LESTOR, Joan. Under-Secretary at the Foreign and Commonwealth Office, 1974–5, and at the Department of Education and Science, 1975–6, resigning her post over public expenditure cuts. Under-Secretary at the Department of Education and Science, 1969–70. Chairman of the Labour Party, 1977/8. Labour MP for Eton and Slough, 1966–83, and Eccles since 1987.

LEVER, Harold. Chancellor of the Duchy of Lancaster, 1974–9. Financial Secretary to the Treasury, 1967–9, Paymaster-General, 1969–70. Created a life peer, Lord Lever of Manchester, in 1979.

MABON, Dickson (Dick). Minister of State at the Department of Energy, 1976–9. Chairman of the Labour Committee for Europe and the European Movement between 1974 and 1976. Labour MP for Greenock from 1955. Joined the SDP in 1981 and sat as SDP Member, 1981–3.

McCAFFREY, Tom. Chief Press Secretary to the Prime Minister, 1976–9. Press officer in Home Office, 10 Downing Street, and Foreign and Commonwealth Office, 1966–76.

McELHONE, Frank (1929–1982). Under-Secretary of State for Scotland, 1975–9. PPS to Tony Benn, 1974–5. Labour MP for Gorbals, 1969–74, Glasgow Queen's Park, 1974–82.

MacKENZIE, Gregor. Parliamentary Under-Secretary of State for Industry, 1974–5, Minister of State, 1975–6. Minister of State at the Scottish Office, 1976–9. PPS to James Callaghan, 1966–70. Labour MP for Rutherglen, 1964–87.

McNALLY, Tom. Political Adviser to Jim Callaghan, 1974–9. International Secretary of the Labour Party, 1969–74. Elected Labour MP for Stockport, 1979; joined SDP, 1981 and sat as SDP Member, 1981–3.

MARSHALL, Walter. Chief Scientist, Department of Energy, 1974–7, Deputy Chairman of the United Kingdom Atomic Energy Authority, 1975–81. Chairman of the UKAEA, 1981–2 and of the Central

Electricity Generating Board since 1982. From 1968–75, Director of the Atomic Energy Research Establishment, Harwell. Created a life peer, Lord Marshall of Goring, in 1985.

MASON, Roy. Secretary of State for Northern Ireland, 1976–9. Minister of State at the Board of Trade, 1964–7, Minister of Defence, 1967–8, and of Power, 1968–9, and President of the Board of Trade, 1969–70. Secretary of State for Defence, 1974–6. Labour MP for Barnsley, 1953–87. Created a life peer in 1987.

MAYNARD, Joan. Labour MP for Sheffield, Brightside, Oct 1974–87. Vice-Chairman of the Labour Party, 1980/81.

MEACHER, Michael. Parliamentary Under-Secretary of State for Industry, 1974–5, Health and Social Security, 1975–6, and Trade 1976–9. Labour MP for Oldham West since 1970.

MELLISH, Robert. Joint Parliamentary Secretary at the Ministry of Housing, 1964–7. Minister of Public Building and Works, 1967–9. Government Chief Whip, 1969–70 and 1974–6. Opposition Chief Whip, 1970–74. Labour MP for Bermondsey from 1946 to 1982, when he resigned from the Labour Party and sat as an Independent until the by-election in March, 1983, which was won by the Liberals. Deputy Chairman of the London Docklands Development Corporation since 1981. Created a life peer in 1985.

METHVEN, John (1926–1980). Director-General of the Confederation of British Industry, 1976–80, and Member of the National Economic Development Council, 1976–80. Director-General of Fair Trading, 1973–6.

MIKARDO, Ian. Labour MP for Poplar, 1964–74, and for Bethnal Green and Bow, 1974–87. MP for Reading, and South Reading, 1945–59. A distinguished leader of the Labour left, he was Chairman of the Labour Party, 1970/71. A close associate of Aneurin Bevan and sometime chairman of the Tribune Group of Labour MPs.

MORRELL, Frances. Political adviser to Tony Benn, 1974–9. Press officer for the National Union of Students and the Fabian Society, 1970–72. Previously a schoolteacher, 1960–69. Leader of Inner London Education Authority, 1983–7.

MULLEY, Fred. Secretary of State for Defence, 1976–9. Minister of Transport, 1969–70, and again, in the Department of the Environment, 1974–5. Secretary of State for Education and Science, 1975–6. Deputy Defence Secretary, 1964–5, and Minister of Aviation, 1965–7. Minister of State, Foreign and Commonwealth Office and for

Disarmament, 1967–9. Chairman of the Labour Party, 1974/5. Labour MP for Sheffield Park, 1950–83. Created a life peer in 1984.

MULLIN, Chris. Editor of *Arguments for Socialism* and *Arguments for Democracy* by Tony Benn; *Tribune*, 1982–4. Political novelist. Labour MP for Sunderland South since 1987.

MURRAY, Len. General Secretary of the TUC, 1973–84. Member of the TUC staff from 1947. Created a life peer, Lord Murray of Epping Forest, in 1985.

ORME, Stan. Minister of State for Social Security, 1976–7 and Minister for Social Security, 1977–9. Minister of State, Northern Ireland Office, 1974–6. Chairman of the PLP since 1987. Labour MP for Salford West, 1964–83 and for Salford East since 1983.

OWEN, David. Minister of State at the Foreign and Commonwealth Office, 1976–7, then Foreign Secretary, following Tony Crosland's death, 1977–9. Parliamentary Under-Secretary of State for the Royal Navy, 1968–70. Parliamentary Under-Secretary of State, then Minister of State, at the Department of Health and Social Security, 1974–6. Labour MP for Plymouth Sutton, 1966–74, and Plymouth Devonport, 1974–81. Founder member of the SDP, 1981, and sat as SDP Member, 1981–3; SDP MP for Devonport since 1983.

PEART, Lord (Fred Peart) (1914–1988). Lord Privy Seal and Leader of the House of Lords, 1976–9. Minister of Agriculture, 1964–8, and Lord President and Leader of the House of Commons, 1968–70. Minister of Agriculture, Fisheries and Food, 1974–6. Labour MP for Workington, 1945–76. Created a life peer in 1976.

POWELL, Enoch. Minister of Health, 1960–63. Resigned as Financial Secretary to the Treasury in protest at the Budget. Conservative MP for Wolverhampton South West, 1950–74. Stood down as Conservative candidate in February 1974 in disagreement over the calling of a General Election. United Ulster Unionist MP for Down South, October 1974–9, Official Unionist Party, 1979–87.

PRENTICE, Reg. Labour Government Minister, 1964–9 and 1974–6. Labour MP for East Ham North, 1951–74, Newham North East, 1974–9. In October 1977 Reg Prentice crossed the floor and sat on the Conservative benches until 1979. In 1979 he was elected Conservative MP for Daventry and sat for Daventry until 1987; he was Minister for Social Security, 1979–81, in the Conservative Government.

PRIMAROLO, Dawn. Secretary of Bristol South East Labour Party, 1979–83. Labour MP for Bristol South since 1987.

RAMPTON, Sir Jack. Permanent Under-Secretary of State at the Department of Energy, 1974–80. Formerly a senior official at the Ministry of Technology and the Department of Trade and Industry, 1968–74.

REES, Merlyn. Home Secretary, 1976–9. Parliamentary Under-Secretary of State at the Ministry of Defence, 1965–8, and Home Office, 1968–70. Secretary of State for Northern Ireland, 1974–6. Labour MP for South Leeds, 1963–83, and for Morley and Leeds South since 1983.

RODGERS, William (Bill). Secretary of State for Transport, 1976–79. Parliamentary Under-Secretary of State at the Department of Economic Affairs then Foreign and Commonwealth Office, 1964–8. Minister of State at the Board of Trade, 1968–9, and the Treasury, 1969–70. Minister of State at the Ministry of Defence, 1974–6. Labour MP for Stockton-on-Tees (Teesside, Stockton from 1974), 1962–81. Founder member of the SDP in 1981 and sat as SDP MP for same seat, 1981–3.

ROGERS, Herbert. Election Agent for Tony Benn, 1951–70. Secretary of the East Bristol Independent Labour Party from 1912. Agent for Sir Stafford Cripps, MP for Bristol East; after the 1914–18 war Herbert Rogers became Secretary of the Bristol South East Labour Party.

ROSE. Sir Clive. Deputy Secretary in the Cabinet Office, 1976–9. Diplomatic Service, 1950–73. Head of the British Delegation to Negotiations on Arms Reduction in Central Europe, 1973–6. Chairman of the Civil Contingencies Unit, 1978/9. President, Association of Civil Defence and Emergency Planning Officers since 1987.

ROSS, William (1911–1988). Secretary of State for Scotland, 1964-70, and 1974–6. Labour MP for Kilmarnock, 1946–79. Created a life peer, Lord Ross of Marnock, in 1979.

SCANLON, Hugh. President of the Amalgamated Union of Engineering Workers, 1968–78. AEU organiser, 1947–63. Member of the TUC General Council, 1968–78 and of the National Economic Development Council, 1971–8. Created a life peer in 1979.

SCARGILL, Arthur. President of the Yorkshire Area of the National Union of Mineworkers, 1973–81. President of the NUM since 1981, and member of the TUC General Council since 1986.

SEDGEMORE, Brian. PPS to Tony Benn, 1977–8. Labour MP for Luton West, 1974–9, and for Hackney South and Shoreditch since 1983. Granada TV researcher, 1980–83.

SHORE, Liz. Deputy Chief Medical Officer for the Department of Health and Social Security, 1977–85. Post-Graduate Medical Dean, North West Thames Region, since 1985. Married to Peter Shore.

SHORE, Peter. Secretary of State for the Environment, 1976–9. Head of Research Department of the Labour Party, 1959–64. PPS to Harold Wilson, 1965–6. Joint Parliamentary Secretary at the Ministry of Technology, 1966–7. Secretary of State for Economic Affairs, 1967–9. Minister without Portfolio, 1969–70. Secretary of State for Trade, 1974–6. Labour MP for Stepney, subsequently Stepney and Poplar, and then Bethnal Green and Stepney, since 1964. Married to Liz Shore.

SILKIN, John (1923–1987). Minister for Agriculture, Fisheries and Food, 1976–9. Government Whip, 1964–6 and Chief Whip, 1966–9. Minister of Public Building and Works, 1969–70. Minister for Planning and Local Government, 1974–6. Labour MP for Deptford, 1963–87.

SILKIN, Sam (1918–1988). Attorney-General, 1974–9. Leader of UK delegation to European Assembly, 1968–70. Labour MP for Dulwich, 1964–83. Brother of John Silkin (see above). Created a life peer, Lord Silkin of Dulwich, in 1985.

SKINNER, Dennis. Labour MP for Bolsover since 1970. Chairman of the NEC, 1988/9. President of the Derbyshire NUM, 1966–70.

SMITH, John. Minister of State in the Privy Council Office, with responsibility for Devolution, 1976–8. Secretary of State for Trade, 1978–9. Parliamentary Under-Secretary of State, then Minister of State, at the Department of Energy, 1974–6. Labour MP for Lanarkshire North, 1970–83, and Monklands East since 1983.

STANLEY, Bryan. General Secretary of the Post Office Engineering Union (later the National Communications Union), 1972–86; member of the National Executive, 1973–8.

STEEL, David. Leader of the Liberal Party, 1976–88, and the joint Leader of the Liberal and Social Democratic Alliance during 1987. Liberal MP for Roxburgh, Selkirk and Peebles, 1965–83, and Tweeddale, Ettrick and Lauderdale since 1983.

STOWE, Kenneth (Ken). Principal Private Secretary to the Prime Minister, 1975–9. Under Secretary, then Deputy Secretary, in the Cabinet Office, 1973–5. Permanent Secretary, Department of Health and Social Security, 1981–7.

THATCHER, Margaret. Leader of the Conservative Party since 1975.

Secretary of State for Education and Science, 1970–74, previously a junior Minister in the Ministry of Pensions and National Insurance, 1961–4. Prime Minister, 1979–1990. Conservative MP for Finchley since 1959.

THOMAS, George. Speaker of the House of Commons, 1976–83, (Deputy Speaker 1974–6). Minister of State at the Welsh Office, 1966–7, and Commonwealth Office, 1967–8. Secretary of State for Wales, 1968–70. Since 1983, Chairman of the National Children's Home. A former Vice-President of the Methodist Conference. Labour MP for Cardiff Central, 1945–50, Cardiff West, 1950–83 (sat as Speaker from 1976). Created a hereditary peer, Viscount Tonypandy, in 1983.

THORPE, Jeremy. Leader of the Liberal Party, 1967–76. Liberal MP for North Devon, 1959–79.

UNDERHILL, Reg. National Agent of the Labour Party, 1972–9. Labour Party official since 1933. Created a life peer in 1979.

VARLEY, Eric. Secretary of State for Energy, 1974–5, exchanging Cabinet jobs with Tony Benn to become Secretary of State for Industry, 1975–9. PPS to Harold Wilson, 1968–9. Minister of State at the Ministry of Technology, 1969–70. Labour MP for Chesterfield, 1964–84. Retired in 1984 to become Chairman of Coalite Group. Created a life peer in 1990.

VAUGHAN, Ron. Official driver to Tony Benn at the Ministry of Technology, 1968–70, and at the Departments of Industry and Energy, 1974–9

WALKER, Peter. Secretary of State for the Environment, 1970–72, and for Trade and Industry, 1972–4. Minister for Agriculture, Fisheries and Food, 1979–83, Secretary of State for Wales, 1987–90. Deputy Chairman of Slater, Walker Securities, 1964–70. Conservative MP for Worcester since 1961.

WEINSTOCK, Arnold. Industrialist. Managing Director of GEC since 1963, of Radio and Allied Industries, 1954–63. Created a life peer in 1980.

WHITELAW, William (Willie). Secretary of State for Employment, 1973–4, previously Leader of the House of Commons, and Secretary of State for Northern Ireland, 1972–3. Chairman of the Conservative Party, 1974–5. Home Secretary, 1979–83. Created a hereditary viscount in 1983.

WHITTY, Larry. Assistant Private Secretary at the Ministry of

Technology, 1965–70. Official of General and Municipal Workers' Union, 1973–85. Since 1985, General Secretary of the Labour Party.

WILLIAMS, Shirley. Secretary of State for Education and Science and Paymaster-General, 1976–9. Member of the National Executive, 1970–81. Parliamentary Secretary at the Ministry of Labour, 1966–7, Minister of State, Education and Science, 1967–9, and the Home Office, 1969–70. Secretary of State for Prices and Consumer Protection, 1974–6. Labour MP for Hitchin, 1964–74, for Hertford and Stevenage, 1974–9. Founder member of the SDP in 1981, President in 1982 and SDP MP for Crosby, 1981–3.

WILSON, Harold. Leader of the Labour Party, 1963–76. Prime Minister, 1964–70, and 1974–6. Resigned in 1976 and did not hold office again. President of the Board of Trade, 1947–51, when he resigned with Aneurin Bevan. Chairman of the Labour Party, 1961/2. Labour MP for Ormskirk, 1945–50 and Huyton, 1950–83. Created a life peer, Lord Wilson of Rievaulx, in 1983. Married to Mary Wilson, poet and writer.

WISE, Audrey. Labour MP for Coventry South West, 1974–9, and for Preston since 1987.

# (II) Personal

BENN, Caroline. Born in the USA. Postgraduate degrees from the Universities of Cincinnati and London. Founder member of the comprehensive education campaign in Britain and editor of *Comprehensive Education* since 1967. Author of educational publications including *Half Way There* with Professor Brian Simon (1970) and *Challenging the MSC* with John Fairley (1986). President, Socialist Educational Association since 1970. Member, Inner London Education Authority, 1970–77. Member, Education Section, UNESCO Commission, 1976–83. Governor of several schools and colleges, including Imperial College, London University and Holland Park School, from 1967. Lecturer, adult education service, 1965-present. Married Tony Benn, 1949. Four children (see below).

BENN, David Wedgwood. Younger brother of Tony Benn; a barrister, worked for the Socialist International and later for the External Service of the BBC. Head of the BBC Yugoslav Section, 1974–84. A writer specialising in Soviet affairs.

BENN, Hilary. Born 1953. Educated at Holland Park School and Sussex University. Research Office with the trade union MSF (formerly ASTMS). A past President of Acton Labour Party, elected to Ealing Council, 1979. Deputy Leader of the Council and Chair of the Education Committee, 1986–90. Chair of the Association of London Authorities' Education Committee, 1988–90. Contested Ealing North in 1983 and 1987 Elections. In 1973 married Rosalind Retey who died of cancer in 1979. Married Sally Clark in 1982. Four children.

BENN, Joshua. Born 1958. Educated at Holland Park School. Founder of COMMUNITEC Computer Training Consultancy, 1984–8. Director of Westway Music Publishing, 1980–82. Former contributor to *Sound International, Beat Instrumental* and computer and electronics magazines. Co-author or *Rock Hardware* (1981). Executive member of Computing for Labour. Employed by the Housing Corporation since 1988. Married Elizabeth Feeney in 1984. One son.

BENN, June. Former lecturer; novelist writing under the name of June Barraclough. Married David Benn in 1959. Two children, Piers, born in 1962, and Frances, born 1964.

BENN, Melissa (Lissie). Born 1957. Educated at Holland Park School and the London School of Economics. Socialist feminist writer and journalist. Joint author with Ken Worpole of *Death in the City* (1986). Contributor to several essay collections on feminism, the media, the police and crime; her work has also appeared in *Feminist Review, Women's Studies International Forum* and several international publications. Contributes to the *Guardian, New Statesman, Marxism Today, Spare Rib*. On the staff of *City Limits*, 1988–90.

BENN, Stephen. Born 1951. Educated at Holland Park School and Keele University. PhD for 'The White House Staff' (1984). Former assistant to Senator Thomas F. Eagleton. Secretary and Agent, Kensington Labour Party. Labour candidate GLC, 1981. Member GLC Special Committee, 1983–6. Chair, Brent South CLP. Member of ILEA 1981–90 and Chair of General Purposes Committee. School and College Governor. Court of Governors, Central London Polytechnic. Vice Chair, Association of London Authorities' Education Committee, 1987–90. Parliamentary Affairs Officer for Royal Society of Chemistry since 1988. Composer. During the period covered by this volume, lived with June Battye, a student at Keele. Married Nita Clarke in 1988. One daughter, Emily, b. 1989.

KHAMA, Sir Seretse (1921–1980). Founder and President of the Bechuanaland Democratic Party from 1962, becoming Prime Minister of Bechuanaland (Botswana) in 1965, and President of the Republic of Botswana in 1966. A barrister educated at Oxford, Seretse had become chief of the Bamangwato tribe in 1925, aged four. He was removed from the British protectorate by the Labour Government in 1950 over objections to his marriage to Ruth Williams, a white British woman, in 1948. Became close friends with the Benns who lent support in the 1950s. Seretse Khama was godfather to Melissa Benn, and Tony Benn godfather to Anthony Khama.

RETEY, Rosalind (1953–1979). A contemporary of Hilary Benn at Holland Park School, graduated from Queen Mary College, London. They married in April 1973. Rosalind contracted cancer in 1978, and died in June 1979 after much suffering which she bore with immense courage. A fund, under the control of students at Holland Park, has been established in memory of Rosalind.

STANSGATE, Lady. Margaret Holmes, born in Scotland in 1897, the daughter of Liberal MP, D.T. Holmes. Married William Wedgwood Benn in 1920. They had three children (the eldest son, Michael, was killed while serving as an RAF pilot during the war). A long-standing member of the Movement for the Ordination of Women, the first President of the Congregational Federation, served on the Council of Christians and Jews, and of the Friends of the Hebrew University. Fellow of the Hebrew University. Joint author of *Beckoning Horizon*, 1934.

STANSGATE, Lord (1877–1960). William Wedgwood Benn. Son of John Williams Benn, who was Liberal MP for Tower Hamlets and later for Devonport, and Chairman, 1904/5, of the London County Council of which he was a founder member. William Wedgwood Benn was himself elected Liberal MP for St George's, Tower Hamlets, in 1906. Became a Whip in the Liberal Government in 1910. Served in the First World War and was decorated with the DSO and DFC, returning in 1918 to be elected Liberal MP for Leith. Joined the Labour Party in 1926, resigned his seat the same day, and was subsequently elected Labour MP for North Aberdeen (1928–31) in a by-election. Secretary of State for India in the 1929–31 Labour Cabinet. Re-elected as Labour MP for Gorton in 1937. He rejoined the RAF in 1940 at the age of sixty-three, was made a peer, Viscount Stansgate, in 1941, and was Secretary of State for Air, 1945–6, in the postwar Labour Government. World President of the Inter-Parliamentary Union, 1947–57.

WINCH, Olive (Buddy). Miss Winch was with the family as a children's nurse from 1928 until 1940, when she left to undertake war work. A life-long friend.

# APPENDIX I
## Her Majesty's Government
## Complete List of Ministers and Offices

## The Cabinet, January 1977

| | |
|---|---|
| Prime Minister and First Lord of the Treasury | Mr James Callaghan |
| Lord President of the Council and Leader of the House of Commons | Mr Michael Foot |
| Secretary of State for Foreign and Commonwealth Affairs | Mr Anthony Crosland |
| Lord Chancellor | Lord Elwyn-Jones |
| Secretary of State for the Home Department | Mr Merlyn Rees |
| Chancellor of the Exchequer | Mr Denis Healey |
| Secretary of State for Employment | Mr Albert Booth |
| Secretary of State for Energy | Mr Tony Benn |
| Secretary of State for Social Services | Mr David Ennals |
| Secretary of State for Industry | Mr Eric Varley |
| Secretary of State for the Environment | Mr Peter Shore |
| Secretary of State for Scotland | Mr Bruce Millan |
| Chancellor of the Duchy of Lancaster | Mr Harold Lever |
| Secretary of State for Transport | Mr William Rodgers |
| Secretary of State for Trade | Mr Edmund Dell |
| Secretary of State for Prices and Consumer Protection | Mr Roy Hattersley |
| Minister of Agriculture, Fisheries and Food | Mr John Silkin |
| Secretary of State for Defence | Mr Fred Mulley |
| Secretary of State for Northern Ireland | Mr Roy Mason |

| Secretary of State for Wales | Mr John Morris |
| Secretary of State for Education and Science | Mrs Shirley Williams |
| Lord Privy Seal and Leader of the House of Lords | Lord Peart |
| Minister for Social Security | Mr Stan Orme |

## Ministers not in the Cabinet, January 1977

| | |
|---|---|
| Attorney-General | Mr Samuel Silkin |
| Solicitor-General | Mr Peter Archer |
| Minister of State for Energy | Mr Dick Mabon |
| Minister for Defence | Mr John Gilbert |
| Minister for Housing and Construction | Mr Reginald Freeson |
| Ministers of State for Foreign and Commonwealth Affairs | Dr David Owen |
| | Lord Goronwy-Roberts |
| | Mr Edward Rowlands |
| Ministers of State for Industry | Mr Gerald Kaufman |
| | Mr Alan Williams |
| Ministers of State for Northern Ireland | Lord Melchett |
| | Mr Don Concannon |
| Chief Secretary to the Treasury | Mr Joel Barnett |
| Financial Secretary to the Treasury | Mr Robert Sheldon |
| Minister of State, Treasury | Mr Denzil Davies |
| Minister of State, Agriculture, Fisheries and Food | Mr Edward S. Bishop |
| Ministers of State for Education and Science | Lord Donaldson |
| | Mr Gordon Oakes |
| Minister of State, Privy Council Office | Mr John Smith |
| Minister of State for Employment | Mr Harold Walker |
| Minister of State for Health and Social Security | Mr Roland Moyle |
| Ministers of State, Home Office | Mr Brynmor John |
| | Lord Harris of Greenwich |
| Minister of State, Prices and Consumer Protection | Mr John Fraser |
| Minister of State for Civil Service | Mr Charles Morris |
| Ministers of State, Scottish Office | Lord Kirkhill |
| | Mr Gregor MacKenzie |

| | |
|---|---|
| Minister of State for Overseas Development | Mrs Judith Hart |
| Minister of State, Department of the Environment | Mr Denis Howell |
| Parliamentary Secretary to the Treasury | Mr Michael Cocks |
| Lord Advocate | Mr Ronald King Murray |
| Solicitor-General for Scotland | Lord McCluskey |

## Changes to Cabinet 1977–9:

Anthony Crosland died in February 1977, and was replaced as Foreign Secretary by David Owen.

Joel Barnett, Chief Secretary to the Treasury, was promoted into the Cabinet in February 1977.

Edmund Dell left the Cabinet in November 1978 and was replaced as Secretary of State for Trade by John Smith.

## The Cabinet, May 1979

| | |
|---|---|
| Prime Minister and First Lord of the Treasury | Mrs Margaret Thatcher |
| Secretary of State for the Home Office | Mr William Whitelaw |
| Lord Chancellor | Lord Hailsham |
| Secretary of State for Foreign and Commonwealth Affairs | Lord Carrington |
| Chancellor of the Exchequer | Sir Geoffrey Howe |
| Secretary of State for Industry | Sir Keith Joseph |
| Secretary of State for Defence | Mr Francis Pym |
| Lord President of the Council and Leader of the House of Lords | Lord Soames |
| Secretary of State for Employment | Mr James Prior |
| Lord Privy Seal | Sir Ian Gilmour |
| Minister of Agriculture, Fisheries and Food | Mr Peter Walker |
| Secretary of State for the Environment | Mr Michael Heseltine |
| Secretary of State for Scotland | Mr George Younger |
| Secretary of State for Wales | Mr Nicholas Edwards |
| Secretary of State for Northern Ireland | Mr Humphrey Atkins |

| | |
|---|---|
| Secretary of State for Social Services | Mr Patrick Jenkin |
| Leader of the House of Commons and Minister for the Arts | Mr Norman St John-Stevas |
| Secretary of State for Trade | Mr John Nott |
| Secretary of State for Energy | Mr David Howell |
| Secretary of State for Education and Science | Mr Mark Carlisle |
| Chief Secretary to the Treasury | Mr John Biffen |
| Paymaster-General | Mr Angus Maude |

# APPENDIX II
## Labour Party National Executive Committees
## 1977 and 1980

1976/7

| | |
|---|---|
| Mr John Chalmers | Chairman |
| Miss Joan Lestor, MP | Vice-Chairman |
| Mr Norman Atkinson, MP | Treasurer |
| Mr James Callaghan, MP | Leader of the Parliamentary Party |
| Mr Michael Foot, MP | Deputy Leader of the Parliamentary Party |
| Mr Ron Hayward | General Secretary |

*Trade Unions' Section*

Mr T.G. Bradley, MP (Transport Salaried Staffs' Association)

Mr J. Chalmers (Amalgamated Society of Boilermakers, Shipwrights, Blacksmiths and Structural Workers)

Mr J. Forrester (Amalgamated Union of Engineering Workers, Technical, Administrative and Supervisory Section)

Mr H.E. Hickling (Union of General and Municipal Workers)

Mr W. John (Amalgamated Union of Engineering Workers, Engineering Section)

Mr A. Kitson (Transport and General Workers' Union)

Mr S. McCluskie (National Union of Seamen)

Mr F. Mulley, MP (Association of Professional, Clerical and Computer Staffs)

Mr W. Padley, MP (Union of Shop, Distributive and Allied Workers)

Mr B. Stanley (Post Office Engineering Union)

Mr R. Tuck (National Union of Railwaymen)

Mr E. Williams (National Union of Mineworkers)

*Socialist, Co-operative and other organisations' Section*
Mr J. Cartwright, MP (Royal Arsenal Co-operative Society)

*Constituency Labour Parties*
Mr F. Allaun, MP
Mr J. Ashley, MP
Mr A.W. Benn, MP
Mrs B. Castle, MP
Mr. E. Heffer, MP
Miss J. Lestor, MP
Mr I. Mikardo, MP

*Women Members*
Mrs Judith Hart, MP
Mrs Lena Jeger, MP
Miss Joan Maynard, MP
Mrs Renée Short, MP
Mrs Shirley Williams, MP

*Labour Party Young Socialists' Representative*
Mr N. Bradley

---

1979/80

| | |
|---|---|
| Baroness Jeger | Chairman |
| Mr Alex Kitson | Vice-Chairman |
| Mr Norman Atkinson, MP | Treasurer |
| Mr James Callaghan, MP | Leader of the Parliamentary Party |
| Mr Michael Foot, MP | Deputy Leader of the Parliamentary Party |
| Mr Ron Hayward | General Secretary |

*Trade Unions' Section*
Mr T.G. Bradley, MP (Transport Salaried Staffs Association)
Mr J. Golding, MP (Post Office Engineering Union)
Mr A. Hadden (Amalgamated Society of Boilermakers, Shipwrights, Blacksmiths and Structural Workers)
Mr N. Hough (General and Municipal Workers' Union)
Mr D. Hoyle (Association of Scientific, Technical and Managerial Staffs)
Mr A. Kitson (Transport and General Workers' Union)
Mr S. McCluskie (National Union of Seamen)
Mr F. Mulley, MP (Association of Professional, Clerical and Computer Staffs)

Mr G. Russell (Amalgamated Union of Engineering Workers)
Mr S. Tierney (Union of Shop, Distributive and Allied Workers)
Mr R. Tuck (National Union of Railwaymen)
Mr E. Williams (National Union of Mineworkers)

*Socialist, Co-operation and other organisations' Section*
Mr L. Huckfield (National Union of Labour and Socialist Clubs)

*Constituency Labour Parties*
Mr F. Allaun, MP
Mr A.W. Benn, MP
Mr E. Heffer, MP
Mr N. Kinnock, MP
Miss J. Lestor, MP
Miss J. Richardson, MP
Mr D. Skinner, MP

*Women Members*
Dame Judith Hart, MP
Baroness Jeger, MP
Miss Joan Maynard, MP
Mrs Renée Short, MP
Mrs Shirley Williams, MP

*Labour Party Young Socialists' Representative*
Mr A. Saunois

# APPENDIX III
## Peace, Jobs, Freedom

*Statement presented by the NEC to the special conference*
*Wembley, 31 May 1980*

Today's conference allows the Labour Party to present to the British People its plans for overcoming Britain's crisis and proposals for action internationally.

In the advanced, industrialised world, including Britain, mounting unemployment – now standing at more than 17 million – is the price of capitalist economic decline.

In the poor, undeveloped countries the despair of poverty and hunger is deepening and threatens peace.

The spread of weapons, spearheaded by the quickening race in nuclear weapons and their proliferation, makes the dangers of a third world war very real.

As peoples and countries become more dependent on each other – highlighted by the crucial dependence of the industrialised world on oil – international co-operation becomes more necessary but harder to secure and sustain.

Britain should be playing a full part in making the world a fairer, safer, more co-operative international community. Under this Government it is not.

With Britain's long traditions in manufacturing skills and innovation, and its important indigenous fuels – coal, oil and gas – the country should be facing the 1980s full of hope and confidence. But this is not the Britain of today.

Instead of confidence, we see deepening social divisions. Instead of an expansion in manufacturing wealth, we face recession, spending cuts, unemployment and growing despair, especially among the long-term unemployed and young people without jobs. Instead of a Government committed to the fair treatment of people wherever they live or whatever their circumstances, we confront a Government determined to uphold the harsh attitudes and priorities of the market place, where the rich get richer and the poor get poorer. We oppose cynical appeals to greed and self-interest enshrined in the last two Tory Budgets.

We denounce the damage being heaped on our economy by blind reliance on monetarist policies and free market economics. We urge the early adoption of Labour's alternative economic strategy based on expansion. We condemn the harm Tory policies are doing in dividing Britain: the employed from the unemployed, the well-off from the less well-off, the healthy from the sick, the increasingly privileged minority from the underprivileged majority.

The Labour movement stands for fairness, equality and justice – and against all forms of discrimination whether on the grounds of race, colour, creed or sex.

We are for a fundamental and irreversible shift in the balance of power and wealth in favour of working people and their families – against propping up the existing order of unfettered capitalism, based on private wealth and privilege.

We are for planning the nation's resources to meet our needs; for public ownership of the means of production, distribution and exchange – against the harsh, impersonal values, inefficiency and waste, of production solely for profit.

We are for democratic socialism – at home and overseas. It is the only sane and sensible path for people to decide their own destinies, to enjoy a fair share of the wealth they create, to live out their lives with a real sense of individual fulfilment, to join freely with others in building civilised communities in lasting peace for themselves and for their families.

For those reasons we urge the British people to reject the Tory drift to catastrophe and support our alternative strategy for peace, jobs, and freedom.

*Labour's alternative*

There can be no going back: a powerful *new* economic strategy is needed, based on public ownership, expansion and democratic planning.

The central features of Labour's policy are:

*First*, the restoration and maintenance of full employment. That is the key to the rest of our proposals for transforming Britain's economy and must be the highest priority for the next Labour Government. Major changes will be needed in our society if we are to create the new jobs which will be needed – in the way we work, in how much we work, in how the fruits of our work will be shared. With the right industrial strategy it must be possible to achieve full employment – when thousands of people are crying out for better homes, more hospitals, more help for the elderly and better schools.

*Second*, we believe in economic expansion. This must now be spearheaded by increased public expenditure – to meet pressing social and community needs and to create jobs.

*Third*, we believe that Labour's strategy of expansion will help to curb inflation. Expansion will make it easier for industry to contain its costs; it will provide workers with rising real wages; it will make it possible for social benefits – such as pensions and child benefits – to be increased in line with prices and earnings. We will also introduce a comprehensive and powerful system of price controls. The closest co-operation between the Labour Government, the party and the trade union movement will be essential to carry out our economic and other policies.

*Fourth*, Labour will work for an international agreement under which all countries are helped and encouraged to expand their economies to the limit of their productive capacity and so stimulate world trade. The expansion of Britain's economy will increase world trade. At the same time, however, we are determined not to allow manufactured imports to continue to destroy our industries and jobs. We will plan our trade in manufactures and our international payments to protect and promote industrial development in Britain. Sensible trade planning can assist Third World development.

*Fifth*, we will introduce strict controls over international capital movements to prevent a flight of capital overseas – and introduce new defences for sterling to help fight off any run on the pound. We shall also work for international agreement to help being about greater currency stability.

*Sixth*, we reassert out belief, based on experience of recent Labour Governments, in the crucial importance of extending public ownership and planning the economy. We shall establish the machinery and take the powers we need to translate our plans into action. Planning agreements must guide the activities of the huge companies which dominate the economy and be backed by the statutory powers – especially discretionary powers over prices – set out in Labour's Programme. We would aim to make substantial progress towards our target of doubling the level of manufacturing investment within our first Parliament.

We will also extend public enterprise to ensure a significant public stake – and a degree of control – in each important industrial sector; and this will include companies in such sectors as pharmaceuticals, medical equipment, micro-electronics, construction and building materials. We will support job creating technology and industrial innovation in consultation with the trade unions involved. An Investment Fund would also be established to channel North Sea oil revenues and funds from the financial institutions, into industry. We will take North Sea oil into public ownership; and we will restore to public ownership, without compensation, the assets of our public sector industries sold off by the Tories.

*Seventh*, we will ensure that there is progress towards genuine industrial democracy in both the public and private sectors; and we shall promote co-operative development in all its forms. We will repeal, entirely, the Tory Employment Bill.

*Eighth*, work-sharing will be needed to combat the economic crisis we will inherit from the Tories – and the loss of jobs which could flow from the unplanned introduction of new technology. Time off for study, longer holidays, earlier voluntary retirement and a progressive move to a 35-hour working week will all have a part to play. This would create more jobs – and give more people proper opportunities to enjoy leisure, rather than enforced, insecure and useless idleness on the dole. We shall expand greatly training and retraining to acquire the skills we need, including a major traineeship scheme for school leavers.

*Ninth*, we are determined to lift the burdens imposed on our economy by the EEC – on food prices, on jobs and on our public finances. We shall amend the 1972 European Communities Act so as to restore to the House of Commons the full control of all law-making and tax-gathering powers now ceded to the European Communities. We will also seek fundamental reforms to the EEC: and we will use every means at our disposal to achieve them, including the use of the veto and withholding payments into the budget. But, should even these measures fail to convince our partners of the need for radical change, the party will be forced to consider again whether continued EEC membership is in the best interests of the British people.

*Tenth*, we accept that these policies cannot be implemented whilst the present unequal balance of wealth and power persists in Britain. We are therefore committed to a whole range of measures involving the strengthening of the powers of the House of Commons, the abolition of the House of Lords, and the introduction of a full Freedom of Information Act to strengthen democracy against privilege and patronage.

*Policy for Peace*

Ways to secure lasting peace and progress towards disarmament must be first on the agenda. A third world war would destroy civilisation – and the danger of its breaking out is growing alarmingly. Following the steps taken by the last Labour Government in such fields as non-proliferation and the Mutual and Balanced Force Reduction talks, Britain must again take a lead in disarmament negotiations. The arms race must be halted, war hysteria dispelled.

Détente, in our view, is essential, coupled with universal respect for the rights of all peoples and nations to self determination. Accordingly we condemn the Soviet intervention in Afghanistan and warn against all military interventions contrary to the UN Charter.

In 1974, we renounced any intention of moving towards the production of a new generation of nuclear weapons or a successor to the Polaris nuclear force; we reiterate our belief that this is the best course for Britain. Many great issues affecting our allies and the world are involved. The Labour Party opposes the manufacture and deployment of Cruise missiles and the neutron bomb and refuses to permit their deployment in Britain by the United States or any other country.

The Soviet Union has already deployed the SS20 missile and NATO has taken a decision to equip itself with Cruise and Pershing 2 missiles. There will be an interval of three or four years before NATO's new weapons are produced and deployed. We regard it as imperative that this breathing space should be used to prevent a further upward twist in the arms spiral.

The Labour Party calls upon the British Government to enter immediately into East/West negotiations, with a view to reaching new agreements that would ensure that Cruise missiles and Soviet SS20s are both withdrawn. Britain is a prime target. It is our conviction that the safety of the British people, and of the people of Europe both East and West including the people of the Soviet Union, will be best secured by multilateral mutual disarmament in the nuclear and conventional fields. The arms race has already begun. It must be halted. We dedicate ourselves to this objective.

The next Labour Government will reduce the proportion of the nation's resources devoted to defence so that the burden we bear will be brought into line with that carried by our main European allies. A Labour Government would plan to ensure that savings in military expenditure did not lead to unemployment for those working in the defence industries. We shall give material support and encouragement to plans for industrial conversion so that the valuable resources of the defence industries can be used for the production of socially needed goods.

Labour will give every encouragement to those working for the cause of international peace. We will establish a peace research institute. Labour believes that a significant contribution to peace and arms control could be achieved by introducing criteria for the limitation of arms sales abroad. The Labour Government used such criteria to cut off the supply of arms to South Africa, El Salvador and Chile and imposed strict limitations on the supply of arms to a number of other countries. For these actions to be fully effective, it is necessary that there should be agreements by other states not to make up such supplies, and we urge that Britain should seek immediate negotiations with other arms supplying states with a view to reaching agreement that would prevent the supply of arms to countries where such supply would increase the chances of international conflict or internal repression. But we should in any case apply these criteria to our own arms sales.

The Labour Party believes that it is vital to breathe new life into the disarmament negotiations. There are great dangers of nuclear proliferation and these muse be reduced. As part of this purpose, we urge the immediate ratification of the Agreement on Strategic Arms Limitation between the United States and the USSR and we regard it as vital that new talks with the purpose of further reducing the number of strategic nuclear weapons held by both sides should be begun at once. We want to see a Comprehensive Test Ban Treaty. We support the UN Committee on Disarmament.

We deeply deplore the fact that so little progress has been made during the last twelve months in the negotiations to reduce conventional weapons. We call upon all the governments concerned to impart a fresh urgency to the negotiations that have been taking place between East and West in Vienna. We will work with all those who want peace, in Europe and elsewhere, to turn away once and for all from the dangerous madness and enormous waste of increasing arms of mass destruction.

Poverty is a fundamental cause of political chaos and even of war. The next Labour Government will give greater emphasis to the North/South dialogue. It will participate constructively in all negotiations seeking to establish a world trading pattern fairer to developing countries. The free market world economy is not in the interests of developing countries. We oppose the International Monetary Fund's austerity measures which are totally unimaginative and inappropriate to the current world recession and to the developing world. Such policies also impose a heavy political and economic burden on third world countries. We again commit ourselves to the UN target for overseas aid of 0.7 per cent of the GNP, with the emphasis to be put on rural development.

We shall campaign for international peace, international cooperation and international development. These must be our priorities for the 1980s and we call on the whole Labour movement, inside and outside Parliament, to fight for these policies.

*The task ahead*

The Labour Party is a democratic socialist party and proud of it.

We believe that millions of people in this country are turning to us for leadership.

We shall defend their interests, present our programme clearly and campaign for it boldly inside and outside Parliament. We must campaign for their support now to turn back from the politics of fear and join with us to create a society built upon hope for peace, for jobs, and for greater democracy.

This support must be built in the constituencies. It means our local parties will need to launch – through leaflets, pamphlets, posters and meetings – a campaign to support the Labour Party and its policies outlined in this document. So we must take the message of this document and the Conference to the country and through the Parliamentary Party to the House of Commons.

We must explain to people worried about unemployment, inflation, housing, cuts in welfare, health, and education services, cuts in the value of social security benefits and pensions, that only through the policies of the Labour Party can these essential services be restored and extended.

We believe that the objectives outlined in this document will attract growing support from the electorate and the task of the party organisation is to see that this support is expressed in active involvement in membership and work for the party.

The ideals and aims of this statement will require not only a Labour Government with a majority in Parliament but one backed by a strong and effective party organisation in the country.

The people and the party want to see an end to the present Tory Government at the earliest opportunity. We want to see it replaced by a Labour Government elected on socialist policies supported and understood by the electorate.

# APPENDIX IV
## Abbreviations

| | |
|---|---|
| ACAS | Advisory Conciliation and Arbitration Service |
| AEA | Atomic Energy Authority |
| AGR | Advanced Gas-cooled Reactor |
| APEX | Association of Professional, Executive, Clerical and Computer Staff |
| ASLEF | Amalgamated Society of Locomotive Engineers and Firemen |
| ASTMS | Association of Scientific, Technical and Managerial Staffs |
| AUEW | Amalgamated Union of Engineering Workers |
| BALPA | British Air Line Pilots' Association |
| BBC | British Broadcasting Corporation |
| BL | British Leyland |
| BNFL | British Nuclear Fuels Limited |
| BNOC | British National Oil Corporation |
| BOSS | Bureau of State Security, South Africa |
| BP | British Petroleum |
| BSC | British Steel Corporation |
| CAP | Common Agricultural Policy |
| CBI | Confederation of British Industry |
| CEGB | Central Electricity Generating Board |
| CGT | Capital Gains Tax |
| CIA | Central Intelligence Agency, USA |
| CLP | Constituency Labour Party |
| CLPD | Campaign for Labour Party Democracy |
| CLV | Campaign for a Labour Victory |
| CND | Campaign for Nuclear Disarmament |
| COHSE | Confederation of Health Service Employees |
| COI | Central Office of Information |
| CP | Communist Party |
| CPRS | Central Policy Review Staff |
| CPSA | Civil and Public Services Association |
| CQM | Cabinet Committee (on Common Market) |

| | |
|---|---|
| CSEU | Confederation of Shipbuilding and Engineering Unions |
| CTT | Capital Transfer Tax |
| CU | Civil Contingencies Unit |
| DATA | Draughtsmen's and Allied Technical Association (subsequently part of AUEW-TASS) |
| DES | Department of Education and Science |
| DFC | Distinguished Flying Cross |
| DHSS | Department of Health and Social Security |
| DOP | Cabinet Committee (Defence and Overseas Policy) |
| DSC | Distinguished Service Cross |
| ECE | Economic Commission for Europe |
| EEC | European Economic Community |
| EETPU | Electrical, Electronic, Telecommunications and Plumbing Union |
| EI | Cabinet Committee (Economic and Industrial) |
| EMS | European Monetary System |
| EMU | Economic and Monetary Union |
| ENA | Ecole Nationale d'Adminstration |
| ENM | Cabinet Committee (Energy) |
| ETU | Electrical Trades Union (subsequently part of EETPU) |
| Euratom | European Atomic Energy Community |
| EY | Cabinet Committee (Economic Strategy) |
| EY(P) | Cabinet Committee (Pay and Prices) |
| FBR | Fast Breeder Reactor |
| FO | Foreign Office |
| *FT* | *Financial Times* |
| GATT | General Agreement on Tariffs and Trade |
| GCHQ | Government Communications Headquarters |
| GEC | General Electric Company |
| GEN12 | Cabinet Committee on South African and Rhodesian Policy |
| GEN23 GEN29 | Cabinet Committees on Official Information |
| GEN73 | Cabinet Committee on Government Holding in BP |
| GEN74 | Cabinet Committee on Nuclear Policy |
| GEN119 | Cabinet Committee on Public Appointments |
| GEN158 | Christmas Emergency Cabinet Committee |
| GKN | Guest, Keen and Nettlefolds |
| GLC | Greater London Council |
| GLRC | Greater London Regional Council (of the Labour Party) |
| GMC | General Management Committee |

| | |
|---|---|
| GMWU | General and Municipal Workers' Union |
| GNP | Gross National Product |
| HSE | Health and Safety Executive |
| IAEA | International Atomic Energy Authority |
| IBA | Independent Broadcasting Authority |
| ICI | Imperial Chemical Industries |
| ICRP | International Committee on Radiological Protection |
| IEA | International Energy Agency |
| ILEA | Inner London Education Authority |
| ILP | Independent Labour Party |
| IMF | International Monetary Fund |
| INLA | Irish National Liberation Army |
| IPC | International Publishing Corporation |
| IRA | Irish Republican Army |
| IRD | Information Research Department |
| IRN | Independent Radio News |
| ITN | Independent Television News |
| IWC | Institute for Workers' Control |
| Jet | Joint European Torus |
| KME | Kirkby Manufacturing and Engineering Company (formerly IPD-Fisher Bendix) |
| LACSAB | Local Authorities Conditions of Service Advisory Board |
| LBC | London Broadcasting Company |
| LCC | Labour Co-ordinating Committee |
| LPYS | Labour Party Young Socialists |
| LSE | London School of Economics |
| MBE | Member, Order of the British Empire |
| MI5 | British Security Service (internal security), formerly Section 5 of Military Intelligence |
| MI6 | British Secret Intelligence Service (overseas intelligence), formerly Section 6 of Military Intelligence |
| MLR | Minimum Lending Rate |
| MoD | Ministry of Defence |
| NACODS | National Association of Colliery Overmen, Deputies and Shotfirers |
| NALGO | National and Local Government Officers' Association |
| NATO | North Atlantic Treaty Organisation |
| NATSOPA | National Society of Operative Printers, Graphical and Media Personnel |
| NCB | National Coal Board |
| NCCL | National Council for Civil Liberties |

| NEB | National Enterprise Board |
| NEC | National Executive Committee |
| NEDC | National Economic Development Council (Neddy) |
| NEDO | National Economic Development Office |
| NF | National Front |
| NGA | National Graphical Association |
| NHS | National Health Service |
| NI | National Insurance |
| NNC | National Nuclear Corporation |
| NPC | Nuclear Power Company |
| NPT | Non-Proliferation Treaty |
| NRPB | National Radiological Protection Board |
| NUJ | National Union of Journalists |
| NUM | National Union of Mineworkers |
| NUPE | National Union of Public Employees |
| NUR | National Union of Railwaymen |
| NUS | National Union of Seamen |
| NUT | National Union of Teachers |
| OECD | Organisation for Economic Co-operation and Development |
| OPEC | Organisation of Petroleum Exporting Countries |
| PLO | Palestine Liberation Organisation |
| PLP | Parliamentary Labour Party |
| PPS | Parliamentary Private Secretary |
| PR | Proportional Representation |
| PRT | Petroleum Revenue Tax |
| PSBR | Public Sector Borrowing Requirement |
| PSF | French Socialist Party (Parti Socialiste Français) |
| PSV | Public Service Vehicle |
| PWR | Pressurised Water Reactor |
| RAF | Royal Air Force |
| RD | Cabinet Committe (Relations with Developing Countries) |
| RNVR | Royal Naval Volunteer Reserve |
| RPI | Retail Price Index |
| SALT | Strategic Arms Limitation Talks |
| SAS | Special Air Services |
| SDLP | Social Democratic and Labour Party (Northern Ireland) |
| SDP | Social Democratic Party |
| SGHWR | Steam-Generating Heavy Water Reactor |
| Sigint | Signals Intelligence |
| SLADE | Society of Lithographic Artists, Designers, Engravers and Process-Workers (subsequently part of NGA) |

| SNP | Scottish National Party |
| SOGAT | Society of Graphical and Allied Trades |
| SPD | Social Democratic Party (Sozialdemokratische Partei Deutschlands) |
| SPG | Special Patrol Group |
| SSEB | South of Scotland Electricity Board |
| SS 20 | Multiple-Warhead Soviet Nuclear Missile |
| STUC | Scottish Trades Union Congress |
| SWAPO | South West Africa Peoples' Organisation |
| TASS | Technical and Supervisory Section (of AUEW) |
| TGWU | Transport and General Workers' Union (T&G) |
| TSSA | Transport and Salaried Staffs Association |
| TSRB | Top Salaries Review Body |
| TUC | Trades Union Congress |
| TUVL | Trade Unionists for a Labour Victory |
| UDI | Unilateral Declaration of Independence |
| UN | United Nations |
| UNESCO | United Nations Educational, Scientific and Cultural Organisation |
| USDAW | Union of Shop, Distributive and Allied Workers |
| USSR | Union of Soviet Socialist Republics |
| UUUC | United Ulster Unionist Coalition |
| VAT | Value Added Tax |
| ZANU | Zimbabwe African National Union |
| ZAPU | Zimbabwe African People's Union |

# Index

Shell oil 3; *see also* Esso
Sheridan, Colonel 404
shop stewards: from Air Products 60;
meeting on strike at Windscale 69; at
Dungeness B power station 318–19
Shore, Liz 79, 302, 614
Shore, Peter 96, 180, 237, 270, 290, 301,
498, 614; on dismissal of PPSs 6; and
National Waste Management
Corporation 33; on Idi Amin 40;
direct elections to European
Parliament 50, 117, 121, 123, 154; on
Permanent Secretaries 51; on
Windscale dispute 74; on shares of
Burmah Oil Company 75; Lib-Lab
Pact 87, 89, 90, 91; and nuclear lobby
100; on nuclear policy 126; on sale of
shares in BP 141; on industrial
democracy 142; and transport of
plutonium 143; and FBR 157; on
White Paper on pay policy 194; at
memorial service for Piers Shore 215;
on sanctions against South Africa
235; on exchange controls 256–7; on
choice of nuclear reactors 263; and
industrial democracy 267; North Sea
oil development fund 276, 280; on
Margaret Thatcher 282; on Kirkby
Mechanical Engineering 299; on pay
policy 326; and inquiry on FBR 342;
on Bingham Report 345; on
Christmas bonus for old age
pensioners 365; on EMS 365, 380; on
pay sanctions 417; on right to strike
in essential services 438; on water
shortage in north-west 442; on
depleted uranium in ammunition 445;
on Election strategy 446; on nuclear
weapons in Pakistan and India 454;
on import controls 457; on Official
Information Bill (Freud) 473; and
leadership of Labour Party 484; on
statutory powers of intervention 486;
on House of Lords 487; as foreign
affairs spokesman 512; on
Commission of Inquiry 559; and
leadership campaign 560, 586; on
defence policy 575; on US raid on
Iran 591
Shore, Piers 213, 215
Short, Edward (Lord Glenamara) 496
'Short money' 496–7, 523, 576, 577;
resolution on 509; Jim Callaghan on

514, 523; *see also* opposition parties,
government funding
Short, Renée 543, 573
Shotton steelworks, closure 414
Shrimsley, Anthony 288
Shrimsley, Bernard 288
Sierra Leone, President 162
Sigint 399
Silkin, John 153, 177, 215, 241, 250,
392, 400–1, 503, 554, 614; on
dismissal of PPSs 6; and devolution
47; and Lib-Lab Pact 89; on Common
Agricultural Policy 201; at Cabinet on
Common Market 206; on House of
Lords 487; *Guardian* on 508; in
elections to Shadow Cabinet 512; as
industry spokesman 512; and
leadership campaign 586
Silkin, Rosalind 215
Silkin, Sam 22, 180, 601n, 614; on
exchange controls 256
Sillars, Jim 8, 173
Simon, William 511
Simonet, Henri 234
Simpson, Bill 136
Simpson, Ernest 2–3
Simpson, Robin 69
Simpson, Wallis 3
Sims, Monica 542
Sirs, Bill 415, 527, 562
Skinner, David 256
Skinner, Dennis 35, 253, 356, 357, 370,
500, 512, 517, 522, 614; on manifesto
43; at Labour Party Conference
(1977) 225; at Anti-Nazi League rally
345; on pay policy 353; on Queen's
speech (1978) 372–3; on alternative
strategy to pay policy 376; on EMS
395, 398; on statement of Jim
Callaghan on picketing 471; on
statutory powers of intervention 485;
on House of Lords 487; after General
Election 503; on appointment of
Front Bench spokesmen 515; at Home
Policy Committee (NEC) 521; on
Benn-Heffer proposals on PLP 524;
on Commission of Inquiry 550–1, 559
small businesses 218
Smiles, Samuel 25
Smith, Mr 81
Smith, Ian 200, 223n
Smith, John 369, 392, 582, 614; on
secondary picketing 438; on import